THE HERO JOURNEY IN LITERATURE

Parables of Poesis

D1571320

Evans Lansing Smith

University Press of America, Inc.
Lanham • New York • London

Copyright © 1997 by
University Press of America,® Inc.
4720 Boston Way
Lanham, Maryland 20706

3 Henrietta Street
London, WC2E 8LU England

Library of Congress Cataloging-in-Publication Data

Smith, Evans Lansing.
The hero journey in literature : parables of poesis / Evans Lansing
Smith.
p.   cm.
Includes bibliographical references and index.
1. Heroes in literature. 2. Voyages and travels in literature. I. Title.
PN56.5.H45S65   1996   809'.93353--dc20   96-30896 CIP

ISBN 0-7618-0508-7 (cloth: alk. ppr.)
ISBN 0-7618-0509-5 (pbk: alk. ppr.)

♾™ The paper used in this publication meets the minimum
requirements of American National Standard for information
Sciences—Permanence of Paper for Printed Library Materials,
ANSI Z39.48—1984

To my children:

Carly, Angela, and Anita

"Here beginneth the marvels"

Contents

Preface

This book completes a tetralogy begun twenty years ago, in 1976, when I first read Joseph Campbell's *The Hero With a Thousand Faces*. All four books develop a mythopoetic approach to literature. This one focuses on basic works of the canon, from antiquity to the present, and the other three focus on the use of five myths -- the apocalypse, alchemy, the descent to the underworld, the labyrinth, and the Great Goddess -- in the literature specifically of the 20th century. All five of those myths are relevant to a discussion of the hero journey, which I define as a circular narrative, beginning and ending in the same place, with an initiatory journey in between. The initiation stage of the journey nearly always involves revelation and transformation. I have stuck to this definition rather rigidly throughout this book, choosing not to discuss works that don't fit the circular pattern of the hero journey cycle. The only deviation from this principle occurs when a small arc of the circle (the return phase) is broken. All of the other works discussed are clearly hero journey cycles, and many employ a basic iconography (doorways, divestiture, eye, river, and mountain symbolism, etc.) which can be established by detailed readings of the various texts. The texts themselves are those typically taught in a wide range of college courses, particularly in the sophomore surveys, but at all other levels as well. I also include various new and strong candidates for inclusion in the canon (Persian, Arthurian, Feminist, Postcolonial, African-American) which are to be found in more recent anthologies of English, American, and World Literature. In the last chapter, on the literature of the 20th century, I have chosen to focus mostly on those shorter narratives typically anthologized, and to refer the interested reader to my other three books, where detailed discussions of the numerous long masterpieces of the modernist tradition are to be found.

Introduction

A year or so after traveling with Joseph Campbell, first in Northern France, to study the Arthurian Romances of the Middle Ages, and then in Egypt and Kenya to pursue the mythologies of the Ancient Near East, I had a dream about him. I was walking down one of the avenues in New York City. When I turned off into a side street, I came to a nondescript doorway, with no address and nothing written above it. On a whim, I walked up the dark stairway to a furnitureless room on the upper floor, inside of which I sat down with Joseph Campbell. He had a bell jar in his hand, a kind of alchemical beaker, hermetically sealed. A vaporous mist hovered over a sediment of earth at the bottom of the jar, into which we both gazed, Campbell with that marvelous smile of delight that so often illuminated his features. As we looked into the jar, the mist slowly and subtly swirled around, and became animated with the delicate colors of the rainbow. Joseph pointed to the rainbow -- the cauda pavonis, or peacock's tail of the alchemists -- and I was led to see in it the emergence of life from the mysterious, invisible forces of the universe, into which the colorful apparition would return at the end of the cycle, evaporated into Prospero's "thin air," like a dream. As we watched the phosphorescent mist swirl above the handful of earth at the bottom of the beaker, a tiny boy slowly became visible, a faery's child, with a nearly transparent body of evanescent light. Again, I was led to understand, with no words passing between us, that this was the alchemical child, herald of the new life which was just then beginning for me.

Looking back at my dream of the homunculus in the beaker, I have come to see it as a call to adventure, initiating my own personal version of the universal archetype of spiritual development, which Joseph Campbell called the hero journey. I've been many years now on the way, devoting much of my time to the exploration of the hero journey in the classic literary works of our tradition. In the summer of 1988, after returning home from my first teaching at a small college in Switzerland, I saw segments of the PBS series, "The Power of Myth," in which Joseph Campbell told Bill Moyers about his days as a student in France during the 20's. With characteristic zeal, Campbell recalled his daily visits to the Cathedral of Chartres, during which he identified every single figure in its biblical pantheon, whether stained in radiant glass or carved in immemorial stone. He became such a familiar figure that one day the sexton entrusted him with an extraordinary task: "Would you like," said the sexton, "to come up with me into the belfry to ring the noontide bells?" Who could say no? Campbell ascended the famous steeple into the belfry, where, with a magnificent breeze whistling through the stone windows, he climbed onto one side of a see-saw plank to begin the rocking that rang the enormous bull-throated bells beneath him.

As I listened to Campbell share this precious memory of his youth with the TV audience, equally precious memories of my own returned: I had heard that story before, when, during a travel-study tour of Northern France in the fall of 1977, organized by the Mann Ranch in California, Campbell told it to me as we sat together on the bus heading into Chartres at twilight. It was near the end of a really terrific week, which had included visits to Rouen, Amiens, Mt. St. Michel, the standing stones of Carnac, the Medieval forests of Brittany, the Chateaux country on the way to Chartres, and then on to Paris. Campbell beamed with delight in his window seat beside me, looking out at a host of chateaux entirely invisible to me: he had piercing blue eyes, and knew the terrain well, where to look beneath a cluster of trees, or behind a tiny copse in the distance, for the noble relics of the Middle Ages. We'd had lunch on the grounds of one of the chateaux earlier in the day, sitting beside the still pool that surrounded the pinnacled pile, which was perfectly reflected on the surface of the water: spires, towers, turrets, crenellations, copes, barbicans, chimneys, battlements, windows, and arched doorways were all perfectly replicated, though pointing downwards, in the serene mirror of the pool's surface. The castle shimmered, above and below the water line, a dazzling white surrounded by a bevy of immemorial oaks. It was as if we had stepped through a hole in the hedge into another world, or as if we had passed through a door of glass into the mysterious chambers of Glastonbury Abbey, where Arthur and his court danced the morris.

Our group had stopped earlier in a little pub in the woods of Brittany, to have a cup of cider, some cheese, and to enjoy the fine hospitality of our perfectly darling old French host, a diminutive white haired dwarf with a mystical sense of humor. After several glasses of cider, we strolled down the long path outside the pub, which led into the woods where Vivian had beguiled Merlin -- a picture of which he had carved into the cedar panels of his bar. Stopping beneath a tremendous flowering hawthorn, the old man said to me: "Il y'a beaucoup de choses qui n'existe pas" ('There are many things which don't exist!'), and I could well believe him. Deep inside the woods, we all sat down in a circle, sitting on logs and fallen tree trunks amidst the briars and a scattering of Amanita muscaria mushrooms -- "Don't eat those," Campbell said, "or we'll never get to Paris!" Joseph Campbell then told Merlin's story: of how the old man fell in love with Vivian, the sorceress, who coaxed his magic spells out of him, then used them to imprison the old wizard in a tower of white thorns, in which he remained eternally invisible. Only the sound of his voice -- whispering with the wind that blew gently through the trees of the vast forest -- came to those knights who wandered through the forests of Broceliande, in quest of love or the Holy Grail. As Campbell finished his story, with hounds bellowing in the distance, the sun broke free from the mist, and its shafts penetrated the tall trees surrounding our silent little group. It continued to shine on the shimmering surface of the little pond where we had lunch, Campbell leaning against a standing stone on the shore, with the Lady of the Lake retrieving excalibur in the water behind him: I imagined I saw her hand extended from beneath the rippling surface, waving the dazzling steel three times in the air, before returning to the depths.

To visit Mt. St. Michel, we stayed at the little hotel down the road where Eisenhower had set up offices after the Normandy invasion. In Rouen, I'd seen where machine guns had gouged gaping holes in the Cathedral, and an old woman had taken me in to her burned out basement to thank me for liberating France! (I conveyed her gratitude to my father.) In the peaceful hotel near Mt. St. Michel, Campbell sat quietly in a corner after breakfast (very unlike his normal gregariousness) before his slide-illustrated lecture, for which he said he was "composing his images." The evening before, a few of us had gone out after dinner to see the Mount at night, rising mysteriously above the dark swirl of the treacherous tides, pinnacle and archangel invisible in the darkness above. We drove together with a National Geographic photographer working on a story there, and walked up along the cobbled streets of the village to the colossal arch leading into the monastery and cathedral. One leaned back against the stone barricades to gaze up at the huge, fluted, columnar arches, which supported the massive weight of the monastery, and which eerily dissolved into the intangible darkness of the endless night above. "It's the impenetrable inner Self," a bandy legged and feisty little Australian analyst whispered to me, as I stood with thighs trembling in the wind. (Fred had received his Jungian calling from a hallucinatory crow, which sat on his right thigh for years, refusing to fly away until he began his training analysis). My trembling returned later in Paris, when a small group of us walked over to Notre Dame, and then down by the river, after a lengthy dinner (with lots of wine): the sight of the powerfully vaulted nave and apse of the

Cathedral, seen from behind, and below, along the shores of the Seine, with the flurry of flying arches supporting the weight, overwhelmed me. The trembling didn't stop until one of our companions, an older woman who ran a philanthropic foundation in California, simply melted on the stone steps climbing up from the embankment: she'd had far too much wine!

As I watched the Bill Moyers interview, it occurred to me how appropriate that my education should have led me to Joseph Campbell's work. All of my liberal arts studies at Williams College seemed in fact to lead up to that climactic tour of France, and to a second tour some months later in Egypt and Africa. I had taken courses in most of the various disciplines which Campbell synthesizes: I had studied psychology, sociology, religion, classics, literature, and art history with a wide range of marvelous men. In a sense, Campbell was all in one, and studies in mythology helped me bring together everything Williams had so prodigally bestowed upon me. Suddenly, while sitting in the breakfast room of a little hotel down the road from Mont St. Michel, listening to Campbell lecture and looking at his glorious collection of slides, everything in my education came together -- the labyrinth on the worn pavement at Chartres, the Chateaux reflected in still pools, the beguiling forests of Brittany, and, above all, the marvelous Arthurian tales which Campbell recited like a masterful bard of the Celtic tradition.

Campbell believed that certain archetypal symbols, or mythic images (like the Great Goddess, the maze, and the underworld) tend to recur in art, religious narratives, dreams, and literary works. These symbols elusively cut across temporal, disciplinary, and cultural boundaries. Hence, an illiterate youth of the 1960's might dream (as I did, before reading Homer) of escaping from a cave of cannibals after a shipwreck by clinging to the long hair of a yak. Hence also an old man might dream shortly before his death (as my wonderful step-Grandfather David Van Alstyne did) of being at a royal banquet in the great hall of an English estate where all the guests were seated, headless, and waiting for the servants to bring their heads to them on large silver platters! Grandpa Van was blind when he told me this dream, and had just sung me the songs he had learned in the French ambulance corps during the Great War, which interrupted his years at Williams. The dream made me think of *Sir Gawain and the Green Knight*, in which the decapitation that occurs during a Christmas feast at Camelot is a symbol of rebirth.

Campbell came close to being a kind of Renaissance man: vigorously trained in the precise details of one particular discipline, but well aware of its relevance to several. Like Marsilio Ficino or Pico della Mirandola, his work integrated philosophy, theology, painting, and literature into a single domain of study. Yet he was also a gentleman:

friendly, amusing, erudite, and energetic -- an athlete in fact who enjoyed whiskey before dinner. One could simply relax with him, as I was fortunate enough to do on several occasions: on the bus to Chartres he avoided larger topics by simply delighting in the Chateaux scattered around the countryside. At lunch in a game park in Kenya, he roared with laughter when a monkey snarled at me and stole a banana as I backed off. We had spent the whole morning in a jeep, bouncing around in the waste land, looking for game: the mere existence of life in that brutal environment seemed unlikely, but we saw a herd of wild elephants washing in a muddy river, a lion lolling in the dust beneath the meager shade of a bush, and a noisy crowd of sacred baboons huddled nobly together in the branches of a huge sycamore. In the evening at the Samburu Lodge, an archetypal aviary invaded the well manicured lawns, with the snow capped peak of Mt. Kenya gleaming slightly pink in the distance. Campbell recognized the birds from his study of African masks, and, after dinner, treated us to long slide-illustrated lectures on the gradual emergence of Homo Sapiens Sapiens from the long lineage stretching back to the early Hominids: Archaic Homo Sapiens, Homo Erectus, Homo Habilis, and Australopithecus (some 5 million years of evolution). My favorite picture of the sequence was taken by Jane Goodall: it showed a tribe of gorillas pounding their huge chests and stampeding through the dense underbrush in response to a dazzling clap of thunder and lightning.

Campbell was equally relaxed and fun in Egypt, where I saw him blow a kiss to the gods, as we rode in horse drawn traps by the Temples of Luxor and Karnac. On another morning, he waved to a crowd of cheering teenagers on a field trip, laughing boisterously with them as we emerged from the magnificent underground tomb of Sethos I. Later that night, in a bar on an island near Aswan, I laughed as he talked over whiskey about Freud's tendency to faint in Jung's presence. Our visit to the Valley of the Kings the next day traced the archetypal model of the hero journey cycle: beginning and ending on our floating hotel (the SS Osiris) moored on the eastern bank beneath the Temple of Luxor, and exploring the tombs beneath the rocky mountains on the western bank in between. (The descent through the maze of doorways, corridors, stairways, and chambers to the grandly painted cathedral ceilings of the tomb rooms beneath the mountains was one of the highlights of the trip, and permanently shaped my view of the symbolism of the hero journey in literature). Crossing the river to the yonder shore, on a little ferryboat, with faluccas sailing all around us, little boys peddling roses in paddle boats, and women drying their wash on the rocks, I asked Campbell about the Oriental idea of liberation from the wheel of life. If Nietzsche was right, I mused, and life is an endless cycle of eternal repetition, then the idea of liberation must be an illusion. "O no," he said

xiii

vehemently, "It's very real," and left it at that. But he returned to the topic of Nietzsche that night, sitting at a small table with a beer on the boat, after judging a costume contest (the actress Dina Merrill won for her performance as a harem girl).

The SS Osiris then took us up the Nile for excursions to the temples of Dendera and Abydos, Karnak, Esna, Edfu, and Kom Ombo, where policemen roamed the streets in front of the glowing Temple swatting hordes of children with long papyrus reeds. We flew from there to Abu Simbel, looking down on large conical hills of volcanic rock rising mysteriously from between what looked like dried up river beds. After reading Thomas Mann's great biblical tetralogy, some years later, I thought of Joseph transported to the prisons of the Pharaoh on a boat like the SS Osiris, and once I imagined seeing the deep well into which he had been thrown by his jealous brothers. At the Temple of Dendera, I walked way back into a small chapel to look up at the ceiling, which bore a relief sculpture of the Sky Goddess Nut: her back arched over the earth and her four limbs stretched out to demarcate the cardinal points of the compass, she swallows a solar disk at sunset which then travels its stations of the cross through her body, to be reborn at dawn from her womb. It's the most concise representation I know of the mysteries of death and rebirth associated with the Great Goddess, a mythic figure found in a wide range of literary masterpieces.

Our trip ended at the pyramids of Giza outside Cairo. The city itself is an unimaginable pandemonium: huge crowds of people cramming themselves into buses that never seem to stop, either to load or unload, with men dangling out the windows the whole way; cattle carts and donkeys fouling the traffic in the narrow streets of the old city; and everyone honking maniacally, relentlessly, for no other reason that the pure joy of it. At the pyramids, there were camel rides, and Campbell's man let him ride way out into the desert, like Lawrence of Arabia surveying the infinity of sand surrounding him. After the ride, the camel man -- clad in a long Egyptian caftan -- surprised Campbell by announcing that he was from Kansas, and would Campbell please take his picture while he held the camel's reins! Those long blue or white caftans are marvelous: near the Valley of the Kings, a genuine Egyptian guide held a mirror up to the sun for us, as we stepped gingerly down a stairway into a tiny tomb beneath the desert. Looking up, one saw the guide deflecting the brilliant rays of sunlight down into the tomb, the walls of which were colorfully painted with bright images of Isis and Osiris.

Let me conclude with a few thoughts about why Campbell is so important. When I first began teaching at Midwestern State University, a very nice minister came up to me after class to ask what religion I preferred: well, I said, I was raised an Episcopalian, turned to Hinduism and yoga during my 20's, practiced Tibetan Buddhism during my 30's, and was now interested in the angelology of Islamic mysticism. He looked completely astonished, and I suddenly realized that all he wanted to know was whether I was a Baptist or a Methodist (I don't think Catholic was an option -- another student in the class had solemnly informed us that the Pope wasn't Christian). One of the things which Campbell's work laid foundations for is a republic of religions, in which all play their individual roles as the various masks God wears in a global community. Another concept inspired by Campbell's work concerns the idea of interdisciplinary studies, which embrace the many perspectives appropriate to the study of literature. There are no dogmas of exclusion in the study of literature, broadly conceived: we can all learn from each other in the free range of discourse our departments foster. Finally, there is the notion of a discipline itself: the commitment one makes to one particular field of study, sticking it out in spite of any disappointments and obstacles that present themselves during the journey.

Campbell's model of the hero journey -- an archetypal narrative structure to be found in a wide variety of world literature, myths, religious tales, and rituals -- has exerted a major influence on literary criticism. But, quite surprisingly, no books have traced the narrative structure of the hero journey, and the archetypal motifs that accompany it, with a strict focus on literary history, from the Ancient World to the present. There have been books on the hero journey for kids, the hero journey for women, the hero journey in dreams, and numerous articles on the hero journey in myths and rituals. There have been theoretical books on the hero journey as narrative, books on the nature of the hero and heroine, hundreds of books on the general theories of mythology which have sprung up in our time, and anthologies of quest narratives in contemporary literature. But, oddly enough, no book that focuses in a disciplined way on the history of literature, as this one does. My intention is to fill that gap with discussions of major works of the canon, from Homer to Welty, in separate chapters on the major periods of our tradition, from the Ancient World to Modernism.

The circular structure of the hero journey is well known: it involves three stages (separation, initiation, and return), with threshold crossings and guardians, helpers, trials, and ordeals, all leading to a transformation of the consciousness of the hero, heroine, and the society they live in. My trips with Joseph Campbell followed the pattern perfectly: the two large circles (the one to France beginning and ending in Heathrow Airport outside London, and the other to Egypt beginning and ending in the Kennedy Airport outside New York) circumscribing numerous smaller hero journey cycles beginning and ending in bus or ferryboat, from which we went into the dolmens of Carnac on the Brittany coast, into the forests of Brittany where Vivien wove a tower of white thorns around Merlin, down the road at twilight to the colossal cathedral of Mt. St. Michel, into the temples of Luxor and Karnac, across the river to the tombs in the Valley of the Kings) -- all punctuated by Campbell's lectures and casual conversations along the way.

During the hero journey in literature, certain key images tend to recur -- images like threshold crossings (doorways, corridors, staircases) and rituals of divestiture -- and it will be our task to chart the iconography these images establish. The key stage of the adventure is the initiation, during which two things typically occur: revelation and transformation. Something fundamental about the world, the society, and the self is typically revealed at the climax of the journey, with a resulting transformation of the world, the community, and the self. One particular moment of revelation occurred for me during that ferryboat ride to the Western bank of the Nile, across from the Temples of Karnak and Luxor, when we discussed the concept of liberation. The revelations of the monomyth typically have to do with fundamental structures, of the world, the society, and the psyche, structures which I will discuss as archetypes of the aesthetic imagination in my conclusion. For I take it that the hero journey can be approached as a metaphor not only for the transformation of the society and the self, but also as a metaphor for the processes by which stories are created (poesis) and interpreted (hermeneusis). Harold Bloom suggested something similar in his famous essay on the internalization of the quest romance in the poetry of Wordsworth and others during the Romantic era. But no one to my knowledge has recognized (and documented) the fact that the hero journey has always been an image of the mysteries of the processes of literary creativity, both of writing (poesis) and reading (hermeneutics). Odysseus, Gilgamesh, the Ancient Mariner, Marlow, the Knight at Arms, and the woman in "The Yellow Wallpaper" are terrific storytellers, and all of them must read the text of the world, revealed by their journey, in order to tell and understand their stories. By the same token, their audiences (the Phaiakians, the people of Uruk, the Wedding Guest, the Company Accountant) must all undertake the journey too, which becomes a symbolic allegory of the intricacies of reading and interpretation. The following chapters focus on the literary history of these parables of poesis and hermeneusis.

Chapter 1:
The Ancient World

The oldest literature in our tradition comes down to us from the Sumerians, the first civilized people of the Tigris-Euphrates river valleys, and the first writers to rely on the hero journey as the basic narrative structure of their sacred stories. The Sumerians date back to about 3500 B.C.E., and were a non Indo-European people whom we must credit with the origins of language, writing, crafts, architecture, statecraft, irrigation, agriculture, and etc. (not to mention the art of brewing beer). Their rule in Mesopotamia lasted until about 2000 B.C.E., when their cities fell prey to the Akkadian Semites of Ur. The Sumerian language survived, however, much like Latin, as the high culture idiom of the area, and by about 1750 B.C.E. their sacred narratives were recorded, translated, and collated in cuneiform tablets which mix Sumerian and Semitic usages. These tablets record our oldest mythological and literary legacies: in the materials devoted to Gilgamesh and Inanna, we find the earliest versions of the Flood, the Creation, death and resurrection, crucifixion, and the imagery associated with the Garden of Eden (woman, tree, serpent, and fruit). All of these motifs probably had a long oral and visual history (via story telling, sacred rituals, and illustrations on clay seals), extending possibly as far back as 3500 B.C.E.

Gilgamesh, as we know from eight short Sumerian tales, was a King of Uruk around 2700-2500 B.C.E., but his "Epic" was not integrated until an Akkadian composition of the Old Babylonian period of about 1750 B.C.E. The material devoted to Inanna is still being dug up and deciphered, mostly from the stunning remains of the library of Asshurbanipal at Nineveh, the Assyrian capital destroyed by the Babylonians in 612 B.C.E. and left in the rubble beneath the sands of the desert for nearly 2000 years! They were dug up in 1853 during excavations conducted for the British Museum by Austin Layard and added to by other tablets excavated by a Turko-Persian team in !849-50, and then later by tablets discovered by an American team led by John Peters of the University of Pennsylvania in Philadelphia in 1888-

89. Among the 40,000 pieces of tablets now scattered in museums all over the world, we have the oldest versions of the hero journey in our literary tradition. These stories (of Gilgamesh, Enkidu, and Inanna) may well have been passed along trade routes orally via Syria and the Ionian Islands into the Mediterranean basin of the Homeric epics, and hence down through the ages to survive in the archetypal adventure stories of the Arthurian romances of the Middle Ages.

In the material devoted to Inanna and Gilgamesh, we have, in each case, three separate hero journeys recording the trials, ordeals, and initiatory transformations appropriate to the three basic stages of life: youth, maturity, and old age. With respect to Inanna, these are the three phases Robert Graves designated as aspects of the Triple Goddess (virgin, mother, and hag) and symbolized by the three phases of the moon (crescent, full, and waning). But as we will see, the *Epic of Gilgamesh* records the similar passages in the complete life cycle of the male, so that, taken together, the stories associated with the two provide a comprehensive and invaluable vision of the combined totality of the heroine and hero's journey.

The Descent of Inanna

To begin with the stories about Inanna, Queen of Heaven and Earth. This material, recently gathered together in a superb volume by Wolkstein and Kramer, gives us a precious and primordial paradigm of female development throughout the three basic life stages of virginity, maternal maturity, and old age. The last two phases of development are expressed in clearly demarcated heroine journey cycles, while the first phase of adolescence is reflected upon in a short non-cyclic myth called "The Huluppu Tree." This tale parallels the story of Enkidu in the *Epic of Gilgamesh*, in that it records the primordial emergence of a civilized order out of a state of primitive wildness, but reflects upon this process from the perspective of the feminine. The emergence of civilization is symbolized by three stages in the life cycle and 'hero journey' of the tree itself: in its virgin state it is a wild tree growing by the banks of the Euphrates in the fresh early days of the Creation; in its cultivated maturity it is a tree tended in the garden of the goddess Inanna; and finally in death it becomes the throne bed of the royal couple after Gilgamesh has driven the Anzu bird from its branches, the demonic goddess Lilith from its stem, and the serpent from the coils of its roots.

In its most primitive and pristine virgin state (which corresponds to the girlhood of the Goddess), we see the tree "in the very first days" planted by the banks of the Euphrates, from whose primal waters it derives its sustenance. The passage to the next phase of being is precipitated by a natural crisis: a whirling South Wind tears the tree up by the

roots, and the flood waters carry it downstream. These are, metaphori-
cally, the rough winds that shake the darling buds of May, those tempestuous passions which afflict adolescence as it prepares for the transition to adulthood. The description of the tree by the fresh waters of the
river remind one of Joyce's river Liffey at its source in the Wicklow
mountains, when it is a sparkling freshet of rapidly dancing stream water, i.e., Anna Livia Plurabelle, the heroine of *Finnegans Wake*, in her
virginity.

After the flood waters subside, the Huluppu tree is retrieved by
Inanna, who plants it in her holy garden in Uruk, and sits dreaming in
its shade of the day when she will have a shining throne and bed. Like
Enkidu in the Gilgamesh epic, the tree's transition from its natural origins in the wild to a cultivated plant in the gardens of the city has been
presided over by a feminine deity. Inanna, as we will see, takes the
place of the temple harlot in preserving a fragment of her own wild
girlhood from the floodwaters of biological maturation; it is a piece of
herself that will then, with proper care and cultivation, become the basis
of her new identity. This development also suggests the progression
from the hetaeric to the agricultural modes associated with the feminine
and civilization in Bachofen's discussion *Das Mutterrecht*.

After ten years of cultivation in the garden of Inanna in Uruk, new
trouble begins to brew for the young goddess queen and her Huluppu
tree: a serpent nests in the roots, the dark maiden Lilith inhabits the
trunk, and the Anzu bird roosts in the branches, brooding upon its
fledgling demons. Since these three beings will not leave, Inanna must
solicit male help, for the first time in her life, to drive the demons away.
Utu, the sun god, refuses, but Gilgamesh, her brother, accepts the task.
These three demons represent a kind of return of the repressed energies
of the earlier primitive stage of the tree's life cycle in the wilderness
beside the Euphrates, but those primal, instinctual drives have taken
new forms, one's associated with Dionysian revelry and passion un-
tamed by cultivation. Lilith, particularly, is associated with unbridled
sexuality, a kind of pre-civilized hetaericism not submissive to masculine authority.[1] She was Adam's legendary first wife, who left him to
breed demons of death beside the Red Sea after Adam insisted on being
on top during intercourse. She is, that is to say, adolescent womanhood
wildly sowing her oats in furious rebellion against all authority which
would restrain her energies. She has little to do with children, preferring
to murder babies in childbirth than to assist in their delivery. If impreg-
nated, abortion, not marriage, would be her first thought.

The serpent and the Anzu bird suggest other emerging but wild
powers of the feminine during adolescence: the one rooted in the earth
has the power to shed its skin to be reborn, but it is also secretive and
wily, imbedded in the hidden mysteries of the earth, which only pro-

found, even catatonic introversion can intuit. The eagle bird, on the other hand, is flighty and excitable, capable of piercing cries of spiritual ecstasy and transcendent flights of the mind, yet still nurturing during long hours of sedentary brooding over eggs that will hatch into the as yet unimaginable future. This suggests a kind of manic-depressive dynamic of the young womanhood of Inanna, an unstable oscillation between high flying enthusiasm, and terrible fits of melancholic brooding over the future.

None of these three creatures are negative in themselves: what is needed is not repression and conquest of their energies, but integration and transformation. As Erich Neumann writes, the notion of a "patriarchal victory" over the "luciferian dragons" activated by the emergence of the earth archetypes of the Great Goddess is no longer "at the disposal of modern men and women" (33; my trans.). What is required is not the "conquest of the evils, rather their redemption, not patriarchal victory, rather a transformation of that which is below."[2] What we find however in the Sumerian material is a kind of mixture of matriarchal and patriarchal approaches to the problem of what Hurwitz calls the "dark aspects of the feminine." Since Lilith, the Anzu bird, and the serpent would apparently be inconvenient bed or throne partners, Inanna solicits the help of her brother Gilgamesh (not the help of a lover) to drive the creatures away. This maneuver brings the Huluppu tree towards its third and final phase of development. This too is the first task of young manhood in relation to the feminine: to help her cope with her demons -- here to drive them away, *not to destroy them* (it was Nietzsche who said to be careful in the casting out of your devils lest you cast out your angels as well!). He must preserve their energies yet make sure they do not sabotage the creation of throne and bed for the young goddess, his sister. Gilgamesh therefore strikes the serpent, scares the Anzu bird off into the mountains (where the women both of Dionysian times and of today still go to retrieve the wild freedom of Artemis), and provokes Lilith to smash up her home and flee to the "wild, uninhabited places" from which she came (Wolkstein and Kramer 9). Then Gilgamesh carves a throne and a bed out of the wood of the Huluppu tree for his sister Inanna, while she gives him a staff and ring of royal rule. In these final forms the tree reaches the last stage of its cultivation, yielding (like the giving tree) the wood that through its death serves as the prop of royalty and of procreation: Inanna is now ready to assert the full power of her womanhood.

Before she can do so, however, and especially before her marriage (which will come only *after* her full development), Inanna must go on her first complete heroine's journey. "The Huluppu Tree" recorded the stages in the emergence of civilized life from its primitive roots in a gathering culture precedent to the high Neolithic of the Ancient Near

East. These stages corresponded roughly to the developments in childhood, which prepare the individual for the journeys to come. In the next stage, Inanna must acquire the rudiments of wisdom and retrieve the basic arts of civilization from Enki, the god of the waters. This heroic cycle will take her from Uruk, to Abzu and the sacred precincts of Eridu, and back to Uruk. During the journey, Inanna will steal the royal, divine, and human powers necessary to a fully functioning civilization and return them to her people in Uruk. At this point in her life, Inanna represents the Goddess as a patron of civilization, like Athena.

The journey begins when Inanna has reached physical maturity, yet is untried and unattached. Being single, she initiates her journey, simply deciding, as she leans against an apple tree in sheepfold marveling at the beauty of her vulva, to set forth in search of her maternal grandfather, Enki. He is in possession of the holy laws of heaven and earth., and he receives her so amicably that they get staggering drunk on Sumerian beer. During this marvelous binge, Enki bestows upon his favorite granddaughter the priesthood, godship, kingship, and the numerous powers and skills affiliated with her full maturity. These include all the basic arts, rites, judicial skills, powers of speech, lovemaking techniques, musical talents, and crafts of civilization. There is a delightful sense of Enki's participation in his own beguiling here that reminds one of Vivian's theft of Merlin's magic at the end of the old Druid's life. Inanna gathers the arts together into the Boat of Heaven and wisely departs before the beer wears off.

The whole episode is a wonderful example of the elixir theft motif as the climax of the heroine's journey. It shows us Inanna making full use of her education -- taking advantage of her male elders and having a good time along the way! The task now is to retain and exploit her newly won powers for the benefit of the community to which she returns as patron goddess. In order to do this she undergoes what Joseph Campbell calls the magic flight, fleeing with the treasures hard to attain and defending herself against the demons sent in pursuit by the sobered up Enki. This involves return threshold battles which suggest the dark turmoil of the educational process of winning the runes of wisdom. At this point she encounters the dark side of her male mentor, the wise old man turned dragon, unwilling to relinquish his powerful lore to a young woman.

Enki sends a sequence of six monsters after Inanna (*enkum* creatures, *uru* giants, *lakama* monsters, shrieking *kugalaga*, *enumun*, and watchmen of the Iturungal canal), but they are repulsed by Inanna's faithful steward Ninshubur (who will return to play a crucial role during Inanna's descent into the great below). Each monster represent an aspect of the shadow side of the wise old man, and in turn the abusive potentials of Inanna's own animus. The seventh monster to attack is Enki himself, only when he catches up to her, his monstrous aspect turns beneficial, as he grants his granddaughter full rights to the powers stolen, celebrates her new role a patron goddess of Uruk, and acknowledges a newly formed alliance between the cities of Eridu and Uruk (a political treaty which, psychologically, corresponds to a reconciliation between the unconscious and the ego).

Now firmly enthroned in a position of authority and power, with her own clearly defined selfhood, Inanna is ready for courtship and marriage. This seems the proper way of proceeding: selfhood first, a pre-requisite to marriage. The courtship of Dumuzi and Inanna is beautifully related in the Sumerian poem. Inanna must choose between the shepherd and the farmer, inclining originally to the farmer and rejecting Dumuzi. The situation suggests the conflict between Cain and Abel in the Old Testament, only here a Goddess must determine whose offering will be accepted! Out of this quarrelsome triangle, love is born, and the conflict between shepherd and farmer dissolves into a celebration of renewed fertility symbolized by the sacred marriage of Dumuzi and Inanna.

The courtship is one of the most beautiful love poems in world literature, but as it does not enact the heroine's journey cycle, I will now proceed to the third phase of Inanna's development: the mid-life passage into the underworld and the reconciliation with the powers of death and with the dark aspects of the feminine driven away earlier by Gilgamesh. This journey is recorded in the most famous of the Sumerian poems, "The Descent of Inanna to the Great Below." The departure is again self-initiated; Inanna simply "opens her ears" to the great below. She then abandons her seven temples in the seven cities of ancient Sumer, and adorns herself elaborately with the seven symbols of her royal power: crown, neck and breast beads, breastplate, golden bracelet, lapis measuring rod and line, and royal robe. This clothing scene is the prototype of all subsequent armings of the hero, a standard convention of the monomyth from ancient to modernist literature, just as Inanna's stripping down at the seven gates of the underworld will be the archetype of all subsequent divestitures in the long history of the hero journey. Here, the clothing with which Inanna adorns herself represents the formidable security of the Queen's worldly position, aspects of her ego or persona that will need to be stripped away before she can fully open her ear to the wisdom of the great below (the Jungian unconscious).

When she arrives at the gates of the *kur* (the Sumerian underworld), Inanna tells the threshold guardian, Neti, that she has come to participate in the funeral rites of Gugalanna: known as the "Bull of Heaven," he is the husband of Ereshkigal, Queen of the *kur*. Inanna asks for the beer of the funeral rites to be poured into the cups (can she beguile her dark sister Ereshkigal as she had Enki?) and then has each article of clothing stripped from her as she passes through each of the seven gates of the underworld, until she stands naked and bowed low before Ereshkigal in the throne room of the Queen of the Dead. Ereshkigal fastens the eye of death upon her, and the words of wrath and guilt are spoken against her: Inanna is turned into a rotting corpse and hung up like a piece of butchered meat from a hook on the wall.

The imagery of being stripped down, of having all that one had struggled to achieve brutally taken away, leaving one naked in the presence of death, is absolutely basic to the threshold crossings of the hero journey (all the way up to Thomas Pynchon's *The Crying of Lot 49*). Perhaps the imagery suggests the psychological trauma of mid-life, the breakdowns and divorces, the loss of jobs, libido, and prestige, those changes that feel like hell and remind us that we are only rotting corpses all 'hung up' about one problem or another. Any identity crisis can precipitate the hero journey at any time in life, of course, and always involves a death experience, during which the old vestments of the personality are stripped away, leaving a sense of nothingness.[3] But the mid-life problem is represented in "The Descent of Inanna" with a concision and intensity nearly unsurpassed in the history of world literature.

It is characteristic, however, of the polysemous nature of myths, that we might also see Inanna's descent as a cosmological image, representing the cyclical disappearance of Venus, the morning and evening star associated with the goddess and so important to literary history all the way up to the Hesperus and Vesperus trope in Tennyson's *In Memoriam*. In the Sumerian context, the seven gates through which Inanna passes represent the seven spheres of the planets, spheres through which the soul ascends, shedding its material sheathes after death; and through which it descends, before birth, from the spiritual realm into incarnation. In addition to this astronomical mysticism, we might also relate Inanna's descent to the fertility mysteries of the date palm (as Jakobson suggests), or see in these images of the cyclical death of Venus the vestiges of an actual ritual of suttee burial (as Joseph Campbell suggests).[4] Each approach to the symbolism of the seven gates (psychological, cosmological, social-political) yields a comprehensive unity characteristic of myth: our star begins to set at mid-life, our date palms to bear fewer fruit, and rituals of mourning and burial become, increasingly, a part of our yearly calendars.

The mythic journey here, however, reminds us that there is a passage through death, and a return journey to be made, perhaps as perilous as the departure from life. The sacred narrative of Inanna reminds us that what smells like death and feels like hell may actually be the labor pains of delivery. In "The Descent," Inanna instructs her faithful servant Ninshubur to solicit help if Inanna fails to return in three days time. Ninshubur goes first to Enlil and then to Nanna (Inanna's father and paternal grandfather) to petition for help in beautifully poetic prayers, thrice repeated. Both relatives on the male line refuse, self-righteously blaming the goddess for her own troubles. Only Enki, Inanna's maternal grandfather, the third deity summoned by Ninshubur, agrees to send help. Enki fashions two little asexual creatures (a *kurgarra* and a *galatur*) from the dirt between his fingernails, gives them the food and water of life, and instructs them to go to the underworld, where they will find Ereshkigal, Queen of the Dead, with her breasts uncovered and her hair swirling around her head like leeks (she is giving birth!). Once in the *kur*, the creatures are instructed simply to repeat the six lamentations Ereshkigal utters during her labor (everything hurts -- inside, outside, belly, back, heart, and liver!), until she stops and offers them a gift as reward for moaning and groaning in cadence with her agony (excellent advice for fathers here). The fingernail-fashioned emissaries then request the corpse of Inanna, which comes back to life after they sprinkle the bread and water of life upon it.

It is fascinating to speculate that what we have here is a eucharistic meal (bread and wine) associated with death and rebirth, along with a kind of crucifixion (Inanna is hung up on a peg for three days and three nights, after judgment is passed against her by Ereshkigal). In fact, when you consider the sacred marriage rituals in the courtship of Dumuzi, and the funeral rites in this section of "The Descent of Inanna," we have right here in Sumerian literature all the basic prototypes of the sacraments of the Church: Baptism, Confirmation, Marriage, Funeral Rites, Communion, and Crucifixion all in place by 2000 B.C.E. at the latest! The archetypal core of meaning shared by the sacraments of both the Sumerian and the Holy Roman theologies is death and rebirth, and the revelation of their mysterious unity. This revelation is in fact the climactic moment of the heroine's journey. Gugalanna's funeral, the original impetus of the descent, has here modulated into the moment of his birth, and the keening of Ereshkigal's lamentation becomes the crying of childbirth. As the Bull of Heaven, Gugalanna represents the moon, which dies each month to be reborn, just as Inanna as the evening star descends periodically into the dark domain of Ereshkigal (the *kur*) in order to be reborn. Sumerian cosmology situates the *kur* right above the primal waters from which all life comes, the *kur* monster having carried Ereshkigal down there when she was a maiden. It is appropriate then to find Ereshkigal at first mourning and then giving birth, since in her domain of the underworld, birth and death are flip sides of the same coin.

Inanna's return to the upperworld after Ninshubur effects her rescue, with the help of Enki's creatures, suggests a kind of power struggle
between matriarchal and patriarchal authorities. There is also a kind of
threshold battle to be fought during the return which parallels the stripping and death of Inanna during the descent. Inanna is only allowed to
return to her temples if a replacement is found to take her place in the
underworld. Terrifying demons of death, called the *galla*, accompany
Inanna on her return to choose her replacement. The *galla* neither eat,
drink, make offerings or libations accept gifts, enjoy love, or have
children. Sylvia Perera interprets them as the powerful energies of the
female shadow side activated by the journey into the unconscious (they
remind one of the "Schalengewalten," demonic forces activated by the
En-sof's turning inward towards the great darkness, which Gershom
Scholem describes in his recital of a kabbalistic myth (qtd. in Neumann
34)). The witch like hatred of the *galla* poisons everything around
Inanna with implacable jealous rage, showing us what happens when a
woman who has gone down into the darkness is overwhelmed by the
dark powers resident there (she becomes a fearsome Lilith).

These demons first allow Ninshubur, Inanna's servant, and her two
sons, Shara and Lulal, to go free, possibly because they dress in sackcloth, tear out their hair, and grovel in the dust at Inanna's feet when she
returns. Only Dumuzi, Inanna's husband, makes the fatal mistake of
remaining seated on his throne when his wife returns from her hellish
journey -- he fails to grovel and groan in acknowledgment of her suffering. Hence, the *galla* smash him up with axes, pour the milk out of
his churns, break his reed pipe, and send him wailing off into the
wilderness, where Utu the sun god changes him into a snake, and he
tries to wiggle out of the crisis. The entire episode is a wonderful distant reflection of a distraught husband unable to deal with menopause
and extreme PMS, both of which catapult Dumuzi into his own mid-life
hero journey (to be examined below).

The conflict between husband and wife, however, between king
and queen, also adds a political or cultural dimension to the heroine's
journey. Earlier we noted that the fathers in Inanna's family tree (Enlil
and Nanna) refused to help retrieve her from the underworld. Only
Enki, her maternal grandfather, responded to her need. This later confrontation with Dumuzi, much of whose power has been conferred upon
him by his wife through marriage, would seem to relate to the earlier
conflicts between Inanna and the patriarchal order: Dumuzi apparently
would like to remain on the throne provided him by his wife, while she
undergoes the terrible ordeal of the descent, but he is ultimately chas-
tened by the dark powers of the feminine deities Inanna and Ereshkigal.
If the conflict between husband and wife reflects a myth of marriage
crises at mid-life, it may also reflect the larger problem of a culture in

transition from a matriarchal to a patriarchal orientation (the poetry is a mixture of earlier non Indo-European Sumerian and later Semitic languages). It is interesting then that Inanna's journey results in a renewed equilibrium between masculine and feminine potencies quite unlike the complete denigration of the Goddess in the Hebrew Old Testament.[5]

This equilibrium is established by forcing Dumuzi to depart on his own mid-life journey to the underworld. Unlike Inanna, he must be forced off his throne (Inanna had gone willingly, setting her ear to the great below in sympathy with the grief of Ereshkigal). Another difference between the journeys is the intensity and violence of the threshold battle inflicted upon Dumuzi by the demons unleashed by his wife's return (Inanna had simply allowed herself to be stripped down, while Dumuzi resists the descent and flees). After Inanna fastens the eye of death on Dumuzi, while he stubbornly remains seated on his throne, the demonic *galla* smash him around and set off in pursuit as he flees to the steppes. It is interesting to note that Dumuzi begins his mid-life journey with a return to nature (like those middle-aged males Robert Bly, Sam Keen, and others tell us about, pounding drums in the forest and embracing trees) and with an archetypal dream which prefigures the basic tasks of his journey. Dumuzi lies down among the canals beside the frogs in the rushes and dreams of the reeds and tall trees rising terribly all around him. The single reed trembles sympathetically for him; the double reeds are taken away; and his churn, drinking cup, and shepherd's crook are shattered.

Upon waking, he takes this dream to his sister Geshtinanna for analysis: she becomes his therapist, ready to help him handle the revelations of his vision quest into the wilderness. As Jung noted, it is quite typical for analysis to be initiated by a powerful dream brought into the sessions by the analysand. It is also perhaps typical for this first dream (which contains the diagnosis and prognosis of the development to follow) to have been precipitated by a violent marital conflict and a related career crisis (Dumuzi gets knocked off his throne, i.e., loses his job and wife, so that his libido is turned inward on two accounts). Out of the stress of this situation, a numinous dream comes bubbling up from unsuspected depths, in compensation for the devastation of the ego and persona. Dumuzi has instinctively retreated to the rivers of life, where the rushes and the reeds whisper to him (as they did to Psyche during her marital crisis).

Geshtinanna goes through all the details of the dream systematically, seeing them as delineating a series of catastrophes to be inflicted upon Dumuzi by the demons unleashed upon him by his wife (the idea that women are incapable of violence should receive its final quietus here!). These catastrophes may also be seen as the disruptions of that stage of life which we simplistically refer to as retirement: Dumuzi's means of livelihood is destroyed, his shepherd crook broken, his lambs lost to the eagle, and the sheepfold rendered a "house of desolation ... given to the winds" (76-77). In addition, the natural pleasures of life lose their savor: the "drinking cup falls from its peg ... The churn lies silent; no milk is poured. / The cup lies shattered" (77). Such poignant images of the loss of li bido and the impotence of age! Gone the butter churn and the pouring of milk, images of sexuality used earlier to consecrate the sacred marriage. Only dread and the nameless anxieties of the wind remain.

To make matters worse, Dumuzi is betrayed by an old friend who informs the *galla* where to find him in the ditches of Arali. Dumuzi prays again to Utu, who turns Dumuzi into a gazelle as he flees first to Kubiresh, then to the refuge of the goddess Old Belili, and finally to his sister Geshtinanna's sheepfold, where he is captured and broken to pieces. One might see Dumuzi's behavior as typical of the male under marital stress, taking refuge with feminine family members, first his grandmother and then his sister. Dumuzi's response is similar to Cupid's in the tale of "Cupid and Psyche," in which Cupid retreats to his mother's home at the first sign of conflict in his relationship with Psyche. Dumuzi does him one better by retreating all the way back to the Great Mother herself, the source of all being, as if his conflict with Inanna had activated the deepest archetypal layers of a mother complex which is ultimately projected onto his sister Geshtinanna, in whose "sheepfold" he finally takes refuge (the Sumerian sheepfold being a euphemism for womb suggests an incestuous level of attachment). It is then the purpose of the *galla* sent after Dumuzi by his wife to sever these apron strings: Dumuzi is forcibly removed from the sheepfold and, in a classic instance of the divestiture motif of the hero journey, stripped of holy crown, royal garments, royal scepter, and holy sandals, leaving him bound and naked like Inanna in the underworld. These images powerfully express the pain of a man forced to relinquish worldly attachments and regressive yearnings simultaneously.

We do not have an account of Dumuzi's descent to Ereshkigal, for which he is now prepared. Instead the song ends with the magnificently poetic lamentations of three women (one thinks of the triple goddess, or of the three mourning women at the tomb of Jesus): Dumuzi's mother, wife, and sister. These personify the three fates and the three aspects of Dumuzi's own inner feminine principle, which serves here as impetus of his individuation journey. Inanna arranges for Dumuzi and his sister Geshtinanna to alternate terms in the underworld -- perhaps, as Jakobson suggests, an image of the cycles of the grain (Dumuzi) and the vine (Geshtinanna meaning grapevine). Dumuzi thus becomes the first of those dying and resurrecting gods (consorts of the Triple or Great Goddess) discussed by Frazer in *The Golden Bough*. His relationship with his sister Geshtinanna in particular is very beautifully wrought, and it parallels the earlier brother-sister relationship between Gilgamesh and Inanna. Taken together with the complex wife-sister relationship between Isis and Osiris in Egypt, these ancient prototypes of the hero and heroine's journey give us precious archetypal images of male-female sibling relationships (left relatively untouched by Christine Downing's recent book on sisters). In the Sumerian material, the relationship is important at puberty and then again at mid-life: Gilgamesh drives Inanna's demons away in the former, while Geshtinanna interprets Dumuzi's dreams and does time for him in the underworld in the latter. Our Sumerian cycle ends with Inanna's return to the temples she had left at the beginning of the descent, bringing our journey full circle, and restoring the goddess to a power deepened by the wisdom of the abyss.

Gilgamesh and Enkidu

The material combined in what we know as the *Epic of Gilgamesh* records the trials, ordeals, and initiations appropriate to the three basic stages of life's journey (youth, maturity, and old age) which parallel the heroine journey cycles of Inanna. Three separate but interrelated cycles of the journey occur in the *Epic* to provide a complete picture of male development. The first of these has to do with Enkidu, who represents the crisis of primitive masculine virginity at the point of transition into adulthood. Enkidu is created in response to the oppressive rule of Gilgamesh, King of Uruk, who dominates the male population by claiming first rights with all the virgins of the village! This grates on the nerves of the men, who get together to pray to Anu for relief. Anu responds by requesting that Aruru, the goddess who created Gilgamesh, now create an equal to challenge him. She does so by first conceiving an image in her mind, meditating upon it, and then fashioning her image in clay pinched from the waters and dropped into the wilderness far outside the city gates.

This is the first instance in the long lineage of hero journeys that begins with a state of political oppression which initiates the compensatory action and constitutes the call to adventure. Enkidu is also the root of a large genealogical tree of wild men of the woods, a root that will later branch off in characters like the Green Knight and Calogrenant (or Merlin) in the Arthurian tales of the Middle Ages. Enkidu has long womanly hair and a body matted with a cattle-like hide; he is completely uncouth, eating grass and roaming with gazelles and herds of wild game, tearing up traps set for them by hunters. Ontologically and phylogenetically, Enkidu represents primitive manhood, in a gathering stage of pre-civilized innocence, before even the emergence of hunting rituals: he is the wild child lurking in all male hearts, personal and collective, and his fall into the civilized ways of adult life still retains the power to move us deeply.

For Enkidu, the transformative call to adventure comes from a harlot whom a trapper arranges for him to meet, breasts bared, at the drinking hole where the wild herds congregate. She is the prototype of the women at the well of the Middle Ages, who stand as threshold guardians and guides on the journey into the wisdom of adulthood. She is also the instrument of the 'trapper' who in turn is an instrument of the will of the gods. What male is not trapped by his own thirst, to be subsequently bound by the conventions of civilized life and the domestic round? The harlot makes herself naked and gratifies the eagerness of Enkidu's thirst with six days and seven nights of love, numbers which suggest the creation of a new world and life for Enkidu: the wild animals now flee from him, and his newly forming human thoughts weaken and bewilder him (he is, for the first time, "sicklied o'er by the pale cast of thought," as Hamlet was too at the same time of life). The harlot then becomes his guide, and her words to Enkidu (that he has become wise and godlike, curious echo of Eve 's role in the much later Hebraic Garden) identify her in the archetypal role as both temptress and psychopomp (like Homer's Kirke), who transforms, recreates, and instructs the hero in the ways of his new life. She is, in short, a civilizing force, like Athena, or Inanna, a feminine muse of the arts and crafts of a highly developed culture.

It is important then that the symbolism of clothing is employed to represent Enkidu's transformation: the harlot divides her clothing in half to dress him, then leads him into the shepherd's tent, where he is anointed with oil and clothed as a man. We have moved, that is to say, quite eloquently and quickly, in a concise progression from the Paleolithic hunter-gatherer, to the herders of the Semitic region, with a new suit of clothes to signify the development. One further step takes us into the city of Uruk, where Enkidu is drawn by the challenge of subduing Gilgamesh. "I have come to change the old order," Enkidu announces, in a phrase destined to become a stock cliché of world politics. Meanwhile, Gilgamesh, who has dreamt twice of the coming of Enkidu, prowls the streets of Uruk, ready to take the bride before the bridegroom. Enkidu blocks his way, and they wrestle like bulls, breaking doorposts before swearing friendship in a particularly amicable version of the threshold battle. Notice the motif of the doorway, which we will find surfacing again and again in the iconography of the hero journey. After breaking doorways, Enkidu is escorted through a gateway into his new life in the city. This journey, then, reverses what will later be the standard direction of the cycle, from city into forest, which is the direction of the second hero journey in the *Epic*, when Gilgamesh and Enkidu go to the land of the Cedar Forest.

This second journey, like the first, begins with a sense of oppression, but of a different nature, no longer political but internal, a matter of mood and of what the Jungians call an *abaîssement du nîveau mental,* a depressive lowering of the spirits which activates the unconscious. Enkidu and Gilgamesh are both apparently oppressed by idleness and a sorrowful awareness of mortality, which then compels them to undertake a quest for famous deeds that will preserve their names for posterity. These deeds, as it turns out, are appropriate to the second phase of the male cycle, which involves those mature achievements that fulfill his destiny, establish worldly power, and contribute to the growth and stability of the community. For the purpose of the second journey is to defeat Humbaba, the ferocious giant who guards the cedar woods. The two heroes will then deforest the mountains, and return to Uruk with wood to be used for building the temple. In so doing, Gilgamesh and Enkidu will open and protect trade routes into the dangerous mountains of the North.

The preparations for the journey are elaborate, and they establish the conventions of epic poetry. First the warriors procure divine assistance from Shamash, who promises Gilgamesh the protection of the eight winds, a pledge reinforced by the prayers of the queen Ninsun. Special weapons (axes, swords, and bows) are then forged and advice given the hero by a public council. All of these preparations anticipate such famous scenes of the arming of the hero as those which occur in the *Odyssey* and *Sir Gawain and the Green Knight*. The arming and propitiation of divine energies prepare the psyche for its ordeals, and activate the much needed reservoirs of courage and fortitude essential to the accomplishment of the task at hand. We still find such ceremonials performed in locker rooms, both athletic and military, all over the world.

Once armed, the heroes journey three days and cross seven mountains, before arriving at the threshold gateway into the great forest, through which they pass to reach the foot of the green mountain, a dwelling place of the gods (both the gate and mountain icons will become *de rigueur* in the subsequent history of the hero journey). We should remember that the Sumerian word for mountain, *kur*, also means underworld; we find this symbolic affiliation all the way from the Egyptian netherworld of the *Tuat* to the fairy hills of Celtic folklore in such medieval works as *Sir Orfeo*. At the foot of the green mountain, Gilgamesh digs a well before the setting sun and pours fine meal on the ground (much like the propitiatory invocations performed at the entrance to the Kimmerian underworld in Book 11 of the *Odyssey*, or by Jason summoning Hecate in *The Voyage of the Argo*). This ritual yields a sequence of premonitory dreams: of fighting a wild bull, of being struck down by a mountain, and of a truly apocalyptic scene of tempest, lightning, fire, and death.

Enkidu interprets the first two of these dreams as favorable omens of victory, but the third is left unglossed. The intensification of dream activity is a characteristic feature of the hero journey, one which suggests the dissolution of the ego into the deep currents of the imagination, so that the center of awareness shifts towards the archetypal depths of the soul. The hero journey always involves an internal dimension of meaning, in which external events become symbolic of psychic states of altered consciousness. Whenever life pushes us into crisis, the big dreams begin to boil up from the cauldron of the unconscious to serve as guides and props. Many of these dreams stick with us all of our lives, as real as any event recorded by the waking brain. In the Gilgamesh material, these crisis dreams occur in incremental groups of three, which lead up to a climactic revelation of more than merely personal significance (here the apocalyptic vision of the end of all time). The dreams move through increasingly dreadful images of annihilation: from bull, to mountain, to cosmic cataclysm. These images prepare Gilgamesh for action in the external world: the day after the dreams, he defeats the giant guardian of the mountain herds, Humbaba, by extinguishing his mysterious "seven splendors." Gilgamesh then clears the forest all the way from the mountain to the land of the Euphrates, and the heroes return home triumphantly bearing the elixir won by the ordeal -- the cedar wood from the "land of the living" that will be used to build temple and palace (much as the wood of the Huluppu tree was used to build throne and bed for Inanna).

The return to Uruk completes the cycle of the second hero journey in the *Epic*. It represents the culmination of Gilgamesh's worldly career and the attainment of the goals appropriate to the first half of life: no longer the tyrannical, lust-ridden adolescent stealing brides, he is now a responsible contributing member of the adult community. The transition is signified, once again, by a change of clothes: on his return to Uruk, Gilgamesh sheds the stained clothing of the journey and puts on his royal robes and glorious crown -- a linkage between homecoming and splendid reinvestiture which anticipates the biblical clothing symbolism in the story of Joseph and the Gnostic imagery of the royal mantle in the "Hymn of the Pearl" (see below). But this homecoming quickly leads to a new departure, in this case precipitated by the death of Enkidu, who is cursed by the gods for killing Humbaba and the Bull of Heaven, which is sent by Ishtar to avenge her rejection by Gilgamesh when he returns from his journey to the mountains. As so often in the hero journey, the call to adventure, which disrupts our daily lives and initiates the separation from the domestic security of a familiar environment, is death, and it leads to a quest beyond the worldly power of mature manhood for the everlasting wisdom of old age.

The tablets of the *Epic of Gilgamesh* devoted to the death of Enkidu elaborately delineate the circumstances leading up to the departure of Gilgamesh on his third and final heroic quest. He must first resist the Circean seduction of Ishtar, the goddess of love who has a habit of changing her lovers into animals (Gilgamesh would be her seventh victim). She offers him fertility and the complacency of worldly power, which Gilgamesh must now reject in order to proceed along the path of individuation. He must not retreat into the lair of middle age, for those who do, Ishtar seems to tell us, become less than human: the poisonous lust of complacency in the sheepfold of the goddess, the myth says, breaks the wing of birds, buries lion hearts beneath seven pits, sadistically spurs the stallion to exhausting performances, makes shepherds wolf like and devours them with their own dogs, and transforms the gardener into a blind mole burrowing through the dark alleys of desire. All of these metamorphoses recounted by Ishtar are metaphors for the various perils of mid-life, and they show the dark side of those mistaken anima projections that destroy the lives of so many males in our culture, whose crisis leaves them crippled, stifled, sado-masochistic, and groping blindly for the meaning in their suffering. Gilgamesh escapes this fate by spurning the spurious allure of Ishtar, who here represents not so much some external female temptation, as those regressive tendencies in the male which drive him towards some more or less infantile state of gratification or frustration. In taking a stand against Ishtar, Gilgamesh is taking a stand against those forces within himself which would imprison him and prevent further growth.

Since hell, however, hath no fury like a woman scorned, Ishtar responds by soliciting revenge from her father Anu, king of the gods, whom she asks to release the Bull of Heaven to destroy Gilgamesh. In a fascinating anticipation of *Genesis* (still nearly one thousand years in the future), Anu warns that if he in fact releases the Bull on the people of Uruk there will be seven years of draught and famine. Ishtar replies that she has saved sufficient grain to feed the people for seven years (A female Joseph!). Gilgamesh and Enkidu destroy this Bull in an apocalyptic battle before the gates of Uruk, during which a sequence of bull snorts unleashes a series of cataclysms, like the blowing of the trumps in St. John's *Apocalypse*. Enkidu then humiliates Ishtar by throwing a bloody bull thigh in her face, but Gilgamesh responds rather more respectfully by fashioning a famous icon of gold plate and lapis lazuli horns out of the remains of the Bull, such as the glorious one excavated from the Royal Cemetery of Ur (Campbell, *Atlas* 2.1.78-83).

The psychological message of this scene seems to be that there is a price to be paid for, and a means of propitiation of, the spurning of anima enticements in mid-life. The price has to do with the willingness to accept the continued strife and conflict of our relationships, rather than relaxing into the cheap comforts of some promised relief (like divorce or some superficial affair). For this task the courage to endure seven year famine of emotional drought is required, suggesting a need to overcome one's infantile yearning for maternal tenderness and support from one's mate or some other source. Gilgamesh *must* undergo the pain and anxiety of separation from the feminine (within and without) in order to proceed to the third heroic quest of masculine individuation. Resisting the feminine, in whatever form she takes, is the first step to further growth at this point of life, and it is as anxiety and pain ridden a step as the first step away from the mother in childhood, which in a way in reenacts.

It is a kind of death, in fact, which involves deprivation and loss. Enkidu is struck down shortly after slaying the Bull, and he quickly sickens and dies over a ten day period. We also begin to lose our dearest friends during mid-life. This case is particularly painful, since Enkidu dies cursing his life. But a vivid dream vision of the underworld provides some guidance (if not exactly consolation) and helps reconcile him to the inevitable. He passes through those stages of the death and dying process which Elizabeth Kübler-Ross called the final stage of growth (anger, denial, depression, acceptance, and joy). After the death sentence is passed against Enkidu by a council of gods (which Enkidu witnesses in a dream), he becomes enraged and curses the cedar wood of the gateposts, for which he had urged Gilgamesh to slay Humbaba; he also curses the trapper who tricked him by the water hole, and the harlot who seduced him. As his anger turns to depression and grief, he weeps before the sun god Shamash, who then calms Enkidu by reminding him of the good things in his life (to balance the scales of judgment). It is only after this initial reconciliation with death that Enkidu is granted his great dream vision of the underworld, as if to suggest that the ego must be both annihilated and pacified before the archetypal reservoirs of the unconscious bubble up from below to sustain us in our hour of need.

The dream anticipates Enkidu's final hero journey to the land from whose bourn no traveler returns, and gives him some sense of orientation that will help him endure the traumatic transfiguration of the psyche which we call death. This ultimate metamorphosis is imagined as a transformation of Enkidu: a bird with a vampire face, lion's foot, and eagle claw lacerates and smothers Enkidu, changes his arms into wings covered with feathers, and then leads him into the palace of Ishalla, the Queen of Darkness.[6] All of the people in this palace are clothed like birds, but see no light; the king and even the gods now become servants, and a procession of acolytes and high priests perform ecstatic incantations, while Belit-Sheri records her judgments of the souls in a book of the dead. The dream is terrifying, but, as the text says, "we must treasure the dream whatever the terror; for the dream has shown that misery comes at last comes to the healthy man, the end of life is sorrow" (93). Enkidu then dies after reviewing his entire life in a powerful hymn of lamentation.

It is the death of Enkidu that initiates the last hero journey in the *Epic*, which is really a search for "everlasting life," in the form of that mature wisdom of old age that enables the blessed among us to accept life and death on its own terms. Gilgamesh laments the loss of his friend bitterly for seven days and nights (as if undoing the Creation) until the worm fastens on the corpse. His despair and fear of death then lead to his departure for Dilmun, the land called Faraway, where Utnapishtim has lived ever since the Flood. This journey is the archetype of all successive journeys to the otherworld in our literary tradition; along with the "Descent of Inanna," it provides our first images of the *nekyia*. The threshold crossing occurs in the mountain passes where Gilgamesh strikes and scatters lions prowling around him in the moonlight, and then encounters man-scorpions who guard the gates into the great mountains of Mashu (gateway and mountain imagery coalescing again to form the archetype here). The peaks of these mountains reach up into heaven, while the bases sink down into the underworld. The scorpions at the gates have a stare that kills (remember Ereshkigal's *eye* of death fastened on Inanna in the *kur*), and beneath the mountains are the twelve leagues of darkness that Gilgamesh must traverse in order to reach the garden of the gods at the edge of a distant sea. The darkness below the mountains is as terrifying and thick as the light of the garden beyond is joyous and radiant. After eight leagues in the darkness, Gilgamesh screams, after nine he feels a light wind, and after eleven a slight glimmer of light appears at the end of the tunnel. After twelve leagues, light streams out as Gilgamesh emerges into a garden by the sea, with bushes bearing gemstones, agate, and pearls of instead of thistles and thorns. Here lives the radiant woman of the vine, Siduri, tending her golden bowls and vats and covered with a veil. She is the one who will direct Gilgamesh to the yonder shore where Utnapishtim lives.

As an image of the natural cycles of death and rebirth, the journey through the darkness beneath the mountains to the garden of Siduri reflects the diurnal passage of the sun (Shamash, the sun god, greets Gilgamesh at the end of the twelve leagues of the night). As a psychological image, however, it bears a striking resemblance to the near death narratives now being recorded and analyzed in great numbers by a variety of specialists in different disciplines.[7] The epic and the clinical versions of the death journey have a great deal in common: most fundamentally we have the image of biological death in the form of the scorpions, then the journey through the dark tunnel towards a radiant realm of light, and the greeting by a numinous being who serves henceforth as guide and guardian of the revelations which ensue. As a mythological image crucial to the historical development of the genre, the *Epic* anticipates the wanderings of Odysseus, which bring him to the island of another daughter of the sun, Circe, who offers a potent wine and then directs Odysseus across the sea of death to a meeting with another sage of the otherworld, Tiresias.

Such paradisal landscapes presided over by beings of light and feminine soul guides will punctuate the entire history of literary voyages to the otherworld from Homer, to the Grail and fairy legends of the Middle Ages, to the stories of Ambrose Bierce in the 19th century, to the novels of Hermann Broch in the 20th. Such promises of ultimate wisdom, peace, and knowledge as we will find in the *Epic of Gilgamesh*, we shall find many more times in the revelatory initiations of the hero journeys to come. Common to both the literary and the clinical line is the encounter with an ancestral figure, whose omniscience or immortality radiates that peace which passes all understanding. It is to such a figure, Utnapishtim, that Siduri now directs Gilgamesh.

He is first directed to Urshanabi, the ferryman to the yonder shore and prototype of Charon, but, in an inexplicable fit of rage, Gilgamesh smashes up the tackle of the ferryboat, and must therefore cut 120 stakes to be used as punting poles to cross the waters of death. Urshanabi guides Gilgamesh to Dilmun the land of the Faraway where Utnapishtim lives immortally. Gilgamesh tells the story of his journey and then asks about the living and the dead. All Utnapishtim can do is communicate images of impermanence: only the nymph of the dragonfly sheds her larva to see the sun in its full glory. The message is essentially Buddhist (all is sorrowful, all is empty), and it echoes the preacher of Ecclesiastes (all is vanity). But the message also gives us our first image of the butterfly as a symbol of resurrection. Aware of the fact that the message is a frustrating one to Gilgamesh, who has traveled such a perilous journey in search of everlasting life, Utnapishtim decides to tell the story of how he obtained immortality: "I will reveal to you a mystery," he says, "I will tell you a secret of the gods" (109).

The revelation of the secret mysteries of the gods constitutes the climactic moment of initiation in the hero journey, and here the revelation comes in the form of a story, a very famous first version of the Flood myth we know from *Genesis,* only considerably earlier. The fact that the ultimate revelation of wisdom comes in the form of a sacred narrative suggests an early and close relationship between the hero journey and *poesis*, the making of poems and stories, as if the journey is somehow a self-reflexive representation of the creative process itself (the story is about itself coming into being): the journey here is a story which yields another story, and that story itself bears life giving and sustaining powers. Gilgamesh will later lose the flower that restores youth to old age, but nothing can take the story away -- it becomes a talisman of mythic power, specifically of the power to reveal those mysteries of wisdom that somehow bestow meaning upon our latter years and days, in spite of the full awareness of our fragility and brevity. The *story* is the flower which the wily serpent cannot eat; the *story* is the flower through which we learn to shed our skins to become new beings.

The actual plant with the power to make the old young lies at the bottom of the sea. After hearing the story of the flood, and then falling asleep for seven days in his failed attempt to win immortal life, Utnapishtim instructs Gilgamesh to go to the washing place and to throw off his animal skins. There he washes his long hair as clean as snow, the sea carries away his skins, the sparkle of his eyes is renewed, and he is given a fresh set of clothes which will show no sign of age until he reaches Uruk. Once again the symbolism of divestiture and adornment of the body with sacred garments marks a crucial turning point in the transformations ordained by the hero journey. The animal skins which Gilgamesh sheds here represent the body discarded at death, and the fresh suit of immortal clothing represents the robe of glory of the later Gnostic tradition, i.e., the spiritual body of a transfigured existence to be put on after the resurrection according to St. Paul.

After this ritual baptism (which discards the body of the Old Adam), Gilgamesh then retrieves the magic youth-bestowing plant from the ocean floor, and resolves not to eat it immediately, but to take it back home for the elders of Uruk: no longer the self-seeking hero out for his own glory, Gilgamesh has now achieved that concern for others which is the mark of the wisdom of old age. After retrieving the plant, however, he loses it, while sleeping on his return journey, to a serpent, which immediately sheds its skin after eating the fruit. (Fruit and serpent become symbols in the cylinder seals of this period, symbols which suggest a sacrificial meal that included the consumption of an ambrosial beverage carried in a pale of the gods).[8] After losing the flower, the only elixir left is the story Gilgamesh returns to Uruk to tell: "He was wise, he saw mysteries and knew secret things, he brought us a tale of the days before the flood" (117).

The Egyptian Books of the Dead

Every tourist who visits Egypt goes one morning across the river Nile at Luxor, from the eastern to the western bank, to walk up into the Valley of the Kings, where the tombs of the great Pharaohs lie beneath the sun roasted mountains, and then finishes the day returning by ferry or falucca to the eastern bank for the son et lumière at the Temple of Karnac. In so doing, those tourists are traversing the path of the ancient hero journey of the soul, following the sun from the eastern shore of its rising, to the western shore of its setting, back again at dawn to repeat the diurnal cycle. The Egyptian version of the monomyth must be pieced together from the innumerable representations of the soul's journey through the underworld to found illustrated on the walls of the great tombs, and in the pages of the papyri of the Books of the Dead, buried with less fortunate members of the society who could afford paper, but not granite versions of the soul's guidebook to the afterlife. Although incomprehensibly archaic, our knowledge of these early forms of the hero journey cycle comes largely from the images in the tombs, and from three versions of the Book of the Dead: the great work called "Coming Forth by Day," already antiquated by about 3500 B.C.E., when the priests added new chapters and edited old ones, and later adapted by the Theban priests of the New Empire in about 1650 B.C.E. into two compilations, known as "The Book of That Which is in the Tuat," and the "Book of Pylons," sometimes called the "Book of Gates" (Budge 174). It is to these books, tomb paintings, relief sculptures, and a variety of papyri (such as the Papyrus of Ani in the British Museum) that we owe many of the motifs of the heroic descent to the underworld to be examined in the following chapters.

While the entire topic of Egyptian mythology is notoriously complex, there are single simple images which condense the basic themes into the context of the hero journey cycle. One such image is to be found on the ceiling of a chamber in the back of the Temple of Hathor at Dendera, from Hellenistic times. We look up at a sculpted relief showing the Goddess Nut arching in a kind of cat posture with her hands and feet extended to anchor each of the four quarters of the composition (which symbolize the four cardinal points of the compass). She devours a solar disk that travels through her body, which is both the tomb into which the sun descends nightly, and the womb from which it is reborn at dawn; for we also see the solar disk emerging from the loins of the Goddess and projecting rays of life downwards towards the earthly image of the cow-eyed Goddess Hathor. The image represents the whole cycle of life, a hero journey presided over by the Goddess, in whose womb and tomb we all live and die, including the Gods, and in whose body the mysteries of death and transfiguration take place. The image was one of the great idées fixe of Ancient Egypt, with several other noteworthy examples -- including a stone relief mandala from the British Museum depicting three solar disks, with winged uraeus serpents, passing through the womb of the Goddess (Jung, *Mandala* Fig. 47); and, perhaps most famously, the grand cathedral like tomb of Seti I, which shows not one but two images of the solar journey through the wombs of two Goddesses, placed back to back on the immense ceiling, each with ten solar disks traveling through their bodies, and with two additional disks, one at the mouth, and one emerging from the womb (Hornung 474). The twelve disks represent the twelve stages of the diurnal journeys of the sun, both through the underworld below, and through the heavens above. For ultimately, "ascent and descent fall together": "Both, the depths of the womb of the Goddess above us and the abyss of the underworld beneath us, are the same realm, in which, following the path of the sun, all constellations and all being renews itself" (Hornung 475; my trans.).

One last, and particularly beautiful hieroglyph, containing the entire hero journey cycle of soul and sun in a single image, is to be found inscribed in the sarcophagus hall of Ramses III. There we see the Pharaoh's name inside a sun disk formed by a double uroborous (two snakes biting their tales), which is itself encircled by twelve stars alternating with twelve suns. The two Goddesses of the Hours ("Stundengöttin") lie prone with arms raised in worship on either side of the circular cartouche, within which we find the the Pharaoh's name, "Mes", meaning born, and, along the inner circle of the double uroborous forming the cartouche, twelve goddesses lying prone with arms uplifted to worship two more large solar disks. A bearded mummy with two large uraeus cobras on either side stands on top of the outer edge of the circle, which represents the complete hero journey cycle of sun, star, and Pharaoh, all constantly being reborn into new life (Hornung 466).

The texts which normally accompanied these images on the walls, ceilings, and sarcophagi of the Kings, were taken from the Books of the Dead, both of which traverse complete cycles of the hero journey, from sundown to sunup, through the twelve chambers of the underworld, the Tuat. These are notoriously complex books, so that I can only focus on some of the motifs commonly to be found in the hero journey cycles which follow the Egyptian prototypes, from Ancient times all the way up to the present: images of the night-sea journey, mountains, doorways, divestiture, decapitation, serpents, star, sun, and moon all converge here for the first time as standard icons of the journey. The first hour of the night from the Book of Pylons establishes a basic iconography of the hero journey, of which we will find many more examples: it shows a boat traveling up a river between two mountains towards a door guarded by a large serpent standing on its tail -- boat, river, moun-tain, twilight, serpents, solar symbolism, and doorways are all motifs long to be associated with the monomyth. The serpent sheds its skin to be reborn, like the sun emerging from the darkness, and it is therefore to be found guarding the pylons of each chamber of the underworld. Certain spells and incantations recited over the serpents are typically to be found inscribed in the elaborate hieroglyphic margins beside the pylons which separate the chambers of the underworld (Wilkinson 138). The pylon of the twelfth hour is particularly ornate, including two poles surmounted by bearded heads representing the sun god, the two uraeus serpents of Isis and Nephthys, an enormous long serpent stand-ing on its tail, and two mummies at the two twisting corners of the doorway passage (Budge 203). The fact that certain spells and incanta-tions are needed to pass through these twelve doorways connects the whole idea of the hero journey with poesis, for, from the very begin-ning, the descent to the underworld required the composition of espe-cially inspired, important poems to record and facilitate the journey.

Variations on threshold imagery occur throughout the twelve hours of the Egyptian night sea journey, often in association with other archetypal motifs frequently to be found in association with the mono-myth. The second hour, for example, shows four dead men and twenty prisoners with hands tied behind their backs, on the left bank of the river: these are the enemies of Ra, who attempt to impede his passage (Budge 180), and their presence establishes a basic metaphor of the hero journey linking the underworld with bondage, captivity, and im-prisonment. Souls will be bound or set free by descents ever afterwards, by such heroes as Jesus, Aladdin, Orpheus, Hermes, and Lancelot. Variations on the threshold imagery of doorways occur in the third, fourth, and sixth hours of the Book of Pylons: in the third we see the twelve holy gods of the Tuat, each in his shrine, with the doors open, and a huge snake lying across the tops (Budge 182); in the fourth we see a long sepulchral building with nine chapel doors, each containing a mummified god lying prone (Budge 186); and, most significantly, in the sixth hour the pylon opens into a chamber with Osiris seated at the top of nine steps, the Lord of the Staircase (Budge 189). Separate chambers and staircases will continue to be associated with the hero journey from Aladdin to the films of Bergman, Cocteau, and Murnau. Since Osiris is the Lord of death and resurrection, the ascent at the sixth, darkest hour of the soul's journey symbolizes the resurrection to come, a theme most thoroughly treated in the tenth, eleventh, and twelfth hours of the Book of Pylons. In the tenth, we see a winged ser-pent precede the solar barge (a symbol we know from the plumed Mayan serpent Quetzalcoatl), and, on the left bank of the river, we see two pedestals: a baboon with a five pointed star above his head on one, and, on the other, a right (solar) eye pectoral, known as the wedjat or eye of Horus (Budge 197; Wilkinson 43). Baboon, eye, and star all serve as heralds of the dawn: the baboons gather in large clusters to greet the dawn with raucous cries in the trees of the Sudan; the star is the morning star (Hesperus) which we see in Sumerian myth as a symbol of rebirth; and the eye of Horus plays a special role in the resurrection magic that resuscitates Osiris, slain by his brother Set. Taken all together, the eye, star, and doorway form an icon of the journey to and return from the underworld that we saw in our discussion of the Sumerian Goddess Inanna.

The last dramatic hour of the journey, the twelfth, depicts the completion of the night-sea cycle: it shows the god Nu holding up the sun barge after it passes triumphantly through the last doors of the Tuat, and emerges into the light of day (Budge 203). A scarab beetle pushes a large solar disk upwards towards the outstretched arms of Nut, the sky Goddess whom we saw on the ceiling of the temple at Dendera, devouring and giving birth to the sun. She is shown here standing on the head of Osiris, who forms a kind of island above the boat by bending completely around so that the tips of his toes touch the back of his head. It is worth pointing out that this elaborate yoga posture may be taken as an icon of the entire hero journey cycle, which has now come full circle. This dramatic moment of the return from the underworld in the twelfth hour became a kind of fixation for the Osirian cults. Their most typical symbol of the resurrection shows a pillar (symbol of Osiris) surmounted by an ankh sprouting arms raised in worship from the cross beneath the loop and supporting a solar disk. Three baboons on either side of the sun lift their arms up in a similar gesture of praise, as do the two kneeling Goddesses on either side of the pillar, Isis and Nephthys, sisters of Osiris and instrument of his resurrection (Clayton 137). The baboons, as we have seen, appear also in the tenth hour of the Book of Pylons -- they celebrate the return of the sun god with their characteristic pandemonium; the pillar is the one Isis made from the erica tree in which Osiris was entombed in the palace of Byblos -- it is a kind of doorpost, much like the symbol of Inanna in Sumerian myth. The twin sister Goddesses, Isis and Nephthys, are the same we saw pushing the sun across the sky in the insignia of Ramses III -- they represent the dual powers of the womb and the tomb. The cross finds its prototype here in the ankh on the pillar -- when Christians want to 'say' resurrection, they draw a cross, just as the Egyptians did thousands of years before.

Threshold imagery remains an important feature in other papyri and Books of the Dead which depict the soul's hero journey into the afterlife. In the Book of That Which is in the Underworld, from the tomb of Seti I, the solar barge is shown passing up the river by enigmatic doorways on the shores in the seventh, eighth, and tenth hours of the night. In the seventh hour, four goddesses guard the entrances to four tombs of Osiris, with two heads on either cornice, and mounds of sand inside each for the dead souls of god to lie upon (Budge 232-35). The heads may well represent human sacrifices associated with the building of the tombs and the descent to the underworld, and they come to form a characteristic feature of sacred architecture all over the world, as we know from such Romanesque doorways as Dysert O'Dea and Clonfert in Ireland, both with numerous heads over the arches (Cunliffe 84), or the heads of the exfoliating green men on the portals of the south transept at Chartres or the north choir door at Freiburg im Breisgau (Anderson 82-88). We will also find the decapitation theme again during Sir Gawain's journey to the Green Chapel, and in many Russian folktales. In the eighth hour of the Book of the Tuat, nine decapitated heads dangle from a hieroglyph meaning "servant," with another hieroglyphic for the word "linen" in front of them, and with six doorways surrounding them. Each doorway leads into those circles of the underworld through which Ra must wander, and passage through each of the doorways is predicated upon reciting sacred incantations. The beings of each circle then answer through these doorways, in the voices of bees, weeping women, men who moan, and lamenting bulls (Budge 239-40). I emphasize the linkage between doorways and hieratic speech because it suggests the kind of linkage between the hero journey and poesis which will persist all the way up through Ambrose Bierce to Joseph Conrad. The Papyrus of Ani, on the second floor of the British Museum, makes the connection between poesis and the heroic passage through a sequence of seven doorways quite clear: the entire scroll is covered with the sacred hieroglyphics of liturgies, prayers, hymns, and incantations with make up the poem as a whole.

Images of poesis are also central in what is perhaps the best known climax of the hero journey of the soul in all of Egyptian mythology: the last judgment scene. In all of these scenes, the God known as Thoth records the judgment in the book of life (prototype of John's vision of the Apocalypse). As the god who invented letters and writing, Thoth later becomes Hermes in Hellenistic syncretism, the guide of souls to the underworld and the archetype of the writer. In the very ancient papyrus illumination from the Book of the Dead of Kenna, from the 19th Dynasty, Thoth is the sacred baboon tending the two scales of the judgment, one of which holds the heart of the deceased in a canopic jar, and the other the feather of truth (Maat). A chimera with crocodile snout bisecting the balance beam of the scales between nodules 3 and 4 (there are eight total) will swallow any soul whose heart, by virtue of its 'sins' or attachment to the world, is heavier than the feather. Joseph Campbell suggests an analogy between the lower three nodules and the kundalini chakras of eating (Muladhara), sexuality (Svadhishthana), and power (Manipura), attachment to which imprisons the soul; while the upper four nodules represent the higher life of the heart (Anahata), throat (Visuddha), brow (Ajna), and crown (Sahasrara) chakras (*Inner Reaches* 65, 84; *Mythic Image* 330-90). In the very famous Papyrus of Ani from the British Museum, Thoth is Ibis, not baboon headed. He stands prominently with quill in hand recording the judgment, to the scales of which the dog-headed deity of mummification, Anubis, escorts the soul of Ani, clad in brilliant linen. The whole climax of the journey, the image seems to suggest, is an act of poesis, as the story of the soul is written down by the god of scribes and writing: if nothing else, the descent to the underworld produces another chapter in the huge Book of Life, at which Thoth remains at work throughout all eternity.

Odysseus

Homer's *Odyssey* has been the focus of a innumerable commentaries. James Hillman discusses the way wounding opens up the ego to the archetypal depths of the psyche, and he suggests that the scar of Ulysses (a thigh wound inflicted during a boar hunt in his youth) indicates the special relationship Ulysses has to the feminine, death, or the sea of the unconscious. This unique balance enables Ulysses to bypass the normal senex-puer conflict in favor of a unique harmony between the archetypal or human realms ("Puer Wounds" 100-128). For Joseph Campbell, the *Odyssey* dramatizes the reemergence of the goddess during the 8th century B.C., after a long period of repression by the heroic patriarchs of Troy ("The Great Goddess" 84). Murray Stein also focuses on the collapse of the patriarchal orientation of the persona after the Trojan War, taking the return of Odysseus to Penelope as a model for the mid-life crisis. His interpretation focuses on the roles Hermes plays in the *Odyssey* (guide, thief, protector, or companion) as aspects of the "liminality" of the mid-life transition (*In Mid-life* 129).

None of these commentaries, as valuable and indispensable as they are, have developed in detail the full range of Odysseus' experience of the feminine in the poem, an experience which follows the pattern of the progressive integration of the anima. Jung wrote that this assimilation occurs in four stages: the instinctual (Eve), the romantic (Helen), the spiritual (Mary), and the sagacious (Athena). What we find in the *Odyssey* is precisely this paradigm of integration, in which the four stages of the anima are represented by Circe, Calypso, Nausicaa, and Penelope.[9] Furthermore, each encounter with the archetypal feminine in the poem re-enacts the death and rebirth mysteries celebrated at

Eleusis, leading towards the final integration of the anima into human life, symbolized by the reunion of Odysseus and Penelope.

The encounters of Odysseus with the archetypal dimensions of the feminine occupy Books V-XII of the *Odyssey*, in which Odysseus tells the story of his sea-adventures to Alkinoos and the court of the Phaiakians. Yet the entire progress of the narrative presses towards the reunion of the wanderer with his wife Penelope, a painstakingly diffi-cult achievement which takes up the last twelve books of the poem. This suggests that the final goal of his individuation process is the inte-gration of the anima in fully human terms, and a reconciliation of the unconscious night-sea world of his oneiric wanderings with the domes-tic concerns of daily life. Hence the narrative traces the gradual trans-formation of the Odyssean anima from its most primitive to its most civilized levels. Although in an actual analysis these levels are always mixed up together, and the notion of a final goal seems inadequate, Homer's poem establishes clear differentiations between facets of the anima, and posits a final destination as the lodestar of psychic growth.

This becomes clear when we chart the peregrinations of Odysseus according to their chronological order--the narrative order is compli-cated by the fact that Odysseus doesn't begin his story until Book V, af-ter the first four books launch his son Telemachus on a journey in quest of his father, and after most of his adventures have occurred. The actual order of the sea-adventures, then, is skewed by the aesthetic frame-tale device, which transforms a straightforward plot into a reflective flash-back (Isn't this also an accurate metaphor for the way analysis pro-ceeds? For the way it provides a context for our stories and gives them shape and significance?). Discussions of the mythological and psycho-logical significance of the *Odyssey*, therefore, almost always recon-struct the story of the wanderings by beginning at the beginning, whereas Homer begins nearly two-thirds of the way towards the end of Odysseus' journey. We don't actually see Odysseus in the poem until his imprisonment on Ogygia, Calypso's island, and we don't hear the whole story until he is forced, by grief and a request to reveal his iden-tity, to tell it to Nausicaa's family. I want to emphasize this: is it not true that analysands often don't reveal themselves until midway in their initiatory journeys, and often only then under the duress of grief, im-prisonment, and longing?

With this in mind, let's begin with a focus on the four central fe-male characters in the poem, in order to discuss in more detail the ac-tual dynamics of the integration of the anima in the poem. These four figures of the feminine, in the chronological order of their appearance in the sea-adventures, are Circe, Calypso, Nausicaa, and Penelope. Circe, as you remember, lives in a mandala like stone hut in the center of a solitary island. Karl Kerenyi suggests that her name means circle, "a fitting name for a daughter of the Sun, since the solar movement is circling" (10-11). We will return to this notion of circling below; but for now we should note that as daughter of the sun, she is an apt initial epiphany of the Self, a sort of first dream that propels Odysseus on his journey to Hades. Rather than approach her directly (another indication of Homer's psychological savoir-faire), Odysseus sends a scouting party, who see her surrounded by "wolves and mountain lions ... mild / in her soft spell, fed on her drug of evil" (171). They hear her singing "in her beguiling voice, while on her loom / she wove ambrosial fabric sheer and bright / by that craft known to the goddesses of heaven" (171). Then she invites the men to "a meal of cheese and barley / and amber honey mixed with Pramnian wine, / adding her own vile pinch, to make them lose / desire and thought of [their] dear father land" (172). The "vile pinch" is of course the drug which changes them into swine, though with human mind intact, penned in a pigsty to eat "acorns, mast, and cornel berries--fodder / for hogs who rut and slumber on the earth" (172).

Circe, therefore, is an anima of a complicated sort (is there one who isn't?). As daughter of Helios, she is associated with the light of the Self, which illuminates all psychic events, and gathers them into its magnetic circle of reference. Yet being surrounded by wolves, lions, and pigs, with wild bucks ranging freely on her island (one of which Odysseus shoots for a ritual feast), she also represents the Lady of the Beasts, a kind of Artemis figure at home only in the solitary wilderness of distant islands. She mediates between the spiritual domain of the heavens and the earthy, primitive kingdom of animal life, yet she still lives far from the "fatherland" of domestic life. In addition, as Joseph Campbell has shown, she is associated with Aphrodite (*Occidental Myth* 161), and her allure reduces men to the most primitive levels of sexual need and instinctual craving (Stein, Chapter Five). Yet the land around her is traversed by "wide watercourses" (169), and like Athena she sits weaving at her loom, and is therefore rudimentarily connected with the basic arts and crafts of a civilized world. I say rudimentarily, because, in spite of the complexities and contradictions in her nature, Homer appears primarily to mean to present her as a primitive goddess, one who lives alone, without social relations, surrounded by animals. He tells us that "No farms, no cultivated land appeared" on her "wilderness" island (168), and the acorns she feeds her "men" is the food J.J. Bachofen associates with the most primitive stages of civilization and the feminine.

The contrast with Calypso, the next goddess on the itinerary, is therefore calculated and instructive. For although Calypso is also solitary and asocial, she is associated with vegetative life and the rudimentary arts of agriculture and viniculture, unlike Circe, who was primarily

symbolic of a more primitive stage of human development associated
with hunting and gathering (bucks and acorns). Odysseus stays with
Circe for just one year, and with Calypso for seven, an indication of his
progressive growth from what Bachofen calls the hetaeric or Aphroditic
stage of sexuality towards the matronly level of married life that will
climax with Penelope. Yet Calypso is still a "dangerous nymph" (224)
who lives and sings alone on a "distant island" (83), far from the normal intercourse of men and the gods--in the fairy realm, that is to say,
of the nymphs of the unconscious. Hermes remarks upon this distance
when he arrives on Ogygia: he explains that "Zeus made me come, and
not my inclination; / who cares to cross that tract of desolation, / the
bitter sea, all mortal towns behind / where gods have beef and honors
from mankind?" (84).

It is noteworthy here that the process of gradual disentanglement
from the snares of the unconscious begins, in the poem as in analysis,
not with the ego, but with the unconscious itself: it is Zeus and Athena,
archetypal figures associated with the Self, who initiate Odysseus' escape from the allure of Calypso. That is to say, individuation is very
largely an act of grace, although surely Odysseus' continual longing for
home has contributed the psychic energy necessary to catalyze this
movement in the Self: he sits for seven years on his "stone seat" facing
"seaward--tear on tear / brimming his eyes" (85). By night he submits
to the snares of Calypso and her dreamlike pleasures, though by day he
"fights shy of her and her desire", sitting on the "rocky shore ... with
eyes wet / scanning the bare horizon of the sea" (85). As Hillman has
noted, it is this longing for home, this *pothos*, which distinguishes the
Odyssean wanderings of individuation from the random peregrinations
of the picaresque, and establishes the special connection to the feminine
and her archetypal depths.

Hence Calypso is a step forward in the progressive integration of
the anima. Homer's imagery reflects this development, for although like
Circe Calypso sits weaving at her loom, passing "the golden shuttle to
and fro" and "singing high and low / in her sweet voice" (83), the imagery here focuses "upon the hearthstone [with] a great fire blazing"
(83), whereas in the case of Circe there had only been "a smoke wisp
from the woodland hall" with no sight of the hearth (169). The detail is
significant: as Bachofen notes, "All civilization and culture are essentially grounded in the establishment and adornment of the hearth"
(107), and with the transition from Circe to Calypso, Homer has initiated the domestication of Odysseus in relation to the feminine which is
a central theme of the poem. [10] Calypso is not surrounded by animals
and bestial men as Circe was, but by trees, birds, trellised vines, and
beds of flowers (83).

That is to say, in Bachofian terms, the anima has here progressed from the Aphroditic towards the Demetrian, from "swamp generation to the *laborata Ceres* (the tilled soil)" (191). And at precisely this point the return to "religion and law" which Bachofen associates with the "transition to agriculture" occurs (191): Zeus intervenes by sending Hermes as an emissary of Athena's will to return Odysseus to the polis (Ithaca) and Penelope. He must therefore be wrested from the arms of the reluctant nymph Calypso, who attempts to detain her mortal lover by offering him immortality. Odysseus' reply to this temptation is the classic statement of the Western attitude towards the transcendentalism of the East: faced with all the adversities of the sea, with death, old age, and shipwreck, Odysseus simply replies, "Let the trial come" (87). Thereby he rejects the siren call of disengagement from life, and the retreat into the archetypal, just as he had done earlier when he left the island of the sun (as Joseph Campbell points out in *Occidental Myth* 173).

Hence, his next encounter with the archetypal feminine occurs in the context of city life, though still at one step removed from the normal conditions of a purely human civilization. Calypso's island had been a sort of Elysium, with four springs bubbling up near one another or streaming outwards from their maternal source like the four rivers of Eden (83), far from the normal vicissitudes of human life.[11] Nausicaa, the third of Odysseus' encounters with the divine feminine, shares this distance from life with Calypso, but since she exists in a social context (having as her parents a King or Queen who rule an elegant kingdom of seafarers), she stands just at the gateway or return threshold which will lead Odysseus from the dream kingdom by the nymph-bestudded sea to his home in Ithaca.

Odysseus first sees Nausicaa on the seashore, where she has been advised by Athena, who came to her in a dream, to wash her laundry in the streams that run into the sea in preparation for her marriage. Odysseus, "far gone in weariness and oblivion" after a night recuperating from his shipwreck and three day swim, is awakened by the sound of the girls playing ball and emerges from a small grove of olive trees under which he had spent the night.[12] All the nymphs flee at the sight of this lion like man, "rain-drenched, wind-buffeted ... Streaked with brine, and swollen" (103). Nausicaa, however, husbands much in her mind, apparently knows a good thing when she sees it. She gives him clothes and oil, and instructs him to bathe in the river, from which he emerges refreshed and reborn, shedding the god-like splendor Athena has endowed him with. Nausicaa then returns home to her father with her prize, and Athena wraps a cloud of invisibility around Odysseus to protect him from the curiosity of the locals, and which she removes only when he throws himself at the mercy of Alkinoos by sitting abruptly down in his hearth.

It is important to note at this point that Athena has replaced Hermes as the psychopomp or tutelary spirit of the hero. This shows that Odysseus is beginning to leave the archetypal realm of dreams, nymphs, nekyias, and wanderings associated with Hermes, and to make his way back to the polis of daily life, of which Athena is the goddess. While in the realm of the unconscious, a male deity had served to guide him through the labyrinth of the archetypal feminine; as Odysseus makes his way back to his Kingdom on Ithaca, a feminine deity becomes his guide and protector.

Yet the world Nausicaa inhabits, as civilized and refined as it is, with its contests, banquets, and courtly behavior, is still more divine than human, and her offer of marriage with Odysseus represents the familiar temptation of the hero to remain in the magic circle of the archetypal realm, rather than to make his way back into the normal sufferings of human life. Although the Phaiakians inhabit a civilized island, where the plow has "parceled out the black land" (99), Skheria is still just one step removed from the Calypso's Elysium, somewhere between the archetypal and the human realms. Apollonius of Rhodes tells us that "the sickle used by Cronos to castrate his father Uranus" lies buried under its soil, that "Demeter of the underworld ... lived there once and taught the Titans to reap corn for food," and that Macris, who "took the infant Dionysos to her bosom and moistened his parched lips with honey .... came to the remote Phaecian land, where she lived in the sacred cave and brought abundance to the people" (174, 178).

Its palace is a kind of Yeatsian Byzantium, with "high rooms ... airy and luminous / as though with lusters of the sun and moon" and "with an azure molding / of lapis lazuli" (113). Its orchard (which Homer describes at length--again in contrast to the primitive condition of the other islands of the Odyssean itinerary) occupies "four spacious acres planted / with trees in bloom and weighted down for picking: / pear trees, pomegranates, brilliant apples, / luscious figs, and olives ripe and dark" that grow from trees whose fruit never fails, in winter or in summer (114). Furthermore, after Odysseus is finally escorted home to Ithaka by the Phaiakians, Poseidon turns their ship to a stone mountain and thereby cuts off normal commerce with the world beyond. It seems that the divisions between the archetypal and the human need to be strictly demarcated, or at least that the gods would have it so.

Odysseus, however, is able to bring a rich treasure hoard back with him, gathered from his oneiric wanderings on the godly sea. The Phaiakian sailors deposit him, sleeping and laden with bronze and gold, on his native shores, beside the cave of the Naiades. These are "immortal girls" whose mystic cave contains "winebowls hollowed in the rock /

and amphorai" to which bees bring honey. There are great looms of
stone where "the weaving nymphs make tissues", clear springs in the
cavern that flow forever, and two entrances: "one on the north allows
descent of mortals, / but beings out of light alone, the undying, / can
pass by the south slit; no men come there" (233). In a sense, Odysseus
is still dripping with the ambrosial dew of archetypal seas, still very
near to the wild heart of the immortal psyche. In order to make his way
back to Penelope, he must again bypass the magical allure of the sea-
nymphs, who signify the hypnotic pull of the anima into the depths of
the unconscious, and who are most dangerous just when the hero is
about to return to the domestic world of waking reality.

Again guided by Athena, who disguises Odysseus as a beggar,
Odysseus goes to the swineherd's hut, where he is reunited with his old
father, Laertes, and later with his son Telemachus. As Joseph Campbell
shows, this father son atonement, spanning the three generations, and
embracing past, present and future, is an earthly analog of immortality:
the scene presents the "high moment of the merging of the two worlds
of Eternity and Time, Life and Death, Father and Son" (*Occidental
Myth* 176), a reconciliation of opposites that will be repeated after the
slaughter of the suitors reunites Odysseus and Penelope. Their union, as
Campbell has shown (*Occidental Myth* 164), reenacts the sacred marriage of the sun and the moon, and hence is the climax of the integration of the anima: each stage (Circe, Calypso, Nausicaa, Penelope) is
progressively more humanized, more willing to be fully assimilated,
yet bearing the seeds of future trials and further growth. In the reunion
of Odysseus and Penelope, the two worlds of the unconscious and conscious minds are joined in a moment of achieved individuation --
which, as subsequent legend has it, simply yields to further wanderings,
and the final consummation, in a land far from the sea, of death.

If this outline of the plot of the sea-adventures of Odysseus suggests a linear movement in the integration of the anima towards the
mythic ideal of individuation, one should remember the tendency of
analysis to revolve in vicious circles around an unredeemable core of
suffering. Homer, in fact, incorporates this experience of compulsive
repetition as a structural principle in the *Odyssey*, so that the narrative
can be seen as proceeding in a circular, as well as in a linear way. The
ending and beginning point of each circle of the sea-adventures is a
goddess, and the nuclear core of the revolving wheel of the complex is
the death and rebirth experience which accompanies each epiphany of
the anima in the poem. Hence the narrative circles back to the beginning, as Telemachus, with whom the *Odyssey* begins, returns to Ithaca
in synchronistic harmony with his father at the end of the book, when
the sun (Odysseus) and the moon (Penelope) wheel around to their sacred 20 year marriage at the Winter Solstice.

Perhaps a diagram will help make this conjunction of circles and lines, of male and female, of eternal return and temporal progression, more clear. The chart below summarizes the sea-adventures as we have reviewed them above, and incorporates the return to Ithaca:

1. Lotos	Sirens	Elysium	Naiades
2. Cyclops	Skylla	Prison	Hut
3. Aeolus	Helios	Immortality	Atonement
4. Giants	Charybdis	Shipwreck	Slaughter
5. Circe	Calypso	Nausicaa	Penelope

At the bottom of each column (reading vertically) you see underlined the names of the archetypal feminine figures with whom each set of sea-adventures climaxes. Each of the women, therefore, is both the end of one set of coherent episodes, and the beginning of the next, one infernal and/or paradisal circle leading directly to the next, in the linear progressive manner outlined above (so that we seem to be getting somewhere, both in the story and in analysis, but are actually revolving in repetitive circles that move up a level towards some final center, perhaps the olive bed where Odysseus and Penelope lie at the end of the book).

Reading across the horizontal columns from left to right, the coherence of the four sets of episodes becomes clear. At level 1 there is the siren call of the beyond, which Joseph Campbell describes as "the allure of paradise, or, as the Indian mystics say, the 'tasting of the juice': accepting paradisal bliss as the end (the soul enjoying its object), instead of pressing through to non-dual, transcendent illumination" (*Occidental Myth* 172). The danger here is the danger of the Lotos Eaters: forgetting home and human life in favor of the blissful Elysium offered by Calypso, and the paralyzing awareness of the eternal return in the honeyed cave of the Naiades. It is the danger of the archetypal inflation that comes with that first big dream that sets the course of the entire analysis. As Campbell writes, and as all analysts and analysands know, one is forced by the current to press beyond this initial delusion, even if it takes a captain to drag us back onto the boat for home (how many transcendental excursions in the 60's ended just in this way: with a call from the draft board?).

What comes next, in the second horizontal column, is the depressive side of the manic inflation: the hours spent in the cave of the Cyclops, who gets drunk, devours men, and blocks the entrance way to daylight with an enormous stone no mortal can roll away. Here the only hope is that peculiar combination of Herculean power and Hermetic cunning characteristic of Odysseus: he sheds ego by calling himself Noman, rams the pine shaft into the Cyclops' eye, and ties himself and his men to the bellies of the sheep so they can pass undetected the next morning when Polyphemous rolls away the stone. At each station of the four adventures along the way of line 2, we see a repetition of this threshold combat, which combines imprisonment, dismemberment, and/or disguise: the many headed dragon, Scylla, devours six men as Odysseus passes below its cliffside caves in his boat; Odysseus feels trapped in the cave of Calypso's desire; and finally, disguised as a beggar in the swineherd's hut (Noman again), Odysseus formulates his stratagem of vengeance on the suitors.

Following these vivid images of physical death and imprisonment comes the revelation of the transcendental spheres of the spirit, beyond the pairs of opposites, in line 3. At this stage, Odysseus meets Aeolus, the Lord of the Winds (pneuma=spirit), and lands on the shores of the Island of the Sun, where, because he falls asleep while his men eat the sacred oxen, he is finally shipwrecked and left alone on the sea. The Island of Helios is analogous to the Solar Door in Hinduism, through which the yogi passes into the beyond, never to return: as Joseph Campbell writes, "had Odysseus been a sage of India, he would not now have found himself alone, floating at sea, on the way back to his wife Penelope, to put what he had learned into play in domestic life" (*Occidental Myth* 173). It is the lure of the absolute, of union with the archetype of the Self. The immortality offered at this stage by Calypso would sever all connections with human life with the passage to the yonder shore. But Odysseus rejects this way, accepting instead the secular, familial analog of immortality which occurs in the Swineherd's hut. Here the three generations are united: Grandfather Laertes, Father Odysseus, and Son Telemachus -- Past, Present, and Future alive in the present moment of the eternal now.

Because Odysseus rejects the way of serene detachment from the vicissitudes of life, he must therefore pass back through the thresholds towards the feminine, which in the *Odyssey* represents the immanence of the divine in daily life, there for those who have the eyes and heart to perceive it. Consequently, he must again submit to dismemberment and shipwreck, just after the exaltation of his transcendental contact with the archetypes (how many times has the sublime wisdom distilled during the analytical or meditative hour given way to the bitterness of renewed torment?). At this stage (line 4), his men are devoured by giant cannibals (the Laestrygonians), and sucked into the whirlpool of Charybdis; Odysseus himself is shipwrecked during his return from Calypso's island, or must slaughter the suitors, in one of the must disturbing scenes of domestic violence following the return of a soldier from the war ever written.

Then comes the long awaited and much enjoyed union with the feminine, that both ends one journey and begins another, as if all the trials of this man of many sorrows simply recapitulate the stages of a relationship, or of an analysis: the allure at the beginning (1), the imprisonment and struggle with the shadow (2), the ecstatic revelation of love's mystical promise (3), the return of the repressed complexes (4), and the climax of the sacred marriage (5). Yet these stages suggest that the integration of the anima requires the ritual repetition of death and rebirth celebrated at Eleusis in the mysteries of Demeter and Persephone: the *Odyssey* is also a "Book of the Dead", for each turning of the circle propels Odysseus through the stages of death outlined in the spiritual cartographies of the Tibetans and the Egyptians. There is the initial siren call of the beyond, a revelation of the Mother Light, followed by the physical and spiritual agonies of death and dismemberment (by Cyclopes and Skyllae); then the revelation of the transcendent spirit reoccurs (Aeolus and Helios), and if, like Odysseus, the dying soul cannot bear the radiance, it makes its way back to mortal life, through the whirlpool of rebirth.

This approach to the cyclical repetition in the poem's episodes parallels the traditional Buddhist view: Odysseus remains bound on the ever-revolving wheel of birth-death-rebirth, circulating in eternal return. Yet precisely because the wheel stays in place, it enables movement forward: it represents the convergence of circular repetition with linear progress, hence giving us an image of the way analysis, and life, move. Joseph Campbell, in fact, sees the key to the *Odyssey* in the death and rebirth mysteries celebrated at Eleusis, in which the goddesses Demeter and Persephone and the pig played as central a role as they do in Homer's epic poem (*Occidental Myth* 171, 176). For Jung, the death and rebirth process was associated with the hero's struggle for freedom from the mother, which involved periodic regression to the depths of maternal embrace and the consequent re-enactment of liberation. As Hillman points out, Freudian views of Odysseus have followed Jung in attributing his wanderings to the nostalgic search for the lost mother ("Pothos" 51-52, 56). However, the most thorough exploration of the death and rebirth dynamic of individuation has come from the transpersonal psychology of Stanislav Grof, whose systematic research with LSD has synthesized Jungian and Freudian views of the structure of the psyche.

Through a focus on what Grof calls Basic Perinatal Matrices (BPM), recollections of the birth trauma stored in the unconscious, we can come to a better understanding of the wanderings of Odysseus, which in a rather detailed way re-enact the dynamic of death and rebirth. Grof charts four such matrices, associated with four stages of clinical delivery: I. Primal Union with the Mother (Intrauterine Experience before the Onset of Delivery), II. Antagonism with the Mother (Contractions in a Closed Uterine System), III. Synergism with the Mother (Propulsion through the Birth Canal), and IV. Separation from the Mother (Birth) (*Realms* Chapter 4). The first matrix "manifests itself as an experience of cosmic unity. Its basic characteristics are ... peace, tranquillity, joy, serenity, and bliss" (105); the activation of the second matrix "results in a rather characteristic spiritual experience of "no exit" or "hell" in which one feels "encaged in a claustrophobic world and experiences incredible physical and psychological tortures" (116); BPM III involves the encounter with death as a "titanic struggle, frequently attaining catastrophic proportions" (124); and the fourth Perinatal Matrix "represents the resolution of the death-rebirth struggle" in which the "suffering and agony culminate in an experience of total annihilation on all levels" (138).

A cursory glance at the diagram charting the wanderings of Odysseus should suggest the relevance of the Grofian schema. In each column, presided over by a particular avatar of the archetypal mother, one notes the fluctuating dynamic of death and rebirth, of violent struggle and resolution, which constitutes the basis of perinatal recollections in the unconscious. Odysseus initially experiences the blissful tranquillity of immortality associated with the Cosmic Union with the Mother. Like the child at the onset of delivery, however, feelings of threatening enclosure and imprisonment soon set in (in the caves of Polyphemous and Calypso, or the Swineherd's hut), that modulate towards the titanic struggles with cannibals, whirlpools, or suitors which Grof records in imagery related to third stage of delivery. The experience of spiritual transcendence and breakthrough associated with actual birth generally comes, in the *Odyssey*, in the middle, after the liberation from the imprisonment of the caves. In Book 5 of the poem however, when Odysseus leaves Calypso, each stage of the perinatal matrices seem to occur in precisely the order of an actual death and rebirth experience.

Odysseus initially experiences Calypso and her cave as a blissful Elysium, where all of his biological needs are gratified. He is surrounded by the radiant beauty of a tropical Greek island and deeply in love with a Goddess. Calypso's cave is a "good womb" at the entrance to which are flower beds and grape vines. At this point he is, as Joseph Campbell is fond of saying, "transparent to the transcendent" and closely in touch with the immortality the Goddess offers him. Yet these blissful sensations soon give way to that sense of frustration and imprisonment which Grof associates with the onset of uterine contractions before the cervix has opened: Odysseus sits chained to his stone beside the sea, mourning his exile from real life, until Hermes comes to announce his liberation. Then Odysseus builds his ship of death, which will ferry him into life on the shores of Skheria, after a shipwreck and desperate three day swim through the stormy Mediterranean: a titanic struggle of catastrophic proportions stirred up by "the Earthshaker,

Lord Poseidon" (90-92). During this struggle, Odysseus receives a tal-isman from the sea-nymph Leucothea, a sort of umbilical sash which he winds around his chest and must cast into the "winedark sea" when he reaches shore (91).

After a tempestuous struggle with the surf, Odysseus manages to swim to shore, and is cast up onto the beach like an exhausted new born, struggling to regain its breath. Any mother or father (who has been fortunate enough to have witnessed his child's birth) will recog-nize the perinatal imagery in this scene! When Nausicaa discovers him the next day, he is, of course, naked, and still "streaked with brine and swollen" like a baby (103). He must be bathed in her stream and anointed with her olive oil, then clothed in the fresh linen she has un-wittingly prepared for him, before he is fit to be presented to the world of her father's court (105-106). It is as beautiful a moment in the *Odyssey* as it is in life: for here the brave child has purposefully left the archetypal realm of the immortals behind, floating on the seas of memoria, to sustain him or her from below, through another go at life's trials. For it seems that at each turning of the wheel, we must die to be reborn, as we struggle to integrate anima (soul) into our lives. There can be no more appropriate guidebook to lead us through this valley of the shadow, towards the green pastures, than Homer's great poem, a myth of analysis, and a book for both the quick and the dead.

A key moment in the epic genre of the hero journey is the descent to the underworld, as we have seen above in our discussions of the Sumerian material associated with Inanna and Gilgamesh. In the *Odyssey* this occurs in Book 11, the so-called *nekyia* in which Odysseus follows Circe's directions to visit the Kimmerian land of the shades of the dead to receive the special wisdom of Tiresias relevant to his des-tiny. Book 11 gives as fascinating glimpse into the Greek conception of the underworld, and it transmits the epic conventions down to Virgil, Dante, and Milton. Furthermore, the cosmology of Hades as delineated by Homer bears a striking resemblance to Jung's cartography of the human psyche, with its separation into personal, historical, and mytho-logical (collective) levels. [13]

To begin our descent with the prescripted ritual invocation of the shades of the dead set forth by Circe (10. 545-583) and performed by Odysseus and his men when they arrive in the land of Kimmerians (11. 1-55). Circe directs Odysseus northwards to the "bourne of Ocean" and "Persephone's deserted stand and grove / dusky with poplars and the drooping willow" (10. 550-51). Here, among "the crumbling homes of Death," Circe describes the convergence of the four rivers of the un-derworld at a place she calls "The Rock" (10. 555-58). Odysseus reaches this site at dusk, when "the sun dipped, and all the ways grew dark / upon the fathomless unresting sea" (11. 12-13), words anticipating Dante's descent at twilight into the dark wood where the straight way was no longer plain. This is the time of day when the sun itself commences its diurnal night-sea journey, something Circe as a daughter of the sun would know about (Romanticism will revision the importance of twilight in the hero journey as a time of dream and desire). In fact, it looks as if we are meant to conceive of the entire necromantic ritual performed by Odysseus in this "realm and region of the Men of Winter" as proceeding under cover of darkness, since Homer seems to describe the Nordic winter when he says "Never the flaming / eye of Helios lights those men / at morning ... ruinous night being rove over those wretches" (11. 15-20). Hence, the journey represents the nadir of the sea wanderings, reiterates the ancient affiliation of the sun and the descent into the underworld (as we have seen in the progress of Gilgamesh through the twelve leagues of darkness), and falls exactly in the middle of the epic of the *Odyssey*. It is the turning point or vortex around which the linked episodes fall symmetrically away before and after Book 11.

These directions to and delineation of the topography of the oracular cite here visited by Odysseus have been taken literally by Professor Dakaris of Ionina University, who since 1958 has overseen the excavations of a cemetery surrounding a Byzantine chapel in Ephyra, a late Mycenean city north of the modern village of Mesopotamon in far Northern Greece. Following leads from the Homeric description of the Kimmerian oracle, and from the writings of Pausanius in the 2end century C.E., Professor Dakaris speculated that Homer knew the specific region of the oracle well enough to describe it in detail. In fact, the rivers Pyriphlegethon, Cocytus, and Acheron join near Ephyra, poplars and willows still grow there today, and, near one of the graves in the cemetery, Professor Dakaris found a fist-sized aperture (about the size of Alice's rabbit hole) through which cool air rushed. Here he began digging, and found under the graves and church a large structure of huge stone blocks, which has now been completely excavated. The work uncovered long corridors, narrow doors, little rooms, and labyrinthine passageways surrounding a central sanctuary of several rooms, with a large vaulted chamber beneath them on the lowest level. Here, deep below the hilltop Byzantine Church, Professor Dakaris situates the primeval oracle of the dead consulted by Odysseus in Book 11 of the *Odyssey*.

Among the artifacts excavated by Professor Dakaris to support his theory are included large bellied earthenware vessels (receptacles for the offerings of sweet milk, honey, wine, and barley); beans, mussels, and pork bones in large quantities (the pig being the sacrificial animal associated with the Goddesses of the Underworld from Greece, to southern India, to Melanesia);[14] large sacks containing the black lumps of hashish used to induce hallucinatory visions of the dead during the 29 day ordeal of darkness involved in ritual; heaps of prophylactic stones thrown apotropaically over the shoulder to ward off spirits; sheep bones found in a trench at the beginning of a long corridor leading to the labyrinthine ante-chambers of the inner sanctuary; a sequence of smaller rooms, just beyond the first of which is a hole in the ground the size of a block of stone for the sacrificial blood of the black ram. Twelve steps lead down this hole to a barrel vault with ribbed arches and a small hole in the top of the ceiling. The soil on the floor of this vault is softened by layers of blood turned to humus.

Following these leads, Professor Dakaris offers a reconstruction of the rites as a 29 day ordeal, the climax of which was a staged epiphany of the dead in a cauldron hung from the ceiling of the barrel vault, accompanied by shadows cast by smoky torches and intensified by clanging noises and the hypnotic invocations of liturgical chanting. After the climactic revelation, a debriefing apparently took place in a room filled with sulfur residues and with a door leading outside and down to the sea. where ritual ablutions may have been performed at dawn of the 30th day. [15]

Many of the details found in Homer would seem to be illuminated by the speculations of modern archaeology. Whatever the actual historical situation revealed by the archaeologists, the mythological symbolism of the ritual invocation is rich. The mixture of sweet milk, honey, wine, water, and blood suggests an ambrosial beverage which confers divine wisdom, such as that "bellyful of the blood-mixed mead" consumed by Wotan in Norse mythology. [16] That the receipt for the offering contained some kind of psychoactive drug seems partially confirmed by the presence of large quantities of hashish in the Dakaris excavations. [17] Also similar to the Norse constellation is the linkage between tree, priestess, and underworld. Furthermore, the symbolic associations of barley or wheat reach as far back as Çatal Hüyük and as far forward as the New Testament, where Jesus says "Except a corn of wheat fall into the ground and die, it abideth alone: but if it die, it bringeth forth much fruit" (John 12:24). And of course the resurrection is assured believers by the Eucharistic feast of wine and wheat, linking death and rebirth with the symbolism of barley and wine found in the *Odyssey*. We should also note the sacrificial importance of the lamb given to "appease the nations of the dead" in Homer, and substituted for the sacrifice of Isaac in the Old Testament.

Proceeding to the actual conversations Odysseus conducts with the dead, and the order of their appearance, we find Homer's underworld divided into three basic levels: a personal level providing information to Odysseus of direct importance to his immediate destiny; a broadly historical level containing the souls first of the famous women and then of the famous men of Greek culture; and then a deeper mythical level of heroic males suffering torments for their deeds. The movement from a personal, to a historical, to a mythological level would seem to anticipate Jung's stratification of the psyche in terms of the personal and the collective unconscious. In the first level, Odysseus talks to his companion Elpenor, most recently dead after a fall from Circe's roof; he comes to request proper burial when Odysseus returns to Circe's island. Then Odysseus sees the shade of his less recently departed dead mother, Antikleia, who tells him that she died of grief in her longing for Odysseus, and that his father Laertes is pining away with a similar grief in a "lowly bed" lacking "rugs, or fleecy mantle ... among the slaves" (11. 191). This suggests that the level of the underworld (as of the unconscious) most immediately accessible to Odysseus is the personal, containing those dead who were actually a part of the hero's family and friends. Furthermore, his conversations with them, as with the blind sage Tiresias, revolve around issues of immediate personal concern to the wanderer: his return home to an Ithaka besieged by suitors.

Tiresias, of course, is the blind prophet of the ancient Greek world, whose powers of omniscience and foresight were conferred upon him by Zeus, in compensation for having been struck blind by Hera for suggesting that women enjoyed sex more than men. Tiresias was an authority on the subject, since he had spent half of his life as a man and half as a woman, having had his sex changed twice on the occasions of inserting his staff between a pair of copulating serpents. Joseph Campbell suggests that Tiresias points back to the oldest stratum of Greek myth, to a matriarchal matrix of symbolism in which no clear dualistic distinctions were made between opposite poles (male and female, life and death, time and eternity) of the one life force. Hence while blind to the phenomena of the sensible world, Tiresias sees the archetypal realm of the pure ideas which are the basis of the created world.

Homer's Hades seems to follow from such distinctions, since his underworld is most broadly divisible, in its second and third levels, into categories of sexual differentiation: after the manifestation of the three shades most directly concerned with Odysseus, the narrative proceeds first to a catalogue of women ("consorts or daughters of illustrious men ... great loveliness of ghosts" 11. 192), and then to a catalogue of the illustrious men, after Persephone "dispersed the shades of women" (11. 197). To clearly separate the two groups, Homer inserts an interruption when Arete and Alkinoos pause to commend the heroism of Odysseus and to promise him abundant gifts and a passage home (11. 195-97). The female catalogue ranges broadly through Greek cultural history, with each shade pausing just long enough at the trough of blood which draws them to Odysseus to declare "her lineage and name" (11. 192). By contrast, the male catalogue begins with three extended dialogues with Agamemnon, Akhilleus, and Aîas, the son of Telamon (all of whom Odysseus knew during the Trojan war years). The catalogue then modulates directly from the historical to the deepest mythological layers of Hades, with glimpses of various heroic figures not contemporary with Odysseus who are suffering torments for challenging the gods: Minos, Orion, Tantalos, Sisyphos, and Heraklês.

The overall cartography of Homer's Hades, then, yields a map strikingly similar to Jung's archaeology of the psyche, with its division of personal and collective levels. Also like Jung is the division between male (animus) and female (anima) archetypes, which are united into a figure who symbolizes the reconciled opposites of the Self -- Tiresias, who then becomes the mouthpiece for the transcendent wisdom of the psyche as a whole. Furthermore, Homer seems to reiterate a partition between personal and collective levels of the underworld in both the female and the male categories, moving in the former from Antikleia, mother of Odysseus, to the historical and mythical mothers of the collective; and in the latter from personal friends of Odysseus (Akhilleus, Agamemnon) to the mythological heroes with whom he had no personal contact (Minos, Heraklês, et. al.). These latter represent the archetypes (the gods within his complexes) which mirror the conscious configuration of his ego. This is most clearly so with reference to Heraklês, who like Odysseus performs a series of labors and endures wanderings inflicted upon him by the gods, including a heroic descent into the underworld. But Tantalos and Sisyphos also present archetypal reflections of Odyssean complexes and sufferings: the object of the former's desire forever recede beyond his reach, just as Ithaka eludes Odysseus just when he nearly reaches home, but is blown away by the bag of wind given him by Aeolus; the relentless efforts of the latter (Sisyphos) to push a boulder up the hill reflect the repeated shipwrecks and misfortunes which delay the final homecoming of Odysseus.

If, then, we approach Homer's underworld in the *Odyssey* as a metaphorical image of the unconscious, the *nekyia* becomes a journey of individuation (of integrating the archetypal dominants and driving powers of the psyche), and thus an integral moment in the overall pattern of the book. Another related approach to the Homeric underworld of Book 11 would be to note that it constitutes what one critic called a "burial place of memory," perhaps functioning as a mnemonic device for the poet, a way of recording and recalling to memory the vast catalogue of the lore and legend of oral tradition. We know something from Lord and Parry about the oral-formulaic devices by which the epic materials of the *Iliad* and the *Odyssey* were passed down by storytellers during the four hundred or so years after Troy, and before reaching the written form in which we now know them. Book 11 may well give us a glimpse into those memory techniques, about which we also know something from Frances Yates, who traces the development of these during the Renaissance in her book *The Art of Memory*. Dame Frances begins her story with Simonides of Ceos (556-468 B.C.E.), a greatly admired lyric poet of Paros, to whom a marble tablet found on that is-land attributes the invention of "'a system of memory aids'" (29). Yates suggests a pre-literate oral stage in the development of these memory aids: "One can imagine," she writes, "that some forms of the art might have been a very ancient technique used by bards and storytellers," such as, one hastens to infer, the Homeric poets (29). She proceeds by noting that "Aristotle was certainly familiar with the artificial memory" systems, which employ what he calls *topoi*, imaginal places the "'mere mention'" of which elicits in the "'trained memory'" the subject materi-als stored therein (31) -- such places (*topoi*) as the caves and islands of the wanderings of Odysseus, or, more to our present point, the under-world caverns where the ancestral shades tell their stories to our hero. Such knowledge stored in the caverns of memory could either be histor-ical reminiscence, or Platonic recollection of the *eidola*, "the recovery of knowledge or sensations which one had before birth" (34). This latter takes us into the deeper realms of archetypal memory, for "Plato, unlike Aristotle believed that there is a knowledge not derived from sense impressions, that there are latent in our memories the forms or molds of the Ideas, of the realities which the soul knew before the descent here below" (36). This is the realm of the informing structures (*eidola*) of what W.B. Yeats called the Great Memory.

This suggests the two levels of memory we have situated above in the strata of Homer's Hades: one of personal and historical significance, and the other of mythic recollection of those "ideas which form and shape life" which Plato called the *eidola*, and which James Hillman places in relation "with Hades himself (*aidoneus*)" (*Dream* 51). The underworld, that is to say, is the ultimate *topos* of memory, a kind of *memoria* conceived of as the deepest and hidden recess of the mind. The movement towards this level is commonly described (in Plato, Augustine, Freud, or Jung) as a movement "from concretely real and actual events to recollections extending far beyond the life of the per-sonal individual" (Hillman, *Myth* 169).

The same movement, we have shown, is enacted by the descent of Odysseus into the land of the Kimmerian shades. Homer shares the im-agery of the cave as a *topos* of memory with Augustine, who in his *Confessions* describes the "'fields and dens and caverns'" of memory as "'innumerably full of innumerable kinds of things'" (qtd. in Hillman, *Myth*: 171). There are in fact other intriguing parallels between the

Augustinian and the Homeric conceptions of Platonic memory: Augustine's "'spacious palaces of memory'" are a *thesaurus inscrutabile* of innumerable images, like Homer's pandemonium of shades in the Kimmerian caves; and just as Augustine must choose those images he requires among those which "'rush out in troops'" by driving away undesired remembrances "'with the hand of my heart'" (qtd. in Yates: 96), so must Odysseus "draw sword from hip, crouch down, ward off / the surging phantoms from the bloody pit" in front of the caverns of Acheron until Tiresias appears. Given these specific parallels, it is interesting to find Frances Yates reproduce Renaissance illustrations depicting "Hell as Artificial Memory" (pl. 7a, 128) with the various caverns of another fresco used to organize images as "Places of Hell" (pl 8a, 129). Apparently, as James Hillman suggests, "the palaces and caverns of *memoria* are also arenas of the inferno" (*Myth* 191).

All of this suggests that there was, from early on, an intimate connection between the mythic descent into Hades and the creative processes of composition, which we are calling poesis. For the descent catalyzes the archetypal forms and stories of racial memory which are the poet's material. In fact, Homer puts a complex allegory of poesis right in the middle of his tale, at the crucial moment when Odysseus names himself, and begins to tells his own story, to King Alkìnoös, Queen Arete, Nausicaa, and the rest of the Phaiákian court. For the Odyssey, (like *The Arabian Nights*, "The Rime of the Ancient Mariner," or *Heart of Darkness*) is largely a frame tale, a story about a person telling a story to another person. Both the teller of tales and the audience are incorporated into the text as characters, and both undertake hero journeys associated with story telling and reading. It is at the exact moment when the frame tale of Odysseus begins, in Book 8, that Homer includes another frame, as the court poet of Skhèria, Demódokos, gets up to recite the story of Ares, Aphrodite, and Hephaistos. This wonderful tale is far more than simply a story of adultery of the God and Goddess of War and Love: it is also a complex allegory of the secrets of the poet's artistry, and of creation in general.

Hephaistos, as the craftsman of the gods, represents the artist, and the secrets of his craft art in general. The world itself was fashioned by an artist, called the Demiurge, who shaped the cosmos following the forms given by God (Foster 43). Aphrodite and Ares came to represent (in the Neoplatonic tradition) two fundamental aspects of the process: creation and destruction, fusion and separation, or, as the alchemists put it *solve et coagula* (Nicholl 28). In the story Demódokos tells, Hephaistos forges a powerful, invisible net to catch his wife Aphrodite (Goddess of Love) in bed with Ares (God of War). As early as Empedocles (5th century B.C.E.), the union of Aphrodite and Ares came to represent the union of "Love and Strife, concord and discord,"

which themselves were conceived of as "the forces, functioning in alteration, that unite and separate the four elements in a universal process
of forms coming into being and dissolving" (Campbell, *Bullfinch* 8).
We recognize the same forces, in modern physics and chemistry, as
those which drives atoms together to form molecules and ignite nuclei
when forced into fusion (Love, concord, Aphrodite); versus that which
separates molecules into the elements from which new compounds may
be formed, and that which splits the atom itself to release nuclear energy by fission (Strife, discord, Ares). Both forces are involved in the
universal processes of creation, as such Renaissance painters as
Veronese knew when they painted scenes of the marriage of Mars and
Venus: the Neoplatonic teachings of Pico della Mirandola and Marsilio
Ficino had, from 1471 on, firmly established the kind of allegorical
treatments of Greek myth inaugurated by Plutarch (50-120 A.D.), who,
is his *Isis and Osiris* declared that the origin of this world are composed
of a mixture of the "contrarious powers" represented by Aphrodite and
Ares (Wind 86-7).

Hephaistos, therefore, synthesizes the two powers which drive all
creation generally, and the artistic opus of poesis specifically. When he
surprises Aphrodite and Ares in his bed (place of origins, place of
death), he holds the whole world in his net (Alpha to Omega).
Aphrodite fuses all things together, while Ares separates, distinguishes,
holds apart. Both processes are basic to artistry, and to epic poetry particularly, which must simultaneously gather together and keep distinct
the numerous elements of its total composition (from the line, to the
oral formula, to the episode). Love and war are also the central themes
of the Homeric epics, beginning with the abduction of Helen and leading to the battle between the suitors who compete for Penelope. Fusion
and fission are also basic to metallurgy and the mythology of alchemy,
which involves breaking matter down into its constituent elements
(solve, separatio), and recombining them to form new molecules
(coagula, coniunctio). Hence the image of Ares and Aphrodite caught
in the net of Hephaistos (who is a smith) is a metaphor for the mysteries
of the forge, in which the operations which either separate or fuse the
materials are performed. There is, in fact, a "close connection between
the profession of smith and the art of the poet and musician": as Eliade
notes, "the smith, in virtue of the sacred character of his craft, the
mythologies and genealogies of which he is the keeper, and his association with the shaman and the warrior, has come to play a significant
part in the creation and diffusion of epic poetry" (*Forge* 98, 88).

The knotting of the net, therefore, represents the Creation, which,
like an epic poem, is woven together from various narrative strands.
Whoever Homer was, we know that his major contribution was to iso-
late the major elements of the Odyssean oral corpus, and then to fuse

them together into an artistic unity, thus imitating the process by which the Demiurge fuses and separates the elements of the creation. Like the nymphs and Goddesses weaving and singing at the loom, scattered throughout the poem, Hephaistos represents the archetype of the poet, and the net his creation. Making a net requires weaving separate strands together, like rope plaiting (see below). It is an old Indo-European image of the creation of the cosmos, which Indian mythology compared to a net of gems, "where in every gem of the net all the others are reflected" (Campbell, *Inner Reaches* 111). Gimbutas links the net motif to the "life giving power of the Goddess" in the early Neolithic generally, and specifically in Boetian, Mycenaean, and Minoan images of the Goddess known in Crete as "The Lady of Nets" (*Language* 81-7). Alternatively, the world is conceived as a web or network of threads binding all things together by the rays of the sun (Coomaraswamy, *Metaphysics* 351). The net is the world of maya, which, by the warp and woof of fear and desire (Ares and Aphrodite), ensnares the transmigrating soul like a captured bird (Coomaraswamy, *Metaphysics* 76). The image of reticulation is also tied up with sewing, spinning, and weaving, as traditional metaphors of creativity (Coomaraswamy, *Traditional* 298), and with the imagery of the knot, or labyrinth: in the Brahma Upanishad, the deity creates the world like a spider spinning his web of a single thread, each knot of the net a reticulated soul. To be free of maya's network is to be "released from all those 'knots (*granthi*) of the heart,' which we should now call complexes," and those who have achieved such liberation are referred to as "the Nirgrantha, 'whose knot is undone'" (Coomaraswamy, "One Thread" 28).

Hence, the revelation of the mysteries of creation lie disguised right in the center of the hero journey of Odysseus, whose story captures the attention of the entire court, like Hephaistos catching the world in the web of his own creation. Like Odysseus, both poet and reader journey through the labyrinth of the world and text, joyfully ensnared by the twistings of the plot, all tied up in knots, until the time for shedding the mortal coils of the maze arises at last.

Demeter and Persephone

The "Homeric Hymn to Demeter" contains one of the most beautiful of all heroine journey cycles. It stands in relation to the *Odyssey* in much the same way as "The Descent of Inanna" stands in relation to the *Epic of Gilgamesh*, for it provides an image of the female journey in counterbalance to the male, covering all the basic stages of feminine growth and development. It particularly focuses on the problems of puberty, mid-life, and old age, all three of which passages involve journeys of a different sort.

The separation phase of Persephone's journey begins with the famous abduction by Hades, Lord of the Underworld, while she is picking flowers in a field with twenty three nymphs attending her. This yields twenty four nymphs total, counting Persephone, which suggests the diurnal symbolism of the hours, a motif we will find again in Wolfram's *Parzival*. As an image of totality, the number implies the all embracing domain of the Great Goddesses of antiquity, and also establishes a cosmic parallel for the Persephone's journey: like the sun, moon, seasons, and hours, she periodically undertakes the descent into Hades. The call to adventure takes the form of a marvelous narcissus flower; when Persephone picks this "lure," the earth opens up and Hades carries down with his chariot and "immortal horses" (2). In some versions, a herd of pigs follows the couple down into the abyss, covering up their tracks, so that Demeter is unable to track her daughter down. These two animals, the pig and the horse, will reappear throughout the ages as symbols of Hades, from the four horsemen of the apocalypse in *Revelation*, to the pigsty which leads the poet to the cemetery in Eliot's "Little Gidding" (50). The chariot will yield to Dante's ferryboat, but eventually find innumerable forms in the literature of the Modern world, from the horse carriage in the "Hades" chapter of Joyce's *Ulysses*, to the automobile Birkin drives off with Ursula in, in *Women in Love*. A thousand and one variations will also ensue on the imagery of abduction as the first phase of the hero journey.

The abduction after picking the narcissus is also, literally, Demeter's call to adventure, as the two heroine journeys (of mother and daughter) are intimately intertwined. She hears the eerie, profound cries of Persephone echoing from mountain peak and ocean bottom. As with the descent of Inanna, it is the act of listening which initiates the separation phase of the journey at mid-life, the time when mother loses the daughter within, and the daughter without. And as with Inanna, the symbolism of divestiture immediately emerges to signal the crisis: after a sharp pain grips Demeter's heart, she tears "the headband round her divine hair," casts the "dark veil" from off her shoulders, and rushes over land and sea "like a bird," searching for Persephone (2-3). In "The Descent of Inanna," in *Epic of Gilgamesh*, and in Egyptian funerary art, the soul in Hades is commonly depicted as a bird, whether it flies up or down. In Farid Attar's *Conference of the Birds*, the legendary Simurgh, image of the divinity, is said to have left an impression of its feathers upon all of our hearts, the memory of which allows the soul to take flight. Birdflight and divestiture will remain archetypal symbols of the hero journey right up to the literature of the present.

Demeter wanders for nine days with bright torches in her hands, before speaking to Hekate, and then to Helios, lord of the Sun, who tells her of Persephone's fate (3-4). The torches will become standard paraphernalia of the Eleusinian mysteries, for which this myth provides the script, and the repetition of the hearing motif (like Demeter, Hekate hears but does not see Persephone being dragged down into Hades) suggests, among other things, the importance of poetry in religious rituals. When Demeter hears of her daughter's fate -- abducted by her "own brother from the same seed" (4), she is overcome by anger and severe grief, which compels her separation from the Olympian gods, and further descent into the realm of mortal mankind. Tearing at her body, she wanders to Eleusis, suddenly aging, so that she now looks line an old woman "barred from childbearing and the gifts of wreath-loving Aphrodite" (4). She has reached menopause, and sits maniacally depressed by a well with an olive tree growing above it. Four daughters from the royal household come carrying copper vessels to fetch the water for their father, and find the old woman sitting by the well. The image of the Goddess at the Well, symbolic of her power as the source of all life, has a noble pedigree and lineage to come: one thinks of Rebecca at the well in the Old Testament; of the Samaritan woman at the well in the New; of the mysterious maidens of the well in Celtic and Arthurian mythologies; of the nymphs of the water Goddess from Northumberland (Green 223); and of the three ladies of the sacred spring at Carrowburgh on Hadrian's Wall, spilling water from urns (Cunliffe 89) -- all prototypes, perhaps, of the Lady of the Fountain in Chrétien's "Yvain". It is a marvelous icon of the creative power of the Goddess, one which we find versions of in "The Horse Dealer's Daughter," by D.H. Lawrence, and *Finnegans Wake*, by James Joyce. But the well is also an entrance to the otherworld, not only in Celtic myth, but also in biblical story of Joseph, and in such tales as "Mother Holle" by the brothers Grimm (Biedermann 377). It is this duality of womb and tomb which Demeter and Persephone, represent.

For when the four daughters of Keleos return with Demeter to the palace, the Goddess takes a job of nursemaid for the young prince, born late in life to Queen Metaneira, who serves Demeter as a kind of surrogate child, to compensate for the loss of her daughter (and hence of her own maternity) during mid-life. When Demeter steps into the palace, the symbolism of torches, divestiture, and sacred springs yields to a common icon of the passage between the two worlds in the heroine's journey: the icon of doorways. When the four daughters lead Demeter through the "portico" to where their mother sits "by a pillar," and then turn to watch the Goddess step across "the threshold," they are awestruck when her head touches the roof and she fills "the doorway with divine radiance" (6-7). The doorway marks the incarnation of the divine into the mortal realm, a descent to the underworld, from Mt. Olympus, for the Goddess Demeter, although an epiphany for humankind. In addition to the emphatic use of such images as the "portico," "threshold," and "doorway," the Homeric poet places the "lady mother" beside a "pillar," which, as Marija Gimbutas has shown, is another archaic icon of the Great Goddess, appearing in association with eggs, caves and crypts, with snake and phallus, as symbols of her womb and tomb (Language 221-35). Arnold Van Gennep suggests that such threshold symbols represent liminality, a state of being betwixt and between, and hence often found in association of rites of passage like marriage (Persephone), mid-life and menopause (Demeter), and death (Hecate). These are precisely the three phases of feminine development which lie at the heart of the Homeric Hymn.

The ritual which proceeds within the confines of the sacred space (a temenos) -- marked off by pillar, portico, threshold, and doorway -- constitute the initiatory phase of Demeter's journey, and it involves the imagery of death and rebirth characteristic of the monomyth. Each night Demeter nurses Demophoön ("the fine son of prudent Keleos" and "fair-girded Metaneira"), breathes sweetly upon him, anoints him with ambrosia, and hides him "like a firebrand in the blazing fire" (234-40)! The scene recalls the wanderings of Isis, who, while searching for her murdered husband Osiris, comes to Byblos and the courtyard with the erica tree growing up around cedar coffin in which Osiris lies entombed. Like Demeter, Isis takes on the task of nursing the young prince, whom she anoints nightly and puts in the fire, meanwhile turning herself into a swallow to flit mournfully around the erica tree (Campbell, *Mythic Image* 21-23). Both Goddesses are interrupted as they perform rituals designed to confer immortality upon their charges (a task which seems appropriate to women who have just experienced the deaths of husband and child), when the Queen mothers burst upon the scene and break the spell in terror for their children. Demeter admonishes Metaneira and then instructs her to build the temple of Eleusis, into which she retreats for a protracted period of mourning, during which she creates famine by withholding the fruits of the earth. Denied the accustomed sacrificial offerings of the harvest, Zeus sends Iris to negotiate with the grieving Demeter, who refuses to "allow the grain in the earth to sprout forth" until she is reunited with her daughter Persephone. To this end, Zeus send Hermes Argeiphontes[18] down to Hades with the mission of retrieving Persephone, whose heroine journey cycle the poem now turns to explore.

Several mythologists have seen in these allusions to the grain symbolic allegories of the cycles of the seasons: Jane Ellen Harrison pointed out that, in the tale Demeter tells the daughters of Keleos, she calls herself Deo, a name derived from the Cretan word for barley grains (272); Karl Kerényi suggests that the child in the fire and Persephone in Hades represent the grain in the oven, or the corpse in the winter earth, from which it emerges reborn in the spring ("Kore"

117); while Gordon Wasson sees in the symbolism of the mown ear held aloft during the Eleusinian mysteries an allusion to the hallucinogenic barley beverage Demeter consumes in the Hymn, a compound of the fungus which grows on wheat. Psychological discussions of the myth (by Downing and Christ, among many others), as dramatizing the entirety of the female life cycle, with a unique focus on the mother-daughter relationship as compensating for the patriarchal emphasis on fathers and sons in the Bible, are all rooted in Jung's analysis in *Essays on a Science of Mythology* and in the work of his female followers (like Esther Harding and Nor Hall). In his lectures, Joseph Campbell focused in great detail on the continuity between the Eleusinian mysteries and the vocabulary of the rituals of the Goddess going back to Mesopotamian times: the pig motif, for example, points as far afield as to the Malekulan mysteries of the Goddess of the underworld (*Occidental* 171), and to the sacred vessels carried by the cherubim of Babylonian provenance (*Mythic Image* 285). Our focus is on the narrative structure of the heroine journey cycle, in the initiation phase of Persephone in Hades, to which we now turn. [19]

After the separation from her mother, Persephone's journey takes her via chariot to Hades, where the initiation stage of the cycle, associated with death and rebirth, proceeds. Hermes confronts Hades with the message from Zeus, which orders the Lord of the underworld to release Persephone, and allow her to return to her mother. As in the *Odyssey*, Book 11, Hermes here plays the role of psychopompos, this time guiding souls out of, rather than into the underworld. It is a role he will perform constantly, throughout the course of literature, all the way from traces of his presence in Psalm 23 (the rod and staff suggestive of the caduceus, and the sill waters suggestive of the crossing of the Styx), to his central role in the fiction of Thomas Mann. Before Hermes persuades Hades to release Persephone, however, Hades contrives to feed her a "honey-sweet pomegranate seed," in order to ensure that "she might not spend / all her days again with dark-robed, revered Demeter" (12). The food of the "pomegranate seed, sweet as honey to eat" (13), as Persephone later confesses to her mother, recalls the forbidden fruit, from the biblical tree of knowledge, "whose mortal taste / Brought death into the world and all our woe" (*Paradise Lost* 2-3). Like the bread and water of life, however, which bring Inanna back to life, the food is a sacrificial offering; for, in Ancient world, honey was "widely regarded as a substance of resurrection magic .... the dead were embalmed in honey," and "To fall into a jar of honey' became a common metaphor" for death (Walker 407). One also hears an echo of the famous Linear B inscription from Crete: "To the lady of the Labyrinth, a jar of honey," which suggests a connection between the underworld and the maze, Persephone and Pasiphae (Campbell, *Occidental* 47).

Hades is referred to in this passage, and throughout the Hymn, as "Aidoneus, Ruler of Many" (12), an epithet which brings up important associations. As James Hillman has pointed out, "the word *eidolon* relates with Hades himself (*aidoneus*), and with *eidos*, ideational forms and shapes, the ideas that form and shape life" (Dream 51). The word *eidos* is Platonic, referring to the doctrine of ideas, the notion that all created forms are modeled on a perfect patterns in a cosmic blueprint designed by God. The heroic descent to the underworld, therefore, typically involves the revelation of the form or pattern guiding one's life, as in the case of Odysseus and Aeneas: both of them discover the secret pattern of destiny (personal and public) while in Hades. It is this revelation of the archetypal pattern, of the form giving shape and significance to life and art, which becomes a key aspect of the initiation phase of the hero journey, in Modernist as well as in Ancient literature. The modernists, for example, created an elaborate vocabulary of form in those works based on the descent to the underworld.[20] For Hillman, therefore, the rape of Persephone "refers to a transition from the material to the psychical point of view" (51), from the raw material of daily life to the archetypal forms of the creative imagination which give that material shape and significance. From this perspective, Persephone's journey is an image of poesis, of the processes of the creative imagination, so that the first thing she does when reunited with her mother, is to tell a story, rehearsing its "every point" (13). Like Gilgamesh, she returns from the underworld with a story, having plundered the archetypal storehouse of images associated with the caverns of memory (Hillman, *Analysis* 171). We should remember, in this context, that for both Virgil and Homer, Hades was a burial place of memory, where the great stories of the race lay like seeds in an underground silo.

Persephone's ecstatic reunion with her mother Demeter is one of the great and most moving moments in the history of the heroine's journey: the powerful horses surge unchecked over sea, rivers, glens, and mountain peaks, and mother rushes to daughter like a maenad tearing through the shady woodland of Dionysos (12). As Joseph Campbell has shown, the theme of the atonement (the union of father and son) often marks the climax of the initiations of the hero journey cycles: the reunion of Odysseus, Laertes, and Telemachus in the shepherd's hut on Ithaka, for example, represents the reconciliation of "the two worlds of Eternity and Time, Death and Life" (*Occidental* 176). The atonement combines with the symbolism of homecoming to represent the soul's arrival at its eternal destination, as we will see again in our discussion of the biblical journeys of Joseph and the Prodigal Son. But, in the "Homeric Hymn to Demeter," the great roles of the atonement are played by mother and daughter, both of whose heroine journeys come full circle with their tender reunion.

The Biblical Hero Journey

The basic narrative structure of the biblical stories, from the Old to the New Testament, is the hero journey cycle; it is the single basic type of the overall structure of the Bible as a whole (from Genesis to the Apocalypse of St. John), which is then variously developed in a series of refigurations in the individual episodes in the stories of Joseph, Jonah, Jesus, and the Prodigal Son). Each version of the hero journey repeats the basic pattern of the overall structure of the Book as a whole, while also illustrating a gradual progression of basic biblical themes.

The biblical paradigm of human history is a hero journey (from *Genesis* to *Revelation*): we begin and end the cycle in Paradise, the Edenic at the beginning and the Earthly Paradise at the end, with the separation and departure being initiated by the serpent's call to adventure. Before the Fall those idyllic conditions reign which characterize domestic security of familiar daily life which must be disrupted in way for the journey to begin. The setting of the garden is described in terms of a symbolic landscape very similar to the description of the island of Calypso in the *Odyssey*: a river in the midst of Eden separates into four rivers (thus dividing the earth into four quarters), so that the mountain garden with its trees of knowledge and of life becomes a symbol of the *axis mundi* or *omphalos*. Both represent the spot where the divine energy pours into earthly form and immediately breaks up into combined pairs of opposites (such as male and female, good and evil, life and death) which taken together form a symbol of totality. As Joseph Campbell has shown, the mythic image of the central axis around which the four quarters of the world revolve and from which they originate is of universal distribution, and probably has its roots in the Ancient Near Eastern cosmologies.[21]

It is the serpent who disrupts this unity and makes Eve and Adam aware of a world of dualities by feeding them the fruit of the tree of knowledge, which promises to make them wise and to open their eyes in order to be as gods (3: 5-6). This temptation initiates the hero journey and separation from the Garden, a transition and threshold crossing in which the symbolism of clothing and doorways plays a crucial role. The first thing Adam and Eve do to signify their awareness of a new condition is to make themselves new clothes out of fig leaves, and the Lord God follows suit by clothing them in "coats of skin" (3: 21). This is a curious and fascinating moment in the hero journey, one open to a variety of mystical interpretations, such as those which come down to us in Gnosticism and Neoplatonism, in which nakedness represents the soul disincarnated, as pure spirit before birth and after death, while clothing represents the soul incarnated in bodily form -- the biblical text says just this, in fact, since God clothes Adam and Eve in a coat of *skins* for the first time after the fall. Gnostic and Kabbalistic commentaries on *Genesis* could therefore suggest that Adam's body was different before the fall, a body of light such as the one Paul says we will put on after the resurrection, while the Fall represents the descent of the soul into the mortal body (a coat of *skin*) of earthly life.[22] Closely related to the symbolism of clothing here is the image of the doorway: God drives Adam and Eve out of the garden shortly after clothing them in bodies of mortal flesh, and then sets the Cherubims and the flaming sword at the east side of Eden to prevent their return. Although no door or gateway is specifically mentioned here, the traditional iconography of the expulsion usually includes a doorway guarded by a Cherubim, such as we find in Masaccio's *Expulsion from Paradise*.

The consequence of the temptation and Fall is human life (none of us would be here if not for the wonderful thing Eve, the mother of all living, did for us in the Garden: she is what the Hindus call *shakti*, the feminine principle which sets life going by overcoming the passive stasis of the male). The trials and ordeals of human history constitute the initiatory phase of the biblical hero journey, the climax or nadir of which is the coming of Jesus and the Crucifixion. His divine presence (*parousia*) constitutes the revelation of the secret meaning of life and initiates the transformation of the human condition, via the absolution of original sin. This makes the return to the beginning possible which brings the human journey full circle: Alpha and Omega meet in The Book of Revelation, when the Earthly Paradise lost in the beginning is restored. This basic narrative frame for the Bible as a whole (the hero journey from Genesis to Revelation) provides the great enclosing circle for the many hero journey cycles between the beginning and the ending books. The variations on the theme are too numerous to treat exhaustively, though taken as a whole, they have immeasurably enriched the vocabulary of mythic motifs affiliated with the monomyth. We can only focus here on a few representative variations of the theme that illustrate the universal motifs and, when taken together, show the progressive development which occurs as we move from Joseph, to Job, to Jonah, and finally to Jesus.

Joseph's hero journey in Genesis begins with a call to adventure coming from within and without: from within it comes in the form of two dreams that exalt Joseph over his brethren, and from without it comes in the form of sibling rivalry after Jacob favors Joseph by giving him the coat of many colors. This combination of inner aspiration and outer envy precipitates the departure, and, when he follows his brothers to Dothan, the threshold battle occurs as the brothers strip Joseph of his coat and cast him into the waterless pit, shortly thereafter to sell him to the Ishmaelites who take him down into Egypt. Joseph is directed to Dothan by a "certain man" who finds Joseph "wandering in the field" of Shechem; this mysterious threshold guardian, who serves as guide and helper, will later appear in works by Thomas Mann and Saul Bellow as Hermes, guide of souls to the underworld, though the biblical account tells us very little about him.

In Genesis, the symbolism of clothing is important from the start: it is Joseph's "coat, his coat of many colors that was on him," that arouses their wrath, as the brothers recognize him approaching from a distance. After being thrown in the well and sold off to the Ishmaelites, the brethren take the coat and dip it in the blood of slaughtered kid, so that they can then provide it as proof that Joseph was devoured in the wilderness when they return to their father Jacob. The rather odd syntax of the King James translation keeps our attention firmly focused on the coat (italics mine):

> And they took Joseph's *coat*, and killed a kid of the goats, and dipped the *coat* in the blood; and they sent the *coat* of many colors, and they brought it to their father; and said, This have we found: know now whether it be thy son's *coat* or no. And he knew it, and said, It is my son's *coat*, an evil beast hath devoured him; Joseph is without doubt rent in pieces. (Gen. 37: 31-33)

Five times in three verses, and then the related image of Jacob tearing his own clothes in grief, with the same verb ("rent") using to describe the dismemberment of the body of the son and the divestiture of the clothing of the father: "And Jacob rent his clothes, and put sackcloth upon his loins, and mourned his son many days" (Gen. 37: 34).

The literary typology of the hero journey will alert us again and again to the important symbolism of clothing to indicate a change of being. We have already seen this in the Sumero-Babylonian material, where the stripping of Inanna symbolized the shedding of the mortal vestments of the body during her descent through the seven gates of the underworld. And so in the story of Joseph the rent clothing and the coat dipped in blood represent a complex image of both incarnation and death: just as Adam must put on a coat of skins in order to begin his life as a human being, so must Joseph's condition be bloodied upon his departure from the paradise of his father. The coat, that is to say, and the descent into the Egyptian land of the dead, represent the spiritual body of light that is bloodied by incarnation and the descent into the material world.

A clue to this interpretation comes to us from the Gnostic version of the hero journey called the "Hymn of the Pearl," which reads much like a mystic gloss of the Joseph story. This hymn is to be found in the apocryphal Acts of the Apostle Thomas, extant in a Syriac and Greek version, products of that Hellenistic world explored by Hans Jonas in *The Gnostic Religion*. In the Hymn, the hero is directed to descend from his father's house down into Egypt to retrieve a Pearl "which lies in the middle of the sea which is encircled by the snorting serpent" (113). Before the hero leaves on his mission, his "robe of glory" or "purple mantle that was woven to conform exactly to [his] figure" is stripped from him (113). While in Egypt he clothes himself "in their garments," temporarily forgets his mission, and falls into an intoxicated sleep until awakened by a letter from the King his father. Once arisen, he charms "the terrible and snorting serpent ... by naming over it my Father's name, the name of our next in rank, and that of my mother" (115). (This magical formula suggests an alternative to the Christian trinity by including a feminine deity, "the queen of the East"). He then seizes the Pearl and puts off "Their filthy and impure garment" before leaving the land of the Egyptians and returning to the light of his home-land in the East (115). Once home, the robe of glory comes to meet the boy, who has forgotten its splendor; he sees in the robe a mirror image of himself, "the image of the King of kings," and "the quivering move-ments of the gnosis" (115). The robe then emanates songs, and the hero decks himself with "the beauty of its colors," and casts "the royal man-tle" over his "entire self" (115). He then proceeds to the "gate of saluta-tion and adoration" that leads to the splendor of the father, so that we see once again the coalescence of clothing and threshold imagery as the hero passes through the doorway into the presence of the Father.

There are essentially two sets of clothing here in the Gnostic hymn: the royal robe of glory worn at the beginning and at the end of the journey, and the impure filthy garments worn among the Egyptians. The robe of glory corresponds to the coat of many colors given Joseph by his father; but Jacob himself got it from Joseph's mother, who would then represent Sophia, the goddess who produces our first body of light when her "shadow image is projected upon the primal waters of chaos" (Quispell 208).[23] The impure garment corresponds to the garment torn from Joseph by Potiphar's wife. As Jonas points out, this impure gar-ment denotes "the body as a passing earthly form encasing the soul," to be exchanged for a garment of light when the soul returns home to the father after death (56). As Jonas puts it, the robe of glory "symbolizes the heavenly or eternal self of the person" with which he is reunited at death: "in the Coptic-Manichaean genealogy of the gods, we find among the divine emanations the 'figure of light that comes to meet the dying,' also called 'the angel with the garment of light'" (122). Joseph's

coat of many colors, therefore, is an image of his divine and angelic
body of light, which must of necessity be bloodied (that is to say, exchanged for a physical body) at the moment of his incarnation and descent into the material world (Egypt) after the fall.

In Egypt, Joseph is sold into bondage and becomes the household
servant of Potiphar, who gradually makes Joseph the overseer of his
property because everything flourishes in his presence (including the
desires of his master's wife). Hans Jonas notes that Egypt was widely
regarded in the ancient world as "the home of the cult of the dead, and
therefore the kingdom of Death .... The Gnostics then turned this evalu-
ation into their use of Egypt as a symbol for 'this world,' that is, the
world of matter, of ignorance, and of perverse religion" (118). The
symbolism of the impure garment, then, is in accord with the symbolism of Egypt as the realm of bodily incarnation and physical desire. In a
scene parallel to the rending of Joseph's coat of many colors by the
jealous brethren, Potiphar's wife "caught him by his garment, saying
Lie with me: and he left his garment in her hand, and fled" (Gen. 39:
11). In the next four verses the word "garment" is repeated four times,
as Potiphar's wife falsely accuses Joseph of seducing her, yielding a total of six repetitions. Four of those repetitions occur in the rhythmical
phrase "he left his garment" (Gen. 39: 12, 13, 15, 18), keeping our attention fixed on the moment of Joseph's being stripped down.

This sequential stripping down of the hero is familiar to us from
Inanna's descent, and what follows for Joseph is a kind of descent as
well, this time into the underworld of the Pharoah's prison a few
leagues up the Nile. [24] After two years in prison, Joseph is summoned
by Pharaoh to interpret his dreams, and the imagery of clothing again
surfaces to signify a transition: "The Pharaoh sent and called Joseph,
and they brought him hastily out of the dungeon: and he shaved himself, and changed his raiment, and came in unto Pharaoh" (Gen. 41: 14).
This is the crucial turning point of Joseph's journey, the nadir of his descent into the land of the dead, during which the dream life of those
around him (the baker, the butler, and the Pharaoh) is intensified and
becomes the means of Joseph's liberation. We have noticed before, in
both the Gilgamesh Epic and the "Descent of Inanna" how the heroic
nekyia tends to activate crisis dreams, and we will find the connection
of the journey and reverie consistent throughout the historical development of the monomyth. This moment that marks Joseph's return to
the upperworld is celebrated by a change of clothing: after successfully
interpreting the two famous dreams of the Pharaoh by predicting the
seven years of famine to follow seven years of plenty, Joseph is made
overseer of Egypt and is freshly clothed "in vestures of fine linen"
(Gen. 41: 42). These new vestments, symbols of royal power like the
me in the story of Inanna, are the fourth change of clothes in Joseph's

journey; the glory of the fine linen anticipates Joseph's final ascent from the underworld, at the moment of his death (a change of clothing left to our imagination).

Hence the nadir of Joseph's descent into the Pharaoh's dungeons emphasizes two aspects of the biblical hero journey: the theme of imprisonment and the importance of dreams. The fact that Joseph is imprisoned evokes the traditional symbolism (from the biblical point of view!) of Egypt as the land of corruption, bondage, and death, i.e. (from the Gnostic point of view) the material world itself, from which the heroic soul must be delivered before becoming the deliverer. That messianic role will be left to Moses, who in Exodus reenacts the main stages of the hero journey cycle, just as Jacob and Joseph had in generations previous: all three go down into bondage from the Holy Land, to move back towards the Promised Land at the end. The notion of this bondage in a foreign country as incarnation, and of deliverance as death, which returns us to the realm of the spirit, becomes so central to the biblical tradition of the hero journey that we find, for example, Dante's one hundred souls singing *"In exitu Israel de Aegypto"* as the Angel ferries them from the banks of the Tiber after their death to the base of the purgatorial mountain (*Purgatorio* 2: 46). The words of their song are from Psalm 114 ("When Israel went out of Egypt"), which had been part of the burial service since the sixth century A.D. (Sinclair 24). Joseph's journey, then, becomes the basic type for the descent of the soul into life and its deliverance from bondage by death and spiritual rebirth.

During Joseph's stay in the dungeon, dreams resurface as a central focus in the hero journey. It seems that the intense suffering and humiliating ordeals of the *nekyia* function as catalysts of such archetypal dreams as those dreamt by Gilgamesh in the cedar forest, Dumuzi hiding in the ditches of Arali, or (as we will see below) by Lucius as he lies beaten and exhausted beside the Adriatic sea over which the full moon rises in *The Golden Ass* of Apuleius. All of these dreams reflect the deepest dynamics of death and rebirth buried in the soul, just as the dreams of the baker and the butler which Joseph interprets in the dungeons of the Pharaoh predict the death of the one and the new life of the other, and just as the Pharaoh's dreams are of famine and fertility. Interpretations, Joseph tells his analysands (the baker and the butler), come from God (Gen. 40: 8), suggesting that dreams carry divine wisdom. The butler dreams of three branches of a vine, and the baker of three baskets of bread, both of which Joseph interprets as the three days before the head of the former will be lifted up, and the head of the latter lifted off (i.e., decapitated!). Three days is, of course, the number of days Inanna spends in the Sumerian *kur*, Jonah spends in the belly of the whale and Jesus in hell. In the Pharaoh's dreams, the numbers seven and fourteen provide the numerological keys: seven well-fed kine and seven lean, seven good ears of corn and seven blighted, and seven years of fertility and seven of famine. The number seven corresponds to the seven gates of the underworld through which Inanna passes, the seven days of Creation, the seven years Jacob spent to first get Leah (whom he didn't want), followed by the seven more years he spends to get Rachel (whom he did want). In the astronomical symbolism of the Gnostics, the number seven is associated with the seven planetary spheres through which the soul passes in its descent into earthly incarnation.[25]

Such number mysticism is also important in the story of Jonah, who spends three nights in the belly of the whale. Jonah's call to adventure comes as "the word of the Lord" which commands him to set out for Nineveh to preach against the wickedness of the people there. As in the Gospel of John, it is the *Logos* in the beginning which initiates the mystery. In this case, Jonah attempts to refuse the call, which turns out only to be another way of beginning the journey. His departure from Joppa to Tarshish precipitates a storm at sea, a typical symbol of the threshold battle which we have seen in the *Odyssey* and will see again in the "Voyages of Sinbad" and "The Tale of Zubaidah" in *The Thousand and One Nights*. During the storm, Jonah goes down into the hold of the ship and falls asleep: imagery of sea, sleep, and forgetting are frequent in Neoplatonic and Gnostic hermeneutics as symbols of the world into which the soul descends at birth, i.e., of the secular world in which the soul loses remembrance of its heavenly origins.[26] Jonah is awakened from this sleep, as is the soul, by death! After the sailors pray for help, Jonah is thrown into the sea, as the brothers had thrown Joseph into the well.

In fact, the "Psalm of Thanksgiving" Jonah recites from the belly of the whale that swallows him for three days and three nights elicits imagery which looks both back to Joseph and forward to Jesus. The language of this psalm suggests that a strict fundamentalist approach to the Bible as literal truth is rejected by the Bible itself. Jonah himself says that the belly of the whale is *not* simply the belly of the whale; it is a metaphor or symbol of the netherworld: "Out of the belly of hell cried I," Jonah says, "earth with her bars was about me for ever" (2: 6); and he refers to the belly of the whale as "the deep, in the midst of the seas" (2: 3) and as "the bottoms of the mountains" (2: 6). These metaphors all suggest that Jonah's journey into the belly of the whale is a symbolic descent into Hades with motifs derived from Mesopotamian and Egyptian prototypes. At least one Midrash has noted that Jonah "typifies the soul of man swallowed by Sheol" (cited in Campbell, *Creative Myth* 13). Sheol is also the "deep," or the "abyss," and hence suggests that Jonah has circled back to the abyss of the beginning, the Tehom of Genesis 1, in order to be reborn. Like Gilgamesh, he has plunged to the depths of the ocean floor to pluck the flower of rejuvenation: an Assyrian seal of 700 B.C. (the time of Jonah) shows Assur, a god of Nineveh (to which city Jonah was journeying) floating above a tree of immortality on the floor of the abyss, guarded by two fish deities (Campbell, *Creative Myth* 13-15). The metaphor of the "roots of the mountains" is also interesting, in light of the fact that both the Sumerians and the Egyptians situated their underworlds (*kur* and *tuat* respectively) at the roots of the mountain ranges bordering the world into which the sun descends at nightfall. Mountainous interiors will, furthermore, be consistently affiliated with the netherworld in the hero journey all the way up to Murnau's film *Nosferatu* in the 1920's, as we will see in the last chapter. Also suggestive of the Mesopotamian and Egyptian influences is the allusion to the "bars" of the earth closing about Jonah forever, for the bars recall the importance of doorways and gates in "The Descent of Innana," *The Epic of Gilgamesh*, and the Egyptian Books of the Dead. From these depths Jonah is raised up by the Lord, after the whale vomits him onto the "dry land" (2: 10).

As we have seen, the descent into the underworld is associated with the revelation of the gods and the transformation of the hero, as he is reborn or resurrected as a sadder and wiser man. The symbolism of revelation and transformation here is a variation on the universal theme of the initiation in the hero journey, but within the specific context of the Bible as a whole, Jonah's story recalls Joseph's descent into the well, and then into the prisons of Egypt; it also prefigures the three days and three nights between the crucifixion and the resurrection of Jesus in the New Testament. In fact, it was a commonplace of typological criticism to illustrate the story of Jonah alongside Christ's harrowing of hell, Joseph thrown into the well, and Daniel in the Lion's Den (Campbell, *Hero* Figs. 5, 11). Jonah, like Jesus, brings a boon of deliverance to the community upon his return from the belly of the whale: the conversion of Nineveh, and the delivery of the word of God. It is during this return phase of the journey that Jonah experiences the characteristic difficulties of reintegration into the world left behind (anger, alienation, confusion) that will become increasingly evident in Romantic and Modernist versions to be discussed below.

In the specific context of the Bible, then, the hero journey of Jonah exemplifies the beliefs, morals, and spiritual mysteries of the Judeo-Christian world: repentance, atonement, salvation, and resurrection. But the symbolism of the journey reaches beyond the ethnic clothing of the folk idea to the universal significance of an elementary idea found in cultures all over the world. We have already noted the metaphor that links the belly of the whale to the Sumerian underworld,

and the night-sea journey to such stories as that of the Sun God Re in
Egyptian myth, who must traverse the twelve chambers of the *Tuat*. In
the Eskimo fable of the Raven swallowed by a whale who invents fire
to burn his way out we also find what we might call the Pinocchio motif of the hero who meets his father (God the Father) in the belly of the
whale (in a kind of atonement theme) and returns bearing gifts of wisdom to his community. A Greek ceramic depiction of Jason regurgitated from the dragon guarding the golden fleece is another instance of
the belly of the whale motif (Campbell, *Hero* Fig. 12), and we shall see
further folktale examples when we come to our discussion of the
Grimm's tale, "The Wolf and the Seven Little Kids."

The essence of this wisdom seems to involve the cultural and personal regeneration achieved by means of a retreat into the womb of the
mother, which Erich Fromm argues is the tenor of the metaphors of the
ship's hold, the sea, and finally the belly of the whale in the story of
Jonah. The result of this uterine journey is a transformation of Jonah
and of Nineveh: from reluctant to obedient prophet, and from moral
profligacy to spiritual reformation. As Mircea Eliade has shown, such
ordeals of initiatory transformation and revelation typically occur in
during rites of passage which dramatize death and rebirth as a return to
and separation from the womb of the mother. Freudians, perhaps,
would note that Jonah seeks to avoid the wrath of God the Father by
entering, symbolically, the womb of the mother (the act which itself
also precipitates the wrath); this might also help explain Jonah's residual anger after the conversion of Nineveh.

Jung charts a similar psychic cartography in his depiction of the
night sea journey as a regression of libido into the matrix of the unconscious, during which the archetypes that will restructure and transform
the hero's existence are activated. Describing what he calls the "Jonah
and the Whale" complex, Jung writes: "The regressing libido ... continues right back to the intra-uterine, pre-natal condition, and leaving the
sphere of personal psychology altogether, irrupts into the collective
psyche where Jonah saw the 'mysteries' (*representations collectives*') in
the whale's belly" (*Symbols* 419-20). According to Jung, the "mystery
he beholds represents the stock of primordial images which everybody
brings with him as his human birthright, the sum total of inborn forms
peculiar to the instincts" (408), i.e., the archetypes. As amplification for
this interpretation of the Jonah story, Jung cites earlier commentaries by
Paracelsus and Rabbi Eliezer which envision the whale's belly as a
"great synagogue" illuminated by "the two eyes of the fish" and by a
pearl suspended form the whale's rib cage that shines like the sun at
noon and shows "Jonah all that was in the sea and in the depths" (qtd.
330). The pearl, Jung concludes, represents the potential for spiritual or

symbolic life as the ultimate goal of the regression of the libido into the
womb of the mother (a very different goal from the Freudian).

Apart from such psychological concerns, it is certainly noteworthy
that one of the supreme results of Jonah's hero journey is a magnificent
poem (*nekyia=poesis*): his Psalm of Thanksgiving is catalyzed by his
descent into the whale's belly on the bottom of the sea, and it is one of
the greatest poetic expressions of spiritual crisis in our tradition. The
complete destruction of Jonah's conscious intentions; the vivid experience of tempest, defeat, and death; that sense of being overwhelmed by
monstrous energies beyond human control; that profound journey into
the realm of mystery beneath the surface of the world -- all these exis-
tential, ontological, and psychological dimensions play a role in the
hero journey and contribute to the aesthetic richness. From the aesthetic
point of view, the descent into the belly of the whale suggests a feminine image of creativity: the poet emerges from the mother's womb
with a poem and a story, that pearl of great price retrieved from the
abyss.

The parable told by Jesus to Luke (a frame tale), known as the
Prodigal Son, picks up many of the motifs from the Old Testament hero
journey cycles, and hence represents a good example of biblical typology, that mode of allegory by which the tales of the Old Testament anticipate their fulfillment in the New. Hence, in the Prodigal Son, the
underworld, or belly of the whale becomes the "far country" into which
the boy travels after coming of age. That the far country represents
Hades is stated clearly by the Father, who twice says that his son "was
dead, and is alive again" (15: 24, 32). The fact that the son feeds with
the swine in the far country (15: 16) also recalls the affiliation between
pigs and Hades in the Eleusinian mysteries. And, as in "The Homeric
Hymn to Demeter," the homecoming and atonement complete the hero
journey cycle, and represent the return of the soul to its heavenly kingdom, so in "The Prodigal Son" do we also find the related symbolism of
re-investment: just as Joseph received special items of clothing to signify his return from the underworld, so the Prodigal Son receives a
robe, a ring, and some sandals from his father, on the occasion of his
homecoming (15: 22). Typologically, the atonement and reinvestiture
looks back to Joseph, and forward to Jesus, whose hero journey (from
heaven to earth and back to heaven) is itself an image of the incarnation
of every man and woman.

Aeneas

In Book 6 of the *Aeneid*, Aeneas comes to the doors to the
Cumaean Temple of Apollo, on the panels of which Daedalus has
sculpted the story of Crete (14-37). Virgil makes detailed note of the

monstrous love of Pasiphae which spawned the Minotaur, the inextricable complexity of the maze, and the thread which Ariadne gives Theseus so that he may penetrate the labyrinth and slay the Minotaur. The Cumaean panels represent central themes of the *Aeneid* as a whole: unnatural lust, problems of artistry and rhetoric, the meanderings of Aeneas leading to the founding of Rome, and the descent into Hades which constitutes the main action of Book 6 (Doob 31). Many critics have noted the death and rebirth symbolism of the labyrinth, and its association with the journey to the underworld.[27] This is a particularly fruitful line of speculation in any literature survey that moves from, say, Homer to Dante, and beyond to Mann and Borges, since we find the descent to the underworld in all of them connected to the maze and its related political and poetic themes. Virgil's evocation of the Temple of Apollo also suggests a labyrinthine structure composed of "a hundred open portals" (48) which "fly open ... of their own will" (90-91) when the god pronounces his oracle. Virgil's emphasis on the imagery of gateways and doors which open magically in this description establish an iconography of the maze which remains standard all the way from Dante to Mann and Borges.

In the *Aeneid*, the *nekyia* of the *Odyssey* is adapted to the more rationalistic temper of the author and his time, so that the descent to the underworld becomes a precise image of the stages of human death and dying. The basic hero journey pattern of descent and return is left intact, but elaborated and structured in such a way as to serve as a kind of *Ars Moriendi* (an Art of Dying text). Other differences from the Homeric text include the replacement of the dialogue with the mother with a dialogue with the father, and a related shift towards the historical future envisioned by Aeneas while in Hades. Both changes reflect the increased centrality of patriarchal values in Augustan Rome, with their emphasis on reason and the practical concerns of Empire building and civil service, as opposed to the mysticism and matriarchal orientation of the *Odyssey*, with its correlative focus on the individual and his immediate personal fulfillment in the present.

That Virgil rationalizes the hero's *nekyia* is evident from the allegorical structure of Hades: outside the entrance to the abyss we find personifications of the causes of death -- Care, Want, Age, Disease, Discord, War, etc. Moving closer to the actual "jaws of Orcus" at the doorway to the underworld, however, we find those mythological monsters whose terrifying aspects embody the unknown forces of the actual moment of death itself. Being unknown, these terrors take symbolic form as Centaurs, Scyllas, Gorgons, Harpies, and other assorted Chimerae. Without "knowing the truth," Aeneas takes these "empty images" literally (much as Hercules had when he drew his sword against them). His guide the Sybil must therefore tell him "How faint these lives" are -- that is to say, they are the "phantoms" representing human fears about the moment of death (what the Tibetan Book of the Dead calls the wrathful deities, projections of the mind of the departing soul), not actualities like Care and Want.

Beyond this point of entrance into Hades, Virgil must of course rely on traditional images of mythic figurations of the unknown, but he continues to adapt these images to a rational vision of actual stages in the dying process. The path from the doorway into Hades leads on to the shores of Acheron, where Charon stands ready to ferry the multi-tudinous dead, clamoring along the banks, to the afterlife on the yonder shore (the river crossing as a symbol of death and rebirth in the hero journey is one we will find many more times in the chapters ahead). These souls are said to be as numerous as leaves that fall in the first frost of autumn, or as numerous as migratory birds that "darken heaven when the cold season comes / And drives them overseas to sunlit lands." This last lovely simile, suggests that the destination of the blessed souls gathered on the shores of the dismal river is the sunnier climate of the Elysian fields, and the comparison of the soul to a bird is one which we have already seen in Egyptian mythology and in Enkidu's vision of the *kur*. In Virgil, only those souls whose bodies have been accorded proper burial rites may pass on across the river, those left un-buried being condemned to "flutter and roam" the limbo of this side of the river for one hundred years. It is at this point that Aeneas sees his helmsman, Palinurus (as Odysseus had seen Elpenor), who requests proper burial. The movement from the known causes of death outside to doorway, to the symbolic ogres of the threshold, to the problem of actual burial, the next stage in the dying process, shows the logic of Virgil's vision.

After the details of burial have been settled, Aeneas is logically ready for the passage over Acheron into the afterlife proper, a passage procured by the golden bough which he brings as tribute to Proserpine, Queen of the Dead. Just at the other side of the river, amid the "form-less ooze" and "grey-green sedge" of the mire (rational images of natu-ral decay after burial), Aeneas encounters Cerberus lying in a cave making the shoreline resound with the ringing of his triple-throated barking. The Sybil stills him with bread soaked in a soporific honey, possibly an allusion to an opiate. We then pass beyond the river into the first level of Hades, where Virgil situates actual souls of the dead (infants, the falsely accused, suicides) in the place occupied by the "wives and daughters of illustrious men" in Homer. This again indicates Virgil's rational approach to his material in providing a justly calculated vision of which souls would go where after death.

Virgil then passes very quickly through a catalogue of women in the fields of mourning, abbreviating Homer's catalogue considerably and restricting the view to those women "whom pitiless love consumed / With cruel wasting," among whom Dido, whom Aeneas abandoned on Carthaginian shores, figures prominently. In a famous scene, she turns away angrily with "savagely glaring" eyes and a "burning soul." This episode has no direct parallel in the *Odyssey*; yet in both instances the heroes talk first with those recently dead, with whom they had close personal contact in life, suggesting that this stage of the descent constitutes something like the life review common to near death narratives collected by contemporary thanatologists.

After the encounter with Dido, Aeneas moves to the climactic moment of his descent, the conversation with his dead father, followed by the vision of those great Romans to come who will build the Empire Aeneas has yet to found. These conversations constitute the revelation phase of the hero's initiation, during which the secrets of his personal destiny are disclosed. In this case, that destiny is of world historical significance, serving partly as a rationalized justification for the Roman Empire. However, the fact that Aeneas returns with his vision of Roman power through the ivory gates of false dreams implies a profound ambivalence felt by Virgil regarding his presumed role as state propagandist par excellence. Be that as it may, the return of Aeneas to the upperworld back through the gateway reiterates the importance of threshold imagery in the hero journey, and completes the full cycle of his descent. What is essential to remember for further analysis of the cycle is the revelation of the basic pattern of the hero's life, of the informing structure which bestows shape and significance upon experience. It is the manifestation of this fundamental idea (*eidos*), which confers meaning upon life, that constitutes the climax of the hero's initiation.

The Golden Ass: Lucius and Psyche

One of the best beloved and most enduring of heroine journey cycles from the Ancient World comes down to us in the book by Apuleius called the *Metamorphoses*, from about 158 A.D., but known to the world as *The Golden Ass*. Like the Bible, a single large hero journey cycle (the story of Lucius, who travels from Rome, to Thessaly, and back to Rome) frames numerous smaller cycles (the most important of which concerns the adventures of Psyche). The story has attracted the attention of numerous critics and scholars, while artists from Marie-Catherine D'Aulnoy ("The Green Serpent" of 1697), to Walter Pater (*Marius the Epicurean* of 1885), and more recently C.S. Lewis (*Till We Have Faces*) have been tempted to create new versions of the story of "Cupid and Psyche." Early on in our century, in 1914, Richard Reitzenstein argued that Eros and Psyche were local deities in Greek cults (von Franz 64), while in 1962 Reinhold Merkelbach linked the story to the mysteries of the Isis cult in Egypt (von Franz 2). The tale has been studied both as an allegory of male psychological development, focusing on the mother complex and the integration of the anima (von Franz), and as an allegory of the psychological development of the feminine (Neumann and Johnson). James Hillman sees the story more generally as what he calls the myth of analysis, an allegory of the psychological creativity and growth characteristic of therapy as a whole. Christine Downing has very briefly discussed the relationship between sisters in the story. That the larger hero journey of Lucius frames the tale of Eros and Psyche, which Lucius hears recited to a young bride abducted by a group of thieves, suggests that von Franz is on target (as usual) with her focus on the psychodynamics of male development. The great age of the story, however, and the fact that it is told by an old woman to a young bride to be, suggests a long history of oral transmission stretching back far beyond Apuleius, so that the tale of Psyche certainly condenses a powerful tradition of matrilineal wisdom.

The novel as a whole begins and ends with Lucius, who travels from Rome to Thessaly and back to Rome. His call to adventure seems simply to be, like Psyche's, curiosity: he wants to find out more about witchcraft and the mystical magic for which Thessaly was renowned. The call seems also to do with a hidden longing for his mother, whose family originated in Thessaly (33). As so often in the monomyth, the threshold crossing into the realm of the unknown is symbolized by two talismanic doorways. The first stands at the entrance to the house where Lucius' aunt Byrrhaena lives, whom Lucius meets after passing "from door to door" around and around the city (50). Byrrhaena immediately invokes maternal imagery, saying Lucius is "'Just like his noble mother Salvia,'" recalling the days when she herself nursed him as a baby, and pointing out that she was more than kindred with Salvia, since she "shared a nipple with her," having "sucked the same nurse, one to each pap" (51). No wonder Lucius blushes! But more profoundly, the image of the two sisters sharing the same breast, and the emphasis on maternal love, immediately introduces the theme of the Great Goddess in the novel. So does the sculptuary in the hallway entrance into Byrrhaena's house: there are four columns at each corner, crowned by "representations of the Palm-bearing Goddess," with a statue of Diana, carved in Parian marble, standing in the middle of the hall, with a stream springing out "in crinkling waves" from under her feet (52).

The symbolism of the four quarters of the globe radiating outwards from a central point, which represents the mysterious origin of all life, is as commonly to be found in the architectural traditions of antiquity (think of the piazzi of Rome) as in hero journey representations of the Great Goddess (think, for example, of Eve, "Mother of all living," in the center of Eden, with the four rivers of paradise flowing outwards from the source). In this case, the Goddess assumes the specific form of Diana, surrounded by the hounds which will devour Actaeon, who is depicted "staring hungrily at the goddess," with the horns of his transformation just beginning to curl up from his brow (52). The image is like the overture of an opera, or the exposition of a sonata, for it anticipates the major themes and action of the novel: the transformation of Lucius into a donkey, and his long journey to regain the good graces of the Goddess (von Franz 31-33). Hence, it is with supreme irony when Byrrhaena, after noticing the "fascinated pleasure" with which Lucius explores the sculptuary of the entrance hall, says to him "'Everything you see here is yours'" (52). Indeed it is, for the statue of the Goddess represents the archetypes of his own unconscious, waiting to erupt and drag him down into the underworld.

A second doorway stands at the threshold entrance into the realm of adventure, and again Lucius is brought to it by a woman, this time Fotis, the delectable chambermaid with whom he enjoys a long night of lovemaking, after watching her cook in the kitchen. This is a marvelous seduction scene, although it is really Lucius who is being abducted: Fotis stands "stirring the stock pot with her rosy little hands moving round and round above it," with "undulating loins" and a mischievous tongue (54). When Lucius asks what sort of "honeyed relish" she is preparing for the man happy enough to "dip finger there," Fotis warns him to "Keep your distance. For if the tiniest spark of that heat grazes you, you'll be scorched to the gizzard, and no one will be able to quench you but myself. For I'm very good at putting choice spice into pot or bed, and making them both equally stirring" (54). Later, when they pick their "nightlong bone" together (56), Lucius compares the disrobing Fotis to a "Venus who rose beautifully from the trough of the sea" (60), an image which anticipates the finale of his hero journey, when he will pray to the moon rising above the Adriatic, and see Isis in a dream vision. The Goddess stands, therefore, at the beginning and at the end of the cycle; she is the Alpha and the Omega, the womb and tomb of our life journey.

I dwell on the details of the kitchen scene not only for their enticing lubricity, but also to remark upon the archetypal motifs of the Goddess which they playfully evoke: the "honeyed relish" Fotis stirs in the stock pot suggests a long standing association between bees and the Great Goddesses of the Ancient Mediterranean. Many of the seal ring impressions excavated by Sir Arthur Evans depict the Goddesses with waspish waists and bee-like heads; Minoan burial sites like the tomb at Pylos were in the shape of a large beehive; and one of the famous Linear B tablets from Knossos offers "a jar of honey" to the "Lady of the Labyrinth" (Campbell, *Occidental Myth* 50, 47). From around 3500-

1750 B.C. in Asia Minor, the dead were embalmed in honey, and eu-
phemistically said to have fallen into jars (pithoi) of honey. The myths
imply the use of bee-balm to restore the dead, a magical ritual presided
over by the various Goddesses of the Ancient Mediterranean world:
Demeter was called "pure mother bee" and offered honey cakes in the
shape of genitalia at the Thesmophoria, while the priestesses of
Aphrodite at Eryx were called bees (melissae) and the Goddess herself
Melissa, or Queen bee, whose male consort was annually sacrificed
(Walker, *Encyclopedia* 407). Her symbol was the golden honeycomb
which was the last gift of Daedalus to Aphrodite (Davenport 58). In her
Prolegomena of 1903, Jane Harrison notes a connection between *poesis*
and *thriambos*, the mad song sung by the inspired priestesses of Delphi,
bee goddesses who (a passage from the Homeric Hymn to Hermes
suggests) became prophetic when intoxicated by a honey mead (441-
42). There is also an archaic connection between the bee goddess and
the bull, both symbols of death and rebirth which Porphyry refers to in
his commentary on the "Cave of the Nymphs" in Homer (qtd. in
Gimbutas 270). An onyx gem from Knossos depicts a bee-headed
nymph with bull horns and a "double-axe shaped butterfly" above her
head (Gimbutas 272).

Apuleius combines this insectomorphic imagery of the Goddess
with another fascinating archetypal symbol of her power: the cooking
pot, or cauldron. There are many cups and cauldrons in the archaic period of Greek myth -- such as the cauldron Medea cooks an old ram in
to renew its life, as she was also said to have cooked Jason himself in as
well! (Matthews 46). The image was widespread, with many variations
on the theme, as we know from another black-figured Attic vase of a
child in a cauldron (Kerényi, *Gods* 23). It survived into the Hellenistic
era of the mystery cults of the 2end and 3rd centuries A.D., as we know
from an alabaster serpent cup (to which attention was drawn during the
1930's) which contains not one, but sixteen people (Leisegang 194f.).
The Pietrosa Bowl of approximately the same period illustrates the entire cycle mystery of death and rebirth, using a syncretic group of
mythological figures thought to be Orphic (Campbell, *Mythic Image*
388). Celtic prototypes include the Grail (as we will see) and
Ceridwen's Cauldron, heated by a fire stoked by the breath of nine virgins blowing steadily for nine months, until the moment for tasting
should arrive. When her apprentice Taliessin sneaks a taste, he is immediately inspired with the power of prophetic song, and, like Lucius,
undergoes a sequence of transformations (Graves 27-28). Cauldrons of
rejuvenation and poetic inspiration are also to be found throughout Irish
and Welsh legendry. The Irish King Matholwch, for example, possessed a magic cauldron into which he cast his dead warriors and
cooked them, so that they could rise and fight again the next day (Green

58). Another scene on the famous Gundestrup cauldron (a large silver vessel of the 1st or 2end century B.C. found in a bog in Denmark) shows the Dagda dipping a warrior into the pot, either to partake of its healing brew, or to be cooked (Cunliffe 108).[28]

The cauldron, therefore, combines the imagery of the mother archetype (loving and devouring) with the motifs of the bee goddess and the theme of transformation, which lies at the core of *The Golden Ass*. After Lucius gorges himself on the honeyed relish Fotis stirs up for him in her stock pot, she gets a little revenge, which brings us to that second doorway I promised you above. Lucius begs her to take him to Pamphile's room, the mistress of the household, who, as his aunt Byrrhaena had warned him, is an accomplished witch. Fotis brings the foolishly curious Lucius, at the first watch of the night, to spy on Pamphile's demonic rites, which he watches through "a chink in the door panel" of her room (82). This is the door which will lead him down through the "gulf of Avernus" over which Pamphile presides, like Hecate (57). The imagery of divestiture combines with the threshold motifs (as in "The Descent of Inanna") when Lucius watches through the "chink in the door panel" as Pamphile takes off "all her clothes" and rubs her naked body all over with an ointment that turns her into an owl. Hoping to emulate Pamphile, Lucius applies the ointment Fotis steals for him, but by reciting the wrong incantation, he is turned into an ass, instead of an owl! While stalled that night in the stables, thieves smash the bolts of the doors down, and steal him to carry their loot,

This begins the long journey of trials and tribulations which Lucius experiences on the road: the adventures become increasingly cruel and sordid, until Lucius finally escapes a perverse Roman matron who wants him to play the bull to her Pasiphae. Exhausted and humiliated, Lucius comes to the final, redeeming initiation of his journey, which involves that revelation and transformation which make the return stage of the journey possible. The ordeals of the road (which include the recitation of the story of Eros and Psyche discussed below) are too numerous to explore in detail, but the revelation of Isis in Book 11 is one of the great moments in the history of hero journey. It occurs after Lucius falls asleep at dusk by the sea, but suddenly wakes up to see "the full orb of the Moon shining with peculiar lustre and that very moment emerging from the waves of the sea" (235), like the Venus he had fancied Fotis to be. He recognizes the moon as "the primal Goddess of supreme sway," although during his prayer to "the august image of the risen Goddess," he addresses her variously as the Queen of Heaven, Ceres, Venus, sister of Phoebus, and Proserpine (235-36). This is the one Goddess in the same four manifestations that Psyche has to integrate during her journey, and they represent a quaternity of powers which taken together constitute the feminine principle in its totality.

The moon itself, as Robert Graves pointed out, represents the same totality in triple form: the crescent virgin, the full mother, and the waning
crone. She rises from the primordial waters of the Creation, which,
flowing through all human beings, beasts, and "even inorganic objects
... increase when she waxes, and decline when she wanes" (235). But
the waters of the sea may also suggest "the standing Gnostic symbol for
the world of matter or of darkness into which the divine has sunk"
(Jonas 117), the world from which the divine Goddess is now arising.
Similarly, the sleep into which Lucius falls before the vision represents,
in Gnostic terms, the nadir of his fall into the material world, while his
awakening indicates the beginning of the soul's ascent and return to its
heavenly home (Jonas 69).

The Goddess, of course, transcends Gnostic dualism, embracing
the opposites within Herself. After Lucius prays to the moon for
restoration of his "lost self" (shades of the Prodigal Son), he falls asleep
again and again awakens to the vision of "a god-like face" emerging
"from the midst of the sea with lineaments the gods themselves would
revere" (236). It is a "resplendent image" of the Goddess, rising out "of
the scattered deep" (a wonderful phrase, suggestive at once of the imagery of dis-and-re-memberment, and of the mythology of the mer-
maid), clothed in the radiance of the night sky (236). The grand tradition of clothing symbolism in the hero journey comes to noble climax
in this revelation of the Goddess. She has an abundance of ringleted
hair, she is wearing a crown of flowers and a mirror like a "miniature
moon" over her brow. The mirror is supported by vipers on either side,
and "blades of corn" are disposed above it. Her garment is white, yellow, red, and pitch black, a quaternity of colors which embody the four
powers of the Goddesses Lucius names in his prayer. The pitch black
cloak is embroidered along the edges and all over its surface with stars,
a full moon is stitched into the center, and a garland of "every kind of
fruit and flower" clings to its fluttering border. She is the night sky,
mother universe, who wears the cosmos like a splendid evening gown,
covering the mysteries of her inscrutable nakedness; she is mother
earth, the source of every fruit and flower that nourishes or sustains
mankind; and she is the mother of the muses, for she holds, in her right
hand, a "brazen sistrum" which emits a triple chord and "shrill sharp
cry" when vibrated. (That same chord can be heard today in the halls of
modern hotels, when the bridesmaids of Cairo come keening to celebrate a marriage.) In her left hand, the Goddess holds "an oblong
golden vessel," the prototype of the Grail, and of all sacred cauldrons
(237).

Such is the splendor of the Goddess, a symbol not only of the
beauty and power of the universe, but also of poesis, for the noble
speech which she now addresses to Lucius is uttered in a "divine voice"

which the prose attempts (successfully) to mimic. She identifies herself as Isis, the one Goddess of the many names, the "natural mother of all life, the mistress of the elements, the first child of time, the supreme divinity, the queen of those in hell, the first among those in heaven, the uniform manifestation of all the gods and goddess" (237). It is a liturgy later to reemerge in the litanies of the Virgin Mary (Stella Maris) of whom Isis is the prototype. Before she ebbs "back into her own essence" (239), she instructs Lucius to eat some roses the next day from the hand of one of her priests, when he will see "the sun of [his] salvation arise" (238), an image which suggests the solar night-sea journey as a cosmic parallel to the lunar cycle. The next day, all of nature sings hymns to "the Mother of the Stars, the Producer of the Seasons, the Mistress of the Universe" (239), epithets which indicate the supreme power of this feminine manifestation of the divine. But it was a swan song, a last glimpse of the archetypal goddess of the Bronze Age world, since she would soon be appropriated by the patriarchal orientation of Roman Catholicism (Campbell, "Goddess" 74-85).

Her mysteries were, however, preserved throughout the course of the Hellenistic era of the Roman period, when those rituals which reenacted the heroic descent to and return from the underworld rivaled the emerging ceremonies of the Christian cult. Apuleius gives us tantalizing glimpses of these rites of passage (the climactic revelation of the initiation phase of the journey), during which Isis appeared "shining on amid the darkness of Acheron and reigning in the Stygian depths" into which the initiates descend (239). These rites were a marvelously syncretic affair, embracing the iconography of a variety of Mediterranean motifs: the six priests in the procession, for example, carry a blazing lamp, model altars, a golden palm tree, a "wand of Mercury," a "vessel of gold rounded into the shape of a woman's breast," a golden winnowing fan, and an amphora (241). These six priests are succeeded by four representations of the "Gods themselves" (241): the dog-headed "messenger of the gods of heaven and hell, Anubis"; the cow-headed "emblem of the Goddess that is fruitful mother of all"; a man carrying "the chest that contained the Secret Things of her unutterable mystery"; and, finally, a man carrying a "venerable effigy of Supreme Deity" (241). (How reminiscent this all is of the accouterments of the Mass and Communion ceremonies of the Christian Church!). These last two items are versions of the sacred vessel, which we will see again as the Grail of the Arthurian processions during the Middle Ages. One can still see the so-called Basket of Isis, from Caligula's Temple of the 1st century A.D., which shows a serpent coiled three and a half times around the top, just lifting its head from the basket, with a crescent moon sprouting a grain of wheat beneath it (Campbell, *Mythic Image* 339). It looks very much like the chest carried by the third priest, but it is the effigy carried by the fourth priest which Apuleius describes in greater detail: it is a golden urn covered with Egyptian hieroglyphics with a spout on one end, and an asp coiling round the whole length of a handle on the other (242). The association between sacred vessels, lamps, and serpents was quite common in the syncretic iconography of the Hellenistic era, and it survived all the way up into Christian times: votive tablets from the Asklepion (Greek, 4th century B.C.E.), ivory images of Hygeia (Roman, 4th century A.D.), and a portrait of St. John the Evangelist blessing a chalice from which a snake emerges (15th century, Piero di Cosimo) attest to the longevity of the icon (Campbell, *Mythic Image* 286-97). Lucius refers to the vessel as "the instrument of my salvation" (242), for the same priest carries the roses which enable him to recover human form, and which initiate the completion of the hero journey cycle, when Lucius returns, transformed, to Rome.

Two more hero journey cycles, however, await the neophyte there. Both seem to involve the standard pattern of separation, initiation, and return which Eliade discusses as the essence of the religious mysteries of all time (*Myths* 195-200). Although it was illegitimate, indeed punishable by death, to reveal the secrets of these mysteries, the hints Lucius gives us concerning the rituals of Isis and Osiris recall the earlier pattern of the Eleusinia, and highlight certain standard motifs of the hero journey. They include, first of all, threshold imagery, when the presiding priest performs "the rituals of opening the doors" to reveal certain books written in elaborate, unknown characters: "hieroglyphically painted animals" and "wreathed and twisted letters with tails that twirled like wheels or spiraled together like vine-tendrils" (248). The notion of an unknown language, expressing inscrutable revelations in a mysterious tongue, is one that will continue to be associated with the revelations of the hero journey, all the way up to Ambrose Bierce. But it is important to point out here that one of those mysteries has to do with poesis, for which the monomyth is a metaphor: all poets strive for that highly condensed, magical language which characterizes great literature, and it is significant therefore that Lucius finds books in the inner sanctum where his journey ends.

The emphasis on the symbolism of letters is important too, for all during antiquity letters were seen as the seed forms of all creation (of worlds and of texts): the Greek word for letters, for example (*stoicheia*), "also carries the meaning *elements* with all the cosmological associations of that term," for the letters are "the basic elements of the cosmic order," and it is from "these units that the material form of the universe, and the natural world, was constructed" (Drucker 56). There exists a variety of mythologies from the Indo-European sphere in which a sacred alphabet serves as a medium of creation. In Egyptian theology, "The real creator was the Word -- the primeval speech which came from God wherein all things got their name" (Clark 63). In some texts Atum was the deity who "delivered the creative Word," "the intermediary between God's thought and the multitude of created things" (Clark 63), while in other texts it is Ptah who creates the gods and the world simultaneously with the creation of "'every Divine Word'" (Clark 65). In the Coffin Texts of the Herakleopolitan Period the creative Word was understood as the 'Command' which establishes the order of the Creation (Clark 63). Clark sums up as follows: "The Egyptian theologians were convinced that the world was governed by ideas, the 'words' of the gods," and they conceived of "God as the mythical first being, as the Divine Word and Creator" (267).[29]

In Hinduism, Prajapati, hatched from cosmic egg, speaks three words (Bhuh, Bhuvah, Svar) which create Earth, Aether, and Sky; while in Tantrism, the Creator, Preserver, and Destroyer of all things is the Goddess Kali, from whom "issue all letters and words (*Sabda*) and the world of things (*Artha*) which they denote. Into Her as Kali they are dissolved" (Woodroffe 236). In the Kundalini Yoga system, the entire Creation evolves from the seed syllable Om (Mookerjee 133). Each of the psychic centers of the body has a seed syllable in the center of a lotus, the petals of which are inscribed with other letters, which all taken together represent the subtle energies of the spiritual body, of which the physical body itself is a gross manifestation.[30] Similarly, in the esoteric traditions of Islamic mysticism, the body of God is itself "composed of the letters of the alphabet" (Massignon, qtd. in Campbell: *Occidental Myth*: 444). This notion corresponds to the kabbalistic conception of the body of Adam having been created by divine speech, a conception illustrated in pictures which show the body with different letters associated with different parts, lined up to correspond to the Tree of the Sephiroth (Poncé 150-54).

In the Kabbalistic *Sefer Yetzirah* (Book of Creation), the Hebrew alphabet is the divine instrument by which God "created the soul of all creation and everything else that was ever to be created" (qtd. Maclagan 30; Poncé 39): "every creature and every word emanated from one name" (qtd. Maclagan 30). As Scholem points out, this word was the Tetragrammaton, the secret name of God from which all Creation and Speech derives (247). An illustration from Athanius Kircher's *Oedipus Aegyptiacus* of 1652 shows the Tetragrammaton in the center of the tree of knowledge, with the seventy two names proposed by the kabbalah written in four letters of seventy two languages on the petals or leaves on the tree (Godwin 63). Kabbalah generally focuses on twenty two letters: three Mothers (Aleph, Mem, Shin) associated with the three basic elements of creation, three seasons, and three basic parts of the body (Aleph-Air-Head, Shin-Fire-Body, Mem-Water-Stomach); seven double letters linked to the seven coordinates of space (four corners, above and below, center), seven planets, seven days of the week, and the seven gates of the Merkabah mystics (Poncé 42); and finally there are the twelve simple letters which incorporate the entire range of sensual experience and the twelve signs of zodiac (Poncé 44). Further correspondences link the letters symbolizing the four worlds of the sephirothic tree to the body of Adam (brain, heart, breath, genitals) (Poncé 53). The golem (an early form of Adam) is created by inscribing the word *Emeth* on the forehead, which brings it to life, while erasing the first letter of that word yields *Meth*, the word for death, and results in its dissolution (a ritual analogous to the Tantric symbolism associated with Kali).[31]

Hence, when Lucius is led through the hidden doorways of the spacious temple into a shrine of books encoding secret wisdom in the highly condensed form of "unknown characters" which swirl around like little labyrinths, what we have is a glimpse of the original elements of the creation, provided by the hero journey. His last cycle takes him once again down into Hades, where all the ladders start, and the imagery here is of the solar journey, perhaps associated with the Egyptian voyage of Ra-Osiris through the twelve chambers of the Tuat (Budge 170-211). We are told that Lucius "approached the confines of death," crossed the "threshold of Proserpine," and saw the midnight "Sun shining in all his glory," before returning to the world at dawn. As usual, his rite of passage and spiritual rebirth is signified by new vestments, a kind of coat of many colors, composed of "twelve stoles," a "vestment of linen embroidered with a flower pattern," and a "costly cape" covered with a myriad of animal shapes (serpents and griffins), known as an "Olympic stole" (250). Decorated "like the sun and draped like a statue," Lucius emerges from his second to last underworld to sing praises, for the rest of his life, to Isis -- "Most holy and everlasting Redeemer of the human race," who bestows "the consoling smiles of a Mother upon our tribulations" (250).

Within this grand hero journey cycle we have a little gem, the tale of Eros and Psyche, which, furthermore, contains several smaller cycles within itself, like a series of Chinese boxes, or Mayan worry dolls. It is a frame tale (Apuleius calls it simply "The Tale of the Old Woman"), a story within a story, one of thirteen such within the novel as a whole. The point is important, for the device of the frame tale puts both tellers and readers of tales into the novel as characters, which suggests that one of the many themes of the hero journey is the process by which literature is written and read. Poesis and hermeneusis occupy a central position as subjects of the monomyth: it is a self-reflexive tale, a story about itself, a mirror held up as much to art as to nature; it is about the collection of and response to significant tales, for both writer and reader must undertake the journey, which becomes therefore a myth of writing and reading.

Psyche's journey begins with an involuntary call to adventure, when her great beauty arouses the wrathful jealousy of Venus, with the result that Psyche is banished from her home. She is sent to a mountain ridge (threshold border between the worlds in Sumerian, Babylonian, and Egyptian myths) where it is said she will become the bride of a "raging serpent" (108), a widespread motif in the mythologies of the Ancient Mediterranean region. Joseph Campbell shows how this archetypal iconography permeated the pre-biblical cultures the Near East and the Indus river valleys, until its message of joyful participation in the rhythms of life and death was transformed by the patriarchs of the Old Testament, of the *Theogony*, and of the Vedas into an image of the Fall (*Occidental Myth* 9-41; *Mythic Image* 281-301). Campbell's work acknowledges the seminal work of Jane Ellen Harrison on the pre-Olympian deities of Greece, and has recently been amplified by Marija Gimbutas, whose *Language of the Goddess* devotes an entire chapter to the icon of the goddess and the serpent (121-37).

Psyche is magically delivered by the wind to a magnificent palace in a paradisal valley, with a "fountain flashing with waters like glass in the middlemost of the grove" (110). As in biblical myth, the fountain is a symbol of the source and origin of all life, as is the sacred vessel of the woman of the well who attends it. Soon after her arrival, doorway symbolism emerges, when Psyche "crossed the threshold" (110) into the halls of the marvelous palace, which is built of gemstones, the finest citronwood and ivory, and, most significantly, golden pillars and silver walls crusted over with relief work (110). The two metals are associated with the Sun and the Moon, the periodic synchronization of which became a symbol of the reconciliation of Eternity and Time, male and female (in the *Odyssey*, in kundalini yoga, in Medieval representations of the Crucifixion, and in the alchemical traditions).[32] The castle of marvels motif will become one of the standard motifs of the initiation phase of the hero journey, for it represents a recovery of the imagined paradise of our infantile domecilia, a place where, as Apuleius puts it, no wish but finds its fulfillment, and no treasure of the world is forbidden (an Eden of the Id, one might say).

But here Psyche loses her virginity, as her mysterious bridegroom comes to her unseen nightly, and the passage into womanhood initiates a second separation phase of her journey. After her sisters cast aspersions on her invisible mate, Psyche succumbs to curiosity, and during one fateful night holds an oil lamp above her husband (who turns about to be Eros himself), a drop of which she spills while fiddling with the arrows in his quiver! The drop burns his wing, and he flies off: first into a tree, and then back home to his mother Venus, where he will enjoy a long, lonely sulk. Several people have defined myth as that which never happened continuing to happen every day, and surely this sequence repeats itself with every relationship, for every marriage is a hero journey. The symbolism of seeing the light, of getting burned, of pricking your finger on forbidden arrow points, of running home to mama have all entered our vocabulary of love, and will remain so forever. The oil lamp is a form of the sacred vessel of the mystery rites (and indeed a symbol of the marriage of the soul with God in the parable of the Virgins), and the quiver of arrows also has a long mythological pedigree and lineage. Many heroes shoot arrows randomly to find brides in folktales (as in the Russian tale of "The Frog Princess" or Antoine Galland's "Prince Ahmed and the Fairy Pari-Banou"), and the arrow itself represents the soul's directed flight to the bull's eye, symbol of the bindu passage, through the Brahma door of the sun, into the otherworld.[33] And indeed, Psyche's ultimate destination will be the eternal realm of the Gods on Mt. Olympus.

Before she gets there, however, she must undergo the trials and ordeals of the journey, after being separated from her home for the second time. When Eros abandons her (an unwed mother to be), her first impulse is to commit suicide beside the river (a constant temptation, aroused by the tendency of Eros to transform itself into Thanatos, during the heroine's journey: it recurs at each stage of her adventure, beside rivers and on tower tops). The river, as always, represents the threshold crossing into the underworld, and here as elsewhere Psyche receives assistance and guidance, just when she needs it most. Pan instructs Psyche to go in search of Venus, her mother in law to be and the source of all her troubles. Along the way, she must encounter Ceres, Juno, and Proserpine, and perform the various tasks, with the assistance of the various helpers, for which the tale is justly famous: the sorting of the seeds (assisted by the ants), the fleecing of the golden rams (assisted by the reeds), collecting a crystal jar full of the water of death (assisted by Jupiter's eagles), and retrieving a beauty creme from Hades (assisted by a talking tower).

Psyche's tasks and helpers have been variously interpreted in the many fine commentaries of our times. For Neumann, the four tasks are also associated with the four elements of the creation -- the ants earth, the reeds water, the eagles air, and Eros fire (126). Both von Franz and Neumann suggest they embody the feminine quest for wholeness (whether of the anima or of the woman). The quaternity of Goddesses represent the diverse archetypes of the feminine, which all men and women must integrate: the maternal Ceres, mother of the grain, whose seeds must be sorted out, and whose helpers, the ants, represent the intuitive wisdom of the collective unconscious; the erotic mysticism of Venus, who also represents the problem of the jealous stepmother (both a person to cope with and a role to be played by many women), and whose helpers, the reeds, represent the patient voices of nature in coping with the threats of aggressive rams, symbols of domestic violence; the dutiful wife, Juno, whose husband's eagles help Psyche to get above it all and gather the bitter waters of death from between the dragons' jaws; and the dread Goddess of Hades, Proserpine, the last passage in the cycle of feminine growth, for which Psyche receives guidance not from nature, but from the tower, an artifact of civilization. All four of these tasks involve four separate heroine journey cycles, all appropriate to what Gail Sheehy has referred to as the "passages" typically to be navigated during a normal woman's life.

Hillman connects the performance of the tasks more generally to what he calls the initiation rites of psychotherapy, ordeals by which the structure of consciousness is transformed: "neurosis becomes initiation, analysis the ritual, and our developmental process leading to the union of psyche and eros, the mystery" (*Analysis* 95). The story is important because it uniquely provides us with a mythic model (incorporating both sexual and spirituality) for our relationships, all of which involve "'an Odyssey of the human soul' -- a tale of union, separation, and suffering and an eventual reunion of love and soul blessed by archetypal powers" (96). Demon and daimon become one, as Eros leads Psyche into the invisible realm of the underworld, activating the archetypal forms which give shape and significance to life. From this perspective, the story represents the activation of the imagination crucial to poesis, for all great literature must combine psyche and love, and lead readers into the realm of the imaginal soul. By shattering the pretensions of the ego, Eros "leads the soul to the Gods and brings some glimmer and sublime horror of the divine into the soul -- for we are at our best and worst in love" (70). The story typifies the tendency of relationships to collapse, constantly, into trouble ("So quick bright things come to confusion," Lysander wisely notes in *A Midsummer Night's Dream*). But this collapse is creative: things must fall apart before they can achieve wholeness, for, as Crazy Jane reminds the Bishop, "'Nothing can be sole or whole / That has not been rent'" (Yeats 255). "Eros is born of Chaos," Hillman concludes, "and will always hearken back to its origins in chaos and will seek it for its revivification. Eros will attempt again and again to create those dark nights and confusions which are its nest. It renews itself in affective attacks, jealousies, fulminations, and turmoils. It thrives close to the dragon" (99).

Psyche's last task, however, may be approached as an image of aesthetic as well as of psychological creativity. The task constitutes one of the most interesting versions of the descent into Hades in the entire history of the heroine's journey. The tower tells Psyche that she must seek out the "ventilation hole of hell" and pass through the "yawning

door" that "leads down an untrodden track" into the "caverns of darkness" (138), a description which sounds much like the kind of oracular
sites Homer may have had in mind for the nekyia of Odysseus. After
passing through the doorway, Psyche encounters five figures before
coming into Proserpine's Palace: Ocnus, a lame man, driving a lame
ass; Charon, the ferryman to the "Farther Shore"; a dead man floating
on the surface of the Styx, who imploringly raises his rotted hands for
help; some old women weaving; and Cerberus, a colossal dog with
three heads, standing guard "before the threshold" of the Palace (the
second doorway down). Psyche receives further instructions: to ignore
Ocnus, the dead man on the river, and the weavers, all of whom will
ask her assistance; to carry two bits of money in her mouth; and to feed
Cerberus a "sop of barley-bread soaked in honey-wine" (138). Corpses
have been excavated from Roman catacombs buried with coins beneath
their tongues to pay Charon for the ferryboat across the river of death,
and the three-headed dog guarding the doorway is familiar to us from
the labors of Hercules and the descent of Aeneas. The weaving women
also suggest the symbolism of the Fates, typically situated in the underworld (as in the myth of Perseus). But the symbolism of weaving,
combined with the image of Ocnus, the lame ass driver, points to something far more rich and strange: oddly enough, the descent to the underworld represents an allegory of creativity in general, and of poesis in
particular.

That Apuleius may have known the tomb painting of Ocnus from
a columbarium in the Villa Pamphili in Rome is suggested not only by
his having incorporated Ocnus into his tale, but also by the fact that he
names the witch who initiates Lucius into the mysteries Pamphilia.
Another image of Ocnus, the rope plaiter, is to be found in the frieze
from an aedicula in a columbarium near the Porta Latina in Rome, discovered by Campana in 1832 (Bachofen Pl. IIIa.). It is the first to catch
the visitor's attention, for it "is situated directly opposite the staircase
leading down into the tomb" (Bachofen 52). This position establishes
an architectural link between threshold imagery (staircase and doorway)
and the descent into Hades very much like the linkage we find
generally in the hero journey. The images have been brilliantly analyzed by Bachofen (51-65). The painting from the Villa Pamphili
shows an old man sitting on a rock with a farmstead in the background
composed of several buildings, one of which, be it noted, is a large
tower-like silo (the model for the tower in Apuleius which gives Psyche
her instructions?). An ass sits at his feet nibbling the rope which he
holds abjectly in his right hand. The relief from the frieze shows the old
man kneeling by a bunch of tall reeds (shades of Psyche's golden rams
in the marsh?); he is plaiting two strands of a rope, the finished end of
which is being nibbled avidly by an ass" (Bachofen 53).

As Bachofen shows, these "hieroglyphs" of Ocnus, like the image of the weaving fates in Apuleius, are symbols of "the creative formative activity of the material principle" (59), which, by dying, the enlightened soul has "transcended" (63). Ocnus himself "appears in the role of an agathodaemon creating and preserving life" (62), which he does by weaving together the two strands of the rope, which represent "the twofold power of nature, the interpenetration of the two sexual principles prerequisite to all generation" (56). The weaving women present an alternative and complementary allegory of creativity. As Bachofen puts it,

> Rope plaiting is frequently symbolic action, based on the same conceptions as the spinning and weaving of the great nature mothers. The symbol of spinning and weaving represents the creative, formative power of nature. The labor of the great material primordial mothers is likened to the skillful plaiting and weaving which lends articulation, symmetrical form, and refinement to crude matter. The organisms all emerge in finished state from the womb of the earth. From their mother they have the subtle web of their body, which she fashioned with unparalleled mastery in the dark womb of matter. (56)

Although Bachofen suggests that it is precisely the realm of created matter which the soul transcends at death, one can also suggest that such images in Psyche's underworld serve as metaphors of the creative powers of poesis. As in the *Odyssey*, poets may be seen as weavers too, as rope plaiters, and song as the web woven from the various strands of the poet's raw materials. In fact, all of the Goddesses Psyche encounters during the course of her wanderings represent the primordial creativity of nature, of which poesis is also an expression: Ceres generates and sustains the life giving grain; Juno maintains the creativity of marriage; Venus represents the powers of human reproduction; and Proserpine, the story tells us, creates that special kind of beauty, characteristic of all great poetry, that comes from the awareness of death. Taken all together then, the tasks of the heroine's journey, which end in marriage and birth, can be seen as depicting the dynamics of poesis: at the end, a story is born, alongside a child named Joy.

Notes

[1]. See *Lilith: Die Erste Eva: Eine Studie über dunkle Aspekte des Weiblichen* by Siegmund Hurwitz, Zürich: Daimon Verlag, 1980.

2. "Umwertung allmählich immer deutlicher, nach der nicht Besiegung des Bösen, sondern eine Erlösung, nicht der patriarchale Sieg, sondern eine Wandlung des Unteren das eigentliche Ziel zu sein scheint" (Erich Neumann, "Die Bedeutung des Erdarchetyps für Neuzeit" 33).

3. See Eric Erickson's *Youth: Identity and Crisis.*

4. For the mysticism of the date palm see Thorkild Jakobson, *The Treasures of Darkness*, and for the mysticism of ritual regicide, see the magnificent pages in *The Way of the Animal Powers.*

5. See Joseph Campbell's discussion of this shift in the import of the imagery of serpent, woman, tree, and fruit in the first chapter of *The Masks of God: Occidental Mythology.* Since that ground breaking work, many other fine studies of the transition from matriarchal to patriarchal symbolism have appeared, such as *The Chalice and the Blade*, Gilda Lerner's *The Creation of Patriarchy*, and *The Once and Future Goddess.*

6. See Edgar Herzog, *Psyche and Death* (Chapter 5), and James Hillman, *The Dream and the Underworld* (148, 150), for discussions of the bird as death demon.

7. In addition to the popular work of Raymond Moody, *Life After Life*, see also the works of Kenneth Ring, Kübler-Ross, Hans Küng, and Carol Zaleski. In two other remarkable studies, Stanislav Grof has charted the iconography of death and dying in LSD therapy, and connected this imagery to perinatal experiences.

8. For pictures of these seals and discussion see Joseph Campbell's *The Masks of God: Occidental Mythology* (Chapter 1) and *The Mythic Image.*

9. Elizabeth Drew discusses the important transformations of the anima in T.S. Eliot's poetry, with a focus on the way the primitive "Belladona, Lady of the Rocks" of *The Waste Land* modulates towards the spiritual Lady of the Leopards in "Ash Wednesday" (101, 106). M.L. von Franz also provides a synopsis of Jung's notion that anima development occurs in four stages (CW 16: 174) in her chapter on individuation in *Man and His Symbols*: "The first stage is best symbolized by the figure of Eve, which represents purely instinctual and biological relations. The second can be seen in Faust's Helen: She personifies a romantic and aesthetic level that is, however, still characterized by sexual elements. The third is represented, for instance, by the Virgin Mary--a figure who raises love (eros) to the heights of spiritual devotion. The fourth type is symbolized by Sapienta, wisdom transcending even the most holy and the most pure" (185).

10. George Lord, for example, focuses on Odysseus' need for rehabilitation before returning to the domestic duties in Ithaca, a rehabilitation which is a crucial role of the feminine in the poem.

11. William Anderson, in fact, notes the connection between Ogygia and Elysium, and the close relationship between Calypso and death.

12. Howard Porter suggests that the olive tree symbolizes the rebirth motif, which he discusses as the central theme of the poem.

13. Jung was reading the *nekyia* section of the *Odyssey* at the time of the formulation of his own approach to the material of the deep unconscious, an approach which I have argued is structured by the myth of the descent to the underworld (see my "Descent to the Underworld: Jung and His Brothers").

14. On the symbolism of the pig, the goddess, and the underworld, see Joseph Campbell, *Occidental Mythology* (171).

15. The details of these excavations and of the speculations of Professor Dakaris may be found in Vandenburg's *The Mystery of the Oracles*, a study of the archeological light shed on all the major oracles of the Ancient Classical world.

16. The striking phrase is from John Heath-Stubbs' terrific poem *Artorius*.

17. Evidence of the possible role played by an LSD derivative of the ergot wheat in the Eleusinian mysteries is persuasively presented in *The Road to Eleusis* by Wasson, et. al.

18. On the Argeiphontes epithet ("slayer of Argos," the thousand-eyed beast the jealous Juno sets to spying on Ino, after turning her into a heifer), see Gary Astrachan's fine article, in *Gorgo: Zeitschrift für archetypische und bild-haftes Denken*.

19. See also Burkert, Meyer, and Kerényi's *Eleusis*.

20. See my articles and books, listed in the bibliography, for details.

21. See *The Flight of the Wild Gander*. Another example of the image would be the symbolism associated with the Hindu *yantra*, a meditation aid in which the *bindu* point shows the place where the divine energy incarnates, to be broken up into the four quarters which enclose a sequence of circles (see Ajit Mookerjee's *Yoga Art* for some splendid examples and commentary). Jung, of course, discusses these *mandalas* as images of psychic totality.

22. On the body of light see Gilles Quispell, who writes "Adam war also, wenn ich mich so ausdrücken darf, vor dem Falle mit einem Lichtleib bekleidet .... So kommt es, neben bei gesagt, daß Adam in gnostichen und manichäischen Quellen als ywsthr Leuchter, bezeichnet wird. (Adam was also, if I may so express myself, was clothed before the Fall with Light Body .... So it comes about that Adam in gnostic and manichaean sources will be designated as the Luminous One" (215-216)).

23. The phrase "ihr Schattenbild in die Urwasser des Chaos projiziert" de-scribes the cosmogonic creation of the body of Adam and of the universe by the Archonten produced by Sophia, who lust after the image of their mother (elsewhere called "die Lichtjungfau," the Light Virgin) which she projects into the waters like an image in a mirror (Quispell 212)).

24. Thomas Mann makes the journey to the prison an Egyptian *nekyia*, having Joseph float to prison down the Nile like Osiris on the solar barge wan-dering through the chambers of the afterlife.

25. See also William Blake's illustrations for *The Book of Job*, where there are twenty one plates divided into three cycles of seven plates each (Damon 5).

26. See Jean Pépin, "The Platonic and Christian Ulysses," Hans Jonas *The Gnostic Religion*, and Kathleen Raine on William Blake's painting of Odysseus and the Cave of the Nymphs, for the symbols of sea, sleep, and forgetting.

27. See for example, Walter Jackson Knight, Mircea Eliade, or Joseph Campbell.

28. The cup, the Grail, and the cauldron are universal archetypes of world mythology. The Chinese sacrificial vessels are splendid if terrifying examples (Campbell, *Mythic Image* 124f. and *Treasures of the Bronze Age of China*). A wide range of images can be found in *The Grail*, by John Matthews.

29. For images of the Creative Word see Maclagan as follows: Book of Kells for John's "In the beginning was the Word" (64); Dogon signs of Egg of Amma ("The Belly of the World's Signs") from which the world is created with four segments as four elements with two character signs for each, and from thence a total of 11, 616 signs for all the creation (76); the *Red Book of Delaware Indians*, in which the world is a syntax of fundamental forms which can be variously combined (79). For the Oriental imagery see Mookerjee: the seed syllable *Aum* (*Yoga Art*. Plate 10) and temple sculpture of *Sabda* (Word) unfolding into a mandala (an image which corresponds to the image of Christ as the Logos surrounded by the four corners of the world represented by the Evangelists) (*Tantric* 85). For Kali, see Mookerjee (*Tantric* Plate 3) and Campbell *The Mythic Image* (Plate 323).

30. See Mookerjee (154-156) or Joseph Campbell's *The Mythic Image* (Plates 312-14; 332-34) for pictures of the chakras and the letters associated with each.

31. See Scholem, "Die Vorstellung vom Golem" for a detailed account of the ritual creation of the Golem. All translations of Scholem's article are my own.

32. See my "Alchemy and Modernism," along with Campbell, *Occidental Myth* 163 and *Inner Reaches* 70-92.

33. See the entire section devoted to "The Sundoor and Related Motifs" in Coomaraswamy's *Selected Papers*, Vol. 1, particularly Figure 18 of the Egyptian World Door and Sundoor" (480), and "Symbolism of the Dome."

Chapter 2:
The Arthurian Romances
and the Middle Ages

Numerous commentaries have focused on the Grail quest as a metaphorical individuation process, the climax of which is always a revelation of the totality of the Self, in such symbols as the mandalas Parzival encounters in the Grail Castle. Edward Whitmont, Emma Jung, and Robert Johnson all agree that the Grail legends of the Middle Ages compensated for the excessive patriarchal orientation of the Church by exalting the feminine. Whitmont argues that the wounding of Amfortas, the Waste Land, and the sorcery of Clinschor reflect a violation of the feminine principle, and that the legends point towards a healing reintegration of the feminine still necessary today. Emma Jung focuses on the split between the masculine and the feminine, between spirit and nature, and between good and evil as psychologically damaging aspects of dogmatic dualities which the reconciliations of the Grail legends tend to heal (Joseph Campbell goes so far as to equate Clinschor and the Pope). Along similar lines, Robert Johnson suggests that Perceval's central task is the integration of the inner feminine which the Jungians call the anima. This involves the reconciliation between opposites which is also a common theme in alchemy, known as the *mysterium coniunctionis*.

Anthropology also offers illuminating perspectives on the Grail legends: Jessie Weston was the first to suggest that the enigmatic symbols in the Grail Castle (cup, bleeding lance, wounded King) may originally have been sexual symbols of regeneration in one of the late Classical mystery cults carried into Northern Europe by Roman soldiers, and gone underground after the Theodosian suppression of paganism in 438 A.D. In such mysteries, the imagery of sexual and vegetal cycles had developed into highly sophisticated symbols of spiritual death and rebirth (such as Chrétien and Wolfram draw upon) which were meant to have a transformative, even redemptive impact upon the psyche of the initiate. The Grail as cup, from this perspective, could find remote ancestors in the *Kernos* mixing bowl of the Eleusinian mysteries, the Orphic bowl of creation called the *Krater*, the initiatory symbolism of the Pietrosa Bowl, and the crucible of the alchemical opus. [1] The import of these symbolic systems may have survived in the secret initiation rituals of the esoteric societies of the Middle Ages (like the Cathars of the Albigensian Crusades in Southern France), of which the Arthurian romances may provide tantalizing glimpses. Heinrich Zimmer, as we have noted, suggests a Gnostic sect and imagery associated with the Marseille Tarot pack.

Finally, the perspective of comparative mythology on the Grail romances has been gloriously illuminating, especially in the great work on the subject by Joseph Campbell, *Creative Mythology*. Campbell argues that Wolfram adapts the religious imagery from a variety of traditions (Christian, Arabic, Oriental, Celtic, Classical, Alchemical) and applies it to the inner mysteries of human development over the course of a complete life cycle. In this view, the symbols in the romances become "archetypal, universal mythic images of spiritual transformation" which transcend theological sectarianism (453). Hence the symbols serve as "paradigms of secular human experiences in depth dimension" (484) which are seen not as supernatural facts (in the way of dogmatic literalism, of whatever creed), but as "inherent in the episodes of men's normal lives" (484). In this sense, Wolfram's *Parzival* looks forward to the mythic method of Mann and Joyce, and is in fact the "first example in world literature of a consciously developed secular Christian myth" (476) which inaugurated a "new age of the human spirit" (480). The redemption of the Waste Land achieved by Gawain and Parzival then, brings about a new era of secular mythology, an age of the Spirit which sees through dogmatic creeds to the universal symbols of human transformation. The Arthurian romances took the symbolic imagery of the hero journeys of the ancient period, transformed it, and passed it along to us, in the incomparable works of the Middle Ages, to which we now turn.

Sir Gawain and the Green Knight

Sir Gawain and the Green Knight is the consummate literary adaptation of the hero journey in Medieval literature. In its concision and structural ingenuity, in the rich splendor and profusion of its precise descriptions, in the symbolic images that tie each minute detail of the whole poem together into an "endless knot," the poem achieves its place at the pinnacle of the romance genre of the Arthurian tradition. It richly rewards critical scrutiny from a great variety of perspectives, four of which will serve as foci in what follows: mythological, anthropological, structuralist, and formalist.

The poem is a treasure trove for myth critics, since nearly every character and detail of imagery suggests a long lineage of mythological speculations rooted in the pre-Christian, proto-literate beginnings of the Celtic and Nordic populations of the British Isles. Having been composed in a Midlands dialect 150 miles northwest of London, the poem was much closer to those frontiers where Christianity still mingled with the diverse elements of pagan mythologies. Its very language bears the imprints of Anglo-Saxon and Scandinavian vocabularies, and its main protagonists and plot lines show connections to Irish myth and saga. This is most readily apparent in the figure of the Green Knight, who can be seen as a personification of the fertility cycles: he is the Green Man, Jack in the Green, or Wild Man of the Woods, a descendant of a vegetation god whose annual death and resurrection was celebrated in village festivals that dramatized his decapitation and revival. In fact, John Speirs argues, we still see his face peering down on us from the roof embossing of Medieval churches, with leaves sprouting from the corners of his mouth, eyelids, brow, and ears (219). In the poem, his green hair and beard are long and bushy, and he is just as vigorously alive after the beheading as before. His armor is embossed with birds and butterflies, both ancient symbols (as we have seen) of the soul, which emerges from the chrysalis of the mortal body at death.

In addition to the Green Man, the Green Knight is also, as Heinrich Zimmer has argued, a symbol of death, with his gruesome grim reaper's battle axe, his beheading trick, and most of all his Green Chapel, which is situated in a valley beside a boiling stream and overgrown with moss like the burial barrows of the Neolithic. One thinks, for example, of Newgrange outside of Dublin, a huge earthen mound with the opening of its long passageway situated in such a way that the first rays of the rising sun on December 21, the winter solstice, penetrate and illuminate the cruciform interior chambers. The symbolism there suggests the death and rebirth of the sun in the womb / tomb of the mother goddess of the earth. Heinrich Zimmer also suggests that the color of the Green Knight is not the color of the crops, but of corpses. Although one detractor of the myth critical approach to the poem has attacked the apparent discrepancies between Speirs (the Green Knight as fertility symbol) and Zimmer (the Green Knight as Death), it is clear that the Green Knight must be both the Green Man and the Grim Reaper in order to embody the polarities of the fertility cycle (Moorman 171-86). Any dynamic mythic image must embody such oppositions, thereby reconciling and transcending them. The fact that the Green Knight carries a holly bob in one hand ("greenest in groves when leaves are bare") and a large Danish axe in another, and that we see him both with head on and head off, draws our attention to the fact that he is a symbol of both life and death, and indeed of the transcendent source of both. This duality is developed also by the two ladies in Bertilak's castle: one of them is identified as Morgan the Goddess, and, in a detailed stanza her ancient and considerably faded appearance is contrasted with the youthful beauty of the lady by her side. The two of them together, therefore, represent the contrary manifestations of the Goddess -- life and death, womb and tomb -- and their opposition corresponds to the opposition between holly bob and axe.

John Speirs sees the seasonal contrast as the essence of the poem's meaning and structure, which is based on an elaborate interplay between opposites that readily lends itself to structuralist analysis. We see this dialectic between life and death not only in the two aspects of the Green Knight, and in the two ladies of the Castle, but also in the historical frame of the poem's beginning and ending stanzas; in the glorious celebrations of the seasonal cycles at the beginning of Fitts 2, 3, and 4; in the richly evoked scenes of Christmas feasting versus the days of fasting as Gawain journeys to the Green Chapel; in the delightful interlacing of sex and slaughter as we move from the bedroom to the hunt in the second Fitt; and, finally, in the imagery of death and rebirth in the climactic scene at the Green Chapel. In the first stanza of the poem the dynamic of death and rebirth is applied to the cycles of history, as we read of the new European nations of Medieval Europe (Rome, Tuscany, Lombardy, and England) rising out of the ashes of the ruined Troy. Each of the first stanzas of the three subsequent Fitts of the poem echoes the theme in marvelous celebrations of the seasonal cycles. The stanzas that begin Fitts 2, 3, and 4 emphasize the continual interplay of life and death in the revolution of the seasons. The splendid details of Christmas feasting at Arthur's and then at Bertilak's court, which frame the fasting months of Gawain's journey, are therefore meant as complementary images of death and life in the historical and seasonal cycles. Nowhere is this dynamic interplay between opposites more beautifully handled than in the interlocking of bedroom and hunting scenes in the third Fitt, where we move from the cozy indoor realm of sleep and sexual dalliance to the detailed descriptions of hunting and butchering simultaneously taking place outdoors. On one level, these scenes move from sex (the origins of human life) to slaughter, but on another we can discern the seeds of the opposite realms within both: the bedroom courtship carries the seeds of death, were Gawain to capitulate to the seduction of the Lady; while the hunting scenes, though dealing with death, are extremely lively, and remind us that the food of the slaughter will nourish the bodies of the living. Hence, the opposites reflect each other and are reconciled: sex leads to birth which leads to death, while butchering animals sustains our lives.

The two fundamental forces of death and life come closest together during the scene at the Green Chapel, where Gawain faces his own version of Doomsday. At the bottom of the valley, across a rushing river, stands the Green Chapel. Gawain waits as the Green Knight comes clattering down the cliff side, after sharpening his blade on a grindstone, generating an astonishing commotion. In this scene, the Green Knight seems almost like the Norse God Thor, who presided over judicial proceedings on the day of the week named after him (Thursday -- "Donnerstag"). Like Thor, the Green Knight is enormous and powerful, carries a huge weapon (much like Thor's hammer, *Mjolnar*), has long hair, and is associated with lightning and thunder (bright bolts fly from his horse's hoofs as he leaves Arthur's court, and the deafening noises when he enters the court and when he sharpens his axe suggest thunder). The judgment and punishment of Gawain at the Green Chapel, therefore, connect the Norse God of Justice with both the courtly testing of chivalric virtue, and the Christian rite of penance and absolution (the language of the confession is much evident during this scene and a source of great amusement for the Green Knight).

We can amplify the figure of the Green Knight farther afield if we follow the lead of such scholars as George Dumézil, whose work situates Norse mythology in an Indo-European context via a study of linguistics and comparative mythology. The image of a God of Justice whose emblem is the lightning bolt is found not only in the figures of Thor and Zeus, but also in Tibetan myth, where, after the lightning bolt dispels the illusions of the phenomenal world, the thunderous lion roar of enlightenment and liberation follows. The word *vajra* in Sanskrit (a very important Indo-European tongue, the sacred language of Oriental India and Tibet) means lightning bolt and diamond, both of which, Joseph Campbell suggests, "may be readily applied to the hammer of Thor" (*Occidental Myth* 481). The pure brilliance of the diamond represents the adamantine quality of the perfected spiritual life, and hence the "power of eternity through which phenomenality is annihilate" (480). It seems significant, then, that the Green Knight's feminine counterpart in the bedroom, his *shakti* you might say, offers Gawain a brilliant red-gold gemstone (the counterpart of the diamond) which shines with the radiance of the sun, and suggests immortal life as the goal of Gawain's journey. There seems, therefore, to be a deeper level of spiritual symbolism beneath Gawain's tests; as Heinrich Zimmer suggests, "themes that must once have been enacted on a higher mythological stage" have been modified to fit the chivalric and Christian context of the poet's audience (81).

All of these levels of meaning merge outside the Green Chapel, where the knot tying these different strands of meaning together is pulled tight. Those strands have all to do with the symbolism of death and rebirth, which operates as much on the level of Celtic mysticism as it does on the level of Christian dogma. As Brian Stone suggests, the

Green Chapel "is exactly like an entrance to the Celtic Other World. But Gawain sees it as an entrance to Hell" (183). The general appearance of the Chapel suggests the kind of burial mound associated with the death and rebirth of the sun and the king as consort of the Neolithic Goddess (whose importance in such ancient monuments of pagan England as the Avebury circle and Silbury Hill has been demonstrated in the books of Michael Dames). Jones uses the words "barrow" and "mound" in his translation of the original Middle English words "berg" and "berge" (lines 2171, 2172, and 2178 in the Tolkien edition), both derived from the Old English beorg (Tolkien 165). The Middle English berg is cognate with the German Berg meaning mountain, so that once again we find the entrance to the underworld situated beneath a mountain, as we have seen in the *Epic of Gilgamesh* and "The Descent of Inanna," and will see again in English folklore, where the entrance to fairyland is often beneath the hollow hills. In *Sir Gawain*, the "berg" is overgrown and hollow within, like the faerie hills, and it has a hole on either end (line 2180), which recalls the Cave of the Naiades in the *Odyssey*. In fact, one might also connect the green girdle the Lady of the Castle gives Gawain to protect him from death with the veil Leucothea gives Odysseus to protect him at sea as he swims towards the shores of Phaiakia. Since Neoplatonic allegory saw mortal bodies incarnated through one end of the cave, and perfected souls exiting through the other, the barrow symbolism here ties in with the themes of rebirth which the poet exploits during the punishment of Gawain at the Chapel.[2]

Gawain initially sees the Chapel as the antithesis to the Christian Chapel where he had confessed himself at Mass earlier in the day, after which the poet wryly declares Gawain to have been "sent out so pure / That Doomsday could have been declared the day after" (91: 1884). Gawain calls the Chapel of his judgment day the "corsedest kyrk that ever I cam inne" (2196): it is a place fit for the Devil to say his matins after midnight. But this apparent opposition between Satanic and Christian ritual is reconciled shortly after Gawain receives his nick in the neck for having kept the green girdle given him by the Lady of the Castle, hence breaking his bargain with Bertilak to exchange winnings at the end of the day. As a result, the Green Knight cuts through the exposed flesh of Gawain's neck so that the shining blood spurts over his shoulder onto the clean white snow. When Gawain sees the bright red blood, he leaps up and declares himself merrier than ever he has been "since he was a child born of his mother" (2320). In the place where he had thought to meet his doom, under the shadow of a pagan temple of the Goddess Morgan Le Fay, he finds rebirth. Gawain is both judged and reborn beside the barrow, and the apparently conflicting ideologies of Celtic magic and Christian dogma are reconciled. For after Gawain does his penance and confesses the sins of cowardice and covetousness, treachery and untruth, the Green Knight laughs and in a playful parody of the sacrament declares well shriven, "as stainless now / As if you had never fallen in fault since first you were born" (110). This last declaration ties together the Celtic and Christian mysteries of death and rebirth, sin and redemption, and links both to the courtly codes of chivalric knighthood. Gawain takes the green girdle back to Arthur's court as a sign of his shame, whereas the knights there take it to signify the honor of a quest fulfilled. Gawain's return leads to the birth of a new brotherhood, the Knights of the Green Garter. Hence, the polysemous symbolism of death and rebirth operates on all of the various levels of the poem's meaning (Celtic, Christian, and Courtly), tying them together into a seamless knot.

If, as the structuralists suggest, the function of myth is to enable us to cope with the irreconcilable opposites of life, then we can note that *Sir Gawain and the Green Knight* is informed throughout by an enriching interplay between the two poles of life and death (keeping in mind that each bears within it the seeds of its opposite):

Life:	Death
bliss	blunder
wonder	wrack
truth	untruth
holly bob	axe
young wife	ancient lady
bedroom scenes	hunting scenes
feasting	fasting
castle	forest
chapel of the mass	green chapel
honor	shame
Guenevere	Morgan Le Fay

Both the structuralist and the myth critical approaches to the poem, therefore, merge at this central point of the poem's dialectic, from which the circumference of detail radiates outward to form the pentangle of the Endless Knot. In addition, both the structuralist and mythic perspectives illuminate a formalist approach, which would begin by noting the intricate unity of part and whole in the poem: each particular combination of opposites listed above reflects the dynamic of the whole, as if the poem were a hologram, or a specific manifestation of the primary imagination, which Coleridge characterized by the "awful omneity of all in each." This unity between part and whole in the poem's imagery is sustained by the elaborate symmetries of poetic structure: the poem begins and ends with the same line ("The siege and the assault being ceased at Troy"); the second Fitt begins in a castle

(Arthur's) and ends in a castle (Bertilak's), with a journey in between, hence reflecting the structure of the whole poem, which begins and ends in Arthur's castle with a journey in between; Gawain sets out for the Green Chapel twice, at the beginning of Fitts Two and Four, both of which Fitts begin with a celebration of the passing of the seasons. So precise in structure is our poet that the stanza in which Gawain crosses himself three times before the appearance of Bertilak's castle on Christmas Eve is number 33, the traditional age of Christ at the time of the crucifixion.

In fact, each stanza is a kind of microcosm of the whole poem, moving forward with a leisurely, rich accumulation of precise detail, with a place for everything and everything in its place, yet leading up to a climactic point in the bob and wheel at the end of each. This rhythm is reinforced by the larger progression of the stanzas of each Fitt towards a central climax in the action: the beheading in the first; the arrival at Bertilak's castle in the second; the incremental repetition of exchanged winnings, leading to the concealment of the green girdle in the third; and the journey to the Green Chapel with the return blow in the fourth. Every part contributes to the whole, into which it is woven to produce the fine tapestry of the Endless Knot.

All of these aspects of the poem (mythic, structuralist, formalist) work together to generate one of the most intricately wrought hero journeys in our tradition, one which clearly exemplifies all the various stages of the cycle. The call to adventure comes with the dramatic interruption of the Christmas feast when the Green Knight hurtles into Arthur's hall. Gawain's departure from the domestic security of Camelot on All Hallow's Eve leads to the threshold crossing battles with wild creatures by forest and ford and with sleet and cold on mountain ridges. The trials and ordeals are cumulative in the exchange of winnings temptations, and lead to the initiatory climax at the Green Chapel. As is typical of the initiation stage of the cycle, it is at the Green Chapel that the revelation occurs, both of Gawain's true character and of the forces directing the action of the plot; and both revelations lead to a transformation of Gawain's sense of himself and the world around him. On the deepest level, this initiation involves a mystical experience of the unity of life and death which underlies the sacramental lore of penance and redemption. Most simply put, the revelation here is of certain weaknesses within his character that Gawain has not previously confronted, a shadow side of cowardice and covetousness which compose new chinks in his armor. His ordeal and initiation have taught him things about himself which he would rather not know, and to which he reacts rather severely, indeed somewhat childishly, as when he blames women for his failings in an outburst of monkish misogyny that says more I suspect about Gawain than it does about the poet.

But Gawain also learns in this scene about the mysterious forces of his destiny or "wyrd": Bertilak reveals the truth about the beheading game, about the exchange of winnings, and about the two ladies in the castle. Morgan the Goddess is the puppeteer pulling the strings, the weaver of the tapestry who sent the Green Knight to Arthur's court and who arranged for Gawain's temptation. She is his fate, his temptress, his judge, and the mother of his new identity. For Gawain returns to the court a changed man, less complacent about his chivalric excellence and notorious courtesy, more aware of his shameful weakness and of his mortality. After the journey comes full circle, returning in the end to its beginning point, Gawain must submit to the humiliation (as he sees it) of telling the courtiers about his failings. In the end, he remains true to his word, even if the truth exposes his inclination to treachery and untruth, a susceptibility ironically celebrated by the birth of the a new order of knights: The Knights of the Green Garter.

I would like to finish our discussion of the poem with a focus on the importance of clothing symbolism, which serves to further connect Sir Gawain's journey with those of earlier, and of later, heroes and heroines. Among the elaborate symmetries of structure and theme noted in the discussion above is the fact that Gawain is armed twice at parallel points in the poem, i.e., at the beginnings of Fitts 2 and 4, when he sets out for the Green Chapel. Four precisely detailed stanzas, accompanied by extended authorial glosses on the significance of the pentangle, are devoted to the arming of Gawain at the beginning of Fitt 2. These stanzas are, in many respects, analogous to those lines which delineate the royal *me* donned by Inanna in preparation for her descent to the underworld in the Sumerian poem. There is, first of all, the deliberate progression through all the parts of the body to be covered, from the royal crown on the head to measuring rod in the hand in "The Descent," and from shoes to legs, thighs, midriff, arms, elbows, and gloves in *Sir Gawain*. The brilliant impression provided by the Gawain poet's description is repeatedly one of radiance: the knight's war gear glitters on the floor, has brightly polished knee-pieces, polished glinting and gay armor on the arms linked with lustrous gold, etc. (stanza 26). Similarly, when Gawain's horse (Gringolet) is brought in, the brilliance of gold strikes the dominant chord: the saddle gleams gaily with golden fringes, the bridle is embossed with bright gold (as are the rest of the equestrian furnishings), and all is "arrayed in red with nails of richest gold, / Which glittered and glanced like gleams of the sun" (stanza 26). The final touches of this portrait -- which Max Müller would have recognized as of a solar deity transformed into a Christian Knight -- include the casque with "burnished neck guard" and the circlet on Gawain's head, which "Threw a gleaming lustre out" (stanza 27). What follows then are the two stanzas on the shield, with the Virgin Mary on the inside, and

the pentangle on the outside, the significance of which is comprehen-
sively glossed by the poet into five sets of five: the five senses, five
fingers, five wounds of Christ, five joys of the Virgin, and the five
courtly virtues.

   Gawain then proceeds on his journey in search of the Green
Chapel, arriving at Bertilak's castle on Christmas Eve, where he is ritually disrobed, so that Fitt 2 is as symmetrically framed by the arming
and disarming of the hero (Fitt 4, as we will see, follows the same pattern) as was the "Descent of Inanna." At the end of Fitt 2, Bertilak's ret-
inue removes Gawain's helmet, sword, and shield -- the last item of particular importance given the power of the pentangle over the other
world (Speirs 230). While still "garbed in his fine garments," Gawain is
then presented to Bertilak, who takes him to a beautifully ornamented
room where servants further strip Gawain of his "battle shirt and splendid clothes" and replace them with "rich robes / Of the choicest kind to
choose from and change into" (stanza 36). This process exposes the
naked flesh, which can still be seen shining like "spring / In all its hues"
beneath the garments the squires give him (36). Much is then made of
this rich robe when Gawain sits before the hearth in gracious languor: it
is called a "magnificent mantle ... a gleaming garment gorgeously embroidered / Fairly lined with fur, the finest skins / Of ermine on earth,"
and it is thrown over Gawain to complete his reinvestiture. It is as if he
were being freshly armed for the battle of love that awaits him in the
bedroom, during the temptation scenes to follow in Fitt 3, in which
clothing symbolism continues to be focused on. When the Lady of the
castle takes him by surprise in his bedclothes, he asks for "better habil-
iment," but she refuses. She herself will be progressively disrobed during the sequence of temptations, until on the third morning she appears
in "a ravishing robe" trimmed with fur that leaves her "fair throat ... un-
veiled" and her breast and back bare as well. Gawain cannot help "gazing on her gay and glorious attire" when he is awakened from his
troubling dreams, and it is on this day that he accepts the green girdle
from her as love token. She removes this girdle from her waist to give
to Gawain.

   During the arming scene which follows at the beginning of Fitt 4,
when Gawain sets off again in search of the Green Chapel as he had
done at the beginning of Fitt 2, the girdle plays a central role as a new
item of clothing. The order and detail of the arming scene in Arthur's
court is greatly abbreviated here in Bertilak's castle: while the poet
points out the symmetry of the two scenes by noting that Gawain's armor has been kept "as fresh as at first," the overall impression of radiance is considerably dimmer, and, in a widely noted opposition, the
green girdle replaces the shield as a center of interest. In this second
arming scene, only three lines indicate the brightness of the armor (as

opposed to nine in the first), and the only parts of the body focused on are the lower parts -- the waist, the "swelling hips," and the "loins" wrapped by the girdle. This is a dimmer and more carnal Gawain than the one who originally set forth from the innocence of Camelot.

This seems appropriate, given the somewhat tarnished image of Gawain's truthfulness at this point (having violated his word by keeping the girdle). Myth critics (following the lead of Max Müller) would perhaps also find the diminution of Gawain's radiance appropriate here, since, if he has a solar ancestor in his pagan pedigree, it would well accord with this stage of the journey into the darkness of winter, when the sun is at its weakest before the restoration of the new year.[3] Hence, as in so many other aspects of the poem, the mythical and the ethical elements coincide with the Christian, since, after Gawain receives his blow on the neck at the Green Chapel, his brilliance is oddly regenerated: we see his "shimmering blood ... glinting on the snow," and he immediately draws and swings "his bright sword." Shortly thereafter, he is cleansed of his sins by absolution and confession, at which point Gawain makes explicit the sense of his diminished brightness when he says that the frailty of the flesh "tends to attract tarnishing sin" ("teches of fylth").

This second arming scene at the beginning of Fitt 4 then moves towards a second disarming scene during the judgment scene at the Green Chapel, where Gawain's faults as well as his neck is laid bare; it is a scene that is meant to parallel the stripping down of Gawain at the end of Fitt 2. In this climactic scene at the Green Chapel, Gawain is asked to remove his helmet, and when he bows his head to receive the blow, we see "the bright flesh bare" at the neck (stanza 90). When the wounding blow is actually delivered on the third stroke, "the naked neck" is again focused on, when the "barb of the axe bites into the bare neck" (stanza 93). This is followed by the ultimate image of nakedness conjured up by the poet's remark that "never had the knight since being nursed by his mother / Been so buoyantly happy" (stanza 93). He is now as exposed as a baby of the mother's breast, and shortly confesses the shame he feels at the exposure by a further act of disrobing: when the Green Knight says to Gawain "that braided belt you wear belongs to me" and is the cause of Gawain's punishment, Gawain "took the knot, with a twist twitched it loose, / And fiercely flung the fair girdle to the knight" (stanza 95). He is now divested of the most important item of clothing donned during the arming scene at the beginning of the Fitt.

The precise focus on this elaborate procedure of arming and disarming Gawain emphasizes the importance of clothing symbolism characteristic of the hero journey: arming for departure, stripping down for initiation, and redressing for the return journey. In fact, the process here seems to recall not only Inanna's detailed preparations and strip-

ping down, but also Joseph's in *Genesis* and in the imagery of divestiture in "The Hymn of the Pearl." Like Inanna, Joseph, and the hero of
the Gnostic hymn, Gawain begins his journey elaborately dressed in
garments clearly meant to provide protection. This armor is stripped
from him in the underworld, exposing him to the temptation of sin and
death; also like Joseph or the hero of the Gnostic hymn, Gawain then
puts on a new suit of clothes (in Bertilak's castle) to indicate his assimilation into the new 'heathen' environment. Recall that Joseph had to put
on Egyptian clothing in the service of Potiphar, clothing which is
stripped from him by Potiphar's wife; similarly, Gawain puts on new
clothes in Bertilak's castle, during which he also is tempted by his host's
wife while lying nearly naked in bed. Further parallels emerge when we
consider the details of the Gnostic gloss on the Joseph story in "The
Hymn of the Pearl," during which the hero must exchange his robe of
glory for Egyptian garments. He then falls into a "deep slumber," only
to be awakened by his father's letter, after which he retrieves the pearl
of great price and discards the "filthy and impure" Egyptian garment
before returning home to be re clothed in his originally splendid mantle.

The parallels to Gawain's journey are detailed and fascinating to
note (we should remember that the title of the Gawain poet's other masterpiece, *Pearl*, suggests Gnostic allegory): like the Gnostic hero in the
hymn, Gawain falls into a deep slumber (from which he has difficulty
awaking on the third morning) after changing his clothes in the alien
land of Bertilak's castle. He seems temporarily to have forgotten the
perils of his original purpose as he is tempted (like the Gnostic hero) by
the lady of the castle. Furthermore, on the last morning of his temptation, the lady offers him a "rich ring . . . With a sparkling stone ...
Which beamed as brilliantly as the sun" (stanza 73). This stone is analogous to the pearl of great price, and symbolizes the hidden mystery of
the soul, which survives temptation and mortality to shine in eternal
radiance. The girdle which Gawain accepts in its place, with its sexual
connotations, suggests the filthy garment of the "Hymn of the Pearl":
when Gawain is punished at the Green Chapel, he fiercely flings the
girdle away, calling it a "false thing, foul fortune befall it" (stanza 95)
("Lo! ther the falssyng, foule mot hit falle!"). After divesting himself of
the girdle, Gawain, like the Gnostic hero, returns to his homeland,
where he is clothed once again in the raiment of chivalric knighthood.

Hence, a network of imagery passed down through generations of
the hero journey narratives has survived in *Sir Gawain and the Green
Knight*, linking Gawain with Joseph and the Gnostic hero of the "Hymn
of the Pearl": we have the symbolic changes of clothing, the imagery of
sleep and temptation by the host's wife, gemstone and pearl, and the
special significance of the Egyptian garment and the green girdle as
symbols of the flesh. While both the garment and the girdle represent

sin and carnality, a further detail associated with the green girdle -- its magical ability to confer invulnerability upon its wearer -- takes it further back in time to Leucothea's veil in the *Odyssey* (which protects the wearer from drowning at sea), and on back further to the robe Gilgamesh receives from Utnapishtim's wife which never ages. The lady in *Sir Gawain* says of the man that binds himself with the belt of green that "As long as he laps it closely about him, / No hero under heaven can hack him to pieces, / For he cannot be killed by any cunning on earth" (Stanza 74). Compare Leucothea's veil in Book 5 of the *Odyssey*: while leaving Calypso's island, a stupendous storm shatters his boat, and while cleaving to the mast the sea nymph Leucothea appears to offer Odysseus her girdle, which she tells him to bind beneath his breast after putting off his garments. After reaching the shores of Skheria, Odysseus must throw the girdle back into the sea with averted face. He is then discovered by Nausicaa, princess at the river who has come to do her laundry: she first washes and then reclothes Odysseus.

In the *Epic of Gilgamesh*, Gilgamesh goes to the land of the faraway in search of immortality, where he (like the hero of the Gnostic hymn and like Gawain) falls asleep and forgets his task. Then he receives the magical robe with its power to restore youth. Here, as in *Sir Gawain*, we have the wife of the host giving a talismanic garment to the hero who eventually returns it. One wonders, indeed, whether the girdle or the pentangle is responsible for Gawain's survival of the ordeal of the Green Chapel, during which he conspicuously wears the girdle: does he owe his salvation to Morgan the Goddess, or to the Virgin Mary? To Celtic magic, or to Christian grace? Such questions must have been vividly present in the mind of the fourteenth century audience recently converted to Christianity, with 'pagan' customs still alive among the peasantry. One also wonders whether the girdle retained its magic when Gawain returned to Camelot -- but such questions the poet has left unanswered, forever.

Sir Orfeo

Much of the symbolism of Gawain's hero journey, with its Celtic, Norse, Christian, and Classical sources, is found in other Medieval versions of the monomyth. As John Speirs suggests,

> Whatever connections -- in their ritual origins or later stages -- there may have been between the different mythologies, Mediterranean, Norse, Celtic, from with the numberless tales circulating in medieval Europe appear to have evolved, the similarities of pattern between them have been frequently remarked on. (140)

The most universal of such similarities is, of course, the narrative structure and attendant symbolic imagery of the hero journey.

In *Sir Orfeo*, from the Auchincleck manuscript dated around 1330, we find the weaving together of Celtic, Christian, and Classical threads into a beautifully embroidered tapestry of symbolic imagery. Written in octosyllabic couplets, which suggest the minstrelsy of the Breton lais, the poem reworks the traditional material of the mortal queen abducted to the underworld (Persephone, Eurydice), which here becomes a kind of Celtic otherworld, or fairy realm of enchantment ruled by a Pluto very much resembling Chaucer's "King of Faerie." Heurodis, the abducted Eurydice of Classical myth, must be retrieved by her grief-stricken, harp-playing husband, Orfeo, but she remains associated with Persephone and the flowers of springtime as well. Grimaldi has discussed Orfeo as a Celtic folk hero, Christian Pilgrim, and Courtly King: as folk hero he undergoes initiatory experiences in the realm of faerie, the forest madness of the lover, and the visions of the faerie dance, hunt, and palace beneath the hills; as pilgrim, his sins of pride and lust are purged during ten years of penitential wandering as an anchorite, and the journey itself suggests the human pilgrimage from Eden, into Exile, and on to the restored Earthly Paradise; finally, as King, Orfeo enacts the fall of princes motif so popular during the Middle Ages, and he learns the value of the law and of obedient servants (in addition, the poem explores the courtly relationships between kingdoms, between subject and ruler, and between patron and poet). All three of these levels of allegory enrich the underlying narrative structure of the hero journey.

The journey begins with madness and grief in the form of a dream vision, followed by the abduction of Queen Heurodis. Hence, from the beginning of the poem, the psychic and external adventures are linked, so that the initiation rite parallels the individuation process. The dream vision occurs beneath an "ympe tree" (a grafted tree) on a fine May morning, when Heurodis has gone with her maids to enjoy the fields full of flowers with blossoms on every bough of the orchard (1. 35-45). Like Persephone in the Homeric hymn, Heurodis is affiliated with springtime and with flowers; like the Eve of Milton's *Paradise Lost*, she dreams of her abduction sleeping beneath a tree in the garden while separated from her husband; and like Guenevere of Chrétien's "Knight of the Cart," she will be abducted to an otherworld with both Celtic and Christian features. While sleeping in her orchard beneath her ympe tree, Heurodis dreams of a king with a crown of precious stone shining as brightly as the sun (1. 125-28) who carries her off on a palfrey to his palace, and then promises to forcibly abduct her the next day after he returns her to the orchard beneath the ympe tree (a curious pun, certainly, on imp or elf, which links faeries to tree spirits). Heurodis has this dream shortly before noon, at a time of day the poet calls "under-tide," a word suggestive of an underworld of time beneath natural time, yet coextensive with it.

Hence, the whole dream anticipates the complete heroine's journey cycle (from orchard to underworld palace and back to orchard), like one of those premonitory dreams which Jungians tell us drive people into analysis and predict the entire course of development that lies ahead. Indeed, this dream precipitates neurotic symptoms, as Heurodis falls into an hysterical fit, thrashing around, rubbing her hands and feet, scratching her face until it bleeds, tearing her body with her sharp nails, and, interestingly in the light of our discussion of clothing symbolism above, rending her rich robe to pieces ("Her riche robe hye all torett" 57). It would be difficult to find a more clinically exact portrait of the ravings of witless hysteria (she refuses to speak until Orfeo manages to get her back into the palace). As Spearing comments in his headnotes to the poem,

> there is a constant association in this poem between the fairy world and psychological derangement or disintegration .... The underworld of the poem can be seen as the dark side of the human mind .... The intangible dark powers within the mind may assert themselves at any moment, in tension or in relaxation, setting a barrier between the sufferer and normality, absorbing him or her into an alternative world, glittering dangerously beneath the apparently solid ground. (48)

Furthermore, as in the story of Joseph, this transition between "alterna-tive worlds" is signaled by rent garments and wounding of the flesh.

The call to adventure and threshold battle coincide in this poem, both emerging from the dream and its connection with psychopathol-ogy. The journey then becomes an image of psychotherapy, a kind of myth of analysis.[4] As Spearing suggests in his commentary on the poem, it is a myth which suggests that a cure is possible "only if the healer has the love and the courage to be willing to go through madness himself, to commit himself, naked and unarmed, to the wilderness and to the underworld and its central citadel" (49). This is the role Sir Orfeo must commit himself to; in order to rescue and heal his wife, he must undertake the journey, which also then represents a kind of myth of marriage, since the fit which possesses his wife Heurodis causes the first conflict between them: "Sethen we first togider were, " she says to him, "Ones wroth never we were" (97-98). It is their first quarrel, and it initiates what Jung called the alchemical marriage, during which the couple is subjected to the full range of corrosive mortifications which break the relationship down to its essential elements, which are then re-combined to produce a more mature union.[5] As in the alchemical draw-ings which illustrate these operations, which show an initially royally robed King and Queen stripped naked for their descent into the crucible of transformation, so in *Sir Orfeo* the scene immediately following the abduction of Heurodis shows us the divestiture of the King: in his grief over the loss of his wife, Orfeo hands his kingdom over to his steward and then strips off his armor to put on a "sclavin" (a pilgrim's mantle) with no "kirtel ne hoode, / Shert, no no nother goode." He then goes barefoot into the wilderness and the poet enumerates the various pos-sessions which have been stripped away in a sequence of anaphoric lines analogous to the stripping of the royal *me* from Inanna: he that once wore variegated grey fur and slept on purple linen now lies moss covered on the hard heath; he that had castle and land now is cast out into the freezing snow; he that was once surrounded by knights and ladies must battle "wilde wormes" (as Gawain had to do); he that had plenty of each dainty morsel must now dig all day for roots to eat (217-232).

These lines vividly evoke the imagery of divestiture characteristic of this phase of the hero journey. Other medieval works often contain similar images of grief and nakedness in the forest madness of the lover: Chrétien's Yvain goes mad and leaves Arthur's court when he re-alizes he has forgotten to return to his wife Laudine after a year's time, and goes raving into the forest, where he strips naked and grovels for roots, rabbits, and stale bread before a courtly maiden revives him with a magic ointment and then reclothes him. Tony Hunt's commentary is equally applicable to Orfeo: Yvain is "the victim of a brainstorm which obliterates his former self and hence prepares for the reconstruction of a new identity" (136). Lancelot too undergoes such a metamorphosis -- both in Malory, when he leaps out the window and runs mad into the forest in response to Gueneve re's insane jealousy; and in the anony-mous Prose Lancelot, in which he has his shield, horse, and armor taken from him in exchange for a "holy man's hair shirt" and is then advised that the five virtues of his youth (virginity, humility, long suf-fering, rectitude, and chastity) are the "wedding garments" which Christ has bestowed upon those "that serve him" (145). One is tempted to note a connection here to the clothing symbolism in *Sir Gawain and the Green Knight* and its connection to the five courtly virtues. At any rate, such amplifications upon the symbolism of clothing could be widely extended with respect to the Arthurian stories (see the various discus-sions in other sections for detail): Parzival, for example, in Wolfram's masterpiece, is sent off to court ill-clad by his mother, kills the Red Knight and takes his armor, and is then clothed in the royal garb of the Fisher King in the Grail castle. That robe surely suggests Joseph's coat of many colors and the radiant mantle of the Gnostic hero of the "The Hymn of the Pearl." Imagery of stripping down also occurs in *The Quest of the Holy Grail* when Perceval gets naked into bed with the devil, who takes the form of a beautiful maiden to intoxicate and tempt him into sex and sleep, so that clothing symbolism there is linked with the themes of imprisonment in the material world (sleep and drunkenness) common to Gnostic works.

In *Sir Orfeo*, we find clothing symbolism in the descriptions of the abductor, King Pluto, who first appears in the dream of Heurodis wearing a crown of precious stones shining brightly as the sun. The radiance of his presence remains his distinguishing characteristic later in the poem, after the grieving Orfeo follows his wife among the faerie dancers into a rock, beneath which he finds the hidden kingdom of Pluto. The word "rock" here suggests a cliff side, so that as in the Gilgamesh epic we once again find the underworld situated beneath a mountain, and like the end of the journey through the twelve leagues of darkness (a three mile journey here in *Sir Orfeo*), the destined landscape is paradisal: a "fair country / As bright as the sun on a summer's day" (326-27). In the middle of a smooth green plain, Orfeo finds a castle with walls as clear and shiny as crystal, inside of which (or through which) he sees spacious dwellings made of precious stone. Every pillar is burnished gold, and darkness never visits the land: "All that land was ever light / For when it should have been thick night / The radiance of the precious stones / Shone as brightly as the sun at noon" (345-48). Orfeo thinks he has found the "court of Paradis" (352) and immediately gains entrance as a wandering minstrel. The whole passage is very reminiscent the journey of Gilgamesh beneath the darkness of the mountains to the garden of Siduri, and shows the continuity of solar imagery in the hero journey cycle. Just as in the Sumero-Babylonian epic the twelve leagues suggests the twelve hours of the night, so Orfeo's journey to the fairy king's castle is search of his wife (Gilgamesh began his journey in search of his dead friend Enkidu) has been seen as reflecting a solar myth: Speirs says that the castle may well have been "in the original myths the abode of the sun god, or the sun itself" (147), and that the "precious stone that ... shines as bright as the sun" on the King's crown suggests that "If ... the original of the Otherworld King was the sun-god, his stone would originally have been the sun itself or its symbol" (143). Indeed, the imagery of a radiant realm of gold and gems as the climax of the hero journey is a constantly repeated motif, from the tales of the Arabian Nights, to the Arthurian legends, to Ambrose Bierce, and on to the narratives of the near death experience (as we will see in the chapters below).

Indeed, in *Sir Orfeo*, the court of Paradise can only be reached after the extreme sufferings of a kind of near-death experience: the fairy kingdom is still the land of the dead. As in *Sir Gawain and the Green Knight*, the description of the otherworld kingdom fuses Celtic, Christian, Classical, and Courtly themes: the faerie hunt and dance are "common features in Celtic legend" (Spearing 42); the porter at the gates follows the Greek legends of Orpheus among the shades of the dead; the image of Heurodis abducted beneath an "ympe tree" implies the seduction of Eve, although Paradise here is to be found beneath the hollow hills; and finally, the exploration of the relations between king and servant, king and queen, king and minstrel, and between kings of foreign but neighboring realms delineates the complex hierarchies of medieval courtly society.

In addition to these concerns, however, another level of meaning in the poem relates to universal issues of human creativity: the hero journey becomes a metaphorical image of the creative processes by which the powers of the poetic imagination are activated, intensified, and executed in a performance which receives royal patronage. That is to say, Orfeo's journey to the otherworld, his *nekyia*, is an image of *poesis*. The intense grief, the psychological derangement, the patholog-ical elements of the dream vision, the physical symptoms, the profound isolation in the wasteland, and the beatific vision of the "court of Paradis" -- all raise the power of his verse to a supernatural level. Alone in the wilderness, Orfeo takes out his harp from a hollow tree on bright clear days and plays at will, so that "Into alle the woode the soun gan shille," as all the beasts and birds gather round "To here his harping afine / So miche melody was therin" (253-54). [6] The word "glee" used to denote the special kind of pleasure to be derived from this kind of harping is derived from the Old English *gleo* for merriment and glad-ness, and is also used in *Sir Gawain* to designate courtly joy, where it is alliterated with *glaum*, the root of our modern word "glamour." In the Middle Ages, and in the ballad tradition glamour was associated with the supernatural appeal of a kind of magical beauty. Hence the special power poetry derives from the otherworld is one of the central themes of the poem: it is a power akin to the glamour associated with Persephone's beauty cream in "Cupid and Psyche." As we will see in the chapters below, this connection between the hero journey and *poesis* is central throughout the history of the monomyth.

The conclusion of the hero journey cycle in *Sir Ofeo* reiterates the symbolism of clothing, as Orfeo returns to his rightful kingdom in beg-gar's rags, like Odysseus, in order to test the fidelity of the steward left in charge. All the townspeople remark upon his long hair, his shaggy beard hanging to his knees, and his shriveled, rough, and blackened skin, still covered with the mysterious affliction the poet calls "mis-sais." One can imagine, in fact, that his face and body have roughly the same appearance remarked upon by Utnapishtim's wife at the approach of Gilgamesh after his long journey to the Land of Faraway, or Land of the Living. One can also imagine how an unpatronized minstrel wandering from court to court might have looked. At any rate, the power of Orfeo's harping changes all that: after shrilly tuning up, Orfeo harps "the blissefullest notes ... That ever any man yherd with ere" (504-505). This leads to his recognition as the lost king, after which he is bathed and freshly clothed in royal garments, as the hero of the Gnostic hymn had been at his homecoming. The hero journey then becomes a discovery of identity, a discovery conferred upon hero and reader by the power of poetry (remember that Odysseus names himself at the court of Alkinöos and tells his story after the harping of the blind poet Demodokos). This discovery of the true identity of the king through the "magical harmonizing and civilizing power of song" consequently helps to "build harmony out of the different classes of society" (Spearing 47, 49), so that the boon brought back by the hero (the power of song) has restorative powers of collective as well as of personal significance.

There is also a deeper level of Celtic mysticism operating in this lovely poem having to do with the coexistence and mutual interpenetration of this world and the other. Whereas in Christian and Neoplatonic or Gnostic thinking there is a rather rigid demarcation between the two realms of spirit and matter, such dualism tends to be blurred in Celtic circumstances. This can be seen when we examine the Gnostic elements in *Sir Orfeo* and note the fact that there are really two hero journey cycles and two abduction scenes in the poem, which are curiously interlaced.[7] In the first, Heurodis is abducted into the faerie kingdom from her courtly home in the 'real' world, but in the second she is taken from the "court of Paradis" in the 'other' world by her husband minstrel, who is described as a kind of Hades figure, "lene, rowe and blak," while Heurodis is a kind of innocent Persephone, "lovesom, withouten lak" (435, 436). This seems a dramatic role reversal: Heurodis is still the lovely young princess, even though she is presumably in the underworld, or land of the dead, while her husband from the land of the living is the dark and threatening Hades come to carry her off: "A lothlich thing it were, forthy, / To seen her in thy company" (437-38), the faerie King says to Orfeo before he agrees to let her go. In this second hero journey (to be completed only, presumably, by the death of Heurodis and her return to the otherworld), it is this 'real' life of ours that becomes the underworld (the land of mortality and of the flesh, black and rough like the animal skins Gilgamesh wears). It is into life, then, that Heurodis is forced to descend, from the paradisal conditions in the faerie court, where there is eternal hunting and dancing among the radiance of never fading gemstones. She represents, in other words, the human soul, *anima mundi*, which, in Gnostic and

Neoplatonic allegory must die into life to be incarnated, and achieve rebirth through death, when the soul returns to its heavenly source.

What is uniquely Celtic, then, about *Sir Orfeo*, is its suggested unity of the two journeys, which are equivalent rather than antithetical. Both courts are simultaneously kingdoms of the dead, and kingdoms of the living, and the soul wanders back and forth, endlessly, between them, just as the eye alternates between castle and reflection, when pondering the facade and image of a medieval chateau reflected in the lake and moat which surrounds it: this world above the water line, and the other below merge into a single image of the same mystery, transcendent yet immanent. As Joseph Campbell puts it, "heroes may ride back and forth over the very ground of the Castle of the Grail without seeing it: and I am told that in Ireland, one may walk around and right past a fairy hill without seeing it. One seems to be walking a straight line, but actually is curving past an invisible fairy hill of glass, which is right there, but hidden -- like the Hidden Truth" ("Peripheries" 15).

Chrétien's Lancelot

Chrétien's "Knight of the Cart" begins where it will end: in the court of King Arthur at Camelot. The call to adventure comes, as in *Sir Gawain and the Green Knight*, in the form of a sudden intrusion: a fully armed knight interrupts the meal to announce that he holds in captivity many knights, ladies, and maidens from Arthur's domains who will only be released on condition that one knight be allowed to accompany Queen Guenevere into the nearby woods and defend her. Arthur's seneschal, Sir Kay, obtains permission to be that knight in a most incongruous way that violates the basic codes of courtly etiquette: he threatens to leave Arthur's service immediately, refusing to relent until the Queen falls on the floor and begs him not to quit. Kay then relents, on condition that Arthur allow him to accompany Guenevere into the woods with the intruder. This agreement causes terrific distress, grief, and dejection among the courtiers, who comment on it as outrageous, arrogant, and absurd. As the Queen is led away miserable and depressed, "every man and woman watching grieved as bitterly as if she lay dead in her coffin, not believing she would ever come back in her lifetime" (187). Gawain then complains that Arthur has done an extremely silly and astonishing thing, and gets permission to ride immediately after the Queen to see how Kay fares in her defense.

I dwell on the details of this departure from Camelot because they serve to emphasize the uncanny and indeed uncourtly way the tale begins: incongruous behavior; humiliation of the King and Queen at the hands of their inferior servant, Sir Kay; King Arthur's irrational and ill-advised decisions to release the Queen into Kay's protection; and a

general sense of astonishment and grief among courtiers, who imagine
their Queen to have been taken off to her grave. All of these details
seem appropriate to the archetypal nature of the call in this case: it is a
tricky abduction into the land of the dead, which already holds many of
Arthur's people captive. Courtly etiquette must always find death an ill-
mannered violation of its codes of behavior. A kind of pathology grips
all in the court, a general weakening of its splendid chivalric ego and
the persona (the King) who defends it. Pathological imagery intensifies
in the scenes devoted to the threshold crossing into the woods, where
Gawain finds Kay's horse with the bridle snapped (a lovely detail, suggesting that all hell has broken loose!), its saddle broken and battered,
and its stirrup cups bloodstained. In Platonic allegory, a riderless horse
would signify the removal of reason from its rightful place in the chariot, from which it controls the drives of appetite and will. The court
then comes upon Lancelot approaching on a horse that drops dead in
front of them from exhaustion; Lancelot gets a new one from Gawain,
which the court then soon finds dead in a field trampled down and littered by broken lances and shields. The climax of these pathologized
details comes when Lancelot agrees later to get on a cart led by a dwarf,
who promises him knowledge of Guenevere's whereabouts in return.
Lancelot hesitates two steps before climbing on the cart, because, we
are told, the cart was used in those days only for criminals guilty of
treason, murder, theft, or violent highway robbery. Anyone put in the
cart would lose all legal rights and be subject to the abuse and slander
which is actually heaped on Lancelot when he and Gawain arrive a castle that same evening.

This supreme public humiliation, and the gruesome details leading
up to it, suggest that a serious deflation of the ego and a complete res-
ignation of the persona is the prerequisite for the hero journey in this
case: it is precisely the wounding of chivalric pride, and the violation of
courtly codes, that gets the story going, and indeed make it possible at
all (if Arthur had remained his courtly self, immune to Kay's humiliations, Guenevere would never have been abducted, and there would
have been no "Knight of the Cart"). From the psychological perspective, this deflation is typical of an onslaught of the unconscious: the dis-
ruption of normal functioning (like the fit Heurodis throws in *Sir
Orfeo*) is "a symbolic or archetypal situation with which every encounter with the unconscious begins: namely, the complete breakdown
of the former activities .... and in this moment the life energy is
dammed up and then generally breaks through in the revelation of an
archetypal image" (*Puer* 27). Neurotic wounding, that is to say, leads to
an activation of the archetypal dreams of the unconscious, represented
in this tale by the underworld into which Guenevere is abducted, and
into which Lancelot descends in order to retrieve her. This loss of the

court's soul (its anima, one might say) will lead to just such an activation of those powerful images of the collective unconscious as the story proceeds. James Hillman calls this radical shift from the ego to the unconscious "soul-making," and suggests that pathological events are indispensable initiators of psychological wisdom: "In the chalice of the wound is soul. This means that psyche is the aim of our bleeding love and that the wound is a grail. The opus is not in Jerusalem; it is right here in our wounds" (*Puer* 116). "Through that little hole of the wound," Hillman continues (with reference to Thomas Mann's *The Magic Mountain*), "the immense realm of the spirit enters" (108). In *The Dream and the Underworld*, Hillman writes of the abduction of Persephone (along with the death of Eurydice the mythic analog of the Queen's abduction in Chrétien's romance) as a death dealing blow that "takes matters out of life and makes them into soul" (96). The abduction signifies a "transition from the material to the psychical perspective" (53), and a subsequent revelation of those archetypal ideas "that form and shape life" (51). Russian formalist criticism calls these archetypal ideas "elementary poetic forms," and argues (with a different vocabulary and set of assumptions) that these forms are activated in stories by a process of "defamiliarizing" (Steiner 50-54), such as we see in the incongruities and humiliations at the beginning of Chrétien's tale.

Whether we call it "soul-making" or "defamiliarizing," the departure from the court in "The Knight of the Cart" leads to the evocation of "elementary poetic ideas" (or archetypes) during the episodes chronicling Lancelot's tests and ordeals in the hero journey. The first ordeal occurs at midnight in the castle where he had arrived in the cart, and it takes up once again the theme of wounding: though warned by the Lady of the castle that no knight who has been subjected to the shame of the cart would even think to lay in the magnificent bed she forbids him to sleep in, Lancelot asserts his right to the privilege. The elementary idea here is the motif of the perilous bed, popularized by the Arthurian legends in tales usually devoted to Gawain (as in *Sir Gawain and the Green Knight* and in the sections devoted to Gawain in Wolfram's *Parzival* that will be discussed below). While sleeping in the magnificent bed to which to which his hostess reluctantly leads him, Lancelot is awakened at midnight by a lance shot down from the rafters like a thunderbolt, which pins him to the bed and bursts into flames. The head of this lance just grazes his side (a bit like Gawain's nick in the neck), and Lancelot's puts the fire out, throws the weapon away, and goes back to sleep (!). Chrétien will pick up the wound in the side later in the tale, when the connection to the five wounds of Christ is evoked as an "elementary poetic idea" or "archetype." The test here, in the perilous bed, is one of courage, and the temptation is of fear; the next test, therefore, is one of fidelity, designed to tempt him with desire: fear and desire, the two temptations of the Buddha beneath the Boddhi Tree, which, as Heinrich Zimmer suggests, comprise the essence of Gawain's ordeals in the domain of Bertilak and Morgan the Goddess. Hence, at the next castle where Lancelot spends the night, an exceedingly beautiful and elegantly dressed damsel offers her hospitality on the condition that Lancelot sleep with her, a condition, Chrétien says, which many people would have been eager to accept. Not so Lancelot: that night, after rescuing the naked damsel from a group of rapists, he is forced to lie with her, but he does so without removing his shirt, and his fidelity to Guenevere stifles the faintest trace of desire in his heart. These two episodes at the beginning of Lancelot's journey, therefore, are not, as some have supposed, gratuitous or random; rather, they serve to establish Lancelot's courage and loyalty, and to prepare him for a higher love (like that of the Boddhisattva's) which transcends fear and desire.

Having passed these tests, Lancelot moves more deeply into the elementary ideas associated with the netherworld: Lancelot comes to a church where "a series of apparent borrowings from the account of Christ's Crucifixion and harrowing of Hell as found in the *Gospel of Nicodemus*" begins (Owen 512). In the cemetery of the church lies a finely sculpted and tremendously heavy sarcophagus bearing an inscription saying that whoever raises the slab will free all the people imprisoned in that land from which no traveler has as yet returned, a phrase often repeated in the text (210). This is Hamlet's "undiscovered country from whose bourn no traveler returns." Lancelot astonishes the monk by raising the slab without the slightest difficulty, hence delivering all the men and women trapped in the kingdom from which no one escapes -- just as Christ delivers us from death by his sacrifice and harrowing of hell (an elementary idea of Christian iconography with a wide distribution in art history). While Chrétien's intentions here are uncertain -- Heinrich Zimmer suggests he was simply unaware of the deeper significance of his images -- it seems to me that he has hit upon the essence of Lancelot's appeal. As both the best of knights, and the worst of knights (because of his betrayal of Arthur, Lancelot combines godly and human traits, and like Jesus sacrifices himself and his honor to save Guenevere from hell), he becomes a kind of savior, a Boddhisattva, in fact, who refuses to renounce the world until all beings have been delivered and achieved enlightenment.

These allusions to Christ become most pronounced during the famous sword bridge crossing, a scene often depicted in Medieval art.[8] After many preparatory ordeals, Lancelot finally arrives at that river separating this world from the next, into which Guenevere has been abducted. It is appropriate that Lancelot arrives at this threshold late in the afternoon. The water rushing beneath the bridge is "black and turbid, as horrid and terrifying as if it were the Devil's river" (225). Two lions are tied to a stone slab at the opposite end of the bridge, which is described as a highly polished, razor sharp, glistening sword. The peril is so formidable that one of the knights in Lancelot's company is moved to offer the following illuminating remark: trying to cross that bridge would be like trying to "return to one's mother's womb and be born again (but that would be impossible)" (226). In the light of Heinrich Zimmer's suggestion that Guenevere (who awaits Lancelot across the river) is the Great Goddess, with whom Lancelot will share the sexual ritual known in mythology as the *hieros gamos*, or sacred marriage, which renews all life and releases it from bondage to death, these remarks seem very cunning, coming from a man who Zimmer also supposes knew little of the psychological and metaphysical import of his symbols!

There can be no question, however, that Chrétien intended a sustained parallel between Jesus and Lancelot: having been previously wounded in the side while sleeping in the perilous bed, Lancelot is now grievously wounded in the hands and feet while crossing the sword bridge. Upon reaching the yonder shore, blood oozing from his wounds, he looks up and sees King Bademagu and his son Meleagant anxiously watching from the window. The wounds now include all the ones associated with Jesus, and complete the portrait of Lancelot as the Crucified Christ (bleeding from palms, feet, and side - speared by Longinus) who redeems mankind from death (remember that Lancelot had done so earlier by lifting the stone slab of the sarcophagus). To reinforce the analogy, King Bademagu promises to heal Lancelot by using "the three Marys' ointment," a clear indication "that Chrétien's mind is turning on the events of the Crucifixion and Harrowing at this point" (Owen 513), since this is the ointment brought to the tomb by three women variously identified with Mary Magdalen, Mary Salome, and Mary mother of James.[9] But the Triple Goddess and her dying and resurrecting consort also evoke those pagan, Celtic associations which Robert Graves discusses in *The White Goddess*. Lancelot's entrance into the underworld is also an entrance into the realm of the Goddess, principally embodied by Guenevere, but also suggested by numerous other little details, such as the lions or leopards which guard the gateway of the castle at the other end of the sword bridge. As Joseph Campbell and Marija Gimbutas have amply demonstrated, the affiliation between the lion and the Great Goddess is one that goes all the way back to statuette of the Goddess giving birth on a lion throne in Çatal Hüyük, of about 6500 B.C.E., which can be traced from there, via the Cretan Seal of the Lady of the Labyrinth, standing on a mountain with lions on either side, of the 16th century B.C.E., on up to statue of the Anatolian Goddess Cybele flanked by lions of the Hellenistic period.[10]

In addition to the motifs of the wounds, the sword bridge, and the ointment of the three Marys, Chrétien makes use of the imagery of doorways and other thresholds throughout the course of the "The Knight of the Cart." The imagery of the entrance to the underworld as a door or gateway is a standard feature of the many Medieval depictions of the Harrowing of Hell. Albrecht Dürer's prints of the scene from 1510 and 1512 may be taken as typical: they show Jesus passing through a sequence of arches (guarded by demons) and stooping to re-trieve Adam and Eve from a sepulchral threshold leading down into hell. The elder Bruegel's painting of "The Just Delivered From Limbo" also shows the entrance into the jaws of hell as a door knocked off its hinges. While numerous precursors of Dürer and Bruegel -- painters of canvas, fresco, and illuminated manuscript -- also deploy the imagery of doorways and demons in their depictions of the Harrowing of Hell, the convention is evident in pagan traditions as well, as we know from our discussion of the descent of Inanna through seven doorways in our first chapter. Virgil, Dante, and Milton all put guarded doorways at the entrance to their underworlds, and, in so doing, transmit the imagery to later generations of poets and novelists for whom the hero journey be-comes a basic narrative structure. The threshold imagery which Chrétien uses extensively in "The Knight of the Cart" seems appropri-ate, therefore, to the iconography of the heroic descent: Lancelot sits on the window ledge of one castle to watch the Queen pass by with a cof-fin; defeats two armed knights at the doorway into the room where the Lady is being raped in the next castle; breaks through a lattice guarded by a knight in the Stone Passage; passes through a bailey gate, cham-ber, barred door, and narrow postern gate in the daunting fortress where he needs to look at the ring given him by the Lady of the Lake to see if he is bewitched or trapped; is escorted by King Bademagu through the tower gateway which the manuscript illuminations depict guarded by lions on the other end of the sword bridge; and finally through the barred window into the room where Guenevere waits for him. One of the means by which Chrétien achieved his "molt bele conjointure" (the "very beautiful linkage" between parts to which he aspires in his pre-liminary remarks to the tale) is, therefore, the consistency of threshold imagery to mark the stages of Lancelot's Harrowing of Hell.

What follows Lancelot's crossing of the bridge and passage through various gateways and windows, however, is more pagan than pious: the elementary motif of the *hieros gamos* (sacred marriage) is climax of this hero journey. Guenevere apparently possesses the omni-science of the Goddess, since she chastises Lancelot for hesitating two steps before climbing on the cart back down the road of trials. Stung by her astonishing reaction to his appearance, still bleeding from the miraculous ordeal of the sword bridge, Lancelot attempts suicide, which in the context of the mythology of the Great Goddess and her ritually slain consort, suggests the death and rebirth of the hero who ventures into the underworld to redeem the soul of the world from death. Jesus, as Sir James Frazer demonstrated many years ago, was of course one many ancient deities of the Near East whose allegiance to the Goddess led to his death and resurrection: we see this archetypal image in the dual manifestations of Mary as the Madonna, giving birth to the Christ child in her lap, and as the Pièta with the Crucified Christ having returned to her lap in death in order to be reborn. [11]

Guenevere, in fact, is adored like the Virgin Mary, as were many of the ladies exalted in the courtly love poetry of the troubadours (in France) and the Minnesänger (in Germany). [12] After tearing through the bars outside Guenevere's window (here the threshold portal is a window, instead of a door, but it still leads into the *sanctum sanctorum*), Lancelot comes to the Queen's bed and "bows in adoration, for no holy relic inspires him with such faith" (247). When he leaves her chamber after a flawless night of love, he bows again, "behaving just as though he were before an altar" (248). For he has experienced a love so sweet that its wonder cannot be spoken of: Chrétien is not simply being coy when he remarks that "The supreme and most exquisite of their joys was that which the tale conceals from us and leaves untold" (247). Although Chrétien is, as usual (for a complexity of tone and meaning is the very signature of his style, once thought to have been so simple) having a little fun here, but there is more to it than that. This is not prudery or coyness alone, but wisdom, for the modesty and restraint of this moment records the mysticism of love in the poetry of the Middle Ages. It is the ineffable joy of the "Liebestod," of love in the domain of death, with the ecstasy which transcends the categories of reason, and about which therefore Chrétien must remain silent. What this silence suggests is the supremely mystical joy of the 'love-death', an oxymoron characteristic of Medieval love poetry. The oxymoron typifies a "mode of speech commonly found in Oriental religious texts, where it is used as a device to point past those pairs of opposites by which all logical thought is limited, to a 'sphere that is no sphere,' beyond 'names and forms'" (Campbell, *Creative Mythology* 188).

While it is true that "the literary expression of courtly love often used the imagery of Christian worship," (as we see Lancelot's idolization of Guenevere), "whilst texts such as hymns to the Virgin might use the terminology of courtly love" (Owen 514), the mingling of the sacred and the profane captures the mood of pagan mysticism appropriate to the sacred marriage which occurs in Guenevere's bedroom. Lancelot has, in a sense, returned to his mother's womb in order to be reborn, being both the son and lover of the Goddess. The blood left behind on the sheets is menstrual, maternal, and mortal, coming as it does from Lancelot's wounds, yet suggesting both the broken hymen of virginity (for their love is ever new, just as Guenevere is ever virgin) and the blood of birth. I think Zimmer was right to suggest a pagan, heretical (perhaps Gnostic or Catharist) initiation rite behind this entire sequence of Lancelot's adventures, which Zimmer finds recorded in the Marseille Tarot pack (177-179). Lancelot endures the public humiliation of the cart (analogous to station XII of the Tarot pack, "The Hanged Man"), and the ordeal of the sarcophagus (station XII, "Death"), in order to achieve the final mystery of union with the Goddess (station XXI, "The World"), which is "symbolic of the life renewing moment that restores the life of the world" (Zimmer 179).

Lancelot's return to Camelot, however, reiterates the Christian allegory in a scene not commented on by Zimmer or, as far as I know, by other critics. For the threshold battle of the return crossing with Meleagant is a typological revisioning of the defeat of Abel in *Genesis*, which is reversed by the victory of Christ on the battlefield of Armageddon. The battle occurs in the presence of all the lords and ladies of Arthur's court on a heath which is dominated by a splendid sycamore tree, planted (we are told) in the time of Abel. Fine emerald green grass (ever fresh) grows beneath the sycamore, beside a spring pearling above a pebbled bed bright as silver, and through a channel as pure and unblemished as burnished gold (279). While the imagery here is Christian, suggestive of the recovery of paradise before Abel's death (with Meleagant playing the role of Cain and the Anti-Christ, and Lancelot the role of the victorious Jesus of *Revelation*), it is a Christianity modified by the archaic Celtic and alchemical motifs of the union of the sun and moon (gold and silver), the sacred tree, the spring of life, and the radiance of the otherworld (all of which we have seen in that other marvelous poem about the liberation of the Queen of Life from the Land of the Dead, *Sir Orfeo*).[13] Lancelot performs his final feat by playing the role of Jesus, however, whose victory reverses the fall and the consequences of the first murder, and reestablishes the paradise of the millennium. Having delivered the courtly souls imprisoned in the land of death, he now defeats the powers of evil for all time -- in order to win the favor of his Queen, Guenevere. The fusion of gold and silver is particularly interesting in this context, for it suggests that union of Eternity and Time, Sol and Luna, King and Queen, which alchemy employed as a symbol of the completed Opus. The conjunction of the solar and the lunar symbolism, in the calculation of the date of Easter, also enters into the imagery of the Crucifixion of the Middle Ages and Renaissance, a point which further enriches the typological linkages between Lancelot and Jesus in the rest of the text: Albrecht Dürer's "Great Crucifixion" of 1498, for example, shows Jesus on the Cross with the three Marys at its base, with a sun immediately to his right hand and a moon immediately to his left (the right side and sun traditionally male, the left side lunar); but the image is an old one, as a glorious page from The Psalter of Robert de Lindesey of about 1220 shows -- it shows a sun above the right arm of the Crucified Jesus, and a moon above his left (Marks and Morgan Plate 3).[14]

Chrétien's Yvain

In Chrétien's tale of the "Knight with the Lion," there are two complete hero journey cycles, which begin and end in Camelot, and in a sense a third, which begins and ends in court of Lunette, the Lady of the Fountain. Three journeys chart Yvain's individuation process, and his gradual development from a vainglorious youth (the first journey), to a mature adult responsive more to the needs of others than to his own (the second journey). In a sense, the interlacing of hero journeys resembles those earlier divisions appropriate to the various stages of life which we discussed in the Sumero-Babylonian myths of Gilgamesh and Enkidu, and Inanna and Dumuzi.

The first cycle begins (as did the "Knight of the Cart") with a sequence of incongruities and inappropriate behavior in violation of courtly codes. King Arthur, to begin with, astonishes his courtiers by retiring to his room with Guenevere after the Feast of Pentecost (actually a lovely symbol of the retreat of the libido from an outer to an inner room of the psyche, i.e., from the conscious ego to the unconscious self). This is so unprecedented that some members of the court are offended and do not "spare their comments" (281). The offense is intensified when the King is detained so long by his dalliance with the Queen that he apparently 'falls asleep' by her side. Calogrenant then begins to tell a story which he might very well never have started in the King's company; for just as Arthur's post-Pentecostal dalliance with his wife is offensive, so the tale Calogrenant begins is "a story that was not to his honor but to his shame" (281). There is something illicit about storytelling like this in the King's absence, but the story seems for that reason all the more enticing, as if the removal of Arthur symbolized the departure of the superego, which makes the uncensored material of the id more accessible. In his commentary on alchemical symbolism, in which the opus is often initiated by the slaying of the King, Edward Edinger points out that "the king refers to the ego -- at least the dominant or ruling principle according to which the ego is structured" (53). The slaying of the King (or in this case his removal into the realm of sleep and sex) therefore represents that "regressive dissolution of the conscious personality" (19) which serves to activate the archetypal imagery of the unconscious, which is the basis for the elementary ideas of fictional plots.

Sleep, sex, and dishonorable, even shameful stories, are all linked together at the beginning of this hero journey cycle. In fact, the dissolution of courtly behavior initiated by Arthur's removal is picked up immediately in the squabbling that erupts between Kay and Calogrenant when Guenevere sneaks out of the King's room to hear the story: Kay is "extremely abusive, wickedly sarcastic and sneering," heaping abuse on Calogrenant as he tells his tale. Calogrenant says to the Queen that he'd "rather have one of [his] eyes plucked out than tell any more of [his] tale today" (283), so shameful is it to him. This corrosive eruption of the court's shadow figure (Sir Kay, who represents the reverse of chivalric politeness) is familiar but nevertheless uncanny; it goes hand in hand with the compelling appeal of the rather dishonorable story Calogrenant must now proceed, under the Queen's orders, to tell. This process of 'defamiliarization' precipitates the juiciest stories (as is witnessed in many dreams which involve a trip or trick that removes a person symbolic of the superego in order to allow the dream material to bubble up in the cauldron). And indeed, Calogrenant's story of his journey through the forest to the magnificent fountain, his humiliation at the hands of the Black Knight who guards the fountain, and the subsequent sequel, when Yvain sneaks off to fulfill the quest which Calogrenant fails, is laced with the kind of alchemical imagery we would recognize as elemental in the vocabulary of European storytelling: the wild man of the woods, the fountain with the tree and Grail cup, the Lady who marries the slayer of her consort -- all suggest a long lineage of mythological symbolism.

Calogrenant first tells his spellbound courtiers that some seven years ago, while traveling in quest of adventure, he came upon a right hand path through a dense forest -- a difficult track full of briars and thorns -- which led to a magnificent castle in Broceliande. That night, he enjoyed the splendid hospitality of a grand old man and his gloriously refined and altogether delightful daughter. Calogrenant tells how he left the next morning and shortly came to a clearing where unruly and ferocious wild bulls were fighting in front of a churlish giant some seventeen feet tall. The giant is huge and hideous, with a head longer than a pack horse, ears like an elephant, brows and eyes like an owl, nose like a cat, mouth like a wolf, teeth like a boar, and so forth! This wild man who guards the entrance to the mysteries of the forest has as his remote ancestor Humbaba, who guards the cedar woods in the *Epic of Gilgamesh*, and more contemporary cousins in the Green Knight, the Loathly Damsel, and such Grimms brothers tales as "Iron Hans" (to whom Robert Bly has recently devoted his sagacious reflections on masculinity). Heinrich Zimmer suggests another medieval source which would identify the wild man encountered here by Calogrenant as one of the incarnations of Merlin, whose magic is ultimately derived from the Celtic mysticism of the forest, into which he retires, wreathed round about by a tower of white thorns, when he dies. It is therefore appropriate, in Zimmer's view, that neither Calogrenant nor Yvain slaughters this giant (as Enkidu and Gilgamesh had slaughtered Humbaba). Rather, they allow themselves to be guided by him on their quests for the magic fountain. This is in keeping with the harmonious acceptance of the natural supernaturalism of the Celtic peoples, who by celebrating the immanence to the spirit refuse to establish a dualism that necessitates a conquest of nature.

Be that as it may, this gigantic shapeshifter and guide of souls encountered on the threshold of the mysteries of the forest directs Calogrenant (and then Yvain) to the tree and fountain, where begin the marvels and the terrors of the initiation. The tree is archetypal, Druidic or Norse in origins, "the loveliest tree that Nature ever managed to create. It keeps its leaves the whole year round" (286), i.e., it is the Tree of Life (like Yggdrasil). In its shade a spring colder than marble boils up, and there is a basin (iron in the Wild Man's account, purest gold in Calogrenant's) hanging from the tree beside a large "slab" (according to the wild man) made of an emerald and four rubies bright as the sun (according to Calogrenant). The Wild Man instructs Calogrenant to use the basin to pour water from the spring onto the emerald slab, and when he does so there is a terrific clap of thunder and a hail storm is unleashed, from more than fourteen directions, which shatters all the neighboring trees. When it dissipates, the branches and leaves of the tree from which the golden ladle hangs are completely covered by birds, who sing an ecstatic pastorale in a magnificently serene and transcendently pacified atmosphere.

All of the elements of this description are archetypal -- tree, spring, golden cup, gemstone, and thunderbolt -- and together yield one of the great moments in the Arthurian tradition.[15] If, as seems certain, Merlin has a Celtic, Druidic background, it is appropriate that the Wild Man directs Calogrenant to this truly splendid tree, since the mythology of the Celts revolved around a kind of archetypal arboretum which formed the very basis of their alphabet, poetry, and religious rituals.[16] Chrétien's tree seems to be a kind of hybrid mix: it is partly the Yggdrasil of Norse myth, rooted in *Nifelheim* and ascending through Middle Earth to branch into the heavens, and the source of Wotan's runic staff acquired during the nine windy days and nights he spent hung from the tree; and it is partly the kind of Persian image of the tree, where angels gather to sing the praises of God, which Chaucer adapted in his *Parliament of Foules*. Furthermore, as Chrétien's story shows, the tree is also Biblical, the place where the opposites of good and evil are reconciled by rituals of transformation: does the spring boil or freeze? is the basin iron or gold? is the slab rock or emerald? All are both and the same, since the tree represents the place where heaven and hell meet on earth, where tempest yields to Paradise, and where iron is transmuted into the philosopher's stone (an emerald tablet in one important alchemical document).[17] It is also the place where young knights endure the rite of passage into adulthood, to be transformed from glory seeking egoists (iron clad heroes) into Christian soldiers in service to the higher community (golden cherubim). In this way, Chrétien changes a mythical into an ethical symbol of transformation, adapting an elementary idea to his courtly concerns.

Archetypally, the tree also has ancient connections with the Great Mother, that loving and terrible goddess who presides over the rituals of death and rebirth (think of Inanna and the Huluppu Tree, Eve and the Tree of Knowledge, Isis and the Cedar). Zimmer suggests a close relation between Chrétien's Lady of the Fountain and Diana of the Sacred Grove at Nemi, Goddess of the Golden Bough, with whom Frazer begins his famous opus. Diana's grove was also guarded by a prowling knight who defended the oak from which the golden bough hung from the knight who would become next guardian and consort of Diana by slaying him. Such a figure seems to be in the background in Chrétien's tale, in which the Black Knight who guards the fountain and tree will be slain by his successor Yvain, who then becomes the consort of the Lunette, the Lady of the Fountain.

Calogrenant ends his tale at the point when he is defeated by the Black Knight by saying to his audience "So I've foolishly told you what I never wished to tell at all," but he is soon compelled to hear Guenevere repeat the entire story of what he sees as his humiliation to Arthur. While Guenevere is doing so, another rather ignominious proceeding takes our tale towards its next step: Yvain sneaks out unobserved to avenge Calogrenant's shame, in order to beat the other courtiers in the race for the glory of the quest, which Arthur initiates by swearing to see the fountain and its marvels within a fortnight. Tony Hunt has commented on Yvain's sly violation of courtly procedure as a symptom of his egotistical immaturity and lust for fame; but Yvain's clandestine departure from court also fits the pattern of 'defamiliarizing' or 'pathologizing' which we have noted in the sequence of shameful moments which Chrétien seems to have woven into his conception of stories and storytelling in this first separation stage of the hero journey (from Arthur falling asleep after the feast, to Kay's sarcastic and rude remarks, to the shameful tale itself and the dishonorable response it evokes in Yvain). This interweaving of the return and departure phases of the hero journey also works beautifully to show how stories serve to motivate an audience: Calogrenant's return to Camelot and recitation of the story of the fountain becomes Yvain's call to adventure, initiating a second hero journey cycle in the text.

Yvain's cycle begins by repeating the stages of the journey up to the arrival of the Black Knight after the tempest is unleashed when the water is poured on the emerald stone. The battle which ensues constitutes a fascinating version of the threshold crossing from the domestic to the daemonic realm of the supernatural. It is a detailed and suitably bloody image of the passage from nature into spirit, which sustains the pathological imagery of wounding (and of doorways and corridors) as a symbol marking the transition from Camelot to the faerie domains of the Celtic otherworld which we saw in "The Knight of the Cart." After a long and fierce battle beside the spring, Yvain delivers a savage blow that severs the Black Knight's helmet and splits his skull down to the brain, spattering bloody bits of gray matter over the shining, but now much dented armor. Mortally wounded, Esclados (the Black Knight) races back to his castle with Yvain in pursuit. Yvain is much concerned, at this point, for if Esclados escapes he will lose the evidence of victory needed to secure his glory and escape Kay's taunting back at Camelot. Driven by this desire for fame, and fear of shame, Yvain risks the narrow passage through the gate of the castle, which contains a hidden blade in the portcullis that crashes down like "a Devil out of Hell," slicing Yvain's horse in half and grazing his heels (293). Esclados escapes through a second gateway into the city, but Yvain is left precariously caught in a hallway between the two threshold gates.

While the imagery here probably draws on the conventional iconography of the jaws of the Devil devouring sinners at the gateway to the palaces of Hell,[18] it is also interesting to note that the scene is an extraordinary variation on the imagery of gateways and corridors which we have traced throughout our exploration of the hero journey cycle. Yvain is now suspended between the daily and the supernatural realms, which are divided by doorways, such as the ones Inanna, Ra, Sir Orfeo, and others had to pass through. That the threshold crossing has something to do with the transition from the material world of the flesh to the spiritual realm of the otherworld is made clear by Chrétien by having Lunette, a beautiful damsel who will be Yvain's helper and guide during this stage of the journey, emerge from a small door in the hallway to give Yvain a small ring that renders him as invisible as "the wood which is covered by the bark that grows on it "(294). The simile is suggestive of the mythical properties of the great tree where Yvain's threshold battle began: like Osiris buried in the cedar of the *djed* pillar, Yvain is now an invisible captive in the realm from only the Lady of

the Fountain (like Isis) can deliver him. Furthermore, invisibility certainly marks, in the clearest possible way, the transition from the material to the spiritual realms. So does the imagery of wounding and death,
accompanied by profound grief and lamentation, which predominates
during this section of the story: while Yvain looks out on the lords and
ladies of the castle, who are crazed with grief beside the bier of
Esclados, the wounds of the corpse open again and the fresh blood runs
clear and crimson. This bleeding is regarded as "positive proof that the
man who had fought the combat ... was now certainly still present"
(296). All this suggests the mortal passage of the dying body into the
invisible realm of that enchanted kingdom from which no traveler returns (Lancelot had also been rendered invisible by a ring as he passed
into the Kingdom of Meleagant). Yvain, however, is blind to the spiritual significance of his experience (though I don't believe Chrétien
was): he is only disturbed by the burial of the corpse and the lamentations of the courtiers because it removes positive evidence of his victory, which he will need to prove himself in the face of Kay's malicious
mockery and abuse (299).

The imagery of wounding now modulates (rather predictably) to
the wounds of Love inflicted on Yvain by the sight of Laudine grieving
over the bloody, mutilated corpse of Esclados: "Having mortally
wounded her husband," Yvain wonders in his love-stricken grief, "do I
think I can be reconciled with her?" (300). Apparently he can be, with
the extended manipulations of Laudine's maid Lunette, who urges the
practical exigencies facing her Queen as reasons for reconciliation: the
arrival of Arthur is imminent, and she will need a man to defend her
fountain and kingdom. Faced with this impending crisis, Laudine, the
Lady of the Fountain, now marries Yvain, the man who had slain her
husband, and who will now become the next guardian of the mystical
tree and fountain. Once again, the mythological imagery is activated by
wounding and grief, since the marriage with Laudine makes more sense
as a union with the Frazerian Queen of the Sacred Grove than it does as
a courtly marriage (though Chrétien takes pains to have it make sense,
as a matter of political necessity, for a woman to acquire, through marriage, a defender of her realm). Though a Freudian reading of this
whole sequence is clearly tempting -- Yvain murders a commanding father figure and forces his way through the 'gates of the castle' in order
to marry his wife -- I find Heinrich Zimmer's mythological amplification more eloquent and productive: like the Queen of the Sacred Grove
of Nemi, with her Golden Bough and ritually slain consort, Laudine
symbolizes the "perennial power of life," that "fairy mistress of the
Fountain of Life," into whose mysteries Yvain is to be initiated by the
sacred marriage (104, 108). Those mysteries have something to do with
the reconciliation of opposites and the transition from the material to

the spiritual: just as the tree embraced the loving and terrible polarities of the natural world, so Laudine enacts within her castle walls the mysteries of the funeral and the marriage ceremonies within the space of a couple of days. These two ceremonies combine the mythical powers of the Great Goddess to take life, and to give it back through the renewed fertility made possible by marriage. Chrétien's tale, then, achieves a somewhat uneasy union of the contrary spheres of "Christian chivalric humanity" and the "world of faerie, the transcendental sphere of the higher cosmic powers" immanent in the forests of Celtic mysticism (Zimmer 128, 108). The task of the tale is to reconcile the domains of the conscious personality of courtly life with the unconscious wellspring of being symbolized by the fountain and the marriage with the Goddess.

Yvain, at any rate, will return a new but not quite fully transformed man, to Arthur's court, having achieved the honor and social prestige which is the goal of the hero journey in the first half of life. His return to Camelot comes after the arrival of Arthur's entourage at the Fountain, which follows the marriage of Laudine and Yvain, when, as Chrétien wryly remarks, "the dead man is completely forgotten" and "His slayer is married to his wife, and they sleep together" (310). This "speedy reconciliation," or "o'er hasty marriage" (as Hamlet would have it), takes just a few days. Yvain's transition is symbolized by a change of clothing, characteristic of the hero journey cycle: Lunette prepares him for Laudine by bathing, grooming, and adorning Yvain in a scarlet robe lined with vair and linked at the neck by a golden clasp worked with precious stones (306). In such attire, Yvain welcomes Arthur and Gawain into the castle, after exacting his revenge on Kay during the siege of the Fountain: knocked off his horse by Yvain, Kay is "overcome with shame, dejected, mortified, and crest fallen" (312).

In Laudine's castle, before Yvain's return to Camelot, a relationship develops between Gawain and Lunette which, though primarily treated by Chrétien as an example of Gawain's legendary prowess as a courtly lover, also conceals within it aspects of mythological symbolism. Lunette is compared to the moon being courted by the sun, personified by Gawain. He is indeed like the sun, Chrétien says, since "chivalry gains lustre from him just as in the morning the sun casts its rays and lights up all the places where it shines" (313). Is Chrétien working with a lost source here? The analogy between Gawain and the sun would intrigue such 19th Century German scholars as Max Müller, whose obsession was with solar heroes whose diurnal and seasonal journeys formed the natural background for the hero journey cycles; and, as we saw above John Speirs suggests solar connections for Gawain, and John Spearing solar connections for Sir Orfeo. At any rate, the marriage of the sun and the moon is an old Bronze Age symbol reaching far back beyond Homer's *Odyssey*, where, as we have seen, the reunion of Odysseus and Penelope occurs at the end of a twenty year cycle referred to as the Great Solar Year, when the new moon and summer solstice coincide. In Joseph Campbell's commentary, the solar principle represents eternity in its transcendence of earthly cycles, while the moon represents time in its immanent cycles of death and re-birth (*Creative Mythology* 163-64). During the Middle Ages, such im-agery is to be found frequently in alchemical illustrations [19], and in the imagery of the Crucifixion (also a symbol of the union of eternity (God the Father) and time (Jesus the Son)). Many illuminations of the Crucifixion place a sun and moon on either side of the cross, and some-times match them with personifications of the masculine and feminine principles in the form of St. John and the Virgin Mary.[20] Perhaps the most famous such example is Dürer's "Great Crucifixion" of 1511, in which we see "Upper left, the sun of the spring equinox; upper right, the full moon of Easter" (Campbell, *The Sacrifice* 53). The calendric logic, having to do with the calculation of the date of Easter on the first Sunday after the first full moon to follow the spring equinox, conceals, in Joseph Campbell's view, a pagan mystery descended from the Bronze Age mythologies of the ancient near and far east (*Inner Reaches* 70), and still widely diffused today, as a Tibetan temple banner of the 19th century suggests. It depicts the deity Yāmantaka, Slayer of the Lord Death, with, "In the upper corners, right and left ... figures sym-bolic of lunar and solar consciousness: lunar being participation in the terrors of this temporal sphere; solar, of disengagement from the same, to rest in peace in what may be thought of as Eternity" (Campbell, *The Sacrifice* 44-45).

It is Gawain who persuades Yvain to complete his first hero jour-ney cycle by returning to the tournaments of Camelot, and in so doing leaving the timeless realms of faerie enchantment into which he has en-tered by marriage. His wife Laudine grants Yvain a year's leave of ab-sence; if he should overstep this limit, she warns, her love will change to hate. To help him remember his obligations, she gives him a ring with the power to confer a kind of immortality upon its wearer, much like the green girdle given Gawain by Bertilak's wife: "No true, loyal lover can be held prisoner or lose any blood or suffer any harm pro-vided that he wears and cherishes it and bears his love in mind" (316). Such a talisman, as we have seen, is the special gift of the Goddess (whether it be Utnapishtim's Wife's robe, Leucothea's veil, or Morgana's green girdle), who bestows it upon her chosen consort (Gilgamesh, Odysseus, or Gawain). Because the hero is traditionally bound to the wheel of time, however, by virtue of his humanity, he cannot simply retreat into the timeless realm of transcendent bliss offered him by the Goddess. Yvain therefore forgets his promise while performing his courtly duties in the temporal realm of Camelot, and a messenger sent from Laudine serves as the second call to adventure, and begins Yvain's second hero journey cycle. This second journey deals with the difficult acquisition of wisdom and maturity, gained through identification with the suffering of others, rather than with the power and prestige gained through the first journey and the conquest of the Black Knight Esclados. This dividing line in Chrétien's tale corre-sponds, then, to the two journeys undertaken by Gilgamesh, the one (to the Cedar Forest) appropriate to the first half of life, and the other (to the Land of Faraway) to the second half.

While in Laudine's castle, Yvain had forgotten the "requirements of the world of ordinary human conduct ... personal relationships ... and contemporary chivalry"; and while in Camelot, he regains his honor but loses the immediate contact with the supernatural energies of life repre-sented by Laudine as the Lady of the Fountain (Zimmer 112). The task now is to achieve some kind of reconciliation between the two realms, a *bele conjointure* between *armes* (honor) and *amour* (love).[21] Such a 'beautiful joining' of various oppositions is the goal of the second hero journey. This second journey begins with a coincidence of inner and outer conditions: on the inside, Yvain remembers his broken promise with grief and great distress, while externally he confronts the humilia-tion of Laudine's messenger, who publicly declares him to be a "dis-loyal traitor, liar and deceiver, who has abandoned and duped" Laudine (318). Since Yvain has proven a "false, treacherous thief" (318) who has betrayed Laudine with his hypocritical deception, he is required to return the ring and forsake the pleasure of her company and love. His attachment to the worldly concerns of his temporal identity has (as in the Gnostic "Hymn of the Pearl") led him to forget the radiance of his life in the otherworld, to which he is now recalled (as the Gnostic hero was by his father's message).

The effect of this public humiliation of a knight who has been basking in the glory of personal fame is as devastating as the return of Inanna from the underworld had been for her husband Dumuzi. Yvain is plunged into profound distress, and, like Dumuzi, his only thought is to flee into the wilderness, "a land so wild that nobody would know where to look for him, and where there was no man or woman or anybody knowing anything more of him than if he were in the pit of Hell" (318). His journey to "Hell," therefore, is initiated by a kind of psychological derangement which leads to his departure into the forests of the unconscious, and to the total disintegration of his courtly persona. Once again, it is the symbolism of clothing which marks this threshold crossing and transformation: Yvain's "head is assailed by so wild a delirium that he loses his senses, whereupon he tears and rends his clothes and goes fleeing across fields and ploughed land" into the woods, where he lives in nakedness and madness (319). Like Inanna, Dumuzi, Joseph, and Sir Orfeo, Yvain begins his journey with a symbolic rending of clothing, only in Yvain's case the divestiture is self-inflicted and dramatizes the pathology of the 'forest madness' of the lover so popular during the Middle Ages.[22]

There is of course the very real potential for rapid and profound transformation in this moment of crisis: only the body that is stripped down to bare bone (and even dismembered or boiled in shamanistic rituals of initiation)[23] can be totally reclothed. As Tony Hunt says, this "brainstorm" obliterates the courtly self in order to initiate change; it is, as D.D.R. Owen remarks, a change from a "chivalric quest of adventure from motives of personal glory," to a Christian quest for "responsible social endeavor" (515). This transformation begins when Yvain is discovered asleep in the forest by three women (two damsels and their Lady). These three women suggest the symbolism of the Triple Goddess of Celtic as well as Christian and Classical origins; they preside over fate and the ritual transformations of consciousness associated with a death and rebirth experience. In Gnosticism, this sleep in the wilderness suggests the soul lost in the material world, from which Yvain is awakened for his return journey to the spiritual realm of Laudine. One of the maidens recognizes the true identity of the sleeping knight, and convinces her Lady of Yvain's usefulness in the defense of her domain against Count Alier, who has plundered her lands. Lady Noroison then remembers an ointment given her by Morgan the Wise that has the power to clear any head of madness and frenzy (an herb which would no doubt be of interest to psychopharmacology!). Morgan the Wise is Morgan Le Fay of *Sir Gawain and the Green Knight*, the mysterious goddess of whom these three ladies represent the courtly incarnation, and the feminine power of transformation behind Yvain's healing. One of the maidens rubs his temples, forehead, and body until the "madness and depression left his brain" (321). Hence, Chrétien's version of what Goethe called the eternal feminine is both the cause and the cure of Yvain's breakdown: as Laudine, the Lady of the Fountain, she drives him mad; and as Lady Noroison and the two maidens, incarnations of Morgan the Wise, she restores his wandering wits and brings him back to life. Her cure would still be available today, had not her maid become so enthusiastic in her application of the ointment onto Yvain's naked body that she used up the whole jar!

Yvain's return to health initiates a sequence of adventures emphasizes his "potential qualities as a husband" (Owen 518), and as a Christian knight in the service of the community (Hunt). He will, during this second sequence of ordeals, defeat Count Alier and reclaim the plundered lands of Lady Noroison; kill Harpin of the Mountain, a giant who is pestering Gawain's niece; rescue Lunette from the Fountain, where Laudine has condemned her to death for conspiracy; and free three hundred maidens from an Isle of Damsels impressed into a kind of slave labor by "two sons of the Devil" (355). This last episode "seems a recollection of some tale of the Celtic Otherworld" which has been adapted to reflect Chrétien's concerns about the contemporary "exploitation of female labor in the developing silk industry of the Champagne" (Owen 519). If so, it would be an early example of a political use of Eliot's mythic method, which sustains a parallel between contemporary history and ancient myth in order to give shape and significance to life. At any rate, Yvain's labors gradually modify his character by reshaping him into a man capable of putting his knightly prowess into the service of others, a capability which Chrétien apparently considered a prerequisite to marriage in a Christian community. Yvain is aided in his execution of these tasks by the lion of the tale's title, which Yvain had liberated from a dragon. In fact, during this entire second episode, Yvain is not known by his courtly name, but simply as "The Knight with the Lion," a fact which suggests the new orientation of his identity.

The episode in which Yvain rescues the lion from the dragon is centrally situated in the narrative, and might have suggested a "figuration of the combat between good and evil," since "medieval symbolism usually equated the lion with noble qualities and even with the Deity" (Owen 518). This nobility is perhaps most commonly evident in the symbolism of the four evangelists found abundantly in medieval illuminated manuscripts, in which St. Mark's symbol is the lion. Owen also suggests a Classical source (Androcles and the lion, as retold by Peter Damian in the 11th century). Heinrich Zimmer mentions the story of Hercules and the Nemean lion, only as a means of contrast with the Celtic attitude towards nature suggested by the lion. For Zimmer, the transformation of Yvain into the Knight with the Lion suggests more than a movement from honor (*armes*) to loyalty in love (*amour*), or from personal glory to selfless service. The lion represents the raw natural energies of life (also manifested in the Lady of the Fountain and the Wild Man) and the intuitive guiding principles of Celtic forest lore (122). In this reading of the lion, the new identity Yvain achieves as a result of his forest madness contrasts with the Christian and Classical attitudes towards nature and the feminine: Yvain lives in harmony with the lion, which he rescues rather than killing (as Hercules, Androcles, and, farther back, Gilgamesh had done). Yvain, therefore, is a character shaped by the Celtic consciousness of a supernatural spirituality resident within the natural world -- not beyond it. As the Knight of the Lion, Zimmer concludes, Yvain represents an achieved reconciliation of Christian, Courtly, Classical, and Celtic elements in the European culture of the Middle Ages.

Yvain returns, finally, to Camelot, to complete his second hero journey cycle: he is wiser, humbled, and more mature, fighting now in the defense of Noire Espine's younger daughter against Gawain, who fights for the elder. The joust ends with a stalemate, and the revelation of Yvain's true identity, after which he returns to Laudine, who now accepts him (perhaps out of necessity, rather than love, some would argue!). This completes the large hero journey cycle begun by Yvain's departure from Laudine's castle. All of the hero cycles taken together give us a complete vision of male development from youth to manhood. Chrétien's third and most famous, though unfinished Arthurian romance (*Perceval*, or *The Story of the Grail*) is similarly divided into separate hero journey cycles. The two which are devoted to Perceval reflect a similar development as the one undergone by Yvain, and the third takes up the character of Gawain.

Chrétien and Wolfram's Parzival

The story of Perceval, as begun by Chrétien and revised and completed by Wolfram von Eschenbach in his masterpiece *Parzival*, has proven irresistible to critics and artists of our time. Emma Jung was, I believe, the first to focus on Perceval's story as an image of the individuation process, and Robert Johnson's simplification and commentary on the story, entitled *He*, as an image of male integration of the anima was a popular best seller of sorts. Joseph Campbell's illustrious career began with graduate studies in Paris and in Munich, where he discovered Wolfram's work, which would be a mainstay of his lectures for many years following. His *Creative Mythology* takes us through the entire story of Parzival, with extended analysis and commentary. More recently, the story has been the subject of such films as Eric Rohmer's *Perceval* and Hans Jurgens Syberberg's *Parzival*. It can only be our task here, therefore, to indicate the main lines of the hero journey cycle in the story, with reference both to Chrétien and Wolfram, and to briefly relate these to the archetypology of the monomyth which we have been developing in previous chapters.

Chrétien begins his "Story of the Grail" with a glimpse of his hero's youth: Perceval lives alone, far from the court, with his mother, who wants to prevent the boy from ever becoming a knight, since his father had been killed during the Crusades (Wolfram begins his poem with two long and complex chapters about Gahmuret, Parzival's father). Perceval's call to adventure comes one fine spring morning, when five gloriously armed knights crash through the "wild, desolate forest" where Perceval is out hunting birds with his javelin. Like Enkidu in the

Epic of Gilgamesh, Perceval passes his young years in the company only of the wild animals and a few local farmers. He is the simple fool (*le bel inconnu* of Medieval romance, the *einfache Mensch* of Mann's *Magic Mountain*, which draws on the Grail legends),[24] raised with a pure heart, innocent of life in the court, knowing only the love of his mother, who tries to keep him from growing up. At first, Perceval thinks the knights are devils, because of the terrific noise they make, but when he sees their "glittering hauberks and the bright, gleaming helmets ... and the scarlet shining in the sunlight" he thinks they are angels, or even God Himself (since his mother had told him that God is Light). In a sense, they are both: devil to the mother who will drop dead after her son resolves to follow the knights to Arthur's court, and angels of destiny to Perceval whose vocation in life is announced by their arrival. The first task in the young man's journey is a kind of internal threshold crisis: he must break the bonds with his mother, a process in which the symbolism of clothing plays a special role. Before collapsing, she dresses Perceval up as a country hick and sends him riding off on an old nag, hoping such attire will deny him access to Arthur's court (there are charming ivory jewel box carvings from France representing Perceval's arrival at court in this get up). She also gives him a crash course in courtly codes: take a kiss and a maiden's ring if she offers it and go to church as often as you can (as yet, he doesn't know what a church is).

On his way to Camelot, Perceval comes upon a Lady alone in a pavilion. She is asleep in bed and wakes up to fight Perceval off, but he kisses her seven times and then steals her ring -- just following mother's instructions! He then devours all the food set out for her before leaving her alone at the mercy of her jealous husband, who returns shortly thereafter. The husband, Orilus, refuses to believe the tale Jeschute tells him, and therefore subsequently subjects her to years of abuse. After leaving Jeschute in her tent, Perceval is directed to Carlisle (where Arthur's court is in session) by a charcoal burner driving a donkey (in Wolfram it is a crude fisherman who prefigures the Fisher King from later in the story). When he arrives a maiden bursts out laughing, and Kay strikes her in the face because a prophecy predicted that she would not laugh for more than six years until the man who would be supreme among the knights arrived at court.

Perceval then sets off to avenge the insult and commits his third youthful folly: he has inadvertently been the cause of his mother's death, the source of Jeschute's sorrows, and will now kill his own kinsman, the Red Knight, who has just challenged the court by throwing wine on Guenevere. Perceval kills the Knight with his javelin, which he tosses through the visor into the eye socket, through the brain, and out the back of the neck. Then, with a squire's help, Perceval takes the fallen knight's armor, which he puts on over the hair shirt his mother had dressed him in. The entire scene is an excellent example of the use of clothing symbolism to signify the transformation of the hero as he crosses the threshold to his new life. Newly attired, Perceval now sets off on the first hero journey cycle in the story. This cycle will bring him the fame Yvain achieved during his first journey to the Lady of the Fountain, while the wisdom and spiritual maturity of the second half of life will have to await the second cycle and the quest for the Grail.

The Red Knight's horse runs away with Perceval and gallops all day long until arriving at a magnificent castle by the sea which seems to emerge directly from the rock: its keep in the center is surrounded by four handsome turrets at each of the four walled corners (it is, in other words, a mandala, or symbol of the inner Self which is the ultimate goal of Perceval's journey). Here lives Gornemant of Gohort, the wise old man (human counterpart of the castle as an archetype of the Self) who will instruct Perceval in courtly ways: like Nestor in the *Odyssey*, he prepares the boy for manhood. The completion of this rite of passage is celebrated by another symbolic investiture: the worthy old man brings Perceval a shirt and breeches of fine linen, a tunic of fine indigo silk woven in India, and then persuades Perceval at last to divest himself of his mother's hair shirt. Then Gornemant fits on the right spur and girds the sword about the waist, both of which ritual gestures signify Perceval's admission to "the highest order created and ordained by God, namely the order of chivalry, which must be free of all baseness" (396).

At this point of the passage into manhood Perceval is "extremely anxious to return to his mother," so he heads "into the desolate forests, with which he was more familiar than with the open country" (397). In the elegant simplicity of mythological language, this desire to return to mother leads Perceval to his wife (the psychological wisdom of these old texts is wonderful): after crossing the wasteland he arrives at the well-situated fortress of Blancheflor, again set by the sea and now besieged by Engygeron and Clamadeu, suitors for her love and land. Blancheflor's castle has been devastated by the siege; it is the typical situation of the wasteland, translated into political terms. The houses and streets are empty and in ruins, the monks and nuns have been terrorized, and the fortress is empty of bread, wine, and ale. All are dejected and grief-stricken, and, when Blancheflor desperately pleads for Perceval's help that night (innocently climbing into bed with him to recite her 'rosary of yew-berries'), she tells him that of the three-hundred or so knights who originally manned the castle, only fifty are left, forty-eight having been killed or imprisoned by her besieger Engygeron, and his seneschal Clamadeu. It is the political wasteland here, which Perceval is called upon to regenerate by arms. The situation has degenerated as a result of neglected love and the abusive politics of marriage during the Middle Ages; it must therefore be redeemed by a love inno-cent of those politics. Perceval agrees to dispatch the suitors on condi-tion that Blancheflor accept his spontaneously aroused love. Hence, in the weeks that follow, Engygeron, Clamadeu, and a list of other knights are defeated and dispatched to Arthur's court, where they are instructed by Perceval to submit themselves to the service of the maiden who laughed when Perceval first arrived. The symbolism behind the politics of this episode relate to the archetypical male task, to reclaim the soul, or anima mundi (in this case Blancheflor) from its imprisonment in the material world. A tremendous rush of renewed life is therefore released by Perceval's liberation of the castle: hall and dwellings ring with jubi-lation, chapels and church bells peal for joy, and all give thanks to God for delivering them from a long a terrible captivity (410).

Their deliverer, however, still has his mother on his mind, and he decides to go retrieve her from the Wild Forest of his youth and then to return as master of Blancheflor's kingdom. No one can detain him, since "he has a greater desire to go and see" his mother than for any-thing else (413). This time Perceval's regressive longing will lead him to the Grail castle, as if there were a spiritual mystery buried in the heart of his mother complex -- a goddess behind the symbolism of the complex represented by the Grail.[25] Perceval again travels all day long, continually praying to God that he might find his mother alive and well, until at last he comes to a rushing river. "Ah, almighty Lord!" he ex-claims, "If I could cross this water, I fancy, I'd find my mother on the other side, if she's still alive" (414). If, in fact, the river crossing sug-gests the Stygian passage to the otherworld, he might indeed find his mother, though among the dead, rather than the living. In psychological terms, his mother still lives in his unconscious, weaving the web of his fate, the source of those complexes which compel his destiny. The river, however, seems impassable: a man fishing in a boat tells Perceval that no boat, ferry, bridge, or ford leads across the water, but that Perceval can take shelter that night in the house where the fisherman lives, close by the river and the surrounding woods. After climbing as instructed through a fissure in the rock, Perceval looks but at first does not see the tower rising splendidly from a distant castle.

Once again, the river crossing and the passage through a rock or cliffside emerge as symbols for the journey into the otherworld, as in Sir Orfeo or Gilgamesh. In Wolfram's version of the story, the fisher-man who appears to guide Parzival in his passage between the two worlds is called the Angler, and we see him on a large lake beautifully dressed, and wearing a hat of peacock feathers which Joseph Campbell suggests the alchemical symbolism of death and rebirth, and the Christian symbolism of the Resurrection (*Creative Myth* 501): "There can be no doubt," Campbell writes,

that Wolfram knew exactly what he was doing when he put peacock plumes in the bonnets of both King Gramoflanz, the
guardian of the Tree -- the World Tree, the philosophical tree,
the tree of the Garden, the tree of Christ's Cross, the Bo-tree of
Buddhahood -- and the wounded Fisher King, whose fishline
from the Great Above to the Great Below is equally *axis mundi*:
awaiting everywhere, with its baited hook, in the waters of this
world, to haul us up to the lotus boat of the radiant Fisher of
Men with the peacock feathers pluming from his cap. (503)

Perceval now proceeds to his night's lodging in what will be in
Chrétien's work the first literary manifestation of the Grail Castle, and
the great climax of this first hero journey initiation in the tale.
Chrétien's account is restrained and relatively simple (when compared
with Wolfram's!). Perceval crosses the bridge to be met by four serving
lads who disarm and clothe him in a new mantle of fine cloth; he is
then lead into a square hall (large enough to seat four hundred men), in
the middle of which he finds a handsome older man seated on a couch
in front of a fire burning brightly between four strong pillars. As
Perceval sits and chats a lad brings the old gentleman an exquisitely
forged sword which will only be broken in "one particular perilous circumstance," and which the old man presents to Perceval. Then a youth
carries a white lance with a crimson drop of blood oozing from its tip
past the old man and Perceval, who refrains from asking about it, since
Gornemant had "instructed him to beware of talking too much" (416).
Two other youths come by, each holding extremely fine candelabra
burning at least ten candles each, and a beautifully adorned damsel
bearing the grail (simply described as a sort of dish) accompanies them.
The grail diffuses so great a radiance that the myriad candles lose their
brilliance, like the stars when the sun rises. It is of pure refined gold, set
with various precious stones. A maiden holding a silver dish (silver
being the complementary color of the moon) follows the grail bearing
virgin; and, finally, two lads carry in a broad ivory table top, which
they set on two trestles made of an ebony which never rots nor burns.
As a haunch of venison in hot pepper sauce is being served, Perceval
sees the grail continually passing in front of him each time a new dish
is served; though he refrains from asking who is served from the grail,
he greatly yearns to know. A desert of dates, figs, nutmegs, cloves,
pomegranates follows, washed down by spiced and mulberry wine.
(The eleemoysnary enthusiasm seems purely French; Wolfram, by contrast, is more involved in the fashion details). Perceval watches as four
strong young men grasp the four corners of the spread which covers the
couch on which the old man sits, and carry him off to bed, the crucial
question left unasked.

As D.D.R. Owen notes, Chrétien does not imply any Christian gloss on the grail, which will come to be associated with the chalice of the last supper. Certain elementary mythological symbols, however, are therefore allowed to speak eloquently for themselves. The number four, for example, with a fifth object in the center, recurs throughout the scene, and suggests the configuration of the mandala (Jung's symbol for psychic wholeness): four serving lads meet and reclothe Perceval; four posts surround the burning fire in the exact center of a large square room where the mystery play passes; four ritual objects (sword, spear, grail, serving dish) pass in front of Perceval while he is dining; four lads set up the serving table and trestle in their midst; and four vigorous youths carry the old man in the middle of the coverlet off to bed. In Jungian theory, the four cardinal points represent four basic personality types and psychic functions (thinking, feeling, sensation, intuition), while the fifth central point in the mandala represents the transcendent function, which generates the archetypal symbols of the Self, and reconciles the polar duality of the two pairs of opposites at each of the four cardinal points. The most frequent example of this archetype in the Middle Ages was the image of Christ surrounded by the four evangelists. Chrétien does not direct our reading towards such allegories, nor does he emphasize the possible pagan origins in the Celtic symbolism of the cornucopia (discussed by R. S. Loomis). Rather, he wisely allows the images to speak silently for themselves, so that they can exert their elusive power undiminished by the strictures of any systematic interpretation. This leaves the symbols free of doctrine. Similarly, the golden grail and the silver serving dish suggest the solar - lunar network of symbols going way back to the ancient Bronze Age mythologies of eternity and time which we saw in the *Odyssey*. Chrétien, rather like Homer in fact, simply allows the motifs the freedom to exhilarate readers without depriving them of their numinosity by appending an allegorical gloss (as our Cistercian monk felt compelled to do).

Wolfram von Eschenbach was tempted to elaborate on this scene in his terrific completion of Chrétien, *Parzival*, in which alchemical lore and Oriental wisdom greatly enrich the symbolism of the Grail feast. Upon his arrival at the Grail Castle, Parzival is greeted by several pages who disarm him on the green lawn within the walls, and then adorn him with a cloth-of-gold cloak from Araby given him by Repanse de Schoye (the maiden whom we will later see carrying the Grail). He is then led by a rude jester into a hall where a hundred chandeliers hang. with as many candles on each, above a hundred couches with quilts, four knights seated on each: all surround the fireplace in the middle, against which we see the old ailing lord of the castle seated in a sling bed. A page then carries a bleeding lance around the four walls of the great hall, and is accompanied by much wailing and weeping. This circumambulation initiates a grand procession: through a steel door at the end of the Hall comes a pair of noble maidens, with garlands of flowers in their hair, wearing brown scarlet gowns, and carrying golden candelabra; a duchess and her companion, similarly dressed, come next, carrying two ivory trestles. Together with the flower maidens, they form a group of four, and bow to the lord. Four more pairs of ladies then enter, all wearing Azagouc robes of green samite, four of them carrying large candles, and four carrying a table top cut from a radiant garnet-hyacinth, which they set on the ivory trestles. This group of eight maidens clad in green then bows to the lord. Two princely ladies, each carrying ingeniously fashioned razor sharp silver knives on nap-kins then enter, preceded by four faultless virgins each bearing a light. This makes a group of six, who bow before the lord seated in the sling in front of the fire, before joining the other twelve maidens. Six more maidens now advance, dressed in brocade of Nineveh, cut parti-wise, like the previous group of six, and carrying vials of pure glass with burning balsam. The Princess Repanse de Schoye, wearing a brocade of Araby and carrying the Grail on green achmardi, follows these six: she and her vessel are said to be the "consummation of heart's desire, its root and blossoming .... paradisal, transcending all earthly perfection" (125). The Grail is then placed before the Maimed King (while Parzival stares intently at Repanse de Schoye, whose robe he is wearing), and the seven maidens join the other eighteen to form a group of twenty five, twelve on either side of the crowned Repanse de Schoye.

This image of Repanse de Schoye standing in the center of the Grail Castle with twelve maidens gorgeously dressed on either side of her is one of the grandest epiphanies of the Great Goddess in our pos-session, rivaling the magnificent appearance of Isis in *The Golden Ass* of Apuleius. Like Isis, Repanse comes to us adorned in astronomical symbolism: she is mother universe, from whose womb are born the twelve hours of the night on her left, and the twelve hours of the day on her right. She bears the mystery of the Grail as a symbol of her own power, and, like the Virgin Mary of the New Testament, or the Sophia of the Old, she complements the male Trinity of the Grail Castle, who might well be seen as incarnations of her consort, in the three stages of life which she bestows upon them: Parzival is the King to be and repre-sents the folly of youth; the crippled Amfortas is the present and ailing King representing midlife; while Titurel is the King of the past, repre-senting the inaccessible wisdom of old age. Altogether we have a qua-ternity surrounding the Grail (Repanse, Parzival, Amfortas, and Titurel), only this quaternity gives the Goddess -- who presides over our birth, sustains our lives, and takes us back into her womb at the end of the cycle -- a central position of importance, hence compensating for the overvaluation of the masculine in Christian dogma.

After this grand procession an elaborate banquet begins: chamberlains with bowls of gold are assigned at the rate of one to every four knights, accompanied by one handsome page carrying a white towel (that's two hundred servants total!. One hundred tables are then set up before each of the one hundred couches on which the groups of four knights sit (totaling four hundred knights). Parzival and the Maimed King wash and a count's son dries their hands with a fine silk towel. Four pages then assist the previously assigned chamberlains and towel bearers at each of the hundred tables of knights (two carve, two serve). Four trolleys bearing cups attended by one clerk enter to serve wine to the hundred tables, one at a time. One hundred pages are then bidden to receive the loaves and abundant delicacies magically dispensed by the Grail, which is again eulogized as "the very fruit of bliss, a cornucopia of the sweets of the world and such that it scarcely fell short of what they tell us of the Heavenly Kingdom" (127).

It should be mentioned here that the image of the feast is a central one to the world's great myths and religions, and hence a frequent occurrence as a symbol of consummation in the hero journey. One thinks initially of the role played by the bread and water of life in both the *Epic of Gilgamesh* and the "Descent of Inanna," and similarly of the importance of food in the burial rites of the ancient Egyptians. Elaborate banquets form the refrain in the epic hero journey of Odysseus, and in Plato these feasts become metaphorical of the riches of philosophical speculation, as in the *Symposium*. The mystery rites celebrated at Eleusis, based on Persephone's heroine journey cycle, chose an upraised grain of wheat to represent the theme of death, rebirth, and spiritual nourishment. In the *Satyricon* of Petronius, as in Fellini's terrific film, these philosophical feasts turn towards travesty and parody; while in Christianity, the Last Supper and the communion ritual of the mass take center stage as symbols of the mysteries of incarnation and sacrifice. We find the symbol of the banquet served by the cornucopia of the Grail all through the Middle Ages. One of the most recent manifestations of the archetype of the feast I know of is the summer meeting of the Eranos group of scholars at Casa Gabriella, on the shores of Lago Maggiore, just around the corner from Ascona in the Swiss Ticino. Since 1933 all of our greatest archetypalists have met there to present papers, from Jung and Heinrich Zimmer, to Joseph Campbell, Henri Corbin, Gershom Scholem, and James Hillman. It is interesting to note the Arthurian symbolism one finds alive and well on those mythical shores where the feast is served each August (Eranos is a Greek word meaning a banquet to which one gained admittance by bringing an intellectual gift): meals are served at a wonderful tree shaded round table above the lake, and partially hidden in the foliage along the path which leads to the round table is a stone dedicated to the unknown genius of the place. On the stone, an image of the Grail is carved, in the form of two triangles joined at their apices.

In Wolfram's *Parzival*, the Grail is in fact the philosopher's stone (an emerald fallen from heaven); it also serves as a kind of cup, or cornucopia. Parzival observes the magnificent feast in silence; "true to the dictates of good breeding, he refrained from asking any question" (127). While he sits musing on this divine spectacle, a page appears carrying a sword with a priceless sheath and ruby hilt, which the crippled lord bestows upon him. This is a "prompt for him to ask a Question" which could rid his host of his "misfortune from on high" (127), but Parzival remains dumb, and the dinner ends. As the Princess and her maidens carry the Grail back through the steel door through which they entered, Parzival glimpses "the most handsome old man he had ever seen or heard of," whose identity Wolfram now withholds from us. He is Titurel, the fourth of the major attendants mentioned above as forming a quaternity with the Grail in the center. In fact, the entire Hall is a magnificent mandala radiating around the Grail and fire in the center, its transcendent still point of the turning world, surrounded by groups of four, which reiterate the mystical quaternity, in the center. There are four knights per hundred tables, which we can imagine symmetrically arranged in groups of twenty five in each of the quadrants of the Hall; there are four knights per trolley bearing golden cups, each of which establishes a new center at each of the tables. The maidens themselves form two groups of twelve on either side of the central Repanse de Schoye. It is a grandly elaborated symbol of universal wholeness.

This revelation of the mysteries of the Grail Castle constitutes the climactic initiation of the first hero journey cycle in the story of Perceval in both Chrétien and Wolfram. From here, Perceval will return to Arthur's court, completing the first cycle of departure, initiation, and return. He will return with a fine worldly reputation, a wife and kingdom, but sadly as a failure in the spiritual realm. After being ignominiously expelled the morning after the Grail procession for not having asked the question that would heal Amfortas, Perceval chances upon a maiden weeping beneath an oak tree and holding the decapitated body of a knight in her lap. She tells Perceval that his host of the previous night was the rich Fisher King, wounded in the thighs by a javelin, and she reprimands him for not asking the healing question. Perceval then names himself for the first time in the story, which leads the mourning lady to reveal herself as Perceval's cousin, and to explain that he had probably been tainted by responsibility for his mother's death, and hence as yet ineligible to heal Amfortas.

No longer nameless, Perceval continues on his way, not now in search of the mother he now knows to be dead, but in pursuit of the knight who decapitated his cousin's beloved. This man turns out to be Orilus, the jealous husband of Jeschute, whose ring Perceval had stolen a while back after first leaving home. Jeschute is now in terrible shape after long abuse from her maniacally suspicious husband: her lacerated flesh shows through a hundred holes in her garment, and her face (pale, wrinkled, and haggard) is stained by the numerous tracks of her tears. All of this is Perceval's fault, the consequence of his youthful indiscretion. After confessing his folly to the lady's husband, now known as the Haughty Knight of the Heath, Perceval knocks him off his horse in a joust and commands him to take care of his wife and then proceed to Arthur's court. Meanwhile, having received a steady stream of knights defeated by Perceval and sent to his court, Arthur has packed up his tents and gone in search of him (Perceval is still known only to Arthur as the Red Knight). When Gawain and Kay find Perceval lost in a love trance at the sight of three drops of blood in the snow (which remind him of Blancheflor), Perceval breaks Kay's arm in a joust (thus avenging Kay's humiliation of the maiden who laughed when Perceval arrived in court) and is then gently enticed into Arthur's tent by Gawain, who can tell Perceval is in love. This completes the first cycle of the hero journey, during the course of which Perceval has literally made a name for himself. But he is still haunted by the depressing awareness of his failings and spiritual blindness. Like many men at midlife, he has all the power and glory of worldly success, but is still poisoned by a spiritual malaise about the unanswered questions in life, and this malaise will lead to his second departure from court. This second hero journey coincides with the annunciation of Gawain's journey, which both Chrétien and Wolfram turn to at this point.

Gawain's call to adventure and departure parallel's Perceval's second journey. Wolfram makes this clear by establishing explicit connections between the Grail Castle and the Castle of Marvels where Gawain will undergo his initiatory ordeals, and by having Parzival and Gawain cross paths at the ford in front of the Castle of Marvels. Wolfram's version is again the more complex, holding a mirror up not only to the elementary themes of myth, but also to the Byzantine politics of medieval Germany. In both Chrétien and Wolfram, Gawain's journey begins when a knight arrives at court and accuses Gawain of having treacherously murdered his master. The knight challenges Gawain to combat in the presence of one King Escavalor, and Gawain then sets off on his journey.

His first trial is to defend a young girl during a tournament, after which he is unwittingly lodged in the castle of the knight who challenged him to combat. While in this knight's castle, Gawain is seduced by the sister and attacked by her courtiers. As a result, when the lord of the castle finds out that his offer of hospitality has been abused by his people (having attacked Gawain), and that the man they have attacked is none other that Gawain, he makes a special deal: Gawain can go free to find the bleeding lance of the Grail King and return in one year for the joust to avenge the death of his master. Gawain departs and endures a series of adventures that focus on his odd relationship with an abusive woman whom Wolfram calls Orgeluse. These adventures reach their climax at the Castle of Marvels and its test of the Perilous Bed, which constitutes an initiation parallel to Perceval's in the Grail Castle. It is to Wolfram's account of this initiatory stage of the hero journey that we now turn.

Orgeluse and Gawain first see the Castle after emerging from a great forest: it is, like the Grail Castle, on the other side of river, and nearly four hundred ladies look down from windows at the couple as they approach the quay. Beside the quay is a meadow with signs of heavy combat. After Orgeluse rudely leaves Gawain behind by crossing the river on a ferryboat, Gawain defeats Lischois Gwelljus in a joust in the meadow. He then strikes a deal with the ferryman to accept Lischois as a toll for the passage (the ferryman usually gets the horse). On the other side of the river, Gawain enjoys the meager but sincere hospitality of the ferryman (named Plippalinot), who then tells him about the Castle and its perilous bed, and the mighty sorcery of Clinschor, who is responsible for the afflictions of the women enchanted there. He then gives Gawain a shield undented by combat and instructs him to leave his horse with a huckster selling priceless merchandise in a booth outside the Castle. From there, Gawain goes to the room where the perilous bed awaits him: it sits on four ruby wheels on a slick floor made of shining jasper, chrysolite, and sardonyx, brought by Clinschor from many lands by wizardry. The floor is so glassy that Gawain can hardly stand upright, and the bed seems continually to thwart his efforts to mount it, until with one great leap he lands squarely upon it. The bed immediately starts crashing around the room (like a reluctant bride, Heinrich Zimmer says!), and after Gawain crawls under his shield he is attacked first by a barrage of pebbles and arrows and then by a magnificent lion, as tall as a horse. All the while, the enchanted maidens of the Castle look on (there are beautiful illuminated manuscripts and an ivory jewel box of this scene). After one of the maidens determines that Gawain is still alive, Arnive, the Queen of the Castle, heals his wounds with ointments given her by Cundrie the Sorceress.

The next morning Gawain awakes and explores the Castle, finding at one side a staircase spiraling around a pillar forged by the subtle arts of Clinschor. As Gawain sits down in an oriel to observe the mysterious images of all the surrounding countryside (which are reflected in the polished surface of the pillar), he is greeted by four queens of the Castle: old Arnive, her daughter Sangive, and two of Sangive's daughter's. These four queens are, we will learn later, Gawain's Grandmother and Mother (both long dead!) and his two sisters. Once again, they suggest the three manifestations of the one Goddess, and form a quaternity which parallels the male dominated quaternity in the Grail Castle. Their domain, as Joseph Campbell points out, is Goethe's Realm of the Mothers in *Faust*, and the spell which afflicts them is the same waste land of "life in death" which surrounded Amfortas and the Grail Castle (492-93).

This magic pillar in the Castle of Marvels is another mythic image with a long lineage in the Arthurian tales. It is a kind of *axis mundi*, or an *omphalos*, a still point of the turning world which Gawain reaches via an ordeal death and transcendence on the perilous bed. Having passed beyond the earthly domain of fear, desire, and duty, Gawain now sits in Buddhistic contemplation of the rapidly evolving and dissolving images of the material world, which he sees reflected in this mirror of Maya (strangely reminiscent of the mirror of Karma in the Tibetan Book of the Dead). In fact, the pillar may well have its origins in Oriental lore, having come to Wolfram via the Abbasidian Khalifate of Baghdad (where the Arabian Nights came into being, to passed along the lines of war and trade during the Crusades), who got it from a famous palace in Delhi (Campbell, *Creative Myth* 503). Unlike the Buddha, however, Gawain is compelled back into the realm of action by his love for Orgeluse, whose image he now sees in the pillar, in the company of another man. More Boddhisattva than Buddha, this love for another sentient being compels Gawain's return to the world, where he will confront Gramoflanz at the mystical tree.

Arnive explains to Gawain that the pillar shines out day and night six miles into the surrounding countryside, all the activities of which are reflected on its surface. Gawain then sees Orgeluse riding to the meadow across the river with Turkoyt, another champion who will soon be unhorsed by Gawain, after he quickly arms himself and crosses the river to confront him. After the defeat of Turkoyt, Orgeluse leads Gawain to "Li gweiz prelljus," a roaring torrent on the other side of which is a garland, hanging from the twig of a tree guarded by King Gramoflanz, which Orgeluse imperiously challenges Gawain to get for her. Gawain leaps the rushing river on his horse Gringuljete (the Gringolet of the Gawain poet), but only the forelegs of the horse make it, so the two nearly drown before crawling out onto the yonder shore (in Chrétien's "Knight of the Cart," Gawain had been washed downstream when he tried unsuccessfully to cross the ford Lancelot had crossed using the sword bridge). After Gawain breaks the twig and sets the garland on his helmet, King Gramoflanz comes riding out unarmed, wearing a peacock feather hat (like the Fisherman who had directed Parzival to the Grail Castle) and carrying a moulted sparrowhawk, which he says is a love token sent him by Gawain's sister from the Castle. Gramoflanz explains that he has killed the noble husband of Orgeluse, abducted her, but unsuccessfully sued for her favor. He now loves Itanje, Gawain's sister, to whom he asks Gawain to take a ring. He then goes on to say that he has taken a vow to fight only two knights at once, and to engage in single combat only with a knight named Gawain, whose father King Lot he accuses of having treacherously murdered his own father "in the very act of greeting" (306). Gawain then identifies himself and they agree to joust on the field at Joflanze in sixteen days time in the presence of Arthur's entire court. When Gawain leaps back across the river Sabins, he is greeted by a penitent Orgeluse, who explains that her animosity stemmed from grief over her slain husband Cidegast, and that she has been testing Gawain to prove his worthiness. Having found him purged and as purified as gold in the fire, she now accepts his request for her favor, and the two lovers return to the Castle of Marvels. Orgeluse explains along the way that the merchandise of Thabrant which stands at the gate was a love gift from Amfortas, who we learn was wounded in the service of Orgeluse (hence the two journeys come together). Orgeluse has since given the precious merchandise to Clinschor, to avoid his necromantic spells, until such time as a man achieves the adventure of the perilous bed and confers his favor on Orgeluse. Having done so, Gawain redeems the Castle of Maidens from its curse, just as Parzival must still redeem the Grail Castle by healing Amfortas.

Back in the Castle, Gawain secretly sends a message to request Arthur's presence at the fields of Joflanze, where he will joust with Gramoflanz to assert his right to the garland from the tree. At the bidding of Orgeluse, he frees the two knights whom he has defeated in the meadow beside the ferry (they had been compelled into the service of Orgeluse to defeat Gramoflanz). He then tactfully informs Itanje of Gramoflanz's love for her, before giving her the ring he had asked Gawain to deliver. A wonderful feast then follows (parallel to the Grail feast), during which the captive lords and ladies of the Castle mingle in love for the first time since Clinschor had cast his evil spell upon them, which had made them blind to each other. Gawain too is healed that night by Orgeluse! After a digression devoted to the reception of Gawain's squire at Arthur's court, and the squire's return with the news that Arthur has agreed to appear at the field of Joflanze on the day appointed for Gawain's joust with Gramoflanz, Gawain sits one morning with Arnive, who now reveals the strange mysteries of the Castle: as is conventional in the hero journey, the initiatory climax involves the revelation of those mysteries which transform and regenerate the individual and the community.

The Castle is the work of Clinschor, who took up magic after being castrated by the King of Sicily for sleeping with his wife Iblis. As a result of being "leveled off between his legs by royal hands," Clinschor went to Persida to study the necromantic arts with which he may cast spells on any people of worthy disposition whose happiness would provoke his spleen. In order to avoid a fate similar to Clinschor's, the King of Rosh Sabins has given Clinschor the Castle. It contains all precious things in such abundance that thirty years of siege could not deplete its stores. Whoever should pass the adventure of the bed becomes the Lord of the Castle, free from the molestation of Clinschor. As such, Arnive now requests that Gawain allow the many subjects forced to live in the Castle by Clinschor's arts to return to their homelands (like Lancelot in "The Knight of the Cart," Gawain frees the courtiers from imprisonment in the otherworld). Gawain's journey then comes full circle when Arthur's court arrives at the fields of Joflanze: Parzival appears simultaneously and since he has also challenged Gramoflanz, Gawain fights Parzival first until they recognize each other. Parzival then defeats Gramoflanz, and an elaborately wrought vision of medieval politics then ensues, with the result that the quarrels all around come to an end, and the hero journey is completed for Gawain by a marriage ceremony. Hence, it is with a sense of political importance as well as psychological healing and mystical revelation that Gawain's triumph allows life to begin anew, freed from the spells of Persian magic, and from the Byzantine complexities of domestic diplomacy on the home front.

Chrétien's account of Gawain's initiatory ordeal is basically the same as Wolfram's, though somewhat simpler. That Gawain's journey takes him into a kind of Celtic otherworld (with forest journeys, river crossing, and meetings with a Triple Goddess and a guardian of the Tree) is emphasized by Chrétien's remark that "No knight who has ever gone that way by road or field has been able to come back; for that's the boundary of Galloway, which a knight can't cross and then return again" (461). This of course is that land from which no traveler returns, i.e., the underworld, here situated in the west of Ireland! The injunction greatly vexes Gawain, who nevertheless crosses over the river to defeat the Haughty Knight of the Rock (Turkoyt in Wolfram), then to be accompanied by the Haughty Maiden of Logres (Wolfram's Orgeluse) to the Perilous Ford, which Gawain leaps over as in Wolfram to confront Guiromelant (Wolfram's Gramoflanz). Like Gramoflanz, Guiromelant is in love with Gawain's sister and also has vowed vengeance upon Gawain for his father King Lot's role in the death of his father. But unlike Gramoflanz, Guiromelant is not wearing a peacock hat and is not defending a tree and garland. It is Guiromelant who in Chrétien tells Gawain that the three queens (four in Wolfram) of the Castle of Marvels are Arthur's mother, Gawain's mother, and Gawain's sister --

which astonishes Gawain since the first two are long dead, another indication that Chrétien has kept the underworldly associations of the
Castle clearly in mind.

The mythological symbols, or elementary poetic ideas, associated
with the Castle of Marvels link Gawain's journey to the many other instances of the otherworld journey we have discussed previously, and
particularly in Chrétien's other romances, "Yvain" and the "The Knight
of the Cart." A progressive humiliation of Gawain at the hands of the
abusive Orgeluse prepares him for the revelations of the Castle in much
the same way that the purgatorial ordeals prepared Yvain and Lancelot
for the consummation of their journeys in Chrétien's other tales. All
three voyages to the otherworld take the heroes into the realm of
archetypal imagery which Jung associated with the collective unconscious. Gawain gets there, we have noted, by taking the road into the
land from which no traveler returns (as does Lancelot) until he crosses
a river with Plippalinot the Ferryman, who conducts souls to the yonder
shore, where they will be judged and tested on the perilous bed. The
imagery here combines Celtic motifs of the land beyond the waves, and
the Classical conventions of Charon and the Styx crossing (the toll here
no longer a coin, but a horse, one of the sacred animals the Celts inherited from their Bronze Age precursors).[26] Plippalinot and his daughter
live off the toll exacted for the crossing, and eat larks captured by their
Merlin hawk: these are the souls of the dead, represented as birds as far
back as the Egyptian papyri of the various Books of the Dead and as the
Epic of Gilgamesh. Bird souls also abound in Celtic legends of the Isle
of Maidens across the waters where the dead are transformed into beautiful swans.[27]

Once on the yonder shore, Gawain enters the castle in each of
whose four hundred windows a beautiful maiden watches, all of them
supervised by a trinity (in Chrétien) or quaternity (in Wolfram) of
Queens. Inside the Castle Gawain endures a kind of death and rebirth
ritual during his night on the perilous bed, a ritual appropriate to a consort of the Great Goddess in her triple form (Virgin, Mother, and
Crone). For surely the imagery of Chrétien suggests the Triple Goddess
of the Celtic world (Sister, Mother, and Grandmother) as much as it
does the three fates of the Classical underworld. Furthermore, the symbolism of the lions who attack Gawain as guardians of the threshold
passage into the realm of the mothers recalls the two lions at the end of
the sword bridge which leads to Guenevere in "The Knight of the Cart."
These lions take us many millennia back to the ancient origins of
Goddess worship during the late Neolithic and Bronze Age of the
Mediterranean world: her earliest image at Catal Huyuk depicts her
giving birth on a throne supported by two lions, an ancient prototype of

the Hellenistic sculpture of Diana, also flanked by two lions (Campbell, "The Great Goddess"). The lion was the traditional symbol of the Goddess and was associated with the sun as a feminine power: the sun pounces on the moon, as the lion does on the bull, and both moon and sun are then reborn from the fires of her womb. Hence the lion pounces on Gawain, in the Castle of the Medieval Goddess, leaving him nearly dead, but reborn and healed the next morning, when the sun rises from the darkness of the night. He emerges from his ordeal transformed, with a new identity as the King of the Castle of Marvels, husband to be of Orgeluse. In Wolfram's version he is healed by Cundrie's magic oint-ment, another powerful symbol of the feminine power to bestow re-birth, and one which we have already seen (in Chrétien's "Knight with the Lion") associated with that other great sorceress of the Arthurian world, Morgan le Fay. In Chrétien, the image of Gawain and the three queens of the Castle parallels the image of Parzival and the three Grail Kings, hence serving to compensate for the patriarchal orientation of the Brotherhood. The symmetry between the two quaternities is strik-ing, and suggests that Gawain achieves in the feminine realm what Perceval achieves in the masculine (psychological, spiritual, and politi-cal regeneration of the waste land): the two quaternities taken together give us an octagonal mandala, a symbol of the fully consummated quest for psychic wholeness which the Grail represents.

The ritual imagery associated with a pagan Goddess of death and rebirth continues in Gawain's next task: the joust with Gramoflanz on the other side of the raging river Sabins, where Gawain must retrieve the garland from the tree for Orgeluse. In Wolfram, Gramoflanz ap-proaches wearing the peacock feather hat (a detail which, as we noted above, links the two episodes of the Castle of Marvels and the Grail Castle). We noted previously the symbolism of resurrection in the iconography of the peacock in Christian and alchemical traditions: in the latter, just after the stage of the opus known as *mortificatio*, a daz-zling array of colors appears in the crucible known as the peacock's tail (Campbell, *Creative Mythology* 501). These alchemical images con-verge with the Celtic and Classical symbols of death and rebirth asso-ciated with the river crossing, and all occur in the context of the sym-bolic tree which Gramoflanz guards. The tree with its guardian (consort of Orgeluse) suggest the King of the Wood episode which begins Frazer's famous study, *The Golden Bough*, in which Diana's consort guards a golden bough hanging from a sacred oak, until he is slain by his successor. In Wolfram, an elaborate variation occurs: Gramoflanz, our King of the Wood, is merely defeated in a joust, and then appeased by marriage to Gawain's sister, and Gawain becomes his successor. As is usual in Wolfram, a complex political and social dimension comple-ments the mythical tenor of his symbols, so that the death and rebirth mysteries associated with Diana and her consort, the King of the Wood, are given a realistic twist, serving also as images of the regeneration and reorganization of the kingdom. Not only does Gawain achieve a personal triumph and transformation, but he also effects a delicate political solution to the debilitating social conflicts of Medieval Germany: he reconciles oppositions between his own and Gramoflanz's family, and in so doing overcomes the long standing conflict between Gramoflanz and Arthur. These reconciliations require a delicate diplomacy, which Wolfram delights in developing thoroughly, creating labyrinthine social complexities only to resolve them by political alliances and marriages that parallel that mystical rebirth which is the traditional theme of the archetypes of the otherworld -- the Goddess, the Golden Bough, the Resurrection, and the alchemical symbol of the peacock. When we add to this the fact that Parzival pulls off a similar political treaty by uniting Christian and Muslim worlds through the baptism of his half-brother Feirefiz later in the story, we have a profound politicizing of mythic materials by Wolfram which Joseph Campbell neglects in his otherwise magisterial *Creative Mythology*.

We must now return to Parzival's second hero journey, during the course of which the complete mysteries of the Grail are fully revealed in the initiation stage of the journey. The call which precipitates his second departure from Arthur's court comes in the wonderful form of the Loathly Damsel, Cundrie the Sorceress, who speaks all languages, knows geometry and dialectic, and has mastered astronomy! Ornately attired -- a hat of peacock feathers significantly links her to Gramoflanz and the Fisher King -- she rides into court on a mule harnessed by the most costly of bridles. Her appearance is conventionally loathsome, and recalls the imagery of Chrétien's Giant of the Woods in "Yvain": she has boar bristle hair and tusks, a dog's nose, bear's ears, lion claw hands, and so forth. Her news is devastating: the honor of the Round Table has been tarnished by the presence of Parzival, whose perfidy is responsible for the continued sufferings of the Sorrowful Angler, since he failed to ask the fateful question. Cundrie lays it on thick, thoroughly humiliating Parzival in a manner that reminds us of the deflating attacks on Yvain and Lancelot in Chrétien's tales. Here, Parzival is a "heartless guest," a "ban on salvation, curse on felicity, disdainer of flawless fame," "sport of Hell's guardians," a "man devoid of honor," than whom none other "was ever more perfidious" (165). This ritual of abuse initiates Parzival's departure in a stage of deep grief and shame, the climax of which is a kind of dark night of the soul, during which Parzival renounces God after five years of wandering, as he makes his way back towards the Grail Castle in order to redeem his former failure.

The climax of his descent into spiritual depression leads to the complete divulgence of the mysteries of the Grail, as if the ego needed

to be completely annihilated before the radiant wisdom of the archetypal Self could be released. This ultimate revelation of those spiritual
mysteries of the Grail which will sustain Parzival during the second,
mature half of life occurs on Good Friday, when the wandering knight,
at the low point of his journey, comes upon the hermit Trevirizent.
Trevirizent is the spiritual counterpart of Gurnemanz, substituting
Christian doctrine for the latter's worldly advice about chivalry. This
doctrine, however, is not strictly dogmatic, since a great deal of pagan
lore about the Grail and its King slips in, which opens up the symbols
to a flood of universal wisdom. It is the hermit Trevirizent who tells us
of Wolfram's source (probably an invention) for the Grail legend, one
Master Kyot, who first read, in Toledo, of the thing called the Grail in
an astrological treatise by the heathen Flegetans. In this text Master
Kyot read that Flegetans discerned in the hidden secrets of the constellations the existence of the Grail, which was left on earth by a troop of
heavenly beings, which the text later identifies as those angels who remained neutral during the war in heaven when Lucifer was cast out by
the Archangel Michael. Master Kyot, Trevirizent continues, pursued the
mystery in many obscure Latin texts, discovering in Anjou the text
which tells the story of the Grail and delineates the pedigree of the
Grail Kings (Titurel, Trimurtel, and Amfortas) and of Parzival himself.
(One should note here how typical it is in the hero journey, as in initiation rites worldwide, for the neophyte to discover not only the ultimate
mysteries of the gods, but also the ancestral mysteries of his own tribe
and family). After a heavy dose of Church dogma, Trevirizent then continues to tell Parzival of the Grail: it is a stone called "Lapsit exillis"
defended by the Templars of Munsalvaesche, and by virtue of the stone
the Phoenix (another alchemical symbol of rebirth) molts its feathers
and the flesh and bones of mortal men are made young again (239). The
chivalric brotherhood appointed to attend the Grail is determined by inscriptions that periodically appear under the top edge of the stone: such
children who are so bidden to the Company are immune from sin and
go directly to Paradise at death.

Of Amfortas, the current maimed King, we soon learn much: during his youth he rode forth in pursuit of Amor, violating the restraints
of holy matrimony. Such ways being unsuitable for those in the service
of the Grail, whose loves are also determined for them by magical inscriptions which appear on the stone, Amfortas is wounded in the
thighs and scrotum by a poisoned lance, wielded by a heathen knight
from the precincts of Paradise, where the Tigris flows. All attempts to
heal the wound have failed: herbs, Pelican blood, the heart and carbuncle stone of the unicorn, and, significantly, the "same twig to which the
Sibyl referred Aeneas, to ward off the hazards of Hell and Phlegethon's
fumes" (245), i.e., the Golden Bough guarded by Gramoflanz!

Amfortas cannot die, living as he does in the continuous presence of the Grail. As a result, the most bizarre remedies from the remote pharmacopoeia of the Middle Ages are resorted too, most significantly the bloody lance, which, when inserted into the wound when the planet Saturn or the change of the moon mark a particularly severe phase of the King's suffering, draws frost from his body around its tip. The frost can only be removed by the silver knives which the wise Trebuchet fashioned, and which Parzival had silently observed on the occasion of his first visit to the Castle. Only by asking Amfortas the question, Trevirizent dramatically concludes, "Uncle, what ails you?" can the wound be healed.

As we have seen throughout this study, it is typical for the initiation phase of the journey to bestow a kind of omniscience upon the hero: all secrets are revealed, and a radical transformation of his character results. Wolfram's Grail Stone magnetically attracts all the wisdom lore of the Middle Ages into the force field of its archetypal energy: from astrology, alchemy, herbal lore, to the cabalistic mysteries of esoteric texts. As the peacock plumes on Cundrie's hat had anticipated, these revelations revolve around the mysteries of death and rebirth, through the power of love and compassion (Wagner's "mitleid" in his opera *Parsifal*). This love involves, as we have seen in both Chrétien and Wolfram, a death of the ego, so that the higher faculties of the Self can be activated.

The Quest for the Holy Grail

The notion of a spiritual reality visible to a chosen few also informs the ecclesiastical version of the Arthurian hero journey, *The Quest of the Holy Grail*, but in that great work, written by Cistercian monk of extraordinary literary skill in about 1220, there is no possibility of reconciling this world and the other: Arthur's Camelot and the Castle of the Grail at Corbenic remain distinct, and in some ways antithetical throughout.

The narrative primarily focuses on the hero journey cycles of four knights: Lancelot, Perceval, Galahad, and Bors. All four of these of these knights eventually achieve revelations, in varying degrees of intensity, of the Grail. Like the four evangelists of the New Testament, each prepares for and approaches the central mystery in a different way. I believe our Cistercian monk meant for us to visualize the four knights with the Grail in the center as a kind of Christian mandala which, in the iconographical traditions of the Middle Ages (based on The Book of Revelation) pictures Christ enthroned in the center with the symbols of the four evangelists surrounding him on each of the four quarters. In fact, the analysis that follows suggests a biblical typology linking

Lancelot to Matthew (Man), Perceval to Mark (Lion), Bors to Luke (Ox), and Galahad to John (Eagle), with the Grail (Christ) in the center. Each represents, from the Jungian perspective, a different slant on the individuation process based on the four personality types (thinking, feeling, sensation, intuition), and the hero journeys in each case involves a shift from an egocentric to a suicentric identity, the totality of the Self here represented by Christ as the Grail. Furthermore, each of the knights has a shadow or outcast side evoked during the quest with which he does the battle of reconciliation or conquest: Lancelot's shadow is Hector, Bors has Lionel, Perceval has Gawain, and Galahad has Melias. All three of the knights who achieve the Grail quest have a common anima figure (Perceval's sister), while Lancelot of course has Guenvere as his eternal feminine side. Perceval's sister plays the role of guide to the higher mysteries of the Grail, sacrificing herself at the end of the quest, while Guenevere's hidden presence restricts Lancelot's final vision of the Grail. In the following paragraphs I will chart the psychological and spiritual journeys of the four knights, showing how the trials and dreams of each effects a transformation of consciousness that prepares them for their own unique glimpse of the Grail in its full radiance.

The journey begins during the feast of Pentecost. The call to adventure is the Grail itself: it appears after a clap of thunder slams all the doors in the palace of Camelot shut, and a radiance seven times brighter than the sun itself dazzles the Knights seated at the round table, as the Grail descends, shrouded in a veil of samite, above the middle of the table. The Knights are stunned into a silence which Gawain breaks to pledge a quest for the Grail, after it disappears from their midst. The keynote in the rest of the chapter is Arthur's grief over the imminent disbanding of the Knights, many of whom he foresees will never return from the quest. As with so many of the hero journey cycles, the separation phase is marked by mourning, depression, loss, and an anxious sense of dread suitable to the initiation of a great journey. Under these circumstances, the threshold crossing into the realm of adventure is not so much an external battle as an internal struggle with all those emotional forces which would have us abandon the journey before it begins. Arthur actually confesses his fears and devastation and asks the Knights not to go; in the hands of our Cistercian monk, the situation is intensified by the implication that in departing from the round table, the knights are actually taking leave of this world and all attachments to it in order to move into the realm of the spirit.

Arthur's grief is emphasized throughout in a rich accumulation of phrases rather unique to the hero's departure: Arthur is "sorely put out"; Gawain's vow, Arthur says, "is a mortal blow to me, for you have deprived me of the best and truest companions a man could find"; the quest "saddens" him so much that he cannot find "the strength to bear this loss"; Arthur falls "silent and the tears that welled unchecked to his eyes for all to see bore witness to his distress of mind"; "Gawain, Gawain," he laments, "you have filled my heart with anguish from which I shall have no relief ... for I have a great dread that those dearest to me will never return" (45). He is so "bitter at their departure" that his grief infects everyone in the court: "they fell to weeping and lamenting" and "the whole court was thrown into turmoil at the news of this departure" (46). When Guenevere hears the news, "her anguish for Lancelot was such that she thought she would die of grief .... There was no more wretched woman than she" (46).

This grief and remorse well reflects the sense of dread that accompanies a departure from the familiar to the unknown: it is a kind of intimation of mortality that awakes the deepest of human fears. Arthur remains "afflicted in mind" during that dark night of the soul, when they all sleep for the last time together in Camelot; he is tormented, "racked in mind and spirit," and he wakes up "in heaviness of spirit" (48). In fact, his "sombre thoughts" plunge him into so deep a grief that he asks Lancelot to "call a halt to the Quest," a shameful request for the King to make, to which he is driven by dread in extremis (49). Lancelot's particular threshold ordeal at the "moment of separation" is to leave Guenevere to a "grief so pitiful that the most hardened man alive could not have looked on unmoved" (51). With "his heart riven at the sight of his lady's hurt," Lancelot must hear her say "you have betrayed me and delivered me up to death," before he can harness his horse and leave (51). When the knights finally do leave, en mass, our author tells us that "Never had there been such weeping and wailing as was set up by the townspeople when they saw the companions setting out on the Quest of the Holy Grail" (51). The mood is indeed apocalyptic, full of the dreadful forebodings of the collapse of the Arthurian era.

I wish to emphasize Arthur's almost uncanny grief and rather shameful trepidation during this departure because it highlights a crucial feature characteristic of nearly all the separation scenes of the hero journey: all involve pathological imagery of some kind, externally dramatized by bloody blows, and internally by psychological derangement. As in Chrétien, some such pathologizing often occurs at the beginning of the tales, and in fact makes them possible. In "Yvain," the King goes to take a nap with Guenevere, a very unusual procedure which leads directly to the telling of a tale of shame and dishonor which then in turn precipitates Yvain's departure and hero journey cycle. In "The Knight of the Cart," Arthur foolishly allows a strange knight to carry off the Queen and then sends the inept Kay to retrieve her, both blunders which initiate the journey. Such lapses of Kingly authority and discretion actually set these tales in motion, suggesting that some relaxation of the superego must occur before the dream story can bubble up from the cauldron of the id (to use Freudian terms). Once the royal censor has been removed, weakened, or humiliated by severe grief, the story begins. What the initial threshold battle at the moment of separation suggests, then, is a removal of those forces of order which would impede the storytelling process. In Chrétien, this involves what the Russian formalists would call a 'defamiliarizing' of conventional codes of behavior that evokes the elemental structures of plot as story evolves into tale.

These penitential humiliations are necessary, as our monk tells us, because no one can begin the Quest "unless he be shriven or seek confession, for no man may enter so high a service until he is cleansed of grievous sin and purged of every wickedness. For this is no search for earthly things but a seeking out of the mysteries and hidden sweets of Our Lord" (47). In psychological terms, the rigidities of persona and ego, and the fierce attachment to life of the instincts, must be dissolved before the archetypal mysteries are manifested. A restructuring of consciousness must occur which involves, initially, "A certain *abaîssement du niveau mental*, i.e., a weakness in the hierarchical order of the ego" which sets "instinctive urges and desires in motion" and brings "about a dissociation of personality" (Jung, *Transference* 9). As M. L. von-Franz puts it, "every encounter with the unconscious begins [with] the complete breakdown of the former activities" of the ego, before the life energy "breaks through in the revelation of an archetypal image" (*Puer* 27). James Hillman calls this breakdown "pathologizing," and links it to the descent to the underworld (Hades) of the dream, where the fundamental forms (*eidola*) that guide and shape life are hidden.

Hence we see the mood of despair and grief at the departure of the knights from Camelot continue during the adventures that follow. Lancelot is quickly knocked off his horse for the first time in his life by his son Galahad, and then subjected to a sequence of humiliations. First, while asleep beside a stone cross, he witnesses, without fully waking up, a procession of the Grail, and then has his armor taken from him. Both images (of being knocked off one's horse and having one's armor stolen) effectively communicate the degradation of the ego which precipitates a spiritual crisis of transformation. Lancelot is then chastised for being harder than stone (obduracy in sin), more bitter than wood (rottenness of sin), and more barren than a fig tree. A hermit tells him the parable of the talents (from Matthew) to show how he has wasted his life in sin. The clothing symbolism is picked up the next day, when Lancelot gets a new horse and new arms, and when, after coming upon an ill-clad corpse in a chapel at noon, another hermit tells the parable of the wedding feast guest cast out for being improperly dressed (again from Matthew): the feast is the table of the Grail, and the wedding garments of the worthy the graces and virtues, and the outcast represents those "lacking their raiment of confession and good deeds" (145). He also gives Lancelot a long lecture on the five lost virtues of his youth which have been stripped from him and replaced by an opposite set of five vices. Lancelot then receives another symbolic change of clothing, a hair shirt, before continuing on his penitential journey. (It is important to note that allusions to the gospel of Matthew are sprinkled throughout the chapter, occurring over nine times, suggesting that link in the author's mind between Lancelot and the Evangelist, whose symbol is a man).

At nightfall, Lancelot comes to a wooden cross at a crossroad and dreams first of a man surrounded by stars and attended by two knights and seven kings, and, secondly, of another man surrounded by angels who descends from heaven to cast out the elder of two knights, in order to endow the younger with lion body and wings that allow him to soar out of this world into heaven. The next day a hermit interprets Lancelot's dream: the elder knight is Lancelot himself and the younger is his son Galahad (both lion and eagle here); the star man of the first dream is Celydone, father of the line of seven kings leading to King Ban, Lancelot's father. On the next day Lancelot comes at noon to a large castle surrounded by five hundred fighting knights, and rides with the black ones, only to be defeated and captured (again for the first time) by the white ones. An anchoress explains the next morning that the black knights represent sin (surprise!) and the white knights represent the hermits who have defeated Lancelot's pride and saved him from the evils of courtly life. The whole tournament, she adds, "was but as it were a figuration of Jesus Christ" (158). The next day the narrative leaves Lancelot in a steep valley by a river with an intractable forest behind him and no horse, his own having been killed by a mysterious black knight who had emerged suddenly from the furiously rushing river. Lancelot, that is to say, having been purged of his pride and worldly attachments (ego and persona) is now ready to cross to the yonder shore where the mysteries of the Self will be revealed.

This cycle of adventures completes Lancelot's humiliations, dream visions, and penitential instruction, all of which serve the purpose of preparing him for the partial revelation of the Grail which will occur later in the tale at the Castle Corbenic. Unhorsed by Galahad, reviled by abusive squires, severely chastised by venerable hermits, defeated for the first time in combat, and left alone in the lonesome valley, Lancelot is ready for the revelations that follow the rape of the ego. Out of this severely depressed condition dream visions have come: of the Grail, of the man with seven stars, of the lion-bodied, eagle-winged man who soared into heaven. In terms of the hero journey, Lancelot's trials and ordeals have catalyzed the archetypal contents of his own personal as

well as collective unconscious, and these ordeals and dreams have effected a dramatic transformation of his consciousness. It is significant
to note that all the symbolic figures in his dreams have been human
(not animals, as will be the case with Bors and Perceval), and that this
seems appropriate, given the many allusions to the Gospel of Matthew,
the symbol of which is Man. Lancelot is, in fact, the most fully human
of the four knights, as is conventional in the Arthurian material.[28] He is
traditionally weighed down by suffering and guilt, unable to leave his
human love for Guenevere behind, yet longing for an equally deep and
fulfilling spiritual vision that will redeem and give meaning to his long
suffering. In this respect, Lancelot is the closest of the four to Jesus
(who remember is both fully human and divine). But now our narrative
of preparatory ordeals turns to Perceval, who is associated with Mark,
and his symbol, the lion.

    Like Lancelot, Perceval begins his journey by being knocked off
his horse by Galahad. He then goes to a chapel where a woman (Queen
of the Wasteland) tells him his mother died when he left home, and re-
hearses the histories of the three great fellowships: of the Apostles, of
the Round Table, and of the Grail. Perceval next comes to an abbey
where he watches the ancient four hundred year old King Mordrain receive communion. A priest tells Perceval that Mordrain had delivered
Josephus, son of Joseph of Arimathea who brought the Grail to Logres,
from the prison of the pagan King Crudel, and that Mordrain is awaiting the coming of Galahad. This mystical vision, after being unhorsed
by Galahad, parallels Lancelot's half-sleeping vision of the candlestick
and Grail beneath the cross at the crossroads. Perceval leaves this abbey
only to be knocked down again by twenty armed knights pulling a
corpse. Galahad appears briefly and disperses these twenty knights,
while Perceval unsuccessfully struggles to regain his horse. That night,
another dream vision occurs: a woman appears to give Perceval a magnificent black stallion that runs away with Perceval after he mounts it,
and carries him at supernatural speed towards a wide river, approaching
which Perceval crosses himself, which causes the black stallion to buck
him off and plunge into the river, where the horse bursts into fiendishly
shrieking flames. Like Lancelot, Perceval finds himself alone at night
in a dense wilderness by the riverside, but when he wakes up he finds
himself on the craggy peak of an island from which he will eventually
be delivered by a miraculous ship (as Lancelot will later be by the
riverside where we have left him).

    While on the peak of the island, Perceval kills a serpent carrying a
lion cub in his mouth, and he is then befriended by the lion in pursuit of
its cub. That night, Perceval dreams of an old woman on a serpent who
reprimands him, and then of a young woman riding on a lion. We learn
later -- from a venerable sage on the miraculous ship that rescues

Perceval from the island -- that the old woman on the serpent represents the Old Testament, and the young woman on the lion the New (Bors will also have figural dreams; we have already seen the younger son as the New Testament surpassing the older father in Lancelot's ordeals and dreams). The next day, another magic ship appears to Perceval, only this one is demonic: a gorgeous maiden on board invites Perceval to come out of the heat of the sun to rest under a tent, where she nearly seduces him; but when he climbs naked into bed with her, he sees a cross which breaks the spell. The boat dissolves in flames, and the venerable sage returns to inform Perceval that the maiden was the devil, the tent the world, and the heat of the day the fire of the Holy Spirit, which she attempts to extinguish with sleep, sex, and death (shades of Gnostic symbols here). Perceval recognizes the incarnation of what Jung called the wise old man archetype (a figuration of the Self) as the Living Bread, and follows his instructions to board the ship, where the narrative leaves him for now.

Perceval's ordeals purge his lingering lust and vulnerability to the wiles of the anima: it surely makes sense for a young virgin knight with high spiritual ideals to dream of the dark side of the feminine which he has repressed. While she appears here as a temptress, Perceval will later find her in positive form as his own sister, in chapters which will fully explore the anima problem in a Christian context. It also surely makes sense that Perceval's dreams and adventures are not dominated, as Lancelot's were, by human, but by animal figures, specifically the lions which become his guardians when he is stranded on the uninhabited island. Like the imagery of the wild stallion, river crossing, ship journey, and enchanted island, which suggest a pagan context associated with the journey to the otherworld, the lion has also traditionally been associated with the pagan Great Goddess: it is the solar beast which devours the moon bull consort, who is then reborn from her womb. We see her "enthroned, giving birth, flanked and supported by lions" in a ceramic figurine from Çatal Hüyük of about 5000 B.C.E., and "six millenniums later, we have a marble image of the same Anatolian goddess (now named Cybele), also enthroned and flanked by lions" (Campbell, "The Great Goddess" 78-79). It is interesting then to find her enthroned in Perceval's unconscious, and again associated with lions, with the sun, and with the theme of transformation and rebirth, since it is on this island that Perceval dies to the world with which she tempts him, and is reborn to the realm of the spirit. While intuitively evoking such deep layers of archetypal symbolism, our Cistercian monk appears to primarily to wish to suggest the typological equation between Perceval and Mark, the evangelist whose symbol is the lion.

Like Lancelot, Perceval is brought to the edge of the shore by his preparatory ordeals, and he awaits the ship to continue his journey to the yonder shore of the spiritual life, which lies beyond his personal, albeit unconscious attachments to the temptations of the world and the flesh. The ship journey will lead into the archetypal realms of the collective images revealed later by his anima, his *soror mystica* (mystical sister). The narrative shifts at this point to Gawain and Hector, who are the coupled foil or dark side to Perceval and Lancelot respectively: they have few adventures and represent the shadow side of the Grail knighthood, its repressed pride and lust. A hermit explains why they have so few adventures when he says "signs will never appear to sinners" because the Grail is "of a spiritual order" (174). Since Gawain is unable to atone for his sins or, in psychological terms, to purge himself of his egotistical attachment to his courtly reputation, he is rendered ineligible for the deeper journey towards the Grail. He does, however, have a dream of three bulls yoked together, one of which bears traces of spots on its white body and is identified with Bors.

The instruction of the white bull, Sir Bors -- the Ox of the evangelistic quaternity -- is dominated by dogmatic lessons on the symbolism of the Mass and Confession, both of which are sacraments of transmutation. An aged monk tells Bors that only confession can purify the knights and make them eligible for the Grail, which changes earthly into heavenly food, just as confession transmutes earthbound affections to a heavenly plane (176). The monk applies an alchemical analogy to describe this process which "promises them gold in lieu of the lead they used to have" (176), bringing to mind Jung's analogy between alchemical operations and the processes of individuation.[29] The monk emphasizes that confession is a change of one's "inner state," making it fit "to receive a different food" (177). Bors leaves this hermit and comes to an abbey where, like Lancelot, he changes clothing to symbolize the transformation of his "inner state." He is given a white frock to wear as "a mark of penance ... to chasten the flesh" (179). Bors removes his own gown and shirt, puts on the frock, and then a "gown of fine red cloth" (179), the color of which, like the color of Galahad's armor, suggests the fire of the Holy Spirit. In the communion scene that follows, the clothing symbolism so often apparent in the hero journey takes on a fascinating dimension. In the presence of the host of the Mass, Bors says "my eyes, being mortal clay, and thus unapt to discern the things of the spirit" cannot see Christ in the bread. Christ then must "*cloak* his true appearance" (180, italics mine) in the sacramental ritual (he will later 'uncloak' Himself during the ultimate revelation of the Grail, when Christ appears naked in the chalice). God clothes himself, in this scene, in the vestments of ecclesiastical ritual, and the climax of the Grail quest is His unveiling, when the full significance of the Mass is revealed. Along with the Confession, the Mass enacts a transformation of consciousness whereby the center of the personality is shifted from the earthly attachments of the ego to the archetypal presence of the Self.

Thus prepared by the hermit's instruction, and by the change of vestments, Bors goes forth to encounter a sequence of adventures and dreams dominated by bird imagery and by women. He first has a vision of a large pelican feeding its dead young at the top of a blasted tree by stabbing itself in the breast and letting the blood revive its fledglings before dying. Then Bors agrees to defend a younger against an elder sister, who has stolen lands given the younger by King Love. The night before the battle he dreams of a large white swan who tempts him with worldly power, and of a small strangely beautiful black rook whom he agrees to serve. On the next day he defeats the elder sister and rides off into the forest where he must choose to defend a maiden against a rapist, rather than rescue his brother Lionel, who is naked and being beaten with a thorn bush. After these adventures, Bors meets a monk on a black horse who gives him false interpretations of his adventures and then leads him to a ruined castle and abbey, where Bors is tempted by a "gorgeously attired lady" who jumps off a tower with twelve maidens when Bors resists her. Bors crosses himself when he sees this terrible group suicide, and the whole shows goes up in smoke (this episode is structurally and thematically parallel to the temptation of Perceval on the miraculous ship). Bors then proceeds to a white monastery where he gets a true interpretation of his dreams and adventures: the pelican is Christ on the Cross reviving a fallen humanity with his own blood and death; the younger sister and the black bird represent the Holy Church, while the older sister represents the enemy and the Old Law. Bors then must go to confront his own brother Lionel, who kills a monk and then another knight. A fireball thrown down from heaven when Bors lifts his sword separates them, and Bors proceeds to the seashore, where he boards the miraculous ship with Perceval.

These chapters devoted to Bors make it clear that the purpose of the trials and ordeals of the hero is a gradual transformation of the psyche in order to prepare it for an encounter with the Self. The dreams and adventures effect that transformation on a personal level, forcing the knights to confront unacknowledged portions of themselves which have been repressed and which therefore return in negative forms; while the sacraments of the Confession and the Mass effect the transmutation on a more collective level. Although the dreams are interpreted according to medieval allegory, they retain that elusive suggestiveness characteristic of Celtic mysticism and living archetypes. In fact, part of the healing power of the dreams is precisely in their reconciliation of dogma and the native dynamics of the individual knights: archetypal dreams are stirred up by each quest, and, along with the instructive rituals of the hermits, gradually prepare the heroes for the final revelation.

In the case of Bors, the dream language relies heavily on bird symbolism, suggesting that he may have been meant as a parallel to the Gospel of John. The issue is complicated, since Bors is initially associated with the white bull or ox of Luke, but later has dreams in which the bird symbolism of John preponderates. One explanation could be that in medieval iconography, the representations of Luke as the Ox often put wings on the oxen, just as the lion of Mark was often winged.[30] Of the dream visions which occur during the quests up to this point, we find Lancelot dreaming of man (Matthew), Gawain dreaming of bulls (Luke), Perceval of lions (Mark), and Bors of birds (John). That configuration would give us four knights with Galahad in the center as the "semblance" of Christ (which is exactly the way one monk refers to Galahad earlier (64)). But clearly the author could not equate Gawain with Luke, since Gawain is disqualified early on in the quest, and since he is not one of the four to see the Grail.

Galahad must be the eagle then, as Lancelot's vision of him soaring with wings over the earth suggests. In fact, Galahad seems as unearthly as the eagle, and it is, as we will see, Galahad who wears the sword of Solomon later on, a symbol of the Logos. Galahad's quest differs in important ways from the other three knights who see the Grail. He undergoes no temptation or penitential ordeal to prepare him for the revelations on the miraculous ship, and, more significantly, he has no dream visions whatsoever. Five days after being knighted he comes to an abbey where Nascien is buried and wins a shield that had been given King Mordrain by Josephus. He then lifts a heavy tombstone, removes the body of a knight from the crypt, and silences a voice that renders its hearers senseless -- three perils which a monk glosses as representing the hardened ways of sin, the subsequent death of mankind, and the "terrible words which they spoke to Pilate, the governor: 'His blood be on us and our children!'" (65). The adventure then, the monk continues, "shows forth the meaning of the Passion of Jesus Christ, while at the same time it symbolizes his coming" (65). Once again, Galahad is both a Christ figure, and a pre-figuration of the second coming. After this adventure, Galahad disperses the seven knights holding souls captive in the Castle of Maidens, which a monk tells him represent hell and the seven deadly sins. Unlike Perceval and Bors, there is no real temptation of Galahad in this scene; he seems irreproachable and so much like Christ that he has no repressed anima problems! As the monk says of the adventure, "even as He sent His Son ... even so did He send Galahad" for the deliverance of those maidens who symbolize the souls of men trapped in Hell (79). From this point on Galahad has only random appearances, though many adventures are suggested, and we do not pick him up again until Chapter Ten, when he joins Perceval and Bors on the Miraculous Ship. There have been no dreams and no temptations for Galahad, but we are now ready to proceed to the initiation stage of the hero journey, in which the highest mysteries which the ordeals have prepared us for are finally and fully revealed.

With the three principle Grail knights together, plus Perceval's sister, the narrative shifts to an examination of the contents of the Miraculous Ship. These contents take us far beyond the personal psychologies of the individual knights, dramatized in the adventures before their arrival on the Ship, into entirely collective levels of archetypal and ancestral symbolism. This progression follows the logic of the individuation process, which moves through autobiographical material to deeper levels of collective significance encoded in archetypal imagery. That is why in the *Quest*, at this point in the story, the visions and dreams are no longer experienced individually, but are shared by all three knights simultaneously. Another important change is that they receive instruction here not from a hermit, but from a woman, Perceval's sister. Hence the feminine in the quest has been transformed from temptress to psychopomp; she reveals the stories behind the mysterious items on the Ship -- its sword and its bed. Perhaps this reflects the conceptions regarding Sophia as the feminine wisdom of God who was with him before the Creation and breathed upon the waters in *Genesis*. The change also, reflects, however, a natural development in the individuation process, as the inner feminine side of the masculine matures, and in so doing becomes a guide to the mysteries of the Self.

Perceval's sister first tells the three Grail knights how the Ship came to Logres when the maimed King was fighting the newly baptized King Varlan, who came on board the Ship and used the magnificent sword to strike the dolorous blow that creates the Waste Land (216). The second use of the sword occurred when Nascien drew it after the Ship took him to an island where a giant lived, at which point the sword broke in two, only to be restored by King Mordrain, whom Nascien later meets at sea. Nascien is punished for his presumption by a flying sword. The final blow caused by the sword, Perceval's sister continues, occurred when King Parlan, the Maimed King who will later appear in the Grail Castle, boarded the Ship to which he was led after losing his way on a hunt, and then drew the sword slightly from its scabbard, at which point a lance pierced his thighs and inflicted the wound that can only be healed by Galahad's coming. Celtic materials are here abundant and not quite thoroughly assimilated into Christian allegory, though in the chapter that follows, the narrator attempts to Christianize the history of the ship, its bed, and its sword.

This occurs in a long chapter in which the narrator pauses to explain the mysteries on board directly to the reader. The bed on board,

and the Ship itself, we learn, were built by King Solomon under the direction of his wife (note again the increased importance of the feminine
in this part of the story). In order to fully tell the tale, the narrator takes
us all the way back to *Genesis*. The bed has three posts that sustain a
canopy: a white and a red post inserted perpendicularly into the frame,
and a green cross post, all of naturally hued, unpainted wood. This
wood, we learn, comes from the Tree of Knowledge in the Garden of
Eden, a sprig of the fruit tree which Eve had taken with her after the
Expulsion and planted while she was still a virgin. The sprig grew into
a magnificent white tree, from which other white trees were grafted;
when Adam and Eve were instructed to make love beneath the original
white tree, in order to conceive Abel, the white tree turned green to be-
token Eve's loss of virginity, and other grafts were subsequently planted
from this green tree. Finally, when Cain killed Abel beneath this very
same originally white and now green tree grafted from the Tree of
Knowledge, it turned blood red.

I wish to emphasize the importance of story and instruction in this
part of the hero journey, since the initiation phase of the monomyth
characteristically communicates its revelations in story form (the hero
journey being in part about the process by which great stories are discovered and set down). It is also very interesting, given the well known
importance of trees in the lore of the Celtic Druids and in Celtic
verse,[31] that our Cistercian monk should develop the image of the Tree
of Knowledge in such extraordinary detail: perhaps it was the residual
element of Celtic mythology in European society (which played such
an important role in the origins and development of the Arthurian romances in general)[32] that contributed to the formation of this fantastic
midrash (one is tempted to call it) about the Tree. In the context of the
history of the hero journey in literature, it is fascinating to note the similarity of this legend to the story of the Huluppu Tree from ancient
Sumer, in which the tree's cycles also reflect the progressive development of civilization in relation to the feminine goddess (Inanna) who
tended the tree.

Though the legend up to this point is to be found throughout
Medieval literature, the tale now departs from the conventional motif in
which Seth plants a seed from the Tree of Knowledge in Adam's
mouth. This seed grows into the tree from which the wood of the cross
is made.[33] Our Cistercian monk goes on to tell how the tree flourished
during Solomon's time. One day, in consolation for the many sorrows
caused Solomon by his unfaithful wife, Solomon was given foreknowledge of the coming of Mary and of the birth of Christ. Racking his wits
to find some way of letting future generations know of his prescience,
he consults his wife (!), who advises him to build the Miraculous Ship

of our tale. She herself then oversees the construction of the bed, using white and green wood for the two posts from grafts, and a slice of bleeding red wood from the original tree. The sword comes from Solomon's father King David, and she tells Solomon to use his wisdom to fashion a magnificent pommel, hilt, and scabbard for it: the hilt is ribbed by the magical spines of a serpent and fish from the Euphrates, which confer insensibility to heat and single-mindedness upon the sword bearer; the pommel is formed of a single stone containing all the colors of the earth; and the scabbard is a brilliant red samite embroidered on both sides with prophecies written by a man who appears in Solomon's dreams. All of this information is written down in a letter to which Perceval's sister directs the knights in the next chapter.

These revelations of hidden knowledge about talismanic objects of profound spiritual significance is, as we have seen, characteristic of the climax of the hero journey, in its initiation stage. These revelations always involve some transformation of the hero or heroine's identity, which in this case implies the process by which the mortal nature of knights is dramatically, and incrementally (since other even more powerful episodes of revelation still lie ahead), spiritualized. As Jung has noted, "the sword is very much more than an instrument which divides. What it means is the transformation of the vital spirit in man into the Divine" ("Transformation Symbolism" 304). This is of course the whole thrust of the Grail quest as conceived by the Cistercian monk, in which the Grail is itself the Chalice of the Communion ritual, in which the whole mystery of the death and resurrection of Christ occurs, along with the transmutation of human nature which occurs as a result of participation in the rite.

What is uniquely interesting in *The Quest* is the crucial role played by the feminine in this fantastic legend about the Tree, the Ship, the Bed, and the Sword, with its rich accretion of archetypal imagery derived from diverse sources, Celtic as well as Christian. In the legend as told by the clerical narrator, Eve, Solomon's wife, Guenevere, and Perceval's sister represent a full range of symbolic images of the feminine associated with the mysteries of transformation implied by the Grail quest. First there is Eve, who unconsciously carries a little piece of Eden into Exile. Although she was of course traditionally blamed for the Fall, this gesture is positive, in that by carrying the sacred branch out of Paradise, "she unknowingly prepares the world's redemption" (Matarasso 298). Like the Tree itself, Eve combines the opposites of life and death, good and evil, and hence becomes a suitable expression of the archetypal mother of all living, which Jung describes as "loving and terrible" ("Four Archetypes" 16). So too, as Matarasso points out, does Solomon's wife combine negative and positive traits: "she stands midway between Eve and Mary. In her feminine guile ... she looks backward to Eve ... and in the part she plays, half-consciously, in" the building of the Ship, Bed, and Sword, "she prefigures the Virgin Mary" (299). One might say that in the typology of the *Quest*, she represents the Old Testament, while Perceval's sister represents the New; Guenevere plays the role of Eve, visible also in the various temptresses in the dreams of the knights. As Matarasso points out, the author of the *Quest* "always assigns his women a positive part in the redemption of mankind .... in Perceval's sister we have the figure of woman redeemed and in her turn redeeming. The very concept of courtly love is presented purified and subordinated" (299). The whole section of the story then is dominated by the anima in its deepest collective sense as an archetype: she is the mother of all, the temptress, the mother of our redemption and transformation, and finally the instructress and guide who directs the knights to the Grail Castle. Hence, the anima passes through all the stages of development which Marie Louise von Franz associates with the individuation process.[34] We last see Perceval's sister sacrificing her life to cure a woman of leprosy; then she is put on a ship that floats to the river where Lancelot is stranded, takes him aboard, and delivers him to Galahad.

The purgatorial ordeals, temptations, and dream visions which make this progressive development of the anima possible are now complete. The gradual process of transformation of the consciousness of the four knights has brought them all to this watershed transition from purgatory to paradise, and that change is signified by the joining together of three of the knights on the Miraculous Ship, their ferryboat to the yonder shore of the Grail Castle, and from there further on to the Holy City. The ship journey effects the final severing of earthbound affections (the natural concerns of the courtly ego and the instinctual drives manifest in the temptation scenes) and the departure for the higher spiritual realms (the sea being the reservoir of archetypal images of the collective unconscious). It is at this point that the narrative returns to Lancelot, left alone on the shores of the river, and to a long chapter to his encounter with the Grail, one of the most intriguing in all of the Arthurian romances. Though he is in fact the first of the knights to actually see the Grail, his experience is a partial one, and he will not accompany Perceval, Bors, and Galahad to the Holy Land. If the four knights can be said to correspond to the four types and functions of Jungian psychology (sensation, feeling, thinking, and intuition), then Lancelot represents the inferior feeling function (from the clerical point of view).

His departure from the earthly to the spiritual realms begins when a voice instructs him to board the first ship he sees coming along the river; when he does so, he finds the sweetly scented corpse of Perceval's sister bearing a letter explaining the circumstances of her death. Lancelot drifts along on board for one month, during which time he is fed like the Israelites by the manna of the Holy Ghost, and he is now called (for the first time in the tale) a "servant of Jesus Christ" (256).[35] This signifies that shift from an egocentric to a suicentric personality which we have seen the other knights undergo as well. Galahad is subsequently directed to the ship, and father and son are reunited for six months of drifting in service of the Lord: this figures the atonement, the union of eternity and time, god and man, Self and ego. After Galahad's departure from the boat, Lancelot drifts another month alone until the ship arrives at the rear entrance to the Grail Castle, at Corbenic. The entrance faces the sea and is guarded on either side by lions; when Lancelot draws his sword to pass between them, a fireball knocks the sword from his hand and so dazzles him that he doesn't know whether it is night or day. He then musters his courage and faithfully passes through the entrance, goes into the Castle, and walks down a long corridor to a locked inner room "with a great light flooding through the opening, as if the sun had its abode within" (262).

This whole sequence reiterates the importance of doorways and threshold imagery in the hero journey, which we will have traced from ancient Sumerian literature to modern films by the end of our own journey. In addition, Lancelot's encounter with the dazzling effulgence of the inner room recalls the solar imagery noted in the stories of Sir Orfeo and Sir Gawain (and on further back to Gilgamesh and the Egyptian material). When Lancelot arrives at this inner room at the end of the corridor entered by the doorway guarded by lions, he prays to be admitted, and when he looks up he sees angels and an old man lifting the Grail at Mass who is having such a difficult time with the weight of the Trinity sitting in the vessel that Lancelot steps forward into the room to help him. But when he passes across this second major threshold in the sequence, a puff of scorching wind passes through his body and knocks him out for twenty four days, one day for each of the twenty four years spent in adultery with Guenevere. Hence the threshold imagery here signifies both a transition from the material to the spiritual, and from the conscious ego to the unconscious Self (Cocteau will use the doorway in a similar way, having Beauty pass unconscious through the doorway into her room in the Beast's chateau). Lancelot is stricken with grief at the fading of the bliss he experienced during his twenty four day coma when he is awakened. He is then divested of his hair shirt and brought "a fresh new linen gown," followed by "a gown of scarlet cloth" which he agrees to put on only after putting the hair shirt back on (265). Noteworthy here again is the convergence of clothing symbolism with the threshold crossing, both being long standing symbols of transformation in the hero journey genealogies.

After Lancelot has crossed these thresholds, glimpsed the Grail, and fallen into a coma, to be reclothed on awakening, the King of the Castle is informed that "that knight who was lying here as dead is risen fit and well, and he is none other than Sir Lancelot of the Lake" (266). This language clearly suggests another kind of threshold crossing implied by the doorway and corridor imagery -- the threshold between life and death which Jesus also traversed. Despised and rejected of men during the Quest, dead and resurrected in the presence of the Grail, yet remaining fully human in his love for Guenevere, Lancelot combines the dual aspects of the Incarnation, human and divine, in himself. In fact, Lancelot is a kind of Boddhisattva, that form of Buddha consciousness which returns with love and compassion to the world of suffering *samsara* even after the ecstasy of release and enlightenment (*nirvana*). But our Cistercian monk does not seem as willing to pursue this analogy between Christ and Lancelot with the same intensity that Chrétien does in "The Knight of the Cart" (see below).

After Lancelot returns to Camelot, we return to the other three knights whose adventures bring them also to the Grail Castle at Corbenic. During five years of wandering, Galahad restores the sight of King Mordrain, cools a spring of giant boiling bubbles in the Perilous Forest, and quenches a fire in the crypt where Simon is buried. Previous to these adventures, Galahad and the other three knights had roamed the countryside, removing the remaining afflictions of the Waste Land. Together they massacred the evil sons of Count Ernol, and fought at the castle where the Lady with leprosy was eventually healed by the blood of Perceval's sister. In the midst of these adventures, a very important episode occurs which confirms the implied linkage of the four knights who see Grail and the imagery of the four evangelists. Perceval, Bors, and Galahad ride into the Waste Forest in pursuit of a white hart surrounded by four lions. The animals run into a small chapel, and while a hermit intones the Mass, the hart turns into a man and the four lions into a man, an eagle, a lion, and a calf (the symbols of the four evangelists evoked during the earlier quests of the four knights). The ecclesiastical bestiary passes on a ray of light through a stain glass window without breaking it -- a favorite image of the Immaculate Conception during the Middle Ages. The hermit then interprets the unveiling of these secrets: the transformation of the hart into a man signifies the "transformation that He underwent on the cross: cloaked there in the mortal garment of his human flesh," Christ won us eternal life, which is "aptly figured by the Hart," the hermit continues, "For just as the Hart rejuvenates itself by shedding part of its hide and coat, so did Our Lord return from death to life when he cast off his mortal hide which was the human flesh He took in the Blessed Virgin's womb" (244).

This fascinating gloss enriches our sense of the symbolism of clothing in the hero journey by linking the Neoplatonic and Gnostic imagery of the soul clothed in the rags of the body at birth -- and divesting itself of those rags at death in order to be reinvested in its original radiance -- with the Christian imagery of the Incarnation and Crucifixion. In addition, the passage evokes the affiliated pagan imagery of the Great Goddess, who weaves the clothing of our flesh in the cave of her womb. As we have seen, this affiliation has a long lineage in the history of the hero journey, stretching all the way back to the "Cave of the Nymphs" in the *Odyssey*, and to the talismanic robe given Gilgamesh by Utnapishtim's wife. Even the symbolism of the Hart has a pagan ancestry, closer to the Bronze age world of the British Isles than to the period of the Gospels. As far back as the magnificent earthen mound known as Silbury Hill, built over many generations from around 3000 B.C.E. in the countryside surrounding the little village of Avebury, we find buried antlers, which, as Michael Dames has shown, formed part of an elaborate sequence of natural symbols of rebirth surrounding the hill (since the stag sheds its antlers in the spring). The Hart also plays a role in the alchemical and Christian iconography associated with St. Christopher, who sees an image of Christ on the Cross between the antlers of a large buck. Shortly after this vision in *The Quest*, knights separate for five years of further penance before being reunited at Corbenic in the Grail Castle.

The configuration of the quaternity continues to play an important role at the Castle Corbenic: at the Mass of the Grail, twelve knights witness four maidens carry the Maimed King into the room, and four angels bring candles, red samite, and the bleeding lance while Josephus comes down from heaven to perform the Mass. These four angels are the celestial counterparts of the four Grail knights who actually see the Grail in the story and of the four evangelists. After Josephus consecrates the host (when a child with a face like fire falls from heaven into the bread), he disappears and Christ himself emerges bleeding from the Grail to "reveal some part of [His] secrets and [His] mysteries" to the worthy knights (276). Christ administers the Mass, instructs Galahad to heal the Maimed King by anointing his wounded thighs with blood from the bleeding lance, and then directs the three knights to board the Miraculous Ship on their long journey to the Holy City of Sarras. In Sarras the Grail is returned to the Holy Temple, Perceval's sister is buried, and after two years (one as prisoner and one as king) Galahad has his final vision: while Josephus recites the Mass of the Virgin, Galahad draws near and looks into the Grail, where he beholds the "source of valor undismayed, the spring head of endeavor" (283) and dies shortly thereafter. Matarasso suggests that Galahad sees the Trinity in its full radiance here, a vision prepared for by an ascending curve of disclosures to the Grail in the story: Lancelot's glimpse of the old man heavily burdened by a "semblance" of the Trinity; the Mass at Corbenic with Galahad, Bors, and Perceval present; and finally the Trinity revealed, face to face, during this last Mass in the Holy City of Sarras (304). This would explain Galahad's immediate death, since no one can look on the face of God and live. Perceval dies a year later, and Bors returns to Camelot, completing the majestic cycle of the hero journey.

The journey overall is divided into two parts by the Cistercian monk: the adventures in the forest form the first part, and the revelations on board the Miraculous Ship and in the Grail Castle the second. In the first part, Galahad represents Christ on earth as a chivalric knight, and the chapter headings show us a quaternity of knights, whose adventures the coming of Galahad to Camelot on Pentecost inspires: Gawain, Lancelot, Perceval, and Bors. This earthly or purgatorial quaternity gives way to a new configuration after the completion of the purgatorial ordeals in the second part of the tale. Gawain (and his companion Hector) drop out of the picture, and Galahad gives way to the Grail as the central focus of the constellation of questing knights, who form now a quaternity associated with the four evangelists: the Grail in the center with Lancelot, Perceval, Bors, and Galahad surrounding it. This gives us two quaternities symmetrically facing each other from across the dividing line of the river, which separates the shores of this world (Camelot) and the other (Corbenic). At the center of each quaternity is the mystery of the Trinity, so that the symbolism of the numbers three and four are combined (as they often are in the alchemical tradition with respect to such problems as the squaring of the circle). The number three occurs elsewhere in *The Quest*, as for example in the three fellowships mentioned earlier (of the Apostles, the Round Table, and the Grail), and in the three women mentioned in connection with the legend of the tree (Eve, Solomon's wife, and Perceval's sister).

Indeed, the narrative is precisely structured around groups of three and four: during the preparatory episodes leading up to the shipboard journeys in part two, each of the four major Grail knights has a sequence of four adventures interspersed with three interludes of clerical interpretation of the adventures. Perceval sees Mordrain at the abbey, is unhorsed by twenty men pulling a corpse, kills the serpent carrying the lion cub on the island, and is tempted by the maiden on the ship. These four adventures then receive three glosses: one from Perceval's aunt, and two from the venerable sage in the ship. Similarly, Bors has four adventures -- he fights for the younger versus the elder sister, rescues a maiden from a rape attempt, is tempted by the demonic princess who kills herself, and fights his brother Lionel. And these four adventures are illuminated by three sessions with a hermit -- one regarding confession and communion, one a false interpretation by a demonic monk, and a third true interpretation. Lancelot has two dream vision adventures, is defeated at a tournament, and is unhorsed by the black knight who emerges from the river, four adventures which are glossed by two hermits and one anchoress. Finally, Galahad gets his shield from an abbey, removes the curse on a sepulchre, defeats the seven knights guarding a castle of maidens, and cleans up at a tournament. Since he is already perfect, we do not need the three episodes of instruction provided the other knights. This gives us a very neat structure involving four adventures for each of the four knights, and three glosses for three of them.

After they join together on the Miraculous Ship, the three knights (Perceval, Bors, and Galahad) share three adventures while in the otherworldly realm on the yonder shore of the river, as opposed to the four adventures each experienced in the earthly realm on this side of the river: they defeat the evil sons of Ernol, see the white Hart and the four lions transformed in the Chapel, and fight and heal the Lady with leprosy. Galahad then performs three miracles before arriving at the Grail Castle: he restores Mordrain's sight, cools the boiling bubbles, and quenches the fire in the cemetery. Hence, the narrative divides itself into two parts, and then subdivides into significant groupings of fours and threes. Taken altogether, these various configurations in the novel form an image of psychic wholeness which Jung felt was symbolized by the mandala, which, "though only a symbol of the self as psychic totality, is at the same time a God-image, for the central point, circle, and quaternity are well known symbols for the deity" (*Mandala Symbolism* 40-41). Hence the quest for the Holy Grail exemplifies the hero journey as simultaneously a quest for psychological wholeness, and a quest for God.

Conference of the Birds

One of the most marvelous of all hero journey cycles comes to us from the Persian world: Farid al-din Attar's "Conference of the Birds," which combines elements of Zoroastrianism, Sufism, and, perhaps Christianity (in its Nestorian form), which spread from Ctesiphon, the Persian capital on the banks of the Tigris, northwards and eastwards from the 7th to 11th centuries. By the year 1000 there were 200 to 250 bishoprics scattered all over Persia, one of which was in Nishapur (between the two metropolitan sees, Rai and Merv, southeast of the Caspian), where Faradin Attar lived and wrote the "Conference" (*Times Atlas* 100). His mystical tale is a glorious classic of the hero journey genre.

The call to adventure comes in the form of a story told at the time of a crisis in the bird community, which is searching for a King. A

Hoopoe appears as the "messenger from the world of the invisible," bringing "knowledge of God and of the secrets of creation," "knowledge of many hidden things," and of "many other secrets" (1004). He is one who has made the journey, a companion of Solomon, and a traveler of "an immense space in the time of the deluge" (1005). Later hero journeys, like the *Popol Vuh* of the Maya-Quiché, will also begin the cycle with a bird messenger. The Hoopoe's call is a kind of story, or song, about the King of Birds, known as the Simurgh, who lives "behind the mountains called Kaf," in a place "inaccessible" to human language, knowledge, intelligence, reason, imagination, perception, or comprehension: "no tongue is able to offer his name" (1005). The mountains recall the journeys of Gilgamesh, the sun god Ra, and Inanna, as does the association between the bird soul and the otherworld, but in Persian and Arabic mythologies, the mountains of Kaf are specifically associated with a celestial region beyond the spheres of the planets, just beneath the heavens proper. In the "Chronicles" of Tabari of the 9th century, emerald cities emanating light, like the Heavenly Jerusalem (four square, each side 12 thousand leagues), and inhabited by angelic, naked, sexless beings, were situated in these mountains. Tradition described Kaf as the ninth sphere of the Ptolemaic system, "the mountain which encircles our universe," and as an emerald formation, the reflection of which provides the greenish-azure tint of our celestial vault (Corbin, "Terre-Céleste 157; my trans.). Kaf is the mountain which marks the "limit between two worlds, the visible and the invisible," the material and the spiritual, the sensible and the imaginal (Corbin 158). It is the place to which the soul ascends at death, or to which the mystical pilgrim travels in vision, crossing the eight lower spheres of the heavens, there to meet its celestial archetype (Corbin 157).

The Simurgh is the King on the mountain of Kaf, an incomprehensible deity in essence, but one which, the Hoopoe tells his conference, has left "an impression of the image of his feather" in all souls (1005). This impression was formed during the first manifestation of the Simurgh, when it fell to earth at midnight in China. Everyone made a picture of the feather, and from these various pictures the different ideologies arose which now create such turmoil upon the earth (1005). These points are basic to a comprehension of the mystical traditions of the hero journey: there is an Imago Dei within all souls, an impression of the feather in our hearts; but the theological systems which arise from the flight of the soul, which that feather makes possible, only cause distortions and contention. The idea that God is One, but religions many, was well known to Farid Attar, as was also the idea that God manifests in two ways: with form (saguna Brahman), and without form (nirguna Brahman). The journey to which the Hoopoe summons the birds will lead from one to the other, and is therefore a daunting call to adventure. It is again important to emphasize that the call comes in the form of a story, a fact which links the hero journey to what we now call reader-response criticism, theoretical formulations about what is involved in the reading process. One factor of that process is the initial resistance readers often experience when beginning a book, and this resistance is expressed in the discomfort the birds feel as they internalize the threshold battle characteristic of the hero journey. To begin the journey, the Hoopoe says the birds must abandon "timidity," "self-conceit," and "unbelief," and that they must wash their hands of this life and submit with grace to the beloved. They must then put their feet upon the Way, but many are daunted and resist the call: fearful of the pain, length, and difficulty of the journey, they hesitate, and begin to make excuses for themselves (1006). The hesitation and the resistance they feel, the need to overcome preconceptions, the summoning of powers of endurance: all of these are central problems in any human activity, reading not excluded.

After the internal thresholds are crossed, the separation phase of the journey begins. It proceeds over seven allegorically named valleys to a world from which no traveler is known to have returned. The valleys are called Quest, Love, Understanding, Independence, Detachment, Pure Unity, Astonishment, Poverty, and Nothingness (1006). The seven thresholds recall the seven gateways of Inanna, and Henry Corbin's translation of the name of the last, "Nakedness" instead of "Nothingness," evokes the process of divestiture which, in "The Descent of Inanna," serves as a metaphor for the stripping down of the soul by death as it journeys towards the divine. Persian mystics also used the seven mountain ranges to represent the seven planetary spheres, each presided over by an Archangelic Intelligence which creates the movement of the sphere by inspiring its Celestial Soul with desire (Corbin, *Avicenna* 46-123). As the New Testament says, many are called but few are chosen: most of the peregrinating birds suffer and die along the way, lost and starving in ocean, mountain, and valley, devoured by animals, hunger, thirst, and fatigue, afflictions which rationalize the decay of the body which is the first stage of the soul's journey into the afterlife (as in Virgil). The use of migratory birdflight as a metaphor of the soul's pilgrimage was widespread among Eastern mythologies, often focusing on the wild goose. Among the earliest relics we have are the ivory geese found along the shores of Lake Baikal in Russia (Campbell, *Atlas* 1.1.72). The fact that they are buried in graves suggests mortuary symbolism associated with the soul's migration, a fact confirmed by the Hamsa goose, or wild gander, which among the Hindus signifies the creative principle of Brahma, "the divine essence, which, though embodied in, and abiding with, the individual, yet remains forever free from, and unconcerned with, the events of individual life" (Zimmer, *Myths* 48). The gander manifests the mysteries of the "divine Self in the body of the universe ... through a song," a point which connects it to the rhythms of poesis encoded within the "melody of inhaling and exhaling" (Zimmer, *Myths* 49).

Arabic and Persian developments of ornithological symbolism was rooted in the Koran (81:19): the appellative of Gabriel ("Rasul Karim") is the same Farid Attar uses for the Hoopoe bird ("Noble Messenger"). For the Muslim mystic, Gabriel was the Archangel of Revelation, which the philosophers called the Active Intelligence, the function of which was to impress the intelligible Forms upon the Contemplative Intelligence, in order, as Attar puts it, "to lift up the reason of all souls" (1007). The Arabic word for the King of Birds, to which the Noble Messenger summons the souls, was Anqa, a feminine noun, which connects the Simurgh to Sophia, the Holy Ghost and wisdom of God, depicted as a dove in Judeo-Christian iconography. More generally speaking, the mythical symbolism of birds among the Muslims is rooted in the Koran (27:16), in which Solomon (with whom the Hoopoe bird speaks) is given "understanding of the language of birds." Pre-Islamic Persians spoke of Karshiptar, a marvelous bird gifted with speech who brings the religion of Ahura Mazda in the Bundahishn (19:16), Zoroastrian scripture. The Simurgh is also typically the goal of the heroic epics of Mazdaism, much like the Firebird of Russian folktale (Corbin, *Avicenna* 193-98). These associations link poesis with hermeneusis, since the composition and comprehension of scripture is connected to birdsong: the word for angel and bird is the same in the Koran, and their principle activity is the recitation of "'dhikr,' rhythmic formulas that correspond exactly to Hindu mantras" (Guenon 301). This angelic language of the birds becomes the basis of poesis, the model for all rhythmic language, the purpose of which is to facilitate access to higher states of consciousness. In Islamic tradition, Adam uses the language of birds, for, while in the earthly paradise, he "spoke in verse" (Guenon 301).

Such elevation of consciousness is represented by the hero journey of the birds in Attar's fable. After thirty of the birds arrive within the precincts of the Simurgh, the revelations characteristic of the monomyth occur in the now familiar form of a passing through a series of doorways. First they come to "the door of this Majesty that cannot be described, whose essence is incomprehensible, that Being who is beyond human reason and knowledge" (1007). This first intimation at the doorway is called the "lightning of fulfillment," and it consumes 100 worlds in an instant, but reveals, simultaneously, a 1000 more, complete with suns, moons, and stars, all of which reduce our sun to the size of a "dancing atom of dust" (1007). This astonishing, almost apocalyptic vision of the vastness of our cosmos (a prodigious enormity of time and space, constantly in the process of creation and destruction) annihilates the puny egos of the little birds, who collapse in horror, and sink down in despair at the threshold of the palace (1007). The light-ning recalls the splendid terror of Hildegard von Bingen's vision from Book 1 of the *Scivias*, in which the universe appears as an egg sur-rounded by tempestuous spheres of fire, lightning, hailstones, and thun-der (814). Closer to Farid Attar's homeland, among the mystical tradi-tions of Tibetan Buddhism (bordering Persia to the east), the lightning bolt was called the vajra, and it represented "the irresistible power of truth by which illusions, lies are annihilated; and again, more deeply read, the power of eternity through which phenomenality is annihilated" (Campbell, *Occidental Myth* 481). The blinding bolt shatters the illu-sions of maya, but, in the same instant, discloses the radiance of the di-amond realm, a sight so astounding that the birds "were amazed and ag-itated like a dancing atom of dust" (1007).

Hence, after the lightning bolt, new worlds are revealed. The door suddenly opens, and its guardian, the Chamberlain, tests the determina-tion of the terrified birds by further shattering the illusions of their egos: do they know they are dust in the wind, their very existence of no significance whatsoever to the King of the universe, for whom "Thousands of worlds of creatures are no more than an ant at his gate" (1007)? The allusion to the ants at the gateway is significant here, for it suggests the lesson given Indra (Indian lord of the thunderbolt) one day by a brahmin boy who appears at the gateway of his magnificent Valhalla, and uses a parade of ants (Indras, all) to demonstrate the in-significant brevity of the life a single universe in the vast procession of time (Dimmet and van Buitenen 320-21). The boy's lesson to Indra is essentially the same as the Chamberlain's to the birds: "O King of Gods," says the brahmin boy, "I have known the dreadful dissolution of the universe. I have seen all perish, again and again, at the end of every cycle. At that terrible time, every single atom dissolves into the primal, pure waters of eternity, whence originally all arose. Everything then goes back into the fathomless, wild infinity of the ocean, which is cov-ered with utter darkness and is empty of every sign of animate being. Ah, who will count the universes that have passed away, or the cre-ations that have risen afresh, again and again, from the formless abyss of the vast waters?" (Zimmer, *Myths* 5-6). This vision shows that the hero journey cycle is a cosmic as it is human: all worlds depart from and return to the primordial waters of the abyss, time and time again. Though "petrified with astonishment" by the vast vistas of time the Chamberlain discloses before their terrified eyes -- which are partially blinded by "the lightning of his glory" glimmering through the door-way, they persist, saying they want to burn in his glory like moths in a candle flame (1007), an ancient Persian symbol of the soul's union with god, and Greek symbol of the soul's resurrection from the cocoon of the flesh.

After these tests, performed at the threshold of the palace, the initiation stage of the journey begins: the Chamberlain "opened the door, and as he drew aside a hundred curtains, one after the other, a new world beyond the veil was revealed" (1000). This sequence combines the symbolism of doorways and divestiture, and leads ultimately to the manifestation of the Simurgh, King of the Birds and the "light of lights" (1008), a formula which in mystical traditions refers to the spiritual source of light, of which a thousand suns are merely minor manifestations. At this point the thirty birds are asked to sit down on a "seat of Majesty and Glory" and are "given a writing which they were told to read through, and reading this, and pondering, they were able to understand their state" (1008). This is a marvelous example of the centrality of reading in the monomyth, for the revelation of letters, or of books (in the act of being both written and read) often forms the climactic revelation of the hero journey, which is in some sense an allegory of poesis and hermeneutics. It is important that the birds be ready to read this book, for without that proper condition of readiness, no meaningful response to any text is possible. Reading, under these circumstances, leads to transfiguration and revelation: at peace and detached from the world, the birds witness the miracle of what Helena (in *A Midsummer Night's Dream*) "an union in partition" (3.2.210), the Neoplatonic mystery of multiplicity in unity.

After reading the text, they see the divine presence reflected in each other's faces, and they realize that "they and the Simurgh" are "one and the same being" (1008), just as Jesus recognized that he and the father were one, on the Cross. It is a realization summed up in Hindu aphorism, Tat tvam asi, "Thou art that" (Campbell, *Occidental* 3), a phrase which expresses the equation between the personal and the universal soul (Atman=Brahman). The atonement is a typical fulfillment of the hero journey, alongside apotheosis and the marriage with the goddess (Campbell, *Hero* 245). Atonement and apotheosis merge here, as the birds see the reflection of themselves and the Simurgh in each other's faces, recognizing the union of thirty birds in one, and recognizing that "they themselves were the Simurgh" (1008). Further revelations of the "secret of the mystery of the unity and plurality of beings" begin to be communicated directly by the Simurgh "without the use of tongues," but with the assistance of reflection: the majestic sun into which they gaze and see both "themselves and him" is a "mirror. He who sees himself therein sees his soul his soul and his body, and sees them completely" (1008). The symbolism of a mirror which contains within its reflections the mysteries of the entire universe is one we have seen before, in the Castle of Marvels to which Gawain journeys in Wolfram's *Parzival*. We also find the mirror as a metaphor of the divine at the climax of the hero journey in the hermetic traditions of the Hellenistic era (Scott, *Hermetica* IV 142-44).

The mirror played a special role in Persian mysticism as a metaphor of incarnation: the soul descends into the material world like an image stepping into a mirror. Henry Corbin and Gilles Quispel pursue the metaphor of the mirror in Gnosticism and Islam: the mirror is an image ("ein Gleichnis") of the creation of consciousness. For Corbin and Quispel, the Minotaur that we find imprisoned in the middle of the maze of mirrors is essentially the image ("Urbild") of the Self, which we see reflected in a sequence of infinite regressions ("Abbilder") upon the surfaces of the octagonal "chamber of mirrors" surrounding the center. According to the tradition of Ibn Arabî, each of these reflections represents one of the seven spheres (celestial earths) of

> a world of pure imaginal perception, a world in which God has created for each soul a universe to which it corresponds, so well that when the mystic contemplates this universe, it is himself, his proper soul, which he contemplates upon there. (Corbin, "Morphologie" 62; my trans.)

In each of these seven spheres we see the reflected image of the self that belongs to that particular world. All seven spheres taken together represent Hûrqalyâ, the world of the archetypes, above this visible terrestrial world, into which the Self projects the forms and images of its reflections, just as a body reflects itself incorporeally into a mirror:

> this world of Hûrqualyâ which is the *mundus archetypus*, not at all the world of Platonic Ideas, rather the intermediary world where the spiritual takes body and shape, and where the material spiritualizes itself into autonomous forms and images, which, our authors never tire of repeating, consist completely free of any other matter than their own proper light, the way images consist of the intangible reflections of the mirror. (Corbin, "Morphologie" 66; my trans.)

In the Gnosis of Iranian mystics like Sarkâr Aghâ, therefore, our incarnation into this world is comparable to the manner in which an image enters a mirror. The soul does not actually descend into the world; it simply projects its reflection into the mirror-maze of materiality:

> Speaking of the manner in which souls make their entry
> into the world, it is necessary to understand, he says, the
> way an image of the human person makes his entry as an
> apparition into a mirror .... No more than the incandescent
> mass of the sun "descends" onto this Earth, do the souls
> (that is to say the selves with the bodies of their spiritual
> archetypes, "descend" materially into the world, "in per-
> son" so to speak. ("Morphologie" 70)

Matter is the mirror which reflects the archetypal forms by which the
Self projects itself into the seven worlds of the *mundus archetypus*. The
center of the octagonal chamber of mirrors is "the place of self contemplation" ("Morphologie" 101).

Hence it is themselves which the thirty birds see in the mirror of
the Simurgh. Having seen before as in a glass darkly, now they see Him
face to face, and know even as they are known. Revelation yields to
transformation, and atonement to apocalypse, a word which bears the
dual meaning of annihilation and uncovering. Along with the ultimate
revelation of "the very essence of the true Simurgh," the birds are transfigured: a "new life" begins precisely at the moment of their "annihilation" in the Lord; they "find" what had been lost (themselves), and everything they had done in life is "washed away" during a baptism much
like the one Dante describes on the peak of the purgatorial mountain.
The birds look just as they did before, but they are "completely
changed" within (1008). (I quote to emphasize the parallel between the
Biblical and the Persian languages of the hero journey here). After
100,000 generations pass, in the blink of an eye, the ultimate revelatory
transformation occurs, as the birds surrendered themselves spontaneously to total annihilation; realizing their own nothingness, stripped
of pride, vanity, and self love, they are "cast down in dishonor and
raised in honor" (1009). The language explicitly recalls St. Paul, posing
questions about the direction of influence among the Nestorian
Churches of the east (from Christian to Persian, or Persian to
Christian?). Like Farid Attar, Paul says that which is "sown in dishonor" is "raised in glory"; that which is sown a "natural body" is
"raised a spiritual body"; that which is "sown in corruption is raised in
incorruption"; for "we shall all be changed ... In a moment, in the twinkling of an eye," when the mortal "puts on immortality" (I Cor. 15:
35f.). This is the same twinkling eye that opened after Inanna passed
through her seven gateways, to stand in the presence of her sister
Ereshkigal, and it is the same eye Isis used to revive Osiris from the
land of the dead. It is a psychological eye, the opening of which (the
goal of the hero journey) enforces a radically new vision of the world.

Notes

[1] For pictures and discussion on these various sacred vessels, see John Matthews, *The Grail: Quest for the Eternal* (46-52; 72-73), Joseph Campbell, *The Mythic Image*, and Hans Leisegang on "the Mystery of the Serpent." Adam McLean has charted the relationships between cauldrons, grails, and alchemical vessels in his article on transformation symbolism (64).

[2] On the Neoplatonic interpretation of the Homeric Cave of the Nymphs, see Kathleen Raine's discussion of Porphyry's influence on William Blake.

[3] Heinrich Zimmer writes that "Gawain, too, betrays unmistakable symptoms of a derivation from the remote past. His strength, for example, increases until noon, and then declines. Indeed, out of deference to Sir Gawain, it was for a while a custom at King Arthur's court to schedule all tournaments for the morning hours of the day. Apparently the knight was a solar god, masquerading under medieval armament, doomed, as ever, to expire every twilight and pass into the 'Land of No Return' (*King and the Corpse* 86).

[4] James Hillman applies the phrase specifically to the story of Cupid and Psyche in his book *The Myth of Analysis*, but we use it more generally here since the hero journey as an image of the psychotherapeutic process (which Jung called individuation) takes a large variety of specific forms which are in themselves variations on the basic structure of the monomyth.

[5] See Jung's *Psychology of the Transference* for a thorough discussion of alchemy as a myth both of marriage and of the individuation process.

[6] The magic flute in Mozart's opera of that title is also made from a tree.

[7] Eugene Vinaver, among others, has noted the importance of the interlace in Celtic design and in the plot structure of the romances of the Middle Ages.

[8] From the relief sculpture of the Cathedral at Otranto, to the ivory jewelry boxes of courtly ladies, to the illuminated manuscripts of the *Prose Lancelot*, all of which can be seen in Richard Barber's *The Arthurian Legends*.

[9] For a comprehensive introduction to the problem of the three Marys in the Gospel and apocryphal traditions, and numerous examples of Medieval images of Mary Magdalen and her ointment jar, see Susan Haskins, *Mary Magdalen: Myth and Metaphor*.

[10] See "Joseph Campbell on the Great Goddess" (78-79), and Marija Gimbutas, *The Language of the Goddess* (108-09).

[11] There are of course innumerable examples of these two scenes in the history of Western art: my personal favorites are the Madonna and Pièta figures sculpted by Michaelangelo, which taken together give us an extraordinarily beautiful portrait of the "loving and terrible" Goddess, mother our life *and* of our death, as envisioned by the Renaissance.

[12] See Joseph Campbell's *Creative Mythology*, Chapter 4, where the contribution of these poets to the mysticism of the Arthurian corpus is celebrated.

[13] See the entries on the tree (212-13), the healing spring (197), and the otherworld (166-68) in the *Dictionary of Celtic Myth and Legend* by Miranda

Green or the section on "Sacred Springs" in *The Celtic World* by Barry Cunliffe. On the Bronze Age symbolism of the union of the sun and the moon as an image of the reconciliation of time and eternity see Joseph Campbell's *The Inner Reaches* (70) and *Occidental Mythology* (163-64). Think also of Yeats' "silver apples of the moon [and] golden apples of the sun" in "The Song of Wandering Aengus."

[14] The meeting of the sun and the moon is a frequent motif in Joseph Campbell's work: in *Creative Mythology* he discusses its role in Homer's Odyssey (163-64), and in *The Inner Reaches of Outer Space*, his discussion ranges from Dürer, to Kundalini yoga, to the sand paintings of the Navajo (Chapter 4).

[15] I remember Lord Kenneth Clark's haughty proclamation, during his otherwise wonderful *Civilization* series on PBS, that the romances of Chrétien were "unreadable," a judgement which I have found absolutely absurd.

[16] Robert Graves notes in *The White Goddess* that "in all Celtic languages *trees* means *letters*; that the Druidic colleges were founded in woods or groves; that a great part of the Druidic mysteries was concerned with twigs of various sorts" (38).

[17] See Edinger who provides the Latin version and translation of *The Emerald Tablet of Hermes* (230-32), Marie Loiuse von-Franz on the *tabula smaragdina* (*Alchemy* 113-14), and Jung's interpretation in *Mysterium Coniumctionis* (218-222). It should also be noted that in the symbolism of the *Kabbalah*, which is closely interwined with alchemical symbolism, the inverted tree becomes a symbol of the emanation of the deity in ten stages of manifestation. Several alchemical pictures portray the stages of the opus as branches on a hermetic Tree of Knowledge.

[18] See, for one example among many, *The Hours of Catherine of Cleves* (Plates 47,48, and 99). Plate 99 is particularly interesting in this context, since, as John Plummer writes, "Not one, but three mouths are incorporated into this awesome vision of the castellated gate of Hell."

[19] Many such images of the King as the Sun, and the Queen as the Moon, can be found in the wonderful anthology of alchemical illustrations collected by Fabricius.

[20] See for example the splendid page from the Psalter of Robert de Lindesey from about 1220, reproduced in *The Golden Age of English Manuscript Painting* (45).

[21] I am indebted to William Kibler and Douglas Kelly for my understanding of these terms in Chrétien's original texts, which were among the topics focused on during our NEH Summer Institute on the Arthurian Romance, held at SUNY Binghamton in 1988. See also William Kibler's Introduction to his bilingual translation of Chrétien's *Knight of the Cart*.

[22] See also Ariosto's *Orlando Furioso* for another splendid treatment of the theme.

23 See Mircea Eliade's classic, *Shamanism: Archaic Techniques of Ecstasy*, for astounding images of dismemberment and reconstruction during what we might call the forest madness of the shaman.

24 See my "The Arthurian Underworld of Modernism" for a discussion of Mann's use of the Grail legends in *The Magic Mountain*.

25 In his *Return of the Goddess*, Edward Whitmont has argued that a revival of the feminine in Western Culture began with the Grail romances of the Middle Ages.

26 See for example the White Horse etched into the chalk cliffs of the Vale of Pewsey in England (Branston 41).

27 See Anthony Roche on the Celtic otherworld in *A Portrait of the Artist as a Young Man*, in which Roche cites "the world of Celtic legend where the children of Lir were magically transformed into swans, and the souls of those who died young took flight to the Otherworld in the shape of birds" (328). The *aisling* conventions associating bird women with the land of faery in Gaelic poetry (329). Mozart's *Magic Flute* also employs the imagery of the bird catcher of souls (Papageno) as a servant of the Queen of the Night. She is modelled on Isis as the Death Goddess in Egypt, who is often depicted in sarcophagi as a magnificently winged bird.

28 Even the recent film by John Boorman picks this up, having Arthur say to Lancelot after the last battle with Mordred, "You are what is best in men."

29 See sections two and three of Jung's article "Transformation Symbolism in the Mass" (293-336) in *The Mysteries: Papers from the Eranos Yearbooks*, edited by Joseph Campbell.

30 See for example *The Book of Kells: Reproductions from the Manuscript in Trinity College Dublin*, plates 20, 50, 59, and others, or *The Hours of Catherine of Cleves*, plate 49.

31 See Robert Graves *The White Goddess* on the relation between the alphabet and tree lore in Celtic poetry.

32 See R.S. Loomis for the classic study of the diffusion of Celtic myths via the minstrel traditions of the Middle Ages into the great literary legacy of the Arthurian stories.

33 For one among many possible illustrations of the legend see the lovely plates devoted to the story in *The Hours of Catherine of Cleves* (Plates 81-85).

34 "The first stage is best symbolized by the figure of Eve, which represents purely instinctual and biological relations. The second can be seen in Faust's Helen: She personifies a romantic and aesthetic level that is, however, still characterized by sexual elements. The third is represented, for instance, by the Virgin Mary -- a figure who raises love (*eros*) to the heights of spiritual devotion. The fourth type is symbolized by Sapienta, wisdom transcending even the most holy and the most pure" ((*Man and His Symbols* 185).

35 T.H. White's *The Once and Future King* devotes an exceptionally beautiful sequence of paragraphs to this episode.

Chapter 3:
The Renaissance to the Age of Reason

As a result of the revival of interest in the Classical world, which found particular expression in the Neoplatonic writings of Marsilio Ficino, the hero journey during the Renaissance became a philosophical allegory of the history of the soul: its separation phase involves its departure (*emanatio*) from spiritual realm of pure ideas (the Platonic Forms); its initiation phase (*conversio*) is the descent into the material world, which it animates with its radiance, but in which it feels imprisoned; and its return phase (*remeatio*) takes it back home to the intellectual realm of the spirit.

A similar allegory later became the basis of the alchemical speculations of the late 16th and early 17th centuries, elaborately illustrated in the Rosicrucian manifestos printed in England and Germany.[1] The imagery there involves the hero journey of the King or Queen: the separation is the fall from the throne; the initiation typically involves dismemberment or drowning; and the return is a resurrection in the hermaphroditic form of the phoenix. The alchemical hero journey basically involves the metaphorical transformation of molecular compounds, which are reduced to base elements, and then recombined and refined to produce the philosopher's stone. The opus, or Royal Art, as it was called, is often symbolized by the marriage of the King and Queen, Sol and Luna, whose relations follow the rhythms of comic hero journey: an initial union (boy meets girl) is broken down in the alchemical bath, in which the variations alchemical operations reduce the couple to base elements, from which the couple emerges renewed in the form of the royal hermaphrodite.

Much of this symbolism lies beneath what Northrop Frye called the argument of comedy, which involves an action that "begins in a world represented as the normal world, moves into the green world, goes into a metamorphosis there in which the comic resolution is achieved, and returns to the normal world" (85). This is the basic form taken by the hero journey cycle in works by Spenser, Shakespeare, Milton, Marvell, Racine, Pope, and Fielding. The last two of these enriched the pattern immeasurably through the development of the mock epic, a device which, by encouraging a fusion of realism and myth, laid the foundations for the Modern version of the hero journey in our times.

Spenser's *Faerie Queene*

The Faerie Queene is a labyrinth of interlaced hero journey cycles, a full consideration of which is beyond the scope of this study. Book 1, however, provides a convenient overture to the imagery of the journey in the work as a whole. Like Shakespeare, Milton, and Pope in the centuries to come, Spenser incorporates the motifs of the maze and the underworld into the cycle, in ways which lay the foundations for the psychological rationalization of the myth to be found in the mock epic, and later in the mythical method. *The Faerie Queene* begins with a hero journey, immediately, in the first canto, when the Redcrosse Knight and Una seek shelter from a tempest in the "covert" of "A shadie grove," just off the "plaine" upon which they are riding (1.1.7). The "loftie trees" spread so broad a foliage as to completely block out "heavens light" (1.1.7), casting an ominous darkness over their descent into the forest, which is reinforced by ending the catalogue of trees which follows with "the Cypress funerall" (1.1.8). Along with touches alluding to the descent into the underworld, Spenser anticipates the association between the forest and the labyrinth by evoking its "pathes and alleies wide, / With footing worne, and leading inward farre" (1.1.7). The couple is quickly lost, unable to "finde that path, which first was showne, / But wander too and fro in wayes unknown, / Furthest from end then, when they neerest weene" (1.1.10), which, as Penelope Doob points out, is a characteristic feature of treading a maze: the path leads at first happily right in to the center, but then veers around to the outermost periphery, until the couple is completely lost -- "So many pathes, so many turnings seeme, / That which of them to take, in diverse doubt they been" (1.1.10). The confusion is typically, in the literature of the late Middle Ages, an epistemological confusion, which Spenser associates with the religious controversies of his day. The Redcrosse Knight resolves to take the path "that beaten seemd most bare, / And like to lead the labyrinth about," but it quickly leads them to the "hollow cave / Amidst the thickest woods" in which Spenser's version of the Minotaur dwells (1.1.11). Una, the one true Church, plays the role of Ariadne, guiding her Theseus (the Redcrosse Knight) into and out of the maze of heresies which the forest represents. The dragon dwelling in "the wandering wood, this *Errours den*" (1.1.13) is the Minotaur of theological controversy, derived from Revelation 9: 7-10, the beast of the Apocalypse, which is also the model of Milton's Sin in *Paradise Lost* (woman above, serpent below the waist). It spews out "bookes and papers" with vile lumps of the regurgitated flesh of its children, and it does so faster than the numerous presses cranked out the religious tracts which Spenser is attacking in this episode, by adapting the myth of the heroic descent into the maze, and the slaying of the Minotaur, to the concerns of the English Reformation.

In the scene that follows, Spenser turns from the maze to the underworld to develop his allegory of the hero journey as a search for the one true Church of England. The enemy is of course the Catholic Church, along with its Popes, Bishops, anchorites, and Priests. After slaying the dragon threatening Una, the couple again look for refuge, this time coming upon "A little lowly Hermitage ... Downe in a dale, hard by a forests side" (1.1.34). We begin to suspect the Hermit who dwells within this "holy Chappell edifyde" (1.1.34) when he tells of "Saintes and Popes, and evermore / He strowd an *Ave-Mary* after and before" (1.1.35), terrible words indeed for an Anglican propagandist. And when, after "drouping Night" comes, along with the "Sweet slombring deaw" of Morpheus, the Hermit retires into his study to consult "His Magick bookes and artes of sundry kindes" in order to seek "out mighty charmes, to trouble sleepy mindes," we know for certain that we are dealing with a popish version of the Renaissance Magus, much feared by Spenser and Marlowe as a master of the black arts of necromancy, though celebrated by Shakespeare, in *The Tempest*, as a benign master of providential magic (1.1.36).[2] His name is Archimago, and he uses "wordes most horrible," "verses," and "spelles like terrible" to summon Hecate, Goddess of the underworld and of witchcraft (1.1.37).

The version of the descent to the underworld which follows is very important for the study of the hero journey in literature, since it develops a psychology of myth (and of dreams) far in advance of, and yet in many ways similar too, the work of Pope, and later of Freud. Archimago uses his incantatory verses to "call by name / Great *Gorgon*, Prince of darknesse and dead night, / At which *Cocytus* quakes, and *Styx* is put to flight" (1.1.37), allusions which firmly establish the realm of dream with the imagery of the classical underworld (some 400 years before Freud's *Traumdeutung* or James Hillman's *The Dream and the Underworld*). Archimago proceeds to summon two spirits "out of deepe darknesse dred," one of which he will use to shape a pleasing female incubus; and the other he sends down to the house of Morpheus, in order to "forge true-seeming lyes" in the form of a dream (1.1.38). Spenser relies heavily upon the kind of water and threshold imagery which we have frequently seen in our history of the heroic descent into Hades: the spirit speeds downwards "through the world of waters wide and deepe" to the very "bowels of the earth full steepe," where

Morpheus has pitched his palace (1.1.39). Tethys, wife of Oceanus, "Doth ever wash" the "wet bed" in which Morpheus lies, steeped in the "silver deaw" of Cynthia, goddess of the Moon (1.1.39). "A trickling streame" and "ever drizzling raine" drowns out all "other noyse," leaving Morpheus to sleep in peace (1.1.41). As we will see, Milton will also conflate the underworld with the primordial waters of the abyss -- the Chaos of classical, and the Tehom of biblical scriptures -- in his poem "Comus." But we have already encountered nearly as many instances of passages by water in our overview of the hero journey as we have instances of threshold imagery, which constitutes a major motif in Spenser's version of the underworld.

On the way down, Archimago's spirit servant comes upon the house of Morpheus, "Whose double gates, he findeth locked fast, / The one faire fram'd of burnisht Yvory, / The other all with silver overcast; / And wakeful dogges before them farre do lye" (1.1.40). The classical sources of this threshold imagery, and of its association with the dream and the underworld, is, of course, Homer's *Odyssey* (19.528-38) and Virgil's *Aeneid* (6.1191-99). Archimago's spirit passes into the underworld, like so many spirits before, through a pair of doorways, "returning by the Yvorie dore" with a "diverse dreame out of his prison darke" (1.1.44), which Spenser refers to as a "fit false dreame, that can delude the sleepers" (1.1.43). The ivory door is the door through which false or illusory dreams pass, the one Virgil chooses for Aeneas to return by with his false dream of Empire. In Spenser, the dream coming through the gates of this underworld is remarkably Freudian: while the one spirit has been retrieving the false dream from the house of Morpheus, Archimago

> all this while with charmes and hidden artes,
> Had made a Lady of that other Spright,
> And fram'd of liquid ayre her tender partes
> So lively, and so like in all mens sight,
> That weaker sence it could have ravisht quight. (1.1.45)

She is surely a creature of delight, fashioned by the repressed desires of the Redcrosse Knight, who now dreams "of loves and lustfull play, / That nigh his manly heart did melt away, / Bathèd in wanton blis and wicked joy" (1.1.47). It seems to him as if "Faire Venus" had stepped into his bed, a "loose Leman to vile service bound" (1.1.48), whose "uncouth sight" and "shameless guise" (1.1.50) inspire the Knight with a "great passion of unwonted lust" (1.1.49). She disturbs his sleep with a "troublous dreame" of "bowres, and beds, and Ladies deare delight" (1.1.55).

All of this constitutes a psychologization of the descent to the underworld which rationalizes the myth and looks forward to *The Rape of the Lock*, and its "Cave of Spleen," inhabited by various female maladies. This process lays the foundations for the transformation of the hero journey in the literature of the 18th century, particularly in the form of the mock epics of Pope and Fielding. But the use of the heroic descent to evoke the psychological and spiritual problems of the human unconscious, during its quest for meaning, also looks farther forward, to Freud and Jung, and to Lawrence and Joyce.

Shakespeare's *A Midsummer Night's Dream*

Shakespeare's *A Midsummer Night's Dream* circumscribes a classical hero journey cycle: the lovers and the rude mechanicals leave Athens, meander through the maze of the forest, and finally return to the city at the end of the play. For the lovers, the journey is a metaphor for the mysteries of marriage and the human heart, while for the working men preparing their play, especially for Bottom, the journey becomes a metaphor for the mysteries of creativity and the powers of the imagination. The forest represents more than the Freudian id, a realm of repressed sexuality and aggression where human beings become bestial; it is also a place of transformation, in which the powers of the imagination replace the dominion of reason. If the city is ruled by the patriarchy of father and King, the woods are permeated by the authority of the matriarchal Queen of the Faeries, Titania. In Shakespeare's hands, the great themes of transformation and revelation associated with the hero journey are all brought to bear upon an emerging philosophy of the imagination, so that the monomyth becomes a metaphor of poesis.

As such, the play establishes an elaborate vocabulary of the imagination which keeps our attention focused on the allegory of poesis which lies at the center of the journey. The call to adventure is typical of the comic tradition: an old father and rigid society blocking the marriage plans of the children, who escape into the woods to sort out difficulties they didn't even know they had, finally to return home, reconciled to each other and to the society which had forced them to flee. During the course of their journey from city to woods and back to city, the great themes of transformation, the reconciliation of opposites, and the powerful duplicities of the imagination emerge as Shakespeare's central concerns.

As in *Sir Gawain and the Green Knight*, numerous oppositions work their way into the action and language of the play, eventually to be comically reconciled at the climax of the hero journey when the lovers return for marriage festivities in Athens. Theseus begins by contrasting the "merriments" of the marriage rites, to be awakened by the "pert and nimble spirit of mirth," with its "pale companion," the spirit of "melancholy," associated with "funerals" (1.1.12-14). He then bids Hermia choose either the chastity of the nun, "For aye to be in shady cloister mewed, / To live a barren sister all your life, / Chanting faint hymns to the cold fruitless moon," or the "earthlier" happiness of "the rose distilled" (1.1. 70-77). The dialectical oppositions between love and hate, animal and human, comedy and tragedy then create havoc during the forest journey, and are compounded by the oppositions between the rude mechanicals and the Athenian aristocrats, and between the fairy kingdom and the world of humanity. The play within the play, performed by Peter Quince and his crew, makes extensive comic use of the grammatical figure associated with the reconciliation of opposites, the oxymoron: we hear of Theseus wonder at the Quince's description of his play as "'tragical mirth' / Merry and tragical? Tedious and brief?" and of his need to find the "concord of this discord" (5.1.55-60). The play itself (Pyramus and Thisbe), of course, combines farcical comedy and tragedy, and its language constantly lapses into such oxymoronic disfigurations as the "sunny beams" of the "Sweet moon" (5.1.264), a figure which recalls Hermia's earlier fantasy of the moon boring through the center of the earth to "displease / Her brother's noontide with the Antipodes" (3.2.55). But the ultimate goal is of a reconciliation between opposites, which is as characteristic of the hero journey -- and of alchemy, in which the mysterious union of Sol and Luna signifies the achievement of the philosopher's stone -- as it is of the genre of marriage comedy:[3] Theseus speaks of the baying of the hounds on the May Day morning as a "musical discord" (4.1.117), and Helena refers to her relationship with Hermia as a "union in partition" (3.2.210). Both phrases epitomize the conjunction of opposites which constitutes the climax of the hero journey. All of these oppositions tend constantly to reverse themselves, in a kind of enantiodromia, which involves the rapid revolution between extremes, as one quality (love, humanity, comedy, life) turns into its opposite (hate, bestiality, tragedy, death) in the blink of an eye.

Shakespeare uses a variety of synonyms to elaborate upon the changes from one extreme to another, and their ultimate reconciliation, wrought by the hero journey: words such as "translated" (1.1.191; 3.1.11; 3.2.32), "transpose" (1.1.233), "changeling" (2.1.23), "change" (2.1.112; 2.2.120), "changed" (2.1.230; 3.1.109), "transformed" (4.1.63), and "transfigured" (5.1.24). One of the principle transformations is of man or woman into beast, and it is important here to remember that the transformation of man into beast is one of the conventional powers of the Great Goddesses of the hero journey as far back as Ishtar in *Gilgamesh*, Circe in the *Odyssey*, and Isis in the *Metamorphoses* of Apuleius (which Shakespeare knew), in which Lucius is turned into a donkey. Bottom, of course, becomes a beloved ass, in Titania's domain; Helena becomes a fawning "spaniel" in the forest, and urges Demetrius to use her as he would his "dog" (2.1.210), while later in the play Hermia calls Demetrius a "dog" and a "cur" (3.2.65); the "crawling serpent" Hermia dreams of at her breast is surely the fickle Lysander (2.2.152), although Lysander himself later calls her both a "cat" and a clinging "serpent" (3.3.260-61), and Hermia compares Demetrius to an "adder" (3.2.73); and, finally, in a forest wildly populated by a variety of species, Helena sees Hermia as a conniving "vixen," a female fox (3.2.324).

While these transformations suggest the violent oscillations between love and hate, which reduce the lovers to animals in the forest, the transformations can also proceed in more subtle directions. A principle theme of the hero journey is the transfiguration of matter into spirit: Demeter puts the baby boy Demoophon into the fire to make him immortal in the Homeric Hymn, just as Isis puts the baby Syrian prince she is hired to nurse in Byblos into the fire each night, while she flits around the erica tree in which Osiris lies entombed. These are the essential images of the mystery rites of the Ancient Mediterranean, which typically evoke that profound transformation of consciousness which marks the passage from the mortal to the spiritual realm. Hence it is curious to find those traditional powers of the Great Goddesses of the mystery rites (hero journeys in themselves) ascribed to Titania, who promises Bottom that she will "purge thy mortal grossness so / That thou shalt like an airy spirit go" (3.1.151-52). With Bottom, she has her work cut out for her, but one can argue generally that all of the lovers in the woods experience a parallel transformation, one which takes them out of the rational, materialistic realm of Athens, into the bewildering labyrinth of the imaginal forest. Theirs is a journey from reason into the dominion of dreams.

Shakespeare uses a diverse vocabulary to evoke those oneiric powers of the imagination activated by the hero journey into the woods: "fantasy" (1.1.32), "fantasies" (2.1.258), "fancies" (1.1.118, 155), "fancy" (4.1.162), "fancy's images" (5.1.25), "dream" (1.1.144, 154; 2.2.153; 3.2.371; 4.1.193, 199, 210-215; 5.1.408); "vision" (3.2.371; 4.1.74, 205; 5.1.406), and, finally, "imagination" itself (5.1.18, 209, 210). The recurrence and variety of these terms suggests that one of the principle concerns of the play is a kind of philosophy of the imagination, one which lays the foundation for the Romantic speculations of Coleridge. For the hero journey, as an image of poesis, catalyzes an intensely activated imagination, producing, yes, delusions and trivial fantasies, but also the more profound visions of a spiritual realm which permeates and transcends the mortal realm of daily rationality. For that reason, Bottom reverts to the language of the New Testament when reflecting upon his dream vision of Titania and her domain: when he says

"The eye of man hath not heard, the ear of man hath not seen, man's hand is not able to taste, his tongue to conceive, nor his heart to report what my dream was!" (4.1.208-211), he paraphrases St. Paul, who, in 1 Corinthians 2:9 uses such language to evoke a spiritual reality, which he refers to variously as "the wisdom of God in a mystery, even the hidden wisdom" (2:7); as "the deep things of God" (2:10); and as the "Spirit of God" (2:11), which speaks not the natural language of "man's wisdom," but in the language of the "Holy Ghost ... comparing spiritual things with spiritual" (2:13). It is a realm which transcends the senses, like the imagination. Hence, when Hippolyta comes to recognize the "constancy" within the changes wrought upon the lovers by their dream visions in the forest, she says their minds have been "transfigured" (5.1.24), a word with immediate biblical overtones for the Elizabethan audience, evoking, as it does, the Transfiguration of Jesus on the mountain, when, as he prays, "the fashion of his countenance was altered, and his raiment was white and glistening" (Luke 9:29).

Such evocative language to describe the activation of the imaginal powers during the hero journey suggests its conventional images of revelation and transformation. It is a revelation not just of the bestiality of men and women in love, but also of the spiritual dimension which sustains their relationships, and which permeates the natural world. For there is both a Minotaur and a Goddess at the center of the maze through which Bottom and the lovers travel. The maze, of course, is an archetypal image of the world of the hero journey, and it is frequently alluded to in *A Midsummer Night's Dream*: in her famous "forgeries of jealousy" speech, Titania mentions the "quaint mazes in the wanton green," and notes that the rapidly changing seasons have produced a "mazèd world" (2.1.99, 113); and Hermia twice declares herself "amazèd" by the fickle affections of friends and lovers in the forest (3.2.220, 345). It may be appropriate, therefore, that Hermia calls Helena a "painted maypole" (3.2.296), for, like the "nine men's morris" to which Titania alludes (2.1.98) there is an ancient connection between the May Day dances and the maze: the "winding and unwinding of the ribbons by which the dancers are connected to the Maypole" suggests the treading of a maze (Coomaraswamy 30), and, in the Morris dances, "the dancers are usually accompanied by a hobby horse, half human, half animal, and possibly a representation of the Minotaur" (Bord 61). Coming, then to the center of the maze, constitutes the climax of the hero journey, and we may find there either the Minotaur of sexual aggression (half animal, half human), or the Maypole, a symbol of renewal, an axis mundi which connects the earth and the heavens, "mortal grossness" and "airy" spirits.

Folk Ballads

Shakespeare and Spenser were both much influenced by various popular forms of the hero journey associated with the folk tradition, about which we know something from the study of ballads, lyrics, and carols. These folk versions of the journey were familiar to Chaucer and to Milton as well, in both of whose works we find variations of the fundamental story of the hero journey into the realm of faerie. One such ballad version is to be found in the tale of "Thomas the Rhymer," based on the legend of a 13th century poet who spent seven years in elfland, where the Faerie Queene granted him powers intimately relevant to poesis: prophecy and true speaking. Versions of the story were published as the "Ballad of True Thomas," printed in "chapbook form from the 16th to the 19th centuries" (Briggs 394). In the ballad, Thomas sees a gay lady riding towards him over the "fernie brae." She is dressed like the Green Knight in "grass-green silk," and fifty nine silver bells hang from her horse's mane (shades of Yeats' nine and fifty swans). Thomas mistakes her for the "mighty Queen of Heaven," until she identifies herself as the "queen of fair Elfland" (Friedman 39). The silver bells that dangle from the mane associate her with the moon in alchemical tradition; her brilliant green mantel and skirt link her to the Celtic otherworld; and her "milk-white steed" suggest the sacred mares of Irish and British folklore. The white mares were sacred to the Great Goddesses of the Celtic world, like the Irish Goddess Macha (Stone 53), the Romano-Celtic Epona (Green 122), or the Welsh Rhiannon, who appears in the *Mabinogion* riding a white horse (Green 176). Rhiannon, like the Queen of Elfland in the ballad, is associated with the underworld, and with poesis: her three magic birds have the power to awake the dead with their singing (Green 176). The marvelous white horse etched into the hillside of Uffington may also link the Faerie Queene and her hollow hills to the mythology of the mare and the Goddess (Cunliffe 50). The cult of the divine mare persisted all the way up until the 12th century, when "Giraldus Cambrensis described the coronation of a king of Ulster, involving the king's sexual union with a white mare, which was afterward sacrificed and sacramentally eaten" (Walker, *Dictionary* 383).

In other versions of the story, and in other ballads, the animal which carries the hero to the otherworld is the deer. In a legend recorded later by Sir Walter Scott, True Thomas follows a hind and a doe off into the forest, at the end of his life, and he is never seen again (Briggs 395). The deer appears again in association with the hero journey to the otherworld in the marvelous ballad known as "The Three Ravens," first published in Ravencroft's *Melismata* in 1611, and then again in Scott's *Minstrelsy* of 1803 (Friedman 23). In the ballad, three ravens tell of a dead knight lying in green field, attended by hounds, hawks, and a "a

fallow doe, / As great with yong as she might goe" (Friedman 24). The
doe is later called the knight's "leman," or lover, and she lifts up his
head, kisses his bloody wounds, gets him up onto her back, and carries
him off to an "earthen lake," where she buries him before dying herself
(Friedman 24). The symbolism here links the deer with both death and
rebirth (since it is pregnant), with the symbolism of sacred springs, so
precious to the Celts (the "earthen lake"), and with the journey to the
otherworld. As Michael Dames has shown, the deer was long sacred to
the Celtic peoples of pagan England; since it sheds its antlers in the
spring, it became a symbol of rebirth. The doe of the red deer family
was called a "hind," an animal naturally associated with the Goddess,
who frequently led men into mystic adventures, nurtured them in
infancy, or carried them off to the underworld in the form of a White
Hind (Walker, *Dictionary* 377). We have also already seen a white stag
associated with Jesus in Arthurian *Quest of the Holy Grail*.

In the ballad, Thomas the Rhymer undertakes his journey to serve
the Elfland Queen for seven years, riding off on her milk-white steed for
forty days and forty nights, through a land with neither sun nor moon.
The couple reaches a threshold typical of the hero journey, here rivers of
red blood, which lead, however, to a "garden green" (Friedman 40), reminiscent of Garden of Siduri Gilgamesh comes to after his long journey
through the twelve leagues of darkness. And as in the Homeric Hymn
to Demeter, there is forbidden fruit in this otherworld, fruit which the
Queen tells Thomas not to eat, because all "the plagues that are in hell
/ Light on the fruit of this countrie" (Friedman 40). She serves him instead two items frequently found in the sacrificial meals of the hero
journey: bread and wine! After the meal, Thomas lies his head upon the
Queen's knee, and the revelation stage of the journey begins: she shows
him the roads of righteousness and wickedness, between which passes
the road to Elfland. The imagery of the crossroads in the underworld has
distinctly Hermetic overtones, since Hermes was guide of souls to the
underworld, as well as guide of travelers, in honor of whom piles of
stones were erected at crossroads. Aeneas comes also to a crossroads
separating the Elysian fields from Tartarus. Also familiar is the clothing symbolism which marks the transformation wrought upon Thomas
by the revelation of the three roads, and by his seven years in Elfland.
He is given "a coat of the even cloth, / And a pair of shoes of velvet
green" (Friedman 41). In one version of the ballad, Thomas is also
given the gift of true speaking, associating poetry and prophecy, so that
his journey becomes a parable of poesis.

Another ballad which records a hero's journey to the otherworld is
known as "Tam Lin," published in James Johnson's *Scots Musical
Museum* at the end of the 18th century (Friedman 42). The ballad involves the symbolism of investiture and the white horse, as a young

lady carefull kilts her "green kirtle / A little aboon her knee" to ride off
the Caterhaugh. There she meets Tam Lin at the well, who appears after
she plucks two of his roses. Magical events typically occur at wells,
pools, and springs in Celtic myth and romance (such as the magical
spring in Chrétien's "Yvain"). Like the fountain, such locales were sacred symbols of the source of life in Celtic mysticism, as we know
from such artifacts as the relief sculpture of the Goddess Coventina,
found by a well at Carrowburgh on Hadrian's Wall (Cunliffe 89). These
images were typically of female nymphs, like the three water goddesses
from the Roman fort of High Rochester in Northumberland (Green
223). This may help explain the girl's curt reply to Tam Lin in the ballad: when he chastizes her for plucking the rose and breaking the wand
by the well in Carterhaugh, she says that "Carterhaugh, it is my ain, /
My daddie gave it me; / I'll come and gang by Carterhaugh, / And ask
nae leave at thee" (Friedman 43). The site was apparently hers originally. The plucking of the rose in this scene recalls Persephone's narcissus in the fields of Nyssa, where she was abducted by Hades, and it
also looks forward to the marvelous scene in Cocteau's film, *Beauty and
the Beast.*

When the green-kirtled lass in "Tam Lin" returns home from
Carterhaugh, she is apparently pregnant, and another image familiar to
us from our study of the iconography of the Goddess in the hero journey surfaces. Janet finds "Four and tweny ladies fair" playing at the ball
and playing at the chess when she returns home. She herself is said to
be the "flower among them all" (Friedman 43). One thinks here of
Persephone picking poppies with twenty four nymphs in the fields of
Nyssa; of the Grail Maiden surrounded by twenty four virgins in
Wolfram's Castle of the Fisher King; or of the twenty four dancing
nymphs Gawain chances upon in the middle of the forest in Chaucer's
"Wife of Bath's Tale." In all three of these tales, the twenty four
nymphs emanate from the Great Goddess standing amidst them: She is
the source of the twelve hours of the day on the one hand, and of the
twelve hours of the night on the other. Chaucer's marvelous tale, in
fact, follows the pattern of the hero journey exactly, and it probably had
a source in the Breton lays of the Middle Ages. Gawain begins and ends
his journey in Camelot, and experiences the revelation of the Goddess
surrounded by twenty four faeries in the middle of the forest.

In the ballad, Janet invests herself in her green kirtle for a third and
final time, when she rides back to Carterhaugh to pluck the roses by the
well once again. When she does, Tam Lin appears and tells his story:
he had fallen off a horse while hunting, when the Queen of Faeries
caught him, and carried him off "In yon green hill to dwell" (45). The
images associate the horse, the mountain, the Goddess, and the underworld as icons of the hero journey, the return phase of which comes for

Tam Lin at the end of seven years, on Halloween night and the following Hallowday. These are now our All Soul's and All Saints day, which
the French called "Toussaint," a time when the borderline between this
world and the other breaks down, and souls journey mysteriously back
and forth. On that night, Tam Lin tells Janet, the "fairy folk will ride"
to Miles Cross, where she will see him riding on a "milk-white steed"
(45). If she pulls him off the horse, and holds him in his arms, while
he turns into an "esk and adder," a lion and a bear, and finally into a
"burning gleed," she will break the spell binding him to the otherworld,
and win his love. The last step in the redemption involves throwing the
burning coal into well water, and then clothing the naked Tam Lin with
a "green mantle" (46). Divestiture and reinvestment merge here with the
symbolism of the magic flight, the crossoads, and the well, which suggests the alchemical mysteries of the smith at the forge (the ore is
transformed into Tam Lin). The entire sequence is connected to the
theme of poesis by the fact that the bridles on the fairy horses ring with
an unearthly music. The uncanny music of the procession is a characteristic element of the fairy's ride, as in this marvelous passage describing
an old woman's encounter with the little people at the beginning of the
19th century: "They rade on braw wee whyte naigs, wi' unco lang
swooping tails, an' manes hung wi' whustles that the win' played on.
This, an' their tongues when they sang, was like the soun' of a far awa
Psalm" (Briggs 158).

Paintings and Engravings

As we have seen from our earlier discussions of the journeys of
Gilgamesh, Inanna, Joseph, The Prodigal Son, Sir Orfeo, and Gawain,
the arming and divestiture of the hero constitutes a key motif in the imagery of the monomyth. During the Renaissance, the distinction between the earthly and spiritual realms, stemming from "two famous
statues of Venus, one draped, the other nude" by Praxiteles (Panofsky
153), was central to Neoplatonic interpretations of the "Twin Venuses"
of the *Symposium*, one celestial (*Aphrodite Urania*) and the other terrestrial (*Aphrodite Pandemos*) (Wind 138). In Ficino and Pico della
Mirandola, both were celebrated as two noble aspects of love, divine and
human (*Amore celeste e umano*) (Wind 139). As Erwin Panofsky
points out, this distinction humanized the moralistic distinction made
during the Middle Ages between Nature (represented by the naked Eve);
and Reason or Grace (represented by the fully clothed Virgin Mary)
(154). Such considerations inform Neoplatonic interpretations of two of
the greatest paintings of the Renaissance: Titian's so-called "Sacred and
Profane Love" of 1515, and Botticelli's "Birth of Venus" of 1480. In
Titian's masterpiece, the Twin Venuses, one naked and one clothed,

who sit on opposite ends of a sepulchre turned into a well, represent a gentle dialectic between "eternal and temporal values," between the "celestial and 'terrestrial'," and between "*Amore celeste e umano*" (Panofsky 151-153; Wind 148). Hence, the Church prominently visible in the less densely foliated landscape behind the naked Venus refers to the heavenly flame of spiritual love, represented by the burning jar of oil uplifted in her left hand, while the Castle in the dense background behind the clothed Venus may refer to the earthly values of courtly splendor, represented by the "vessel full of gold and gems" which she holds on the rim of the well (Panofsky 151). In Botticelli's "Birth of Venus," we see the naked Goddess arriving on the shore line, blown hither across the sea by the passionate wind of two embracing Zephyrs. The Hour of Spring greets her with a glorious floral robe which, however lovely, represents her descent from the "pure celestial beauty" of her naked self at sea, into the clothed form of her earthly splendor as "*Venere vulgare* or *Aphrodite Pandemos*" (Wind 138).

Other standard motifs of the hero journey were widely elaborated during the Renaissance, later during the Rosicrucian Enlightenment, and finally in England among the Cambridge Platonists, who influenced the work of Milton, Marvell, and Pope. One finds, for example, a version of the journey (complete with descent, exile, and return) in Botticelli's wonderful masterpiece "Primavera," which hangs in the Uffizi Gallery in Florence. As Edgar Wind points out, the "entire picture seems to spell out the three phases of the Neoplatonic dialectic: *emanatio-conversio-remeatio*; that is, 'procession' in the descent from Zephyr to Flora, 'conversion' in the dance of the Graces, and 'reascent' in the figure of Mercury" (125). The idea that "an uninterrupted current of supernatural energy flows from above to below and reverts from below to above, thus forming a *circuitus spiritualis*" (Panofsky 132) was, as we have seen, the Neoplatonic interpretation of the hero journey of the soul as far back as the early commentaries on Homer by Plotinus, Proclus, Porphyry, and Eustathius (Pépin 5-9). Like Marvell's poem, "The Garden," the painting is set in an orchard of fruit trees. The Goddess Venus occupies the direct center of the composition, framed by Zephyr on the right border and Mercury on the left. Zephyr represents the force of emanation, by which the spirit is propelled into the material world, and forced out of the heaven of the intellect, which hovers above the labyrinth of fruit trees in the orchard. Mercury, on the left border, represents the process by which the spirit returns from the material to the intellectual world. He stands with left hand on hip and right hand, holding his caduceus, pointed upward into the fruit-laden boughs. As Wind points out, it is "the hidden light of intellectual beauty (*intellectualis pulchritudinis lumen*) to which Mercury raises his eyes and lifts his magic wand" (124), fulfilling the task, set for him by Ficino, of calling "the mind back to heavenly things through the power of reason" (122).

The painting, therefore, is framed on either side by the separation and return phases of the hero journey of the spirit, while the center of the composition is devoted to its initiatory incarnation in the material world. For Neoplatonists like Pico della Mirandola, the world was ambiguous: Pico called "the realm of matter *Il mondo sotterraneo*," a kind of prison where the pure forms or ideas are 'drowned,' 'submerged,' 'perturbed' and 'disfigured beyond recognition' (Panofsky 134-35). However, being infused by the "'presence of the spiritual in the material,'" the sublunary world could not be equated with hell (Panofsky 134). Rather, the figures of terrestrial beauty serve to recall to the mind the pure forms of the supercelestial realm, and, so it would seem, this is exactly the function of Venus, standing in the center of Botticelli's "Primavera," with Zephyr, Chloris, and Flora on one side of her, and the three graces on the other. She represents the earthly and the divine forms of love in one figure, and thus constitutes the central revelation of the heroic descent of the spirit pictured in the painting as a whole. Like Mercury, she stands gracefully with her right hand pointing upwards into a little clearing in the maze of the orchard, and her left hand resting gently on her thigh, a gesture frequently to be found in the images of the Goddesses of art history: the right upward pointed hand signifies transfiguration, the return of the soul to its spiritual home, initiated by the loving contemplation of earthly beauty; her left had, resting on the thigh, represents incarnation, the descent of the soul into the womb of Anima Mundi. The goal, Botticelli seems to suggest, is to achieve balance between the two, in full recognition of the radiance of the spiritual in the forms of earthly life.

At the beginning of the 17th century, there was a revival of the philosophies of the Renaissance, during the Rosicrucian Enlightenment, when the Neoplatonic, Gnostic, and Alchemical worlds came together to create a marvelously syncretic skeleton key to world mythology and religion.[4] Like Botticelli, the beautifully illustrated manuscripts produced at this time (to provide visual emblems of the hermetic secrets) often used the metaphor of the hero journey as a principle of aesthetic composition. The *Rosarium Philosophorum*, from Frankfort in 1550, for example, treads the path of an entire hero journey cycle.[5] The first plate shows the alchemical version of the archetype of the fountain, always symbolic of the source of life in the monomyth. In place of what would be the four rivers of Paradise radiating out from the Garden of Eden in the Bible, we have four six pointed stars at each corner to symbolize the four elements, with a fifth star, in the center above the fountain (between the sun and the moon), to represent the quintessence. In the second plate, the King stands on the sun, the Queen on the moon, and a crested dove descends from the star of the quintessence, as Sol and Luna join left hands, while holding interlacing branches (of the tree of life) in their right hands. The hero journey proper begins in figure 3, which shows Sol and Luna stripped down, still standing on sun and moon: the divestiture motif marks the initiation of the descent, as we know from our studies of Inanna, Joseph, Gawain, Orfeo, Yvain, and many others. In alchemical terms, the divestiture marks the first breakdown of the molecular compound, as it undergoes the various operations in the vas hermeticum. In the *Rosarium*, the hermetic vessel takes the form first of a seven-sided bath, into which the couple sits in figure 4, and then later as a bath on top of a coffin (both representing the alchemical crucible). Figure 5 depicts the conjunction of Sol and Luna, who are shown joined in coitus on the surface of a flowing river in a mountainous landscape. In the numerous hero journey cycles we have examined, the crossing of the river, or the passageway into the mountains, represent the descent into the underworld. Hence, after the lovers sprout wings on what is now the small surface of a pond in figure 5a, the next plate (fig. 6) shows them as a hermaphrodite floating dead on the waters of putrefaction in Hades: "Hier liegen König und Königin tod / Die sele scheydt sich mit großer not" (Here lie King and Queen dead / The soul in great distress is fled). The waters float now on top of a quadrangular sarcophagus, in which the couple is broken down into the four elements ("Hier teylen sich die vier element"), while the soul ascends into the clouds of heaven, in figure 7. These two plates represent the nadir of the marital hero journey, for, in Jung's view, the entire sequence represents not only the journey of individuation and the processes of psychoanalysis, but also the rigorous ordeals of marriage (both follow the rhythms of the descent into hell). After the ego is broken down into the base elements of the repressed complexes of the unconscious, the reconstruction begins, along new lines, as the Self begins to emerge, purified by the trials of the journey. These purifications proceed through the various alchemical operations (all of which, as Jung, Edinger, and von-Franz show, have psychic equivalents) in figures 6-9: from putrefaction, to ablutions of heavenly dew ("der Taum von Himmel"), to the sublimation effected by the return of the soul (which itself undergoes a complete cycle of separation, ascent, and return in the sequence).

Figure 10 marks the new birth of the hermaphroditic couple, who emerge from the coffin to stand together upon a crescent moon, having completed the cycle of their descent. Several archetypal symbols of the hero journey are included in this plate: the couple holds a crested serpent in the left hand, and a cup with three crested serpents emerging in their right. The serpent, in this context, as in the *Epic of Gilgamesh*, represents renewal, the power to shed skins; while the cup represents the Grail, or Chalice, symbol of the highest spiritual fulfillment of the monomyth. Beneath the base of the cup we see the alchemical or cabalistic tree of life and knowledge, with seven branches and thirteen happy faces, while beneath the serpent in the left hand sits a little bird, symbol of the soul's flight coming to rest. The same scene is magnificently illustrated in a famous picture from the *Aurora Consurgens* in Zürich (De Rola Plate 4), which shows the hermaphroditic couple standing in a pile of putrid eagles (representing the morbid memory of their passage through Hades), with a marvelous Phoenix spreading its wings protectively behind them (representing the new life of immortality emerging from the grave of the crucible).

One of the finest of the hermetic manuscripts -- the *Atalanta Fugiens*, published in Frankfort by Michael Maier in 1617 -- condenses the alchemical hero journey cycle to one fine engraving (Emblem XXIV). The journey begins in the city in the left background of the engraving, which represents the domestic concerns of daily life. A bridge diagonally drawn from the mid-background to the left border of the print suggests that separation from the daily realities of city life characteristic of the first stage of the hero journey. It is perhaps via this bridge that the King lying unconscious, being eaten by a wolf, in the foreground, has crossed over to the yonder shore of the mysteries. Or he may have come over in the little sailboat which we see right in the middle of the picture, bow pointing to the right midground of the yonder shore, where the King is seen emerging from a bonfire burning the wolf. Both means of crossing the river are archetypal, familiar to us from the journeys of Gilgamesh, Odysseus, Dante, Lancelot and Gawain, and many others to come. Since the King emerging from the bonfire in the right midground is moving diagonally back toward the boat docked on the shore, and hence towards the city in the background, we have the entire cycle of the hero journey (city, to yonder shore, to city) implied, as the basis of the composition as a whole.

The mysteries of the initiation stage occupy the entire foreground of the print, where the King lies prone on a slight diagonal, head to left foreground, feet pointing back to the right midground's bonfire. The three diagonals (bridge, dead King, resurrected King) function to delimit the three stages of the journey (separation, initiation, and return). The central mystery of the initiation, typical of the monomyth, has to do with death and rebirth, conceived here in terms appropriate to the alchemical operations of solutio, calcinatio, and circulatio.[6] The wolf devouring the King may represent some corrosive applied to the compound in the crucible, in order to break it down to its fundamental elements; after the wolf incorporates the body of the King, it is subjected to calcination in the bonfire on the right midground frame of the print, further reducing and refining the elements of the compound, which are then recombined to produce the renewed substance of the philosopher's stone, which is symbolized by the King emerging from the flames of the bonfire, and moving back towards the river boat and city in the background. But the wolf also recalls the belly of the whale motif, a basic moment in the monomyth found in the Book of Jonah, and in several of the folktales we will look at in the next chapter (particularly in the Grimm's tale of "The Wolf and the Seven Little Kids"). In alchemy, the wolf was often maternal, and her cave both the womb of regeneration, and the tomb of death: one of Goosen van Vreeswyck's plates from *The Green Lion*, for example, shows the wolf mother sitting in front of a pile of bones, but suckling a wild boy alongside her cubs (Fabricius 56). As Jung has frequently noted, the confrontation with the Great Mother, who is as loving as she is terrible, is a characteristic climax of the hero journey of individuation ("Four Archetypes" 14-16). Its prototype may well be the relief sculptures of the Goddess Nut on the ceilings of the Egyptian tombs and temples (like the Temple of Dendera), which show Her devouring the sun god Ra in the evening, and the solar disk traveling through her body, to emerge from her womb in the morning.

Several other alchemical texts from this period follow the complete pattern of the alchemical circulatio (separation, descent, and return), such as the *Philosophia reformata* of Mylius, published in Frankfort in 1622 (De Rola 98-107); the *Sapienta veterum* from the 18th century in Paris (De Rola 108-117); the *Splendor solis* (Fabricius 134-35; Roberts Pl. IX); or the *Janitor pansophus* in the *Museum Hermeticum*, published in Frankfort in 1678, which equates the alchemical journey with the biblical apocalypse (Fabricius 164). Goosen van Vreeswyk's *De Groene Leeuw* (The Green Lion), published in Amsterdam in 1672) uses the symbolism of the labyrinth the represent the alchemical hero journey (Bord 87), which suggests that one of the sources of the symbolism of the maze in Shakespeare (and in Milton, Marvell, and Pope) may have been the hermetic version of the monomyth.

Milton and Marvell

At the beginning of *Paradise Lost*, Milton summarizes the entire cycle of the biblical hero journey (from Genesis to Revelation) in a few short lines: the "fruit of that forbidden tree" initiates the separation from the Garden, leads to the years of exile, "till one greater Man / Restore us, and regain the blissful seat" (1.1-5), coming full circle in the return to the Garden of the beginning. It is, as we have noted earlier, the grand paradigm of the monomyth in biblical terms, which is played out recurrently in the many smaller cycles of individual episodes (Joseph, Jonah, Job, the Prodigal Son, Jesus). Like Shakespeare, Milton repeatedly evokes the myth of the labyrinth in connection with the hero journey of Adam and Eve, which begins with the call to adventure in Eden. Like Spenser in *The Faerie Queene* (1.1.11), and like Shakespeare in *A Midsummer Night's Dream* (2.1.99) and *The Tempest* (3.3.2-3), Milton uses the maze as a symbol of the complexities of nature, art, theology, politics, and science. In "Comus" the maze is equated with Hades as a metaphor of the underworld in which the soul is imprisoned, while in *Paradise Lost*, the labyrinths of nature, human history, science, philosophy, and rhetoric are associated with Satan and the Fall.

In "Comus," Milton uses the labyrinth as a Gnostic image of the underworld in which the fallen soul is "immanacled" (664). The Messianic Spirit sent down by Jove must tread the "perplexed paths" of the "drear wood" (37) and enter the "blind mazes" (181) of the "leafy labyrinth" (278) in order to liberate the Lady from the coils of Comus. Her brothers imagine her as suffering a "wild amazement and affright" (356), and even the Spirit stands "amazed" (565) amidst the "paths and turnings" (569) which surround the "necromancer's hall" (649). For Milton is at pains throughout the poem to equate the maze with the symbolism of Hades, portraying the dark wood as a "dungeon" (349), a "Chaos" (334) of "charnel vaults and sepulchres" (472), and as a "hell" (581) ruled by a "damned wizard" (571) with the assistance of his "grisly legions ... Under the sooty flag of Acheron" (604). These images of the maze and the underworld are used to elaborate on the two primary hero journey cycles of the poem: of the Lady, who travels from home into the woods, and then returns home; and of the Spirit, who descends from heaven at the command of Jove into the dark wood, and then returns to the blessed realm at the end of the poem.

Milton takes pains to establish the archetypal framework of maze and underworld in both hero journey cycles. At the beginning of the poem, the Spirit descends from "regions mild of calm and serene air" downwards into "the smoke and stir of this dim spot / Which men call Earth, and with low-thoughted care, / Confined and pestered in this pinfold here, / Strive to keep up a frail and feverish being" (4-8). Meanwhile, the children whom he has been sent to protect make their way "through the perplexed paths of this drear wood, / The nodding horror of whose shady brows / Threats the forlorn and wandering passenger" (37-39). Those who come under the spell of Comus are then "changed / Into some brutish form" (69-70), and their "native home forget / To roll with pleasure in a sensual sty" (76-77). All of these images reflect a long Gnostic and Neoplatonic tradition, according to which the monomyth represents the fall of the soul into the material world: in these allegories, the material world is represented by such images as Odysseus on the island of Circe, or the prodigal son feeding with the swine (Pépin 4-5), while homecoming embodies the return of the wandering, wayfaring soul to the "beloved fatherland, which, according to the Platonists, denotes the intelligible world, the true fatherland of souls" (Pépin 6). The Gnostics typically employed the allegorical image of the passenger as a symbol of the soul astray in the material world (Jonas 55-58).

To these images Milton adds a wide range of Classical motifs and allusions to enrich his version of the Gnostic journey through the labyrinth of Hades. Comus and his riotous company perform a "wavering morris" dance at Midnight (116), like "dun shades" (127) in the company of the Goddess Cotytto, who "rid'st with Hecat" (135) when "the dragon womb of Stygian darkness spits her thickest gloom" (131-32). The morris dance has long been associated with the treading of the maze in English folklore, as we know from Shakespeare (*Midsummer* 2.1.98-99), as indeed it has been in other cultures as well (Coomaraswamy 30). In these lines, as in many others, Milton refers to the dancers in the dark wood as "shades," a word rooted in the Greek term ("skia") for the shadows of Hades (Hillman, *Dream* 51-54). And the connection of the revelry of Hecate and Cotytto, Classical goddesses of the underworld, with the "dragon womb of Stygian darkness," reinforces the image of the gloomy woods in a way that looks forward to Sin in *Paradise Lost*, who is depicted as the dragon womb of Night guarding the gates of Hell (2.650f.). But the drear wood is also viewed as Chaos, the formless abyss of the void (Tehom) before the Creation in Hesiod's *Theogony* (117) and in *Genesis* (1: 2): the Elder Brother asks the moon to unveil herself "And disinherit Chaos, that reigns here / In double night of darkness and of shades" (334-35). But the moon, like the maiden wandering in the maze of shadows, is "dammed up / With black usurping mists" (337), the kind of atmospheric obscurity associated with Hades since Homer's *Odyssey* (11.16-20). The second Brother in the poem adds the classic Gnostic motif of the prison house to the overall conception of the hero journey through Hades when he declares that he finds "little cheering / In this close dungeon of innumerable boughs" (349).

It is the Elder brother's extended discourse later in the poem which firmly establishes the Gnostic, Neoplatonic allegory of Milton's monomyth. In Gnostic traditions, Sophia (or Anima Mundi, the feminine side of God) fell in love with the material world, and became imprisoned there by the Archons or demons. She was moved in the beginning by desire, and eventually rescued by the Messianic spirit sent to retrieve her. Whether she actually fell into the world, or whether she "projected her Shadow into the mirror of the primordial waters" (Quispell 200; my

trans.), was one of those intriguing questions posed by Gnostic speculation. However that may be, the Elder brother elaborates a similar notion
of the fall of the soul into the material world as an event compelled by
desire:

> But when lust
> By unchaste looks, loose gestures, and foul talk,
> But most by lewd and lavish act of sin,
> Lets in defilement to the inward parts,
> The soul grows clotted by contagion,
> Imbodies and imbrutes, till she quite lose
> The divine property of her first being.
> Such are those thick and gloomy shadows damp
> Oft seen in charnel-vaults and sepulchres,
> Lingering and sitting by a new-made grave,
> As loth to leave the body that it loved,
> And linked itself by carnal sensuality
> To a degenerate and degraded state. (463-75)

The linkage of the words "charnel" and "carnal" in this "charming" passage of "divine Philosophy" (476) is typical of Gnostic conceptions of
the fall of the soul into the sepulchre of the body, seen as a degradation,
defilement, or incarnation which must at all costs be reversed by the return of the soul to its primordial essence.

As we have noted, it was typical of both Gnostic and Neoplatonic
allegory to associate the fallen world of matter with the dark side of the
feminine, represented in the *Odyssey* by Circe, the nymph who turns
men into swine (Pépin 3-5). She is the archetypal sorceress of Greek
myth, practitioner of the arts of black magic with which Comus and his
gang are repeatedly associated in the poem. Like Spenser's Archimago
in *The Faerie Queene* (1.1.34f.), or like Marlowe's Faustus, Milton's
Magus is responsible for the temptation and imprisonment of the soul
during its journey into the woods. Every Hades has its Lord, and
Milton's Comus combines classical allusions with the threatening images of the Renaissance Magus: the Spirit tells the Brothers Comus is
the son of Circe by Bacchus, and that he is a "sorcerer" dwelling
"Within the navel of this hideous wood, / Immured in cypress shades"
(520-21), practicing his mother's "witcheries" (524) and "Doing the ab-
horred rites to Hecate" (535). The cypress is a tree "readily associated
with death and burial," as in Shakespeare's *Twelfth Night* (2.4) or in
Spenser's *Faerie Queene* (1.1.8), but it is also associated with a variety
of Goddesses (Biedermann 87-88), such as Hecate, who is the necromantic witch in *The Voyage of the Argo*. Milton also calls Comus a
"damned wizard," master of "night and shades ... joined with hell in
triple knot / Against th' unarmed weakness of one virgin" (580-82).

Comus is consistently associated with the "charms" (150), "wily trains" (151), "dazzling spells" (154), "blear illusion" (155), and "art" (149) of the Renaissance Magus. But the Elder brother maintains his sister's invulnerability "against the threats / Of malice or of sorcery" (585-86), and vows revenge upon Comus, "that damned magician ... girt / With all the grisly legions of that troop / Under the sooty flag of Acheron" (602-04), one of the four Classical rivers of the underworld. Nevertheless, Comus has managed to "immanacle" the Lady in his pleasure palace, where she sits fettered at his table. The Spirit, now disguised as the shepherd Thyrsis, plans to "quell the might of hellish charms" (613) with an herb called haemony, which, like "that moly / That Hermes once to wise Ulysses gave," is of "sovereign use / Gainst all enchantments, mildew blast, or damp, / Or ghastly Furies apparition" (636-41). These lines reiterate the portrait of Comus not only as Hades, lord of the underworld, but also as the black Magus, master of the hermetic "charms," "enchantments," and foul "spells" (646) cast in his "necromancer's hall" (649).

If the woods represent the maze of the Gnostic underworld, and Comus its dark lord, then the Lady represents Sophia, the soul or Anima Mundi of hermetic tradition, imprisoned therein. She notes that though Comus has "immanacled" her "corporal rind" (664-65), her mind remains free (like Sophia's true being in the fatherland), immune to the "brewed enchantments" of the "foul deceiver" (696). Thyrsis says the beautiful sound of her voice "might create a soul / Under the ribs of Death" (561-62), an image linking her both to Eve and Anima Mundi. Even Comus is enchanted, as were the demons of the material world by the image of Sophia: after she sings her song in the woods, he says "Can any mortal mixture of earth's mould / Breathe such divine enchanting ravishment? / Sure something holy lodges in that breast, / And with these raptures moves the vocal air / To testify his hidden residence" (244-48). Her "virtuous mind" is sustained by "Conscience ... pure-eyed Faith, white-handed Hope," seen as a "hovering angel girt with gold wings" (211-14). Her divinity is central to the allegory of the soul imprisoned in the material world, into which the Spirit descends to retrieve her. In so doing, the Spirit traverses the entire cycle of the Neoplatonic, Gnostic, and Christian monomyths, which begin and end in heaven, with the incarnation and descent in between. The return phase of the Spirit's journey is beautifully evoked by the couplets with which Milton closes his poem, in which the imagery of the Hesperides (the classical islands of the blessed, with three nymphs tending a tree bearing golden fruit), the Graces (dancing beneath rainbows in fields of Elysian dew), the garden of Adonis (whose wounds heal, like Arthur's, while he rests on the island), and the marriage of Cupid and Psyche combine to complete a portrait of Paradise as the eternal goal of the hero journey cycle.

All of this looks forward to *Paradise Lost*. Milton establishes the imagery of the labyrinth early in Book II of the poem, in which some of the fallen angels appear sitting apart on a hillside in Hell, reasoning, "In thoughts more elevate ... Of providence, foreknowledge, will, and fate, / Fix'd fate, free will, foreknowledge absolute, / And found no end, in wandering mazes lost" (2. 561). The very syntax of the lines imitates the coiling and circling of the maze through a sustained chiasmus: we move from foreknowledge, will, and fate in the first line to the reversal of the sequence (fate, will, and foreknowledge) in the second. Milton refers to their discourse as "Vain wisdom all, and false philosophy" (2. 565). Stubborn patience is what is needed to tread a maze, but the maze of Pandaemonium is as inextricable as Dante's *Inferno*. Through this dark valley of vain philosophy "Lethe, the river of oblivion, rolls / Her watery labyrinth" (2. 583-84), imprisoning all who drink from it in an eternity of forgetfulness. Later, in Book IV, the metaphor of the labyrinth is again used to describe the flow of the river of Paradise from its central fountain: Milton doubts "if Art could tell

> How, from that sapphire fount the crisped brooks,
> Rolling on orient pearl and sands of gold
> With mazy error under pendent shades
> Ran nectar, visiting each plant, and fed
> Flowers worthy of Paradise, which not nice Art
> In beds and curious knots, but Nature boon
> Poured forth profuse on hill, and dale, and plain (236-43).

This fascinating passage links the "curious knots" of vegetative root systems with the complexities of that "Art" (poetry) which attempts to describe them. As Coomaraswamy has shown, the metaphors of the maze the knot became intertwined during the Middle Ages and Renaissance in works by Leonardo, Dante, and 2(27).

In Book IX, Satan first thinks of the "mazy folds" of the "sleeping serpent" as a place to hide himself in when he arrives in Eden, and then discovers the serpent sleeping "In labyrinth of many a round self-rolled" (161; 183). After possessing the body of the snake, Satan then moves towards Eve erect upon a "Circular base of rising folds, that towered / Fold above fold a surging maze" (498-99). Eve stands "amazed" when she first hears the serpent's eloquence (614), and "Yet more amazed" when she listens to the story of how eating the fruit elevated the Serpent's powers of reason, speech, and thought. Hence, when the serpent leads Eve to the forbidden tree, Milton compares its motion to the "wandering fire" of the will-o'-the wisp, which "Misleads th'amazed night wanderer from his way" (640). Finally, Adam is "amazed, /

Astonied" when Eve returns to tell her story and urges him to partake of the fruit (889-90).

Penelope Reed Doob suggests that Milton and other Renaissance Humanists "found the scholastic method, with its heavy dependence on Aristotle, labyrinthine in a pejorative sense" (200). Doob mentions the earlier work of Huston Diehl, who saw Milton's use of the maze, in a Protestant context, as emphasizing the importance of God's grace. In fact, Milton's application of the imagery of the maze seems primarily to focus on the pejorative uses of "Vain philosophy," oratory, and rhetoric, with its power to seduce and bewilder. The serpent dazzles Eve in the Garden with his philosophical eloquence, which he attributes to having eaten the fruit:

> Sated at length, ere long I might perceive
> Strange alteration in me, to degree
> Of reason in my inward powers; and speech
> Wanted not long; though to this shape retain'd.
> Thenceforth to speculations high or deep
> I turn'd my thoughts, and with capacious mind
> Consider'd all things visible in Heaven,
> Or Earth, or Middle; all things fair and good: (9. 599-605).

The emphasis here is on the powers of reason, speech, and thought as gifts of the fruit, and each, by implication, becomes associated with the seductive maze of rhetoric which the Serpent represents, and which amazes Eve. When Eve resists the temptation to eat the fruit, it is again to the elevated powers of natural philosophy that Satan turns in his efforts to seduce her:

> O sacred, wise, and wisdom-giving Plant,
> Mother of science! now I feel thy power
> Within me clear; not only to discern
> Things in their causes, but to trace the ways
> Of highest agents, deem'd however wise. (9. 679-683)

Writing at the end of the 17th century, and after having traveled in Italy, where he spoke with Galileo, Milton was apparently uneasy about the emergence of modern science in his time: Newton would articulate the mathematical laws of cause and effect, tracing the operations of the highest agents in the natural world, in his *Principia* of 1684. It is significant that Milton calls the Tree of Knowledge the "Mother of science," refers to the juice of its fruit as "sciental sap" (9. 837), and has Eve celebrate its "operation / Blest to sapience" (9. 796-97). If the plant can give "elocution to the mute" serpent, which, having eaten, "knows, and speaks, and reasons, and discerns," then surely she too might partake of that "sciental sap" which would enable her, a woman, to tread the serpentine mazes of philosophy, rhetoric, and scientific speculation.

The labyrinth proved an equally versatile symbol of the hero journey for Milton's contemporary, Andrew Marvell. In "Bermudas," one of the sailors lucky enough to arrive in the waters of the New World sings "His praise, / That led us through the watery maze" (5-6). Shakespeare may also have linked the journey to the New World and the symbolism of the maze when he has Gonzago speak of the "forthrights and meanders" the Italian conspirators are forced to traverse by Prospero in *The Tempest*. One thinks here also of the Medieval notion of the pilgrimage through life as a treading of the maze, an idea to be found (among other places) on the floor of Ely Cathedral, just a few miles north of Marvell's alma mater. He opens "The Garden" by saying "How vainly men themselves amaze / To win the palm, the oak, or bays" (1-2), a remark which suggests an affiliation between the symbolism of the maze, politics, and poetics. This seems especially apt in Post Civil War England, a labyrinth which Marvell managed to traverse safely, to arrive in the end in the Paradise of the Garden, like the sailor in the New World.

There is, in fact, a complete hero journey cycle traversed right in the middle of Marvell's "The Garden." It is a journey of great importance for the Renaissance, in as much as it records a Neoplatonic ecstasy, during which the soul leaves the body, ascends into the intellectual world, and then returns to the body, enlightened by the revelation of the Platonic Ideas. The spiritual journey occupies the sixth and seventh octaves of the poem. In the sixth, the mind withdraws into itself, where it finds the "resemblance" of "each kind" of created form. It is a process of remembrance, of Platonic recollection, whereby the mind recovers its innate knowledge of the pure forms which are the basis all created things. The seventh octave employs several archetypal images to convey the Platonic revelations of the hero journey cycle. The poet sits at the "fountain's sliding foot" in the garden, "Or at some fruit tree's mossy root" (49-50). Both images (of the fountain, and of the tree) represent the return to the origins of life, a constant of the hero journey symbolism. The tree, furthermore, suggests both the tree of life, and the tree of knowledge, from the Garden of Eden, but with no sense of the Fall. The clothing symbolism so often found in the monomyth emerges in the next line, when the soul casts "the body's vest aside" and "into the boughs does glide" (51-52). Divestiture and ascent converge here as symbols of the transformation of matter into spirit, of the shamanic flight of the soul into the upperworld. This most typically involves the image of the World Tree, a pillar which connects the three worlds (below, middle, and above) (Eliade, *Shamanism* 270). During the Renaissance, the shamanic archetype of all poets, Orpheus, was linked to Neoplatonic theories about poetry, and he was typically pictured sitting at the base of a tree.[7] Having reached the upper boughs of the tree, the soul of the poet "sits and sings" like a bird, combing its "silver wings, / And, till prepared for longer flight, / Waves in its plumes the various light" (54-56). This marvelous image looks back to the journeys of the Gilgamesh and the Egyptian pharaohs, who pictured the souls of the dead as birds; and it looks just as surely forward to the Yeatsian versions of the monomyth: in "Sailing to Byzantium," the soul is "set upon a golden bough to sing" (30), and in "Byzantium," the "Miracle, bird, or golden handiwork" is "Planted on the starlit golden bough" (17, 19).

Racine and Pope

After Milton and Marvell, Racine and Pope provide an excellent bridge into the Modern era, for the image of the maze is important to both. In *Phaedra*, Racine presents us with what I am tempted to call a feminist version of the myth, when, in Act 2, scene 5, Phaedra confesses her love to Hippolytus. Her fantasy replaces Theseus with Hippolytus, and Ariadne with herself, whom she puts in a position of higher power, playing a role nearly equal to that of Hippolytus in the navigation of the maze and the slaying of the Minotaur. For in her revisioning of the myth, the son Hippolytus kills the Minotaur, led through the maze by his lover Phaedra, who does more than simply provide the thread as her sister had done for Theseus in the original version. Phaedra imagines herself leading Hippolytus into the maze, and helping him to slay the Minotaur. The implications of this variation are enormous in the context of the play, in which the political complexities of the kingship of Athens and the psychological complexities of passion within the family both find a fitting symbol of the figure of the maze. The implications are enormous in the context of feminist theory. We must note, however, a final variation on the theme, since Racine has Hippolytus ultimately slain by the bull from the sea, a kind of Minotaur who personifies those labyrinthine complexities of unnatural love and political maneuvering which destroy both treaders of the maze in Phaedra's new version.

Pope's musings on the maze are somewhat more serene, yet no less interesting or profound. In the first stanza of *An Essay on Man*, Epistle 1, Pope calls the world "A mighty maze! but not without a plan" (6). What does he mean? The stanza immediately following provides a clue, for in this section of the poem Pope exploits the cosmology of Galileo and Newton to create an image of the universe as a divine labyrinth which reveals the intricacy and mystery of the mind which produced it. The cosmos is pictured as a stupendous network of interlaced labyrinths, in which "worlds on worlds compose one universe," "system into system runs," while "other planets circle other suns" (1. 24-26). It is all held together by the "bearings," the "ties," the "connections," and "dependencies" of the Great Chain of Being (1. 29-33), in itself a manifestation of Daedalian craftsmanship elevated to a divine level. The intricate network of interrelationships between the various links in the Chain which follows reinforces Pope's notion of the world as an "amazing Whole," comprised of systems, planets and suns, Angels and spheres (8. 247f.), all united by "The great directing MIND of ALL" (9.266).

In *The Rape of the Lock*, the cosmological maze turns once more psychological. Speaking of the "shining ringlets" of Belinda's hair, Pope says "Love in these labyrinths his slaves detains, / And mighty hearts are held in slender chains" (2.23-24). He compares the lovers trapped in "the mazy ringlets of her hair" (2.139) to birds caught in "hairy springes" and fishes tangled by "Slight lines of hair" (2.25-26). The connection between the maze and love is essentially the same as that found in Dante or Racine, only comic. But Pope extends the metaphor in a way characteristic of the mythology of the maze to include politics and life as a whole. The card game of Canto III is labyrinthine, suggestive of the social complexities of Hampton Court in which Belinda is embedded. From a broader perspective, all life is a pilgrimage through a labyrinth, as Pope notes when he says "Oft, when the world imagine women stray, / The Sylphs through mystic mazes guide their way" (1.91-94). This remark works many ways, turning in one direction towards the psychologized realm of the spirits which the Sylphs inhabit, and in the other towards the satirical ethos of the poem as a whole.

Pope's use of the mock epic in *The Rape of the Lock* marks a crucial moment in the history of the hero journey, looking back to Homer and Virgil, and forward to Fielding, Eliot, and Joyce. For the mock epic shares with Eliot's "mythical method" the fusion of realistic details drawn from daily life and symbolism derived from myth. Hence, *The Rape* combines precisely rendered portraits of life in London in the 18th century, with such conventions of the epic hero journey as the arming of the hero, sea voyages and battles, the tutelary guidance of the gods, royal feasts, and the descent to the underworld. Pope's handling of this last convention of the monomyth is particularly important, for it represents a psychologizing of the hero journey which lays the foundations for much of modern literature.

Pope incorporated elements of Neoplatonism and the so-called Rosicrucian Enlightenment into his mock epic. And he does so in ways not only supremely amusing, but also very important for the history of the hero journey in literature. One could say that Pope' precise juxtaposition of the most quotidian details of daily life with the deeper dimension of mythological symbolism looks forward to such masters of the mythical method as Thomas Mann, D.H. Lawrence, and James Joyce. This is nowhere more apparent than in Pope's handling of the arming of his heroine, in preparation for her journey, which begins at home in bed. While sleeping, Belinda receives spiritual guidance from her guardian spirit, Ariel, who plays the role Athena plays in Homer. In Canto 1, Ariel appears to the dreaming Belinda and discourses upon the world of the four elements and life after death, common subjects of the alchemical traditions of Rosicrucians. The name of the guardian spirit clearly acknowledges Shakespeare, whose interest in things Rosicrucian has also been established by scholars.[8] The verse of Pope's poem also looks back to Shakespeare, as when Ariel evokes "the airy elves by moonlight shadows seen, / The silver tokens, and the circled green" (1.31-32), lines which echo Puck's "grove or green, / By fountain clear or spangled starlight sheen" (*Dream* 2.1.28-29). There may even be some of Antony and Cleopatra hovering in the wings when we come to the arming of Belinda in preparation for her trip up the Thames to Hampton Court: unlike the simple sandals of Telemachus or the elaborately allegorical shield of Gawain, Belinda's accoutrements include the common items of the boudoir table, upon which the "cosmetic powers" gathered from India and Arabia lie scattered (1.121-149). The dazzling imagery of exotic mirrors and perfumes may look back to Shakespeare's Cleopatra, but the detailed realism of "combs," "files of pins," "Puffs, powders, patches, Bibles, billet-doux" (1. 136-38) looks forward to such exhaustive examination of the hero's mock epic 'armor' as we find in Joyce's *Ulysses*.

This innovative combination of realistic detail with the conventional formulas of the hero journey -- sea-voyages, epic battles, feasts, the descent into Hades -- continues throughout the poem. The journey up the Thames recalls the voyages of Gilgamesh, Odysseus, and Dante, in which the crossing of the waters marks the transition to the otherworld, but it does so in the language of Rosicrucian mysticism and pastoral poetry (2.47-72). When it comes to epic battles, we have the exactitude of the card game (3.27-100), and the absurdities of the actual rape of the lock, by the diminutive Hades of Hampton Court, our noble Peer (3.146f.). The epic feast does not involve sacrificial offerings to the gods, but the crackling berries of the coffee urn, the clinking of coffee cups, and the gliding of those "grateful liquors" which make the "politician wise, / And see through all things with his half-shut eyes" (3.118-19). The incorporation of such precisely observed details from the quotidian rituals of daily life into the mythical structure of the hero journey is one of Pope's major contributions to literature.

The other related contribution is Pope's psychological approach to the descent to the underworld: nearly two hundred years before Freud and Jung, Mann and Lawrence, we find a poet for whom Hades represents the unconscious mind. In Canto IV, after the rape of the lock (which, as in the story of Demeter and Persephone, precipitates the descent), the "dusky melancholy sprite" named Umbriel (who essentially represents Belinda's bad mood) descends to the "Cave of Spleen," to obtain a "wondrous bag ... Like that where once Ulysses held the winds" (4.82). It is full of "Sighs, sobs, and passions, and the war of tongues" to take back to Belinda (4.84). Like Aeneas, who goes down into Hades holding a branch of the golden bough, Umbriel gains access to the Queen of the Underworld (who has a migraine headache and dispenses hysteria, pimples, cuckold horns, jealousy, and envy) by carrying "A branch of healing spleenwort" (4.56). There he confronts the handmaids "Ill-Nature" and "Affectation," not, like Aeneas, Odysseus, or Dante, the souls of the departed dead, who communicate crucial information regarding their destiny. For Pope not only psychologizes the heroic descent to the underworld -- he also rationalizes it, making it possible for the readers of the Age of Enlightenment to accept the fantastic exploits of myth as metaphors and symbols of the trivial concerns of daily life.

It is likely that Pope's Neoclassical rationalization of the hero journey had its roots in the writings of Lucretius, one of those Roman authors widely admired by the Augustan poets of 18th century England. In his glorious philosophical poem, *On the Nature of Things*, Lucretius sets out to replace "the will of the gods" with explanations of the "rational causes" at work in nature (29). His rationalization leads to a reevaluation of myth as a metaphor for things that happen in this life, not as a glimpse into the world to come: "the depths of Hell," he writes, are "part of our lives" (118), and the torments of the damned signify the normal sufferings of our daily existence. Hence, Tantalus represents "an empty fear of the gods"; Tityus is a "man laid flat by love," and the birds which peck him apart represent the "cares that tear us with desire"; Sisyphus is a politician "Drunk with campaigning," and all the various punishments exist only in this life (118-19). Such rationalizations of the hero journey serve to psychologize myths, and hence to make them acceptable to the educated readers of the Enlightenment.

Fielding's *Tom Jones*

Henry Fielding's novel *The History of Tom Jones: A Foundling* (of 1749) stands at a crucial turning point in our survey of the hero journey in literature. While looking backwards to the traditions of the medieval romance, *Tom Jones* carries the conventional symbolism of the Classical epic (in turn transmitted through the romance) forwards into the future, anticipating a long line of novels in our tradition which combine realistic or historical detail and mythic symbolism. Specifically, it is the so-called mock epic element of Fielding's work, so popular during the 18th century, that serves this Janus function in the history of the novel. For the mock epic, while adapting the conventions of Classical literature and medieval romance to the satirical concerns of the 18th century, implies a sustained parallel between aspects of contemporary life and some mythic model from the antique past, and in so doing looks forward to T.S. Eliot's seminal definition of the "mythical method" in James Joyce's *Ulysses*, as "a means of giving shape and significance to the anarchy and futility of contemporary history" ("Ulysses" 681).

Fielding was, in a sense, one of the first great practitioners of the mythic method in the history of the novel, using a sustained and systematic sequence of allusions to the mythic models of the romance and Classical epic traditions to give shape and significance to the historical details of his magnificently structured plot. That Fielding's primary antique model for the hero journey were the Classical epics of Homer and Virgil is a commonplace of the criticism, as is the awareness of his use of medieval romance conventions. Fielding refers to Homer and Virgil at key points in the novel, as I will show, and many of his digressions at the beginning of the books in the several volumes delineate the author's general attitude towards the romances which he professes denigrate.

In some ways, *Tom Jones* is a fiction devised to illustrate a fiction, or a copy of an archetype: it is a typological figure of the Judeo-Christian paradigm of Fall, Exile, and Redemption (from Genesis to Revelation). Tom's journey (paralleled by Sophia Western and Harriet Fitzpatrick's journeys) begins, like Adam's, in Paradise, for the details of the description of Squire Allworthy's Paradise Hall are clearly meant to evoke an arcadian Eden, an Eden to which, the end of the novel implies, Tom and Sophia will return at some future date (just as the Bible circles back to the restored Paradise at the end of the Book of Revelation). In between Genesis and Revelation is life, the heroic descent into the underworld, as Tom and Sophia move down the mountainside into the Vale of Sorrow.

The first description of Paradise Hall and the Allworthy estate evokes this archetypal structure of the Christian hero journey as an educational "progress" through life, such as we find in Bunyan and in the lithographic sequences of Hogarth. The "House" has an "Air of Grandeur in it, that struck you with Awe," and it is situated significantly on the "South-east Side of a Hill, but nearer the Bottom than the Top of it" and enjoying "a most charming Prospect of the Valley beneath" (42). From the summit of a lawn above the house a "plentiful Spring" gushes "out of a Rock covered with Firs" and forms a thirty-foot cascade that runs down through a "pebly Channel" with "many lesser Falls ... into a Lake at the Foot of the Hill, about a quarter of a Mile below the House on the South Side" (42). A river then issues out of this lake "that for several Miles was seen to meander through an amazing Variety of Meadows and Woods, till it emptied itself into the Sea" (42).

Many of the details of this description are evocative of the mountain of Paradise in Genesis (and of course in Milton's *Paradise Lost*): Adam and Eve descend from the eastward gate of the Paradisal mountain southward into the labyrinthine valley of human life and exile. The four rivers spring from a central fountain in Eden, and make their way eventually to the far distant Sea, a figure for the divine destination of our earthly pilgrimage. Just so will Tom be exiled from Paradise Hall by the wrathful but ultimately merciful and just Allworthy, and just so will he enter the maze of the roads leading to London (the labyrinth, as we will see, is explicitly alluded to later during Tom's journey), where his most severe trials and penance occur and lead to his redemption and eventual return to Paradise Hall.

What Fielding does so masterfully, in terms of this first stage of the hero journey, is to rationally build the tensions within the Allworthy family circle to the point where exile seems inevitable, as the need for a redemptive hero to relieve and reconcile those polarities within the society as a whole (of which the tensions within the Allworthy circle are a microcosm) becomes equally urgent. I say to *rationally* build these tensions leading up to the Fall by way of distinguishing Fielding's novel from the biblical, Classical, and medieval manifestations of the archetype. Fielding prides himself in his ability to logically account for and anticipate the motivations and actions of his characters, building the elements of his plot in such a way that the expectations of the Neo-classical reader, with his distaste for the absurdly motivated episodes of the romance, will be fulfilled. In this respect, Fielding participates in that realistic reformation of the plotting of the 18th century novel noted by Ian Watt, who writes of the novelist's need to create a logical sequence of events linked by cause and effect and in accordance with the reasonable development of the characters.

Fielding does this by leading up to the expulsion of Tom from his little Paradise with a sequence of logically related events. First there is the sequence of thefts and minor infractions committed by Tom that intensify gradually in magnitude: the bird poached from Squire Western's property; the horse and Bible given Tom by Allworthy, which he sells in order to assist the Seagrim family in their distress; Tom's amour with Molly Seagrim, leading to a pregnancy which is initially blamed on Tom; and finally, the wild row that erupts on the night of Allworthy's apparently mortal illness, when Tom gets drunk to celebrate Allworthy's recovery, fights with Blifil and Thwackum, and is later caught in the bushes taking comfort with Molly.

Along with this sequence relating to Tom, we have the building tensions within the Allworthy family circle. Several sets of irreconcilable conflicts complicate Tom's situation: there is the sibling rivalry with Blifil (Tom and Blifil form a kind of Cain and Abel pair); there is the rivalry between his tutors, Thwackum and Square, the former professing a kind of Christianity and the latter the ethics of Aristotle, but both hypocritically competing for the hand (or lands) of Bridgit Allworthy; there is the violent jealousy between the Partridges, aroused by the presence of the woman alleged to be Tom's mother, Jenny Jones; and there is lastly the brutal tyranny of Squire Western, who attempts to force Sophia to marry Blifil in spite of her preference for Tom.

Tom is caught in the center of all this, since Thwackum and Square play him off against the apparent virtues of Blifil in their misguided attempt to win favor with Allworthy and his sister, and Western blows up when he finds Tom has captured his daughter's heart. The climax of all this comes when Blifil, playing the role of legitimate heir, villainously misrepresents Tom's behavior on the night of Allworthy's illness, suggesting the cause of Tom's drunken celebration was the imminent death of his benefactor. This leads logically and predictably to the expulsion of Tom and to his departure on the hero journey to London. Fielding has taken great pains to provide an historical account of the events leading to the separation of the hero and the beginning of a quest which would most likely have had a supernatural initiative in the medieval romances, such as in the Grail quests or in *Sir Gawain and the Green Knight*.

The next stage of the hero journey -- the threshold crossing battle -- is handled with a similar combination of realism and romance. It is characteristic in the hero journey cycle for the transition from domestic security to the realm of trials, ordeals, and initiations to be signaled by a crisis of some sort involving battles, shipwreck, death and dismemberment, etc. In the conventions of the Classical epic and medieval romance, as we have seen, these are often supernatural encounters with a threshold guardian, such as a dragon in Wagner's *Siegfried*, a wild man of the woods in Chrétien's *Yvain*, or the wodwos at the fords in *Sir Gawain*.

In *Tom Jones*, the threshold battle is rationalized, replacing supernatural with realistic characters. Instead of shipwreck, for example, Tom is lost at night in the maze of roads leading to Bristol after leaving the Allworthy environs. The threshold battle occurs at the Public House where Tom meets a regiment of soldiers preparing to defend the

Hannoverian cause against the pretensions of the Stuart family and the
Jacobites. Yet the battle also evokes the first instance in the novel
when the descent to the underworld archetype surfaces definitively, to be
sustained throughout the rest of the book. This basic convention of the
Classical epic (the *nekyiae* of Book 11 of the *Odyssey* and Book 6 of
the *Aeneid*) is rationally adapted to the circumstances of Fielding's
Enlightenment novel: the scene at the Public House is probable and realistic, yet the details of the description evoke the marvelous symbolism associated with the descent to the underworld.

We see this mixture of the realistic and the romantic, of the probable and the marvelous, after Tom is knocked out by an Ensign who
has been casting aspersions on Sophia's morality. The Ensign dis-
charges "a Bottle full at the Head of *Jones*, which hitting him a little
above the right Temple, brought him instantly to the Ground" (376).
When Tom's body is raised up from the ground, "they could perceive
but little (if any) Sign of Life in him" (376), and he "was, at first, generally concluded to be dead" (378). Covered with the "Blood beginning
to flow pretty plentifully from his Wound" (376), and administered a
draught of brandy by the Landlady, Tom is then conducted to a room
upstairs and attended by a surgeon.

All of these details are quite probable, realistic examples of what
Fielding will later refer to as his historical integrity; yet they also
evoke that characteristic moment in the mythic journey (the threshold
crossing) in which the hero descends into the underworld of initiatory
trials and ordeals. While discrediting this specific aspect of the romance
tradition later in the novel (where he reassures the reader that he will *not*
take him on a journey into either an inferno or into fairyland), Fielding
nevertheless manages simultaneously to evoke that tradition in those
same readers, many of whom he assumes to be familiar with the otherworld journeys of tradition. We see this in the events following Tom's
collapse into unconsciousness, when he determines to go out into the
yard to find the room where Ensign Northerton has been confined and to
take revenge. Tom gets out of bed to dress himself, and the description
of his clothing immediately suggests the significance of clothing as a
symbol of transformation noted often in the chapters above:

> He had on ... a light-colored Coat, covered with Streams of
> Blood. His face, which missed that very Blood, as well as
> twenty Ounces more drawn from him by the Surgeon, was pal-
> lid. Round his Head was a Quantity of Bandage, not unlike a
> Turban. In the right Hand he carried a Sword, and in the left a
> Candle. So that the bloody *Banquo* was not worthy to be
> compared to him. In Fact, I believe a more dreadful Apparition
> was never raised in a Church-yard, nor in the Imagination of

any good People met in a Winter evening over a Christmas
Fire in *Somersetshire.* (387-388)

When the soldier on guard duty sees this spectre from the underworld,
"his Hair began gently to lift up his Grenadier Cap," he falls "flat on
his Face," and he begins to tremble violently all over, "convinced that
the Volunteer [Tom] was dead of his Wounds, and that his Ghost was
come in Search of the Murtherer" (388). When apprehended by the rest
of the Company, the soldier begins "roaring like a Bull" that "Spirits or
Devils were handling him; for his Imagination being possessed with the
Horror of an Apparition, converted every Object he saw or felt, into
nothing but Ghosts and Spectres" (389). When roused from his fit, he
says "'I am a dead Man, that's all, I'm a dead Man" (389).

As humorously as these realistic details are presented, they nevertheless cannot help but evoke associations with the journey to the underworld, which will continue to enrich our response to the narrative
from this point on in the novel. After leaving this episode among the
soldiers at the Public House, Fielding's allusions to the conventions of
the romance intensify and contribute greatly to the evocative imagery of
the hero journey archetype. In fact, three subsequent episodes in the
novel are informed by the epic conventions of the descent to the underworld. These episodes include the Man on the Hill, the encounter with
the gypsies, and Tom's arrival in London. Authorial commentary and
details of imagery continue to show that while Fielding ostensibly rejects the "unfortunate" beliefs associate with the otherworld journey, he
nevertheless exploits the mock-epic evocations of the underworld in a
masterful way to communicate thematic concerns and to enrich, almost
subliminally, the response of his sagacious readers.

In the first of these three episodes, after leaving the Inn at
Gloucester, it is a "Midwinter" twilight, getting dark early just around
five o'clock (435), with a full moon rising, when Partridge and Jones
proceed to get lost in the labyrinth of crossroads on the way to
Worcester. While Tom finds comfort in the thought that "the loveliest
Creature in the Universe may have her Eyes now fixed on that very
Moon which I behold at this instant!'" (437), Partridge says that he
would never dare look at the moon "for fear of seeing" his wife, since,
"according to a Book [he] once read," the moon is "the receptacle of departed Spirits" (438). They determine to "keep the Left-hand Track, as
that seems to lead directly to those Hills" which lie not far off from
Worcester, their destination (437). As quaint and amusing as this contrast is (it parallels the relationship between the love-struck Don
Quixote and his realistic servant Sancho Panza), the details of the imagery establish a romantic or mythological context to be applied consistently in the events to follow. We know from Shakespeare's *A*

Midsummer Night's Dream that the moon is associated with the haunted forests of the faery otherworld, and we know from Virgil (and indeed from all of world mythology) that the labyrinth is a symbol of the underworld.[9] Following the "Left-hand Track" is a traditional clue for escaping from a labyrinth, or for penetrating to the center, the task which Tom now embarks on. That Partridge sees the moon as the realm of departed spirits, therefore, ties in with the symbolism associating the labyrinth and the underworld. Furthermore, the notion that the left-hand track leads to hills in the distant also suggests the hollow hills where the otherworld of the faery kingdom is traditionally situated.[10]

The archetypal imagery of the hero journey into the otherworld continues as Partridge and Jones approach the cottage where the Man of the Hill lives. He is a kind of Merlin, a forest sage living in isolation and roaming the hills at night. The cottage lies at the base of a "very steep Hill" that Partridge describes as a "'Mountain; which seems to me to be one of the highest in the World'" (443). Again, while these are realistic details describing the Malvern Hills, the mythic image evoked is that of the World Mountain, or *Axis Mundi*, which rises out of the depths of the underworld in the *Epic of Gilgamesh*, and into the depths of which Inanna descends on her journey into the Sumerian *kur*, as does the Egyptian God Ra during his nightly excursion through the *Tuat*. Fielding firmly evokes (by means of the parody attendant upon the mock-epic) the imagery of the underworld forest journey by filling the head of Partridge with "Ghosts, Devils, Witches, and such like," as the travelers make their way to a candle burning in the window of a cottage, where an old woman finally opens an upper casement window after Tom knocks several times at the "Door" (444). Partridge is "almost dead with the Cold," and he suspects "Witchcraft, nor can the Reader conceive a Figure more adapted to inspire this Idea, than the old Woman who now stood before him" (445).

So we now have Partridge standing "almost dead" before a crone. In the folklore tradition of such tales as "Cupid and Psyche" and "The Devil and the Three Golden Hairs," the old crone is surrounded by thieves associated with the underworld and its master, often the Devil. Hence, in this scene in *Tom Jones*, the old woman's description of her master: "'They call him, *The Man of the Hill*, and the Country People are not, I believe, more afraid of the Devil himself'" (446). Although appeased by the comely appearance of Jones, which relieves her "Apprehension of Thieves" (444), the Man of the Hill shortly cries out for help nearby, and Tom delivers "the old Gentleman" from a group of thieves who run off crying out "with bitter Oaths, that they were dead Men" (447). An old crone, a cottage at the foot of the World Mountain, thieves and travelers who call themselves dead men lost in a labyrinth, a wise old man whom locals suspect of being the Devil -- all these details evoke an archetypal response in the most sagacious and reasonable of readers, even those who, like Fielding himself, profess a distaste for the apparatus of the romance convention of the journey to the otherworld.

As we have seen repeatedly in previous chapters, the *nekyia* culminates in a profound revelation which leads to the transformation of the hero: to both Odysseus and Aeneas a wisdom is revealed in Hades by wise older men (Tiresias and Priam) who direct them in their pursuit of destiny. Even in a tale such as "The Devil and the Three Golden Hairs," the Devil, who is the lord of the underworld, is endowed with a special wisdom regarding the sources of the sorrows of the world. Hence, it is archetypally appropriate that the Man of the Hill in *Tom Jones* is reputed for his wisdom: "'there be few Gentlemen that know more of all Matters than he," the old woman remarks of her master (446), and the tale that he tells Tom contains an abundance of wisdom and guidance to Tom, who is himself making his way through the vale of tears already traversed by the old man.

The description of the old man's clothing, focusing on the "Strangeness of his Dress" (448), is also characteristic of the importance of clothing symbolism in the hero journey, as is his willingness to communicate his wisdom through storytelling. His dress suggests a Merlinesque forest sage, a Wild Man of the Woods:[11]

> This Person was of the tallest Size, with a long Beard as white as Snow. His Body was cloathed with the Skin of an Ass, made something into the Form of a Coat. He wore likewise Boots on his Legs, and a Cap on his Head, both composed of the skin of some other Animals. (448)

One thinks of the importance of Joseph's many-colored coat and its Gnostic symbolism in Genesis, or, further back in the tradition, of the robe prepared for Gilgamesh by Utnapishtim. A further connection to the *Epic of Gilgamesh* is the importance of storytelling as a means of revelation of the hero journey: this section of *Tom Jones* is largely devoted to the Man of the Hill's wisdom tale, which concludes with an exalted affirmation of the beauty of the Creation:

> What Time can suffice for the Contemplation and Worship of that glorious, immortal, and eternal Being, among the Works of whose stupendous Creation, not only this Globe, but even those numberless Luminaries which we may here behold spangling all the Sky, tho' they should many of them be Suns lighting different Systems of Worlds, may possibly appear but as a few Atoms, opposed to the whole Earth which we inhabit? (484)

This Newtonian view of a universe composed of numberless planetary systems looks back to Pope's *Essay on Man*, and forward to Romanticism, and it forms a fitting climax to Tom's journey in this section of the novel.

The next stop on Tom's itinerary is the Inn at Upton, at which he arrives with Mrs. Waters, the lady whom he rescues from Ensign Northerton in the woods near the Man of the Hill's cottage, and who subsequently seduces Tom at the Inn. During the few hours we spend at the Inn, all the major characters of the novel arrive, and we are introduced to others who will play a significant role during the events in London: Mrs. Fitzpatrick, Sophia's cousin, arrives in flight from her tyrannical Irish husband, who is in pursuit of his wife, and Sophia arrives with Mrs. Honour, both fleeing the wrath of Squire Western, in hot pursuit of his renegade daughter. There ensues a confusion of identities as Mr. Fitzpatrick mistakes Mrs. Waters for his wife, and Sophia discovers that her Tom is in bed with Mrs. Waters, and leaves her muff on his pillow for revenge, before leaving. The whole episode recalls the hero journeys of the Athenian lovers into the faery woods in Shakespeare's *A Midsummer Night's Dream*.

The importance of the events here and in subsequent chapters for our discussion is that it complicates and enriches the hero journey theme by adding two female heroines, both on journeys of their own which contrast and complement those of the male characters. Both Sophia and Mrs. Fitzpatrick are fleeing from darkly tyrannical male figures, the father of the former and the husband of the latter. Both their journeys had begun in the paradisal surroundings of Squire Western's estate, and both journeys were initiated by abusive males who have attempted to dominate and confine their women. It is interesting to note here that Tom's journey seems to have been initiated by an excess or abuse of liberty, while the females suffer from the opposite condition of restricted liberty. Both Squire Western and Mr. Fitzpatrick are rather brutal males whose imprisonment and (in the latter case) abduction of the females suggest they are like Hades, who in the Classical myth steals Persephone from her mother Demeter and carries her down into the underworld, the same way Mr. Fitzpatrick steals his wife from under the nose of the maternal Aunt Western. Indeed, Mrs. Western's description of her journey across the Irish Channel to the ruined estate of her husband and his broken down old castle is very much in line with the imagery of the journey to the underworld, with its water crossings and ruined halls of Hades in such works as the epics of Virgil and Dante.

These traditions of the abduction and descent into Hades, however, have come to Fielding, and to the modern novel which *Tom Jones* inaugurates, via those Medieval romances, in opposition to the marvelous and improbable elements of which Fielding professes a "historic Integrity" (607). Yet, as we have noted, Fielding honestly acknowledges his debt to these earlier works by defining the romance novel in general (*Joseph Andrews* specifically) as a "comic epic poem in prose" (7). Hence, in relating the history of Mrs. Fitzpatrick, Fielding actually tells us that he has rationalized the romance traditions of the hero journey by replacing damsels in distress with wives abused by tyrannical husbands, and "Knight Errants" with the noblemen who 'rescue' such wives, in this case Mr. Fitzpatrick's neighbor:

> it was by his Assistance that she had been enabled to escape from her Husband; for this Nobleman had the same gallant Disposition with those renowned Knights, of whom we read in heroic Story, and had delivered many an imprisoned Nymph from Durance. He was indeed as bitter an Enemy to the savage Authority too often exercised by Husbands and Fathers, over the young and lovely of the other Sex, as ever Knight Errant was to the barbarous Power of Enchanters: nay, to say Truth, I have often suspected that those very Enchanters with which Romance every where abounds, were in reality no other than the Husbands of those Days: and Matrimony itself was perhaps the enchanted Castle in which the Nymphs were said to be confined. (607)

The exquisite irony regarding the Nobleman's motives here is pure Fielding, as is his very conscious adaptation of the conventions of the romance tradition to his "historical Integrity." For this passage acknowledges the mythic model of the abducted or tyrannized female as the basic motif rationalized in the plot of *Tom Jones*. Indeed, the analogy between marriage and enchantment looks forward to the psychologizing of myths of relationship in Freud and Jung (though we need actually only look back to Pope's *Rape of the Lock* for a more contemporary example of the psychologizing of myth in Fielding's own time).

While Sophia and Mrs. Western join together on their heroine's journeys, Tom's journey continues to be described in mock heroic terms evocative of the descent to the underworld, a basic myth which Fielding rationalizes throughout the novel. After leaving the Inn at Upton, Tom and Partridge once again find themselves lost on the road at night, when they stumble upon a group of gypsies celebrating a wedding in a nearby barn. The fears of Partridge once again stimulate fantasies of "Ghosts or Witches, or some Evil Spirits or other" (664); only this time Fielding explicitly evokes the parallel to the journey into the underworld. Partridge remarks that he and Tom are lost and that "such Darkness was never seen upon Earth, and I question whether it can be darker in the other World" (665).

This remark leads Fielding to a revealing digression, in which he distinguishes his "history" from the Medieval romance and religious epic, in which the journey into Hell or into a Celtic faeryland is a common feature (I quote at some length since it is so relevant to the hero journey theme in *Tom Jones*):

> Had this History been writ in the Days of Superstition, I should have had too much Compassion for the Reader to have left him so long in Suspence, whether *Beelzebub* or *Satan* was about actually to appear in Person, with all his Hellish Retinue; but as these Doctrines are at present very unfortunate, and have but few if any Believers, I have not been much aware of conveying any such Terrors. To say Truth, the whole Furniture of the infernal Regions hath long been appropriated by the Managers of Playhouses.
>
> However, tho' we do not suspect raising any great Terror on this Occasion, we have Reason to fear some other Apprehensions may here arise in our Reader, into which we would not willingly betray him, I mean that we are going to take a Voyage into Fairy Land, and to introduce a Set of Beings into our History, which scarce any one was ever child-ish enough to believe, tho' many have been foolish enough to spend their Time in writing and reading their Adventures. (665-66)

This digression is so important because, among other reasons, it explic-itly identifies the two conventional myths underlying the hero journey which Fielding sets about to revision in his "History."

What Fielding does with the popularity of these myths of the hero journey (the popularity of which is attested by his last sentence) is a very complex affair of great consequence for the subsequent history of the novel. On the one hand he rationalizes the myth by replacing demons and fairies with wandering Gypsies, hence bringing us into the Age of Reason, which cast a skeptical eye on such Medieval glimpses of otherworlds as inform Dante and many others (as we have seen above).[12] On the other, we have the complexities of the mock-epic, which adapts the conventions of the Classical epic (Homer and Virgil) to a satire of contemporary life. One of the most important of those conventions is of course the descent into Hades (*Odyssey* Book 11; *Aeneid* Book 6), also very successfully applied in Pope's mock-epic poem *The Rape of the Lock*. The mock-epic satire cuts several ways, parodying the literature of the past, belittling the pretensions and follies of contemporary life, yet also sustaining the importance of myth as a means of giving shape and significance to the narrative and to life itself. That is to say, the mock-epic, by drawing a sustained parallel between contemporary life and an ancient model from the past looks forward to Eliot's mythical method, and sets the scene for the many novels in the European tradition which combine realistic details of daily life with symbolic meanings evoked by mythic imagery. By situating his work with reference to Cervantes and Homer, as Fielding does in Preface to *Joseph Andrews* (in which he defines "a comic romance [as] a comic epic poem in prose" (7)), Fielding places himself at the source of a great and enduring tradition.

Fielding himself calls this combination of mythic imagery and realistic detail in *Tom Jones* a mixture of the Marvelous and the Probable (395-407): the novel is a "Heroic, Historical, Prosaic Poem" (152), revising the traditions of the epic hero journey by adapting 'historical' detail communicated in a graceful, elegant, 'poetic' prose style. Hence the demons in this scene become "a Company of *Egyptians*, or as they are vulgarly called *Gypsies*" (666), and the chapter turns to a satire of Jacobite politics. However, the fact that Fielding bothers to inform us of the mythological descent of the Gypsies from the Egyptians keeps our attention on the myths of the underworld which he had disclaimed when opening the episode, since the Egyptians are most famous for their elaborate necropolae and complex portraits of the voyages of the sun god Ra and Pharaoh through the chambers of the underworld (the *Tuat*) in their Books of the Dead, preserved as papyri in the British Museum.

It therefore should not come as a surprise that when Fielding escorts Tom into London, shortly after the encounter with the Gypsies, he continues to focus the attention of his sagacious readers on myths of the underworld. Tom arrives on "one of the shortest" days of the year, around the time of the Winter Solstice, when the sun itself is at the nadir of its yearly descent, and proceeds post-haste to the doorway of Mrs. Fitzpatrick's refuge, where he hopes to find Sophia. At this doorway he encounters a difficult porter, and Fielding's commentary leaves us in no doubt as to the domain into which Tom is now entering during the London episodes: "I have often thought," Fielding writes,

> that by the particular Description of *Cerberus* the Porter of Hell, in the 6th *Aeneid, Virgil* might possibly intend to satirize the Porters of the great Men in his Time: the Picture, at least, resembles those who have the Honour to attend at the Doors of our great Men. The Porter in his Lodge, answers exactly to *Cerberus* in his Den, and, like him, must be appeased by a Sop, before access can be gained to his Master. Perhaps *Jones* might have seen him in that Light, and have recollected the Passage, where the Sybil, in order to procure an Entrance for *Aeneas*, presents the Keeper of the *Stygian* Avenue with such a Sop. *Jones*, in like Manner, now began to offer a Bribe

to the human *Cerberus*, which a Footman overhearing, instantly advanced, and declared, 'if Mr. *Jones* would give him
the Sum proposed, he would conduct him to the Lady.' (690-
91)

Read most superficially, this passage illustrates the typical uses of the
mock epic in the literature of the Enlightenment, using Classical conventions for satirical purposes. Read figuratively, however (any literal
reading of Fielding would, as Martin Battestin says, be an impoverish-
ment of the novel[13]), the passage suggests that Tom stands at the
doorway to the "*Stygian* Avenue" upon which he is ready to embark: he
is about to undertake that descent into the Inferno Fielding ostensibly
disavowed during the episode of the Gypsies.

The image of the doorway as a symbol of transition between two
realms is frequently associated with the mythology of the underworld.
Consider the sixth book of the Aeneid, to which Fielding refers us here,
during which Virgil pauses to describe in great detail the gateway leading Aeneas down into Hades; consider also Dante's gateway in the
Inferno, above which the words "Abandon all Hope, Ye who Enter
Here" are written; or consider Milton's detailed description of the Gates
through which Satan escapes from Pandemonium, guarded by Sin and
Death, in *Paradise Lost*. Figuratively read in this context, the allusion
to the Virgilian *nekyia* here in *The History of Tom Jones* is more than
an ornamental device characteristic of the mock epic: it is a structural
and thematic metaphor, signally Tom's passage from the road of the
previous Books in the novel into the complexities of life in London in
the subsequent Books. London, therefore, becomes Fielding's rationalized version of the underworld of the Classical and Christian epic poem.
Realistic contemporaries replace the supernatural characters of myth; the
sop offered Cerberus becomes a bribe to achieve admission to London
society.

Indeed, everything that follows this crossing of the stygian threshold at Mrs. Fitzpatrick's refuge adapts the "Furniture of the infernal
Regions" Fielding had professed to discard earlier in the novel (666).
All of the characters show their dark sides at this point in the novel, and
nearly all suffer the torments of one or another of the deadly passions
that dominate the circles of hell in Dante's *Inferno*. Tom, to begin with,
has entered a world of duplicity, lust, avarice, poverty, and violence, and
will reach the nadir of his hero journey in the dungeons of the city jail.
He becomes the kept man of Lady Bellaston, exchanging sexual favors
for clothing and money, and ultimately liberating himself from her with
a fake proposal of marriage that his friend Nightengale puts him up to,
with the assurance that it will cause Lady Bellaston to break off all relations with him. Attacked by Mr. Fitzpatrick shortly afterward during

his pursuit of Sophia, he retaliates and is apprehended by hoodlums hired by Lord Fellamar, who take him to prison where he is thrown in the dungeons and accused of murder.

Meanwhile Sophia is also entangled in the labyrinth of deceit and greed, as Lady Bellaston, to whom she has retreated for protection, devises a plot to remove her from Tom's reach by having Lord Fellamar abduct her, a plot foiled by the arrival of Squire Western, who locks Sophia up (just as Tom in confined in jail) and bullies her to accept marriage with Blifil. Meanwhile, her Aunt Western attempts to impose Lord Fellamar on her, reducing her to a terrible state of misery as she endures her own rationalized version of the infernal journey. Like Tom, she is surrounded by characters who are driven by one of the deadly sins charted by Dante: the avaricious passion of her father and aunt, the lust for revenge and jealousy of Lady Bellaston, the cruel desire of Fellamar which adapts extreme means of achieving its object (i.e., rape), and the apparent libertine profligacy of Tom.

All of these seething passions come to a boil in a kind of witch's cauldron of torments. Indeed, the language of many of the speeches of Sophia and Tom reflects their infernal confinement: terms like torment, persecution, and cruelty are repeatedly used for this purpose. Sophia complains of the "Weapons of Deceit" and "Rage" of her aunt (905), which provoke the most extreme "Passion" we ever see Sophia afflicted by in the novel (904). In response to the "cruel Persecution" inflicted upon Sophia by Lord Fellamar in her "unhappy Situation" (902), Sophia says naively that he must be "too noble to have any Pleasure in tormenting an unhappy Creature" (903). and Fielding remarks than "none ever took more of this Persecution than poor Sophia," and that Lord Fellamar "seemed likely to torment her no less than" Blifil had done (888). The point is of course that Fellamar is not too noble. This is the century of de Sade, and nearly all the women in *Tom Jones* suffer the sadism of males (though of course most manage to inflict suffering as well). Fellamar, as said before, goes so far as to attempt a rape of Sophia, rape being a conventional image for the abduction into the underworld. Fielding's vocabulary keeps our attention focused on the inferno theme throughout this section of the novel: Sophia's "Mind dictated nothing but the tenderest Sorrow," and she is possessed by "tormenting Ideas" (898). In short, Sophia says. "'I'm the most miserable, undone Wretch upon Earth" (889).

Tom's vocabulary is no less colorful and explicit in its portrait of the sorrows of a damned man who seems doomed to the gallows, as appropriate a destination for a journey into the underworld as the dungeon. Fielding masterfully accounts for all the "Pangs with which he was now tormented" and the "Misery" of Tom's arrest (874) by combining it with a letter of rejection from Sophia, and with the suspicion that he has committed incest with his alleged mother. This web of circumstance, Fielding continues, is so viciously cruel that "it would be difficult for the Devil, or any of his Representatives on Earth, to have contrived much greater Torments for poor Jones" (875). He then advises those readers who delight "in seeing Executions ... not to lose any Time in taking a first row at Tyburn" (874). This is a rationalized version of the Inferno, acceptable to a contemporary reader of the Age of Reason. Like Sophia, Tom calls himself a "Wretch," but unlike Sophia, he is a wretch "condemned for the blackest Crime in Human Nature" (908) and continually subject to "melancholy Hours" (907), lamentation of "the Follies and Vices of which he had been guilty" (911), "Dejection" and "Torments" (912). It is particularly interesting to note Tom's remark to Mrs. Waters that "few will follow the Miserable, especially to such dismal Habitations"; to which she replies "Why, your Face is more miserable than any Dungeon in the Universe" (910).

The word "dismal" is etymologically related to the Latin "Dis," referring to the ruined halls of Hades in which Pluto lives, and in a rationalized version of which Tom now finds himself. But as I have shown in my book *Rape and Revelation: The Descent to the Underworld in Modernism*, there are many chambers in the mansion of Hades. In addition to the inferno, the underworld is also a place of revelation (a crypt) and transformation (a temenos). Secret wisdom is communicated to the hero after his torments, as we see in the *Aeneid*, when after traversing the torments of Tartarus Aeneas has his destiny revealed to him by his dead father. Similarly, Odysseus receives crucial information and wisdom from Tiresias in Book 11 of the *Odyssey*. Fielding's novel follows this tradition closely, since Tom is eventually released from jail to witness a sequence of startling revelations regarding his true identity and destiny.

In terms of Aristotelian theory, this revelatory stage of the plot involves a recognition (*anagnoresis*) of the true identity of the hero. Accordingly, we soon learn what the sagacious reader has no doubt already guessed, at least in part: that Squire Allworthy's sister, not Jenny Jones, is Tom's mother, and that his father is Mr. Summer, one of the finest men, Allworthy remarks, that the sun ever shone upon -- handsome, genteel, and endowed with "much Wit and good Breeding" (940). The "surprising Discoveries" (950) now come fast and furious: Mrs. Waters, with whom Tom had slept at the Inn of Upton is Jenny Jones, who is revealed not to have been Tom's mother, though the suspicion that she was contributed not a little to his torments in the dungeon; Partridge himself is finally cleared of the accusation of having fathered Tom upon Jenny; Mr. Dowling uncovers Blifil's plot to prevent Squire Allworthy from receiving his sister's death bed confession of maternity on the night when the Squire lay ill at the beginning of the novel; Mr.

Dowling reveals Blifil's role in the attempted prosecution of Tom while in the prison in London; and hence finally, Mr. Blifil's villainy is revealed and punished, precipitating a reversal of fortunes which Aristotle calls *peripiteia* and associates with the resolution of a complex plot.

In the context of our discussion of the universal archetypes of the hero journey, it is significant that this surprising sequence of revelations occurs in a setting which Fielding has taken some pains to identify as a kind of underworld. We can see how *Tom Jones* illustrates the continuity and transformation of this view of the underworld as a place where those archetypal ideas which shape and govern life are revealed. Furthermore, the underworld is imagined here not only as a place where the hidden idea shaping the plot of the novel and Tom's destiny is revealed (underworld as crypt), but also as a place where a certain transformation of Tom's character attends upon this revelation (underworld as temenos): he changes, and as a result his fortunes are reversed from bastard to legatee and lord of Allworthy's and Sophia's estate.

Indeed, much of the vocabulary of this last section of the novel evokes a specifically Christian sense of the kind of transformation precipitated by a Harrowing of Hell: constant allusion is made to the fundamentally biblical paradigm of sin, repentance, and atonement characteristic of such narratives as the story of Jonah and Joseph or the Prodigal Son. Indeed, Tom's reconciliation with Allworthy is meant to suggest the atonement between father and son in biblical terms: Tom accepts his "Punishment" at Allworthy's hands because it has taught him "Prudence," the ability to "discern Follies and Vices more than enough to repent and to be ashamed of" (959). And again, during his reconciliation with Sophia, which is meant to suggest the allegorical climax of the Christian hero's search for wisdom, Tom becomes a "true Penitent" who confesses himself of his sins and says "No Repentance was ever more sincere" (972). Hence, his ensuing marriage with Sophia becomes an allegory of the union between the erring soul and divine wisdom.

As we have seen throughout this study of the hero journey in literature, the underworld is a place where secret wisdom about life and death is revealed. Hence, initiatory descents into Hades have often been said to evoke a so-called wisdom tradition, which is often held in contrast with the so-called fertility tradition of the ritual. In *Tom Jones* the two traditions come together, for in his wise repentance following a sequence of surprising revelations, Tom is eligible for marriage with the Great Goddess of the novel, and this marriage leads not only to a renewal of wisdom, but also to a profound release of life energy resulting from the resolution of tensions between various oppositions in the novel. For the society has been purified of its imprudent and destructive passions just as the individuals have. There has been a harrowing of

hell and a purgation (an Aristotelian *katharsis*) of negative emotions
leading to the new life promised by the marriage between Sophia and a
man whose father's name is Summer. The marriage occurs in the dead
middle of winter, about the time of the solstice, after which we can expect a defeat of the powers of darkness (Blifil cast out) and a return of
the light from its sojourn in the underworld of London.

The Arabian Nights

Many of the most important and enduring motifs of the hero journey were established in the folktale tradition of the ancient world, but,
in many ways, the Arabian Nights and the fairy tale were phenomena of
the 18th century. These marvelous stories capture the most profound
wisdom in a thoroughly delightful form and pass it on to later generations of storytellers. Antoine Galland's French translations of *The
Thousand Nights and One Nights* (1710-17) was one of the great publishing events of the century. A Grub street English version soon followed, reaching its third edition by 1715, and reprinted many times during the rest of the century, reaching its 18th edition by 1793; the
Nights influenced Swift, Addison, Pope, Johnson, Sterne, Gibbon,
Fielding, Smollet, and many others (Dickens, Collins, Wordsworth,
Coleridge, Joyce, Yeats) throughout the course of subsequent centuries
(Caraciollo 2-80). Serializaton of Sinbad and then other stories from the
Nights occurred in the years 1720, 1723, and the 1790's, bringing the
stories to a large popular audience (Caracciolo 2-3).

In fact, if taken along with rise of interest in myth, folklore, and
the folktale -- indicated by the work of Vico in Italy, J. G. Herder and in
Germany, William Warburton , Jacob Byrant , and Sir William Jones
in England[14] -- and along with the rise of the literary folktale in works
by Giambattista Basile in Italy, Charles Perrault, Marie-Catherine
D'Aulnoy, Voltaire, and Antoine Galland in France, and Musäus,
Wieland and Goethe in Germany[15] -- one could say that the tremendous
impact of the fairy tale versions of the hero journey normally associated
with the Brothers Grimm actually had its roots in the 18th century. The
word "fairy tale" first appears in English in 1749 (the year *Tom Jones*
was published), and many of the classic tales appeared in various forms
throughout a century whose major figures were all influenced by them.
Robert Samber's translation of Perrault's *Histoires ou Contes du temps
passé* (Paris, 1697) appeared in London in 1729, thereby introducing
"the tales that have become the most loved in the English language"
(Opie 24). Henry Fielding produced a tragic version of "Tom Thumb" at
Haymarket Theatre in 1730, and in the first chapter of *Joseph Andrews*
(1742) he alludes to "Jack the Giant Killer," a tale printed in chapbook

form in 1711, and later by John Cotton and Joshua Eddowes in 1765. "Tom Thumb" was admired by Boswell, Dr. Johnson, and William Cowper (Opie 32, 50). The whole subject is just now beginning to receive proper scholarly attention, and is changing our view of the literature of the period. The variations on the hero journey offered by this body of work exerted an important and lasting influence on the literary traditions of subsequent centuries.

The first collection of the *Arabian Nights*, the Hezar Efsan, was Persian, translated into Arabic during the Persian humanistic period after the fall of the Ommiade Khalifate (661-750 AD) and the founding of the Persian supported Abbasides at Baghdad, the great cosmopolitan center of the Mohammedan world at this time (750-1258). The men and manners of the tales chiefly reflect the Abbaside Khalifate of Haroun er Reshid (786-809), the last before the gradual diminishment of the Islamic Empire. This was a Golden Age of Islam at Baghdad, a thriving city likened to a terrestrial paradise, and inhabited by many great individuals. The court itself (the presumed patrons of the tales) was characterized by a refined atheism, while the ruler and the lower classes were strictly Muslim. The tales were put down in their 'final form' either in the 14th century, or possibly in 800 A.D., when they may have been translated into Arabic from a Persian translation of an Indian original, then amplified by the addition of many tales from a variety of independent sources in Baghdad (800-1000) and later in Egypt and Syria (1200).

The stories therefore mix Persian and Mohammedan elements, and may possibly also have Oriental Indian and Chinese elements. There are still traces of a pre-Mohammedan allegory of the soul's journey derived from Persian, Babylonian, Egyptian, and Indian mythologies. The gods of these earlier pantheons become the Jinn of the Nights, just as the Celtic deities of Old Europe became the faeries of folklore after Christianization. According to this pre-Mohammedan allegory, the winning of women, power, and gold (so often the basis of the stories) were traditional Indo-European symbols of spiritual fulfillment. The tales as we have them seem to have lost these earlier dimensions of meaning, which of been secularized to entertain a courtly and mercantile audience (much as were the Celtic motifs in Arthurian myth).

The compilation of the tales occurred at the same time when the Arthurian legends were being formulated in Medieval Europe, 1190-1230. During the Crusades, there was of course considerable commerce and conflict between the Christian North and the Muslim Southeast, both religions having originated in the Near East. The world of the Arthurian Romance shares with the Arabian Nights an emphasis on romantic love, chivalric valor in combat and court, enchantments of castle and sword, and heroic quests into the magical realms of supernatural power (forest and desert). In fact, the narrative device of the frame tale, which we know from Boccacio's *Decameron* and Chaucer's *Canterbury Tales*, may ultimately have come from the Arabian Nights.[16] Galland's selection for the court of Louis XIV (1704-1717), had a tremendous impact. His influence can be seen in great works of the 18th Century like Lesage's *Gil Blas*, Voltaire's *Candide*, Defoe's *Robinson Crusoe*, Swift's *Gulliver's Travels*, Johnson's *Rasselas*, and in a variety of pseudo-Oriental romances very popular during this period. In the 19th century, three scholarly editions of the Arabic texts were printed, and the first complete translation was produced by John Payne in 1881 in English, and replicated in 1885 by Sir Richard Burton.[17]

The entire collection begins with a famous frame of great importance for our interpretation of the hero journey as a metaphor of the creative processes of reading and writing: Sharazad tells her stories to King Shahryar, to delay her decapitation. Her tales gradually cure the King of his pathological wrath, having become maniacally jealous when he returns from a visit with his brother, only to find his harem has been unfaithful. As Bruno Bettelheim points out, the telling and the hearing of the tales has a therapeutic result, for both reader and writer. By the end of the 1001 nights of stories (many of which reflect upon the King's plight, providing a healing mirror of his affliction), Shahyar has begun to "reintegrate his completely disintegrated personality," and "murderous hatred has been changed into enduring love" (Bettelheim 88-9). In his book *Healing Fiction*, James Hillman has also pointed out the crucial role stories play in the therapeutic process, which was from the beginning based on patients telling stories to men who wrote them down, using the frame tradition as a model for the case study (in which both teller of tale and listener become characters in a story). George Quasha coins the term "psychopoesis" for this linkage between story-telling and soul-making characteristic of both psychoanalysis and the hero journey in general ("Preface" x).

"The Tale of Zubaidah" from *The Thousand Nights and One Night* is an excellent example of the frame tale technique and of the heroine's journey in the collection. The frame is elaborate, many-leveled: Sharazad tells her story to King Shahyar about a Porter who tells a story to a King which the Porter heard from a Kalandar who tells a story he heard from Zubaidah! Within the same frame, three other tales told by three Dervishes are told. All the tales are generally included under the title of "The Porter and the Three Girls of Baghdad."The narrative effect is one of infinite regress, of Chinese box within box, of hero journey within hero journey. The whole arrangement is a treasure trove of material for reader-response critics, and has also received sensitive analysis in Bruno Bettelheim's *The Uses of Enchantment*, where he focuses on the healing power of stories as the theme of the frame. "The Tale of Zubaidah," embedded deeply in the frame, is an excellent example of the heroine's journey, beginning and ending in Baghdad, with the miraculous adventure of shipwreck on a mysterious island in between two threshold battles. Many of those pre-Islamic symbols associated with the journey of the soul are visible just beneath the dogmatic surface of the narrative.

The story is uniquely concerned with the plight of women in the Islamic world and with the relationships between three sisters. It begins, as many heroine's journeys do, with conflict and crisis. The oppressive circumstances this time are patriarchal: two of the three sisters use the dowry left by the death of the father (another common starting point for the journey) to marry, while the third and youngest increases her inheritance prudently in business. When the two older sisters return destitute, having been abandoned in strange lands by bankrupt husbands who have squandered the dowries, the youngest sister takes them in and treats them generously. When the older sisters build up a second dowry, they marry once again, with the same results: bankruptcy, theft, and abandonment. It is upon their second return to their youngest sister, that Zubaidah resolves to sail to Basrah to do business. Zubaidah prudently divides her money, leaving half at home in case some misfortune ruins her at sea. She is therefore distinguished by her prudence, her independence, her distrust of patriarchy, her generosity, and her good business sense.

The crisis which leads to departure for the sisters is marriage, that event which initiates many a woman's heroine journey. For Zubaidah, the departure is related to her sister's misfortunes, but more than that, it is inaugurated from within, at midlife, by the urge to see more of the world. The threshold crossing involves, typically, a storm at sea (an old symbol for the emotional turmoil of midlife), which drives the ship ten days into unknown seas (an old symbol for the unconscious realm of the spirit). The realm of initiation is a strange city on an enchanted island, which Zubaidah explores (a female Odysseus!). While her sisters wander off into the marketplace, where all the inhabitants have been turned into black stone, Zubaidah makes her way towards the citadel of the King's palace (an archaic symbol of the Self). Here the old symbolism of doorways, corridors, and gemstones surfaces: Zubaidah enters the palace through "a great door of solid gold" with a "velvet curtain" hanging in front of it, and she comes immediately upon the petrified King surrounded by furniture of gold and silver and sitting upon a throne encrusted with pearls that shine "so like a star that I thought I should lose my wits in gazing on them" (105).

The astronomical symbolism becomes increasingly important and points towards an archaic mysticism of revelation: silver is associated with the moon, gold with the sun, and the pearls with stars. Passing through another threshold, "an open door made with two leaves of virgin silver," Zubaidah climbs "a porphyry staircase of seven steps," at the top of which she discovers a bed with a golden dais supporting a "diamond, large as an ostrich's egg" dazzling the hall with the radiance shining from all its facets (105). The passage through a sequence of doorways, halls, corridors, and staircases remains one of the standard icons of the hero journey from the Sumerian descent of Inanna to Cocteau's *Beauty and the Beast*. It connotes both the penetration of the labyrinth and the journey to the otherworld (as either descent or ascent), where the revelations ensue. The diamond at the top of this seven-tiered staircase, surrounded by torches which it outshines "utterly" (106), rep resents, on the one hand, the mystical source of light illuminating the seven planetary bodies which lead up to it and the host of starry torches which surround it. That this source of light is compared to an "ostrich egg" also suggests the kind of Orphic Creation symbolism (in which Night hatches an Egg from which the Universe emerges) to be discussed below in the voyages of Sinbad. What we have here in "The Tale of Zubaidah" is a glimpse into the Gnostic mysticism of the soul's ascent to heaven along the seven steps of the planetary scales, much like the famous apotheosis at the end of Chaucer's *Troilus and Creseyde*.

When night falls, Zubaidah is lost in the labyrinth of the palace, unable to find her way out and circling endlessly around the hall with the diamond (106). This chamber yields first a magnificent Koran (the opened book another symbol of the initiatory revelations of the heroine's journey), "written out in stately gold characters with red devices and illuminations in all colours" (106). Zubaidah then passes through another doorway, when, at midnight, she hears a beautiful young man reciting the Koran in a "sweet and learned voice" inside a little room (106). This is the third doorway specifically mentioned by the text, though we are perhaps to infer many others, unless the palace is designed with open sequences of archways like the Alhambra. The astronomical symbolism merges with the motif known as the sacred marriage in the description of the beautiful boy which follows. This description is the climax of the initiatory phase of the journey. While Zubaidah watches the young man reading from "the Koran with grave attention and perfect eloquence" (106), she poetically attributes each of his features to celestial influence: Saturn gave him his black hair, Mars bestowed the roses in his cheeks, the constellation of the Archer gave the arrows to his eyes, "sagacious Mercury" imparted his sweet intelligence, and "Venus forged his golden heart" (107). The catalogue modestly stops here, but one can infer that the young man is a kind of microcosm, each organ of the body corresponding to a celestial patron in a way reminiscent of the magnificent plate from the *Trés Riches Heures*

of the Duc of Berry, which shows a human body embedded in a man-
dorla with designated zodiacal correspondences between the organs and
the heavens. The young man explains that the petrification of the city
actually resulted from the reverence of his father, who worshipped "fire
and light" and "all the turning stars" (107). This aroused the wrath of
Allah, who turned the city to black stone.

This explanation completes the revelation phase of the journey, in
which the ancient symbolism of the soul's journey, couched in the astronomical imagery of the Near East, has been overlaid with Muslim
piety. The revelation, however, operates on both levels, illuminating
the mysteries of the soul and explaining contemporary conditions.
Zubaidah's task is now to bring her newfound wisdom and her husband
back home to Baghdad. Like Gilgamesh, she succeeds in the former task
but fails in the latter, retaining the wisdom but losing the object taken
from the otherworld during the return threshold battle. Her jealous sisters throw her and the young man overboard in the middle of the night,
and the latter drowns. Gilgamesh also lost the flower of immortality
(which he culled from the depths of the sea) while sleeping. Zubaidah,
however, clings like Odysseus to a spar of wood from the ruined bed,
and is carried ashore. Here she kills a large snake before it catches a
smaller snake. The little snake turns out to be a Jinniyah (one thinks
now of the archaic symbolism of the serpent in the hero journeys of the
Ancient World: Zubaidah too has shed a skin of sorts and imbibed inti-
mations of immortality). The Jinniyah sinks the ship, transports the
riches home, and turns the wicked sisters into two black bitches, which
Zubaidah must lash everyday with three hundred strokes when she completes the cycle by returning to Baghdad. The allegory here revolves
around the sibling and shadow problems, suggesting the sad necessity
of breaking ties with sisters who exploit us, and of exorcising the
greedy bitches within.

Threshold imagery associated with the descent into the underworld
persists in the other three tales, told by the dervishes, typically included
among the frame sequence known as "The Porter and the Three Girls of
Baghdad." All three dervishes have lost one eye, which their stories
must account for. The first dervish tells how his cousin asks him to
take a veiled woman to a burial ground, where he digs under some
stones to uncover "an iron slab the size of a small door" (Dawood 258).
Lifting the slab reveals a "vaulted staircase," down which the cousin and
the veiled woman descend (258). The dervish replaces "the trap-door,"
and leaves the couple entombed, like Romeo and Juliet (259). But when
he returns with his uncle, lifts the iron slab, and descends some fifty
steps of the stairway, he finds his cousin and the veiled woman sitting
in a spacious hall among "sacks of flour and grain," but burned "black
as charcoal" (261). The sad story of the young lovers is then told (they

are an incestuous half brother and sister), before the uncle and the dervish climb "out of the tomb" and replace the stones (262).

Threshold imagery and the descent continue to play a central role in the tale told by the second dervish, who adds vital images of poesis to his story. While working for a woodcutter during his exile in a foreign land, the second dervish starts digging around the stump of a fallen tree in "densely wooded glade" (266). His axe strikes against a "ring of brass set into a wooden slab," which, when lifted, reveals a "flight of stairs" with another door at the bottom (266). This door leads into "the spacious courtyard of a magnificent palace," where the dervish finds a "young woman more beautiful than a priceless pearl and as radiant as the sun" (266). The similes are well chosen, for they evoke the pearl of the Gnostic hymn, and the solar rhythms of the hero journey. The princess says she was abducted by "Jerjees the Jinnee, son of Iblees himself, and imprisoned in this palace" (266). Iblees is the Arabic name for Satan, which suggests a parallel between the princess and Persephone, who was also abducted by a lord of the underworld. Like Orpheus, the second dervish now attempts to rescue the princess, but the Jinnee kills her, and carries the dervish out through the vaulted doorway of the underground palace way up to a mountaintop, where he turns the dervish into an ape.

In Egyptian myth, the god of writing (inventor of hieroglyphs) was named Thoth, and he was often depicted with an ape or baboon head, since the monkey has the power of mimickry (*Larousse* 27). As such, Thoth was associated with the mysteries of poesis. One thinks also here of the monkeys in the *Popul Vuh*, which were associated with poesis and song. It is therefore of great interest to find the ape writing in the tale of the second dervish. He finds refuge with a king and his daughter, and amazes them by composing "six couplets, each in a different script," for which feat he is invested with a "robe of honor" (272). After the ape improvises "half a dozen verses in praise of" the King's hospitality, the King's daughter identifies the ape as the dervish, "an illustrious prince" (273). She then proceeds to perform a second magical act of poesis, an which enriches the climax of the tale with a variety of hidden meanings. For it turns out that the King's daughter is a kind of female Magi, trained from childhood by "an old nurse, a skilled enchantress deeply versed in sorcery" (274). She has memorized "a hundred and seventy codes of magic," and boasts of the power to raze the King's city to the ground "and scatter its stones as far as the Mountain of Kaf" (274). Instead of destroying the city, however, she puts her magical powers of poesis to good use, by turning the enchanted monkey back into a prince! Is it not the civlizing power of poetry to turn all of us from monkeys into men? The princess does so by using a knife "engraved with Hebrew words" to mark a circle in the middle of the palace, and to inscribe it with "talismanic names and magic inscriptions," while standing in the center to recite an incantation (274). The additional detail of the Hebrew letters provides a fascinating glimpse into the syncretic world of myth drawn upon by the Arabian tales, for we know of an ancient form of Jewish mysticism which combined geometric forms and the mystical letters of the alphabet. As Wallis Budge has shown, this tradition merged with other aspects of Kabbalism and Gnosticism in the Ancient Near East to produce several marvelous documents and amulets (Amulets 212-38). In these documents, the letters have a wide range of mystical power, all of which confer a kind of esoteric sanctity upon poesis in general (for poets create worlds by the manipulation of names and letters, just as God did, according to the Kabbalists).

The princess uses the magical letters to conjure up a terrifying Jinnee, who appears in a hideous shape, and who pursues and eventually destroys her. This occurs through a series of transformations, which provide a good example of what Joseph Campbell calls the "magic flight" (*Hero* 196f.). The flight recorded in the second dervish's tale is particularly interesting, since it recalls a similar moment in the Arthurian legends of ancient Wales. The Jinnee turns himself into a lion, a scorpion, an eagle, a black cat, a large red pomegranate, and a whale; while the princess takes the forms of a serpent, a vulture, a wolf, a rooster, and a burning coal. The battle ends with the death of the princess, whose sacrifice, however, leads to the transformation of the ape. The entire episode suggests the Pythagorean notion of transmigration, as the soul passes through a series of incarnations, from animal to man, in its progress towards spiritual perfection. Readers of Arthurian literature will also recall the story of Ceridwen, who sets her apprentice, Taliessin, to stirring her magical cauldron. When he dips his finger to taste the brew, he instantly achieves the omniscience the Goddess had intended for her son. As a result, Ceridwen pursues Taliessin through a sequence of transformations, very like those recorded in the tale of the dervish, right down to the hen and grain, which the hen swallows, only to give birth to the transformed Taliessin nine months later (Graves 27-28). Both images of the magic flight serve to connect the hero journey to the transmigration of the soul, and to the powers of poesis (which involve here the manipulation of magic letters).

Threshold imagery dominates the ascents and descents in the tale of the third dervish. Stranded on a desert island, he finds a trap door the size of a millstone, with a "vaulted stairway" going down to a spacious hall, where a young prince lives. The dervish fulfills a prophecy by accidentally killing the prince. He flees to a kingdom with a lofty palace of brass flowing brightly in the sun, where he finds ten youths, all with one eye, who nightly lament their fate. The dervish forces their story out of them, and they send him to the palace where they were blinded. To get there, the dervish must be sewn into the skin of a flayed ram, and carried in the talons of a roc up to the top of a mountain. The imagery of the soul's departure from the corpse, and its ascent to the mountain heavens by birdflight is a classic motif of Persian mysticism, one that recurs throughout the Arabian Nights. When the dervish reaches the mountain top, he passes through the doorway into a marvelous palace, inhabited by "forty young girls, each as beautiful as the rising moon" (285). Like the hero of the Hymn of the Pearl, the dervish is reinvested, "robed in splendid garments" (286), but unlike the Gnostic, he does not shun the spiritual pleasures of the flesh: Instead, he enjoys each of the girls on each of the forty nights that follow! Afterwards, the women go on a journey, leaving the dervish alone with "the keys of all the forty doors of the palace" (286). Like Aladdin beneath the caves of the mountains, the dervish finds Elysian gardens and palatial halls behind the first three doors. The fourth door opens into an intricate maze, a "great pavilion with forty doors, each opening on a vault stacked with pearls and rubies, chrysolites and emeralds and other precious gems" (287). Doors, within doors, within doors -- the labyrinth was a favorite motif of Persian miniature painting, and it provides a visual image of poesis, reflecting the elaborate intricacy of the tales in the *Arabian Nights*, gathered together in the frame of the book as a whole. Every day the dervish opens another door, "more and more amazed at each new wonder," until he comes to the fortieth, "forbidden door" (287). Behind this door he finds a magnificent black stallion, standing before a crystal manger, between two large braziers burning incense and honeyed aloe wood. As in the Arthurian story of Percival, the stallion is demonic, and carries the dervish wildly through the air.

All seven of the famous voyages of Sinbad follow the structure of the hero journey exactly, beginning and ending in Baghdad, with the initiatory voyages constituting the main action of the tale. Though these tales have been adapted to a sophisticated cosmopolitan audience, much concerned with courtly manners and economic conditions, they preserve a deep reservoir of metaphysical import. In "The Second Voyage of Sinbad the Sailor," the impulse to adventure is simply a "desire" to visit "far countries and strange people" that enters Sinbad's head in the midst of a "life of unexampled pleasure" (187). As so often in the hero journey, the real threshold crossing is associated with dream: when Sinbad lies down to sleep by a clear stream on an island where his ship anchors briefly, the fellow travelers sail off without him, leaving him stranded on the island. Walking around the island, Sinbad finds "a gigantic dome of shining white" which turns out to be an enormous rukh egg. That night the tremendous bird blots out the sun and lands to brood upon the egg. Sinbad ties his turban to the rukh's talons, so that when it flies screaming up to "the vault of Heaven" the next morning, it carries Sinbad with it, and then swiftly plummets to drop Sinbad in a "wide and deep valley" entirely surrounded by steep unscalable cliffs.

The gigantic egg of this episode, brooded upon by the dark wings of the bird of night, from which Sinbad is elevated at dawn to the vault of Heaven, is an archaic symbol of the Creation, one which the Orphics later adapted in their cosmology. In the Orphic creation myth, "black winged night, after being courted by the Wind, brought forth an egg, out of which Eros or Phanes emerged" (Biedermann 112). Sinbad has penetrated to the origins of all life at this point: mother universe is an enormous dark winged bird to whose body he is clasped. One thinks of the Egyptian Isis, Nut, Mut, or Nekhebet, all of whom were ornithomorphic symbols of the mother Goddess. The name of the vulture goddess, for example, is Mut, and means "mother" (Wilkinson 85); Nekhebet, who "was represented in the form of a woman with the head of a vulture," was also "the mother of the Sun-god" (Budge 439-40). It is significant, therefore, that the rukh carries Sinbad up to the morning sun after its night of brooding. The heavenly ascent of the hero, often in the talons of a bird (as in the myths of Ganymede or the Navajo Twins), represents the rebirth of the sun, and constitutes the initiation of the hero into the mysteries of the spiritual realm.

From the realm of the heavens, however, Sinbad plummets into the valley of the shadow of death, surrounded on all sides by steep, unscalable cliffs. As Sinbad looks around the deep valley, he sees no way out, but discovers huge piles of diamonds guarded by "innumerable black snakes, thicker and longer than palm trees, each one of which could have swallowed a large elephant" (190). There are no fruit trees or delightful streams in the valley, only unfriendly rocks, so that Sinbad faces death by starvation. He retreats at night into a narrow cave, but after rolling a stone against the entrance, he sees "a terrible snake, rolled about her eggs," and shrivels up like a "dead leaf" and falls "senseless to the ground" (191). The motifs associated with the descent to the underworld are clear: valley, cave, stone, serpent, and the death-like sleep into which Sinbad falls. But the cave is as much womb as it is tomb, a paradox common to the hero journey from the *Odyssey* to *Sir Gawain and the Green Knight*. For in the depths of the cave, Sinbad encounters the Orphic image of Creation for the second time: a serpent coiled around her eggs. Eggs commonly depicted in the tomb paintings and sarcophagi of Ancient Rome represent the creative rhythms of "becoming and passing away" (Bachofen 26). We know that as far back as 1000 B.C., Phoenician mythologies attributed the Creation to a "watery slime called Mot" which was twisted into a shining egg by the swirling winds of night (Eliot 62). The Orphics pictured these winds as the serpent Ophion, which "coiled seven times about the World Egg until it hatched and split open," but the famous image is surely much older and perhaps Middle Eastern in origin, close to the shores where Sinbad journeyed (Eliot 82).

Hence, when Sinbad emerges the next morning from the cave, and rolls "away the stone" (191), two symbols of death and rebirth have been combined: the world egg has hatched after its serpentine incubation, and the cave has modulated from tomb to womb. The rolling away of the stone we recognize not only from the Homer, when Odysseus tricks Polyphemus into rolling away the stone so his men can escape, but also from the Bible, where in the New Testament accounts of the Resurrection, the stone which blocks the sepulchre where Christ lies buried is miraculously removed by the Angels. It now remains for Sinbad to rise up from the valley of the shadow of death, and he does so in the most marvelously symbolic manner. He sees a group of men high up on the cliffs throwing slabs of slaughtered sheep down into the valley. The diamonds on the valley floor pierce the carcass, so that when rukhs and eagles swoop down to carry the meat up to their nests in the craggy cliffs, they carry the diamonds with them. The "jewelers" on the cliffsides then frighten the birds away and pick out the diamonds stuck to the bloody pieces of meat. Sinbad, of course, cunning man, fills his pockets with diamonds and ties himself with his turban to a bloody "quarter of mutton," so that when the rukhs swoop down they carry the intrepid sailor up the tops of the cliff (192). When the merchants see Sinbad climb out from under the carcass with "face and clothes all bloody," they are furious; they see not the miracle or resurrection in front of them, but a business deal gone bad. But Sinbad appeases them with some diamonds, and they take him back to their city and send him back to Baghdad, completing the hero journey cycle.

The diamond is an old symbol of the soul. Along with other precious gems (like the ones Aladdin garnishes from his cave garden, or the emerald we will see in *Sir Gawain and the Green Knight*), the diamond "typifies adamantean quality both of truth and of the true spirit" (Campbell, *Occidental Myth* 481). Lodged in the bloody carcass of the lamb, it represents our own souls, stuck to the bloody corpse we all carry around with us. That the diamond is attached to the body of the slaughtered lamb in the story is surely significant as well, since in Judeo-Christian times the lamb becomes a symbol of the Messiah and of resurrection. Curiously enough, the diamond is also "a symbol of Christ the Savior," whose coming was announced in the prophecy of *Physiologus* in Amos 7: 8-9: "Behold, I will set a diamond in the midst of my people Israel" (Biedermann 95). Sinbad, twice reborn from the caves of the night, to ascend the sky like the sun ("the diamond, like rock crystal, corresponds to the sun" (Biedermann 95)), represents the power of the soul to shed its skin like the serpent. His seven voyages represent a complete sequence of incarnations, at the end of which the hero is liberated from the wheel of life, returning to the holy city of Baghdad forever.

Sinbad's other voyages typically involve threshold symbolism and other imagery associated with the descent to the underworld. In his third voyage, he comes to the "great ebony door" of a "towering palace," passing through which he enters a spacious courtyard littered with "a great heap of bones" (129). There is an open oven door at the far end of the courtyard, surrounded by "pots and pans of enormous size, and many iron spits for roasting" (129). Here Sinbad is overcome by sleep (like the soul of the Gnostic trapped in Hades), to be awakened at sunset as a "colossal black giant" passes through the "doorway" into the infernal courtyard. This giant is another precursor of the Wild Man of the Woods in Arthurian legend: he has a camel's lips, ears that hang over his shoulders, fangs like the tusk of a boar, and nails like the claws of a lion (130). A gruesome meal ensues, as the giant skewers one of the men, like a "fatted ram," and roasts him on a spit inside the great oven. The cannibalism and the oven suggest not only the imagery of such tales as "Hansel and Gretel," or "Vasilisa the Beautiful," but also the archetype of the sacred vessel, often associated with sacrificial meals. Examples would include the Chinese cauldrons, the Gundestrup bowl, and images of the Hell cook in "The Garden of Earthly Delights," by Hieronymous Bosch. The means of escape from this particular hell cook recall the *Odyssey*: after the giant falls asleep, Sinbad and his snatch red hot spits from the oven, and stab their "sharpened ends" deep into the eyes of the snoring monster.

Two more images of the heroic descent emerge after Sinbad escapes from the giant and his infernal oven. The first involves a "serpent of prodigious size," which encircles Sinbad's men in "a knotted coil" after they fall asleep on the next island they come to (132). Once again, the symbolism of the sea, sleep, the serpent, and the maze of mortal coils combine to form Gnostic imagery of the descent of the soul into the underworld of matter. After the serpent devours one of Sinbad's men, the second image of the nekyia surfaces: Sinbad climbs a tall tree and then collects some wood to make a "coffin-shaped box, complete with lid," in which he takes refuge, enduring a long, terrifying night, as the serpent writhes and hisses around the coffin. Hence, the coffin becomes a symbol of that liberation conferred by death upon the soul, which sheds its skin like the serpent to escape the mortal coil of the body. It is a symbol we will see again in Melville's *Moby Dick*.

The symbolism of the descent becomes even more explicit during Sinbad's fourth voyage. When the wife Sinbad marries on a strange island dies and is buried, tradition dictates that he must be entombed with her, in a kind of reverse Suttee ritual! After "a stone was rolled away from the mouth of a deep pit," and his wife's corpse is thrown in, Sinbad is lowered down on a "long rope, together with seven loaves of bread and a pitcher of water" (141). We recognize the age old symbolism of the bread and water of life, which we have seen during the descents of Inanna and Gilgamesh (the former revived by the bread and water of life, and the latter having seven loaves baked for him while he sleeps seven days and seven nights in Utnapishtim's land of the faraway). We also perhaps may recognize elements of the near-death experience in the detailed imagery of Sinbad's escape from the "charnel cave" into which he is lowered with his wife (142). The cavern is filled with skeletons and stinks of rotting flesh. Sinbad survives by killing the next Suttee victims, and eating their food for many weeks. He is awakened one day by the sound of a small animal scurrying among the bones and corpses, and he follows the animal towards a "tremulous speck of light" at the far end of the cave, where the animal escapes through a narrow tunnel. Sinbad crawls through the tunnel on all fours, eventually emerging into the dazzling light of the open sky, like a contemporary cardiac patient revived on the operating table. Sinbad brings with him as many "jewels, pearls, and precious ornaments" as he can gather from the corpses and tie together in their "shrouds and garments" (143). As in the Valley of Diamonds, with the huge gems stuck into the rotting carcasses of the rams, these stones represent the adamantine light of the soul, which survives death. That Sinbad choose one particular "rare pearl" to offer the captain of a ship which rescues him also recalls the Gnostic Hymn, during which the son had been sent to retrieve a pearl from a serpent in the depths of the sea.

Archetypal and thanatological symbols of the underworld continue to enrich Sinbad's last two tales, but with some significant variations. After the adventure in the Cavern of the Dead, Sinbad's sixth voyage leaves him shipwrecked on an island, surrounded by his dying companions. One by one he washes the dead and wrapped them in winding sheets made from the fabrics scattered on the shore (153). After burying them all, Sinbad despairs, and digs himself a "deep grave by the sea" (153). But as he lies in preparation for death, it occurs to him that he should make one last effort to live. Near the wreckage and graves on the shore, Sinbad finds a marvelous river flowing from a gorge in the mountains, and plunging into a "vast rocky cavern" (152). Like the river of the dead we will see in "An Occurrence at Owl Creek Bridge," the banks are "covered with glittering jewels, and the bed was studded with myriads of rubies, emeralds, and other precious stones; so that the entire river blazed with a dazzling light" (152). The description recalls the glittering gardens of the otherworld in the tales of Aladdin, Gilgamesh, and Orfeo, as much as it does the paradisal landscapes evoked by the survivors of the near-death experience. Reasoning that any river with a beginning must also have an end, Sinbad makes a raft, loads it up with sacks of rubies, pearls, and other stones, and lets the current carry him swiftly off into the "brooding darkness of the cavern" (154). Using imagery that suggests both perinatal and thanatological motifs, the tale describes the narrowing of the passage, as Sinbad bumps his head against the rocks, and sinks into a "death-like sleep" (154), as he had done in the Cavern of Serpents in the Valley of Diamonds. Like a new born infant, or like a post-mortem visionary, Sinbad emerges from the dark tunnel into the light of a pleasant mead-owland, beneath an open sky, completing the fourth explicit cycle of death and rebirth recorded by his hero voyages. Like Gilgamesh passing through the twelve leagues of darkness, beneath the dismal mountains, Sinbad is reborn on the yonder shore, and soon hastens home, where he orders that his "story be inscribed on parchment in letters of gold" (155). An act of poesis serves as the climax of this fourth heroic descent, and distinguishes it from the others.

The last of the voyages concludes again with the imagery of the cave, mountain, and river as symbols of the underworld, but adds a crucial variant to the complex. The seventh voyage brings together several of the most precious images of Arabic Persian mysticism. These are all associated with the celestial ascent of the Prophet Mohammed, his Miraj Namah, during which he is taken up through the spheres of the planets by the Angel Gabriel. But the Prophet's ascent has much older prototypes, in the Assyrian story of Etana, a king taken up to heaven on the back of an eagle, during his quest for magic herb for his childless wife (Curtis and Reed 201); and in the Persian legend of the Simurgh, who carries the soul to the mountains of Kaf in Farid Attar's great mystical poem, *The Conference of Birds* (Corbin, *Avicenna* 198). Kaf (as we have seen) is the cosmic mountain where the Cinvat Bridge takes souls from earth to heaven at death, or, alternatively, the 8th heaven of the fixed Stars in Ptolemy, or 9th Sphere of Emerald Cities which surrounds all the others.

Sinbad arrives at this mountain in the last of his voyages after being rescued from a rushing river by an old man wielding a net. He has been on a raft for "three days and nights," after which he sinks into "a dead faint" in the face of a tremendous cataract (158). The "venerable old man" who rescues him, wraps him in warm garments, washes and feeds him, is a fisher of souls. Like Jesus in the New Testament, or the Fisher King of the Arthurian Romance, or like Orpheus the Fisher (Campbell, *Creative Myth* 24), the old man and his net represent that power which delivers rescues souls from the watery abyss. Shortly after Sinbad's rescue, he is taken up to a mountain top by one of the men in the town where the old man lives: one day each year "All the men grew wings upon their shoulders and for a whole day flew high up in the air, leaving their wives and children behind" (160). The winged man drops Sinbad on the top of a high mountain, where he sees two youths coming towards him, their faces shining "with an unearthly beauty," and holding staffs of red gold. They identify themselves as "worshippers of the True God," and one the youths gives Sinbad his staff, and directs to a "certain path upon the mountain" (160).

As Henri Corbin has shown, the epiphany of such angelic messengers, who orient the perplexed soul on its journey to the East (which represents its return to its heavenly homeland), is a recurrent feature of the mystical recitals of Islamic mysticism (*Avicenna* 308). And so, here in Sinbad's last journey, the angels direct him to his final homecoming, when the soul takes rest at last. The journey ends Sinbad's cycle of voyages, the key to which is the Oriental notion of metempsychosis: the idea that the human soul passes through a sequence of incarnations towards its ultimate liberation from the wheel of life. Each of Sinbad's seven voyages represents another turning of the wheel, another incarnate cycle of death and rebirth, as the soul progresses finally to its homeland, in the celestial city of Baghdad.

Perhaps the most enduringly famous of the tales from the Arabian Nights is the story of "Aladdin and the Wonderful Lamp," which circumscribes two complete hero journey cycles. The first begins in "a certain city of China," when Aladdin, a poor tailor's son, is lured out of the streets and gardens of the town by a dwarfish Moor who appears near the "entrance to the market," a threshold symbol leading to the unknown. We are told that Aladdin's mysterious guide is a powerful magician from Morocco, "deeply learned in astrology and the reading of faces" (370). In one sense, the crisis in Aladdin's life, which causes his idle vagabondage in the city, and eventually precipitates his hero journey, is the death of his father, a typical catalyst of the separation phase of the monomyth in life and art. The death of Aladdin's parent coincides with the onset of puberty, a rite of passage in itself typically associated with the hero journey and rendering the archetypal search for the father all that much more intense (we find characters from Telemachus to Hamlet in similar circumstances). Aladdin's hero journey also involves the timeless task of finding a profession, and the Moor in fact lures Aladdin into his care with the promise of apprenticeship as a merchant.

As usual in the hero journey, Aladdin's preparations involve the symbolism of clothing, and his departure the symbolism of doorways. The mysterious Moor from Morocco takes Aladdin to a merchant and asks for his "costliest robe," and Aladdin skips for joy as he picks out "a robe of striped and shining silk, a white turban decorated with gold, a Kashmir belt, and boots of bright leather" (375). His "transformation" renders him "more beautiful than the moon" (376), an allusion which evokes the marvelous mythology of the lunar rhythms (cosmic model

of the hero journey cycle) that Mann will make so much of in his portrait of Joseph. Thus invested, like Telemachus in his sandals, like
Inanna with her royal accoutrements, or like Joseph in his coat of many
colors, Aladdin is ready for his journey and threshold crossing. This occurs the next morning, when Aladdin goes to the door of his house to
await the Moor, and then walks off through "the gates of the city" to
the "notable houses and handsome garden-girt palaces which lie beyond"
(377). These gates mark a threshold which leads from domestic security
of the city to the "mountain, at the end of a deserted valley filled only
with the presence of God," which is the Moor's destination. He persuades Aladdin to continue the harsh journey by offering him a version
of the forbidden food of the underworld: magical "fruits and cakes"
which seal Aladdin's fate (377).

His descent proper begins, here in the deserted valley of the mountains, with the necromantic rites performed by the Moor, who instructs
Aladdin to collect some wood for a fire, over which he sprinkles incense
and mutters "spells in an unknown tongue" (378). As in Egyptian,
Sumerian, Babylonian, and Biblical myth, the "roots of the mountains"
(as Jonah puts it) are associated with the netherworld, as are the spells
in an unknown tongue, which recall the special connection between the
nekyia and poesis most evident in the Egyptian Books of the Dead, in
which each chamber of the Tuat is inscribed with poetic spells and
hymns to facilitate the passage, but also in all necromantic and funereal
rituals, which typically involve magnificently charged language, in the
form of prayers, hymns, invocations, and memorials to the dead. At the
bottom of the chasm the Moor's spells opens up, Aladdin sees a huge
marble slab with a copper ring in the middle, doorway to the underworld, which can only be opened after he grabs the ring and recites his
lineage, naming himself, his father, and his grandfather (for the underworld is typically the domain of the ancestors). Aladdin is so terrified of
the passage that at first he takes the "skirts of his robe in his teeth" and
runs away, a detail which reminds us of the frequent linkage of doorways and divestiture in the heroic descent (378).

Further threshold imagery follows, as Aladdin descends twelve
marble steps to a second "double door of red copper studded with bolt-
heads of the same" (379). This door swings open of its own accord after
Aladdin lifts "his robe to his belt" (380), and then passes through a
"monstrous cavern, divided into three communicating halls" (379). Like
the Egyptian and Sumerian nether worlds, the Arabian is built out of
connecting chambers separated by doorways: in the first there are twelve
jars, of bronze, silver, and gold, and filled with gold liquid, dust, and
coins. Clothing details arise again when Aladdin is instructed to hold
his "robe close about" his waist, in order to avoid touching any of the
jars; the number twelve probably evokes the astrological mythology of

the sun's journey through the signs of the zodiac (in which the Moorish magician is highly skilled); and the linkage of the precious metals suggests the metallurgical mysticism of the planets (sun-gold, silver-moon, copper-Venus) that we saw in the alchemical hero journeys of the 17th century. A third door lies at the end of the third chamber of jars which leads through a magnificent garden of trees heavily fruited with gemstones infinitely varied in color: "diamonds, pearls, nacre and moon-tones, rubies, carbuncles, hyacinths, corals, carnelian, emeralds, beryls, jade, prase, aquamarine, sapphires, lapis, turqoise, lazulite, amethyst, jaspers, sardonyx, topaz, amber, agate, opal, aventurine, chrysolite, cymophane, hematite, tourmaline, peridot, jet and chryso-prase (381). A mysterious midnight sun scatters its rays "through these jewels on to the garden, and the trees burnt as with magic fire" (381). The principle colors catalogued are white, red, green, blue, yellow, and "unknown" (381), which, along with the sun, gives a total of seven illuminations, corresponding to the planetary bodies of the Ptolemaic system: for in the Hermetic tradition, the metals were subterrestrial embryos of the heavenly bodies.

A subterrestrial or paradisal garden of gemstones as the destination of the heroic descent is a frequently encountered motif in the monomyth: we have seen it before, in the *Epic of Gilgamesh* (Siduri's garden by the sea, which Gilgamesh reaches after passing through the twelve leagues of darkness beneath the mountains), in the story of Sinbad (diamonds in the valley of serpents, surrounded by mountains), in "Sir Orfeo" (Pluto's underworld palace of gemstones reached by a hole in a rocky hillside), and we will see it again, often (as for example in Hoffman's "Mines of Falun" or Ambrose Bierce's "Owl Creek Bridge"). The garden of gems is also a motif frequently found in a wide variety of folkloric versions of the hero journey: in "The Twelve Dancing Princesses," for example, the hero breaks off branches from a silver, a gold, and a diamond tree (Ulanov 35). In Persian and Arabic cosmologies, mountain ranges held other related themes from the mystical traditions of Mazdaism and Islam: these traditions describe a "land of emerald cities" hidden within, or at the summit of, a mountain called Qâf; the cities are illuminated entirely by the emerald, glowing in the place of sun and moon (Corbin, "Terre Céleste" 157). It is an imaginal terrain, between the realm of the senses and the pure forms of the intellect, and it represents the intermediary world where the soul ascends to the infinite light of the heavens, or, alternatively, where the soul comes face to face with his spiritual archetype, "the celestial person in which the terrestrial self takes its origin" (Corbin 157; my trans.). Spiritual mystics of the Islamic tradition came to situate this city of emeralds (Hûrqalyâ), in the mystical mountains of Qâf, in the universe of the imagination, the mundus imaginalis: it is known as "âlam al-

mithâl, world of the archetypal images, or yet again the world of
correspondences and symbols, that is to say, that world which symbolizes *with* the world of the senses which it precedes and *with* the
world of the intellect which it imitates" (Corbin 159; my trans.). It is
essentially a world of the imagination, if we conceive of the
imagination as the soul's primary organ of perception, "with just as
much reality and truth as the sensible world perceived by the senses, or
the intelligible world by the intellect" (Corbin 161; my trans.). The
emerald city within the mountains of Qâf is, like the caves Aladdin
enters in the desolate valleys between the mountains, is the place where
the soul "finds everything which is the object of its desire" (Corbin
161; my trans.).

Entering these caves at the climax of Aladdin's journey therefore
involves images of both descent and ascent, as the soul goes down into
the underworld along the twelve steps beneath the marble slab, traverses
the three chambers of the cavern behind the large copper door, and then
ascends the thirty steps to terrace and niche containing the magic lamp.
The descent represents the death of the body, its passage through the
twelve spheres of the zodiac; the ascent the resurrection of the soul and
its return to its divine source, which resides beyond and above the
spheres of the creation. Ladders and staircases had been used as symbols
of the journey of the soul all over the Ancient Near East, particularly in
Egyptian tombs and funerary papyri, in which we find Osiris depicted as
the Lord of the Staircase (Wilkinson 150; Campbell, *Mythic Image*
451). The thirty steps of the staircase leading up to the lamp niche may
be lunar, for we know that the ladders of Set, Osiris, Buddha, and the
Pharaoh had fourteen steps for the waxing moon, and fourteen for the
waning (Walker 525). Later authors, like Wyndham Lewis, would come
to associate Aladdin's cave with the unconscious, and the wizard with
"that old magician Sigmund Freud" (Caracciolo 47), but it was much
earlier that the indigenous traditions of Muslim mysticism associated
the city of gems in the mountains with the archetypal images of the
soul, the mundus archetypus, a world of hidden symbols, where "the
soul suddenly visualizes its own archetypal Image, that Image whose
imprint it simultaneously bears within it, projects, and recognizes outside of itself" (Corbin, *Avicenna* 32).

Aladdin's return from this world involves a threshold battle at the
doorway leading now upwards towards reincarnation, rather than downwards towards transfiguration. He encounters the old wizard, standing
high above him at the top of the twelve steps behind the copper door,
who becomes enraged when Aladdin refuses to give him the lamp, and
throws incense upon the smouldering fire in order to imprison the boy
beneath the marble slab, which "rose of itself and returned to its place"
as the earth quakes (382). Our narrator, Shahrazad, reiterates the sym-

bolism of the descent to the underworld, at this point, by closing the second "door into the garden" as well, trapping Aladdin on the staircase between the copper door and the marble slab: "He was buried alive with all that useless gold" (383). It is conventional for revelations to occur at the nadir of the descent, and this occurs during an aside in which the narrator reveals the wizard's true identity as a black magician skilled in the arts of "sorcery and spells, geomancy and alchemy, astrology, fumigation, and enchantment" (382). It was through these arts that he learned of the existence of the magic lamp, buried in the mountains outside the "city of Kolo-Ka-Tse in China" (382), and it is this lamp, as the world well knows, which now effects Aladdin's resurrection, and the completion of his first hero journey cycle.

We have already encountered the lamp as a symbol of enlightenment in the story of Psyche. Lamps may also have been associated with funerary rituals (and therefore with the descent to the underworld) as symbols of the eternal flame: legend records the discovery of a lamp miraculously burning for centuries in the tomb of Tullia, Cicero's daughter, and, in the alchemical tradition, a perpetually burning lamp illuminates the sealed tomb of Christian Rosencreutz (Walker, *Dictionary* 143). That the lamp is also a form of the Grail is suggested by the meal it magically serves up to Aladdin and his mother, after he returns home from his journey. A traditional symbol of the sacred is the cornucopia, the horn of plenty or dish, which we saw distributing favorite dishes to the knights gathered in the Grail castles of Chrétien and Wolfram. But we have also seen the sacred vessel as the lamp of the mystery rites in the processions of Isis and Osiris: in *The Golden Ass,* one of the priests carries the urn, with handle and spout covered by hieroglyphs, which Apuleius refers to as an "effigy of Supreme Deity" (241). In "Aladdin," the vessel is also a lamp, with the Ifrit inside who serves a meal on "a great tray of massive silver which held twelve gold dishes of scented and hot-tasting meats, six warm loaves as white as snow but gilded about their sides, and two large flasks of old clear excellent wine" (386). The combination of gold and silver we recognize as symbols of the union of Sol and Luna, Eternity and Time; the ritual celebrating this moment is the Eucharist, with its foods symbolic of resurrection, wine and bread; and the occasion for the feast is Aladdin's homecoming, traditional symbol of the completion of the soul's hero journey (as in Inanna, Gilgamesh, the *Odyssey,* Sinbad, Joseph, and the Prodigal Son).

But Aladdin's homecoming leads inevitably to a second complete cycle, one which begins again with the symbolism of doorways. The call to adventure which initiates this second journey is love and marriage: on a certain day, heralds run through the streets, warning all citizens to "hide immediately behind the closed doors" of their houses, in order to avoid seeing "the marvelous Badr al-budur, youngest of the moons of God, daughter of our Sultan's glory" (390). Those who "dare disregard this order and peep through doors or windows" will be executed by sword, stake, or scaffold (390). Aladdin, however, is overcome by "an irresistible desire to see the Princess Badr al-budur," and runs to the hammam (where she is going to take her bath) and hides "himself behind the greet door, in such a position that he might look through the crack of it and see the Sultan's daughter passing to the bath" (390), rather like Actaeon spying on Artemis bathing in her forest pool, or like Lucius peering through the crack in the door of Pamphile's bedroom. For it is an equally fateful moment: so astonished is Aladdin by the vision of "beauty for the first time," and by the discovery that "all women were not old and ugly like his mother," that he is turned "to stone behind the door" (391). It is this drama at the doorway that initiates the hero journey of marriage, as Aladdin begins the lengthy and clever negotiations which lead eventually to his departure from his mother and union with the Princess.

These negotiations require the assistance of the Ifrit in the lamp, who, must first disrupt the Sultan's plans to marry his daughter to a wazir by abducting her on the wedding night and taking her from the palace to Aladdin's humble abode (Badr al-budur's heroine journey also begins with marriage!). Then the Ifrit provides the processional dowry displays the Sultan requires as proof of Aladdin's worthiness to marry his daughter, and both displays involve numerical symbolism associated with the mystical rites of marriage. In the first procession, Aladdin sends "forty dishes of solid gold, filled to the brim with jeweled fruit," like those which he plucked from the trees in the garden beneath the mountain, carried by "forty girl slaves, each as fair as the moon, and guarded by forty handsome young negroes, strong, well-built, and magnificently dressed" (408). These enter the Sultan's palace in pairs of black and white, and form a crescent in front of his throne after setting their burdens of gold down, prostrating themselves, and removing the gauze coverings from the forty dishes with a single movement (409). Then Aladdin's old mother advances to the "centre of the glittering crescent" and negotiates her son's marriage with the King sitting opposite on the throne: for he is the Grand Patriarch of the Universe, and she is the Great Mother, analogous to Isis in the vision of Apuleius, the Goddess from whom those opposites of black and white, male and female, upon which all life is predicated, proceed. The female slaves are consistently compared to "summer moons," and their black attendants to kings (410).

The astonished Sultan then summons Aladdin to court, as a member of his royal family, and Aladdin prepares a second symbolic procession. Like Joseph summoned to Pharaoh's presence from his prison on the Nile, Aladdin puts on a "robe more magnificent than the greatest

king of earth has set aside for the greatest occasions" (411). It is robe of
many colors which, along with the symbolism of the Sultan and marriage, signifies the soul's re-investment in and reunion with the spiritual splendor of its celestial source, to which it returns after its long sojourn in the prison of the material world, a distant, poverty stricken
suburb of heaven. The bathing ritual Aladdin performs before putting
on this magnificent robe is elaborately evoked, and recalls the metallurgical symbolism of the bath in the alchemical marriage of the
Rosarium Philosophorum: the hammam is "made all of jade and transparent alabaster, with pools of rose carnelian and white coral. The or-
namentation was a cunning pattern of large emeralds," and its inner
hallway is "paved with a close-set pattern of jewels" (411). Aladdin
emerges from flower scented waters with flesh glowing like Gawain's in
the Castle of the Green Knight, or Parzival's in the Castle of the Grail,
for the bath signifies that purification of the flesh which allows the radiance of the spirit to shine through. He then summons the Ifrit, and
orders a grand processional: a pure bred Arabian stallion for him to ride,
with "forty-eight graceful slaves, richly, cleanly, and elegantly clad" to
walk in two groups of twenty four; two files of twelve in front of him,
and two files of twelve behind, all forty eight with bags containing five
thousand dinars of gold hanging about their necks (412). Aladdin rides
in the centre of the procession, with a diamond feather in his turban
streaming "back like light itself" (413), and four slaves at his sides
holding "the cords from the housing of his horse" (412). One can't help
but recall here Black Elk's Great Vision of forty eight horses of four different colors streaming in from the four cardinal points of the compass
to the rainbow tent in the centre of the universe, a symbol of totality
and wholeness based on the two numbers (4 and 12) traditionally associated with the earth and the heavens, the marriage of which constitutes
the essence of mystical teachings.

It is, of course, after the marriage that the hero and heroine journeys proper begin. The mysterious Moor reappears on the scene after
using his geomantic skills to find out about Aladdin's marriage. His
magic involves the kind of manipulation of geometric and hermetic figures which we know through such works as the Fausts of Marlowe and
Goethe: he takes some divinatory sand from his cupboard, sits within a
red circle inscribed on a square mat, and marks what he calls "the male
and female points" (421), a figure suggestive of the interlocking triangles of Solomon's Seal, or the Star of David (a recurrent motif in
Goethe's hermeticism). After reciting geomantic spells to form the various figures of the horoscope, the sorcerer learns of Aladdin's good fortune, and sets off to destroy it. He does so by peddling brand new
lamps, which he persuades Aladdin's innocent wife to exchange for the
magic lamp with the Ifrit inside. Having stolen the lamp, the Moor

uses it to abduct the Princess and the palace to Morocco, so that when the Sultan wakes up the next morning and looks out the window, his daughter is gone.

The abduction motif, as we know from the Homeric Hymn to Demeter, from "Sir Orfeo," and from Chrétien's "Knight of the Cart," initiates the descent of the hero into the underworld to liberate the heroine from the lord of death. Hence, after being arrested by the Sultan's police, Aladdin is given forty days to find the Princess, and wanders off into open country. He comes finally to "a great river" (427), looking into the obscure depths of which brings thoughts of suicide, as it did for the desperate Psyche. The river marks the threshold crossing into the otherworld, where Aladdin goes after rubbing his magic ring. The Ifrit in the ring takes him to Morocco, where the Moor has transported the Princess and the Palace. There he manages to retrieve the lamp from the magician by putting drugging him, and he then takes the Princess and Palace back to China, completing the second hero journey cycle of the tale. An interesting detail of this abduction and retrieval cycle links it to the Arthurian tale, "The Knight of the Cart": the Sultan "announced by heralds, with a sound of pipes and drums, that he freed all who had been cast into prison as a sign of public rejoicing" (432). The liberation of prisoners effected by Aladdin's retrieval of the abducted Princess by the Moorish magician is very close to Chrétien's tale, in which Lancelot retrieves Guenevere from King Bademagus (Bad Magic), and along the way liberates all the captives in his kingdom by lifting a marble slab from a tomb with his name on it (shades of Aladdin's marble slab, which he lifts after reciting his name and lineage).

Aladdin's hero journey ends with one final test: the ordeal of his wife's fertility problems, a motif which frequently inaugurates a whole new cycle. Concerned by the fact that she has not yet conceived, the Princess sends for "an aged female saint named Fatmah," who instructs her to hang an egg -- taken from the Rukh's nest, on the highest peak of the Caucasus -- in the middle of the crystal dome in the hall of windows (433-34). She must then meditate upon the egg for many days, after which her "interior nature will undergo modification and the dead shall live" (434). But Fatmah turns out to be the Moorish magician's vengeful brother in disguise, who is attempting to ruin Aladdin's happiness: for, when summoned to retrieve the Rukh's egg, the Ifrit refuses, and reveals his true identity as a servant of the "most holy Rukh," whom the Ifrit refers to as "the Father of Eggs" (435). However, since Fatmah, the disguised sorcerer, requested the egg, and not Aladdin, the Ifrit is able to obtain it for the young couple, after hearing the old woman describe the remedy (436). The symbolism of the egg here brings us back to where we began this section, with the story of Sinbad, who was shipwrecked on an island with a huge Rukh egg in the center, and another island with serpents coiled around eggs in caverns. Sinbad reached that second island by tying himself onto the foot of the Rukh. The Rukh in Aladdin's tale may be related to the Simurgh of Persian folklore, most famously in Farid Attar's *Conference of the Birds*: it is a kind of phoenix whose home beyond the seven mountain ranges symbolized the soul's celestial dwelling place. Stories of the hero's abduction by the mystical bird, and subsequent flight into the heavenly mountains, form a widespread network of variations on the archetype (from the Greek Ganymede to Navajo myth), one of which may have been quite common in Persian and Arabic cultures, as Henry Corbin has argued in his analysis of a tapestry depicting the Simurgh with hero in claws, which he reproduces as the frontispiece of the English translation of his "Terre Céleste et Corps de Résurrection."

One also thinks of the Hamsa, or wild gander, in Hindu mythology, the bird form of Brahma, which, "as the animal mask of the creative principle," one could call Father of the Eggs, whose flight over the Himalayas signifies the transcendence of the soul: "That is why the Hindu ascetic, the mendicant monk or saint who is supposed to have become free from the bondage of rebirth, is said to have attained the rank of 'gander'" (Zimmer, *Myths and Symbols* 48). Aladdin's Rukh, the Father of Eggs, also lives in the mountains, and the subsidiary Ifrits manifest his inscrutable spirituality in a form accessible to human cognition. In meditating upon the egg hanging from the crystal dome in the middle of the hall of windows (there are ninety-nine windows, with the aperture at the apex of the dome representing the hundredth), Princess Badr al-budur is meditating upon the Incarnation, upon the ineffable source of all sublunary life, and becoming fertile thereby, spiritually and physically. The dome itself is one of the great architectural symbols of the Near and Far East: it encloses the world within and beneath, while, passing through the solar door at the apex, the soul achieves liberation, like an arrow piercing the bull's eye, like the Rukh returning to its nest, like a hero returning home from his or her journey (Coomaraswamy, *Traditional Symbolism* 447).

Japanese Journeys and Slave Narratives

Matsuo Basho (1644-1694) was the son of a samurai and lived in Kyoto, Ueno City, and Edo (Tokyo) as a poet and Zen Buddhist priest under various names, the last (Basho) from the banana tree given him by his disciples in 1680. Buddhism came into Japan in about 552 A.D. when a Korean King gave the Emperor Kimmei a packet of sutras and a golden Buddha. A gradual assimilation ensued with the older Shinto traditions and aspects of Chinese Taoism, both of which focus on the immanence of the divinity in all things, especially in nature. In

Shintoism, the resident spiritual powers of natural sites were called kami, and they were worshipped in the new system as Boddhisattvas. The process was very similar to what was happening in Europe at nearly the same time, when Christianity spread northwards and churches were built on sites originally sacred to pagan Celtic and Norse deities.

At Nara, the first Buddhist capital, in 712-20 A.D., a royal decree lead to the compilation of the mythologies of old Japan in a genealogi-cal context (Creation, Izanagi, Izanami, Amaterasu) called the Kojiki ("Records of Ancient Matters") and the Nihongi ("Chronicles of Japan"); while in 752 A.D. a colossal bronze Buddha was built at the Todaiji Temple. At Kyoto (then Heian), 794-894, the teachings of two monks established the kami as Boddhisattvas, and incorporated aspects of Tantric Buddhism from the Indian university at Nalanda. Then from 894-1185 during the courtly medieval period we find the troubadours of Fujiwara Court described by Lady Murasaki in *Tale of Genji* (978-1015). Finally, during the Kamakura period (1185-1392) there is a swing away from delicacies of courtly love and a development of four vigorously Japanese forms of Buddhism, one called Zen founded by Eisai (1141-1215) based on Chinese Ch'an school. From 14th century onward a mixture of these ideas led to a profound interest in the various arts as a means of expressing the essence of Japanese Buddhism: from the native Shinto and Chinese Taoism a faith in the goodness, har-mony, and spiritual mystique of the natural order; from Confucius an emphasis on the dignity and discipline of the social order; from Buddhism a sensitivity to the sufferings and sorrows of all life; and from Zen an emphasis on disciplined spontaneity.

A great masterpiece of this synthesis was Basho's *The Narrow Road Through the Provinces* (1689f.), which traverses a complete hero journey cycle and incorporates numerous haiku poems along the way Haiku were meant to record flashes of enlightenment, of the revelation of the divine in nature, in homely images of daily experience without philosophy. They were composed of 3 lines of 5,7,5 syllables, and each record "epiphanies" as in Romanticism, Joyce, and the Imagistes. Basho combines these with the poetic diary and pilgrimage forms popular since 8th century: these included traveling to temples, historical shrines, old friends, crossing mountain passes, rivers, barriers, and gates analogous to archetypal hero journey of transformation of conscious-ness during moments of revelation. That he comes home like "one come back from the dead" connects his story to the nekyiae of the European hero journey cycles.

Another great masterpiece of Japanese literature of the 18th cen-tury which follows the pattern of the hero journey is "The Love Suicides at Amijima," by Chikamatsu Monzaemon (1653-1724). In 1614 the early Tokugawa period in Japan began, with the first shogun after long series of feudal wars set up in Edo (Tokyo), and the divine right emperor relegated to puppet power in Kyoto. A process of national unification began, in which Basho also played an important role with his spiritual pilgrimages which cover the whole island. Isolation from the rest of world by law retained the integrity of native tradition, until 1853-54, when the American naval expeditions of Admiral Perry forced the country open, followed by the Meiji Restoration in 1868. During this period religious life was a mixture of Buddhism and Shinto, and the social order was Confucian, an orderly division of samurai, farmers, artisans, and merchants. Both Basho and Chikamatsu were popular among rising merchant classes, the former for pastoral nostalgia, the latter for exploration of the conflicts between passion (ninjo) and duty (giri) (rather like Racine and the Neoclassical drama) in the new urban context of the merchant classes and the gay quarters. Chikamatsu's plays set off a plague of copy cat love suicides (shinju) during early 18th century, very much as Goethe's *Sorrows of Young Werther* did in Europe.

Chikamatsu's middle work was in Kabuki style, his early and late work in the puppet theatre style (joruri). In Joruri, one puppet master chants all the parts, while three other black veiled expressionless masters manipulate the life sized puppets of the principal characters: Kamiya Jihei the merchant lover, Tahei his rival, Osan his wife, and Koharu the courtesan, etc.. Traditional joruri, like the No Drama, told classic tales, but Chikamatsu was the first to focus on the ordinary lives of the merchant classes for tragic material (rather like the Naturalism of Ibsen). And in this his historical importance is analogous to the Western evolution from mythic to secular literature.

In both the Eastern and the Western traditions, this involved a fusion of mythological symbolism and realistic representation, a technique which Pope called the mock epic, and which T.S. Eliot would call the mythical method, in 1922. In Chikamatsu the result is a precise and painfully detailed portrayal of the financial, social, and psychological aspects of Jihei's problems, arising from his excessive attachment to a prostitute in the gay quarter: the absence of money, the collapse of the family business, the pawning of the clothing and mounting bills, the violation of family life caused by adultery and divorce, with the social scandal, and the depression, jealousy, and hysteria of the members of the love triangle. All of this is set against a recognizably realistic setting of home, office, and city, with street, bridge, and neighborhood names still in use today. But beneath the realistic details lurk motifs associated with the archetype of the descent to the underworld. Imagery of doorways and divestiture is particularly dramatic in the scene where the father-in-law (Gozaemon) attacks his daughter for pawning her clothes to support her husband Jihei's obsession. Opening the drawers of her wardrobe, Gozaemon finds them "Stripped bare," and he lashes out that Jihei would "strip the skin from" the bodies of wife and child to pay for his prositute (463). Oddly enough, the Narrator then adds threshold imagery to the divestiture motif, by remarking that "Even if Jihei could escape through seven padlocked doors," he cannot escape the wrath of Gozaemon (463). Both the divestiture and the doorway motifs converge here (seven doors, as in the Sumerian descent), to form an archetype which we may as well call the Inanna complex!

But the further backdrop to the play's mythological imagery draws on the popular forms of Buddhist belief and the universal symbols of the hero journey. This involves images of the Buddhist descent to the underworld, with the passage over the six threshold bridges (Tenjin, Oe, Little Naniwa, Funairi, Temma, Kyo) to finally cross the Onari bridge (the name of which means "to become Buddha") to Amijima, the yonder shore of nirvana where the suicides occur. The word "Ami" means "net," a symbol we last discussed in the story of Hephaistos, Aphrodite, and Ares. Here it is the net of karma, implying punishment or reward for one's actions in a former life, and the net of redemption, offered by the Amida Buddha, who confers liberation from the Wheel of Reincarnation. The archetypal motifs of the journey include the symbolism of divestiture, bridge and river crossings (Persian Chinvat), the dissolution of body into four elements, the shroud of silk weaving two worlds together, the crows that guide the souls of the dead, and the elaborate burial posture of Koharu (head north, face west).

Similar motifs associated with the hero journey emerge in the slave and captivity narratives beginning to surface in European and American literature around this time. During the 18th century in America and England, a new genre of literature began to emerge: the slave narrative. The autobiographies of such men and women as Equiano Olidah and later, in the 19th century, Frederick Douglas and Linda Brent, follow in moving detail classic yet realistic versions of the hero journey cycle, moving from freedom, to slavery, and returning to freedom. The realistic details of these autobiographies are enhanced by a very important variation of the mythical method or mock epic: biblical typology, according to which the events in one's life retrace the hero journeys of bondage and liberation recorded in scripture. Drawing parallels between historical experience and biblical prototypes became a way of giving what T.S. Eliot would later call "shape and significance" to the narrative. In this section I would like to briefly discuss the archetypal framework of the hero journey, established by citations of scripture, in three slave narratives, including (perhaps surprisingly) one written by a white woman, Mary Rowlandson, and another from the 19th century, written by Linda Brent.

Mary Rowlandson was born in England in 1635, daughter of John White, with whom she came to Salem, then to Lancaster, Massachusetts. Her father founded the town, and her husband Joseph Rowlandson was its first minister. In 1676 the Indians attacked and abducted Mary into captivity. John Winthrop, governor of Massachusetts Bay Colony, saw New England Puritans as forming a Christian Utopian community like the New Jerusalem promised in *Revelations*. The purpose of the spiritual autobiographies, therefore, was to examine their lives and histories for signs of God's Providence on the one hand, or the influence of Satan on the other. What we find, therefore, in Mary Rowlandson's account of her adventure, are multiple allusions to various biblical types of the descent to the underworld. The journey in itself follows the biblical paradigm of the monomyth: paradise, paradise lost, and paradise regained.

In the 1620's the Wampanoag chief Massasoit generously aided first Colonists, but by 1676 his son, chief Metacomet (King Phillip in narrative) fought in alliance with Algonquins in Massachusetts and Rhode Island to protect their land by forcing the advancing Englishmen out. On February 20th, 1676, the burning of Lancaster led to Mary Rowlandson's captivity and journey ever more deeply into the wilderness during a sequence of "removes": to Princeton MA, to New Braintree, MA, to Petersham, MA, to Orange, MA, to Northfield, MA, to South Vernon, VA, to Keene, NH, to Chesterfield, NH, to Hinsdale, NH, and circling back to Lancaster to complete an entire geographical version of the hero journey cycle.

The central metaphor of the *Captivity and Restoration of Mrs. Mary Rowlandson* (1682) is the descent to the underworld as developed by multiple citations of scripture, in which various typological equivalents of exile and bondage serve to give shape and significance to her story: Among these are Luke 15 (The Prodigal Son, fatted calf, swine and nuts), Isaiah 43 (the passing of the waters), Psalm 137 (By the rivers of Babylon), Job's afflictions, and lamentations, Daniel 6 and 3 (in the lion's den and the three children in the furnace), Psalm 23 (the valley of the shadow), Exodus: honey out of rock and salvation of the Lord).

The language throughout is taken from the Jewish periods of bondage and exile in Egypt and Babylon: Mary is captive, a slave, among enemies, devils, imps, heathen, and pagans in the wilderness, afflicted, and so forth, all types of the descent. One of these metaphors is of the "maze" (263), a standard metaphor of Christian pilgrimage through the world of "amazement and great perplexity" (266). While the language of her restoration has to do with such basic Biblical concepts as "redemption" "fulfillment" of the Promise, and "deliverance" through "chastening". The whole to indicate God's ruling hand in history, his Providence.

Another captivity narrative, written later on the 19th century, by Linda Brent (also known as Harriet Jacobs), uses many details of the hero journey. Her terrific book, *Incidents in the Life of a Slave Girl*, forcefully reminds us that the hero journey is not just a literary convention: it is something that happens to people, to all of us in fact, with varying degrees of intensity, and in a thousand and one different ways. Linda Brent's story begins with a kind of abduction, one which recalls the story of Demeter, Persephone, and Hades. After her father dies, Linda is taken into Dr. Flint's household, and he soon becomes a very satanic master indeed, seducing Linda and compelling her, on a daily basis, to have sex with him. He is portrayed in the darkest terms of cruelty and tyranny, and he plans to lock Linda up into a small shed he builds for her five miles from town.

The loss of childhood innocense is poignantly evoked by having Linda remember the days before her abduction, when she picked flowers in the field, like Persephone among the poppies in the Homeric Hymn to Demeter. Dr. Flint plays the Hades figure who destroys the "flowering vines" around Linda's "flowery home" (973). He is evoked as a "crafty man" who fills the mind of the young girl with "unclean images," "violating the most sacred commandments" that prohibit adultery (969). The vocabulary which Brent uses consistently associates Dr. Flint with the underworld: words like "tyranny," "fiend," "cruel bondage," "sin and sorrow," "degradation" eventually lead to an identification between Flint and the Christian Hades, Satan, that "hoary-headed miscreant" and "old sinner" (973). His wickedness permeates the world around him, so that all of the Southern States become infernal: slavery is a "wild beast" cooped up in a "den full of dead men's bones and all uncleanness" (973); and the South is a land of "shadows ... too dense for light to penetrate," a place where "each is tortured in his separate hell" (974). The slaves are compared to pigs living in an "atmosphere of hell" and hatred (976), and the members of the KKK are the terrifying demons of Linda's nekyia (982).

Eventually, Linda finds refuge from this underworld, but only by retreating to another. She hides in a garret atop a small shed near her grandmother's house, where she suffers the torments of Hades: darkness, cramp, and heat. Like Persephone, however, Linda escapes, liberated from the inferno with the help of her grandmother (who plays the role of Demeter in the story) and a team of white abolitionists from the North. Her heroine's journey out of the underworld where the "demon Slavery" rules occurs via boat, as Linda reenacts the night-sea journey in real life (1000). Symbolic images of liberation long associated with the nekyia emerge spontaneously here, at the end of the narrative. Linda goes on deck at sunrise, as the boat completes its slow ascent of the Chesapeake Bay. The first rays of the rising sun redden the sky and set the waves sparkling. While these images recall motifs associated with the solar journey by boat, through the twelve leagues of darkness, which take us way back to Egypt, Greece, and Sumeria, Linda Brent uses them as symbols of her regeneration and deliverance from captivity: she has "escaped from slavery," and now steps off the boat into "the beautiful glow" of a new day (1000).

Popol Vuh

While probably of ancient origin, the Maya-Quiché Indian council book known as the *Popol Vuh* was first written down in the Latin alphabet in the middle of the sixteenth century, and later translated into Spanish in the early eighteenth century by a Dominican priest, Francisco Jimenez, who used the Latin manuscript preserved in a church in Guatemala. Like the Sumerian "Descent of Inanna," the book was performed, as well as read, during ritual ceremonies. The story of the journey of One and Seven Hunahpu's descent to Xibalba, the region of the dead, circumscribes a fascinating version of the hero journey, one which incorporates many of the archetypal motifs of the monomyth.

The call to adventure comes in the form of four owl messengers sent from the twelve lords of Xibalba to summon the twins, One and Seven Hunahpu, who are playing in the ball court known as the Great Abyss at Carchah. This call coincides with the death of their father (a frequent catalyst of the hero journey in life and literature), and clothing symbolism soon follows, as the twins arm themselves with playthings, yokes, rubber ball and arm guards (1287). These twins, Hunahpu and Xbalanque, control the morning star aspect of their father, Venus, and they later become the sun and the moon. The cycles of all three astronomical bodies, as we have seen (in the descent of Innana, for example, Goddess of the Morning and Evening star), provide cosmological prototypes of the hero journey: that the father has just died suggests that passage of the planet Venus into the underworld which will eventually come full circle in the completion of its diurnal and synodical revolutions. The owl, of course, is universally associated with death and the underworld, but may have had connections to fertility as well among the Aztec and Mayans , and would thus be the aegis of both phases of the journey, departure and return, for they will later assist Ixquic (the pregnant wife of Hunahpu) in her escape from Xibalba (Miller and Taube 128).

The threshold symbolism which delineates the twins' descent into Xibalba comes in the form of two quaternities. First the twins go down a steep cliff to cross a sequence of four rapids with appropriately demonic names (Neck Canyon, Churning Spikes, Blood River, and Pus River). These vividly recall the four rivers of Hades in the Classical tradition (Styx, Acheron, Phlegethon, Cocytus), which Dante too traversed in his *Inferno*, and which were the inverse of the four rivers of Paradise (Pison, Gihon, Hiddekel, and Euphrates). After crossing the rivers the twin come to a crossing of four roads (Red, Black, Yellow, and White), the color symbolism of which is a frequent feature of Native American cosmologies (to be found in the creation myths of the Navajo and the visions of Black Elk). Choices at crossroads also typically occur in European folktales, in which one brother will choose one of three roads leading to the successful completion of the journey. Here, both brothers descend the Black Road to Xibalba, the land of the dead, where they are greeted by two practical jokes: manikin woodcarvings which they mistake for the lords of death, and a bench, burning hot, upon which they burn their butts when invited to sit (rather like Perithoos in Hades, Demeter on the Mirthless Stone of the Eleusinia, or the Perilous Seat in Arthurian myth).

After these tests come the images of chambers and doorways which we are so familiar with in our survey of the hero journey. The twins come to what is called the Dark House, where "heaps and piles of tests" begin (1289). As in the rituals associated with the abduction of Persephone into the underworld of the Eleusinian mysteries, torches and forbidden fruit play a central role in the initiation phase of the journey: the twins are brought one torch and two cigars, already lit, which they are told to return still smoking in the morning. Much like the Pharaohnic journey through the chambers of the Tuat in ancient Egypt, the twins must then pass through a sequence of four more houses, each with a trial inside: Rattling House, cold, clattering with hail, whistling with draft; Jaguar House; Bat House; and Razor House, with blades ripping and slashing (1290) -- this last, like the crossing of the river of the Churning Spikes, recalling Lancelot's sword bridge in Chrétien's "Knight of the Cart." The twins return to the lords of Xibalba, One and Seven Death, after navigating the passage through these five chambers of the underworld, but because they consumed the torch and the cigars along the way, they are condemned to death, sacrificed, and buried at the Place of the Ball Game Sacrifice (1291).

Countless images of the Mesoamerican world portray the Ball Game, which for many became a "metaphor for the movements of heavenly bodies, particularly the sun, moon, and Venus; the ball itself may have been understood as the sun journeying in and out of the underworld," so that the game suggests the rhythms of life, death, and regeneration archetypally associated with the stages of the hero journey (Miller and Taube 43). Human sacrifice and decapitation were undoubtedly central to the mysteries of the game (shades of the Green Knight!), as some balls had skulls embedded in them to create a hollow center (Miller and Taube 44). After the twins fail the tests of torch and cigar in the five houses of Xibalba, One Hunahpu is decapitated, and his head put in the fork of a calabash tree, which immediately bears so much fruit that the gods can't immediately find the skull (1291). An injunction forbidding anyone to pick the fruit or go beneath the tree is issued, and almost immediately violated by a maiden who will play the role of Eve in the myth. Some of the Mesoamerican images of the sacrifice (in the Dresden and Borgia Codices) depict a tree emerging from the skull or belly of the victim, at the top of which a bird sits devouring a serpent which emerges from the tree. The skull therefore becomes a symbol of the fertility of the maize Goddess, Mesoamerican images of whom bear an astonishing resemblance to a painting called "The Dream of the Virgin" painted by Christoforo Simone in 1350. The painting shows Mary lying asleep with the tree of the Crucifixion sprouting upwards from her womb, surmounted by a pelican feeding its young with blood from its breast (Campbell, *Atlas* 2.1.36-7).

Other striking parallels between biblical and Mesoamerican motifs emerge in the account of the heroine's journey of the maiden we spoke of, who immediately heard the injunction not to eat the fruit of the calabash tree. Whether these parallels are archetypal, or whether they indicate the impact of the Spanish missionaries who first recorded the myths, is perhaps impossible to say. The maiden's name is Blood Woman, and her call to adventure is her father's story: when Blood Gatherer tells his daughter the account of the strange origins of the fruit of the calabash tree, she is immediately inspired to undertake the journey. This is an important point, for it represents the role played by storytelling in the monomyth, since one archetypal response to hearing a story is to begin a journey of one's own. When Blood Woman goes to the Place of the Ball Game Sacrifice, where the calabash tree stands, a bone tells her not to pick the fruit, but she insists by sticking out her hand towards the "round thing in the branches" (1291). As she does, the bone spits its saliva into her hand (Freud light your cigar!), resulting in what we would recognize as an immaculate conception or virgin birth, for she returns home with the reincarnating twins in her pregnant belly (1292).

The image of a deity who fathers himself upon a virgin would have raised the hackles on the necks of the missionaries who recorded this story (if they didn't put it there themselves), as would the image of the woman eating the fruit of a forbidden tree. For Blood Woman is twinned herself, both Eve and Mary, and the tree is both the Tree of Knowledge and of Life. Would any of those missionaries have known images like the one we find in the Vatican Library today, which shows Eve at the base of a tree on one side, and Mary on the other -- one side the Tree of Knowledge, with a skull hanging from its branches, and Eve feeding its fruit to Adam; and the other side the Tree of Life, with a crucifix hanging in the branches, with Mary distributing the communion wafers that grow on it (Campbell, *Power of Myth*)? Before Blood Woman leaves the tree, she receives some interesting spiritual instruction from the spitting skull bone in the fork, the revelation of hidden mysteries being a characteristic of the initiation phase of the heroine's journey. The instruction has to do with a basic biblical theme, the atonement of the father and the son, through the mediation of the virgin mother: the spittle is "just a sign," the skull tells Blood Woman, a symbol of the survival of the father in the son, for "The father does not disappear, but goes on being fulfilled" (1292). The tree of death becomes the tree of life, as serpent yields to crucifix, Eve to Mary.

Blood Woman's return to her father brings one hero journey to fruition, but quickly begins another one, when Blood Woman is unable to say who is responsible for the child in her belly. All she can say, in the way of virgin mothers, is that the child is fathered by "no man whose face I've known" (1292). As a result, her father and the lords of Xibalba order that she be taken away for sacrifice by the Military Keepers of the Mat, who are further instructed to bring her heart back in a bowl.[18] Hence begins the Snow White episode of her journey, what the folklorists call the infant exile motif: the four owls take her off, bringing the White Dagger along for the sacrifice, but taking pity on Blood Woman when she tells them that "What's in my belly generated all by itself" when she came to marvel at the head of One Hunahpu in fork of the tree growing at the Place of Ball Game Sacrifice (1293). In the story of Snow White, the hunter kills a deer to find a surrogate heart to return to the wicked Queen, but in the Popol Vuh, the owl messengers use cochineal sap to form a surrogate heart in a bowl, and Blood Woman decrees that from henceforth the cochineal sap heart will serve as surrogate during the sacrifice, replacing the human hearts of the past (1293). This is a familiar development in world religion, the replacement of human offerings with a surrogate (ram, bull, or cochineal sap). Blood Woman's offering is cooked and dried over the fire, and savored by the lords of Xibalba, while the owls secretly release her from the underworld "through a hole onto the earth" (1294). In this way, we read, "the lords of Xibalba were defeated by a maiden" (1294), a formula which applies also to Mary, who by giving birth to Jesus defeated death forever, one of the most characteristic results of the hero journey.

One of the other consequences of the monomyth has to do with the origins of song, writing, and the arts in general: for the hero journey functions on one level as a metaphor of poesis. The twins who are eventually born from Blood Woman's womb are intimately associated with poesis, and the end result of their heroic descent to and return from the underworld is a shaman song called "Hunahpu Monkey" (1298). When Blood Woman returns from Xibalba, through the hole in the earth, she brings the twins with her, and they are born shortly after she takes refuge with an old woman named Xmucane, who, though she identifies herself as the mother of One Monkey and One Artisan, is in fact the mother of One and Seven Hunahpu, the same from whom the twins took their leave at the beginning of their descent to Xibalba. And so, in this marvelously strange but timelessly human way, the hero journey of the twins comes full circle, as they are returned to the mother from whom they departed in the beginning. The Old Woman is the Alpha and the Omega, you might say, the beginning and the end, the womb and the tomb. But in our tale, she has adopted Monkey and Artisan as surrogate children to compensate the loss of her twins, and hence refuses at first to accept Blood Woman into her home.

To win grandmother's acceptance, Blood Woman (like Psyche, like Vasilisa the Beautiful) must perform certain tasks, having to do with fertility: she must gather a netful of corn from a barren stalk in the garden, which she does by reciting a prayer to "Cornmeal Woman," the great Goddess of the Harvest, who would correspond to Demeter (Ceres) in Greek and Roman myth. This feat wins her acceptance with grandmother Xmucane, but the twins now must undergo the familiar trials of sibling rivalry, as the older brothers (One Monkey and One Artisan) abuse them. These two older brothers are the archetypes of all poets and singers: "great flautists and singers ... and writers and carvers" (1296). The twins Hunahpu and Xbalanque succeed in deposing them by turning them into monkeys one day, after sending them up a tree to retrieve some birds (1297). This image immediately recalls the role played by Thoth, the ibis or baboon headed deity in Ancient Egypt, who became the great patron of all writers and poets. Our tale ends, then, with an image of poesis, as all flutists and singers among the ancient people pray to the monkeys, prototypes of mimesis, progenitors of poetry.

Notes

[1] Some of the influential titles and historical events in this area include George Ripley's *Cantilena* (1490), Petrus Bonus's *Pretiosa margarita novella* (1546), Cornelius Agrippa's *De occulta philosophia* (1533), John Dee's *Monas hieroglyphica* (1564), Ben Jonson's *The Alchemist* and Shakespeare's *The Tempest* (1610-11 -- perhaps written for the marriage of Elizabeth and Prince Frederick of Heidelberg in 1613) -- the *Fama Fraternitatis* and *Chymische Hochzeit* (1614-16), Robert Fludd's *Utruisque cosmi historia* (1617), Michael Maier's *Atalanta Fugiens* (1617), Mylius's *Philosophia reformata* (1622), the *Sapienta veterum* from the 18th century in Paris, the *Janitor pansophus* in the *Museum Hermeticum* (1678), John

Milton's *Il Penseroso* (1645), Henry Vaughan's *Silex Scintillans* (The Sparkling Flint) (1650), Thomas Vaughan's translation of the *Fama* (1652; Reprinted 1923), Henry More's *Conjectura Cabbalistica* (1662), Abbé de Villars, *Le Comte de Gablis* (1670), Ralph Cudworth's *The True Intellectual System of the Universe* (1678), and Alexander Pope's *The Rape of the Lock* (1712-14). Studies and bibliographies of the subject may be found in Bonnefoy (211-222), Nicholl, Roberts, Eliade, von-Franz, Faivre, Smith, and, particularly, Frances Yates. Recently, Umberto Eco has attempted (not altogether successfully) to heap this material together in his novel, *Foucault's Pendulum* (in which several hero journey cycles occur).

2 See Dame Frances Yates, *The Occult Philosophy in the Elizabethan Age*, for the distinction between the handling of the Magus in Spenser, Marlowe, and Shakespeare.

3 Jung, for example, devotes all of his volume, *Mysterium Coniunctionis*, to the symbolism of the union of opposites in alchemy, which he takes to represent the achievement of harmony within the Self. Edward Edinger discusses the coniunctio symbolism in his article on *Romeo and Juliet*, and in *Anatomy of the Psyche: Alchemical Symbolism in Psychotherapy*, Edward Edinger also reserves the coniunctio to last, as representing the fulfillment of the journey of individuation.

4 On the transition from Renaissance to Rosicrucian hermeticism, see Frances Yates, *Giordano Bruno* and *The Rosicrucian Enlightenment*.

5 The complete plates and commentary may be found in Jung, *The Psychology of the Transference*, to which the figure numbers in the parenthetical citations refer.

6 Edinger's book includes individual chapters on the alchemical operations.

7 As for example in pictures by Francesco di Giorgio, Francesco del Cossa, Cima da Conegliano, Marcantonio, Veneziano, and Bassano, reproduced in by Giuseppe Scavizzi in Warden (125-145).

8 See for example Dame Frances Yates, *Majesty and Magic in Shakespeare's Last Plays*, and *The Occult Philosophy in the Elizabethan Age* (Chapters 12, 14, 15), or Charles Nicoll, *The Chemical Theatre*.

9 Virgil describes the labyrinth carved over the gates leading into Hades in Book 6 of the Aeneid (Fielding will later evoke the same Virgilian imagery of the gateway to Hades when Tom arrives in London, as we will see below).

10 See for example "Sir Orfeo," and the imagery of the mountains and the underworld in the Sumerian and Egyptian traditions discussed earlier.

11 See Heinrich Zimmer's discussion of Merlin in *The King and the Corpse*.

12 Carol Zaleski, Patch, and others provide very thorough itineraries of the otherworld theme in Medieval literature.

13 Pointed out in his article on the gypsies, "Fielding's Parable of Government."

14 See Feldman and Richardson, *The Rise of Modern Mythology*, for selections from these and other mythologists of the period.

15 See Jack Zipes, *Spells of Enchantment*, for a brief historical introduction and selections of tales.

16 On Chaucer, see Katherine Gittes, "*The Canterbury Tales* and the Arabic Frame Tradition."

17 I am indebted to Joseph Campbell's edition of *The Portable Arabian Nights* for this introductory material, but I use the complete edition of the tales translated by Mathers from the French of Mardrus. For excellent discussions of the bedvilled problem of the collection and translation of the Nights, see Robert Irwin and Peter Caracciolo.

18 The root of the word "popol" is mat, a symbol of rulership associated with noble and priestly dwellings, divination, marriages, councils, and community dances (Miller and Taube 111). As a finely woven product, the mat recalls the symbolism nets and weaving, representations of fate and the rhythms of life and death, male and female, night and day.

Chapter 4:
Romanticism to Naturalism

In his folkloristic commentary on the fairy tales collected by the Grimms Brothers, Joseph Campbell broke the interpretation of the myths and tales down into the cosmological, social-political, metaphysical, and psychological categories.[1] All of these levels of interpretation can be applied to the hero journey, as we have seen, and in fact many of the traditional symbols of archetypal wisdom come down to us in those tales which had such an impact on the literature of the 19th century (particularly on the short stories of Hoffman, Hawthorne, and Tagore). The process of transformation and transmission is a continuous cycle from the oral to the literate, back to the oral and then again into literature. Of the many possible stories from the folk tradition which follow the hero journey pattern, we can necessarily choose only a few, selected from the German and Russian collections.

Jacob and Wilhelm Grimm collected the stories first published as *Nursery and Household Tales* from simple folk of farm and pub, like Grandmother Viehmann, and chose to stick closely to the original materials, having inherited from the Romantics (Novalis, Schiller, Wordsworth, Scott) a veneration for folk poetry. From 1812 on, with their first publications, a new concern for exactitude in recording the tales, and a zealous energy in collecting tales from all over the world developed. In 1806, while working on their collections, Napoleon rolled through Kassel, and the brothers hoped that the "reawakening of the long forgotten literature would contribute to the return of a better day" (Campbell, "Folkloristic Commentary" 836).

The Grimms brothers thought the tales were the detritus of Old Germanic beliefs. But in 1859, Theodor Benfey demonstrated the Hindu origins of much of the mythic material in the tales via the translation into German, Italian, French, and English of the Latin translation in 1270 of the *Panchatantra* from a Hebrew translation of an Arabic translation of the 6th century A.D! This links the tales back to the same mythogenetic ground from which *The Arabian Nights* emerged. In addition to the Oriental sources, the pre-Christian Celtic mythologies of Old Europe made their way into the Arthurian Romances of the 12th-14th centuries. This mixture of material then enriches European literature by Chaucer, Boccaccio, and many others. The current view is that the tales are the product of two major forces: psychological continuity, and diffusion, during which the archetypal motifs are transformed and reshaped. The diffusionist view is the basis of the Geographic-Historic method perfected in 1907 by the Finnish School, a method of systematizing the vast quantity of material and tracing the key motifs to their source. What began during the Romantic period as a nationalistic endeavor, has evolved into an international effort to collate and interpret the tales.

Folktales

A simple tale like the Grimms Brothers "The Wolf and the Seven Little Kids" operates on many levels. The hero journey cycle is complete, taking the little goats in the story from their home, into the wolf's belly, and back into their home. The adventure begins when the mother leaves home for the village, and tells the kids not to let the wolf in while she is gone: they can recognize him by his rough voice and black feet. In a typical pattern known among folklorists as incremental repetition, the wolf comes to the house three times in the mother's absence, gaining entry on the third try by disguising his rough voice and covering his black feet with white flour. All of this action (preliminary to their departure) occurs in a setting now familiar to us: the doorway to the little cottage, which will be the kids' entrance to the underworld. When the kids mistake him for their mother, the wolf crashes through the doorway and eats up all the little goats, except for one who hides in the clockcase. Then the wolf goes outside to nap beside the well.

The threshold battle takes the kids from home into the belly of the wolf, and hence follows a familiar pattern that takes us back to Jonah (or indeed to the Raven of Eskimo fable) in the belly of the whale and on up to Pinocchio, who is reunited there with his father Gepetto. Both Raven and Pinocchio burn their way out of the belly, the former inventing fire to do so, and then teaching the Eskimos the use of fire when he emerges from the whale (Campbell, *Hero* 247-48). The discovery of fire in these analogous tales is an archetypal symbol of enlightenment on the same order as the theme of atonement in the tale of Pinocchio: the revelation of the mystery of fire, and the discovery of the Father as the source of life, constitute the journey's initiation. In "The Wolf and the Seven Little Kids," the goats are rescued by their mother, who hears the whole story from the kid who hid in the clockcase. She then instructs him to get a needle and thread and some scissors, and proceeds to cut open the belly of the sleeping wolf. When the kids hop out one by one, the mother tells them all to get a stone and put it into the belly of the wolf, which she then sews back up and returns to the house with her children. The wolf wakens with a terrible thirst and drowns in the well when he leans over to drink, and the weight of the stones plunges him into the water.

The symbolism of death and rebirth couldn't be clearer: we have a kind of C-section delivery which transforms the tomb of the wolf's belly into a womb. Beneath the simple moral of not letting strangers into the home, a deeper metaphysical wisdom of the soul's journey permeates the story, like waters from the well of life (the pit here also a place of death and life, as it was in the Joseph story in Genesis). On a psychological level, the image of the devouring parent lurks in the background, whether it be the devouring father or the mother whom the kids mistake the wolf for (a Freudian would point out that by killing father wolf the kids are reunited with mother goat!). A curious parallel from Greek mythology confirms this interpretation and provides a telling instance of the survival of ancient motifs in the oral traditions of the European world. In the story of the Olympian Gods, the old Father Chronos devours his children (he has seven of them total) one by one, until his wife Rhea substitutes a stone for Zeus and subsequently forces Chronos to regurgitate the other children. Goya painted a famous picture of Chronos devouring his children which he is said to have kept in his dining room, possibly to cut back on the expenses of feeding guests whose appetites would be diminished by the sight of the painting! Now the name Chronos suggests time, which devours the same children which it generates. The little kid who survives in our several millennia later hides in a *clock* case, and the kids who are rescued substitute stones for children in the same way Rhea did to rescue Zeus. Our little märchen is a well-spring, then, of motifs of extremely ancient pedigree, and it serves to instruct its auditors about far more than the boundaries that divide home from the world at large. For here is a tale that reveals the mysteries of birth, life, time, and death in a way that reminds the soul of its ultimate journey.

Another tale from the Grimms collection which preserves and transmits the millennial wisdom of the generations is "The Devil and the Three Golden Hairs," which is a fascinating oral-folk version of the descent to the underworld. The hero of the tale is marked at birth as one who will marry the King's daughter, a prophecy which provokes the usual effort of the King to rid himself of the child (the infant exile motif).[2] He does so by purchasing the infant from its poverty stricken parents, placing the child in a box, and pushing the box out onto the lake, hoping the box will sink and the baby will drown. Instead, it floats over to the Miller's cottage, who, being childless, brings the baby up with his wife. Like Moses floating in his basket down the Nile, or Perseus floating in the coffin with his mother Danae, the motif of the infant exile evokes the trauma of birth and the sociological tensions between the classes: to wash up onto the shore is to be born into a life of conflict between the powerful and the powerless.

The King tries for a second time to rid himself of the boy when he reaches puberty, the age when the initiatory rites of passage are typically performed. These rites (vividly described by van Gennep and Eliade) often involve the separation of the boy from his parents and a journey into the forest. In "The Three Golden Hairs," the King sends the boy to deliver a letter to the palace which unbeknownst to the boy instructs the guards to murder him; but that night as the boy sleeps beside an old woman in the robber's hideaway in the deep forest, the thieves take pity on him and change the letter, so that instead of being killed when arriving at the palace the next day, he marries the King's daughter as foretold. This second journey hearkens back to those oral traditions of the exchange of letters in European lore, the same which Shakespeare drew from in *Hamlet*. When the King arrives at the palace to discover the marriage, he furiously tries for a third time to rid himself of the boy by sending him to get three golden hairs from the head of the devil.

This set of three incremental repetitions is then matched by three questions which the boy encounters during his second forest journey to the devil's cottage: the first town he comes to is afflicted by the withering of a tree which used to bear golden apples; the second town by the drying up of a fountain that used to flow with wine; and the riverman at the crossing to the yonder shore by the curse of eternally rowing back and forth across the river. All ask the boy what they need to do to reverse their afflictions, and he promises to return in a few days time with the answers. We have encountered both the tree and the fountain before as archetypal symbols in the hero journey, and here both suffer from the pervading conditions of the waste land, which emanates from the tyranny of the King. It is the young lad's universal challenge to reform the conditions inherited from the older generation, and thus to revive the waste land. The crossing of the river is particularly interesting with respect to the archetype of the descent to the underworld upon which the tale is based, for, as we will learn, the riddle of all of the afflictions is well known to the devil who lives on the other side of the river.

When the young boy arrives at the devil's cottage, only the old Grandmother is at home, and she takes pity on the boy, turning him into an ant, hiding him in her skirts, and promising to get both the three golden hairs and the answers to his three questions from the Devil.

Freudians take note: the boy has literally returned ad uterum into the folds of the maternal skirts, from which he will be reborn the next morning after the mysteries have been revealed. These revelations take the form of three dreams which the Devil interprets, for, as James Hillman has eloquently shown, the dream and the underworld are intimately related. Hades is the granary where the seed forms of the archetypal imagination are stored; hence, the Devil, lord of the underworld, knows the answers to the riddles of affliction which preside in the waste land (from a Christian perspective, it certainly seems appropriate that the Devil know the source of these evils). The Old Woman coaxes his knowledge out of him indirectly: while the boy remains hidden in her skirts, she plucks a series of three golden hairs from the Devil's head. Each time, when he wakes up, she says she has had a nightmare, and recounts in sequence the stories of the ferryman, the town with the dried-up fountain, and the town with the withered apple tree. And each time the Devil provides the solution, which the boy takes with him the next morning, along with the three golden hairs he had originally come for. The gold symbolizes light and the imaginal wealth of the underworld, which expresses itself through the archetypal forms of dreams. This Devil is not purely Christian, since he knows the answer to all things (the underworld is a place of knowledge and destiny) and can be tricked into revealing that wisdom. But still, the young boy must never see the Devil directly: he is in the skirts when the Devil arrives and wakes up after the Devil has gone, as if to suggest that there are some manifestations of spiritual power which we as humans had better not attempt to face in their unmitigated power.

The boy sets off on the return journey homeward, after the revelations of the initiatory phase of the journey. First he tells the ferryman to give the oar to the next person who comes along, who will then be the one stuck rowing back and forth forever and ever. The curse of endless repetition which can be passed on magically from one victim to another is a very old one in the lore of the Indo-Europeans, suggestive of the fables of the Gallo-Roman gods of the wheel which Joseph Campbell traces all the way back to the Hindu *Panchatantra* (*Creative Myth* 413f.), and which the Sanskrit scholar Theodor Benfey found traces of in the Grimms tale (Number 54). These tales combine the search for a special treasure, like the three golden hairs, with a sequence of special questions, like the ones the afflicted ferryman and townspeople ask, the answering of which entails the transmission of the curse (this time ultimately to the King). Equally archaic are the afflictions of the fountain and the tree: the frog under the stone in the middle of the fountain and the mouse eating the roots of the golden apple tree. With the removal of the former, the fountain flows once more with wine, and with the removal of the latter, the tree immediately yields its golden apples. There are Norse precedents for both images, which themselves hearken back to Classical sources and beyond: the dragon which guards the well of Nifelheim and the snakes and deer which gnaw the roots of Yggdrasil, the world tree, as well as Freya's tree of golden apples which confer immortality upon the gods, look further back to the dragons of the Hesperides in Greek myth which guard the golden apples of immortality (Campbell, *Mythic Image* Plate 174), and beyond that to a wide variety of fountains and trees which comprise the totality of the archetype (Eliot 108-111). By removing the afflictions and answering the questions, the boy in "The Three Golden Hairs" is performing the typical Arthurian task (and indeed the task we typically ask of all our adolescent males) of redeeming the waste land.

When he returns to the palace and gives the King the three golden hairs, he has completed his cycle of journeys, which can be linked together in clusters of three: three efforts to get rid of him, three questions, and three golden hairs. He has successfully navigated the return phase of the cycle by retrieving some special boon (the golden hairs) symbolic of his new-found wisdom, and he is therefore now well prepared for the rigors of marriage and kingship. His first action tests his new sense of justice: when his step-father greedily asks where the boy found the large bags of gold he has brought back on his donkey, the boy lays a trap for the old tyrant by sending him to the riverside. When the ferryman hands the King the oar, the King takes the ferryman's place and inherits the curse of Charon: he is rowing that boat right now, and will continue to do so as long as people die.

Several beautiful Russian tales collected during the 19th century by Alexandr Afanas'ev record feminine versions of the folkloric descent to the underworld and the encounter with the Great Goddess who rules there. Many of the motifs of heroine's journey originating in the Ancient Near Eastern world were transmitted along lines of trade into Northern Russia via the Crimea. That many of the tales in this splendid collection take their protagonists to the Black Sea is significant, for it indicates a long tradition of oral transmission during which the rich variety of mythological motifs of the Mesopotamian and Mediterranean worlds, not to mention India, Persia, and the Orient, survived the Christianization of the Ancient world during the reigns of Constantine and Theodosius by taking on new forms in the folktale. After Theodosius proclaimed Christianity the official state religion of the Roman Empire in 438 A.D. -- to the exclusion of all other forms of worship -- the archaic motifs of the ancient world passed on into the secret mystery rites of such heretical groups as the Gnostics, on the one hand, and on into the rich treasury of folklore on the other. The result is a magnificent collection of Russian tales enriched by a deep reservoir of mythological imagery which flowed into Russia from the Turkish world and beyond during the many waves of cultural interface in the Crimea.

One of the finest of these tales is the little piece called "Vasilisa the Beautiful," which preserves the archaic lore of the Great Goddess and the mysteries of the descent to the underworld. The heroine's journey begins, typically, with the death of a parent, in this case the mother, who leaves her daughter Vasilisa a little doll. After the father remarries, the Cinderella complex is activated: a wicked step-mother and wicked step-sisters torment their more beautiful sibling and constantly pass the work on to her. This is the domestic crisis that leads to Vasilisa's departure from home; she is sent into the forest to get some light from the witch Baba Yaga, so the sisters can sew at night. Like many a Romantic hero, Vasilisa sets out at twilight into the dark Russian forest. Three horsemen pass her along the way, a black, a red, and a white, until at last she arrives at Baba Yaga's hut. It stands on chicken legs and is surrounded by skulls on sticks and by a fence made of human bones. Vasilisa carefully unhooks the fence's latch (made of finger bones) and enters the hut. Baba Yaga comes crashing through the forest shortly thereafter, riding a mortar and holding a pestle in one hand, and sweeping up her tracks with a broom in the other. Like Psyche, Vasilisa must perform a sequence of tasks (separating poppy seeds from the dirt) or be eaten.

Vasilisa has clearly entered the realm of the dead, but it is a realm where the Goddess presides. At first Baba Yaga appears to be a devouring Goddess, with the skulls and bones of Russians whom she has eaten surrounding her hut. But the fact that she is riding a mortar and carrying a pestle is a significant representation of her nurturing, Demetrian side, for she is associated with the grain (an old symbol of death and rebirth, very much alive in the New Testament), which must be ground (die) in order to make bread (to rise again). Her poppy seeds connect her with the oriental visions of the underworld drifting up along trade routes from Turkey. Hence, what we have in this little tale is a Northern version of the mysteries of Demeter and Persephone. After the virgin Vasilisa performs the tasks enjoined upon her by the old hag, she is allowed to ask just one question: who were the three horsemen she saw on her way to Baba Yaga's hut? My three servants, Baba Yaga answers, the black horse of the Night, the red horse of Dawn, and the white horse of the Day. These are the three powers of birth, life, and death traditionally associated with the Triple Goddess, and they all em- anate from Baba Yaga in her cosmic domain.

Baba Yaga's gift to the brave Vasilisa is equally symbolic: she gives her a skull on a stick with bright beams of light radiating from the eye sockets. Among the most fascinating forms of the archaic divinities of the Ancient world are the little eye goddesses that take us as far back as the Sumerian descent of Inanna, in which Ereshkigal, the Goddess of death, kills Inanna with the "eye of wrath" (Wolkstein and Kramer).[3] The light that shines through the sockets of the skull suggests the mystery of that life which transcends death and illuminates the darkness. The skull thus serves as a symbolic token of the mysteries of death and rebirth embodied by the Goddess, and it is therefore appropriate that Vasilisa uses the light shining from the eyes of this skull to guide her homeward through the dark woods of the Russian forest. She is just about ready to throw the skull away at the threshold of the forest, which she reaches at dawn, when it speaks to her and tells her to take it home and place it in full view of the family. Here the skull fulfills another task crucial to a complete understanding of the role played by the Great Goddess in the heroine journeys of the ancient world: she becomes a Goddess of Justice, blind in this case. When the sisters and wicked stepmother walk into the room, the light blazing through the sockets follows them relentlessly and eventually incinerates them as punishment for their treatment of Vasilisa.

Baba Yaga, therefore, is not only a Goddess of death and rebirth, not only a cosmic Goddess of the diurnal cycles of the sky, but also a Goddess of Justice. The wisdom which Vasilisa achieves on her journey is many layered, and represents an intimation of totality, from the feminine perspective. The skull with which she returns is a talisman of this wisdom, and can be seen as a representation of her initiation into the mysteries of her own femininity. The Russian tales are particularly enriched by such images of the Goddess inherited from both native and Ancient Near Eastern sources. These images revolve around the creative and destructive sides of the Goddess, and constitute the central revelation of several hero journey cycles in the tales. In "Two Ivans, Soldier's Sons," for example, Ivan follows a fleet-footed stag into a meadow, and then crosses a little stream with two ducks floating on it (the stag is his guide and the stream his threshold crossing). He shoots one of the ducks, and takes it with him into the white stone palace which he finds after riding a long while on the yonder shore of the stream. When he sits down to eat the duck after roasting it in the oven, a lovely maiden appears out of nowhere and demands Ivan's magic horse. His refusal to give it turns her into a wrathful lioness (sister of one of the dragons Ivan had slain earlier in the story), and she devours the champion whole. Ivan's twin brother is alerted to the crisis when his handkerchief turns to blood, and he too goes in pursuit of the fleet-footed stag, crosses the stream and shoots a duck, cooks it, and denies the lovely maiden who appears and demands his magic horse, But when she turns into the wrathful lioness, the second Ivan draws his sword and forces her to regurgitate his brother. Although the brother is dead and beginning to rot, Prince Ivan sprinkles him with healing water and the water of life, and then returns home to end the cycle.

The imagery here of the Goddess who both devours and bestows life is analogous to the image of the Wolf in the Grimms tale, from whose stomach the little kids are reborn. And we know that the lion is among the oldest of the animals sacred to the Great Goddess of the Ancient World: she is the sun-lion which pounces on the moon bull, which dies to be reborn from the fire of her womb every month. The image takes us as far back as 6000 B.C. at Çatal Hüyük, where we find a Goddess giving birth on a throne with lions on either side of her (Gimbutas 107). The image survived right down to Roman times, as evidenced by a sculpture of the Anatolian Cybele flanked by lions (Campbell, "Great Goddess" 79). In Ancient Egypt, we have the myth of Tefnut, daughter of the son god Re, who departs into Nubian desert, where she takes the form of a savage lioness, drinking blood and puffing fire from her eyes and nostrils (Clark 228). Along the same lines, the special attachment which the lioness in "Two Ivans" has to the magic horse which she furiously requests of the brothers may imply the patriarchal theft of the sacred horses of the goddess in the Hellenic world (Campbell, *Occidental Myth* 155).

Another image of Baba Yaga as the devouring Goddess occurs in the wonderful tale, "Ivan, the Cow's Son," a completely developed hero journey cycle with many mythological motifs of great interest. It concerns the coming of age of three sons all born when their mothers (the Queen, the Scullery Maid, and a Cow) eat some meat from a golden pike that swims in the castle moat. At adolescence they undertake a journey to the Black Sea, where they find a white hazelwood bridge and a little hut standing backwards on chicken legs by the road. Ivan the Cow's son tells the hut to turn around straight, and the three brothers find a feast inside and spend three nights there. On each day, Ivan the Cow's son takes the place of his cowardly brothers to slay the six-headed, nine-headed, and twelve-headed dragons which come surging up from the sea when he goes out to the hazelwood bridge, taps with his stick, and smashes the magical dancing pitcher which appears at his feet. After the third battle with the twelve-headed dragon, his brothers take him for dead, because the bridge is soaked with blood and Ivan asleep in the stables. After the two brothers leave, Ivan wakes up, turns himself into a fly, and listens on the stove of the hut as Baba Yaga appears and tells her three daughters (the wives of the three dragons) how Ivan killed their husbands.

Baba Yaga, then, is the one Goddess from whom the three manifestations of her power emerge, all avatars of what Joseph Campbell calls "The Serpent's Bride" (*Occidental Myth* Chapter 1). The revenge they plan revolves around key symbols of the archetypal powers of the feminine: the first daughter turns herself into a poisoned well with a silver cup floating on the surface; the second into a poisoned orchard; and the third into a hut and perilous bed that will kill anyone who tries to sleep on it. In case these measures fail to kill the three brothers, Baba Yaga resolves to turn herself into a giant boar and swallow them whole. We have seen the well before as a symbol of the source of life in the Arthurian tale of "The Lady of the Fountain," only here the well is negative, and we have seen the connection between the Goddess and the fruit tree (another symbol of the source of life) in such earlier prototypes as the Sumerian "Huluppu Tree" and the Semitic Tree of Knowledge in Genesis. What is new here is the bed into which the third sister turns herself, a representation of the two poles of the Goddess as the place where life begins and ends. Baba Yaga then transforms herself into one of the most ancient avatars of the Goddess of the Underworld: the wild boar. Several of the archaic consorts of the Great Goddess of the Ancient Mediterranean world were associated with the boar (Attis, Adonis, Osiris, Odysseus, and also, as we have seen, Sir Gawain). In each case, the boar represents (as it did also in the Eleusinian mysteries of Demeter and Persephone) the mystery of death and rebirth (Campbell, *Occidental Myth* 171).

Hence, after Ivan thwarts the revenge plans of the three sisters by smashing the cup in the well, the fruit on the orchard trees, and the bed in the hut, Baba Yaga still manages to devour the two brothers who follow the left-handed path at the crossroads the next day. Ivan follows the right-handed path to a village of blacksmiths, whom he instructs as follows: when the huge wild boar comes charging into town, the twelve blacksmiths get her to stick her long tongue into the burning forge by promising to feed her Ivan the Cow's Son. When she does so, they pin the tongue down and prod her mercilessly with red-hot irons until she vomits up the two brothers and their horses! The devouring tomb of the boar's belly has become the womb of rebirth. To this central image is added the alchemical symbolism of the forge, so that in the background of this story we must also acknowledge those mysteries of metallurgy so beautifully explored by Eliade in *The Forge and the Crucible*, in which he discusses the related theme of humans sacrificed in the furnace (62f.) (shades of Sinbad). In "Ivan the Cow's Son," the two brothers are inside the boar when she is incinerated, and eventually emerge from her out of the flames. I think also in this context of the famous alchemical picture by Michael Maier (*Atalanta Fugiens*, Emblem 24), which shows a wolf put in the fire of the forge after eating a King, and the King emerging reborn from the flames (Fabricius Fig. 89). After their rebirth from the fires of the forge and the belly of the boar, the three brothers return to their kingdom, completing the hero journey cycle.

Others among the Russian tales present a rather gentler portrait of the Goddess revealed during the hero journey. In "Frog Princess," three sons shoot arrows to find wives, and Prince Ivan's arrow is retrieved by a frog which he must marry. She sloughs her skin at night to take human form, on one occasion attending a feast thrown by the King to see which of his three new daughters-in-law can dance the best. Prince Ivan's frog princess sits at dinner stuffing the bones of her meal up one sleeve and the wine from her cup up the other. When she is called upon to dance, she whirls around and around, waving her hands in the air. From her right sleeve, lakes and woods appear, while from her left sleeve, various birds begin to fly about. When she stops dancing, "all that she had created vanished" (121), as if she were the Shiva Nataraja, dancing the world into and out of existence (Zimmer, *Myths* 151-75; Coomaraswamy, *Dance* 66-78). What a lovely way for a Goddess to enact her two central roles, life giving and life destroying. The frog of course is an old symbol of the lord of the abyss from the waters of which all life emerges, and is hence appropriately linked in this tale with the world creative powers of the divine feminine. In an extraordinary sequence of images, Marija Gimbutas shows that the archetype of the "Frog Goddess of Death and Regeneration" may be as old as the Upper Paleolithic, when engravings of females with frog legs first appear as symbols of regeneration. Egyptian myth even preserves a Goddess Creatrix (like our Frog Princess), Haquit, who was portrayed with the head of a frog (251-56).

Another archaic symbol of the creative power of the Goddess in Old Europe which has thrived in Russia is the egg, to which Gimbutas devotes an entire chapter (Chapter 19). That the egg can symbolize both the womb and the tomb, as Gimbutas argues (218), is evident in the splendid little Russian tale called "Dawn, Evening, and Midnight," which is a fully realized hero journey. Three brothers (triplets born to a poor widow on the same night at the times named in the title) set off to find three princesses whom a whirlwind has abducted, nobody knows whither. They come first upon a little man the size of a thumb with a cubit long beard and preternatural strength. The old man thrashes the first two brothers nearly to death when they slaughter one of his rams, but Dawn manages to fasten him by the beard to an oaken pillar with a big iron stake (as in the Grimms "Rose Red"). When the three brothers go to see, however, the little old man has torn himself free, and they follow a trail of blood to a deep hole which leads down into "the other world" (460). Karl Kerényi has shown that dwarfs, trolls, and gnomes are typically servants of the Goddess, as for example the dactyloi who assist Rhea as she gives birth to Zeus in the mountain caves of Ida on Crete (*Gods* 171). Hence, when Dawn convinces his brothers to lower him down into the hole, his nekyia and the revelation of the mysteries of creation begin.

Underground, Dawn finds three kingdoms, of copper, silver, and gold, each presided over by the three abducted princesses. After drinking from a phial of the water of strength, Dawn defeats the three-headed, six-headed, and twelve-headed dragons which guard, respectively, the copper, silver, and golden kingdoms. Before leaving their kingdoms with Dawn their deliverer, each princess waves a red handkerchief and rolls her kingdom up into an egg (Fabergé, no doubt), which she then puts in her pocket! Evening and Midnight then pull their brother and the three princesses back up through the threshold hole, and all return to their home kingdom to complete the cycle. When they arrive, each princess takes her egg out of the pocket and rolls it into an open field, so that "straightway three kingdoms appeared, a copper, a silver, and a golden one" (462). The three goddess have thus fulfilled their dual role, recreating those worlds which they destroyed in the underworld, by rolling the egg or waving the handkerchief: the egg has become both the womb and the tomb.

E.T.A. Hoffman

Many of the motifs found in the folktales find their way into the short fiction of the 19th century, particularly in the works of Hoffman, Hawthorne, and Tagore. The archetypes of the maze, the goddess, and the descent to the underworld play a key role in the "Mines of Falun" by E.T.A. Hoffman, for whom the hero journey becomes a metaphor for poesis (the creative dynamics of writing), and for hermeneusis (the creative dynamics of reading). In "The Mines of Falun" Elis, the romantic protagonist descends into the mines of the Metal Queen, lured downwards by the mysterious old miner Torbern, who leads him through a "gate" ('dem Tore') on the road to the mines (930; 176). Torbern is a what van Gennep would recognize as a threshold guardian, and what Karl Kerényi would call a "Seelenführer," or psychopomp. Elis follows Torbern bravely to "the enormous gulf, like the jaws of hell itself," from which stupefying vapors rise, as if from a "hell-broth ... brewed down below" (930). He compares the mine entrance to the place where "Dante went down and saw the Inferno" (930), and the miners themselves look like "diabolical creatures" (931). When Elis first goes down to work in the mines, the "uncanny" Torbern appears like a "black shadow" to strike his hammer with the force of "distant thunder," before disappearing "amongst the black labyrinths of the chasms" (934). Later Elis sees the "desolate crags" at the entrance to the Inferno as a "numberless horde or horrible monsters, the dire brood of hell" (936). Hence, Hoffman's evocation of the underworld draws from

Dante, Norse legend, and Classical myth: Torbern is a Virgilian guide, leading Elis into the Inferno; he is a type of Thor, swinging his hammer to strike fire and thunder; and he is a type of Hades, albeit servant to his Persephone, the Metal Queen who rules down below, and to whom Elis is irresistibly drawn.

For the labyrinthine underworld of the cave is also the archetypal domain of the Earth Goddess. Eliade suggests that the cave was assimilated to the labyrinth and the goddess from prehistoric times ("Terre-Mère" 75), and the configuration linking the maze, the underworld, and the goddess -- which takes us back to the mythologies of Egypt and Sumer -- has been amply illustrated by Di Stasi and Gimbutas. By the same token, the "ores extracted from mines are in some ways *embryos*" (42), and "the kiln where enameling material was smelted (*schmelzofen*) was designated by the name of matrix or maternal bosom (*Mutterschoss*)" (38). Hence, Elis ultimately collapses into the arms of "the mighty queen" of the caves, who draws him "to her breast" (936). The alchemical dimensions of mining and the imagery of the Great Goddess emerge later in the story, when Elis resolves (on his marriage night) to go down into the caves in order to retrieve the "queen's heart," which he imagines as a "glorious red carbuncle" which is the maternal source of all "hearts and souls" (938). Like the image of the Goddess herself, the metallurgical operations leading to the forging of the philosopher's stone in alchemy are natural symbols of creative processes of poesis, a point Joyce would later make clear in *A Portrait of the Artist as a Young Man*, which closes with Stephen resolving to "forge in the smithy of my soul the uncreated conscience of my race" (253).[4] Other feminine symbols of creativity in "The Mines of Falun" include the notions of cooking and brewing (the vapors rising from the "hell-broth" brewed down below (930)), old Germanic symbols of the union of the loving and terrible aspects of the Goddess to be found for example in "Hansel and Gretel," or in the image of the "Black Witch" ('Schwarze Köchin') in *The Tin Drum* by Günter Grass.[5] As Eliade notes, "The comparison of human work, in which fire was used (metallurgy, forging, cooking, etc.), with the growth of the embryo inside the mother, still survives, obscurely, in European vocabulary (cf. *Mutterkuchen*, placenta, *Kuchen*, gâteau)" (38-9). Hoffman emphasizes the erotic, creative symbolism of the caves and the Metal Queen by surrounding her with "innumerable beautiful maidens" from whose hearts roots, plants, and metal flowers grow (928).

From such pre-literate roots, the imagery of the maze, the underworld, and the goddess gradually emerged as metaphors of the intricacies of reading and writing in the literary tradition: Doob has delineated the development of the myth of the labyrinth from Ovid to Chaucer; J. Hillis Miller has applied the metaphor of the maze to narratology; and, more recently, I have shown how these three archetypes serve as tropes of poesis and hermeneusis in Modernism. In "The Mines of Falun," amidst the "richest veins" of the bottomless caves ruled by the Metal Queen, Elis comes to assume that "none but he understood the secret signs, the significant writing, fraught with hidden meaning, which the queen's own hand had inscribed on the rocks, and that it was sufficient to understand those signs without bringing to light what they indicated" (938). The problem is simultaneously one of psychogenesis, in which old persona dies so that a new self may be born; of hermeneusis, which requires understanding ("verstehen") the "secret signs" of a "significant writing" ("die geheimen Zeichen, die bedeutungsvolle Schrift") (189); and of poesis, for the story gives us a glimpse of the "the queen's own hand" engraving ("hineingrabe") the sacred symbols of the underworld on the parchment of her preference ("Steingeklüft," clefts in the rock) (189).

The German word for writing in this passage preserves the same pun we have in English (engrave): "Grab" of course means grave, as in tomb, and "graben" can mean to dig as well as to engrave. The word "hineingrabe" is therefore resonant: it signifies engraving letters into stone or metal, digging into the earth, and, oddly enough, the process of "going into" ('hinein') a grave ('grabe'). The same pun emerges at the end of the story, where Elis links the Metal Queen with a "cherry-coloured sparkling almandine, on which the tablet of our lives is graven" (938). The word for her writing on the tablet is again "graven" 'eingegraben' (938; 190). To engrave suggests a process of memorial-izing, and the underworld has traditionally been conceived of as what MacDonald calls "the burial place of memory." By this curious twist of language, Hoffman strikes upon the term for writing which links poesis and hermeneusis with the descent to the underworld, very much in the way Thomas Mann would later do, in the "Prelude" to *Joseph and His Brothers*, in which he compares the "Feast of storytelling" to the "descent into hell" ('Höllenfahrt') (33), and in *The Magic Mountain*, in which Naphta says that the grave "comprehends all hermetics," and that it is the "crystal retort wherein the material is compressed to its final transformation" (511).

Rabindranath Tagore

Rabindranath Tagore came from a Brahman family of writers and thinkers, inherited the divided consciousness of colonial India (Imperial England / native India), was educated Calcutta and England in Sanskrit, English, Bengali, and during the Bengali renaissance attempted an East /

West synthesis into a global culture of "the Universal human spirit" (qtd. Davis et. al. 1246). "The Hungry Stones" is a frametale, told by a nameless narrator on a train to two young men. It is about several nights he spent in a ruined Persian palace, where he had visions of an imprisoned princess, and of a mad lunatic, who warns him about the fatal allure of the spirits inhabiting the palace. Throughout the story we find a fusion of what Adolph Bastian called "völkergedanken" and "elementargedanken" (Campbell "Great Goddess") -- folk ideas native to Indian culture, and the elementary ideas of the hero journey archetypes. Fusing the two, Tagore creates a powerful allegory of poesis.

The folk ideas, native to the Oriental Indian traditions of Hinduism and Buddhism, include the notions of moksha (release), maya (illusion), kama-mara (love and death), and the vajra (the lightning bolt). The mad lunatic who has previously fallen prey to the spell of the Arab ghost imprisoned in the Persian palace greets each dawn with the words "All is false! All is false!" a standard refrain in Hindu and Buddhist prayers to this day, indicating the illusions of maya created by the temptations of fear and desire (kama-mara), which bind most of us to the wheel of incarnation, but which the Buddha transcended beneath the Boddhi tree. The traditional symbol of the Buddha's enlightenment in the Tibetan schools is the vajra, the lightning bold which shatters the illusions of the phenomenal world of maya; hence, the long last night the protagonist spends in the palace is punctuated by flashes of lightning which give him a "momentary glimpse of the fair damsel" (1251). After this revelation, the protagonist finds himself in the typical Indian quandary of seeking moksha, release from the wheel of life, driven by the fears and desires revolving around the Arab girl in the ghostly palace: "'Is there no means whatever of my release?'" he asks the mad old man who screams "All is false!" every morning, with the answer being that yes, there is, through listening to the "history" of the young Persian girl (1254).

In addition to these "völkergedanken" native to the local traditions are the "elementargedanken," universal archetypes of world religion, folktales, myth, and literature (such as the Wise Old Man, the Nekyia, the Maze, and the Great Goddess). The symbolism of the descent to the underworld (the nekyia) begins with the "nightmare" and "weird fascination" the protagonist experiences in "the solitude of the deserted palace" (1248). The solitude is inhabited by the "invisible" shades of the Persian past -- harem girls flitting among the fountains, corridors, staircases, and river palisades of the ruins of the palace, which is some 250 years old (1249). It is the land of the Persian dead, and many of the archetypes of Hades surface in the narrative: in addition to the icon of the ruined mansion inhabited by the ancestral shades (cf. Dante, Virgil), there is the river crossing (de rigueur for the nekyia since Gilgamesh,

Odysseus, and Dante), the tortuous ascent of stairways, and the ensuing passage through doors, corridors, and chambers (1250), which is as characteristic of the maze as of the underworld (cf. "The Descent of Inanna" or The Egyptian Books of the Dead (Budge 170-262)). This passage gives the protagonist access to an "intangible, inaccessible, unearthly vision" (1250), as he treads the pathways of a "bewildering maze of alleys in the enchanted dreamland of the nether world of sleep" (1252).

This amazing "nether world" is inhabited by a woman who lures the hero more deeply into the labyrinth, and she seems to demand the heroic task of liberation. In "The Hungry Stones," the protagonist hears the harem girl calling at "dead of night" from "below the stony foundations of that gigantic palace, from the depths of a dark damp grave" (1252). Tagore conflates the imagery of the maze, the underworld, and the goddess in this as in many other passages in the story: beneath the stairs, "the doors and windows and corridors and verandas and rooms" of the "vast desolate hall" through which the protagonist wanders (1250), far below the palace in her "dark damp grave" (1252), the goddess lies in prison. Like the Gnostic Sophia, imprisoned in the labyrinthine underworld of matter (Quispell 211), or like the Hindu jiva, trapped in that realm of illusion (maya), which is generated and sustained by fear and desire (kama-mara), the harem girl longs for release (moksha) (Zimmer 205-06; 263-68; 460-61). The story is replete with archetypal symbols of the creative and destructive powers of the Goddess: rose water fountains and clear water reservoirs (1248); "joyous maidens" who evoke the nagas and apsaras of Hindu folktale and myth; the gurgle of springs "gushing forth in a hundred cascades," which suggest the goddess is the source of life (1249); the new moon and bright star (1252), reminiscent of the archaic affiliation between such goddesses as the Sumerian Inanna and the Greek Aphrodite with the planet Venus; her "pain and craving and ecstasy," suggesting erotic fascination (1252); and the fruits and wine (1251) symbolic of the mother archetype, which is both nurturing and devouring, "loving and terrible" (Jung 16). The palace itself as a "living organism slowly and imperceptibly digesting" the narrator, suggests the devouring aspect of the mother archetype (1248), who is both "Muse" and "witch" (1249), and whose attendant reptile is also typical: a "mysterious serpent" twisting her "stupefying coils" around the hapless protagonist (1252). She is finally a "famished ogress" eager to swallow him up (1254), like the Hindu Goddess, Kali (Campbell, *Mythic Image* 351).

The configuration linking the maze, the goddess, and the underworld in "The Hungry Stones" is archetypal: the Malekulan myth of the descent, for example, revolves around the encounter with a

Devouring Ghost, who sits beside a cave and stone, with which she is identified (a hungry stone!), and who traces half of a maze in the sand at her feet, which the peregrine soul must complete in order to successfully navigate the passage to the afterlife (Campbell, *Mythic Image* 463). Numerous Bronze age funerary monuments consist of huge stones engraved with spiral labyrinths at the entrance to such tombs of the Goddess as the ones to be found on Malta, in the Mediterranean, or at Newgrange, in Ireland (Gimbutas, *Civilization* 172-81, 30, and *Language*, 51-63; Di Stasi (94-110). The oldest myth we know tells of the Goddess Inanna passing through the seven labyrinthine gateways of the underworld (Wolkstein and Kramer 52-89). From such pre-literate roots, the imagery of the maze, the underworld, and the goddess gradually emerged as metaphors of the intricacies of reading and writing in the literary tradition.

Tagore employs the archetypes of the descent, the maze, and the goddess as metaphors of psychogenesis, poesis, and hermeneusis. In "The Hungry Stones," the narrator (Mr. Collector or Srijut So-and-So, as he calls himself) discovers a post-colonial identity which transcends the boundaries of the Raj. He says that he could discern, amidst the "curious apartments" of the ruined Persian palace, "the fragments of a beautiful story, which I could follow for some distance, but of which I could never see the end" (1251). These "dream fragments" suggest the endless lines of a story which the protagonist must seek the conclusion of; and the story concerns an abused, elusive, and imprisoned woman whom the protagonist must liberate. He can only do so in a story which is replete with birdsong and supernatural music, conventional symbols of poesis. Amidst the vast and desolate corridors of the palace, the protagonist hears "a strange tune on the guitar ... the distant note of *nahabat* ... the song of the *bulbuls* ... the cackle of storks in the gardens, all creating round me a strange unearthly music" (1250). The songs transform Mr. Collector "into some unknown personage of a bygone age, playing my part in unwritten history" (1251) -- "unwritten," but sung, dreamt, and intimated by the act of poesis, which the supernatural tunes of birdsong and wailing woman compel, so that the story becomes itself an act of hermeneusis, an interpretation of the birdsong.

As a traditional symbol of the "angelic language" of such Islamic texts as the Koran (Guenon 299-303) and Farid Attar's *Conference of the Birds*, the birdsong suggests a divine dimension of the "unwritten history" which Srijut's descent compels him to tell. The bulbul is a songbird like Keats's nightingale, traditionally found in Persian poetry. But the inarticulate wailing of the Arab girl's ghost infuses the story with a demonic undercurrent. In addition to the birdsong, he must translate her "hard, harsh, mirthless laugh," and her "violent wringing

sobs" (1254). The song of bulbul and "the passionate cry" of the
madwoman compel the Collector to tell his tale, rather like the Ancient
Mariner's encounter with the Spectre Woman on the Ship of Death did;
but in order to do so, the protagonist as poet must become a
protagonist as reader, and "hear the history of a young Persian woman
who once lived in that pleasure-dome" (1254).

Nathaniel Hawthorne

Nathaniel Hawthorne's stories often employ the narrative structure
of the hero journey, and frequently link the journey to the problems of
poesis. "Young Goodman Brown" follows the classic outlines of the
monomyth, ending where it began, in the little Puritan town. It has a
clear call to adventure and departure sequence (at twilight when
Goodman Brown steps out the doorway into the street), clear threshold
battles going and returning (conflicts with the Devil, the guardian of the
realm), and clear initiation rites (in the forest 'baptism'), which reveal
hidden knowledge which transforms the protagonist.

The journey begins at sunset in the doorway of the home where
Goodman Brown lingers with his wife Faith, who thrusts her "pretty
head into the street" and detains her husband with a kiss and begs him
to stay home with her. The doorway remains in focus after they part,
when Goodman Brown looks back home before turning a corner to see
"the head of Faith still peeping after him" from their "threshold" (276).
The first six paragraphs of the story are simply, but symbolically, set
in the doorway, which, as we have seen in our survey of the hero
journey, is a standard icon for the crossing into the netherworld. In this
case, the netherworld is set in the forest (as it has been from the *Epic of
Gilgamesh* to the Arthurian Romances). The threshold guardian is the
devil himself, whom Goodman Brown encounters on the dreary path
leading into the gloomy forest. The "fellow-traveler" looks like
Goodman Brown's father, he has "the indescribable air of one who knew
the world," he has traveled from Boston with supernatural speed, and he
carries a staff "so curiously wrought, that it might almost be seen to
twist and wriggle itself, like a living serpent" (277). While Hawthorne's
primary intention seems to be to portray this mysterious stranger as a
devil (considering the overall context of the story), four of the motifs
mentioned in the portrait allude to the Greek god of travelers and guide
of souls to the underworld, Hermes: his association with travel and
twilight, his supernatural speed, his shape-shifting abilities, and his
serpent-twined staff.

Hawthorne wrote two collections of stories "for Girls and Boys"
based on Greek mythology, *A Wonderbook* (1852) and *Tanglewood
Tales* (1853). Hermes appears in both books in a form very close to the

way the strange dark figure is presented in "Young Goodman Brown."
In "The Miraculous Pitcher," Hermes appears at sunset, as he does in
"Goodman Brown," carrying "the oddest-looking staff" with "Two
snakes, carved in the wood" which the old man in the story (Philemon)
thinks he sees "wriggling and twisting" (1263). When Quicksilver (as
Hawthorne invariably calls Hermes in these tales), lets his staff fall
inside the cottage, it "seemed to get up from the ground of its own
accord" and hop over to the wall, while the "snakes continue to
wriggle" (1264). The narrator suggests that "old Philemon's eyesight
had been playing him tricks again" (1264), just as the narrator of
"Young Goodman Brown" suggests (in very similar language) that the
fact that the "curiously wrought" serpent on the dark traveler's staff
"might almost be seen to twist and wriggle itself" may be attributable
to "ocular deception, assisted by the uncertain light" (277). Likewise, in
"Circe's Palace," the motifs of travel and the caduceus identify Hermes
when Ulysses encounters Quicksilver on Circe's island, and the narrator
notes that "he carried a winged staff, around which two serpents were
wriggling and twisting" (1400). All three epiphanies of Quicksilver use
the same words ("wriggle" and "twist") to describe the serpents on the
staff which identify him as Hermes, while in "The Pomegranate-Seeds,"
Hawthorne simply refers to Quicksilver as "our old friend" and briefly
mentions his "snaky staff" (1430). We may therefore reasonably
conclude that Hawthorne had Hermes as much in his mind in describing
the "dark figure" in "Young Goodman Brown" as he did the devil.
Hermes, be it remembered, is a god of travel, dreams and illusions, and
a guide to the underworld, all of which figure largely in the story.

The threshold battle here is internalized, a matter of conscience, as
Goodman Brown resists going with the devil further into the forest
until the devil reminds him that both his father and grandfather were his
"good friends," and that the deacons, selectmen, governors, and
ministers of New England are among his "general acquaintance" (278).
After Goodman Brown sees Goody Cloyse, the "pious and exemplary
dame" who taught him the catechism, walking with the minister and
Deacon Gookin on their way to the Sabbath in the Forest, his resolve
is weakened. When he sees his wife's pretty pink ribbons floating down
from the clouds above where she has presumably been demonically
transported, it is broken, and he runs howling off down the wild and
dreary road into "the heart of the dark wilderness" (283).

But the wilderness is not only a place of temptation and sin: it is a
temenos, a place of poesis, where the powers of imagination and dream
are intensified. Hawthorne repeatedly evokes the sounds of the forest in
the most poetic and rhythmically periodic of sentences: Goodman
Brown hears "the murmur of the old forest, whispering without a
wind;" "a stronger swell of those familiar tones" of the village;" and the

wind tolling "like a distant church-bell;" (283). All the sounds finally converge into a rather magnificent midnight music:

> He paused in a lull of the tempest that had driven him onward, and heard the swell of what seemed a hymn, rolling solemnly from a distance, with the weight of many voices. He knew the tune; it was a familiar one in the choir of the village meeting-house. The verse died heavily away, and was lengthened by a chorus, not of human voices, but of all the sounds of the benighted wilderness, pealing in awful harmony together. Goodman Brown cried out; and his cry was lost to his own ear, by its unison with the cry of the desert. (284).

Hawthorne reiterates this vision of the forest music later, when the hymn is resumed:

> Verse after verse was sung, and still the chorus of the desert swelled between, like the deepest tone of a mighty organ. And, with the final peal of that dreadful anthem, there came a sound, as if the roaring wind, the rushing streams, the howling beasts, and every other voice of the unconverted wilderness, were mingling and according with the voice of guilty man, in homage to the prince of all. (285-86).

We have already noted how in Coleridge and Whitman (and will see again in Bierce and Conrad) the sea journey and forest evoke a powerful supernatural music composed of mystic tones which it is the poet's task to render and decipher. Similarly, in Hawthorne's wonderful tale, the hero journey precipitates a potent, periodic prose that approximates the power of music. The voices converge into the "harmony" and "unison" of a church "hymn" or "dreadful anthem," added to which we have the carefully delineated symbolic images of the "verses." What the underworld of the forest yields, then, is a prose poem, as the hero journey becomes an allegory of poesis.

For the underworld is also a place of dream and imagination, a rich reservoir of archetypal forms. Among the symbolic images revealed at the climax of the journey in the initiation stage in the forest is the infernal altar where the 'baptism' or 'marriage' sacraments welcoming Goodman Brown and Faith into the demonic congregation occur. The image of the pulpit takes the form of a mandala:

> At one extremity of an open space hemmed in by the dark wall of the forest, arose a rock, bearing some rude, natural resemblance either to an altar or a pulpit, and surrounded by four blazing pines, their tops aflame, their stems untouched, like candles at an evening meeting. The mass of foliage, that

had overgrown the summit of the rock, was all on fire, blazing high into the night, and fitfully illuminating the whole field. Each pendent twig and leafy festoon was in blaze. (284)

Two men lead Goodman Brown, and two women lead a "veiled female" up to a basin hollowed in the rock above which the "dark figure" of the devil presides. Here, the secret revelations of the initiation will occur. Curious to note, Hawthorne has shaped a precise mandala out of his altar: the rock stands in the center of a quadrangular form created by the four blazing pines that surround it, and in the center seven figures stand around the basin of blood, with Goodman Brown and his wife being central. One thinks of the alchemical basin into which the Solar King and Lunar Queen descend, to undergo there the torments of the various operations which transmute base metals into gold. One also thinks of the mandala most common to Christian iconography (of which Hawthorne's image is clearly an infernal parody): the image of Christ in the center of a page surround by the symbols of the four evangelists on each corner. Some of these are even closer to Hawthorne's icon: illuminated pages from several Medieval English manuscripts show the crucified Christ in the center, with a male and female personage on either side at the foot of the cross, surrounded by the symbols of the four evangelists at each of the four corners (Marks and Morgan Plates 3, 20, 25, 40). In "Young Goodman Brown," we have the devil in the center (instead of Christ) with Goodman Brown and Faith on either side of the basin (instead of say, the Virgin and St. John), surrounded by the four blazing pines (instead of the four evangelists).

For Jung, all of these mandalas symbolize the totality of the Self, which embraces and transcends the opposites warring within the psyche: male and female, conscious and unconscious, persona and shadow. The sacred marriage represents the union of these opposites, what Jung called the *mysterium coniunctionis* in alchemy. What Goodman Brown is unable to assimilate, however, is the dark side of human nature, revealed to him by the devil. Goodman Brown is invited to "penetrate, in every bosom, the deep mystery of sin, the fountain of all wicked arts" and together with Faith to receive the mark of baptism, so that "they might be partakers of the mystery of sin, more conscious of the secret guilt of others, both in deed and thought, than they could now be of their own" (287). One of the many ironic ambiguities in the story is that by refusing the baptism of sin, and hence the awareness of his own guilt, he fulfills the very words of the devil, henceforth more conscious of the "secret guilt of others" than of his own. He ends his days obsessed with this secret guilt, which he sees in every breast other than his own. The obsession and revelation of the forest journey

permanently transforms him: "A stern, a sad, a darkly meditative, a dis-
trustful, if not desperate man, did he become from the night of that
fearful dream" (288). As in every hero journey, revelation has led to
transformation, only when Goodman Brown completes the cycle by
returning to his village, he brings with him no redeeming boon, and in
this respect he looks forward to the ambiguities of the modern
monomyth.

Another story by Hawthorne, "The Birthmark," explicitly portrays
poesis as an alchemical hero journey through a sequence of doorwarys.
In the story, a brilliant young scientist (Aylmer) attempts to remove a
birthmark from his wife's cheek by the power of alchemy. He becomes
obsessed with the birthmark shortly after his marriage, seeing it as a
"symbol of his wife's liability to sin, sorrow, decay, and death" (766).
To him it is a "symbol of imperfection" (766) and "the visible mark of
earthly imperfection" (765) which he hopes to correct. But to the
narrator, the mark is a "faerie sign manual" variously interpreted
"according to the difference of temperament in the beholders" (765).
That is to say, the birthmark is a sign in an allegorical system of
significations, which, according to the traditional patterns of Biblical
exegesis, can be interpreted on from moral, psychological, and aesthetic
perspectives.

The moral level has to do with Hawthorne's condemnation of scientific materialism, with its ultimately destructive attempt to dominate
and improve upon nature. Aylmer's first love is for "natural philosophy" and its promise of leading its "ardent votaries" in a Platonic ascent
to "the secret creative force and perhaps make new worlds" in an assertion of "man's ultimate control over nature" (764). Aylmer draws on the
accumulated knowledge of "the elemental powers of Nature" in his efforts to treat what he sees as his wife's affliction. His "treatment of
Georgiana" involves secluding her in the inner chambers surrounding
his laboratory, and subjecting her to subtle infusions of floral distillates
extracted by various alchemical operations. He tells Georgiana about "
the long dynasty of the alchemists, who spent so many years in quest
of the universal solvent by which the golden principle might be elicted
from all things base and vile" (774). His primary efforts involve the ex-
traction of an "elixir vitae ... that should prolong life for years" (772):
it is an "elixir of immortality" which is also "the most precious poison
that ever was concocted in this world" (773). Aylmer obtains his
knowledge of the secret arts of alchemy from "the works of philosophers of the middle ages, such as Albertus Magnus, Cornelius Agrippa,
Paracelsus" who "perhaps imagined themselves to have acquired from
the investigation of Nature a power above Nature, and from physics a
sway over the spiritual world" (774).

It is this quest for perfection and "ultimate control over nature" (764) that is most severely chastised in Hawthorne's condemnation of the science of alchemy. His moral concern about the technological materialism of our scientific age constitutes the first level of allegorical meaning in the story, for administering the potent distillate to Georgiana leads to her death. As she herself recognizes, "the stain goes as deep as life itself" (768), and a denial of imperfection is a rejection of life. It was a concern Hawthorne returned to again and again, as in the story "Rappaccini's Daughter" and in the character of Chillingworth in *The Scarlet Letter*. Indeed, Hawthorne shared these apprehensions about science with other writers in the 19th century like Keats and later Yeats. But Aylmer's attempt to remove the birthmark is not only an allegory about the catastrophic consequences of the scientific enterprise to improve upon and dominate nature; it is also a psychological allegory.

This second level has to do with the complex psychodynamics of marriage, best understood by Jung's notion of alchemy as a metaphorical image of the psychology of the transference. In Jung's view, every marriage involves at least four 'persons:' the husband and wife, and the anima and animus, forming a quaternity in "The Birthmark." According to this view, every marriage constellates the mutual projection of unconscious images onto the partner: that of the husband's anima onto his wife, of the wife's animus onto the husband, and the corresponding reception of the projections along with their reactions to the projections by the husband and wife. The "alchemical marriage" for Jung involves the breaking down of these mutual misconceptions through recognizing their source in the unconscious, a withdrawal of the projections, and an acceptance of the marriage partner for what he or she really is. It is a painful and laborious process of many years involving an alchemical breakdown of the personality into its base elements, out of which a new 'individuated' identity can be forged.

Jung's visual metaphor for this process is taken from the sixteenth century alchemical text the *Rosarium philosophorum*, which depicts the relationship between the alchemist-adept and his 'mystic sister' (soror). He diagrams the complex pattern of relationships as a quaternity, with commentary (95). The direction of the arrows indicates the pull from the masculine to feminine and vice versa, and from the unconscious of one person to the conscious of the other, thus denoting a positive transference relationship. The relationships have therefore to be distinguished, although in certain cases they can all merge into each other, and this naturally leads to the greatest possible confusion. Hawthorne names Aylmer's apprentice Aminadab, which spelled backwards yields 'bad anima.' On the literal level of the allegory, the apprentice "seemed to represent man's physical nature; while Aylmer's slender figure, and pale, intellectual face, were no less apt a type of the spiritual element"

(770). Aminadab is then on one level the shadow figure corresponding to Aylmer's refined persona as an intellectual: the apprentice, in Jung's typology, represents the sensation and feeling functions opposite to Aylmer's intuitive and thinking functions. In addition, however, the naming of Aminadab suggests that Aylmer's relationship with his new wife Georgiana is archetypically stained by a negative anima projection, which in turn indicates an imbalance in his relationship with his own shadow side, or unconscious blackness. Aminadab's "visage was grimed with the vapors of the furnace" (769), yet on the positive side he spontaneously recognizes that it would be a mistake to remove the birthmark.

Aylmer's fixation on Georgiana's birthmark is the symptom which disturbs his relationship with her and initiates the alchemical marriage. His unwillingness to accept his wife as less than perfect, and his readiness to exalt her one flaw to archetypal status as a symbol of feminine evil suggests that he has projected a 'bad anima' onto his wife. It is a complex image darkening irrational idealizations with exaggerated notions of evil: his wife should be perfect, he reasons, yet she is fatally flawed by an innate capacity for sin and decay. Georgiana, on her side, accepts the projection in her willingness to undergo the ordeal of having the little mark removed, even though she knows it penetrates as deep as life itself. She buys into her husband's stereotypical condemnation of feminine imperfections precisely because she in turns projects her animus onto him. After reading his scientific journals she "reverenced Aylmer and loved him more profoundly than ever" with a love bordering on "worship" (775). She sees his love as "honorable ... so pure and lofty that it would accept nothing less than perfection" (777), and therefore "with her whole spirit she prayed that, for a single moment, she might satisfy his highest and deepest conception" (777). Her exalted estimation of his love suggests a view obscured by the animus, and in acting out his corresponding anima projection upon her, she sacrifices herself on the altar of his religiously inspired alchemy.

Their marriage, then, illustrates all of the possibilities for the greatest natural confusion outlined by Jung's interpretation of the relationship between the alchemist and his mystical sister in the *Rosarium philosophorum*: husband and wife, husband and anima, wife and animus, anima to animus, and so forth. The ultimate goal of the alchemical marriage, a renewed fully individuated Self capable of recognizing and withdrawing its projections, is of course not achieved in the story. Georgiana dies in the end. Nevertheless, the ending elicts that possible reconciliation of opposites Jung associated with the alchemical *conuinctio*. The Self, in its capacity to embrace the totality of the conflicting impulses of the psyche, facilitates the union of opposites. In the story, such a conjunctions arise in the image of the elixir Aylmer distills as a 'precious poison' both deadly and medicinal, in Georgiana's perfect yet defective beauty, in Aminadab as the earthly opposite of his spiritual master, and in Aylmer's exclamation that both "Matter and spirit -- earth and heaven" have done their part in the alchemical operations upon his wife (780).

The archetypal figure compelling the opus is Aylmer's negative anima complex, behind which one discerns the lineaments of a goddess. Aylmer devotes his "toilsome youth" to an exploration of "the elemental powers of Nature" which he personifies as feminine (769). He extracts "rich medicinal virtue, from the dark bosom of the earth" and he attempts to "fathom the very process by which Nature assimiliates all her precious influences from earth and and air, and from the spiritual world, to create and foster man, her masterpiece" (769). That is to say, behind his complex is an archetype, and behind the archetype a goddess: the "great creative Mother" who is the sole subject of his research (769). She is "loving and terrible" (to use Jung's definition of the Mother archetype), producing poison and antidote, combining earth and spirit, marring perfection with blemishes of evil. In as much as Hawthorne lost his father at the age of four, and spent the major portion of the next 33 years of his life as the solitary reclusive child of a widowed mother, I think it safe to assume the centrality of the Mother complex in his psychological make up.

From this perspective, "The Birthmark" can be seen not only as an allegory of the evils of science and the complexities of marriage, but also as an allegory of poesis: it is a sort of Kunstlerroman, an autobiographical portrait of the artist as alchemist. Like the alchemist, who attempts to create gold out of base metals, the writer transforms the ordinary into art. In *A Portrait of the Artist as a Young Man*, James Joyce uses the metaphor of the communion ritual for this process, whereby the priest of "eternal imagination" "transmute the daily bread of experience into the radiant everliving body of art" (221). In *The Tempest*, Shakespeare uses the image of the Magus to symbolize the artistic power of poetry to sublimate spiritual forms from base materials. Hawthorne's definition of alchemy as the "quest of the universal solvent by which the golden principle might be elicited from all things base and vile" (772) echoes Shakespeare's definition of love in *A Midsummer Night's Dream*: "Things base and vile, holding no quantity / Love can transpose to form and dignity" (1.1.232-33), and his portrait of Aylmer would seem to owe much to Prospero.

The spirit display Aylmer evokes for Georgiana, for example, resembles Prospero's wedding masque for Ferdinand and Miranda in *The Tempest*, and like that masque suggests the power of the poetry to body forth "the forms of things unknown" and give shape "to airy nothing" (*Dream* 5.1.15-16). To release Georgiana's "mind from the burden of actual things," Aylmer conjures "Airy figures, absolutely bodiless ideas, and forms of unsubstantial beauty" and also "The scenery and the figures of actual life ... with that bewitching, yet indescribable difference which always makes a picture, an image, or a shadow so much more attractive than the original" (771). Such scenery, figures, and forms of beauty are of course the stuff of dreams and art. Unlike the impressions of actual life, which are opaque, the images of art figured forth in the mind of the reader are "transparent to the transcendent" (Campbell 57), suggestive of symbolic meanings beyond themselves. They are one step removed from the actual towards the imaginative, from whence derives their universal appeal.

The progressive change in the setting of "The Birthmark" reflects this progressive descent, through a sequence of doorways, into archetypal depths of the imagination. The story begins in the outer rooms of the house, those closest to the normal concerns of domestic life. Aylmer then dreams of "attempting an operation for the removal of the birthmark" (767), and shares the resulting plan to "seclude themselves in the extensive apartments occupied by Aylmer as a laboratory" (769) with Georgiana. That is to say, the domestic concerns of daily life have been disrupted by a call to adventure sounding from the daemonic depths: the "spectres" of Sleep have broken forth from "the dim region of her sway ... affrighting this actual life with secrets that perchance belong to a deeper one" (767). When Aylmer leads Georgiana "over the threshold of the laboratory," the birthmark glows so intensely that Aylmer convulsively shudders, and his wife collapses into a "deathlike faintness" (769). This transition from the actual into the dream kingdom of death corresponds to the battle of the threshold in the hero journey, which for Hawthorne is a journey not only into the realm of sin, decay, and death, but also into the realm of the imaginative.

The "smoky, dingy, somber rooms" of the laboratory have been converted into "a series of beautiful apartments not unfit to be the secluded abode of a lovely woman" (770). It's real anima territory, permeated by a "penetrating fragrance," darkened by "gorgeous curtains," suffused by "a soft, impurpled radiance," and shut off from the world in the "infinite space" of "a pavilion among the clouds" (770). Aylmer feels "that he could draw a magic circle round her within which no evil might intrude" (770), as if he has sealed her off in the "vas hermeticum" of the alchemists, the temenos of sacred space within which the rites of purification will be performed. In these rooms, Aylmer begins the opus, administering "agents powerful enough to do aught except to change [her] entire physical system" (773), and entertaining her with some small vanities of his art.

That art, Hawthorne implies, is shared by alchemist and poet. Georgiana relieves the "tedium of the hours" spent in seclusion from the real world by reading the volumes in Aylmer's library, the most engrossing of which is the "large folio from her husband's own hand, in which he recorded every experiment of his scientific career" (774). This volume, I would suggest, is a guarded autobiographical allusion to Hawthorne's own extensive *American Notebooks,* in which he recorded the observations and fantasies that provided the prima materia of his romances. Like his alter ego Aylmer, Hawthorne also "handled physical details as if there were nothing beyond them; yet spiritualized them all, and redeemed himself from materialism by his strong and eager aspiration towards the infinite. In his grasp the veriest clod of earth assumed a soul" (774). Both artist and alchemist transmute the daily bread of actual life into the radiant golden body of art, helping earth to make soul.

This taste of her husband's craft induces Georgiana to impulsively cross the last threshold that separates her from the heart of his mystery. She secretly follows him into the innermost chambers of his laboratory, where the "furnace ... seemed to have been burning for ages" beside the "distillery apparatus ... retorts, tubes, cylinders, crucibles, and other apparatus of chemical research" (776). This unexpected intrusion leads to their first quarrel: "Would you throw the blight of that fatal birthmark over my labors?" Aylmer demands; "Go, prying woman, go!" (776). It is difficult not to see in this "prying woman" the Psyche of Apuleius' *Golden Ass* who holds up the lamp to her demon lover, exposing him to the light of conscious scrutiny, and leading him to abandon her in the magical pavilion where he has secluded her from mortal life. It is also difficult not to see this scene as typically marital, and perhaps autobiographical: the wife here prying into the secrets of the artist's heart by reading his journals, and Aylmer (Hawthorne) responding with the wounded rhetorical question "Have you no trust in your husband?" (776).

This portrait of the alchemist as scientist, husband, and artist, then, operates on the polysemous levels of allegory. The inner chambers of the laboratory represent the laboratory, the secrets of the heart, and the workshop of the artist. All three figures combine Shakespeare's lunatic, lover, and poet into the single character, and the story dramatizes the destructive attempt to control and dominate nature, the integration of the contents of the personal and collective unconscious during the alchemical marriage, and the dynamics of poesis. All three figures fail "to look beyond the shadowy scope of time, and, living once for all in eternity, to find the perfect future in the present" (780). The scientist fails by his reluctance to accept the limitations his ignorance imposes upon his enterprise; the husband fails by his inability to accept the mortal frailties of his wife; and the artist fails by replacing reality with an imaginary Utopia that obscures the defective perfection of actual life.

Another story, "Rappaccini's Daughter," suggests a similar constellation of moral, psychological, and aesthetic aspects in its portraiture of the anima. It tells of a young student of letters (Giovanni Guasconti) who takes lodgings near the University in Padua. His window looks out over the enclosed botanical garden of the renowned and feared Dr. Rappaccini, whose daughter, Beatrice, Giovanni sees wandering amongst the extraordinary splendor of flowers. "Was this garden, then," Giovanni wonders, the Eden of the present world? " (979) and was Beatrice its Eve, her Father its Adam? It becomes soon apparent that the flowers are malignant, so poisonous that butterflies and birds drop dead in their presence; even the flowers Giovanni throws to Beatrice from his window wilt and die in her hands. For she has been raised as "the human sister" to the most poisonous flower in the garden, which she tends like "one sister performing the duties of affection to another" (980). It gradually emerges that Dr. Rappaccini is plotting to unite Beatrice with Giovanni, but to do so he must establish Giovanni's immunity to his poisonous daughter by secretly administering strong doses of the malignant fragrances before allowing him direct access to the garden and physical contact with Beatrice.

These make Giovanni progressively lethal to outsiders. When he discovers that he has been poisoned and cut off from the world, he blames Beatrice. He calls her the "Accursed one!" and the "poisonous thing" who has made him "as hateful, as ugly, as loathsome and deadly a creature as thyself -- a world's wonder of hideous monstrosity!" (1002). Giovanni then administers an antidote to Beatrice, which will result in her death. He fails to recognize that the plot was not her's, but her father's, who says to the two lovers, as Beatrice lies dying, "My science, and the sympathy between thee and him, have so wrought within his system, that he now stands apart from common men, as thou dost, daughter of my pride and triumph, from ordinary women" (1004). He had meant her to be "terrible" and "beautiful" and to transcend "the condition of a weak woman, exposed to all evil, and capable of none" (1005). As she dies, she replies that she "would fain have been loved, not feared," and she asks Giovanni a rhetorical question: "Oh, was there not, from the first, more poison in thy nature than in mine?" (1005).

Beatrice, then, is the victim of the anima projection both of her father, Dr. Rappaccini, and of Giovanni, her first love. Her father had meant to sever her ties with an evil world by secluding her in the garden of his love. We never hear of her mother, and can assume an intense relationship between father and daughter. A Freudian interpretation is tempting, and the film version in "The American Short Story" series bites the bait by having Giovanni dream of a seductive tryst with Beatrice which ends with a glimpse of Beatrice being kissed delicately by her father. This interpretation puts Giovanni in the Oedipal role of the son who must steal Beatrice from her father's sexual love. From a Jungian point of view, Rappaccini is the portrait of the father who, in the absence of his wife, has imprisoned his daughter in an anima fantasy that has cut her off from all normal human intercourse.

By the same token, Giovanni's fascination with Beatrice displays all the symptoms of an anima fixation: in fact, Hawthorne says that Giovanni snatches "from her full gaze the mystery which he deemed the riddle of his own existence" (990). From the first he is captured by the "witchery" of her "girlish womanhood" (994). Though "worthiest to be worshipped" she exhibits "a frightful peculiarity in her physical and moral system" (994). By falling in love with her, Giovanni "felt conscious of having put himself, to a certain extent, within the influence of an unintelligible power" which he cannot resist (986). The description of Beatrice, in fact, almost exactly parallels Jung's delineation of the mother archetype as "loving" and "terrible:" on the one hand she is "associated with things and places standing for fertility and fruitfulness: the cornucopia, a ploughed field, a garden" (15). She is "all that is benign, all that cherishes and sustains, that fosters growth and fertility" (15). But, Jung adds, "On the negative side the mother archetype may connote anything secret, hidden, dark; the abyss, the world of the dead, anything that devours, seduces, and poisons, that is terrifying and inescapable like fate" (16).

Beatrice is all this to Giovanni. She "instilled a fierce and subtle poison into his system" that he sees as the "wild offspring of both love and horror" (986-87). It is clear that Giovanni's anima is also his (and Hawthorne's) muse, for her proximity kindles the fires of Giovanni's dream life and gives "a kind of substance and reality to the wild vagaries which his imagination ran riot continually in producing" (986). In her presence "There came thoughts, too, from a deep source, and fantasies of a gem-like brilliancy" (993). He is attracted, repelled, and inspired all at once, compelled by a "lurid intermixture" of "simple emotions" that produces "the illuminating blaze of the infernal regions" (987). She leads him, as her namesake did Dante, into the underworld his love, dread, and creativity. Hers is "an Eden of poisonous flowers" (995), created by a "cold and purely intellectual" father who "would sacrifice human life" in the name of his godlike science (982).

In terms of the threshold iconography of the hero journey, it is significant to note the role played by windows and doorways throughout the story, for it is through a sequence of these that Giovanni descends into the garden. During the entire first half of the story, Giovanni is seen sitting at his "window" (the word occurs nine times in the first ten pages) looking down at Beatrice in the garden below. She and her father are then consistently portrayed emerging from (979, 991), appearing (984) or "vanishing beneath" (986, 994), and watching "within the shadow," of a "sculptured portal" at the end of the garden. When Giovanni is finally tempted to leave the window and go down to meet Beatrice, he follows Lisabetta, his concierge, who "led him along several obscure passages, and finally undid a door" (900) which forms a "private entrance into the garden" (989). This descent -- through a sequence of doorways and corridors -- leads Giovanni to his lethal anima, wandering the maze of the "infernal regions" her father has imprisoned her in (987)

Such a portrait of an anima wounded by the father, which in turn poisons and inspires the son it is tempting to interpret as Hawthorne's mother complex, behind which we glimpse in turn the archetype of the "great creative Mother" ("Birthmark"). The psychopathological complex of the feminine portrayed in these stories combines the imagery of beauty, sin, death, disease and creativity characteristic of all of Hawthorne's art. His opus, therefore, records the stages of the individuation process of a great spirit and artist. The descent of his characters into the archetypal depths is a metaphor of individuation and an allegory of poesis. His stories are "flowers of evil" in the sense that they spring from the root systems of the underworld, brought to flowering by the anima. One wonders then if the scarlet "A" on the breast of Hester Prynne could not stand for "Anima," "Artist," "Alchemist," as well as for "Adultery." At any rate, Hester, like her feminine prototypes in the stories, lead Hawthorne into the "unconverted wilderness" where his stories were conceived.

In *The Scarlet Letter*, "A" may stand for "Apocalypse" as well as "Arist." The hero journey has an apocalyptic destination in the novel, and Hawthorne replaces doorways with the famous scenes on the scaffold to mark the major stations along the way. The theme of apocalypse is one of the most enduring and central in all of American literature, from Michael Wigglesworth to Thomas Pynchon. Along the way, its development engaged the great figures of the American Renaissance -- Emerson, Melville, Poe, and Hawthorne. In *The Scarlet Letter*, allusions to the Book of Revelation determine the basis of the novel's theme and structure to an extent not fully recognized by other critics of the novel, who have failed to recognize that Hawthorne attempts in this work a comprehensive refiguration of the Biblical apocalypse. By focusing on the root meaning of 'apocalypse' as an uncovering of hidden or buried secrets, Hawthorne raises hermeneutical and epistemological questions relevant to the debates about Emersonian transcendentalism and its relation to theology raging during Hawthorne's time.[6]

Visions of the end derived from Scripture were, as is well known, a standard feature of the intellectual community of Hawthorne's New England, particularly so in the context of the so-called Second Great Awakening, which emphasized the necessity of religious reform as a means of millennial hope. David Bjelajac has charted the apocalyptic visions in the sermons of the time with reference to Boston's rejection of Jacksonian democracy, its internal debate regarding Emersonian transcendentalism, and the painting of "Belshazzar's Feast" by Washington Allston. The painting, left unfinished at the artist's death, depicts the prophet Daniel, who points to the mystical writing on the wall that interrupts the King's feast and predicts the fall of Babylon and the liberation of the Jews. The subject was traditionally interpreted as "an Old Testament type for the Last Judgement" and as one of those "apocalyptic texts prophesying the end of time" and the building of the New Jerusalem (Bjelajac 22). This millennialism "pervaded nearly every social and religious group in America during Allston's life" (23), particularly among those New Englanders alarmed by the materialist secularism of Jacksonian democracy. The subject had previously been treated by Benjamin West's painting of 1776, when the painter may well have intended a reference to King George and the fall of the British Empire (Bjelajac 45). West's painting illuminates the mystical letters on the wall with a supernatural aura much like Hawthorne's lighting effects used to describe the letter in the sky during the second scaffold scene in *The Scarlet Letter*.

Hawthorne saw Washington Allston's painting sometime after 1844, when it was first exhibited in the Boston Athenaeum. He remarked that the "imperfect beauty" of its unfinished state demonstrated "that the deeds of the earth, however etherealized by piety or genius, are without value, except as exercises and manifestations of the spirit" (qtd. Bjelajac: 16). Elizabeth Palmer Peabody, Hawthorne's sister in law, believed that Allston's scriptural paintings "could function in the same direct manner as the handwriting on the wall" as a warning to prepare "for the more spiritual revelation of Christ" (148-149). She also argued that the Old Testament should be taught in Unitarian Sunday schools (which had decided not to) because if it was interpreted "spiritually or symbolically then it retained its usefulness as a moral guide for both the individual and the nation" (Bjelajac 156).[7] This notion was common to the New England Federalist who accepted the Puritan notion that American history "would lead the way to the second coming of Christ" (157), and who also found him or herself at odds both with Jacksonian democratic secularism and Emersonian transcendentalism, which suggested that "it was unnecessary to introduce God's supernatural grace or the Holy Spirit into the formula of religious conversion" because of the inherent divinity of man (Bjelajac 180).

Such issues and such an approach to scripture are of central importance to an understanding of *The Scarlet Letter*. Hawthorne was indeed very likely suspicious of American millennialism, as Foreman and others suggest, but I will argue below that he shared the suspicions regarding transcendentalism expressed by the painter Washington Allston, who may well also have been, along with Elizabeth Peabody, influential in his decision to employ the apocalyptic typology of the Bible in *The Scarlet Letter*. In addition to the image of the end of the old world and the creation of the new, there are four other Biblical themes derived from Revelation which play crucial roles in the novel: the notion of unveiling, prophecy, the last battle, resurrection and judgement. These five aspects of Revelation, often mixed together, form the basis of the novel's structure and theme, as is most clearly evident in the famous scaffold scenes, which are the skeleton of the plot.

In the first of these scenes, Hester Prynne stands before the Puritan fathers of Boston in order to accept their judgement regarding her sin of adultery. While she stands alone upont the scaffold, holding the infant Pearl beneath the scarlet letter on her breast, the Puritan fathers look down on her from the balcony above and plead with her to reveal the name of the child's father, her partner in sin. They call upon Arthur Dimmesdale, the charismatic young minister and concealed father of the child, to persuade Hester to uncover the secret betokened by the scarlet letter, but she remains silent. Hence, the novel begins shortly after the commission of the original sin, which is covered over by a second sin, Hester's concealing of the identity of the father, and Dimmesdale's reluctance to reveal himself as such. The word apocalypse, of course, means literally "to uncover" or "reveal" that which has been veiled or covered over. In the New Testament, the word for "to cover" (katakalypto) is logically related to the word for "to uncover" (apokalypto), and is occasionally linked with the notion of "the covering of sin by loving action" (Bromiley 406). Hence, the plot of The Scarlet Letter is impelled from the beginning by the need to uncover what has been concealed by Hester's loving protection of Dimmesdale, a need pursued primarily by Roger Chillingworth's efforts to discover the identity of the child's father.

It is during the second scene on the scaffold that the explicitly apocalyptic basis of the novel's plot is clearly related to the Book of Revelation. Compelled by the maddening burden of his guilt, Dimmesdale leaves his study one night and goes to climb the scaffold where Hester had hidden his sins from the world seven years earlier. During "this vain show of expiation" (148) Dimmesdale feels that "the doom of his existence was stealing onward" and that the lantern he sees being carried toward the scaffold would soon "reveal his long hidden secret" (150). He feels a "great horror of mind, as if the universe were gazing at a scarlet token on his naked breast, right over his heart" (148). It is the "uncovering" or "revelation" (an apokalypsis) of this "long hidden secret" (150) that Dimmesdale both fears and desires at this point. Hester and Pearl are then seen walking home from the death bed of the Governor, and Dimmesdale invites them to climb up onto the scaffold with him. When Pearl asks him when they will all stand there together again, Dimmesdale, as yet unwilling to undergo a public exposure at noontide, says "At the great judgement day! Then, and there, before the judgement-seat, thy mother, and thou, and I, must stand together! But the daylight of this world shall not see our meeting" (153).

Immediately after this explicit allusion to the Last Judgement of the Book of Revelation, a meteor sheds an awful and "unaccustomed light" that illuminates all visible things "with a singularity of aspect that seemed to give another moral interpretation to the things of this world than they had ever borne before" (154). Such supernatural celestial phenomena announcing the universal judgement are of course common signs of the Last Day (in Matthew 24:30 Jesus says "then shall appear the sign of the Son of man in heaven ... and they shall see the Son of man coming in the clouds of heaven"), which Hawthorne sees in this scene as an unveiling of hidden things: "They stood in the noon of that strange and solemn splendor, as if it were the light that is to reveal all secrets, and the daybreak that shall unite all who belong to one another" (154). The meteor, then, prefigures revelation, judgement, and the reunion of the dead after the general resurrection. Hawthorne tells us that such "meteoric appearances" were interpreted "as so many revelations from a supernatural source" betokening the "doom" or "destiny of nations" (154-155). The word "doom" here carries the dual sense of an end and a destiny, of annihilation and revelation as two sides of the same coin (a symbolon). Shortly afterwards, Hester and Arthur see Chillingworth "at no great distance from the scaffold" and notice the "malevolence" of his expression, here fully revealed, or uncovered for the first time in the novel: "Certainly, if the meteor kindled up the sky, and disclosed the earth, with an awfulness that admonished Hester Prynne and the clergyman of the day of judgement, then might Roger Chillingworth have passed with them for the arch-fiend" (156). After this vision of Chillingworth as the Anti-Christ from Revelation, the meteor vanishes, "with an effect as if the street and all things else were at once annihilated" (156).

Here then is the sense of a universal cataclysm ("all things else were at once annihilated") combined with the notions of the revelation of hidden secrets, of death and judgement, of the final battle with the "arch-fiend," and a hint of resurrection which characterizes Hawthorne's allusions to the Apocalypse throughout the novel -- Dimmesdale feels "a tumultuous rush of new life" when he takes Hester's hand on the scaffold (153). Hawthorne's primary concern in this scene, however, is not metaphysical or theological: in the attempt to decipher "the awful hieroglyphics" inscribed upon the veil of clouds by the meteor (155), Hawthorne delves deeply into the epistemological issues central to the novel's treatment of the theme of revelation. His focus is on the hermeneutic problem raised by the hieroglyphical letter in the sky: "Nothing was more common, in those days," Hawthorne writes, "than to interpret all meteoric appearances ... as so many revelations from a supernatural source" (154). The task of interpretation, however, often fell upon

> some lonely eyewitness, who beheld the wonder through the colored, magnifying, and distorting medium of his imagination, and shaped it more distinctly in his afterthought. It was indeed a majestic idea, that the destiny of nations should be revealed, in these awful hieroglyphics, on the cope of heaven. A scroll so wide might not be deemed too expansive for Providence to write a people's doom upon .... But what shall we say, when an individual discovers a revelation, addressed to himself alone, on the same vast sheet of record! In such a case, it could only be the symptom of a highly disordered mental state, when a man, rendered morbidly self-contemplative by long, intense, and secret pain, had extended his egotism over the whole expanse of nature, until the firmament itself should appear no more that a fitting page for his soul's history and fate. (155)

This passage emphasizes the shaping power of the subjective imagination in the hermeneutic task, raising the post-Kantian dilemma "that what a man knows is not an objective external world but simply the internal structure of his own mind projected upon an essentially indeterminate ground" (Irwin 241). Hence Hawthorne attributes Dimmesdale's perception of the meteoric "A" as a token of his sin to

> the disease in his own eye and heart .... Not but the meteor may have shown itself at that point, burning duskily through a veil of cloud; but with no such shape as his guilty imagination gave it; or, at least, with so little definiteness, that another's guilt might have seen another symbol in it. (155)

The syntactical twisting here betokens Hawthorne's sense of the epistemological dilemma, complicated later in the chapter when he tells us that the sexton had also seen "A great red letter in the sky,--the letter A, -- which we interpret to stand for Angel," since Governor Winthrop had died during that "visionary" night (158). What Providence inscribes upon the "scroll" of the "firmament" is subject to a multiplicity of conflicting and uncertain perceptions, as if the "veil of cloud" has been so partially uncovered as to render any interpretation of the letter suspect and relative. Each reader of the "awful hieroglyphics" deciphers them differently. As John Irwin notes in his book on the symbol of the Egyptian hieroglyphics in American literature, "For Hawthorne and Melville, the ambiguous character of the hieroglyphics was their prime significance. The hieroglyphs were the linguistic analogue of an enigmatic external world whose shape was various enough to sustain almost any interpretaion that man projected on it in the act of knowing" (239).

It is important to note here that Hawthorne sees the hermeneutic task as an attempt to decipher the hieroglyphic of nature. Nature, in fact, is imagined during this episode as a Book authored by Providence. The heavens are a "scroll" to "write a people's doom upon," a "vast sheet of record," and a "fitting page for [the] soul's history" (155). Surely these details are significant when seen in the context of the Book of Revelation, in which the world is seen precisely as book, the seals of which must be broken before it can be read. The "A" in the sky may as well stand for Apocalypse, but it represents a partial uncovering, the mysterious import of which remains subject to the distortions of a diseased mind. One has the feeling that Hawthorne in fact denies analysis of any sort access to the ultimate revelation, which may be fully uncovered only by grace on the Judgement Day.

Earlier in the novel, Dimmesdale says as much to Roger Chillingworth, his alchemical physician, who, as a natural philosopher, argues that no secrets are inaccessible to analysis. As Hester's betrayed husband, Chillingworth has attached himself to Dimmesdale in order to delve into the secrets of his heart, and uncover the identity of Pearl's father. "Would it be beyond a philosopher's research," Chillingworth asks of Dimmesdale and the other Church fathers, "to analyze the child's nature, and from its make and mould, to give a shrewd guess at the father?" (116). Pearl, in fact, is later termed a "living hieroglyph" who requires "a prophet or magicician skilled to read the character of flame" (207). That is to say, she is analogous to the letter A on Hester's breast and to the letter A in the sky: she is the hieroglyphic signature of her father, whose identity Chillingworth claims to be able to "read" in her "character of flame." The Church fathers, however, reply that such a presumption of the hermeneutic power of "profane philosophy "would be sinful .... Better to fast and pray upon it [the mystery of Pearl's father]; and still better, it may be, to leave the mystery as we find it, unless Providence reveal it of its own accord" (116).

This dialogue pits philosophy against theology on the hermeneutic question of revelation. Chillingworth represents the agnosticism of modern scientists, and their techniques of empirical analysis. Hawthorne says that these

> Skilful men, of the medical and chirurgical profession .... sel-
> dom ... partook of the religious zeal that brought other immi-
> grants across the Atlantic. In their researches into the human
> frame, it may be that the higher and more subtile faculties of
> such men were materialized, and that they lost the spiritual
> view of existence amid the intricacies of that wondrous mech-
> anism, which seemed to involve art enough to comprise all of
> life within itself. (119)

Chillingworth's alchemy is similarly called a "ponderous and imposing
machinery" (119), suggesting that Hawthorne intends us to see him as a
prototype of the 'mechanistic' science just then emerging in the 17th
century when the story is set. This was a science struggling to free itself from the occultism and magic of the Renaissance, and in so doing
it laid the foundations for modern scientific method.[8]

Interestingly enough, Chillingworth also anticipates modern
pscyhoanalysis: in his treatment of the ailing Dimmesdale, he assumes
that the Reverend's "bodily infirmity" has "its groundwork" in the psyche, Dimmesdale's "thought and imagination" (124). Hawthorne's description of Chillingworth's method could be seen as a prophetic portrait of the psychoanalyst, fifty years before Freud's *Traumdeutung*:

> the man of skill, the kind and friendly physician--strove to
> go deep into his patient's bosom, delving among his princi-
> ples, prying into his recollections, and probing every thing
> with a cautious touch, like a treasure seeker in a dark cavern
> .... If [the physician] possess native sagacity, and a nameless
> something more,--let us call it intuition ... if he have the
> power, which must be born with him, to bring his mind into
> such affinity with his patient's, that this last shall unawares
> have have spoken what he imagines himself only to have
> thought; if such revelations be received without tumult, and
> acknowledged not so often by an uttered sympathy as by si-
> lence, an inarticualte breath, and here and there a word, to in-
> dicate that all is understood ... then, at some moment, will the
> soul of the sufferer be dissolved, and flow forth in a dark, but
> transparent stream, bringing all its mysteries into the day-
> light. (124)

Hawthorne opposes this analytic science. Chillingworth is the "arch-
fiend" in the novel with whom Dimmesdale, as a Christian soldier, does
battle on the last day. As Douglas Robinson points out in his study of
Apocalypse in American fiction,

Without opposition, the apocalypse is nothing: spatial
(earth-heaven) and temporal (present-future) oppositions are
decided eschatologically by the moral opposition between
good and evil, between God and Satan--the cosmic battle
(polemos) that both precipitates and enacts the end. (10)

Typically, Hawthorne extends the moral and metaphysical implications
of the polemos into the epistemological realm. Chillingworth's notion
that all hidden secrets can be made accessible to knowledge by the
methods of 'philosophical' analysis is opposed in the novel by Reverend
Dimmesdale, who, in his ministerial capacity, is Christ's representative
on earth. In a private conversation between Chillingworth and
Dimmesdale, Hawthorne pursues the conflict. After picking some
grotesque weeds from a man's grave in the cemetery, Chillingworth
imagines that "They grew out of his heart, and typify, it may be, some
hideous secret that was buried with him, and which he had done better
to confess during his lifetime" (131). (The weeds, that is to say, are a
"type" or emblematic hieroglyph concealing yet expressing the mysteries of the heart). Dimmesdale responds by saying the poor sinner was
unable to confess in this lifetime, and calls Chillingworth's notion that
all hidden secrets should be brought to light by his science a "fantasy"
(131). Dimmesdale then counters with the theological perspective on
the issue of revelation:

There can be, if I forebode aright, no power, short of the
Divine mercy, to disclose, whether by uttered word, or by
type or emblem, the secrets that may be buried with a human
heart. The heart, making itself guilty of such secrets, must
perforce hold them, until the day when all hidden things be
revealed. Nor have I so read or interpreted Holy Writ, as to understand that the disclosure of human thoughts and deeds, then
to be made, is intended as a part of the retribution. That surely
were a shallow view of it. No; these revelations, unless I
greatly err, are meant to promote the intellectual satisfaction
of all intelligent beings, who will stand waiting, on that day,
to see the dark problem of this life made plain. A knowledge
of men's hearts will be needful to the completest solution of
that problem. And I conceive, moreover, that the hearts holding such miserable secrets as you speak of will yield them up,
at that last day, not with reluctance, but with joy unutterable.
(131-132)

That last day is of course described in the Book of Revelation, here
imagined as the day "when all hidden things will be revealed," particularly "the secrets buried with a human heart" (remember the linguistic association of "buried" or "covered" sins mentioned above). Only

"Divine mercy" can bestow such knowledge, uncover the sins buried with the heart, and make plain the "dark problem of this life." "For now we see through a glass darkly," Paul says in I Cor 13:12, "but then face to face." The Greek word translated as "darkly" in this passage is "ainigmati", the root of our enigma, and this captures exactly the hermeneutic problem at the base of the epistemological debate between Chillingworth and Dimmesdale: as the Reverend's name suggests, to be alive is to be lost in the maze of of dark wood (a dim dale), where any effort of interpretation must remain tangled in enigma until the Apocalypse. The notion of apocalypse here focuses on its root meaning of "uncovering", which involves the hermencutic task of deciphering the hieroglyphic language of the novel.

Other passages from the New Testament correspond to Dimmesdale's sense of a deferred uncovering, available through grace on the last day. Jesus says of the coming of the Kingdom "there is nothing covered, that shall not be revealed, and hid that shall not be known" (Matt. 10:26). This statement occurs four times in the Gospels (see also Luke 8:16 and 12:2, and Mark 4:22), and clearly prefigures the apocalypse as an uncovering of hidden things: in the verse cited from Matthew, the Greek word translated as "revealed" is "apokalypthsegai," literally "will be uncovered" (10:26). Chillingworth's response to this theological perspective is characteristically scientific: he says of these covered secrets "Why not reveal them here?" (132). This is a significant statement of his point of view in the epistemological conflict, and a prefiguration of the last scene on the scaffold at the end of the novel. This famous scene involves a literal uncovering of hidden sin, as Dimmesdale removes his shirt, exposing what some parishioners see a scarlet letter A branded on his chest. The context of the verse cited from Matthew may even have informed Hawthorne's conception of this scene: Jesus is enjoining the people not to fear those who may kill the body for speaking the truth, and after the prophecy of a day of uncover-ing, he says "What I tell you in darkness, that speak ye in light: and what ye hear in the ear, that preach ye upon the housetops" (Matt. 10:27). In Luke, the remark is a warning to speak out against the "hypocrisy" of the Pharisees by proclaiming the truth spoken in dark-ness "upon the housetops" (12:3). This is of course exactly what Dimmesdale does on the scaffold in the chapter called "The Revelation of the Scarlet Letter:" he publicly, at noontide from the elevation of the scaffold, acknowledges the guilt he had seen God revealing to him in the darkness during his "visionary" night on the scaffold. And he does so by a literal apocalypse, an uncovering that reveals his hidden sin, and betokens his hypocrisy.

Just as episodes in the Old Testament were taken as prefiguring their fulfillment in the New Testament by typological criticism, the scenes on the scaffold in *The Scarlet Letter* stand in relation to each other as type and anti-type, the end fulfilling and completing the beginning. What was covered in the first episode of Hester's public punishment -- the identity of the father -- is uncovered during the last episode, when the unhappy family stands united at last. The end of the novel is prefigured in its beginning, and all along the way through the dark wood: the Alpha and the Omega of Revelation 22:13 have been brought together. Hawthorne sets this scene in the context of the millenial hopes for renewal in the New World so important to the mythologized view of America as the New Jerusalem. It is Election Day, when, as Hester says, "a new man is beginning to rule" and the population rejoices "as if a good and golden year were at length to pass over the poor old world" (229). Dimmesdale's sermon is infused with "a spirit as of prophecy" as "it was his mission to foretell a high and glorious destiny for the newly gathered people of the Lord" (249). Hawthorne contrasts this mission with the apocalyptic seers of Israel, who "had denounced judgements and ruin on their country" (249).

After the sermon, Dimmesdale proceeds to the scaffold, but he must fight off Roger Chillingworth before he is able to climb it. Their final conflict is clearly to be seen as the last battle between Christ and Anti-Christ. In this scene, Dimmesdale enacts the role of the Crucified Redeemer, while Chillingworth is seen as the "wretched and wronged old man opposing it with all his might! -- with all his own might and the fiend's" (253): "old Roger Chillingworth thrust himself through the crowd, -- or perhaps, so dark, disturbed, and evil was his look, he rose up out of some nether region, -- to snatch back his victim from what he sought to do!" (252). The crowd is stunned into silence, and waits upon "the judgment which Providence seemed about to work" (253); they seem to know that "some deep life matter--which, if full of sin, was full of anguish and repentance likewise--was now to be laid open to them" before the "bar of Eternal Justice" (254). Then Dimmesdale proceeds to uncover the "red stigma" searing his "inmost heart:"

> With a convulsive motion he tore away the ministerial band from before his breast. It was revealed! But it were irreverent to describe that revelation. For an instant the gaze of the horror-stricken multitude was concentrated on the ghastly miracle; while the minister stood with a flush of triumph in his face, as one who, in the crisis of acutest pain, had won a victory." (255)

The imagery of the triumphant agony of the crucifixion is unmistakable here, and the immediate effect of the apocalyptic revelation is the defeat of Chillingworth, who kneels down beside Dimmesdale "with a blank, dull countenance, out of which the life seemed to have departed" (255).

After Dimmesdale collapses on the scaffold, Hester "partly raised him, and supported his head against her bosom" (255). While at the beginning of the novel, when proceeding to her own humiliation on the scaffold, she had been seen as a Madonna figure, "with the infant at her bosom" like the "image of Divine Maternity" (56), here she is pictured as the Mater Dolorosa, the Pieta with the crucified one on her lap. In the middle of the novel, of course, she had been seen by the Church Fathers at the Governor's Hall as the "scarlet woman, and a worthy type of her of Babylon" (110), referring of course to the Whore of Babylon from the Book of Revelation. It is therefore certainly true, as Nina Baym says, that Hester is "a kind of archetypal mother-goddess" (19). Specifically, she is an avatar of what Jung called the "mother archetype," a loving and terrible figure combining the opposites of life and death within itself. She is Dimmesdale's "better angel" (201), offering him new life in the forest scene, the temptress leading him into a "world of perverted spirits" (222), and "the angel and apostate of the coming revelation" (263).

The novel in fact ends with Hester's prophetic vision of the future, prophecy being a crucial element of the Apocalypse of St. John, and, as Paul puts it in Acts 2, a sign of the coming of the end (here both of the novel and of the world): "your young men shall see visions, and your old men dream dreams: And on my servants and on my handmaidens I will pour out in those days of my Spirit; and they shall prophesy" (17-18). We should recall that this prophecy comes just after the description of the descent of the Holy Ghost at Pentecost, that Dimmesdale is endowed with the Pentecostal gift of tongues, "symbolizing the power ... of addressing the whole human brotherhood in the heart's native language" (142), and that Dimmesdale had "a spirit as of prophecy" come upon him during the Election Day sermon just before his own end (249). Hester's prophetic powers, however, are revisionary, feminist in fact.[9] Although she acknowledges she is not herself the "destined prophetess" she imagined she might be when young, she anticipates a new and better world in her belief

> that, at some brighter period, when the world should have grown ripe for it, in Heaven's own time, a new truth would be revealed, in order to establish the whole relation between man and woman on a surer ground of mutual happiness .... The angel and apostate of the coming revelation must be a woman, indeed, but lofty, pure, and beautiful; and wise, moreover, not through dusky grief, but the ethereal medium of joy .... (263)

Hence, the ending of *The Scarlet Letter* combines the imagery of judgement and resurrection, the last battle, prophetic visions of the end of an old world and the coming of the new, and the uncovering of hidden secrets associated with the Apocalypse. But it is an open ending, leaving basic questions unanswered. The uncovering of Dimmesdale's shame on the scaffold is itself problematic. Though "Most of the spectators testified to having seen, on the breast of the unhappy minister, a SCARLET LETTER," its origin is explained by "various explanations, all of which must necessarily have been conjectural" (258). Some see it as the product of Dimmesdale's penitential flagellation, others see it as a stigma produced by Chillingworth's necromancy, and others still as the "awful symbol" produced by the "wonderful operation of his spirit upon the body" (258). Others more generously deny there having been any mark whatsoever on Dimmesdale's breast, and read his death in Hester's arms as a parable "to express to the world how utterly nugatory is the choicest of man's own righteousness" (259). Hawthorne leaves the reader to choose among as many theories regarding the origin of the letter as there have been throughout the novel regarding its significance. The letter remains to the end a hieroglyphic symbol of mysterious and indeterminate meaning, calling into question our ability to ojectively decipher the world around us.

As readers, we are left in the midst of the maze, in the middle of the "dark problem" of life. "For now we see through a glass darkly [ainigmati]" (Paul, 1 Cor 13:12); alive before the coming of Christ on the Last Day, our vision must necessarily be enigmatic, partial, distorted. Only with the Apocalypse of the end will all hidden things be revealed, so that we may see the truth face to face. Hawthorne's conclusion to the novel is in this sense strictly doctrinal, favoring Dimmesdale's view that Chillingworth's analytical hermeneutic cannot gain access in this life to what will only be made known during the revelation on the Last Day. I think it is quite true to point out, as John Irwin does, that what we see in the 19th century is a gradual "movement from an interest in an otherworld of absolute values to an interest in how the mind knows the physical world to an interest in how symbolization in a sense creates our 'world'" (318). Certainly one sees in *The Scarlet Letter* a mingling of metaphysical and epistemological concerns in the various efforts to interpret the significance of the hieroglyphic letter. Yet Hawthorne's stubborn insistence on the ambiguous and indeterminate nature of his symbols stands strictly in line with theological notions that the true hidden meaning of life can never be known without the intervention of divine grace, without genuine Apocalypse. This notion counters the Emersonian idea that the hieroglphic emblems of the world are immediately accessible to such divinely inspired democrats as the poet, without the mediation of divine grace.

There is no "end" in Hawthorne's novel, no cataclysmic annihilation, and no final revelation agreed upon by all. What is missing from his apocalypse is precisely the end of the world scenario so much at the heart of the Biblical Book of Revelation. Instead, what Hawthorne seems to imagine is what Douglas Robinson calls "a Protestant dream of historical apocalypse--a dream of a transformation of history in history that would consummate and so give meaning to history" (2). This is most forcefully suggested in Dimmesdale's last Election Day sermon, with its vision of a truly New England, one with a "high and glorious destiny" (249). Significantly, Dimmesdale's prophecy lacks those denunciations of "judgements and ruin" character-istic of the apocalyptic visions of "the old prophets of Israel" (249). Hawthorne seems to want to have it both ways: Apocalypse as a secular image of the American Dream of transformation of history within his-tory by history, and Apocalypse as the sacred revelation of hidden mys-teries achieved through divine grace on the Last Day. The former secu-larized view is represented by Chillingworth, who argues that hidden se-crets should by revealed now "here" in this life (132), as indeed they are on the scaffold at the end of the novel. The latter sacramental view is represented by Dimmesdale; his "revelation" of the scarlet letter at the end of the novel is left ambiguous, with the sense that its signficance will only be made plain by the final revelation of which it is but the type.

In this respect also, *The Scarlet Letter* seems a peculiarly American breed of apocalypse, which, as Robinson argues, characteris-tically has it both ways: "American iconoclasm is iconically mediatory; images of nature are negated apocalyptically not in order that they might be thrown out, but that the writer might incorporate and trans-form them into the mediate ground for visionary contact" (8). This ten-dency yields what Robinson calls a "ternary logic of intercession, in place of Hegel's binary logic of supersession .... to allow writer and reader to perceive the opposites (earth and new earth, present and future) in opposition without subsuming or supplanting them" (8). Hence, in the American breed of apocalypse as Robinson sees it, this world may in fact obstruct our access to ultimate revelation; it is not, however, "destroyed by fire but is itself converted into the mediatory icon of Christ, the self-unveiling veil that reveals by standing between" (9). The veil is to be made transparent by a shift in vision effected by art, not to be destroyed by cataclysm.[10]

From this perspective, the uncovering of the scarlet letter in the penultimate chapter is tantalizingly partial, exactly that revelation within history which transforms its witnesses but does not finally, ul-timately annihilate or illuminate them. The revelation does not end the world, but neither does it resolve its own enigma. The novel retains the "veil" of the world without destroying it. Its last image is "iconically mediatory:" Dimmesdale's sacrificial confession on the scaffold is that "self-unveiling veil that reveals by standing between" (9). It is a revelation within history that momentarily provides us with a glimpse of a more ultimate uncovering: it is a type of Apocalypse.

S.T. Coleridge

"The Rime of the Ancient Mariner" is a classically constructed hero journey: it begins and ends with the Mariner telling his story to the Wedding Guest outside the Church, with the revelations of the story in between. The story itself also follows the pattern, beginning and ending on the English coastline, with the circuitous navigation of the polar journey in between. While the allegorical intentions of the poet have been, and will remain, one of the intriguing mysteries of the poem, many of its symbols and structural devices can be illuminated with reference to the traditional iconography of the hero journey: the call to adventure, initiatory symbols of death and rebirth (associated with the Goddess and the serpent), and threshold battles departing and returning are all clearly present in the poem and reflect some of its basic themes. For the poem is both autobiographical and representative of its age, struggling with the paradoxical powers of the Imagination as curse and as salvation. In addition, the poem uses the hero journey as a symbol of poesis (the process by which a poem is written), and as hermeneusis (the process by which a poem is read).

This is apparent from the beginning in Coleridge's use of the frame tale device: the poem begins with a nameless narrator telling a story about a man telling a story to another man (the Ancient Mariner stops one of three wedding guests, whom he holds spellbound with this "glittering eye" in order to recite his tale). The "Rime" therefore is a poem about telling and listening to stories; both writing and reading can be seen as hero journeys. For the Wedding Guest (as reader), the "glittering eye," haunting images, and hypnotic rhythms of the Mariner's tale function as a call to adventure, almost, indeed, as an abduction, since the Wedding Guest resists, resents, and is often terrified by the tale which he cannot help himself from hearing. His initial resistance turns to fascination as the Mariner describes the ship leaving the harbor (a pleasant and accurate image as any for the departure phase of the hero journey and for the commencement of any particular act of reading). The threshold battle for the Wedding Guest, then, is his initial resistance to the Mariner's domination ("Wherefore stoppeth thou me?"), a battle fought several times during the course of the poem when the Guest interrupts the Mariner, often in fear or protest ("The Wedding Guest he beat his breast, / Yet he cannot choose but hear"). In between, of course, lie many revelatory initiations (largely effected by the powerful current of symbolic images which we will examine below),

which ultimately have a transformative impact on the Guest, who is
left a "sadder and wiser man" by the Mariner's tale.

The hero journey proper is the tale told by the Mariner, which
begins and ends on English shores beneath a church and lighthouse top
of the hill. The imagery of the departure into unknown realms of ice,
fog, moonlight, and mist immediately engage the reader's imagination,
while the threshold crossing is marked by the rounding of the Horn and
the shooting of the albatross, the single act that precipitates the major
events of the poem. It can therefore be seen as an enigmatic symbol of
poesis, a mysterious and guilt-ridden act which opens the floodgates of
the deep imagination, for all the marvelous symbols of the poem are
made possible by the slaying of the albatross. With its death, the ship
enters the mysterious waters of the underworld, down around the south
pole. It is a region of the imagination, of the dead, and of spiritual
beings. For among these waters the boat appears, transfigured by the
imagination, as "a painted ship / Upon a painted ocean." The waters are
also Stygian, the dream imagery being related to the underworld. We
read that "The very deep did rot," "The death fires danced at night," and
that a "Spirit" plagues the ship from "Nine fathom deep." It is at this
point, in the third part of the poem, that the Ship of Death appears,
and, along with it, a cluster of symbols which readers familiar with the
iconography of the hero journey to the underworld will recognize: the
Moon, the Evening Star, Bird-Song, and the Serpent.

As the mariners lie dying of starvation and thirst, a "strange
shape" appears outlined against the circle of the sun setting on the
western horizon; it is the Ship of Death, with its rigging flecking the
sun with the bars of a "dungeon-grate" and its two crew members, "The
Spectre-Woman and her Death-mate." Like all the epiphanies of the
Great Goddess in the history of the hero journey, this "Spectre-Woman"
embraces the opposites of the womb and the tomb: "The Nightmare
LIFE-IN-DEATH was she." With her red lips, free looks, and golden
locks, she represents the erotic allure of LIFE; but with her skeletal
mate rolling dice at her side, she represents DEATH. She appears at
twilight, the time of love and death, while a "hornéd Moon, with one
bright star / Within the nether tip" rises above the "eastern bar." We've
seen this "hornéd Moon" and star before: the two horns of the crescent
moon are associated with the bull-consort, sacrificed and resurrected, in
monthly cycles, symbolizing the two poles of life and death over which
the Goddess presides; the "one bright star" is the same evening beacon
of death and rebirth which the Sumerians named Inanna. Along with
these spiritual symbols, it is important to note that the "Spectre-
Woman" also represents those deep powers of the imagination (she is
called a "Nightmare") which are activated by the hero journey. When
she disappears, the fifty-four sailors die one by one, leaving the Mariner

trapped in a solitary underworld, "Alone, alone, all, all alone, / Alone on a wide wide sea!" After enduring "the curse in a dead man's eye" for seven days and nights, the Mariner looks "upon the rotting sea" while the Moon shines and beholds "the water-snakes" coiling in flashes of blue, green velvet black, and gold in the shadow of the ship. As we have seen as far back as in *The Epic of Gilgamesh*, the serpent (often in association with the Goddess) symbolizes the power of life to shed its skin and be reborn. Hence, when the Mariner blesses the water-snakes, the Albatross falls from his neck and the process of his redemption begins.

While the imagery of the descent to the underworld continues in the next sections of the poem, it begins to exert a purgatorial effect on the Mariner. Although he imagines that he "had died in sleep, / And was a blesséd ghost," the rain begins to fall and the dead sailors take up the ropes and strange sweet sounds rise "slowly through their mouths" as they cluster around the mast. These images suggest resurrection and poesis: the underworld is a place where dead sailors rise again, and where sweet syllables find articulation, a place in fact of bird-song (as it had been since Ancient Egypt and Sumer). For the Mariner hears the "sky-lark sing" and "all the little birds that are" filling the sea and air "With their sweet jargoning!" We have seen previously how in the dream of Enkidu from the *Epic of Gilgamesh* and in the iconography of the Egyptian Books of the Dead souls in Hades were pictured as birds. In Coleridge, then, Hades is the place where poems are born, since throughout the poetry of Romanticism bird-song and poetry are equated (as in Shelley, Keats, Browning, and later Hardy, Hopkins, and Frost).

All of these symbols (Serpent, Bird-Song, Moon and Star, Goddess and Death) comprise the initiation stage of the Mariner's hero journey, the final revelation of which occurs just as the ship returns to English shores. Here too the initiation has to do with the spiritual dimensions of Romantic poetry, and with the faculty of the imagination as a means of apprehending the divine. When the ship is driven into the "harbor-bay" of the Mariner's "own countree" by the supernatural powers of the sea, he has come full circle and begun the return phase of the hero journey. The same "kirk" and hill rise above the harbor which he had left in the beginning of the tale, but before the return can be completed a final revelation and threshold crossing ensues. Seraphs rise out of each corpse on the deck, lovely, heavenly lights which wave a signal to the land. Although they do not speak, their deep silence sinks "Like music" into the Mariner's heart. It is presumably the music of these silent Seraphs and the bird-song of the spirits earlier in the poem that Coleridge has attempted to transcribe into the meter and rhyme of the ballad. It is a music activated, like the mythological symbols of the poem, by the hero journey of the poet, who has been transformed by the experience. As the Mariner crosses the return threshold, a rumbling maelstrom sinks the ship, leaving the old man floating "Like one that hath been seven days drowned," another allusion to the descent to the underworld in the poem. He is rescued from the whirling water by a Hermit, Pilot, and boy. Though he is then shriven of his sins, the Mariner has been transformed by the revelations of the journey, and never fully reintegrates himself into the society he left at the beginning. He is condemned rather to wander "from land to land" and compelled to retell his "ghastly tale" whenever his "agony returns."

Endowed with "strange power of speech," the Mariner is set apart from his fellow men, and thus represents a particularly Romantic version of the hero as poet. But the reader-listener is also presented as a hero, and the journey becomes an allegory of reading. The Wedding Guest is unable to return to the domestic ceremonies, and is left sadder and wiser by the recitation of the poem. He is "Turned from the Bridegroom's door" at the end of the poem, a detail which reminds one of the significance of doorways as symbols of the journey throughout the history of the hero journey. The poem is a doorway (for both poet and reader) leading away from the domestic world into the daemonic realm of the imagination. And, as in the night-sea journeys of Odysseus, Jonah, or Sinbad, the daemonic realm is where the archetypal forms of the imagination are revealed.

Herman Melville

Melville weaves many of the motifs associated with the hero journey to the underworld into his magisterial masterpiece of American literature. Edward Edinger has suggested that "Melville was writing out of the universal archetypal theme of the night sea journey, or descent to the underworld" (*Moby Dick* 21), but his fine Jungian commentary focuses more on psychological interpretations than on a literary analysis of the specific references in the text to the Homeric nekyia. Melville's descent is not only a matter of the activation of the archetypal images of the American unconscious, and not only a matter of encountering the demons of repressed guilt. Melville's hero journey also serves, in part, as an allegory of creativity, whether of writing (poesis), or of interpretation (hermeneusis).

The detailed allusions to the archetypal nekyia begin immediately, when Ishmael arrives in New Bedford on a dark Saturday evening in December. Searching for a place to spend the night, Ishmael wanders through the "dreary streets" like a "candle moving about in a tomb" (9). Threshold imagery quickly surfaces, as Ishmael walks through a door, "which stood invitingly open," into a Negro Church, where a service is in progress. He trips over "an ash-box in the porch," which chokes him with "flying particles" like "ashes from that destroyed city, Gomorrah" (9). He then picks himself up and passes through a "second, interior door" to encounter what seems like "the great Black Parliament sitting in Tophet," with "A hundred black faces" sitting in the pews, and a "black Angel of Doom [who] was beating a book in a pulpit" (10). The preacher's text is appropriately infernal: since Tophet is a scriptural symbol of hell, a "valley south of Jerusalem where children were offered as burnt sacrifices to Molech" (Edinger 25), his text "was about the blackness of darkness, and the weeping and wailing and teeth-gnashing there" (10). (The pun on "wailing" is typical of Melville's humor, which permeates these early chapters of the book). Leaving the Negro Church, Ishmael comes to another door, that of the "The Spouter-Inn:--Peter Coffin" (10). Shivering in front of the door, Ishmael compares himself to Lazarus, "stranded there on the curbstone before the door of Dives," an allusion which reinforces the connection between the threshold imagery of doorways and the descent into Sheol (11).

Finally entering the inn, another sequence of threshold passages is evoked. First is the "dusky entry" leading into the inn, where a weird painting composed of "masses of shades and shadows" seems to "delineate chaos bewitched," or "the Black Sea in a midnight gale," or "the unnatural combat of the four primal elements" (12). (Melville would have made a finely satiric critic of abstract expressionism!). The painting, it so turns out, is prefigurative, depicting as it does a whale in the act of being impaled on the three masts of a ship in a gale. Passing beyond this painting through a "low-arched way" leads Ishmael to yet another threshold: that of the bar at the end of the public room, a den shaped like a "right whale's head," tended by "another cursed Jonah," who stands beneath the "vast arched bone of the whale's jaw" (14). The image linking the doorway to the massive jaws of a monster in this description recalls the many medieval illuminations of the gateway to hell, in which the doorways are composed to the monstrous jaws of the devil. The wild bunch of seamen just home from a four year voyage on the Grampus head straight for the "whale's mouth," where "the wrinkled little Jonah" (16) pours them all tumblers of abominable "poison" (14). The threshold imagery will come up again, much later in the novel, when Melville compares the whale's jaw to a "portcullis" (341, 365), and when, during the final chase, he describes Moby Dick's yawning mouth as "an open-doored marble tomb" (550).

The sequential passage through a series of doorways in New Bedford to the Spouter Inn ends when Peter Coffin leads Ishmael by candlelight up a staircase and into the room he will share with Queequeg. At this point, two more images archetypally associated with the nekyia emerge: divestiture and the labyrinth. As in the Sumerian "Descent of Inanna," in which the Goddesses is stripped down as she passes through each of the seven gateways leading into the underworld, Ishmael gradually sheds his clothing, in anxious anticipation of the arrival of the savage harpooneer: first he puts on and sheds the coarse poncho he finds in the cold room; then he takes off his "monkey jacket" and stands in the middle of the room; then he takes off his "coat," pausing to ponder things awhile "half undressed"; and then finally he jumps out of his "pantaloons and boots" to tumble into the huge bed (22). As in the Sumerian descent, this ritualized divestiture leads to an epiphany of death, for Queequeg now appears, coming into the room after midnight, carrying his shrunken heads like a "cannibal," and so terrifying Ishmael with the bizarre coloring of the tattoos covering his body, that Ishmael says it "was the devil himself who had thus broken into my room at the dead of night" (23). The corresponding imagery of re-investiture comes up later in the novel, in an uproariously funny chapter called "The Cassock," during which a sailor staggers off with the whale's penis, "as if he were a grenadier carrying a dead comrade from the field" (430). He then proceeds to strip, spread, and dry the pelt, in order to cut two arm holes into it and slip himself into the sheathing, as into a raincoat. Melville remarks that the sailor now "stands before you invested in the full canonicals of his calling," because only "this investiture alone will adequately protect him," as he cuts the blubber up into fine pieces called "bible leaves" (430-31), a metaphor which anticipates the important imagery of the whale as a book. Melville concludes this marvelous example of the symbolism of investiture (so frequent in the hero journey) with a bawdy and blasphemous pun: "what a candidate for an archbishoprick," he writes, "what a lad for a Pope" (431)!

Back in Peter Coffin's Inn, Queequeg gradually undresses, after which he performs a fascinating ritual: he takes a little "Congo idol" out of his bag and sets it up in the empty fireplace to create a "little shrine or chapel" (24). He spreads some wood shavings with a bit of ship biscuit on top in front of the idol, and then he kindles the pile "into a sacrificial blaze" (24), a ritual that initially strikes Ishmael as appropriately heathenish and infernal. The "queer proceedings" are accompanied by "some pagan psalmody or other" (25). Ishmael soon comes to accept the eccentricities of Queequeg's rituals, acknowledging them to be a universal expression of the religious impulses of the human spirit. In fact, Melville may be seen in relation to the science of comparative religion which developed so rapidly during his century, for he amplifies his basic themes throughout *Moby Dick* with reference to a wide range of mythological allusions, derived from a variety of world cultures (Hindu, Persian, Greek, Roman, Christian, Native American, Siamese, etc.). Many of these allusions have to do with the theme of death and resurrection, of the descent into and return from the underworld. Hence, it is with a shock of recognition that one notices the parallels suggested between Queequeg's ritual and the Last Supper, a Christian rite which also involves the symbolism of bread, fire offerings, and divine cannibalism. Like Queequeg, the Catholic clergy typically burns incense in a church before offering a piece of bread (ship's biscuit!) to its own idol (the Crucifix), and the laity is then asked to eat the body of the deity ("Take, eat, for this is my body which was given for you"). While Melville doesn't expatiate upon the images in quite this way, he nevertheless exhibits his extraordinary tolerance for a wide range of human religious beliefs throughout the course of his narrative.

One must assume that when Ishmael gets up the next morning to go to Father Mapple's church, that he will participate in some such version of the communion rite. Before he does so, however, Melville evokes another image primordially associated with the heroic descent into the underworld, that of the maze. Waking the next morning in the huge bed, Ishmael finds Queequeg's arm thrown over him in a "most loving and affectionate manner" (27). Upon closer examination, Ishmael finds "this arm of his tattooed all over with an interminable Cretan labyrinth of a figure," very much resembling the "odd little parti-colored squares and triangles" of the quilt (27). As we have seen throughout our study of the hero journey in literature, the maze is frequently employed as a metaphor of the nekyia, as in Spenser's *Faerie Queene*, Shakespeare's *Tempest* and *Midsummer Night's Dream*, or Milton's "Comus." It is a motif that emerges consistently in *Moby Dick* in association with the descent, as we will see. In addition to its Cretan source, Melville seems to have associated the maze with Egypt and the pyramids, as in the poem called "The Great Pyramid" (Edinger 68). Later in *Moby Dick*, the labyrinth will be associated with the "maze of currents" Ahab charts during the quest for the whale (200), a quest which threatens to "lead us on in barren mazes or midway leave us whelmed" (243). The metaphor comes up again when a seahawk steals Ahab's hat, "wheeling and screaming round his head in a maze of untrackably swift circlings" (540), and when, during the final chase, Moby Dick is harpooned, and "gets "corkscrewed in the mazes of the line" (560). For the whale is certainly the Minotaur in the midst of the maze, though initially the monster turns out to be a rather gentle savage (Queequeg), one who even appears in Father Mapple's church later on Sunday morning.

The first thing Ishmael sees in Father Mapple's church is appropriately linked to the descent motif: a grim collection of plaques commemorating sailors lost at sea, "marble tablets, with black borders, masoned into the wall on either side of the pulpit" (36). The text for Mapple's sermon is one also traditionally associated with the nekyia:

for, as we have seen in Chapter 1 of this study, the story of Jonah represents the biblical archetype of the descent into Sheol, a typological prefiguration of the harrowing of hell in the New Testament. As noted in Chapter 1, the belly of the whale may figure what Edinger calls "heroic incest -- a purposeful descent into the maternal womb, the depths of the unconscious, for the purpose of transformation and rebirth" (36). Freudians like Erich Fromm, who saw Jonah's descent as a regression into the "mother's womb" (22), would certainly agree. But for the Rabbinical tradition, the descent into the belly of the whale combined the symbolism of the nekyia with that of the synagogue, a place where God's ultimate mysteries are revealed. Ginzburg, for example, cites a Jewish legend in which the whale shows Jonah Gehenna, Sheol, and the source of the "river from which the ocean flows" (Edinger 40). This is entirely characteristic of the symbolism of the heroic descent, which typically involves rites of initiation, during which the ultimate mysteries of the world are revealed, sometimes in the form of a god or goddess who represents the source of all life (as here in the Jewish evocation of the river from which the ocean flows).

Other images of the heroic descent, in the early chapters of *Moby Dick* include the crossing from New Bedford to Nantucket, on the little packet schooner, and the description of the whaling ship itself, the famous Pequod. The former falls into that same general category of archetypal symbols of the nekyia as the longer quest for the whale does: the water crossing to the yonder shore, as evinced by the Gilgamesh poet, by Homer, Dante, Charlotte Brontë, Coleridge, Ambrose Bierce, Mark Twain, and numerous others. An instance of death and resurrection occurs on the schooner crossing, as Queequeg rescues an obnoxious greenhorn from drowning, after he is knocked overboard by the boom. Queequeg dives into the "freezing foam," and then again "perpendicularly" down under the surface of the waves, after which he "rose again [...] dragging a lifeless form," which he then restores on board ship (63). The alliterative linking of the verbs "rose again" and "restored" emphasizes the images of death and resurrection, in association with the night-sea journey of the hero, which are central motifs throughout *Moby Dick*. The description of the Pequod, which follows shortly afterwards, amplifies the affiliation between the sea quest and the nekyia, for the boat is itself seen, quite literally, as a ship of death. It is a "cannibal of a craft, tricking herself forth in the chased bones of her enemies," for it is entirely inlaid with whale ivory. Not only the thews, blocks, tiller, sheaves, but indeed every inch of the bulwarks are fashioned out of ivory. The boat is "garnished like one continuous jaw, with the long sharp teeth of a sperm whale, inserted there for pins," so that in stepping aboard, the sailors literally step down into the jaws of death, and pass on into the skeleton of the ship's interior, swallowed up like Jonah by that "cannibal of a craft" (71).

But Melville's Hades is more than a place of retribution and repressed guilt; it is also a temenos of the imagination, where the powers of poesis are intensely activated. Ishmael begins to see everything around him as metaphor, portent, and revelation. This becomes evident later in the novel, precisely at the next point when the symbolism of the nekyia is revived, during the first lowering of boats to chase a herd of whales. Before the pursuit begins, Ishmael sits in dreamy reverie, inspired by the calm serenity of the sea. He is stitching a mat with Queequeg, and he comes to see the mat as a symbol of fate: the "fixed threads of the warp" represent "necessity"; the woof Ishmael casually weaves represents "free will"; and Queequeg "carelessly" striking the threads of the woof into place represents "chance" (218). The "completed fabric," therefore, figures forth human destiny, the revelation of which typically marks the climax of the initiation phases of the hero journey. Such revelations result naturally from the activation of the deep imagination, effected by the trials and ordeals of the quest, so that the hero is enabled to perceive the metaphorical nature of the ordinary details of daily life: "the least heedful eye," as Melville puts it, comes "to see some sort of cunning meaning in almost every sight" (541). Hence, Ishmael repeatedly meditates upon the significance of weaving during his journey, an archaic image of fate which we have found previously in the stories of Odysseus, Psyche, and many others. While wandering in an island grove to see the "strange hieroglyphics" carved on a whale's skeleton, for example, Ishmael sees the sun as "a flying shuttle weaving the unwearied verdure," and he wonders aloud, as the "figures float forth from the loom" of creation, at which the "weaver god" endlessly weaves "(459). But the creative aspect of the symbolism of weaving also implies the destructive imagery of fate, as in the description of the line coiled in the tubs of the whaleboats, which is threaded through all the oarlocks, and becomes an image of the web of fate, in which the mariners are caught: it is "a halter around every neck," which pulls them into the "jaws of death" (287).

It is appropriate, therefore, that Ishmael's reverie upon the mysteries of fate be immediately followed by the first lowering of the boats, in pursuit of the first sperm whale of the novel. This first hunt is delineated in terminology which evokes the descent into the underworld. Ahab appears with his mysterious crew of stowaway Orientals, lead by Fedallah, the harpooneer, "funereally invested" in a jacket of "black cotton," his hair "braided and coiled round and round upon his head," like the harpoon line coiled in the tubs at his feet, and attended by his cohorts, "aboriginal natives of the Manillas; -- a race notorious for a certain diabolism of subtilty, and by some honest white

mariners supposed to be the paid spies and secret confidential agents on
the water of the devil" (220). These are all images relevant to the
demonic aspects of the descent into hell, as is the metaphor Melville
uses to evoke the powerful emotions inspired by the chase, which he
compares to those felt by a "dead man's ghost encountering the first
unknown phantom in the other world" (228). Particularly relevant to
descent motif is the archetypal imagery Ishmael uses after his boat is
swamped, and the mariners spend an anxious night adrift at sea. After
the Pequod rescues the half-drowned whalemen, the next morning,
Ishmael remarks, oddly, that his "death and burial were locked up in my
chest" (233); he then compares himself to "Lazarus [...] after his
resurrection," and to a "quiet ghost with a clean conscience sitting
inside the bars of a snug family vault" (233).

Similar imagery associated with the underworld journey follows
soon afterwards, in the chapter called the "Spirit Spout." It begins with
the "coffin tap" of Ahab's wooden leg, while he paces the deck after
days of serene weather, during which the sea has the "devilish charm" of
world from which all life has vacated (238). At midnight a white spout
appears in the distance. The sailors are filled with a "sense of peculiar
dread at this flitting apparition," as the Pequod sets forth, night after
night, its "urn-like prow" churning the "desolate vacuity" of the
midnight sea (238). Strange forms dart through the water beneath the
bow, and "inscrutable sea ravens" perch amidst the halyards on the
stern, hooting "as though they deemed our ship some drifting,
uninhabited craft; a thing appointed to desolation," as it rounds the
Cape of Good Hope (239). Ishmael sees the eerie fowls and fish as
"guilty beings" who have been "condemned to swim on everlastingly"
amidst the "demoniac waves" (239). When a ship called the Albatross
appears shortly after rounding the Cape, therefore, it is entirely
appropriate that it be compared to "the skeleton of a stranded walrus"
(240), and that the Pequod's pursuit of the whale be evoked as the
"tormented chase of that demon phantom [...] that swims before all
human hearts" (242), leading them ever deeper into a futile web of
"barren mazes" (242).

All of these images establish the theme of the descent into the
underworld, in affiliation with the penetration of the maze, as archetypal
analogies of the hero journey in the novel. This network of what
Melville calls "linked analogies" (321) continues to be applied to the
pursuit of the whale and other creatures, like the spirit spout and the
giant squid, which is described as a "white ghost," or an "apparition of
life" (283). The network of infernal motifs becomes quite literal when
the men lower boats for the second chase, on which occasion the
harpoon line becomes a web of death, coiled around each sailor like "a
halter around every neck," pulling them down towards the "jaws of

death" (287). The image of the spiral, here in the form of the harpoon lines, coiled in the tubs and around the sailors, is linked by analogy to the web of fate, chance, and free will, which Ishmael earlier saw woven into the mat. As an image of intricate artistry, the mat and the coil are also linked to the various metaphors of poesis evoked by Ishmael's hero journey, and with the image of the maze, which is formed by spirals and coils doubling back upon themselves, in an elaborate network of repetition and allusion. As we will see, Melville ultimately uses the hero journey as a metaphor for writing (poesis) and reading (hermeneusis), both of which involve the intensification of the intellect and imagination.

One of the characteristic features of the hero journey, from its beginnings, is precisely this power to activate the archetypal configurations of the human imagination. Hence, the second lowering of the boats in pursuit of the Sperm whale activates three archetypes long associated with the hero journey: God's battle with the monster, the sacrificial meal, and the image of the devouring mother goddess. Chapters 61 to 70 describe, in powerful detail the killing, stripping down, and eating of parts of a large sperm whale. It's a long bloody business: the harpoons and lances mutilating the bloody body of the whale, the ravenous sharks beaten off from the bleeding carcass by the harpooneers, the grotesque but precisely ritualistic dismemberment of the whale, and Stubb's consumption of a raw steak prepared for him at midnight by the ship's cook. The details of the killing of the whale are accurately realistic, and stand on their own as a tremendous feat of American naturalist writing. But beneath the realistic surface of the description lurks that long line of mythological images of God's battle with the monster, which Melville takes pains to evoke. Several of these are explicitly discussed in Chapter 82 (Vishnu, Perseus, St. George, and Hercules), but in a rather tongue in cheek fashion, since Melville rather playfully pokes fun at his own obsession by suggesting that St. George's dragon must have been a whale.

Scholarship has richly amplified the image of the battle with the monster for us. Mary Wakeman, for example, has shown how the allusion to Jahweh's battle with a sea monster variously referred to as Leviathan (Isaiah 27:1), Yam (Job 26:12-33), and Rahab (Isaiah 51: 9-10; Psalm 89: 10-11 -- possible source of Ahab's name?) is analogous to the Hindu myth about Indra's battle with sea monster called Vritra, which concerns the release of the embryo of the sun from the primordial waters. Wakeman therefore suggests that the battle is a metaphor of creation, by which a cosmos is shaped (by the god) from a chaos (represented by the sea monster). The battle, that is to say, is an image of poesis, of making, whether it be of worlds, people, or poems. Marie Louise von Franz and Barbara Sproul also pursue the image of the battle with the monster as an image of creation. Barbara Walker focuses on the Mesopotamian prototypes of the biblical battle, noting that Marduk's dismemberment of the female sea monster Tiamat, in the Babylonian creation myth (known as the *Enumu Elish*) is linked by analogy to Jahweh's encounter with the "face of the deep" in Genesis 1:2. The Hebrew word for the "deep" is Tehom, linked etymologically the Babylonian goddess Tiamat, and to the Egyptian word Temu, the oldest female deity of the deep, mother of the four primal elements of the creation (*Encyclopedia* 998). To complete the amplification of an archetype so important to the history of the hero journey, there is no better source than Joseph Fontenrose, who in his book called Python, examines the extensive Greek variations on the theme of the combat myth, and connects not only to Mesopotamian and Hindu variants, but also to the mythologies of China, Japan, and the Americas. The key point here is that the myth is about the way new worlds are fashioned from the body of the dismembered monster: Marduk quite literally makes the world from the corpse of Tiamat, rather in the same way as Odin and Vili make the world from the dismembered body of the dead frost giant, Ymir, in Norse myth (Crossley-Holland 3-4). Hence, Melville won't let us forget that the oil extracted from the Sperm whale provides the 'light of the world,' when used in the lamps and lanterns of the 19th century.

Closely related to the archetype of the creative battle with the monster is the theme of the sacrificial banquet, a motif already very familiar to us from our perusal of the Ancient and Medieval examples of the hero journey. Banquets and sacrificial feasts (often of a ritual nature pervade the *Odyssey*; Persephone feasts upon pomegranate seeds in the Homeric Hymn to Demeter; Parzival's first visit to the Grail castle involves one of the most elaborate banquets in the history of the hero journey; and, finally we find ritual feasts in the otherworld at climactic moments in such folktale versions of the journey as "Hansel and Gretel," "Vasilisa the Beautiful," "Jack and the Beanstalk," or "Beauty and the Beast." In addition to these literary references, the dismemberment and devouring of the whale in *Moby Dick* evokes those hunting rites, stemming way back from Paleolithic times, by which the sacrificed body of the food animal was propitiated and deified. The purpose of these rites was to ensure that the animal would return again from the dead, during the next hunting season, in order once again to offer itself as food, sustaining the lives of the human community by offering itself in death. It is an image we know well from the Last Supper, in the New Testament, where Jesus offers his body and blood, so that others may live, a moment of 'divine cannibalism' reenacted every Sunday in Catholic and Protestant Churches all over the world! Hence, when Melville uses the underworldly imagery of the "marble sepulchre" to describe the "vast white headless phantom" of the dead whale carcass floating off into the distance, he calls it a "great mass of death" (317), thereby linking the consumed corpse of the whale to the "mass" of the Last Supper. While this pun may or may not have been intentional, there is no doubt that Melville deified Moby Dick, or that a complex typology of biblical motifs became an important aspect of the way his presents the whale.

One of these motifs certainly has to do the archetype of the sacrificial meal, an archetype closely related to the imagery of the devouring goddess, which surfaces explicitly for the first time in this section of the novel. Ishmael speaks of "the universal cannibalism of the sea," noting that the sea is a "fiend to its own offspring [...] sparing not the creatures which itself hath spawned" (281). As an horrific example of this terrible fact, Melville gives us the absolutely abhorrent image of sharks devouring their own entrails, which "seemed swallowed over and over again by the same mouth, to be oppositely voided by the gaping wound" (310). As grotesque as this passage is, the mythological image of a parent devouring itself, or its own children points towards the kind of fundamental revelation about the nature of life which is one of the goals of the initiation stage of the hero journey: the problem is that life feeds on life, and that the same energies that produce life, ultimately devour it. Though this metaphysical fact is frequently represent by the image of the female who eats children (Baba Yaga, the Witch in "Hansel and Gretel"), it can also be represented by a devouring father, as in the folktale about the Wolf devouring the seven kids, or in the myths of Tantalos or Chronos devouring their own children. While Freud and Jung focus on the psychological implications of the devouring parent, we must also note the clue which the name Chronos gives us, which helps interpret the entire cluster of myths: does not Time both produce and devour all things, as things eternally come into and pass out of existence? For Melville, time is the sea, the great goddess from whom all life comes, who sustains all life with her fish, and who consumes all life at the end of the cycle.

In the third whale chase of the book Melville turns from the imagery of the descent into the underworld and the devouring goddess of the sea, to the imagery of the nurturing mother and the maze, as a basic variation on the hero journey theme. Indeed, the leit motif of the maze is announced right from the beginning of the novel, when Ishmael awakens to find Queequeg's arm "tattooed all over with an interminable Cretan labyrinth of a figure" (27); and the motif is frequently evoked in the chapters that follow -- as when Melville refers to the "maziness of design" on the "bone sculpture" of the "Hawaiian savage" (277); when Ahab charts the "maze of currents and eddies" on his map" (200); when Ishmael refers to the "barren mazes" of the world, which the pursuit leads the human heart into (243); or when Ishmael compares the complex respiratory system of the whale to "a remarkable involved Cretan labyrinth of vermicelli-like vessels," and declares that "the anatomical fact of this labyrinth is indisputable" (380). These allusions to the maze archetype lay the foundation for the magnificent chapter called "The Grand Armada," in which Ishmael and Queequeg chase a whale into the midst of a large herd, as the Pequod passes through the straits of Sunda.

These are the straits which separate Sumatra from Java, and Melville uses the imagery of doorways to mark this important threshold crossing: the straits are compared to a "central gateway opening into some vast walled empire," unlike the "domineering fortresses which guard the entrances to the Mediterranean, the Baltic, and the Propontis," but nevertheless a "gate," patrolled by the marauding Malay pirates, who pursue the Pequod as it passes through (389). Melville touches upon the imagery of the inferno, by describing the pirates who guard the threshold gates as "atheistical devils [...] infernally cheering" Ahab on (393), but he then modulates to the metaphor of the maze, in his glorious description of the huge herd of whales moving through the straits at the same time. Emerging from the threshold, the frightened whales gather together in a vast group of concentric circles, bulls on the outermost rings, and mothers in the innermost. The Armada is described in terms which consistently evoke the imagery of a circular labyrinth, composed of a sequence of broken spheres: the herd is a "vast fleet of whales hurrying forward through the straits; gradually contracting the wings of their semicircle, and swimming on, in one solid, but still crescentic centre" (392). As the whales become more confused by the chase, they swim in "vast irregular circles," which fill Ishmael with "amazement" and consternation, after a whale his boat harpoons drags him into the center of the labyrinth (395). The boat passes "through their complicated channels and straits," moving from the "circumference of commotion" and the "tumults of the outer concentric circles," into the "enchanted calm" in the centre of the maze (396-97). Here, in the center, Ishmael looks down into the water at the "long coils of the umbilical cord of Madame Leviathan," to which a young cub is tethered (399). It is a peaceful scene, though "surrounded by circle upon circle of consternations and affrights," which Melville personally compares to the "ponderous planets of unwaning woe" which revolve around his own center of joy (399). But when one of the outermost whales panics, after being harpoon and dragged, the "revolving outer circles" begin to collapse upon the "innermost fold," breaking up all the intermediate rings (398). The wounded bull dashes inwards "among the revolving circles," becomes entangled in a loose harpoon line, and flings the sharp iron wildly around, stirring his companions in the herd into a frenzy

(400). At this point the entire labyrinth begins to collapse upon the little whale boat in its center, as "in more and more contracting orbits the whales in more central circles began to swim in thickening clusters," eventually caving in, "tumbling upon their inner centre" (400). Ishmael's little boat struggles through the constricting straits of the collapsing maze towards its "outer circles," while the panicking whales reverse the movement, and randomly make for its "centre" (401).

The language of contraction which attends upon this revelation of the mother whale at the center of the maze picks up on the perinatal imagery Melville had used in a previous chapter, to describe Tashtego's "deliverance, or rather delivery" from the casing of the whale's skull, into which he had fallen while tapping its oil (353). His delivery is effected by what Melville calls "the obstetrics of Queequeg" (353), who performs his "agile obstetrics on the run," as the head begins to sink beneath the waves (354). Queequeg's "Midwifery" involves, therefore, a "running delivery" of Tashtego, who would otherwise remain "coffined, hearsed, and tombed in the secret inner chamber and sanctum sanctorum of the whale" (354). This linkage of the underworld, the maze, and the Great Goddess (both as womb and tomb) into a vivid vocabulary of perinatal diction and imagery is a familiar one to those who know the history of the hero journey: we have seen it in the *Odyssey*, and it will recur again in Ambrose Bierce. And indeed, the mythological iconography linking the maze with the Great Mother is extensively explored by such writers as Eliade ("La Terre-Mère" 75-76), di Stasi (105-08) and Gimbutas (316-17). But what particularly draws me to this passage devoted to the Grand Armada is the evocation of the maze as a series of collapsing or broken concentric circles. Such was the form of the maze during the Middle Ages, at places like Chartres, with its famous floor labyrinth (Doob 132), and the churches at Bayeux, Sens, Châlon-sur-Marne, and St. Martin (Bord 96-102), and such was the form of the maze in the *Timaeus*, which Plato describes as a symbol of the soul fallen into the body, and tangled up in circles "broken and disordered in every possible way, so that when they moved they were tumbling to pieces and moved irrationally, at one time in a reverse direction, and then again obliquely, and then upside down" (Doob 278). Since this passage fits the movements of the boat and frightened whales in the Armada so perfectly (the concentric circles broken, the whales revolving inward, and upside down in the form of the mother whales beneath the surface, while the boat radiates outward to escape), and since Melville alludes to Plato at several points in the narrative, the *Timaeus* may well be one of the sources for his conception of the maze at this point in the novel.

At later points, the metaphorical resonance of the quest is derived less from the maze, than from the descent into hell, an archetype frequently evoked by the hero journey. Demonic imagery particularly dominates Chapter 96, which is devoted to the "Try-Works," in which the blubber is boiled down to oil. The furnace kilns look (and smell) most infernal at midnight, when Ishmael takes his dreamy turn at the tiller. Ishmael says that the smoke has "a wild Hindoo odor [...] such as may lurk in the vicinity of funeral pyres. It smells like the left wing of the day of judgment; it is an argument for the pit" (432). The smoke blackens the faces of the wild harpooneers who stoke the fires. They stand in front of the forge like "Tartarean shapes," and they narrate "unholy adventures," while the ship carries "her red hell further and further into the blackness of the sea and night" (434). Ishmael suggests that the ship, "laden with fire, and burning a corpse, and plunging into that blackness of darkness," is a symbol of Ahab's "monomaniac" soul (434) -- an important metaphor, since it anticipates the psychologizing of the hero journey in the work of Jung and Freud. Indeed, Melville links the entire scene to the metaphors of the dream and the underworld: after Ishmael falls asleep at the tiller, he awakens overcome by "A stark bewildering feeling, as of death," and he sees the heathenish harpooneers, who are dancing in front of the furnace, as "devils in the forking flames" (435). Seen through the lenses of midnight reverie, the entire ocean becomes "the dark side of this earth" (435), and Ishmael's descent into its darkness qualifies him to "sit down on tomb-stones and break the green damp mould with unfathomably wondrous Solomon" (436). His nocturnal meditations conclude with the magnificent image of the flight of the eagle, which is symbolic of the entirety of the hero journey: Ishmael reflects that there are "some souls that can alike dive down into the blackest gorges, and soar out of them again, and become invisible in the sunny spaces" (436). Most souls, however, had better not stare too long into the fire, lest they lose themselves in "a woe that is madness" (436).

Melville keeps our focus on the symbolic imagery of the descent into the underworld with masterly little flourishes of the pen, which recur throughout the final chapters of the novel. He evokes the dreaming "shades and shadows" of "almost final waters," as the Pequod passes through the Bashee Isles into the Pacific (490-91); he describes the ship blacksmith's calling to the sea as a passage to "another life," attainable "without the guilt of intermediate death"; and he evokes the Pacific as a place where the smith can see "wonders supernatural without dying for them," and "bury" himself in a life "more oblivious than death" (494). Ahab's dream of hearses, while lashed overnight to the rotting carcass of a slaughtered whale (Chapter 117); the ghostly typhoon that drives the ship into the "blackness of doom," as the masts burn in the "sulphurous air," Queequeg's tattooes burn "like Satanic blue flames," and the men look like "running skeletons in

Herculaneum" (510-12); the weird sound of the seals, "wailing like ghosts," which the sailors hear "in the deep darkness that goes before dawn," while passing through "unfrequented waters," and which the Manxman says are the "voices of newly drowned men" (526-27); the "falling phantom" of the night watchman, as he plunges from the mast head to his death (527); the burial at sea of a young mate from the Delight, whose corpse splashes the Pequod with a "ghostly baptism" as it strikes the sea (542); the final image of the great whale dragging the boats down into the "infernal world" beneath the maelstrom on the surface -- all of these powerful images keep our focus on the symbolism of the nekyia, clustering together into the most significant and sustained mythological motif in the novel.

This cluster is composed of the archetypes of the inferno, the battle with the monster, the sacrificial meal, the loving and terrible goddess of the sea, and the labyrinth -- all linked by analogy with the hero journey. As difficult to grasp and digest as many of the book's revelations are -- like Melville, one resists the urge to popularize profundities, for surely that man who attempts to interpret Bottom's dream is but an ass -- the hero journey also serves as a kind of allegory of both reading (hermeneusis) and artistry (poesis). We find, throughout the novel, images of 'readers' in the text, involved in acts of interpretation similar to our own; so also do we find images of artists within the text (weavers, smiths, carpenters, scrimshaw sailors, engravers), engaged in activities similar to Melville's own. Melville frequently uses the imagery of the hieroglyph and the maze to relate these aspects of the symbolism of the hero journey to the creative processes of reading and writing. We have already seen how he uses the "maziness of design" on a Polynesian whalebone as a symbol of artistry, one very appropriate to a book of *Moby Dick's* complexity, and as a symbol of reading itself, since the labyrinth of the book is one in which many readers have gotten happily lost. We must now turn to the related symbolism of hieroglyphs and cabalistics, which also become analogies of both reading and writing in the novel.

In the 1820's a Frenchman named Jean-François Champollion used the bilingual Rosetta stone (now in the British Museum) to decipher the 'picture' language of the Egyptians, known as hieroglyphics. His discovery came in the middle of a period of intense interest in all things Egyptian, which in American life manifested in the form of exhibitions, traveling side shows of mummies, architectural monuments, and in scholarly debates about the metaphysical and scientific significance of the hieroglyphic writings. As John Irwin has shown, these debates profoundly influenced the literature of the American Renaissance (Emerson, Poe, Thoreau, Melville, Hawthorne, Whitman, and later Twain). The debate revolved around the traditional notion that the hieroglyphics composed the alphabet of a sacred script, or divine language, and the newer scientific approach to the images as the basic elements of a natural script, or human language. Fundamentally, the study of the Egyptian hieroglyphs influenced Emerson's formulation of an essential doctrine of Transcendentalist aesthetics: that the world itself is a vast book composed of living hieroglyphics, in which all natural things represent those spiritual realities which they symbolize. The job of the inspired poet is therefore twofold: first, to learn to read and properly interpret the hieroglyphical language of the natural world, in order to perceive the spiritual significance of all things; second, to create a poem or book composed of symbolic images drawn from the natural world which serve as images of the spiritual energies from which it is ultimately derived, and of which it is a manifestation. These are the two tasks of reading, or interpretation (hermeneusis), and creative composition (poesis) which we find symbolically represented by the problem of the hieroglyphics in numerous masterpieces of American literature, and particularly in *Moby Dick*.

Throughout the novel, Melville consistently relates the whale not only to the nekyia and the maze, but also to the Egyptian imagery of pyramids and hieroglyphics. In Chapter 86, he refers generally to the "mystic gestures" of the flukes, which the whale waves in the air before diving, and further remarks upon the "Free-Mason signs and symbols" etched upon the tail, by which the whale "intelligently conversed with the world" (388). These signs and symbols must of course be interpreted by the world, if they are to successfully read, a process akin to Champollion's decipherment of the hieroglyphics, which are alluded to in Chapters 68 and 79. The former concerns the strange markings on the skin of the sperm whale, markings which Melville compares to cross-hatching "in the finest Italian line engravings," to the "mysterious cyphers on the walls of pyramids hieroglyphics," to "the old Indian characters chiselled on the famous hieroglyphical palisades on the banks of the Upper Mississippi," and finally to the "numerous rude scratchings, altogether of an irregular, random aspect" inscribed by icebergs on the rocks of the New England coast (315). This rapidly expanding cluster of images associated with the hieroglyphics recalls Thoreau's meditation, in *Walden,* on the patterns created by sand flowing down a railroad embankment over the snow, during a spring thaw, patterns which he takes to illustrate "the principle of all the operations of Nature" ("Spring" 568): the circulatory, skeletal, and respiratory systems of the human body; the intricate network of rivers and tributary streams and brooks; and the patterns created by trees and leaves, as the central arteries exfoliate into smaller branches, twigs, and capillaries (565-68). "What Champollion," Thoreau concludes by asking, "will decipher this hieroglyphic for us" (568), thereby implying that his task is the same as Melville's in *Moby Dick*: i.e., to read the script inscribed upon the whale's back, by natural forces, in order to intuit its spiritual significance. In many ways, this problem is the essence of the hero journey.

The hermeneutic task of 'reading' the whale is a consistent theme throughout the novel. The earlier chapter on "Cetology" the uses the language of bibliography ("Folio," "Octavo," "Duodecimo") to classify the whales by groups, according to their size (137-48). Like the previously mentioned connection between the cut slices of whale blubber to "bible leaves," this marvelously suggestive metaphor implies that the whale is a kind of book, to be read and classified by genre. Melville returns to the analogy linking the whale, the book, and the hieroglyphic in his magnificent description of the whale's brow, in Chapter 79: "Champollion deciphered the wrinkled granite hieroglyphics," Melville writes, "But there is no Champollion to decipher the Egypt of every man's and every being's face" (358). He then suggests that if Sir William Jones could read thirty languages, but "could not read the simplest peasant's face in its profounder and more subtle meanings, how may unlettered Ishmael hope to read the awful Chaldee of the Sperm Whale's brow? I but put that brow before you. Read it if you can" (358). Here Melville links the hieroglyphics with the cuneiform script of the Chaldeans, and the Sanskrit of the Hindu's, deciphered by Sir William Jones in . All three mystic languages are inscribed upon the whale's brow, and it seems Ishmael's hopeless task to read in those sacred languages, and to decipher the significance of the signs and symbols scratched on to the skin of the whale's noble brow. Elsewhere in the book, Melville adds Hebrew to the list of sacred languages which must be deciphered during the quest. This occurs in the chapter called "the Doubloon," in which Ahab, Starbuck, Stubb, Flask, the Manxman, Queequeg, and Pip all get a chance to 'read' the "cabalistics" inscribed on the edge of the coin (441).

The cabala is a profound branch of Jewish mysticism, based on deciphering the hidden meaning of the letters, syllables, words, and names of the Old Testament. The "cabalistics" on the gold doubloon encircle symbolic images of three mountain peaks (surmounted by a flame, a rooster, and a tower), with a segment of the zodiac arching over the whole. Each of the men reads something different into the letters and images -- many renderings, "but still one text," as Stubb puts it (444). Ahab sees himself in the imagery of the doubloon, and remarks that the coin is like "a magician's glass," which "to each and every man in turn but mirrors back his own mysterious self" (442). Stubb, with the help of an almanac, sees the sun passing in turn through each sign of the zodiac as an image of the complete life cycle of humankind.

Queequeg compares the "signs of the Zodiac" to the hieroglyphics on his thigh bone, rather like Pip, who sees the doubloon as the ship's navel. Flask calculates the number of cigars he might buy with the doubloon. Each man in turn, therefore, reads the cabalistics and zodiacal hieroglyphics in his own way. The mysterious script, like the whale, like the book, allows a multiplicity of interpretations, some of which are mirrored in the text. Starbuck's response is perhaps the most interesting, because it focuses on a biblical model of hermeneusis: the writing on the wall in the Book of Daniel, in which the mysterious letters which appear during the feast must be interpreted by the prophet as omens of doom for Belshazzar. "The old man seems to read Belshazzar's awful writing," Starbuck murmers, as Ahab scrutinizes the coin (442). Then he says, "let me read," and proceeds to interpret the cabalistics on the coin as symbols of "vale of Death" (442).

These responses focus on the central issues associated with the hieroglyphs and cabalistics in the novel: the issues involved with the creation and interpretation of texts. In the Book of Daniel, "the fingers of a man's hand" appear, during the feast, and Belshazzar, the king, sees only "the part of the hand that wrote" (5:5). The letters so inscribed upon the wall terrify the king, who offers a reward to "Whosoever shall read this writing, and shew me the interpretation thereof" (5:7). Since Belshazzar's wise men "could not read the writing, nor make known to the king the interpretation thereof" (5:8), Daniel is summoned to "shew the interpretation" (5:12). He is renowned for his knowledge, understanding, interpretation of dreams, and the "shewing of hard sentences" (5:12), and is therefore brought before the king, since, as the king repeats, the "wise men, the astrologers, have been brought before me, that they should read this writing, and make known unto me the interpretation thereof: but they could not shew the interpretation of the thing" (5:15). Belshazzar says he has heard that Daniel "canst make interpretations" (5:16), and the prophet answers that he "will read the writing unto the king, and make known to him the interpretation" (5:17). The reiteration of the phrase (five times) is not only reflective of biblical poetics: it also keeps our atttention on the essential issues of the scene, those having to do with the divine mysteries of writing and reading. Daniel reads four letters of the "writing" that "was written" by the hand upon the wall: Mene, Mene, Tekel, and Upharsin (5:25).[11] Melville later refers specifically to this "writing" when, during the terrible typhoon, he notes that sailor's seldom swear "when God's burning finger has been laid on the ship; when his 'Mene, Mene, Tekel, Upharsin' has been woven into the shrouds and cordage" (510), as omens of doom. This passage links the divine act of poesis (God's hand writing on the wall) with weaving, an important metaphor of artistry elsewhere in the novel. Both in the Bible, and in *Moby Dick*, therefore, the hero journey, and the prophet's task, involve both poesis and hermeneusis, implicating the mysteries of writing and reading in a single image.

Another scene which includes both aspects of the symbolism of the hieroglyphics in the novel occurs when Queequeg orders a coffin, on the lid of which, after recovering from a bad cold, he carves "all manner of grotesque figures and drawings" (490). These figures copy the "twisted tattooing on his body," which itself "had been the work of a departed prophet and seer of his island, who, by those hieroglyphic marks, had written out on his body a complete theory of the heavens and the earth, a mystical treatise on the art of attaining truth" (490). As John Irwin has shown, the idea that the Egyptian hieroglyphics composed a mystical scripture persisted right alongside the more scientific interpretations developed by Champollion. In Melville's marvelous formulation, Queequeg himself, like the whale's brow and skeleton, becomes a book to be read and deciphered, "a wondrous work in one volume" (490), as of course we all are. The tantalizing problem, however, is that Queequeg's hieroglyphic tattooing composes "mysteries not even himself could read" (490), a verb which returns our attention to the problem of hermeneutics in the novel. Because we are all mortal, Melville muses, "these mysteries were therefore destined in the end to moulder away with the living parchment whereon they were inscribed, and so be unsolved to the last" (490). These lines link writing with reading, poesis with hermeneusis, suggesting that the processes by which the hieroglyphs are inscribed upon the "living parchment" of the body, or carved onto the lid of the coffin, are as mysteriously inscrutable as the processes by which that "wondrous work in one volume" is "read" (490). Both processes are represented by the trials and ordeals, the revelations and transformations, of the hero journey itself.

Hence, the cabalistics inscribed upon the doubloon, like the hieroglyphics engraved upon the whale's brow and skeleton, and upon Queequeg's skin and coffin, are images of creation and destruction, of the dual artistry of reading and writing: who or what, after all made the whale in the beginning; who or what marked its brow, or Queequeg's flesh, with the inscrutable language of the living hieroglyphics; and who will read this writing on the wall, and make known the interpretation thereof? The only certain answer is that Melville himself made the whale, just as he created the Cannibal: by writing the book, he sets brow and body meticulously before us, to read as we can. From this perspective, the whale in particular, and the hero journey in general, becomes a metaphor for poesis, that mysteriously creative process by which the poet imitates the creative powers of the universe, by bringing a world into being, in the form of a book. In this sense, art is a mirror held up to itself, a mirror which therefore reflects the entire world upon its mercurial surface. Some such simile is implicit in the earlier discussion of the hieroglyphics on the whale's skin, which are compared to the etchings of an Italian engraving: the whale, that is to say, grandly magnifies the creative processes of human artistry. Put another way, *Moby Dick* is a whale of a book.

Walt Whitman

The association between the heroic descent into the underworld and poesis persists throughout the 19th century. In "Out of the Cradle Endlessly Rocking," for example, Walt Whitman dates his vocation as a poet to a night in April when, as a young boy, he left his bedroom and walked down into the "twining and twisting" patches of briar and blackberry along the seashore and heard the song of the mockingbird grieving for its lost mate. This poetic vocation the poet associates with a first experience of love and death, and with the solitary singing of the mockingbird. The poem which records the vocation is structured along the lines of the night-sea journey (from bedroom down to the shoreline late at night), suggesting an allegorical connection between poesis and the hero journey. The poet hears the mockingbird lamenting the loss of its mate, just as the boy laments the loss of his brother, and from this moment the "thousand songs" which the poet will sing start "to life within" him (392). The motif which will be the basis of all these "thousand warbling echoes" is the "low and delicious word" sung by sea and bird both, "Death, death, death, death, death" (393). The sea, furthermore, is the "fierce old mother" to whom the boy returns, the "savage old mother incessantly crying" (392). She is the Goddess of Death and Life, with her old symbol the waning moon hanging low on the horizon above her head. The poet's "thousand responsive songs" are "awakened from that hour" (393) when he journeyed down to her shores at midnight and heard the bird-song of the dead.

Whitman's "When Lilacs Last in the Dooryard Bloom'd" also uses the hero journey (and the symbols of star, forest, and bird) to represent poesis. It does so by adapting certain musical forms, in which Whitman was much interested throughout his life. If one was to translate the basic structure of the hero journey into a musical form, the result would be the sonata, which ends where it begins, with a development section in between. The exposition in sonata form corresponds to the first stage of the hero journey; it states the one or two basic melodies which will be transformed by orchestration and harmonic modulation in the development section. The development in sonata form corresponds therefore to the second stage of the hero journey, while the recapitulation and coda circle back to the beginning of the sonata just as in the return stage of the journey the hero circles back to his or her point of departure. The basic structure of the hero journey, sonata form, and Whitman's poem is the therefore the same:

Separation	Initiation	Return
Exposition	Development	Recapitulation
Lilac, Star, Bird	Swamp, Funeral	Lilac, Star, Bird

Whitman's poem begins with an exposition analogous to sonata form, "lilac," "star," and "bird" (sections 1-4) replacing melodies A, B, and C, and then proceeds to develop these basic motifs in the middle section of the poem, which follows the journeys of Lincoln's coffin across the land to Illinois, and of the poet down into the cedar swamp (sections 5-16). In this development section, the basic motifs of lilac, star, and bird are intertwined in a manner similar to theme and variations in music, but they are contained and developed within the structure of sonata form, so that the poem ends where it began with a recapitulation of the three basic motifs at the end of section 16: "Lilac and star and bird twined with the chant of my soul, / There in the fragrant pines and the cedars dusk and dim" (467).

The journey of the poet down into the "fragrant pines" of the cedar swamp is analogous to the descent to the underworld and parallels the journey of Lincoln's coffin to the grave. As one critic has pointed out, the description of Lincoln's funeral draws heavily from the Egyptian iconography of Osiris, Lord of the Underworld.[12] The association, for example, between the coffin and the "yellow-spear'd wheat, every grain from its / shroud in the dark-brown fields uprisen" which it passes during the train journey approximates rather exactly the depictions of Osiris lying in a coffin with spears of wheat shooting out from the corpse. So also may the processions, dirges, torches, bells, and perfume be associated with the rites celebrating the descent of Osiris to the underworld. The fact that Whitman chooses a fragrant cedar forest for the poet's journey in the poem may also be significant in the Egyptian context, since the coffin Osiris was made of a cedar tree in Abydos which emitted a powerful incense. All of these motifs are chosen as symbols of resurrection, including the imagery of the evening star, which Whitman had watched passing into the "netherward black of the night" a month before the tragedy of Lincoln's death (Section 8; 461). As we have seen in the first chapter, the evening star is also a conventional icon of the hero journey; it symbolized the Sumerian Goddess Inanna, who, like Osiris, went down into the netherworld to return three days afterwards.

The poet's descent into the cedar swamp parallels Lincoln's journey and is saturated with the imagery of the netherworld. The descent begins at twilight, as the poet lingers with "the lustrous star" of his "departing comrade" to wonder how he shall sing "for the dead," what "perfume" he shall bring to the grave, and what "pictures" he shall "hang on the chamber walls" (Sections 10-11; 462). The perfume will be the lilac sprig, and the pictures and song those created by the poet in the ensuing stanzas, which portray the vast "unconscious scenery" of America, and which translate the song of the "gray-brown bird" amidst the cedar swamp. Hence, the poet's descent into "netherward black of the night" forest parallels the descent of Lincoln and the evening star, and becomes a symbol of poesis. In Section 14, the poet flees into "the hiding receiving night" with "the knowledge of death" on one side of him, and "the thought of death close-walking the other side of me" (464). His journey takes him "Down to the shores of the water" on a path that runs by the swamp "To the solemn shadowy cedars and ghostly pines so still" (464). The terrain is mythological, "ghostly," "solemn," and "secluded." And it rings with the "sacred knowledge of death" communicated by the "carol of the bird," which Whitman calls a "carol of death." It may be significant to note that Isis, the Egyptian angel of death, often depicted on sarcophagi, and ultimately responsible for the resurrection of Osiris, was portrayed as a woman with magnificent wings spread above the coffin. In Section 14 of Whitman's "Lilacs," death is a "*Dark mother*" whose "*sure-enwinding arms of cool-enfolding death*" (464-65) gather the dead into their embrace (the interior ceiling of nearly all Egyptian coffins and sepulchres show Isis or Nut, arms extended to embrace the dying god).

The song the bird sings "From deep secluded recesses, / From the fragrant cedars and the ghostly pines so still," is a carol celebrating "*lovely and soothing death*," as a "*strong deliveress*" (464-65). The netherworld is a place where poems are born, where the bird-songs of the souls of the dead may be heard -- hawk cry for the Egyptians, "sky-lark" and "all the little birds that are" for Coleridge, and "grey-brown bird" (or mockingbird) for Whitman. The poet records the "pure deliberate notes spreading filling the night," as "panoramas of visions" disclose the world of the dead in Section 15. For, as we have seen, the underworld is also a temenos of the imagination, the powers of which are activated by the journey. Whitman sees "as in noiseless dreams" the armies of the Civil War, with the "torn and bloody" bodies of the "battle corpses" vividly evoked. He remains among the dead, as he had during his years as a nurse in Washington, until "the powerful psalm in the night" passes, and the visions with it, so that the journey may come full circle. At the end of the poem the poet returns to its beginning, just as the hero returns to the point of departure, and just as sonata form ends with a recapitulation. Lilacs come back in the spring, the evening star becomes the morning star, and the song of the "hermit bird" records the endlessly passing cycles of the journey.

Mark Twain

Mark Twain's *Adventures of Huckleberry Finn*, generally regarded as a masterpiece of American naturalism, is structured exactly along the lines of the hero journey, beginning and ending in the same town, with the trip down the river and the revelations of the underworld in between. Huck's journey begins when his ghostly father Pap abducts him from the secure domesticity of Widow Watson's home, and takes him to the ramshackle hut in the woods. What follows is a sequence of realistically rendered episodes of life along the Mississippi, which are nevertheless structured by the mythological motifs associated with the journey through the land of the dead. What brings all of the random episodes together, as we will see, is in fact the theme of death, as Huck travels through the dark shadowland of American life along the river.

Allusions to the mythology of the Hades journey begin with Huck's ingenious escape from his abusive and drunken father, who routinely beats the boy during fits of delirium tremens. One day when Pap leaves home, Huck stages his own mock murder so successfully that everyone in town thinks he is dead. The symbolism of the doorway is the first archetypal motif to surface in this scene, when Huck takes an axe and smashes up the door of the hut, hacking it up "considerable" to make it look like robbers have forced entry (656). Then he fetches a pig and hacks its throat with the axe, lying it down of the ground to bleed on the site of the 'murder,' and leaving a trail of its blood along the path down to the river, to make it seem that the robbers have dragged Huck's body down. To add to the illusion, he drags a bag full of rocks along the path to create the impression of his dead body having been heavily dragged along. To complete the picture Huck tears out some of his hair and sticks it to the bloodied axe, and then slits a whole in a bag of cornmeal to leave a little track of grain leading off to a nearby lake (in order to simulate a motif of theft).

All of these details, curiously chosen as they are, have a mythological background associated with the nekyia. Pigs were ritually sacrificed during the Eleusinian mysteries celebrating the descent and return of Persephone (Harrison 152-54); and in one version of the myth, a herd of pigs covers up the tracks left by Hades after he carries her down to the underworld (Kerenyi, *Gods* 243). The climax of the ceremonies apparently involved the elevation of a grain of wheat, and Demeter, of course, was a Goddess of Grain, which, as a symbol of death and rebirth, survives in the New Testament. So Huck has followed a worn path down into Hades, and in spending "three days and nights" (662) on the island in the Mississippi where he takes refuge, he is fulfilling the archetypal commandment which stipulates that the crucified deity shall spend three nights in the dark before his resurrection. During that time, many of the details of the narrative allude to the underworld: Huck thinks of himself as a "corpse" (661), the thunder rolls grumbling "towards the under side of the world" (672), and when Jim finds Huck he thinks he has found a "ghos," and to avoid harm says he "'awluz liked dead people'" (288). It should be noted that in many traditional iconographies (Celtic, Greek, Norse) the realm of the dead was an island. The island is also inhabited by snakes that Huck chases through the "grass and flowers" (662), eventually finding a snake-skin at the top of a ridge (675), and birds, whose pattern of flight Jim interprets as an omen of death (668). Now the serpent's sting has long been associated with the mysteries of death and rebirth (as in *Gilgamesh* and Genesis), and birds have been the traditional denizens of the underworld since Enkidu's dream and Egyptian tomb iconography.

A more realistic representation of the underworld comes during a night when Huck and Jim explore the river after a flood, and find a house of the dead floating along in the darkness. From this moment on, nearly all of the episodes in the novel reflect naturalistic scenes of death and violence, as Huck navigates the dark and often criminal "underside of the world" (672). First Jim finds a dead man in the floating house who is "too gashly" to show Huck (673; Chapter 9). We later learn it is Pap, a significant detail since in earlier epics, like Virgil's *Aeneid*, the hero encounters his father (or some other relative in near death narratives). Then Huck and Jim sneak up onto a wreck carrying murderers and thieves, who are planning to kill one of their group (Chapter 12). After they lose their own and steal the robber's raft, Huck get lost in a fog so dense that he says he has "no more idea which way I was going than a dead man" (704; Chapter 15). When the dense fog causes them to miss the town of Cairo (an old necropolis, be it noted), Jim blames it on "'dat rattle-snake skin'" (Chapter 16; 716).

As the raft continues to float down the Mississippi, the allusions to death and the underworld continue to predominate the realistically rendered narrative episodes. Shipwreck is a standard icon of the hero journey, and after a steamer smashes their raft, Huck and Jim swim ashore to Colonel Grangerford's house. His family is embroiled in a violent feud with the Sheperdson's which spills over into Church and leaves many dead, while the poems and paintings of the Colonel's daughter are entirely devoted to the dead, including the famous parody, "Stephen Dowling Bots" (725; Chapter 17). The subsequent episodes devoted to the phony Duke and Dauphin represent the criminal underworld of the confidence men of the 19th century, but mortal moments continue to prevail: in the squalid Arkansas town where the

Duke and Dauphin do Shakespeare and cheat the audience, Colonel Sherburn shoots Billy Boggs, and Jim is painted "a dead dull solid blue, like a man that's been drownded nine days" (779; Chapter 24); and during the Wilks family scam, the Duke and Dauphin impersonate the dead brother Peter to get the inheritance, and a long passage is devoted to the corpse in the parlour, the funeral sermon, and the subsequent exhumation during a lightning storm in the graveyard (823; Chapter 29).

It comes therefore as no surprise that when Huck reaches the Phelps farm, from which his return home will be effected, the language of death and rebirth continues in its position of prominence as the central metaphor of the hero journey. When he arrives at the farm on Sunday, Huck remarks that

> there was them kind of faint dronings of bugs and flies in the air that makes it seem so lonesome and like everybody's dead and gone; and if a breeze fans along and quivers the leaves, it makes you feel mournful, because you feel like it's spirits whispering -- spirits that's been dead ever so many years -- and you always think they're talking about *you*. As a general thing it makes a body wish *he* was dead, too, and done with it all. (839; Chapter 32).

This passage, along with the many details previously cited, highlight the mythological background of the novel, fusing it with the foreground details to create a uniquely powerful canvas of the hero journey to the underworld in 19th century America. When Huck hears the "dim hum of a spinning wheel," he says "I knowed for certain I wished I was dead -- for that *is* the lonesomest sound in the whole world" (839), but when the Phelps family returns, it is the theme of rebirth from the underworld that strikes the first note: Aunt Sally tells the story of Tom's uncle Silas, who "turned blue all over and died in the hope of a glorious resurrection" (841; Chapter 32). When Aunt Sally finally makes it clear that she mistakes Huck for Tom Sawyer (whose impending visit they are awaiting), Huck says "it was like being born again, I was so glad to find out who I was" (844; Chapter 32). That a spinning wheel initiates these ruminations is surely significant, since the wheel and weaving are both archaic symbols of the cycles of life, death, and rebirth.

And so it is that the return phase of the hero journey begins. Huck's true identity is eventually revealed by Aunt Polly, after the arrival of Tom Sawyer, and after an elaborate plan to free Jim fails (we later learn he has been freed by Widow Watson's will). This revelation leads to a comic reversal of Huck's fortune, who finds that Pap has died and that his inheritance is in the safe keeping of Judge Thatcher. He is then adopted by Aunt Sally, and the return of the hero from the "under side of the world" to "sivilization" is complete.

Charlotte Brontë

Charlotte Brontë's *Villette* begins with that sense of domestic security generally characteristic of the first stage of the hero journey, and quickly moves towards the crisis which catalyzes the separation and departure of the heroine. In this case the threshold crossing takes us over the English Channel (which the narrator, Lucy Snowe, compares to the Styx) to the Continent, and eventually to the little Continental city of Villette, where Lucy Snowe takes up residence in the girl's school which is repeatedly described as an underworld. Her journey is pre-Jungian descent into the archetypal structures of the imagination, as well as a spiritual progress à la Bunyan (Lilly 597). While Fielding's primary interest lay in a rationalization of the myth of the heroic descent into the underworld, Charlotte Brontë seems primarily concerned with a feminine psychologization of the quest romance.[13]

The novel opens with a portrait of domesticity, though with the odd undercurrents that will eventually drag narrator and reader down into the depths of the psyche. It is the "ancient town of Bretton" where Lucy Snowe tells us she visits her godmother Mrs. Bretton twice a year. Lucy is much pleased by the peaceful atmosphere of the large rooms, with "the well-arranged furniture, the wide clear windows, the balcony outside, looking down on a fine antique street, where Sundays and holidays seemed always to abide" (61). While not the Paradise Hall of *Tom Jones*, this little domicile suggests all those comforts of home which are apparently only precariously available to Lucy at home. However, that it is meant to be perceived as paradisal is made clear when Lucy compares the home in Bretton to "a certain pleasant stream, with 'green trees on each bank, and meadows beautified with lilies all the year round'" where Christian and Hopeful sojourn in Bunyan *Pilgrim's Progress* (62).

This relative security and peace is first disrupted by the arrival of a harbinger of darker things to come in the form of a little girl named Paulina, whose situation in life prefigures Lucy's own. She is being left in the care of Mrs. Bretton by her father Mr. Home, on the occasion of the death of her mother, "a very pretty, but a giddy, careless woman, who had neglected her child, and disappointed and disheartened her husband" (62-3). The night of Paulina's arrival is stormy, with a rain lashing the panes, and an "angry and restless" wind (63). Crisis, death, and tempest: all images we have seen frequently associated with the call to adventure in the hero journey, and indeed, Lucy comes to see the little girl in terms which prefigure her own journey to France. The child's "infant visage" evokes the "furrowed face of adult exile," and the room she inhabits seems "haunted" by her ghostly white-clad figure, on the "moonlight nights" when Lucy observes her praying like "some precocious fanatic or untimely saint" (69).

Exile, the encounter with the supernaturalism of a Catholic sensibility, and, even more significantly, the problem of "an overheated and discursive imagination" which Lucy Snowe here pleads "guiltless of" all prefigure Lucy's coming journey to Villette. In addition, however, is the obsession little Polly (as she becomes known in the Bretton home) displays first with the image of her absent father, and then with Graham Bretton, the young man of the household with whom she quickly develops a relationship. While we learn literally nothing about Lucy Snowe's father (on that score she is suspiciously reticent), we will find her later fascinated by Graham Bretton, who reappears in Villette, where little Polly will be replaced by Ginevra Fanshawe as her rival for Graham's affection. Polly's 'father complex' then, which quickly modulates to a fixation on Graham, and the repressed jealousy Lucy consequently feels for Polly, anticipate the central issues of Lucy's journey.

Her heroine's journey is initiated by death: first we learn that her parents have, apparently, died, since Lucy refers to a "heavy tempest" after which she returns home from Bretton, during which time she "must somehow have fallen overboard .... the ship was lost, the crew perished" (95). Her metaphor (sustained throughout the novel) seems to conceal a "bereaved lot" (95) which reduces her to "a faded, hollow-eyed vision" in "mourning-dress" (96). This circumstance compels Lucy to "self-reliance and exertion" (95), i.e., she has to provide for herself. She does so by accepting a position as nurse to the invalid Miss Marchmont, "a woman of fortune" who lives in a "handsome residence" in which Lucy soon becomes "much confined" by the demands of the "rheumatic cripple" (95).

It is the death of Miss Marchmont that finally compels Lucy to escape this confinement and begin her journey. This occurs on a night during which the wind wails at the windows with "an accent keen, piercing, almost articulate to the ear" (97) in a "subtle, searching cry" like the voice "of the Banshee" (98). The call to adventure then, comes from a folkloric death spirit, common in Scotland and Ireland, and will lead Lucy into the underworld. Part of the call, however, is the repressed yearning for romance, stirred up in Lucy by Miss Marchmont's love story, which she tells Lucy the night before she dies. It concerns the premature and tragic death of Frank, who was killed while riding to visit Miss Marchmont on a wild and wintry night when he fell off his horse and was dragged to death by the bridle, Hippolytus like. Hence, a sense of unbridled passion accompanies the spirit of death on this night which compels Lucy Snowe's separation from Miss Marchmont and her departure to London.

After a brief stay in London, Lucy impetuously decides to journey overnight to the Continent, following the prompting of some inner voice which serves as her guide. Accordingly, she sets out from her little London inn at night to the wharf, where a coachmen makes her "alight in the midst of a throng of watermen" (110) who contend for Lucy and her trunk, then row her off over a river "Black ... as a torrent of ink" (111). As the watermen row her along the "sable flood," beneath ships with provocative names like "The Phoenix," Lucy thinks "of the Styx, and of Charon rowing some solitary soul to the Land of Shades" (111). Upon boarding "The Vivid," she is cheated by the watermen. Hence, Charlotte Brontë treats the threshold crossing as a descent to the underworld: the English Channel becomes the Styx, and Europe the underworld. D.H. Lawrence will evoke the same myth for the crossing of the channel in *Women in Love*, and Thomas Mann will have his hero, Gustav von Aschenbach, similarly cheated by a sordid gondolier in *Death in Venice*. It is indeed curious to note, that in both Modernist works, the figure of Hermes -- guide of souls to the underworld, messenger of the gods, god of thieves and travelers, a "bringer of dreams" (14), and "a gate keeper" (15) -- plays a central role.[14] The same is true of *Villette*, as we will see.

One of the characteristics of the god Hermes is his association with travelers who lose their way, and the chance coincidences which lead them back onto the right track.[15] On board "The Vivid," Lucy meets her first guide, one Ginevra Fanshawe, a young English girl returning to school abroad in the little French town of Villette, where Lucy determines to go the day after her arrival on the continent. The continent at night appears to her "like a wide dream-land" (117), and it is interesting to note that Hermes is not only a guide of souls to the underworld, but also a god of those dreams and visions which he can evoke with his magic wand.[16] Throughout the rest of *Villette*, these hermetic associations linking the dream and the underworld will remain relevant, as Lucy's imagination continues in the same highly activated state witnessed by her first vision of the European Continent, a vision which leads her to remark that "Day-dreams are delusions of the demon" (118).

From the extreme sea-sickness (the threshold battle of the channel crossing) of her night-sea journey, to the night spent in the confining quarters of a small French inn, Lucy continues her journey by carriage to Villette, arriving again under cover of darkness in the strange city. The details of her arrival extend the allusions to the underworld during the channel crossing: she calls the little city an "unknown bourne"

(122) (perhaps echoing Hamlet's famous description of death as the "undiscovered country from whose bourn no traveler returns" (3.2.1)), and laments the "thick fog and small dense rain -- darkness that might almost be felt" as she passes "through a gate where soldiers were stationed" (122). The imagery of darkness, fog, and the city gate links the scene to many of the heroic descents into Hades examined in earlier chapters, and look forward to a consistent recurrence of doorway imagery in the rest of the novel, as we will see.

In this arrival scene, another characteristic motif of the *nekyia* is soon evoked, as Lucy gets lost in the labyrinth of city streets. An Englishman appears to guide her towards a refuge for the evening; he turns out later to be John Graham Bretton, so the coincidence is a significant anticipation of the nature and development of their relationship. Dr. Bretton does not go so far as to chaperone Lucy to her final destination, only to direct her in such a manner that she soon loses her way. Indeed, her guide is only a ghostlike presence beside her in "the double gloom of trees and fog," yet Lucy determines to "follow his tread .... through continual night, to the world's end" (125), ironic words suggestive of the infernal nature of her destination. After traversing the Park, the "true young English gentleman" directs Lucy down a broad street to some steps which descend between two lamps down into a narrower street below, at the bottom of which, he says, she will find her inn (125).

One remembers the association of night and fog in the Homeric description of the Kimmerian land of shades at the beginning of Book 11 of the *Odyssey*, and the imagery of mist surrounding the epiphanies of Hermes (the young god of travelers and of the dead), both in the Homeric Hymn and most particularly in Thomas Mann's *Buddenbrooks* and *Death in Venice*. In addition to these archetypal motifs, Brontë has Dr. Bretton instruct Lucy to "descend" into a narrow street "below" the grand avenue. As Lucy proceeds, however, she is frightened by two shady and mustachioed men who come "suddenly from behind the pillars" of a large "portico" at the entrance to some large "palace or church" (125). She suspects these men are thieves, and their association with theft and with doorways is relevant to the cluster of Hermetic imagery in the novel, since Hermes is both a god of thieves, and, as the Homeric Hymn says, "a gate keeper" (15). It is fascinating to reflect that Thomas Mann will use the city landscape in a similar way to evoke the mythic descent into Hades (a journey to which Gustav von Aschenbach will be called by a strange character who appears briefly between the pillars leading into a cemetery), as will Jean Cocteau in his film *Orphée*, in which, as we will see below, the imagery of doorways, avenues, and piazzas plays a central role.

The two men who emerge from behind the pillars of a portico in this scene scare Lucy into losing her way; she must retrace her steps until she comes "to an old and worn flight" of steps which she descends into a narrow street (126). But instead of finding an inn at the bottom of the street, she comes to a "light burning over the door of a rather large house, which turns out to be the "'Pensionnat de Demoiselles,'" which Ginevra Fanshawe had mentioned to Lucy during the channel crossing, a coincidence Lucy attributes to Providence and to a Fate which masters her will and directs her actions (126). After she has "rung the door-bell" and stood waiting beneath the "door-lamp," the portresse opens the doors and conducts Lucy to a salon; here she sits "with her eyes fixed on the door -- a great white folding door, with gilt mouldings" (126). All remains quiet, with the "white doors ... closed and motionless" until Madame Beck, the headmistress of the school, appears suddenly at her elbow: "No ghost stood beside me, nor anything of spectral-aspect" (127), Lucy then assures us, but spectral apparitions will play a central role in the novel from this point onwards.

The imagery of portals and doorways (words for which have occurred eight times in this sequence of passageways into the "strange," "foreign," "unknown," and "odd" world of the Pensionnat), and the presence of Hermes in his various aspects continue to inform the novel. Madame Beck epitomizes the truly "un-English" nature of this "foreign land" (132), as she presides over her bevy of young female students: "she haunted the house in her wrapping gown, shawl, and soundless slippers" (133-34), spying on students and faculty alike, and taking great pains to surreptitiously examine every detail of Lucy's clothing while she lies sleeping in the dormitory on her first night. She so impresses Lucy with this rigorous "'Surveillance'" (135) that Lucy is lead to pronounce Madame Beck "the right sort of Minos in petticoats" (134).

Minos, of course, is one of the Classical judges of Hades; the other, Rhadamanthus, will be alluded to later in the novel by Dr. Bretton; furthermore, the centrality of espionage, "trickery and deception" in the novel (Lilly 610) indicates the presence of Hermes the thief.[17] Hence we can infer that in entering the world of dormitory and classroom, Lucy is descending into a world in which Madame Beck glides on "'souliers de silence' ... through the house watching and spying everywhere, peering through every key-hole, listening behind every door" (136). In the Homeric Hymn, Hermes slips "through the keyhole" of his cavern home "like an autumnal breeze in outer form, or airy mist" (146-47). In *Villette*, doorways remain crucial symbols of transition, as when Lucy stands between two doorways on the day which marks a transition in her life from menial governess to school teacher: Madame Beck has summoned her to fill the spot vacated by an ill professor of English, and pauses to scrutinize Lucy in a "large square hall between the dwelling-house and the pensionnat" (140). "'Will you,' said she [Madame Beck], 'go backward or forward?' indicating with her hand, first, the small door of communication with the dwelling-house, and then the great double portals of the classes or school rooms" (141).

Choosing to go forward through the "great double portals," Lucy advances "to the closed school-room door" (142), which she opens in order to enter the battleground. The classroom is in itself a kind of hell, waiting to be harrowed during "the first few difficult lessons, given amidst peril and on the edge of a moral volcano, that rumbled [Lucy remarks] under my feet and sent sparks and hot fumes into my eyes" (146). A trinity of demons ("Mesdemoiselles Blanch, Virginie, and Angélique" (143)) needs to be dispelled, the last indeed exorcised by incarceration in the closet which Lucy skillfully locks her in on the first day! The doorway symbolism surfaces again later when Lucy overhears a distressing scene in the cabinet of the Portresse. Standing "close by the door" of the cabinet, "that door half-unclosed," Lucy overhears the "soft, deep, pleading tone" of Dr. John, who emerges distraught by "Some mortification, some strong vexation," which Lucy observes while hidden by "the open door" (168). She infers the presence of some "torturer" in the house who has the Doctor "in her power" (169), but we don't realize until later that this tormentress is Ginevra Fanshawe, not the Portresse who presides Cerberus like over her little cabinet, demanding her sops for admission into what appears to be an inferno of frustration for Dr. John.

Other infernal settings in the school include the garden where Lucy takes refuge behind the building, and the attic in which she is locked by M. Paul Emmanuel to learn the lines of a play to be performed during a Fête. The garden has its ghost, as every underworld must. This one is a nun buried beneath "a Methuselah of a pear-tree, dead," at the foot of which lies a "slab, smooth, hard, and black," which legend reports to be "the portal of a vault, imprisoning deep beneath that ground ... the bones of a girl whom a monkish conclave of the drear middle ages had here buried alive, for some sin against her vow. Her shadow it was that tremblers had feared, through long generations after her poor frame was dust" (172). During the "verge of twilight" (173), Lucy takes refuge in an alley adjacent to this tree and tomb, a place forbidden to the pupils and appealing to Lucy for its "seclusion," "gloom," and "shady" isolation (174).

Here she sits one night "on the hidden seat reclaimed from fungi and mould," and lapses, while thinking of her childhood and future, into a "catalepsy and a dead trance" (175). Her calm is interrupted by the occasion of "a small box of white and colored ivory" being dropped from a dormer window of the boy's school across the alley, which

proves to contain violets and a love letter which Lucy reads, and which
a frantic Dr. John soon races through the "garden door" (179) to
retrieve. In so doing, he penetrates "the 'forbidden walk,'" and encounters Lucy "like some ghost" sitting on the seat retrieved from the
rot of the garden (180). Hermes, it should be remembered, is a
messenger god frequently associated with love affairs ("the ever smitten
Hermes" Keats calls him), and with twilight. It is also relevant to note
his association with the medical profession: his caduceus staff is still to
be found on apothecary shops in France, and the mercury of the
thermometer is one of many manifestations of his presence in Thomas
Mann's *The Magic Mountain*. Hence, the appearance of Dr. John at the
twilight hour in mad pursuit of a love message dropped into Lucy's
haunted garden retreat all reinforce the association between Hermes,
guide of souls to the underworld, and Dr. John, established earlier in the
novel.

    Another setting associated with the realm of shades is the attic in
which Lucy is locked up by M. Paul to learn her lines for the play that
is performed during the festival held each year for parents and teachers.
Lucy is cast at the last minute to play one of the male characters, and,
with his usual irascible and imperious manner, M. Paul confines Lucy
all day long to the attic to prepare for the role. The gesture is fully
characteristic of M. Paul, who, while occasionally appealing for his
directness and honest naiveté, is generally presented as the Hades of the
novel, the "savage" lord of its underworld: his hair is dark and "shorn
close as raven down" (277); "a more despotic little man .... never filled
a professor's chair" (278); he is "dark, acerb, and caustic" (281); and he
is subject to terrifying fits of "surplus irritation" in the classroom,
capable of reducing all those present to tears (412). Indeed, he is nearly
Satanic, as ubiquitous and invisible as the devil himself: a "dreadful"
little man, Lucy says, "a mere sprite of caprice and ubiquity: one never
knew either his whim or his whereabout" (322).[18]

    It is appropriate then, that on the day of the festival play, he
should lock Lucy up in a darkened attic like Persephone abducted by
Hades. On this occasion M. Paul is described as "A dark little man .... a
harsh apparition, with his close-shorn, black head" (197). With a
"vexed, fiery, and searching eye," he reenacts the abduction by dragging
Lucy up into the attic: "Without being allowed time or power to
deliberate," Lucy tells us, "I found myself in the same breath convoyed
along as in a species of whirlwind, up stairs, up two pair of stairs, nay
actually up three (for this fiery little man seemed as by instinct to know
his way everywhere" (203). The repetition of the adjective "fiery" during
this description adds a devilish touch to M. Paul's character which is
adhered to throughout the course of the novel, as in a later scene when
he chastises Lucy during an evening study hall for wearing 'worldly'

clothing: during that later scene in "The Watchguard" chapter, M. Paul is described as "flint and tender" which "struck and took fire directly" (416) as his eyes "blaze" and he waxes "hotter" at Lucy (417).

Accordingly, the attic room in "The Fête" is presented as an inferno in which the demonic M. Paul locks Lucy, before he "vanished" (203): "it was hot as Africa; as in winter, it was always cold as Greenland"; it is "tenanted by rats, by black beetles, and by cockroaches"; and "the ghostly Nun of the garden had once been seen here" (204). Here Lucy is condemned to spend her "holiday, fasting and in prison" (205), until her "throne was abdicated" when M. Paul repeats his abduction, only in the inverse direction, "down -- down -- down to the very kitchen. I thought I should have gone to the cellar" (206).

But the genuine inferno turns out to be the dormitory in which Lucy sleeps, and in which a kind of nervous breakdown begins which will inaugurate another transition in Lucy's life. During "The Long Vacation" (Chapter 15) in September and October, Lucy is left alone in the haunted halls of the school building. These early fall months are the ones associated in the folklore of Brittany and Northern France with "Toussaint, in the Black Month," i.e., November 1st, when "the storytelling begins" about "the year's trafficking between this world and *that*" (Byatt 382-83). It is around this time that Lucy had arrived a year previous in Villette, and which now marks, in many details of the narration, her most literal descent into the otherworld.

Confined to the "lifeless," "vast and void," "desolate premises" of the school and its "forsaken garden" (228), Lucy is left alone to care for a deformed child. Its "warped" body, "aimless malevolence," and "propensity to evil" require a "constant vigilance" that crushes Lucy "with a deadlier paralysis" than she has yet experienced (229). This paralysis yields to a "peculiarly agonizing depression ... succeeded by physical illness" (231). Afterwards, "the equinoctial storms began; and for nine dark and wet days," Lucy tells us she "lay in a strange fever of the nerves and blood" (231). Sleep then brings "an avenging dream," an "unknown anguish" with "the terror, the very tone of a visitation from eternity" (231). The dream comes "Between twelve and one" and night, and is compared to a cup "mixed for mortal lips" with a "black, strong, strange" brew "drawn from no well, but filled up seething from a bottomless and boundless sea" (231). Lucy tells nothing more of the content of the dream; only that "Death challenged me to engage its unknown terrors" (232).

It is fascinating to note some of the mythological details suggested by this linkage of the dream and the underworld. The fact that Lucy's ordeal occupies "nine dark and wet days" curiously evokes the Norse myth of Odin, who, in his quest for the runes of wisdom, "hung for nine days and nights on the World Tree," enduring "something which closely resembles the visionary experience of death and resurrection" (Davidson 47). Lucy's metaphorical account of her visionary dream of death as drinking from a bitter cup also suggests Odin's winning of the mead, a "drink of inspiration" mixing honey and blood which "could give to him who drank the power to compose poetry, or to speak words of wisdom" (Davidson 46-7). To seek this hidden knowledge, Odin "also consulted the dead" (Davidson 47), as Lucy seems to do in this dream.

It is a dream that intensifies her poetic powers of vision and wisdom, and which precipitates a modern *nekyia*. For one evening shortly afterwards Lucy succumbs to the "solitude and stillness of the long dormitory": "the ghastly white beds were turning into spectres -- the coronal of each became a death's head, huge and sunbleached -- dead dreams of an elder world and mightier race lay frozen in their wide gaping eye-holes" (232). This powerful vision of Lucy's ancestral dead (the Brontë's Haworth lies in the North of England, a region still bearing abundant remnants of Nordic influence) inspires a panic of escape, as she resolves to get "out from under this house-roof, which was crushing as the slab of a tomb" (232), and to go forth into the city. These details explicitly identify the school as the underworld, a tomb lying beneath the stone slab of the roof, so that there can no longer be any doubt about Charlotte Brontë's myth of choice for the novel as a whole: first Lucy escapes England by crossing a channel compared to the river Styx, only to be imprisoned in the dormitory and attic of a school which is compared to a tomb.

The metaphor continues when Lucy collapses in the street on the same night, after visiting the confessional of the local cathedral, significantly located on the "Rue des Mages" (235), i. e., Street of the Magus. Leaving the cathedral, Lucy gets lost in a labyrinth again, becoming "involved in a part of the city with which I was not familiar; it was the old part, and full of narrow streets of picturesque, ancient, and mouldering houses" among which she "got enmeshed in a network of turns unknown" (235-36). At this point the tempest intensifies, and while trying to "reach the porch of a great building near ... the mass of frontage and the giant spire turned black and vanished, " after which Lucy "seemed to pitch headlong down an abyss" (236).[19]

The abyss into which Lucy pitches here is a psychological underworld of dream and "trance," "Memory" and "Imagination" (237). It is a heroic journey of the "Spirit" separated temporarily from "Substance" (237), much like a shamanic initiation. As Lucy wakes up from her "swoon," she wonders "into what region, amongst what strange beings" has she wandered (237). All seems "spectral" in this liminal condition; she "should have understood what we call a ghost, as well as I did the commonest object," Lucy tells us (237). While "Still half dreaming," Lucy examines the pale walls, on "which a slight but endless garland of azure forget-me-nots ran mazed and bewildered," and she sees herself in a gilded mirror, "spectral; my eyes larger and more hollow, my hair darker than was natural, by contrast with my thin and ashen face" (238) and her fingers "now so skeleton-like" (239).

The details here (Lucy is "mazed and bewildered," "spectral," "ashen," "skeleton-like," and apprehensive of ghosts) clearly suggest a very literal descent into an underworld which Lucy attempts to pass off as "a dream, a fever-fit" (239). But as she gradually ascends from the depths of her swoon, what at first seemed "an unknown room in an unknown house" slowly resolves itself into the little "manoir" in which Dr. John Graham Bretton and his mother have taken up residence, just outside the city gates of Villette. Dr. John had chanced upon Lucy after her collapse near the cathedral, and returned home with her. He does not immediately recognize her as the Lucy Snowe of his adolescent years in Bretton, and only gradually is this important discovery revealed to the reader through Lucy's eyes. Such revelations, based on dream-like states of mind and serendipitous occurrences, are characteristic of the sort of hero journey presided over by Hermes, god of travelers, dreams, death, and love. Indeed, many commentaries have linked Hermes with the kind of synchronistic events (chance revelations of meaningful but acausal connections between internal states of mind and external events) which abound in *Villette*.[20]

But the sense of revelation appropriate to the initiation stage of the hero journey goes deeper, in this section of the novel, into "what lies below," where the "secrets of the spirit He gave" manifest themselves in the form of a visionary experience (252). In an extraordinary passage (one written afterall for a secularized Protestant audience), Lucy audaciously attempts to communicate an encounter with an Angel, the climax of her personal *nekyia*. Appropriately enough, it is Azrael, the Islamic angel of death, which Lucy evokes. Since divine disclosure is so characteristic of this stage of the hero journey, I give Lucy's vision below, as it modulates from the healing angel of the pool of Bethesda, to the avenging angel of death:[21]

> Thousands lie round the pool, weeping and despairing, to see it, through slow years, stagnant. Long are the 'times' of Heaven: the orbits of angel messengers seem wide to mortal vision; they may en-ring ages: the cycle of one departure and return may clasp unnumbered generations; and dust, kindling to brief suffering life, and through pain, passing back to dust, may meanwhile perish out of memory again, and yet again. To how many maimed and mourning millions is the first and sole angel visitant, him easterns call Azrael. (252)

The renewed acquaintance with Dr. John Graham Bretton, catalyzed by Lucy's descent into the abyss of her own unconscious (the climactic revelation of which is the epiphany of Azrael), begins a transformation in her life, as she is temporarily liberated from the sepulchral prison of Madame Beck's school for girls. Lucy briefly enjoys the healing company of Dr. John and his mother, and diverts herself with such amusements as the concert hall and gallery. But when she returns to Madame Beck's establishment in an early November drizzle, that same "heavy door" which she had anxiously awaited the opening off a year before crashes to, as if "an axe had fallen" (306), and she is confined once again in Hades, like Persephone returning after her springtime idyll. Every Hades needs its ghosts and demons, as a counterbalance to the angels (hence conferring an intimation of wholeness), and the narrative is quick to provide them after Lucy returns to her deathly domicile.

The ghost appears in the garret to which Lucy retreats to read her first letter from Graham, and the demon materializes during the dramatic performance of a famous actress which Lucy witnesses with the good Dr. John. To read the letter from Graham, Lucy must procure a key and ascend to the "worm-eaten door" of "the black, cold garret" into which she 'dives' after shutting the "garret door" (324). The door symbolism resurfaces, and the choice of the verb ("dived") is significant, since it provides another image of the underworld in the novel consistent with earlier metaphors of descent: her "bereaved lot" (95) in Chapter 4 ("Miss Marchmont") had been described as falling "over-board" during a "heavy tempest" and drowning in a "rush and saltness of briny waves" (94); during the channel crossing, Lucy had "faltered down into the cabin" beneath the deck, where she became "excessively sick" (118); and the room where she convalesces with the Brettons (Chapter 17: "La Terrasse"), following her plunge into the abyss, is described as "a cave in the sea," a "submarine home" where dolphins and mermaids cavort with the "half-drowned life-boat man" beneath "the upper world" inhabited by Graham and his mother (254-55).

All these settings invoke the cold dark dangers of the depths into which Lucy now dives in the garret to read Graham's letter. There Lucy senses the presence of "wicked things .... evil influences haunting the air" of the "vast solitary garret" (325). From the "direction of the black recess haunted by malefactor cloaks" something glides out to "the middle of that ghostly chamber" which Lucy describes as "an image like -- a NUN" (325). She runs downstairs for help and returns with Madame Beck and Dr. John, who attributes the "visitation bearing a spectral character" in the "dismal, perishing sepulchral garret -- that dungeon under the leads smelling of damp and mould," to Lucy's "highly nervous state" (329). The Nun, he concludes, is a "case of spectral illusion: I fear, following on and resulting from long-continued mental conflict" (330). Lucy too ends up wondering "whether that strange thing was of this world, or of a realm beyond the grave; or whether indeed it was only the child of malady, and I of that malady the prey" (333).

The fact that, as we will later learn, the ghost is a combined product of both worlds (i.e., of this world's practical trickery and of Lucy's exacerbated imagination), and that during this scene the letter from Dr. John is apparently briefly stolen, suggests the presence of Hermes in the haunted, sepulchral garret -- Hermes, god of thieves, messengers (from the gods of the unconscious), of souls descending to Hades, and of dreamlike ("spectral") illusions cast by his magic wand. The nun, of course, is an underworldly reflection of Lucy's own condition: both are buried alive between the walls of the school, and both frustrated by forbidden and repressed desires. Hermes, however, is also (for Thomas Mann at least) a patron of the arts of writing (which involve trickery, deception, and illusion). Hence the demon who surfaces in the next chapter of *Villette* is more an archetypal reflection of Lucy's creativity than she is of any buried sexual desire.

The epiphany of the demon in "Vashti" parallels that of the Angel Azrael in "La Terrasse." After the episode in the garret, Dr. John and his mother plan some therapeutic relief for Lucy. Graham calls to take her to the performance of a tragedy by a fading but once famous actress of the day. The occasion turns quite literally into an inferno, as a fire breaks out in the theatre shortly after midnight, at the climax of the tragedy. All during the performance Lucy had noted the demonic nature of the actress: "in each of her eyes sat a devil," Lucy tells us. "These evil forces bore her through the tragedy .... how wildly they shook her with their passions of the pit! They wrote HELL on her straight haughty brow. They tuned her voice to the note of torment. They writhed her regal fact to a demoniac mask" (339). It is "a mighty revelation" of a woman "torn by seven devils: devils which cried sore and rent the tenement they haunted, but still refused to be exorcised" (339). The background of the scene etches her white figure "like Death" (339), and, during the climax, Lucy says that Vashti's "hair, flying loose in revel or war, is still an angel's hair, and glorious under a halo. Fallen, insurgent, banished, she remembers the heaven where she rebelled" (340).

I emphasize the details of the narration here because they illustrate the aesthetic coherence of this novel, which continually returns to the myth of the underworld to provide shape and significance to individual scenes, and to relate them to the whole. Brontë might well have chosen some other play for the performance, and might well have chosen not to bring the infernal elements of the description out into such sharp relief.

The fact that she didn't indicates the importance of the myth of the descent for the novel as a whole, and in its parts. For this fallen angel is clearly meant to be seen as the counterpart of the earlier vision of the Angel; taken together, Angel and Demon, both revealed splendidly during the heroine's journey, give a sense of wholeness, of a fully rounded archetypal framework for the discovery of Lucy's identity. One without the other would be an incomplete portrait of the human psyche, and would indicate a failure of integration. As an actress playing the role of a biblical Queen who challenges the patriarchal order, Vashti clearly represents the deepest impulses driving Lucy in her quest for psychic integrity.

After the Vashti performance, Lucy spends seven long weeks entombed in the seclusion of the school, which she calls a "snow-sepulchre" (348). Her time is mostly spent awaiting the post hour, "much as a ghost-seer might wait his spectre" (353). She begins to emerge "thin as a shadow" (350), like a "long-buried prisoner disinterred" (356), following a letter from Mrs. Bretton. But the letter summoning her back to life eventually yields the depressing revelation of Dr. John Graham Bretton's increasing interest in Paulina Home de Bassompierre, the little Polly of the beginning of the novel who now returns as "The Little Countess." This revelation of Graham's new romantic interest compels Lucy to bury the letters John had written her, which she chooses to do at the base of the old pear tree in the garden beneath which the nun is buried. After digging out a hole near its root, Lucy wraps the box with the letters "in its winding sheet" (380), then sits leaning against the tree, "like any other mourner beside a newly sodden grave" (381). This ritual catalyzes another manifestation from the "realm beyond the grave" (333), as the Nun reappears as "a tall, sable-robed, snowy veiled woman" (381).

All that is now needed to complete the tableau is a dark and domineering Hades figure, a Lord of the underworld to match its demonic Angel and Queen. In Volume 3 of the novel M. Paul assumes this central role. Like Vashti, M. Paul is frequently associated with the fires of hell. In Chapter 28, "The Watchguard," during an evening study hall, his "sudden despotism" imposes itself by ardent, "fiery action" (414). When Lucy angers him by moving away from the work-desk where he sits down beside her, "flint and tinder that he was! he struck and took fire directly" (416). While reading "'un drame de Williams Shackspire; le faux dieu" (416), Lucy's cool response provokes him into a "blaze" as he "waxed hotter at the north pole to which he had voluntarily exiled himself" (417) at the far end of the room.

The next day, during the fête in his honor, he sits "enthroned on his estrade" (423) like a little Lord Hades, peering into the dark, "barren places of the spirit" of all those before him:

yes, and its perverted tendencies, and its hidden false curves --
all that men and women would not have known -- the twisted
spine, the mal-formed limb that was born with them, and far
worse, the stain or disfigurement they have perhaps brought
on themselves. (424).

It is certainly appropriate for Hades to peer into the shadow side of
things, yet Lucy finds M. Paul "wicked" for doing so (428), and her
description of him harps on his infernal characteristics: "he was
spiteful, acrid, savage; and as a natural consequence, detestably ugly"
(428). He is a "wicked venomous man," a "hissing cockatrice," a
"monster of malice" who "fiendishly" smiles into his handkerchief
while attacking Lucy for apparently neglecting to make a present for
him on his festival day (428-29). She herself begins to feel "hot and
angry" (429) when she descends later that evening into the school room,
only to discover "the freakish, friendly, cigar-loving phantom" (431)
snooping into her desk.

The sense of ubiquity, penetration of intellect, despotism, fire, and
darkness had been well established in the novel before this chapter, and
continues afterwards in the chapter called "M. Paul." Though a
temporary truce had been proclaimed after Lucy finally presented him
with his festive gift, M. Paul soon reverts to his former self: he
remains "acutely irritable; and besides, his veins were dark with a livid
belladonna tincture, the essence of jealousy" (437). Because his
"absolutism verged on tyranny," Lucy compares him to Napoleon
(438), a fantasy that suggests a projection of the archetype of the Self.
As Persephone was by Hades, so Lucy is confined in the broiling
quarters of the underworld by this tyrannical little king.

After a particularly unpleasant lesson, M. Paul forces Lucy to
remain in the classroom to be lectured at. During this scene, the
imagery of the inferno is enriched by alchemical associations: M. Paul
acts upon Lucy like "corrosive aquafortis" (439), and he sits her down
beside an overheated, glowing stove: "this salamander -- for whom no
room ever seemed too hot -- sitting down between my desk and the
stove -- a situation in which he ought to have felt broiled, but did not --
proceeded to confront me with -- a Greek quotation!" (442). Aggravated
to the point of "fever," Lucy marvels that "he was not hot, with the
stove close at his back," she wonders about "the natural history of
salamanders," and she concludes that "sitting in an oven did not agree
with me" (446).

The salamander is frequently depicted in alchemical illustrations as
a symbol of the philosopher's stone being purified through the
operation of *calcinatio*: "'Our stone is an astral fire ... which as a true

salamander receives its nativity, is nourished, and grows in the
elementary fire'" (qtd. in Edinger 100). Jung discusses "the 'central fire'
by whose warmth all nature germinates and grows, because in it dwells
the Mercurial serpent, the salamander whom the fire does not consume,
and the dragon that feeds on fire" (441). Here we should remember that
M. Paul literally feeds on fire (his cigars a constant presence in the
novel), and that Hermes (the Mercurial serpent) is the archetypal patron
of alchemy. Most interestingly, Jung notes that "the union of
consciousness (Sol) with its feminine counterpart the unconscious
(Luna) ... produces poisonous animals such as the dragon, serpent,
basilisk and toad" (144), a "milder form of which is the salamander" (n.
264, 144). M. Paul had first been described in Volume Three as a
"basilisk" perched on his throne (423), and is frequently experienced as
"venomous" and "acerbic.".[22]

The relevance of the alchemical imagery here is that it provides
another metaphor for the goal and purpose of the heroine's journey: like
the descent into Hades, "the entire alchemical procedure for uniting the
opposites ... could just as well represent the individuation process of a
single individual" (Jung 555). The central tasks of the individuation
process, those of reconciling opposites within the psyche and of
integrating the archetypal contents of the unconscious, are symbolized,
then, by alchemy and by the descent into the underworld, which
accounts for their presence in this wonderful novel about a woman in
quest of her Self. Since the Self embraces the totality of the identity --
conscious and unconscious, male and female, light and dark -- Lucy's
journey necessarily involves wrestling with the tensions between these
polarities within. Externally, these polarities are personified by the
many gender crossings in the novel in which the opposites merge: Lucy
dresses as a man during the performance of a play, Colonel de Hamal
dresses as a dead nun, Madame Walravens has a silver beard, M. Paul is
moody and more at home with women than with men, and etc.[23]

Before discussing the importance of the reconciliation between
opposites in relation to the overall structure of the novel, however, we
must conclude our analysis of the descent to the underworld in one final
scene. In Chapter 34, entitled "Malevola," Lucy is sent off by Madame
Beck on an errand that takes her "deep into the old and grim Basse-
Ville" (479). She is to deliver a basket of fruit to "Numéro 3, Rue des
Mages," where she must insist on seeing "Madame Walravens herself,
and giving the basket into her own hands" (478). Lucy sees a storm
gathering towards the twilight hour that pleases her because it "petrifies
a living city, as if by eastern enchantment; it transforms a Villette into
a Tadmor" (479). All the details here are carefully chosen to suggest a
kind of mythic resonance: the "grim Basse-Ville" evokes 'lower' world

of the ancient city, just as the address conjures up sorcery in this 'petrified' quarter of "eastern enchantment."[24]

The "Rue des Mages" turns out not to be a street, but a "part of a square," over the quiet and grassy slabs of which tower the "dark, half-ruinous turrets of the Cathedral, that "venerable and formerly opulent shrine of the Magi" (479), outside of which Lucy had collapsed into the abyss previously in the novel. The houses surrounding the square are now imagined "perhaps to stand cold and empty, mouldering untenanted in the course of winters" (479), and the description following reiterates the imagery of the land of the dead: "I saw, in its whole expanse, no symptom or evidence of life, except what was given in the figure of an infirm old priest who went past, bending and propping on a staff -- the type of eld and decay" (480). This old man propped up on his magic staff ("Thy rod and thy staff shall comfort me" (!)) is, as we will see, the old priest who will reveal the secrets of this necropolis to Lucy: he is a Catholic psychopomp whose guidance Lucy will reject.

As the episode progresses, the symbolism of doorways and corridors associated with earlier netherworld journeys resurfaces. The "infirm old priest" comes out of the very house to which Lucy has been directed; he is a kind of threshold guide and guardian, and soon becomes instrumental in providing Lucy access to Madame Walravens. At first, Lucy "paused before the door," until "a very old woman" with a "cantankerous" aspect and "wearing a very antique costume" reluctantly decides to open "the door to admit" her (480). The threesome then stands in the doorway for some time, until the old priest, by addressing the portresse "not in French, but in the aboriginal tongue of Labassecour," manages to persuade her to allow Lucy "to cross the inhospitable threshold" (480).[25] Doorway and clothing symbolism combine in this passage to evoke much of the resonance of mythic imagery associated with the otherworld.

Once ushered into the salon, Lucy sits in a large antique but "desolate" room "in the shadow of the coming storm" (480). She peers into a smaller room within, attached to this larger room, and amidst the "deep gloom" she discerns the "outline of a picture on the wall" which turns out to be a kind of *trompe l'oeil* doorway (481):

> By-and-bye the picture seemed to give way: to my bewil-
> derment, it shook, it sunk, it rolled back into nothing; its
> vanishing left an opening arched, leading into an arched
> passage, with a mystic winding stair; both passage and stair
> were of cold stone, uncarpeted and unpainted. Down this
> donjon stair descended a tap, tap, like a stick; soon, there fell
> on the steps a shadow, and last of all, I was aware of a
> substance.

> Yet, was it actual substance, this appearance approaching
> me? this obstruction, partially darkening the arch? (481)

The deceptive, illusory conjuration of this ancient apparition in an
arched corridor with "donjon" stairs hidden by a painting that serves as a
doorway is completely consistent with the imagery of the otherworld
journeys of the rest of the novel, and hence provides that pleasing sense
of aesthetic coherence (*integritas*) which Joyce called *claritas* in *A
Portrait*. In addition to aesthetic integrity, there is also that pleasing
sense of variety and contrast which Fielding discussed in *Tom Jones*,
since this is yet another of the novel's many *nekyia* passages, yet it is
unique, and in many ways serves as a kind of climax to the series.

   While the previous items in the *nekyia* series were informed by
allusions to Classical and Christian myths, the journey to Madame
Walravens is permeated with the aura of the Celtic folklore and folktale
traditions of Northern Europe. Though the folkloric element is
predominant in this scene, Classical, Christian, and Celtic aspects of
the otherworld are actually fused together inseparably (as in the
Arthurian romances of the Middle Ages). The ghostly apparition that
emerges behind the arched doorway hidden by the painting leads Lucy to
"comprehend," as she says, "where I was" (481):

> Well might this old square be named quarter of the Magi --
> well might the three towers, overlooking it, own for godfa-
> thers three mystic sages of a dead and dark art. Hoar en-
> chantment here prevailed; a spell had opened for me elf-land --
> that cell-like room, that vanishing picture, that arch and
> passage, and stair of stone, were all parts of a fairy tale.
> Distincter even than these scenic details stood the chief figure
> -- Cunegonde, the sorceress! Malevola, the evil fairy. (481)

Madame Walravens enters holding a "wand-like ivory staff" with a great
abundance of blazing jewels "on her skeleton hands" (481):
"Hunchbacked, dwarfish, and doting, she was adorned like a barbarian
queen" (482). The radiance of the jewels in the gloom suggests many of
the tales from *The Arabian Nights*, such as the "Second Voyage of
Sinbad" and "The Tale of Zubaidah," in which the jewel is a symbol of
a special quality of wisdom having to do with immortality. Her ivory
wand and occult association with a "dead and dark art" recalls the
importance of witchcraft in the infernal journeys of initiation and temptation in such medieval romances as *Sir Gawain and the Green Knight*
or *The Quest of the Holy Grail*, in both of which the dark, dead arts of
the underworld are associated with a wicked priestcraft in its efforts to
seduce wandering Protestants (think also of the false Duessa and the
many wizards of Spenser's *Fairy Queen*).

These associations suggest the conventional critique of the Catholic church by English Protestants; but, as we will see, there seems a deeper more aesthetic, indeed, more psychological rationale beneath the polemic of these images. For though Madame Walravens and her familiars continue to be presented in terms of a malevolent sorcery associated with Catholicism, it is beneath her roof that many of the secrets of the novel are to be revealed. When Madame Walravens curtly rejects Madame Beck's ritual offering of the fruit basket (is Lucy the fruit offered?), the storm breaks loose with a "peal of thunder ... and a flash of lightning .... The tale of magic seemed to proceed with due accompaniment of the elements. The wanderer, decoyed into the enchanted castle, heard rising, outside, the spell-wakened tempest" (482). The Spenserian overtones here yield to the "mystic interest" of the room in which Lucy is left to contemplate the "picture which moved, fell away from the wall, and let in phantoms" (483). The picture had appeared to be a Madonna previously, before it vanished to reveal the phantom Queen Madame Walravens, that "sullen Sidonia, tottering and trembling like a palsp incarnate" who returns through the picture door "muttering venomously as she vanished" (482).

It now proves to be "a woman's portrait in a nun's dress" (483), whose story will be told by the old priest who had procured Lucy's access to the house, and to whom she had confessed during the earlier episode in the cathedral. It is "quite a little romantic narrative, told not unimpressively, with the accompaniment of the now subsiding storm" (484) and having to do with a former pupil of the old priest who turns out to be none other than M. Paul. M. Paul had as a young man of about twenty years old fallen in love with Justine Marie, the subject of the portrait on the door that had moved to "let in phantoms" (483). Left only with "debts and destitution" after the death of his once wealthy father, M. Paul was forbidden consideration as a suitor by Marie Justine's family. Lucy proceeds to tell us that "that old witch of a grand-dame I had seen, Madame Walravens, opposed the match with all the violence of temper which deformity made sometimes demoniac" (485). Marie Justine had withdrawn into a convent, and died shortly thereafter "in her novitiate" (485). Ironically, the family that had spurned M. Paul is subsequently ruined by the death of Marie Justine's father, who had lost all his money speculating on the Bourse. M. Paul then had restored his own fortunes through diligent application, and had undertaken to support Marie's family, including the wicked old Madame Walravens, and in so doing had remained faithful to the memory of the dead love of his youth.

What Lucy retrieves from this particular journey into the underworld then is a story and a revelation: that "plan" which had brought her to the Rue des Mages had seemed to "crude apprehension the ordinance of chance, or the sequel of exigency," but is revealed actually to be the "arrangement" of a power pulling strings from behind the scenes who knows Lucy and "all [her] concerns" (486). M. Paul we have seen repeatedly described in terms suggestive of Hades, Lord of the Underworld, and now we discover his Persephone, the young girl long dead though ever dear and ever present in his mind. Will the Lucy bearing fruit (remember the association between pomegranate seeds and Persephone's confinement in Hades) be the next offering to these mystical Romanists, practitioners of a "dead and dark art" (481).

It is fully characteristic of the hero journey in general, and of the descent to the underworld in particular, for a revelation of the secret arrangement informing one's destiny to occur during the initiation stage of the cycle. In fact, James Hillman suggests an etymological tie between the name Hades and the Platonic notion of the *eidola*, those "ideational forms and shapes, the ideas that form and shape life" (51).[26] That this revelation also often occurs in the form of a story, like the one Lucy hears and returns to the upperworld with, is also fully characteristic of the *nekyia*: recall the story Utnapishtim tells Gilgamesh, the stories Odysseus hears Tiresias tell in Hades, the many narratives Dante hears during his descent in the *Inferno*, or the "strange power of speech" with which the Ancient Mariner returns to tell his story.

Such revelations are crucial to what Jung called individuation, that process by which the ego confronts and assimilates the totality of the psyche, reconciling its internal oppositions, and integrating the archetypal contents of the unconscious mind. It is basically a process of identity formation, for which the hero journey and the descent to the underworld stands as a universal symbol. What makes this integration of the total contents of the psyche possible is the archetype of the Self, which is often symbolized in dreams by images of the center, such as the square in the center of the old city on the Rue des Mages, the destination of two of Lucy's heroic descents in the novel, both situated at climactic moments of transition and transformation. This suggests that there is a more complex psycho-logic beneath the images of the cathedral and its 'parsonage' where the old priest lives than the polemic against Catholicism would imply. The cathedral, in fact, is a symbol of the Self, as is the square in the center of the city which it overlooks: it is the place where the opposites originate and come together, and the place where the secret arrangement of Lucy's journey is revealed.

The episodes surrounding the cathedral curiously resemble a dream of Jung's about an impressive tree on an island beautifully situated in the center of an otherwise unappealing part of the city of Liverpool. "It was night, and winter, and dark, and raining," Jung writes of the dream (197), and the real city was reached by climbing up some steps from a marketplace that reminded him of "the *Totengässchen* ('Alley of the Dead')" in Basel (198). On top was a plateau with the quarters of the city "arranged radially around the square. In the center was a round pool, and in the middle a small island" which blazes in sunlight while everything around it is "obscured by rain, fog, smoke, and dimly lit darkness" (198). Jung then recounts having painted a picture to capture the essence of the dream and then a second picture a year later "with a golden castle in the center" (197). Underneath the second castle Jung wrote "'*ecclesia catholica et protestantes et seclusi in secreto. aeon finitus.*' (The Catholic church and the Protestants and those hidden in the secret. The age is ended.)" (Jaffé 92). Jung recounts this dream at the end of a chapter of his autobiography in which the myth of the descent to the underworld emerges as his own personal myth. The climax of Jung's *nekyia* was the discovery of the mandala, a circular design based on Oriental art which Jung came to see as a symbol of the goal towards which everything in the individuation process is directed. It is a symbol of the Self, "the principle and archetype of orientation and meaning" (199).

Ambrose Bierce

Ambrose Bierce's "An Occurrence at Owl Creek Bridge," of 1891, is a story that looks forward to the Modernist fusion of realism and myth just around the corner. Born into a poor family, Bierce became a Civil War major, twice wounded and much cited for his bravery. As a journalist in London and California after the war, he achieved fame for his bitter satire and for stories which fall into two groups: vividly realistic tales about the Civil War, and tales of the supernatural. Both elements are fused in "An Occurrence," which typically focuses on an individual in the short time before his death (having been gravely wounded twice during the War, Bierce may well have had first hand knowledge of this crisis, now known by thanatologists as the Near Death Experience). The little tale follows the hero journey pattern exactly, moving from the gallows to the river crossing and back to the gallows, and it internalizes many of the mythological motifs which we have traced in our history of the monomyth.

The journey begins where it will end: on the gallows of a bridge above the river, where Union soldiers prepare the execution of Peyton Farquhar, a Confederate soldier who had sabotaged the Yankee army. The setting is as realistic as it is symbolic, for the bridge and river crossing are ancient symbols of the journey to the other world, from Gilgamesh, to Odysseus, to Dante. Bierce psychologizes the prototype by having Farquhar notice details of the world around him (a piece of driftwood, the sight of the railroad running off into the yonder forest, the last thoughts of his wife, the golden sunlight of dawn on the "sluggish stream," the progressive expansion of time, and the fantasy of wriggling out of the noose to escape across the river) that will surface in the death dream vision to follow, just the way Freud argued residue from the waking hours ("Tagesreste") are transformed at night by the dream work.

These details are transformed by the intense activation of the imagination which occurs at the moment of death, when the archetypal symbols of the mind come to the surface. As so often in the hero journey, death is the catalyst which distills these symbols and initiates the revelations of the voyage. For Bierce, the mythological motifs, activated by the hero journey of death, spontaneously evoke the iconography of birth in a way that anticipates the recent work of thanatologists like Kenneth Ring and Raymond Moody, comparative theologians like Carol Zaleski, and transpersonal psychologists like Stanislav Grof, whose work on the birth trauma is particularly relevant to a study of the hero journey pattern in general, and to "An Occurrence at Owl Creek Bridge" in particular.

The connection between the death and the birth traumas is vividly clear as Peyton Farquhar's journey begins. At the instant when the sergeant steps aside from the gallows, allowing the body to swing free from the gallows, Farquhar imagines himself falling straight downward to the bottom of the river. He then struggles to free his hands and swim upward to the distant "gleam of light" on the surface of the water. The image suggests the light at the end of the tunnel which the thanatologists record as a common aspect of the near death experience, and which Stanislav Grof suggests has its roots in the birth trauma. The excruciating pains of the neck, brain, heart, and entire muscular system as Farquhar struggles for the surface are equally perinatal, as is his final emergence from under the water: "He felt his head emerge; his eyes were blinded by the sunlight; his chest expanded convulsively, and with a supreme and crowning agony his lungs engulfed a great draught of air, which he instantly expelled in a shriek!" All of these details closely approximate the birth trauma at the moment of delivery: the struggle to emerge from the vaginal canal, the struggle for the first breath, and the blinding light of the new world. Birth, apparently is our first hero journey, as death will be our last.

What follows is the kind of preternatural keenness of the senses and altered awareness of time which characterizes the imaginal perceptions of people near death: Farquhar sees every little drop of prismatic dew and blade of grass on the opposite shore, and hears the humming of gnats, dragonflies, and waterspiders as an "audible music" analogous to the symphonic harmonies often reported by patients pronounced clinically dead. We should note that the dragonfly played a key role in the nekyia of Gilgamesh, where it symbolized both the brevity and the transcendence of life. But the music also reminds us that the underworld is a place of poesis, as well as an inferno of torment. After Farquhar hears this supernatural music, his body begins to whirl around and the soldiers on the bridge begin to fire their rifles, initiating the journey in earnest, as Peyton struggles to gain the yonder shore of the river, just as Odysseus and Gilgamesh had struggled for the shore during their journeys. Perinatal imagery surfaces again, as the pain in his neck becomes suffocating and the whirling of his body speeds up until he is "spinning like a top." As the rifles fire and cannon ball smashes the trees across the creek, Farquhar sees only "circular horizontal streaks of color" and his whirling body is caught up in a "vortex" with a velocity so intense as to be nauseating. Like the journey down the dark tunnel towards the light, the image of vortex may ultimately have its origins in the contractions of the vaginal corridor which propel the child out of the womb (Grof 102-03). In either case, Bierce has internalized the mythological motif of the river crossing, common instances of which in the hero journey also include Lancelot and Gawain, who cross the rushing river to the realm of the dead in Chrétien's "Knight of the Cart."

The yonder shore (whether symbolic of the biological delivery of birth or the spiritual liberation of death) is traditionally paradisical, glittering with golden sunlight and gemstones, like the Garden of Siduri in *Gilgamesh*, the underground caves of Aladdin, the valleys of Sinbad studded with diamonds, the gleaming halls of Alkinoos in the *Odyssey*, or the kingdoms of the otherworld in *Sir Orfeo* and *Pearl*. Hence, Bierce follows the prototype of the hero journey by describing grains of sand on the yonder shore of Owl Creek as "diamonds, rubies, emeralds," and the trees as "giant garden plants" arranged in a "definite order" and suffused by a "strange, roseate light" from which an "aeolian" music emanates. Many of the near death experiences recorded by Moody, Ring, and others provide similar glimpses of an edenic landscape; it is one of the principle features of the "otherworld topography" which Zaleski uses to link modern and medieval narratives of near death (Chapter 7). Stanislav Grof suggests that such visions hearken back to the resolution of the birth trauma, which may be expressed "in visions of radiant, blinding light that has a supernatural quality" (143).

Peyton Farquhar's nekyia now takes the form of the forest journey, as he travels along the railway paths into a "wild region" replete with "uncanny" revelations. The pathway is "untraveled," that country from whose bourn no traveler returns, and it seems free of "human habitation." The revelations characteristic of the initiation phase of the hero journey take the form here of "great golden stars ... grouped in strange constellations" as if they have been "arranged in some order which had a secret and malign significance." The woods surrounding the path ring with "whispers in an unknown tongue." All of these details are archetypal figurations of the revelations of the underworld, a place where the eidola (basic forms and ideas) which govern life are revealed. Those fundamental patterns suggestive of a secret order and arrangement behind the visible phenomena of the physical world surface as Farquhar plunges ever more deeply into the forest. The climax of the revelation is an epiphany of his wife as a sort of Goddess, as Peyton reaches his home. As in the Gnostic journeys we discussed in the first chapter, in relation to the Homeric and biblical material, homecoming represents the return of the soul to its spiritual kingdom. Farquhar sees his wife at the bottom of the verandah steps (images of thresholds, ascents, and corridors surface again in the iconography of the hero journey here) smiling with an "ineffable joy" and standing in an attitude of "matchless grace and dignity." As he springs towards her, he is knocked out (just as Lancelot had been when he stepped towards the Grail in the Castle of Corbenic) by a "blinding white light," and the scene returns to the gallows from which his body hangs swaying with a broken neck.

The entire sequence has occupied that space of a few seconds in between life and death which the Tibetan Buddhists called the Bardo. The Tibetans called the blinding white radiance at the climax of the soul's postmortem journey the "mother light," and, like Ambrose Bierce, they categorized the visions of the hero journey of death as phantoms of the mind projected onto the void of emptiness. Those archetypal forms, or mythological motifs, which are activated by the transformations of consciousness at death (river crossing, paradisal yonder shores, constellations of secret order, homecoming, the radiance of the mother) the Tibetans classified as aspects of the Chönyid Bardo. Bierce combines these mythological motifs with a fierce realism in a way that looks back to the mock epic and forward to the mythical method of Modernism. We have not seen the last of forest journeys, river crossings, revelations of hidden order, or secret rites performed at midnight in strange, alien tongues.

Notes

[1] These categories and much of the rest of this introductory material (I add the aesthetic category) come from Joseph Campbell's "Folkloristic Commentary" to *Grimm's Fairytales*, reprinted in *The Flight of the Wild Gander*. For more recent translations and historical commentary on the tales, see the work of Jack Zipes.

[2] On the 'infant exile' motif and its relationship to the birth of the hero see the selections from Raglan, Rank, and Dundes brought together in *In Quest of the Hero*.

³ A convenient collection of eye goddess figurines and icons is to be found in Laurence di Stasi's *Mal Occhio*. See also Gimbutas, *The Language of the Goddess*, Chapter 6.

⁴ See my books, *Ricorso and Revelation*, and *Figuring Poesis* for the symbolism of alchemy in Joyce and several other Modernist and Postmodernist authors.

⁵ I discuss the imagery of the Goddess in *The Tin Drum* and other works of the Postmodernist period in *Figuring Poesis*, forthcoming from Peter Lang.

⁶ Douglas Robinson develops an elaborate methodology for the study of the image of the end of the world in our tradition. Oddly enough, the text he chooses as representative of Nathaniel Hawthorne's handling of the theme is *The House of Seven Gables*, a novel which fits in nicely with his hermeneutic, but which is not Hawthorne's most explicitly apocalyptic novel. The most thorough discussion of Hawthorne's typological use of Revelation in *The Scarlet Letter* that I know of is Clifford Foreman's dissertation, which approaches the subject in terms of "two competing typologies. The typology connected with Dimmesdale's three ascents of the scaffold points towards the ultimate 'Revelation' of the last chapter and the last judgement, deflating the Puritan's vision of their interprise. But Hester's Emersonian typology suggests that the revelation of sin can be escaped" (3427-A). Lois Zamora devotes only one paragraph to her discussion of apocalypse in American literature to *The Scarlet Letter*, which she sees as dramatizing a "strongly felt dialectic between millennial and cataclysmic versions" of apocalypse (115). Her article generally, however, is a fine and concise overview of the theme, and her anthology of essays on the subject a useful survey of apocalypse in other areas of American culture. Henry Lindborg focuses less on St. John's Revelation than on the apocalyptic Book of Enoch. Finally, Charles Swann accurately associates Hester's prophecy at the end of the novel with the Second Coming, but does not develop the observation into a thorough study of the novel.

⁷ Arlin Turner's chapter on "The Peabodys" in his biography of Hawthorne omits any detailed discussion of Elizabeth Peabody's ideas and their possible impact on the novelist, prefering to see her instead as a kind of infatuated invader of Hawthorne's privacy.

⁸ The definitive study of alchemical and occult philosophies in the late Renaissance and early 17th century in England is by Frances Yates, who shows how the Rosicrucians provided the foundation for the emergence of modern science. D.H. Lawrence also notes that Chillingworth "belongs to the old medieval school of medicine and alchemy" (148), and that he is "the magician on the verge of modern science, like Francis Bacon, his great prototype" (149).

⁹ Charles Swann notes that Hester is "more subversive than is usually recognized in that she desires and prophesies a radical subversion of the patriarchal structures of her society" (264), and that "she looks forward to the

Second Coming of Christ--only this time as a woman. Angel and Apostate indeed of a coming Revelation!" (266). Clearly, this suggests a feminist Hester, one favoring a "radical (but reasonable) re-ordering of theological language" (266).

[10] For a deconstructive, Neo-Freudian discussion of the veiling imagery in Hawthorne see John Irwin (265-70, 274-75, 280-85).

[11] More on Whitman's interest in things Egyptian is to be found in John Irwin's *American Hieroglyphics*.

[12] See Bloom's article "The Internalization of the Quest Romance."

[13] See my *Rape and Revelation* for a detailed study of the descent to the underworld in these and a large variety of other Modernist works.

[14] See Karl Kerényi: *Hermes: Guide of Souls*. for a discussion of Hermes as a guide of souls to the underworld. The quotations in this sentence, and in the notes below, refer to the line numbers in the translation of the Homeric Hymns by Apostolos N. Athanassakis.

[15] As in Book 21 of Homer's *Odyssey*; in the Homeric Hymn, Hermes is referred to as a "bringer of dreams" (14).

[16] The Homeric Hymn to Hermes refers to the god as a "weaver of schemes" (155), "a cattle rustling robber" (14), and as the "chief of robbers" (175 and 292). Norman O. Brown discusses in details the aspects of trickery, deception, and thievry associated with Hermes as a god of the marketplace in his book *Hermes the Thief*. The most detailed artistic development of this cluster of motifs in relation to art occurs in the works of Thomas Mann (for which see my *Rape and Revelation*).

[17] D.H. Lawrence's remark that "in *Wuthering Heights* we feel the peculiar presence of Pluto and the spirit of Hades" (118) would also apply to *Villette*. In fact, it would seem possible that Lawrence may owe an otherwise unacknowledged debt to the Brontë sisters: in addition to the parallel between the Styx and the English channel noted above, we also find the first epiphany of Hades in *Women in Love* in the chapter called "Class Room," just as the Hades of *Villette* (M. Paul) is seen most often in the class room. Additionally, many of M. Paul's odd personality traits suggest that he is a precursor of Loerke in *Women in Love.*.

[18] It is a commonplace of Jungian dream interpretation that alien parts of a city suggest the underworld of the unconscious, and that impressive buildings like the cathedral in this scene are symbols of the Self. See for example Jung's *Memories, Dreams, and Reflections* (197) or *C.G. Jung: Word and Image* (92-94).

[19] See first of all Jung's essays on synchronicity in *The Structure and Dynamics of the Psyche*, and secondly such illuminating discussions as that provided by Robert Aziz.

[20] The Angel, that is to say, unites the opposites of life and death, like Rilke's "terrible" angels of the *Duino Elegies*. Such moments of achieved equilibrium between the opposites signifies, for Jung, crucial revelations of

the Self, that totality towards which the individuation journey compels us. For a fine recent discussion of the symbolism of the angel in literature, see Massimo Cacciari.

[21] See figure 2-6 in Edinger for an illustration of "The Starry Salamander That Lives in the Fire" from Michael Maier's *Atalanta Fugiens* of 1618.

[22] See Christina Crosby for an excellent discussion of gender issues in the novel, which she argues subjects conventional forms of gender differentiation to intense scrutiny and revision.

[23] In fact, many of the details remind me of the city in "The Tale of Zubaidah" in *The Book of the Thousand Nights and One Night* (alluded to so often in *Villette*), where a young woman sails to a city where the inhabitants have been petrified for worshipping false idols (just as Lucy will see the unholy trinity in this house of eastern enchantment, Numéro 3,-- Madame Walravens, the Priest, and the ghostly daughter of the portrait -- as idol worshipping catholics). She hears the story of the city told in a magnificent palace in the middle of the city which would correspond to the vision of the cathedral in this episode as a "Shrine of the Magi" (it is furthermore interesting to note that the idol worshippers in the "Tale of Zubaidah" are Magians, who worship fire).

[24] It is curious to note how often the underworld is associated with a strange and suggestive language unknown to the traveler: see below for discussions of "The Rime of the Ancient Mariner," "Occurrence at Owl Creek Bridge," "Young Goodman Brown," and *Heart of Darkness*.

[25] My books, *Rape and Revelation, Ricoroso and Revelation*, and *Figuring Poesis* all explore the notion that the descent to the underworld precipitates a revelation of those basic forms which give shape and significance to life and art to many works of the modernism and postmodernism.

Chapter 5:
Modernism

T.S. Eliot's seminal definition of the "mythical method" as "a continuous parallel between contemporaneity and antiquity" with the result of "giving a shape and significance ... to the futility and anarchy which is contemporary history" (Ellman 681) yielded works by such writers as Joyce, Mann, Broch, and Proust, who fuse realistic details and mythic symbols. As I have shown elsewhere, the single most important mythic symbol for the modernists was the descent to the underworld.[1] In the wide range of modernist works in which the myth occurs, the central theme is the revelation of those fundamental ideas which give shape and significance to life and art, ideas for which the modernists developed a complex variety of terms.[2] Many of these works follow the narrative cycle of the hero journey, adapting the vocabulary of motifs associated with to the new concerns of the mythical method.

Typically, the hero journey in Modernism adapts the mythologies of the maze, the apocalpyse, the Great Goddess, and the descent to the underworld. The underworld has four fundamental meanings in these quests: it can be seen as a crypt, a temenos, an inferno, and a granary. As a crypt, the underworld is the place where the hero confronts the ancestors (as in the *Odyssey* or the *Aeneid*). They then communicate the accumulated wisdom of the generations, or reveal the basic pattern and meaning of the hero's destiny. For Modernism, this often involved incorporating the themes, styles, or techniques of the literary ancestry of the European tradition, usually in the form of allusions and citations (as in Pound's *Cantos*, Joyce's *Ulysses*, or Eliot's *Waste Land*). As a temenos, the underworld is a place of transformation: the hero is fundamentally changed by the journey, and returns a different person. In Modernism, this often involves a discovery of one's artistic vocation (as in Joyce's *Portrait*, or Mann's "Tonio Kröger." The Modernist descent is also frequently seen as journey into an inferno (as in Conrad's *Heart of Darkness* or Mann's *Death in Venice*), where the sufferings and torments reflect the catastrophes of contemporary history. However, the underworld remains a place of revelation, where the fundamental forms of the archetypal imagination are activated. In this last sense, the hero journey takes one down into a granary, a place where the seed forms of the mind are stored. Hence, the hero journey in Modernism almost always involves a complex vocabulary and iconography of form, expressed in a variety of key phrases and words.

Eliot simply used the phrase "formal pattern" in association with the "box circle" and lotos pool of "Burnt Norton" (14). Thomas Mann used such terms as "fundamental types" ('Grundtypen') (*Doctor Faustus* 488; 647), "pious formula" ('fromme Formel') and "timeless schema" ('zeitlose Schema') ("Freud and the Future" 422; 493), and "given forms" '(gegebene Formen'), "pattern" ('Muster'), "prototype and abstract" ('Urbild und Inbegriff') and "archetype" ('Urbild') (*Joseph* 81, 123, 23; 94, 149, 29). In *The Death of Virgil*, Hermann Broch created a wide range of synonyms, such as "crystalline archetype" ('kristallische Urbild') (444; 418), "symbol of all symbols" ('Sinnbild aller Sinnbild')(89; 85), and "first image of all archetypes" ('Urbild aller bilder') (481; 453). C. G. Jung (who was much interested in the underworld and alchemy) derived his notion of the archetypes from the Platonic notion of the "eidola," a term which James Hillman has recently associated with the name Hades, and defined as "ideational forms and shapes" (51). Borges referred to these elementary ideas in fiction as "ancient forms, forms incorruptible and eternal" 'formas antiguas, formas incorruptibles y eternas' (*Labyrinths* 70; *Obras* 117), while Julio Cortázar used the term "figuras" to refer to geometrical archetypes like kaleidoscopes, polyhedrons, and crystals in his novel *Hopscotch*, a novel which relies heavily on "The nekias of today" (180) and on the "delicate alchemies" (379) involved in the reduction of material compounds to their elemental substances (429). These archetypal forms are in fact often represented in Modernism by geometrical configurations : In *A Vision*, Yeats uses the gyrating cones; in the *Joseph* novels, Mann uses the circle, the square, the triangle, and the sphere (124); Borges uses the diamond in "Death and the Compass," the wheel in "The God's Script," and the labyrinth in many stories; and, in Doris Lessing's *Briefing for a Descent Into Hell* (a novel like Leonora Carrington's about a psychotic breakdown), these fundamental figures of the mind are evoked by the symbolism of a "circle in the square" in the center of a ruined city (54), which becomes the "inner pattern or template" of the outer city (94).

Thomas Mann

When Thomas Mann came to write his four-volume novel based on the Joseph theme, he would make extensive use of the basic motifs of the hero journey: myths of the Goddess, the maze, and the underworld. The tetralogy begins with a meditation on the underworld in its "Prelude: Descent into Hell" ('Vorspiel: Höllenfahrt') and returns to the leit-motif of the descent when Jacob journeys to Mesopotamia, when Joseph is thrown into the well, when he is thrown into the Pharaoh's prison, and again when Joseph is married to Asenath. Mann's conception of the nekyia draws extensively from "the doctrines of the East ... Avesta, Islam, Manichaeanism, Gnosticism, and Hellenism" (23). In the "Vorspiel," Mann shapes an elaborately wrought metaphor of the nekyia as an allegory of poesis, focusing on the storyteller's descent into the "lower world of the past" (3) in search of those "prototypes" ('Urbilder') upon which all stories are based: the Flood (16-19), the Tower of Babel (19-20), the Garden of Eden (20-23), and the Fall (27-30). The original "prototype and abstract" ('Urbild und Inbegriff') of all these stories, Mann concludes, was the Gnostic version of the nekyia as the descent of "the youthful being made out of pure light" ('Jünglingswesen aus reinem Licht') into the underworld of matter, and the subsequent "Fall" of the Messiah to rescue the first man (24-27; 29). All stories have their origins in the one to which Mann circles back to here: the "romance of the soul" ('der Roman der Seele'), its descent into and return from the material world, which Mann calls the "pure and original form" ('reine Wahrheitsform') (25; 31) of the subsequent journeys (of Jacob and Joseph) into the underworld, upon which the tetralogy focuses. Mann's "Höllenfahrt" in the "Prelude" then, circles "back to the beginning, the origin of the world and the heavens and the earthly universe out of confusion and chaos, by the might of the Word" ('zurück zum Angang, zur Enstehung der Welt, der Himmel und des irdischen Alls aus Tohu und Bohu durch das Wort') (9;14), in order to effect the revelation of those prototypical and original forms which are the basis of poetic re-creation.

In the first volume of the tetralogy the prototype takes the form of Jacob's journey to Mesopotamia, which both Hatfield and Campbell have suggested corresponds to the descent to the underworld (*Mann* 103-107; "Thomas Mann"). The volume begins with Ishtar (the Sumerian Inanna), the evening star which Joseph contemplates while standing beside the well (35f.). And indeed, the nekyia is never far from Jacob's mind, which applies the myth to the whole of his experience, and by extension to all Hebraic myth making, as in the ecstatic summation of the theme inspired by his son Joseph's fear of falling into the well:

> Jacob could not think of those depths without connecting them in his thought, to their enrichment and consecration, with the idea of the lower world and the kingdom of the dead -- that idea which played an important part, not indeed in his re-

ligious convictions, but probably in the depths of his soul and in the power of his imagination: that primitive mythical inheritance of all peoples, the conception of the underworld, the realm of Osiris the dismembered one, where he ruled, the place of Namtar, the god of plagues, the kingdom of terrors, whence came all evil spirits and pestilences. It was the world whereinto the constellations descended at their setting, to rise again at the appointed hour, whereas no mortal who trod the path to this abode ever found the way back again. It was the place of filth and excrement, but also of gold and riches: the womb in which one buried the seed corn, out of which it sprouted again as nourishing grain; the land of the black moon, of winter and the parching summer, whither Tammuz the shepherd in his spring sank down and would sink each year, when the boar killed him, and all creation ceased and the weeping world lay sere, until Ishtar, goddess and mother, made pilgrimage to hell to seek him, broke the dust-covered bolts of his prison, and mid laughter and rejoicing, brought forth the beautiful and beloved out of the pit and the grave, to reign over the new season and the fresh-flowering fields. (57-58)[3]

I quote at length because this passage at the well side is a kind of overture, a veritable wellspring itself, announcing all the central episodes and motifs of the tetralogy to follow, and acknowledging the primacy of the myths of the descent in all of Mann's work.

For both Esau and Jacob conceive of their journeys as nekyias. After the blessing is stolen, Esau wanders off into the "lower world" of the southland, and refers to himself as "the sun-scorched son of the lower world" (86). Jacob too is sent off into Mesopotamia, "into the unknown, never to return, into exile, into the underworld" (88), where he will experience both the riches of the seed corn harvest, and the revelations of Hades when he dreams of the ladder at El-Beth. Before these enrichments, however, Jacob must be stripped down (like Ishtar during her descent) by Eliphaz, who "had him plucked so thoroughly that nothing was left but his life" (89). The great dream vision known as "Jacob's Ladder" follows this stripping down, and it is replete with the kind of threshold imagery of doorways staircases that is characteristic of the journey (from Inanna to Aschenbach): Jacob sees the angelic forms ascending "fiery unnumbered steps" (90) to the "narrow flaming fiery arch that was the gateway of the palace with pillars and lofty pinnacles" where the most High is enthroned (91). The dream revelation occurs "within the circle of stones" which Jacob subsequently calls "the gate of splendor" (92), a metaphor which evokes the threshold symbolism of the hero journey.

The synopsis quoted at length above also announces the end of the tetralogy in its beginning, for like Ishtar and Demeter, Jacob, the grieving parent, will finish the novel with the journey to retrieve his lost son, "the beautiful and beloved, out of the pit and the grave" which is Egypt. The whole story, Mann suggests in Jungian fashion, resides in the collective imagination of humanity ("in den Tiefen seiner Seele und Einbildungskraft"), as one of its most archaic mythical forms ("uralt mythisches Erbgut der Völker"). A similar synopsis of the myth is positioned as an overture near the beginning of the second novel of the tetralogy, *Young Joseph*, when Joseph in Chapter 3 tells his brother Benjamin stories of how Tammuz, Adonis, Osiris, and Ishtar (Inanna) descended to the underworld. For Joseph too will enact the mysteries of the Egyptian Osiris, the Sumerian Ishtar, and the seed corn of Demeter when he is thrown into the womb-tomb of the well, when he is taken down into Egypt, when he descends the Nile on a barge, like Osiris, to the Pharaoh's prisons, the kingdom of the dead, and when he marries Asenath. His version recounts how Astarte (the Sumerian Inanna) shed clothing at the seven gates before standing naked in front of Ereshkigal, the Queen who is keeping Tammuz in the realm of the Dead. In Joseph's version (which is a condescending Hebrew synthesis of many myths), Ereshkigal then locks Astarte in the lower regions, but Astarte responds Demeter like by withholding the fruits of the earth, so that, as in the Homeric Hymn, the Gods above must intervene by sending a messenger to intervene between the jealous Queens and retrieve Adonai with an arrange that still requires him to spend a third of the year in hell (304). Mann returns again and again to this central myth of the Ancient Mediterranean world (as will also his ephebes, from Grass to Pynchon), though we know now more about the original story in its earliest Sumerian versions, and hence can see Mann's playful attribution of demeaning jealousy to the two Goddesses (who most definitely do not fight over a man in the prototype translated by Wolkstein and Kramer) as a comment on the way the patriarchal and provincial Hebrews viewed the cultures around them (Egyptian and Mesopotamian), to whom they owed so much.[4]

Hence we are prepared, when it comes time for young Joseph's descent into the well as the climax of the second novel in the tetralogy, for a recurrence of the cluster of images associated with this basic prototype of the imagination (prison, womb, well, dark night of the moon, tomb, evening star, etc.). Mann calls the well into which Joseph's brothers throw him "the entrance to the underworld" ('dem Eingang zur Unterwelt') (390; 431), and it becomes the place where Joseph becomes aware that he is reinacting to the original stories of his ancestors, and where the revelation of the archetypal forms governing his life occurs: he senses the "transparency of the ancient pattern" ('durchsichtig und urgeprägt') (390; 431), and the more miserable he becomes, "the more deceptively his present mirrored itself in its heavenly prototype" ('desto täuschender spiegelte seine Gegenwart sich im Vorbildlich-Himmlischen') (391; 432). The riches, then, revealed by the descent of the son into "the nether-earthly sheepfold, Etura, the kingdom of the dead" ('unterirdische Schafstall, Etura, das Reich der Toten') (390; 432), are the archetypes. When Joseph takes up his tasks as Potiphar's servant in Egypt, he again recognizes the "uncanny" ('geheimnisvoll') repetition of the "pattern" ('auf Wiederholung des Vorgelebten anlegt') as life pours itself "into the forms of myth" ('mythischer Formen') (551; 611). When Jacob learns of Joseph's abduction, he also compares himself to the Sumerian Innana and her passage through the seven gates of the underworld, and recognizes the repetition of "the mythical pattern" ('mythischem Muster') (436; 481). And when Mann picks up the theme in the last volume of the tetralogy, he again conflates the Sumerian version of the shedding of Inanna's veils, as she goes down into the sheepfold, with the mangling of Osiris, Tammuz, and Attis. Joseph refers to the time of his imprisonment as "The hour of unveiling, of putting off of ornaments ... the hour of the descent into hell" ('denn die Stunde der Entschleierung und des Ablegens der Schmuckstücke war da, die Stunde der Höllenfahrt') (854; 961). When he eventually returns from the Pharoah's prisons, he says that his descent is a variation of the "general and the typical" ('das Allgemeine und die Form eine Abwandlung erfahren'), which the translation calls "the established pattern" (937; 1055). Joseph then explicitly suggests that "typical and the traditional" ('die Form und das Uberlieferte') are revealed in and come from the underworld: "the pattern and the traditional" Joseph says, "come from the depths which lie beneath and are what bind us" ('Denn das musterhaft Uberlieferte kommt aus der Tiefe, die unten liegt, und ist, was uns bindet') (937; 1056).

These passages establish a rich vocabulary linking the archetypal forms of the poetic imagination with the "eidola" revealed by the descent into Hades: forms, prototypes, the typical and the conventional, patterns, and primordial images. These images, found in Mann's last masterpiece, recall the symbolic descent of Gustav von Aschenbach in one of Mann's early masterpieces, *The Magic Mountain* and *Death in Venice*. Both follow the pattern of the hero journey very closely, and pick up on the long tradition of threshold imagery associated with the descent into the underworld and the treading of the labyrinth.

The imagery of the Cretan maze forms one of those leit-motifs found throughout the course of Thomas Mann's work. Lotti Sandt cites Mann's interest in *Der Palast des Minos* by Sir Galahad, and suggests that the sanitarium in *The Magic Mountain* "becomes the Palace of Knossos (Crete), the Labyrinth with the sign of the Double Axe, where

Minos and Rhadamanthus rule and where Ariadne lives" (72; my trans.). Hence, when Hans first approaches the plateau where the sanitarium sits, he sees "a long building, with a cupola and so many balconies that from a distance it looked porous, like a sponge" (8), and once inside it he finds it difficult and tiring to negotiate so many rooms and corridors. As Sandt notes with regard to the Palace of Knossos, "Since the Palace revealed a vast multitude of rooms and corridors, the word Labyrinth would be applied to other buildings of a similarly bewildering kind" (73). As we will see in our discussion of Borges, Cocteau, and Eco, the iconography of a bewildering array of corridors, alleys, doorways, hall-ways, stairways, and rooms remains characteristic of the iconography of the maze throughout Modernism.

Another symbol of the Cretan palace found in *The Magic Mountain* is the symbol of the "double axe," which Hans encounters on the shoulders of the two woodcutters he meets while walking up the "zig-zag" meadow path in the "Hippe" chapter (118). Sandt notes that "with the appearance of the double-ax" (78) his "journey through the labyrinth takes its beginning" (347). It is also noteworthy that, for Mann, the maze is a realm of dream, song, and memory (as it is also for André Gide and James Joyce). As Hans winds along the "zig-zag" path, he begins to sing "folk-ditties, out of collections of national ballads," and then he collapses beneath a sturdy pine, where the trembling of his head "called up to him the memory of his dead grandfather" (118). It is curious to note that Joyce also associates the maze with song and poetry, when Stephen Dedalus paces the pavement outside the university, timing his steps to the fall of verses. Treading the maze, then, becomes a metaphor of poesis. Furthermore, the repeated refrains of the ballads which Hans sings often mimic the repetitive progress through a maze, combining both circular and linear movement. Even Hans' choice of "the left-hand path" in his efforts to return to the sanitarium is a characteristic device for treading the labyrinth which we will see in Borges. Additionally, we have the impeded, exhausting, and painful manner of moving through the maze: Hans crosses a bridge and begins to bleed from the nose, which halts his foreword progress and costs him "nearly half an hour of going to and fro between bench and brook, snuffing water up his nostrils" (119). At this point he is so exhausted that he lies down and has the dream vision connecting his schoolboy chum Pribislav Hippe to Clavdia Chauchat, who will keep him imprisoned in the labyrinth of death and desire for seven years. After the dream, Hans descends the "winding path" to the Kurhaus, where he assumes his seat at Krokowski's lecture on the liebestod. He sits down right behind Clavdia, "the Lady of the Labyrinth" (Sandt 347).

In *Death and Venice*, the aging Gustav von Aschenbach also finds himself ensnared in the "labyrinth" (55) of disease and desire into which he is drawn while pursuing the beautiful young boy, Tadzio, through the "labyrinthine little streets" (71) of Venice. As in Racine's *Phaedra*, the labyrinth here becomes a symbol of the underworld of human desire, and the networks of obsessive-compulsive behavior created by its repression. It is also characteristic for the maze to be represented as a city withholding a dire secret in its center (as it is also in Kafka's *Castle* and in the stories of Borges): Mann's Minotaur is compounded both of desire and disease, the secret course of which is being withheld by the tourism authorities of Venice, and which is revealed to Aschenbach one Sunday after Mass by the acrid smell of disinfectant surrounding a fountain in the center of a dark piazza deep in the heart of the Venetian maze.

Mann depicts the labyrinth of Hades into which Aschenbach has journeyed as a complex urban network of alleys, canals, piazzas, and porticos, focusing on the threshold imagery characteristic of both the maze and the underworld. The entrance into the maze begins with the symbolism of the doorway at the beginning of the story, an icon which Mann forces us to notice. Standing across the street from the North Cemetery in Munich, Aschenbach dwells upon the "hieratic designs" and upon the "symmetrically arranged selection of scriptural texts in gilded letters" inscribed on the portico of the mortuary chapel where the stranger stands (379). As Aschenbach reads these "formulas" and ponders their "mystical meaning," a strange "red-haired" man suddenly appears "standing in the portico, above the two apocalyptic beasts that guarded the staircase" (379). Aschenbach wonders "Whether he had come out of the hall through the bronze doors or mounted unnoticed from outside" (379). In either case, the setting of hallways, staircases, and doorways establishes the archetypal iconography of the maze and the underworld; and the "hieratic designs" of the "scriptural texts" and "formulas" inscribed above the doorway into the cemetery connect Aschenbach's journey to the problems of hermenuesis and poesis, which are intensified by the descent into the underworld that follows.

For the pilgrim who appears and vanishes so mysteriously between the doors of the cemetery's portico is endowed with many attributes associated with Hermes, who is simultaneously guide of souls to the underworld, traveler, thief, patron of poesis, and catalyst of dreams. He appears in the doorway wearing a "broad straight-brimmed hat, with a rucksack on his back, and carrying an "iron shod stick" (379), reminiscent of the caduceus. He inspires Aschenbach with a longing to travel," which immediately takes the form of an hallucinatory vision of primordial Venice (380). Initially, Venice is seen as a kind of Freudian underworld of the id, a picture of "Desire projected ... visually," of a world of repressed, "latent" impulses (380). But the personal recollections of lost youth gradually modulates towards more archetypal levels of the unconscious, as Aschenbach passes through the various stages of his journey to Venice. Along the way he encounters two Charon figures, who will ferry him across to the yonder shores of Hades. The first is the goat-bearded man who takes the coin for the crossing of the Adriatic, on "an ancient hulk belonging to the Italian line, obsolete, dingy, grimed with soot" (388). The second Charon is the illicit gondolier who rows Aschenbach across the lagoon to the Lido, in "that singular conveyance ... black as nothing else on earth except a coffin" (392). Mann emphasizes details associated with the journey by water into the underworld: the gondola inspires "visions of death itself, the bier and solemn rites and last soundless voyage!" (392); and the gondolier combines elements of both Charon and Hermes, for Aschenbach sees him as a ferryman, a thief, and a guide of souls "down to the kingdom of Hades" (394).

Aschenbach has, therefore, figuratively stepped through the doorway of the cemetery in Munich to commence his journey to the underworld, after the sight of the stranger inspires a restless urge to travel. Images of doorways, corridors, alleys, canals and other motifs associated with Hades dominate Mann's portrait of Venice, into the depths of which Aschenbach is propelled by his obsession with the young Polish boy, Tadzio. On the Sunday after Mass, the afflicted Aschenbach watches hidden in the "vestibule" as the crowd of worshippers streams "out through the portals" of San Marco into the dazzling dove-filled piazza (420). He then compulsively follows the Polish family beneath the clock tower into the Merceria and on through the maze-like passages of the city: over bridges into "filthy cul-de-sacs," along "narrow" passages into Byzantine "courtyards," hiding "behind a portico or fountain" when the family steps into a gondola, then continuing the chase deep into the "silence of the labyrinth" ('der Stille des Labyrinths'), rounding the corners of gloomy gardens with "Moorish lattices" and watching beggars descend the marble steps of a church to the stagnant water of the canal (420-21). On another afternoon, the threshold imagery continues, when Aschenbach pursues "his charmer" into "The labyrinthine little streets, squares, canals, and bridges, each one so like the next" that he soon loses "his bearings" (433). Slinking beside walls, lurking behind buildings, Aschenbach follows Tadzio down "narrow alleys" and over a "small vaulted bridge" into an "archway" where the family disappears from sight (very similar sequences occur in the films Bergman and Cocteau). The disappearance of the beloved leaves Aschenbach trapped in the maze of the underworld. After searching in "three directions," he settles down on the "steps of a well" in the middle of a "little square" cornered by palatial houses with "vaulted windows" and "little lion balconies" (434). Earlier in the novella, Aschenbach drank pomegranate juice (Persephone's fruit!), while sitting of the porch of the Hotel (423;

427); here, in the middle of the labyrinth, he consumes the fruit of Hades, "overripe" strawberries, and dies the next day. As in the "Homeric Hymn to Demeter," the consumption of the forbidden fruits of the underworld imprison the wandering soul therein.

We also find echoes of the labyrinth in the winding sentences Mann weaves, the syntax of which mimics the complex turnings of a progress through the maze. As in Melville, the maze becomes a metaphor for both reading (hermeneusis) and writing (poesis).The translators handle this problem with long sequences of periodic and cumulative sentences broken up into complex and compound clauses, separated by semi-colons, and punctuated by interrupting, introducing, and modifying phrases. One example among many would be the first sentence of the second chapter, which is structured by four complex and compound nominative clauses (themselves containing sequences of relative clauses), separated by semi-colons, which introduce the simple main clause with a colon: our hero is announced as "Der Autor," "der geduldige Künstler," "der Schöpfer," and "der Verfasser," and his major works are titled and aphoristically delineated, before we finally arrive at his name, Gustav von Aschenbach, and reach the main verb of the sentence in its last word -- "geboren" (357-58). Other good examples would be the long sentences describing the winding paths by which the cholera epidemic makes its way from the Ganges deltas to Venice (407), or the sentences in the long paragraph devoted to Aschenbach's dream of Dionysus ((410-11). We are moving here towards Hermann Broch's multi-page sentences in *The Death of Virgil*, which also relates the metaphor of the maze to linguistic and poetic problems.

The great climax of Aschenbach's hero journey to Venice comes in the form of a dream vision of the God Dionysus, drawn directly from *The Bacchae* of Euripides.[5] That Aschenbach's imagination is feverishly intensified throughout his journey indicates that activation of the archetypal images of the unconscious which is the basis of all acts of poesis. His dream vision of King Pentheus decapitated and devoured by the Maenads and his own mother surely reflects the imminent dissolution of Europe into the barbarism of the First World War. It also personifies the fulfillment of repressed desires (both erotic and thanatological) that Freud associated with dreams; and it manfiests the deeper workings of the mythical levels of the unconscious which preoccupied Jung. As such, the dream vision constitutes that revelation of the mysteries of forbidden life typically forming the initiation stage of the hero journey (as in Hawthorne and Conrad). But it is a revelation associated with various aspects of poesis, as when Aschenbach sits composing an inspired essay at the beach, while watching Tadzio cavort on the shore, like a young Apollo; or when Aschenbach muses upon the philosophical speculations of Plato in the Phaedrus. For the journey leads not just to death, but also to the "immensity of richest expectation" associated with the imaginal realm of Hades (437).

Joseph Conrad

Conrad's *Heart of Darkness* circumscribes a complete hero journey cycle, both in the tale itself and in the manner of its telling. Hence, the hero journey becomes a metaphorical expression of both the processes by which stories are written and by which they are read: the storyteller's is a hero journey, but so also is the reader's a hero journey. This Conrad accomplishes by utilizing the frame-tale narrative, just as Coleridge had before him, and Chaucer before Coleridge, and the anonymous compilers of the Arabian Nights before any of the moderns. On the frame level, a nameless narrator tells us a story about Marlow, who tells the narrator and others a seaman's tale while waiting on a cruising yawl for the tide to change at the mouth of the Thames, where the frame begins and ends. The revelations of the tale in between transform the listeners in a manner similar to the way the Wedding Guest had been changed by the telling of the Mariner's tale. The tale which Marlow tells to the nameless narrator also circumscribes a complete hero journey cycle, beginning and ending in Brussels, with the initiatory journey up the Congo in between.

Let us begin with a brief analysis of the frame-tale cycle, which begins and ends at the mouth of the Thames on the cruising yawl. The time is twilight, and we are in between the flood and the ebb tides. The sun is setting as the narrator sets the scene for the telling of the tale: Gravesend is off in the distance, and a magnificent sunset commences while a Lawyer, an Accountant, the Director, the narrator, and Marlow sit on the decks of the *Nellie*, the maritime company's pleasure boat. The language of the narrator establishes a historical and literary context for the telling of Marlow's tale, thereby extending its significance. For the stark contrast between the narrator's style, and the style of Marlow's monologue suggests that it is not only the characters of Marlow's tale who undergo the hero journey, but also the language itself and the culture which produced it. The stylistic shifts indicate the collapse of the Victorian attitudes associated with the British Empire at the end of the 19th century, and a departure into the unknown realms of the future, represented by the style of Marlow's narration. As the sun sets, it becomes clear that it is setting on the Empire as well, so that the solar night-sea journey so much beloved of the anthropology of the 19th century can be seen as symbolically indicating the onset of an historical hero journey, as England leaves the old world behind and moves uncertainly towards the threatening world of the future.

The literary style Conrad gives his nameless narrator indicates this imminent transformation of the Empire. The phrases of an English sensibility moulded by the Romantic and Victorian movements of the 19th century linger on the narrator's tongue as he describes this symbolic sunset: the day ends in a "serenity of still and exquisite brilliance," the sea shines "pacifically, the sky is a "benign immensity of unstained light," and the mist over the marshes looks like a "radiant fabric" draping the shoreline in "diaphanous folds" (546). While the landscape painted here may show the influence of Impressionism (as Ian Watt argues), the language itself is Romantic, in the manner of Wordsworth or Constable: the world is 'serene,' 'pacific,' 'benign,' 'unstained,' and 'radiant' in a 19th century manner which the historical events just around the corner would shatter forever. As the narrator continues his reflections on the setting sun, thoughts of the history of the Empire come to his mind in grand Victorian phrases: the old "unruffled" river rests in "tranquil dignity" "at the decline of day" after having done "good service" for centuries; it is a "venerable stream," regarded by the narrator with "reverence and affection," "in the august light of abiding memories; its service has been "unceasing," and the men who have departed from its mouth to the "uttermost ends of the earth" are depicted as "knights-errant of the sea," "bearers of a spark from the sacred fire" on ships described as "jewels flashing in the night of time" (546). It would be difficult to find a passage that more concisely expresses the ideals of Victorian culture in such precisely chosen words as "august," "venerable," "reverence," "sacred," and tranquil dignity." These are not words that would spring to the lips of British soldiers enduring the miseries of the trenches in the Great War soon to come. They are the words of a dying world, about to set forth on a profound journey of transformation.

Nor, therefore, are they the sort of words chosen by Marlow, whose voice replaces the narrator's just after the glorious splendor of the sunset yields to the gloom of dusk. Marlow immediately objects to the narrator's evocation of the "Knights" errant, and he replaces the "immensity of unstained light" with the "flicker" that yields to the darkness. Marlow's sense of history goes back beyond the chivalric years of British power to the period of the Roman conquest, when British shores were wild and primitive, and the language which Marlow uses points towards the pessimistic mood of early Modernism, and to the heroic skepticism regarding high ideals characteristic of our century. The "dignity" and "reverence" of the narrator's Thames yields to Marlow's savage world of "cold, fog, tempests, disease, exile, and death." The narrator's "august light of abiding memories" yields to Marlow's "a sea the color of lead, a sky the color of smoke." And the narrator's generals and "knights-errant" heroically planting "the germs of empires" yield to

Marlow's cynical "legionaries" seduced by the "fascination of the abomination" and consumed by "the growing regrets, the longing to escape, the powerless disgust, the surrender, the hate" inspired by a "detestable" reality.

It is this new voice which initiates the hero journey of the language in our century, as it departs from the cozy securities of a Romantic-Victorian vision of the world and sets forth on a quest for a new language adequate to the historical traumas of the times. Marlow's listeners are perhaps captivated by the spell of this new voice, just as the Wedding Guest was captivated by the glittering eye and ballad rhythms of the Mariner. Like the Wedding Guest, the narrator resists and interrupts the tale to protest at key moments, and finds himself watching "for the sentence, for the word, that would give me the clue to the faint uneasiness inspired by this narrative that seemed to shape itself without human lips in the heavy night-air of the river" (566). Already, Marlow's tale is working to transform the narrator's perception of the river: the first change is indicated when the "benign" and "unstained" radiance of the river yields to the faintly infernal "Flames" flickering on its surface just after Marlow begins his tale, "small green flames, red flames, white flames" (548) (The description may owe something to the water snakes the Mariner sees). Later, as the tale progresses, all light departs from the river: it is no longer tranquil, august, serene, pacific, or venerable, but incomprehensible and "heavy." For Marlow's tale is a new kind of story, the understanding of which requires a hero journey on the part of the listener, who must leave old habits and traditions behind in order to discover the clues which unlock the mysteries of a new form of art: his tale is not "typical," with the "meaning of an episode . . . inside like a kernel, but outside, enveloping the tale which brought it out only as a glow brings out a haze, in the likeness of one of these misty halos that sometimes are made visible by the spectral illumination of moonshine" (547). The narrator's response to Marlow's tale also indicates his bondage to an old manner of interpretation, one going back perhaps via Coleridge to Shakespeare, both of whom were taken with the imagery of moonshine as a symbol of the sacred mysteries of the human imagination.

But the "halo" which the narrator hopes to see enveloping Marlow's tale will be gone by the end of its telling. For, as in all hero journeys, the listeners are transformed by Marlow's narrative. The end of the recitation circles back to the beginning, with the narrator sitting silent on the *Nellie*. Even the narrator's language indicates that we have come full circle, for he returns to the phrases which he had used to describe the river at the beginning, but gives them a new twist which indicates the transformation of consciousness wrought by the revelations of Marlow's tale. The "tranquil waterway" that the narrator sees "leading to the uttermost ends of the earth" both at the beginning and end of Marlow's tale (546; 608), now leads not backward into the past of chivalric knighthood, but forward "into the heart of an immense darkness" (608). Hence, the hero journey structure of the frame can be seen as a mythic model for the dynamics of reader-response, moving from that resistance and misconception at the beginning of the tale, which result from old habits of style and reading inherited from tradition, through the revelations of a new form of art, to which the reader gradually adapts, and finally towards the transformation of our sense of reality at the closure of the reading event.

The tale which effects this transformation upon its listeners is also structured precisely along the lines of the hero journey cycle, beginning and ending with Marlow in Brussels, with the revelations of the trip up the Congo in between. Marlow's call to adventure comes significantly in the form of a serpent (as it did for Adam and Eve) which Marlow saw as a child on an old map of the Congo, in which the river twists its way into the dark continent, fascinating the boy "as a snake would a bird" (549). The more current impulse behind the journey is the realistic need for employment, which takes Marlow to a trading company office in Brussels with a "concern" in the Congo. These offices are described in terms already quite familiar to us from our survey of the iconography of the monomyth: they are found in a building on a "narrow and deserted street" lined by houses with "innumerable windows" and "imposing archways right and left" (550). The threshold imagery is emphasized as Marlow slips through a pair of "immense double doors standing ponderously ajar" and walks up an "ungarnished staircase" to open "the first door" he comes to at the top of the steps (551). This leads into a waiting room, in which a third "door opened," and a "skinny forefinger" beckons Marlow into the "sanctuary," where he will receive his commission. As in modern films by Murnau, Cocteau, Bergman, and Weir, this sequential passage through alleyways lined with windows and large gaping archways, up staircases to door leading into an inner chamber is as often repeated in contemporary as in ancient versions of the hero monomyth.

The door at the top of the staircase leading into the waiting room of the Company offices is further distinguished by its pair of threshold guardians: two women knitting black wool, a younger woman, and an older who has a wart on her cheek, wears spectacles, and emanates an "uncanny and fateful" air. The pair suggest the Eleusinian duad (Demeter and Persephone) and the two women of the Castle of Bertilak in *Sir Gawain*. They are certainly Goddesses, or Witches, weaving the thread of fate like their Classical counterparts, and accoutered by the typical signs of the witches of folklore (wart, nose, spectacles). In another phrase emphasizing the threshold imagery characteristic of the journey, Marlow tells us that he often thought of these two, while off in the Congo, as "guarding the door of Darkness" (551).

Through this sequence of doorways, Marlow passes on to his trip up the Congo on a French steamer, first to the "seat of the government" at the mouth of the river, then on up by sea-going steamer thirty miles or so to the Company's station, and then finally by caravan overland some two-hundred miles to the Central Station on a "backwater surrounded by scrub and forest" (560). Here further progress is impeded by the want of rivets which Marlow needs to repair his steamer, which he finds has been sunk in the river which will take him to his final destination: the outpost (the Interior 'station') of the mysterious Mr. Kurtz, whom it appears to be Marlow's mission to retrieve. The steps and stages of the journey are marked by this sequence of stations, where the trials and ordeals typical of all hero journeys are enacted, with the ultimate effect of transforming the consciousness of the hero and preparing him for the revelatory initiations at its climax.

Marlow presents his journey throughout the tale as a descent to the underworld, drawing on Classical, Christian, and Arthurian allusions to the myth. He called Brussels a "whited sephulchre" and a "city of the dead," with the doorway of the Company office guarded by the fates of the underworld. The metaphor is sustained when Marlow travels up the "streams of death" which lead from the seat of the government to the Company station. The station is presented as "the gloomy circle of some Inferno," inhabited by the "devils" of "greed," "violence," and "hot desire" (556). Its topography is equally infernal, as Marlow descends a steep pathway beside a "vast artificial hole" into a "narrow ravine" through which some rapids roar with "an uninterrupted, uniform, headlong, rushing noise" that fills the "mournful stillness of the grove" (556). Many of these details (the broken rings of the valleys and circles of Hell, the terrible noise of the river, and the mournful silence) come certainly from Dante, but also suggests the presence of a wide range of allusions to Hades characteristic of many another hero journey. For example, when Marlow offers one of the dying slaves chained beneath the trees a "good Swede's biscuit," he is being compassionate as well as reenacting the Classical prototype of the coin offered Charon for the Stygian crossing. Conrad combines vividly rendered realistic details with archetypal import in a manner typical of the mythical method of Modernism. This method allows a certain freedom for its practitioners, who, as Ian Watt notes, cannot be pinned down to any single scheme of mythographic allusion, but are allowed to draw freely from the vast well of analogies established by the tradition of the hero journey.

When Marlow leaves this "grove of death" (566) to trek overland to the Central station, Arthurian and folkloric allusions begin to surface, alongside the sustained metaphor of the doorway. The manager of the station, for example, orders "an immense round table to be made" as a means of avoiding the "constant quarrels of the white men about precedence" (561), the very same motives which compelled Arthur to create his famous round table. The white men who wander aimlessly around the station seem like "a lot of faithless pilgrims bewitched inside a rotten fence" by the spell of ivory, and hence resemble the enchanted denizens of the otherworld in many folktales and Arthurian fables, whose redemption is the hero's task. As we will see, the image of the "rotten fence" will come up later in the description of the Interior station from which Kurtz operates. While no actual gateway is mentioned in the current description of the Central station, the manager's peculiar smile, which comes at the end of speeches "like a seal applied on the words to make the meaning of the commonest phrase appear absolutely inscrutable" (560), seems to Marlow to be a "door opening into a darkness he had in his keeping" (561). The manager is another sort of threshold guardian, analogous to the witches "guarding the door of Darkness" at the beginning of the journey (551).

The imagery of bewitchment, as characteristic of the folktale as of the Arthurian romance, continues as Marlow finally leaves the Central station and heads upriver, after discovering that the steamer had probably been sunk as part of a conspiracy to destroy Kurtz. Many of the revelations of this journey, in fact, have to do with that darker side of human nature normally encountered by any entrance into the world of business, but which Marlow seems to blow up a bit out of proportion. Like Young Goodman Brown, he will be constantly exposed to the evil side of civilization, here to the greed and deception behind the imperialistic colonization of Africa. But the revelation goes deeper than this to a sort of cosmic intimation of the principle of all evil, which Marlow describes during his journey to the Inner station as "the stillness of an implacable force brooding over an inscrutable intention" (571). Only the forest strikes a more positive note, as it represents "the earliest beginnings of the world," as if Marlow's hero journey were compelled by the nostalgia for the lost paradise which we have seen previously in the *Epic of Gilgamesh*, and will see again in such works as Cortázar's *Hopscotch*.

The central revelations of the hero journey in the *Heart of Darkness*, however, involve that evil principle which presides inscrutably behind the face of historical events. These occur in the hut where Kurtz has erected his 'Inner station.' Conrad grew up in a Russian occupied Poland, his father having been sent into exile at one point. I would not be at all surprised if scholarship doesn't someday reveal the influence of the hero journey in Russian folktales on the *Heart of Darkness*. I say this because the hut where Kurtz lies dying, and where the central initiatory revelations of the journey occur, is described in almost exactly the same way as Baba Yaga's hut was in the little tale called "Vasilisa the Beautiful" which we looked at in the previous chapter. Another clue to the possibility of this influence is the fact that the young admirer of Kurtz who greets Marlow at the Inner station is a Russian boy, "son of an arch priest" (588) who has made Cyrillic notes in a nautical manual Marlow had found farther down river. While this boy chatters away, Marlow examines the hut which Kurtz inhabits through field glasses: it is surrounded by numerous stakes with shrunken heads on the tops turned inward toward the station (like the skulls on the fence surrounding Baba Yaga's hut). Ants ascend the stakes to devour "shrunken dry lips" twisted and smiling "at some endless and jocose dream" (591). Kurtz seems imprisoned in this hut and the passage to him "beset by as many dangers as though he had been an enchanted princess sleeping in a famous castle" (579), another reference to the folkloric background of the tale.

It is ultimately Kurtz's proclamation about the "horror" of life in his dying words that constitutes the essential revelation of Marlow's journey. But while in the jungle surrounding the hut, Marlow witnesses demonic ceremonies analogous to the ones Goodman Brown attended. These ceremonies constitute a kind of initiation for Marlow, rituals of revelation and transformation which Conrad uses the Classical term "mysteries" to evoke throughout the novella. The reader may recall that the term is used in Classical scholarship to designate the ritual descent to and return from the underworld celebrated yearly in the Eleusinian mysteries of Demeter, Persephone, and Hades. This certainly is one of the suggested allusions of the term as used in *Heart of Darkness*, along with such related terms as "unspeakable rites" (585), "the inconceivable ceremonies of some devilish initiation" (583), "an unfathomable enigma, a mystery" (578), "an extravagant mystery" (575), "ceremonies" (551), and "a vast grave full of unspeakable secrets" (595).

Marlow at first says "there's no initiation either into such mysteries" (548), but Kurtz, no longer a neophyte in these mysteries, is referred to as "an initiated wraith from the back of Nowhere" (584). The scenario of his initiatory penetration of the mysteries is described in vigorous detail by Marlow in a passage that has much in common with the devil's Sabbath in "Young Goodman Brown" as the climax of the journey. It occurs after midnight "deep within the forest" where "red gleams" waver by a fireside camp. There is drumming and "A steady droning sound of many men chanting each to himself some weird incantation" that has the sound of "the humming of bees" (597). It is a "mysterious frenzy" which has awakened Kurtz and "driven him out to the edge of the forest, to the bush, towards the gleam of fires, the throb of drums, the drone of weird incantations" (598). Marlow tracks him down and, in the depths of jungle, sees "the inconceivable mystery of a soul that knew no restraint, no faith, and no fear, yet blindly struggling with itself" (599). The "satanic litany" continues, "strings of amazing words that resembled no sounds of human language" (599), much like the hymnal Goodman Brown hears roaring through the forest, or the "whispers in an unknown tongue" Peyton Farquhar hears during his own descent into the shadowland (72). These are all images of those powers of poesis activated by the hero journey.

Marlow's job is characteristic of the hero journeys of Arthurian fable: he must "break the spell -- the heavy mute spell of the wilderness -- that seemed to draw him to its pitiless breast by the awakening of forgotten and brutal instincts, by the memory of gratified and monstrous passions" (598). The "mysteries," put in this way seem to suggest a Freudian underworld, and it is certainly marvelous to note the nearly simultaneous appearance of *Heart of Darkness* and *The Interpretation of Dreams* in the year 1900. From this perspective, the revelations of Marlow's journey have to do with the cauldron of instinctual drives which Freud threatened would eventually erupt and boil over in *Civilization and Its Discontents*, a prophecy which seemed to have been fulfilled by the Great War. But there is also a Jungian dimension to Conrad's jungle land of the id, because Marlow's experience leads him to the conclusion that "'The mind of man is capable of anything -- because everything is in it, all the past as well as all the future'" (573), a description which appears to suggest the collective unconscious and the mystery of the archetypes with which the novella is replete. In either case, the metaphor of the dream as an expression of the basic dynamics of the human imagination and as essential to the hero journey is one which Conrad shares with both Freud and Jung, since Marlow repeatedly refers to his experience in terms of dream and nightmare.

After Marlow breaks the spell and forces Kurtz to return to the steamer, the return phase of the journey continues to allude to the mythological paradigm of the descent to the underworld. Marlow feels as if he "were buried in a vast grave full of unspeakable secrets" (595), and after Kurtz dies with the famous proclamation of "The horror!" upon his lips, Marlow undergoes a near death experience resulting from a fever. Like Gilgamesh, or like the Eldest Lady who loses her beloved on the return from the enchanted island, the threshold crossing of the return stage of the hero journey involves the loss of that talisman which it had been one's goal to retrieve, but also the recovery of the wisdom which that talisman (as well as the bitter experience of its loss) conveys. Marlow loses Kurtz to the powers of darkness like Gilgamesh loses his flower, but he brings back with him a story which encapsulates the wisdom of the monomyth. In an extraordinary passage, Conrad seems to suggest an analogy between the story and the near-death experience. After Kurtz is buried, Marlow says "then they very nearly buried me," and proceeds to recount his wrestling match with "death" (602). As always in the hero journey, it involves revelation, this time of Marlow's destiny, and of "that mysterious arrangement of merciless logic for a futile purpose" which is life (602). The "arrangement" may be "futile" and "merciless," but it is a "logic" nevertheless, one that intimates the basic pattern of Marlow's destiny. The revelation of this logic costs Marlow a descent into the "impalpable grayness, with nothing underfoot, with nothing around" (602); yet, he surmises, it may be that "all the wisdom, and all truth, and all sincerity, are just compressed into that inappreciable moment of time in which we step over the threshold of the invisible" (602).

As James Hillman has so wonderfully shown, the Hades of Classical myth was associated with the revelation of those fundamental ideas (*eidola*) which shape and govern life, and this seems to be one essence of the hero journey which Conrad picks up in this passage. But in addition to the Classical, Christian, folkloric, and Arthurian paradigms of the journey which the text alludes to, Conrad also weaves allusions to the Buddha's journey into the novella as a whole, and into Marlow's near-death narrative in particular. The nameless narrator twice refers to Marlow as a Buddha -- at the beginning as a "Buddha preaching in European clothes and without a lotus-flower" (548), and at the end as a silent "meditating Buddha" (608). That the allusion is more than ornamental can be shown by a careful reading of Marlow's near-death revelation, which bears strong imprints of Buddhist thinking. In the legendary saga, the Buddha achieves enlightenment after his years in the forest when he sits beneath the Boddhi tree and is assailed by the triune powers of the world, Kama-Mara-Dharma (Love-Death-Duty). When he remains unmoved by the demons of desire, hatred, and duty, enlightenment follows: the illusory nature of all being (*maya*) is dissolved into the emptiness (*sunyata*) of nirvana . It is the 'nothingness' (*sunyata*) of the mind at the moment of death which Marlow evokes ("nothing underfoot," "nothing around") as a realm beyond the power of Kama-Mara, beyond "the great desire of victory," and beyond "the great fear of defeat" is how he puts it (602). The "ultimate wisdom" revealed by his passage bestows a "careless contempt for the evanescence of all things" (602) characteristic of the Buddhist attitude toward life. Indeed, Marlow's description of his near-death experience as a "passage through some inconceivable world that had no hope in it and no desire" (603) seems to indicate a more powerful presence of Buddhist thinking in Conrad's life than critics have yet acknowledged.

The last job of the Buddha is to return to the world with his teachings, a job which he distrusted as much as Marlow seems to distrust his own ability to complete the hero journey cycle by returning to Brussels. He is permanently alienated when he does, like the Mariner, a

360 *The Hero Journey in Literature*

sadder and wiser man condemned to tell his story forever. Marlow finds himself back in the "sepulchral city" (603), but unable to rejoin the general stream of common humanity. His last task is a visit to Kurtz's fiancé, a task in which the threshold iconography of the hero journey comes to the fore once again. The "Intended's" house is in a street "as still and decorous as a well-kept alley in a cemetery," where Marlow finds himself one twilight standing "before the high and ponderous door" (604) which recalls the "door of Darkness" at the beginning of his tale (551). Once again we see Marlow waiting in a room with "three long windows from floor to ceiling" until "A high door opened -- closed" and the fiancé walks into the room (605). She too is a creature of Hades, a "tragic and familiar Shade" (607) to whom Marlow whispers the famous lie (that Kurtz had her name on his lips when she died). With this lie Marlow finally returns to the world of illusion in which we all must live, completing one of the most remarkable hero journey cycles of all literature, and a great "masterpiece of early Modernism," as Ian Watt puts it.

James Joyce

It was the publication of James Joyce's *Ulysses* that inspired Eliot's famous and influential definition of the mythical method: in Joyce's novel, we find elaborately detailed, realistic portraits of daily life in Dublin enriched by allusions to Homer's *Odyssey*. The novel follows the hero journey structure exactly, tracing Leopold Bloom's peregrinations across the city of Dublin from the morning when he gets out of bed, to the early hours of the next morning when he returns to it. In between ensues a sequence of revelations and encounters loosely modeled on Homer. But the allusions to the Homeric nekyia in such chapters as "Hades" and "Circe" is complemented by a wide range of allusions to Arthurian and Celtic myths about the otherworld in Joyce's earlier work.

In the little story called "Araby" from the *Dubliners* collection, for example, the adolescent protagonist goes on a journey at twilight across the city which includes many aspects of the descent myth of the hero. His call to adventure is an encounter with a girl across the street, Mangan's sister, who tells him she cannot attend the upcoming bazaar, but that he might bring her a gift if he wishes. The boy's encounter with Mangan's sister evokes many of the motifs associated with the hero journey, particularly the imagery of doorways and the iconography of the Goddess, incarnated here in the Catholic iconography of the duality between Eve and Mary: on the one hand, She is the mother of all living, but also (and primarily) the mother of death and sin; and on the other she is Mary, mother of our spiritual life and redeemer of the sins of Eve, the consequences of which she reverses -- hence the Eva / Ave antinomy, which is simply a doctrinal formulation of the essence of the loving and terrible mother Goddess, who is both womb and tomb in the pagan tradition. The Catholic iconography colors the perceptions of the hero of the story, a nameless boy whose journey into life is initiated by the sight of a girl simply called Mangan's sister, standing in the doorway of a neighbor's home at dusk. Joyce's description of this 'epiphanic' moment is repeated three times in two pages of a short story set largely on Saturday evening, which was consecrated by Masses honoring the Virgin (the only ones Joyce returned to the Church to witness in later years). The triune repetition of the image of Mangan's sister in the doorway emphasizes the threshold imagery of the hero journey, and it ndicates the impact of the iconography of the Virgin on the boy's consciousness: she is illuminated from behind by a light from within the house which touches her boy at three points: at the nape of her curved neck, bowed downward toward the boy standing at the railings beneath the steps; at the hand which she gently rests on a spike from the railing; and at the lower edge of her petticoats, just visible beneath her dress. The position of the boy at the base of the steps suggests the posture of worship at the railings of the altar, and the curved luminous neck and spike reinforce the associations of between Mangan's sister and the Virgin. However, the hand resting on the subtly phallic spike and the petticoats visible lower down convey sexual connotations associated with Eva. Hence, the girl is perceived as a mixture of the two mythological images which the boy has imbibed from his religious education.

It is this epiphany of the girl standing at the top of the steps in the doorway of her home which initiates the hero journey in the story. It is twilight when he leaves home clutching "a florin tightly" in his hand, after a threshold battle with his drunken uncle, who comes home late and attempts to discourage the boy from departing at all. But the boy wins the battle, and his journey takes him in a southeasterly direction on a "deserted train" that "crept onward among ruinous houses and over the twinkling river" (34). As so often in the hero journey, the passage takes us over the river, an icon of the transition to the otherworld. He leaves the "bare carriage" and enters the bazaar "through a turnstile, handing a shilling to a weary-looking man" (34). The atmosphere of the bazaar to which the coin gives him access is both infernal and erotic: it is silent and "the greater part of the hall was in darkness;" "great jars that stood like eastern guards at either side of the dark entrance to the stall" where a young lady flirts suggestively with two Englishmen (35). The imagery of forbidden doorways surfaces again here, guarded by strangers and accompanied by a secretive linguistics is indeed "eastern," a standard feature of Sumero-Egyptian underworlds, just as the large jars standing at the entrance are sepulchral and almost canopic. There are el-

362   *The Hero Journey in Literature*

ements of the Arthurian otherworld as well: the boy imagines that he is carrying a chalice like a Grail through a throng of foes, and his arrival at place where a young woman is beset by the 'evil' powers of an oppressor (the two Englishmen seducing or being seduced by the Irish maid at the bazaar booth) is typical of the Arthurian quest.

The profane implications of Mangan's sister crystallize around this figure of the shop girl whom the boy encounters at the bazaar. As in the earlier scene with Mangan's sister in the doorway, the boy stands looking at the woman while she talks with two men with English accents, making him feel all the more excluded. Joyce adapted the content of their bantering from one of the epiphanies he collected as a young artist in the making in which a girl flirts with a man in Church whom she calls very "wicked." In "Araby," the word "fib" replaces wicked, a word which retains the sexual implications of "wicked," because of its context of flirtation, and which considerably extends the theme of the loss of the boy's innocence to include such issues as the way his literary, political, and religious educations have lied to him about life in Ireland. Although it is not certain which female the boy feels more betrayed by at the end of the story, it is certain that Joyce meant Mangan's sister and the salesgirl at the bazaar to be seen as complementary opposites of the Eva / Ave complex which conditions the boy's misunderstanding of women. The revelations of this initiation phase of the journey overpower the boy, so that we do not actually complete the cycle in the story (though it can safely be assumed that the boy will eventually return home). He is left standing in "anger and anguish," like Young Goodman Brown unable to cope with what he learns about himself and the world around him.

Another story in *Dubliners* which makes use of the iconography of the hero journey is "An Encounter." It concerns a truant excursion several boys make one day shortly before the summer holidays. Their plan is to skip school one morning (a very simple call to adventure, Spring Fever), to meet on the Canal Bridge, and "to go along the Wharf Road until we came to the ships, then to cross in the ferryboat and walk out to see the Pigeon House" (21). This itinerary suggests Charon's ferryboat crossing to the yonder shore, or the Celtic voyages by ship to a land beyond the waves, and is typical of the monomyth. Their destination, the Pigeon House, suggests the country inhabited by bird souls which forms a standard feature of Sumerian, Egyptian, and Celtic underworlds: as Anthony Roche notes in his commentary on Celtic motifs in Chapter 4 of *A Portrait* (where Stephen experiences his vision of the bird-girl on the Strand), "the souls of those who died young took flight for the Otherworld in the shape of birds" (328). The young Dubliner in "An Encounter" hides his books "in the long grass near the ashpit at the end of the garden where nobody ever came," and sits waiting on the

Canal Bridge (our threshold crossing) until a boy named Mahony joins him and demonstrates the slingshot which he brings along "to have some gas with the birds" (22). (Ashes, the end of a garden where no-body comes, dead birds gassed: all suggest the underworld).

After walking along the river to the quays, the juvenile narrator says "We crossed the Liffey in the ferryboat, paying our toll to be transported in the company of two laborers and a little Jew with a bag" (23). This stygian crossing takes them to the shipyards and to Ringsend (my und.); the day turns "sultry" so they buy biscuits, chocolate, and raspberry lemonade" from the little groceries among the "squalid streets" (24). The "field" they then reach, with its view of the river Dodder, is not Elysian, but it is infernal, since it is here that their encounter with a seedy and sadistic pervert occurs. He appears "shabbily dressed in a suit of greenish-black," and he looks "fairly old for his mustache was ashen-grey" (24). Like the shades imprisoned in the maze of Dante's inferno,[6] the man walks painfully past the boys some fifty paces, then turns around to "retrace his steps," tapping the ground all the while with his stick like a blind man. As always, this underworld is a place of revelation, for the moribund old shade speaks through "great gaps in his mouth between his yellow teeth" about "sweethearts," dwelling obses-sively on the details of their hair and hands (25-26). The boys will not get to see the Pigeon House, for the man holds them captive in what Doob calls "the inextricable prison-labyrinth of hell," and hence they are unable to pass beyond the *Inferno* to the vision of "souls like a flock of birds" in Dante's *Purgatorio* (306).

In addition to his "ashen" mustache and "greenish black" suit, the man's speech is also characteristic of the souls of the dead as presented in Dante's *Inferno*. In the circle of the lustful, the souls whirl around and around driven by the cyclone of desire, while the souls of the eighth circle (into which Dante and Virgil descend via the whirling circular flight of Geryon) are driven by demons revolving round and round their various circles for all eternity. The man's repetitious speech in "An Encounter" mimics this spiraling aspect of the infernal maze: as if "magnetized by some words of his own speech, his mind was slowly circling round and round in the same orbit" (26). Joyce takes pains that we notice this allusion to Dante's labyrinth of hell: after speaking of the sweethearts, the man goes off to masturbate near the end of the field, and then returns to speak obsessively of whipping boys: "His mind, as if magnetized again by his speech, seemed to circle slowly round and round its new centre" (27). The man remains trapped in the circles of the lustful and the hostile, performing his obsessive rituals of sin and atonement, circling repetitiously in his field, pandering to any pair of boys who might pass by (Virgil and Dante?). The revelations of this shade are purely infernal, the "unfolding" of "some elaborate mystery" (27). The boy sits listening as the "elderly pederast," as Stanislaus Joyce calls him (Anderson 465), leads him "monotonously through the mystery," before escaping to "the top of the slope" (28). In spite of the perverse aspect of this encounter, the word "mystery" repeated in the passage accords well with its traditional meaning as a process of revelation in an underworldly setting (as in the Eleusinian mysteries). The climax of the Classical mysteries involved an epiphany of a god, so that again it is interesting that the boys call the man "a queer old josser" (26), since "in Pidgin English the term 'joss' means a 'god' or an 'idol'" (Anderson 466n.). As in "Araby," the return phase of the journey is implied, but omitted by the narrator, as if to suggest that the initiatory revelations have so permanently transformed the consciousness of the protagonist that he will be unable to complete the cycle by returning home.

In "The Dead," the concluding tale in *Dubliners*, a mature version of the journey across the city takes place with similar undertones of the nekyia: Gabriel Conroy and his wife Gretta leave the family Christmas party late at night in a horse drawn coach that takes them across the Liffey to their hotel -- horse and river crossing being old conventions of the journey to the yonder shore of the dead. What takes place in the hotel room has long been the subject of critical debate; with respect to the conventions of the descent, however, it is important to note that the hotel room becomes a burial place of memory and desire, as Gretta lapses into nostalgic yearning for the young man who died out of love for her. Her "evocation of this figure from the dead, a boy in the gasworks" (219) propels Gabriel into "a fever of rage and desire" (217) reminiscent of the oscillations between desire and rage in the monotonous monologues of the queer old josser in "An Encounter" (in which, by the way, Mahony vowed to "have some gas with the birds" (22; my unds.)). The "figure from the dead" was named Michael, angel of the apocalypse and last judgment. After listening to Gretta's story about him, Gabriel passes beyond the purgatory of his lust, shedding "Generous tears" of sympathy for her, as his soul approaches "that region where dwell the vast hosts of the dead" (223). The story concludes with its grand epiphany of the snow falling on the sea and graves of western Ireland, last refuge of the Gaelic speaking Celts.

The imagery of the hero journey to the underworld continues in *A Portrait of the Artist as a Young Man*. Stephen Dedalus experiences his vocation as an artist during a walk on the strand which combines Celtic, Christian, and Classical conventions of the hero journey. Chapter Four of *A Portrait* provides us with a finely modeled version of the monomyth, though, like the stories in *Dubliners*, the return phase is implied but not completed. The walk begins when Stephen sees the

Jesuit father who is urging a priestly vocation "slowly dangling and looping the cord" of the "crossblind" like a noose (154). The setting and the words chosen throughout the passage (the word grave several times) connect the Jesuit director to the underworld: he stands "in total shadow" in the "waning daylight" (154) at the end of summer; the "curves of the skull" (154) are touched by the light; he speaks "gravely" (154) and leans his chin "gravely" upon his hands (157); Stephen perceives his "shadowed face" as a "spectre" (155), and he repeatedly notes "the gravity of the priest's voice" (157). The imagery is consistent all the way up to the end of the passage on the Strand, when Stephen sees the vestments of a priestly vocation as the "cerements shaken from the body of death" (169) and "the linens of the grave" (170), while he sees the Jesuit college as "the grave of boyhood" (170) from which he has now arisen.

Stephen's pagan resurrection, and the departure phase of the hero journey, begins when he leaves the College and wanders restlessly through Dublin towards the Strand. It is a journey from the hell of the Church to the otherworld of Celtic song and mysticism which also invokes Classical images of the nekyia, such as the crossing of the river Styx. As Stephen descends the steps of the Jesuit college, he remembers the "sluggish turfcolored water" of the bath at Clongowes (161), and he then "crossed the bridge over the stream of the Tolka" (162) in the twilight "glow of the dying day" (163) before reaching home, the other inferno from which he must escape. The precise delineation of Stephen's restless pacing through Dublin also evokes the related imagery of the labyrinth in which Daedalus was imprisoned. Stephen waits outside the university for his father, pacing the pavement back and forth from Byron's pub to Clontarf Chapel, like Icarus imprisoned in the labyrinth, and timing his footsteps to "the fall of verses" (164). This halted and impeded progress, always returning back again to the same place, connects the treading of a labyrinth with the writing of a poem. By setting "off abruptly for the Bull," Stephen seems to take it upon himself both to slay the Minotaur imprisoned in the center of the maze and to take flight from the ties binding him to the endless and pointless peregrinations around the city of Dublin which Joyce thoroughly delineates in *Dubliners*, *A Portrait*, and *Ulysses*.

Stephen escapes the maze of church and family by leaving home at dusk and crossing the Liffey going out of town just as a group of boys from a Christian school come back, heading into town. Before crossing the bridge, Stephen hears the "fitful music" of an "elfin prelude" which evokes Celtic motifs: the music brings the pattering feet of wild rabbits and deer to Stephen's mind, those same animals which so frequently appear as guides to the otherworld in Celtic myth and Germanic märchen. This "elfin prelude" inspires a "wayward instinct" as Stephen rejects "the oils of ordination" and turns seaward at Dollymount, passing on to a "thin wooden bridge" which shakes and trembles (165), rather like the sword bridge of Arthurian legend, for as in Chrétien the water below is rapid and "swirling" (166). Stephen pauses a full page to meditate upon the bridge, before passing to "firm land again" (167). For this river crossing marks a point of no return for Stephen, and suggests that his "symbolic voyage to the Otherworld" (Roche 324) will take him both out of a strictly Christian context, away from home, and out of Dublin (the cerements of church, family, and nation which he must shed).

For it is during the walk on the strand that Stephen receives his vocation as a "priest of the eternal imagination" (221), a calling "from beyond the world" (167) that will lead to his rejection of the Jesuit way and to his departure from Dublin for Paris at the end of the novel. Anthony Roche has beautifully shown that this calling from "beyond the world" is Celtic, and associated with poesis, with its mystical is-lands populated by enchanted swan women, and with its emphasis on song and nature. Stephen has, therefore, escaped a Christian hell only to wind up in the Celtic afterlife! That the revelation of the form Stephen's life is to fit should occur here in the otherworld also corresponds to the Classical tradition: both Odysseus and Aeneas find their futures revealed in Hades. In addition, this Celtic otherworld is a realm associated with song, bird imagery, and the dominion of the Goddess.[7] As always in Joyce, the actual topography of Stephen's journey coincides with an imaginal, mythical landscape, as Stephen leaves the city and a Catholic vocation behind and merges with "the strange light of some new world" inspired by song and inhabited by children and presided over by a girl "whom magic had changed into the likeness of a strange and beautiful seabird" (171).

While Roche emphasizes the Celtic motifs linking song, seabird, and woman, the Classical and pre-Classical associations of this epiphany of the Goddess are equally important. In Homer's *Odyssey*, for example, after inspiring Telemakhos with "a new dream of his father," Athena "left him / as a bird rustles upward, off and gone" (1. 357-60). As in Joyce, this Homeric epiphany has to do with the destiny of the hero and the atonement with the father, coming at a crucial turning point in the action and in the hero's life. Also pagan, and indeed both pre-Christian and pre-Classical, is the connection between the Goddess and the crane: Stephen notes that the "long slender bare legs" of the girl on the beach "were delicate as a crane's" (171). This simile opens up long vistas into the mythological past: Karl Kerényi, for example, in-cludes several Greek ceramic portrayals of Goddesses with cranes; we have also the famous crane dance of Delos, "a labyrinthine dance in cel-ebration of their [Theseus and his men] escape from Crete" (Stephen also taking wings now, turning his mind to unknown arts to escape the maze);[8] and Robert Graves' *White Goddess* has a Minoan image of what he would call the Triple Goddess surrounded by cranes on its cover. We can push further back to the earliest 'Venus' figurines of the Paleolithic with necks elongated into bird shapes and then to the "Geese, cranes, and swans" from the Upper Paleolithic discussed by Gimbutas as standard icons of the "Bird Goddess" (Chapter 1). The connection between the transformative mysteries of death and rebirth associated with these myths was one of great importance to Joyce's conception of Hermes and Thoth, the Ibis-headed patron of the magical arts of writing in ancient Egypt.

What I want to emphasize here, however, is the linkage between various birds and the Goddess (a linkage we also find in Frost's "Never Again Would Birdsong Be the Same" and in Lawrence's novels),[9] suggesting that she is not simply to be seen as a fertility icon, but as a muse of the spiritual life as well. In the Catholic tradition, this is indicated by the iconography of the Annunciation (connected here to Stephen's call to the artistic life as a "priest of the eternal imagination"), in which the Holy Ghost impregnates the Virgin in the form of the descending dove. Hence Joyce tells us that the girl Stephen sees on the beach has "slateblue skirts "which dovetailed behind her," and that her "bosom" was "slight and soft as the breast of some darkplumaged dove" (171). Slateblue is the Virgin's color; the dove her bird; and, finally the moon her planet.

As evening falls, Stephen climbs to the crest of a dune to gaze out upon the "rim of the young moon ... like the rim of a silver hoop embedded in the grey sand" and hovering over "the low whisper of her waves" (173). As David Miller puts it, "the Church's official theology of Moon-symbolism is clear and straightforward: Mary is the Moon" (86). Such symbolism, in the Church, originates in the book of Revelation, in which Mary stands on the crescent moon clothed in the radiance of the sun, imagery passed along by such artists as Dürer in his magnificent Apocalypse series and title page. Once again, however, the lunar imagery in this passage evokes an extremely archaic pedigree of Goddess symbolism originating with the Venus of Laussell (c.20,000 B.C.E.), who holds the horns of the crescent moon in her right hand, her left placed upon the mystery of her womb (Campbell, *Animal Powers* 1. 47f.). Such imagery comes down to us and into the Catholic Church via the Egyptian iconography of Isis standing on the crescent moon, as described in the magnificent vision of Apuleius in *The Golden Ass* of the second century. Lunar symbolism in relation to the Goddess also saturates the work of Lawrence.

Hence, what Joyce has done in this passage is to combine the Eva / Ave duality in a single archetypal figure who transcends the Catholic dialectic with the substitution of a third term which subsumes without negating either pole. The resounding yes to life and to art which the vision of the girl on the beach inspires in Stephen echoes the inspiration of Dante by Beatrice and looks forward to Molly's famous last words in *Ulysses*. In *A Portrait*, the vision comes to Stephen directly from "the wild heart of life" (171) and gives him the courage to "greet the advent of the life that had cried to him" and to celebrate her "call" to a life of "error" and "ecstasy" in a wild outburst of song (172). Behind the biblical associations of such words as "advent" and "call" in this passage, we can glimpse the pagan affiliation of the Goddess and song, as evidenced throughout Homer's *Odyssey*, in which we see Kirke, Kalypso, and the Sirens weaving their haunting songs over the wine-dark sea. The initiation into the mysteries of the Goddess is an initiation into the arts of poetry, and the hero journey is a parable of poesis.

Which brings us to the final details of Joyce's portrait of the Goddess as a young girl: her affiliation with the basic elements of life, fire and water. David Miller has shown how, in the "lunar poetry of Christian piety" devoted to the Virgin Mary, "These apparently opposite elements and qualities are one" (89). Hence it is curious to find that Joyce's girl on the beach, who stands gazing out to sea beside a stream, "gently stirring the water with her foot hither and thither" (171), also has a "faint flame" trembling on her cheek, and that as Stephen turns ecstatically away from her to stride across the strand, "His cheeks were aflame; his body was aglow" (171-72). These elements seem to issue from her "wild heart," the source of life and art, and the basic elements to be "transmuted" by the alchemy of Stephen's priestly craft, which demands a descent "into some new world, fantastic, dim, uncertain as under sea" (172). The essential revelation of the journey then concerns Stephen's aesthetic vocation and the dedication of his powers to the Goddess of life. As in Lawrence, the passage combines biblical, alchemical, Celtic, and Classical motifs, all associated with the breakdown of life to its fundamental elements, and a recreation of the world, the poet, and the poem.

D.H. Lawrence

We find a similar configuration of elemental patterns of the imagination in the wonderful little story by Lawrence called "The Horse Dealer's Daughter," in which the imagery of fire and water is once again evoked in relation to a plain collier girl who assumes the form of the Goddess in the life of the young doctor, Jack Ferguson, who rescues her from the pond in which she attempts to drown herself after the collapse of her family. The story offers a complete hero journey cycle, taking us from the house to the pond and back to the house. The essence of the journey, however, is not so much the aesthetic vocation, but the entry into marriage, a major rite of passage which always entails a hero and heroine journey.

The departure phase of the journey begins when Ferguson visits the house just after the death of the father, when the horses and furniture are being taken away, and the three brothers ponder their future. They wonder what will become of their sister Mabel, who wanders around the house in sullen, ineffectual solitude. The language of this first section emphasizes the crisis conditions which characteristically inaugurate the journey: the breakfast table is "desolate" and "desultory;" the brothers are imprisoned in an "air of ineffectuality" and the sister is "sullen;" all are frightened by "the collapse of their lives" and look around "with a glazed look of helplessness" in a "stupor of downfall;" and a "helpless silence" sets in "of futility and irritation." This is Eliot's waste land, wholly characteristic of the kind of conditions (death, collapse, oppression) which initiates the hero journey cycle. In this case, the call to adventure comes from Jack Ferguson, the town doctor, whose arrival sparks a new energy and sense of hope. The action now moves "through the passage and down to the back door," where the doctor departs, Mabel soon to follow, for the introduction of the doorway signals the departure phase of the journey.

After the doctor leaves the house, he sees Mabel in the churchyard scrubbing her mother's tombstone, who has left the house as well. She has entered a kind of underworld, secluded "under the shadow of the great looming church, among the graves ... as in another country." This otherworld is psychological as well, as Mabel goes into a kind of trance, "mindless and persistent" and so "intent and remote, it was like looking into another world." Jack watches her "as if spellbound" as he walks by the graveyard, and the "vision" of her "portentous" face seems to "mesmerize him." What Lawrence has done here is to psychologize the heroine's journey, as both Mabel and Jack leave the little world of the "fettered, daily life" behind to enter the strange hypnosis of "another country." Words like "mesmerize" and "mindless" suggests the influence of psychology on Lawrence's conception of the journey as a common aspect of our daily experience, in which multiple descents into the unconscious mind typically occur.

Ferguson later watches fascinated as Mabel descends a hill outside of town and walks straight into a pond at the bottom. The setting and language of this section of the story focus on realistic details with mythic overtones suggesting the descent into the underworld. It is during the twilight of a cold winter afternoon that Ferguson races "down" the hill during the "dusk of the dead afternoon," when everything is "deadened, and wintry." The cold is "deadening," the houses seem "extinct" under a sky of "smouldering ash," and Ferguson sees the town as a "hellish hole." As he runs "down" into the "sodden hollow" in the "falling dusk," he sees Mabel's small "black figure" moving "straight down the field towards the pond" at the bottom of the "hollow." He watches amazed as her "small black figure walked slowly and deliberately towards the center of the pond," and then he hastens after her, running "straight down ... into the depression" and on into the "dead water" of the pond. To rescue her, slips into the rank mud, and falls under the hideous, acrid water of the "dead cold pond" which "clasped dead cold round his legs." Lawrence clearly intends us to see Ferguson's journey from the town down into the pond as a modern nekyia, and he typically uses repetition ("down" three times, "dead" six) and variations on a theme to reinforce his vision. But the repetition also works subtly upon the reader, hypnotically pulling the reader down into the land of the dead along with the characters in the story.

But when Ferguson and Mabel reach the bottom of the pond, it turns suddenly from tomb to womb, as images of rebirth begin to replace images of death. When Ferguson emerges grasping the hem of her black dress, he gasps like an infant struggling for its first breath, "and knew he was in the world." He then laboriously pulls Mabel out of the "foul earthy water" and carries her up the hill to her home. The verbs chosen ("rose" twice, "risen" and "restore" once) suggest the resurrection, while the struggle for breath and the total immersion in the water suggest baptism and birth, both Christian symbols of the new life into which Mabel now leads Jack. She is portrayed throughout as a kind of Goddess of death and rebirth, whose elements are the same we saw in Joyce: fire and water.

The elemental motifs of fire and water predominate during the scene when Jack resuscitates Mabel on the floor of her empty home. After he strips her of her sodden clothes and puts blankets in front of the fire, she comes to. Although Jack remains repulsed by the smell and feel of the "dead, clayey water" in her hair (451), he warms up quickly when, noticing her nakedness, Mabel assumes Jack loves her, and draws her down to him by clinging to his knees. She looks up at him with "flaring, humble eyes of transfiguration," her face suffused by a "delicate flame," and her body so hot to the touch that "A flame seemed to burn the hand that grasped her soft shoulder" (453). Along with the heat of freshly kindled flame, however, Mabel continues to exude water: a "strange water" rises in her eyes as if from "some slow fountain," so that what results is a commingling of fire and water in the form of the "hot tears" (a phrase twice repeated in two lines) that wet Jack's throat and stir the embers of his heart, which "seemed to burn and melt away in his breast" (454). Before going up stairs to change, Mabel's "eyes again slowly filled with tears" as Jack kisses her, and as he watches a tear fall, "his heart flared hot" (455). It therefore seems natural that in this maternal alembic of transfiguration, during which the personalities are broken down to their base elements in order to be reconstituted in the compound of a new relationship, the first thing Jack does is put fresh coal on the fire and light the gas lamp, and the first thing Mabel does is offer to heat up some water for tea (456).

The symbolism of divestiture and reinvestment as representations of the transformation of the hero and heroine are characteristic features of the journey, as we have seen many times before (as in the stories of Joseph, Gilgamesh, Inanna, the Prodigal Son, et. al.). Stripping down the ego to the nakedness of the spirit, the soul dies to be reborn. Lawrence's word for this process is "transfiguration," the movement from the flesh to the spirit in biblical terms, but for Lawrence, transfiguration actually refers to a union of the flesh and the spirit, effected by marriage. The essential myth of marriage in all of Lawrence's work is the monomyth; during the course of the journey, the ego of the lovers collapses into the underworld, to emerge renewed, like the Phoenix from its ashes. The tomb of the pond becomes the womb of rebirth, as Mabel and Ferguson circle back home, completing the cycle of the heroine's journey. Only now the fire is no longer "sinking," but regenerated by the coal Ferguson puts on, and the house is lit by the light of the gaslamp, which he ignites with the "matches he found on the mantelpiece." As in so many of the German Märchen of the 19th century, and as in so many of the hero journeys of all time, homecoming represents the fulfillment of the cycle: the end becomes a new beginning.[10]

Charlotte Perkins Gilman

The archetypes of the maze, the goddess, and the descent to the underworld play a key role in "The Yellow Wallpaper," by Charlotte Perkins Gilman, for whom the archetypes become metaphors for poesis (the creative dynamics of writing), hermeneusis (the creative dynamics of reading), and psychogenesis (the creative dynamics of individuation).

The configuration linking the maze, the goddess, and the underworld is archetypal, to be found for example in the Malekulan myth of the descent (Campbell, *Mythic Image* 463), in numerous Bronze age spiral labyrinths engraved on stones at the entrance to temples of the Goddess, abundantly illustrated by the anthropological meditations of Lawrence di Stasi (94-110), and the archaeological studies of Marija Gimbutas (*Language*, 51-63; *Civilization* 172-81, 301). The oldest myths we know tell of the Goddess Inanna passing through the seven labyrinthine gateways of the underworld to stand naked in the presence of her sister Ereshkigal (Wolkstein and Kramer 52-89), or of the journey of the Egyptian soul through the chambers and doorways of the Tuat, under the aegis of the goddess Isis (Budge 170-262). Eliade suggests that the cave was assimilated to the labyrinth, the underworld, and the goddess from prehistoric times ("Terre-Mère" 75).

From such pre-literate roots, the imagery of the maze, the underworld, and the goddess gradually emerged as metaphors of the intricacies of reading and writing in the literary tradition. The same basic archetypal configuration is to be found in "The Yellow Wallpaper," though with a twist. The narrator's breakdown and deepening depression lead to a journey by boat to an old rental home where she is to undergo a rest cure. Several broadly folkloric motifs associated with the otherworld surface during her stay in the ruined rental home, such as the mushrooms she sees in the wallpaper (universally present in such fairy tale illustrations of forest journeys as Ivan Bilibin's picture of Baba Yaga (62) for the tale of "Vasilisa the Beautiful") and the host of "creeping women" held behind the wallpaper by an uncanny spell (like the enchanted ladies in Castle of Marvels in Wolfram's *Parzival*). The "nightsea journey" through the underworld (Frobenius 85) -- a characteristic image of the descents of Gilgamesh, Odysseus, Aeneas, and the Ancient Mariner -- comes full circle at the end of the story, when the narrator says, on the last night of her rest cure, that the family will "take the boat home tomorrow" (1221).

Other motifs of the descent to the underworld (doorways, eyes, sisters, and the spouse substitute) take us back further in time, beyond the male journeys, to our oldest archetype of the nekyia -- the Sumerian "Descent of Inanna," from about 1750 B.C.E. The protagonist hallucinates "strangled heads and bulbous eyes" (1222), which recall the "eye of wrath" which kills Inanna; and the "faint figure" of a mysterious woman (1218) behind the "florid arabesque" (1218) of the yellow wallpaper recalls Ereshkigal. As the narrator descends more deeply into the "sub-pattern" of the labyrinthine paper (1219), she becomes imprisoned by her efforts to liberate a mysterious woman, so much so that when her husband arrives on the morning of her departure, she says "I have locked the door" (1222). He calls for his sister Jennie to fetch an axe "to break down the beautiful door," and then he says "very quietly indeed, 'Open the door, my darling!'" (1222). She tells him there is a key "by the front door," and when he retrieves it and enters the room, he stops "short by the door," and then faints, horrified by the sight of his wife crawling amidst the wallpaper on the floor (1222).

I emphasize this drama at the doorway here (in which the word "door" occurs six times) for its archetypal nature, evoking as it does a long lineage of mythological, literary, religious, and folkloric prototypes which link doorways, the maze, and the descent into the underworld. In the numerous paintings of the Harrowing of Hell, those by

Dürer and Brueghal for example, Jesus stands at or passes through a sequence of arches and doorways to liberate Eve (and Adam) from Hell. the goddess lies in prison. Like the Gnostic Sophia, imprisoned in the labyrinthine underworld of matter (Quispell 211), or like the Hindu jiva, trapped in that realm of illusion (maya) which is generated and sustained by fear and desire (kama-mara), the woman in the wallpaper longs for release (moksha) (Zimmer 205-06; 263-68; 460-61). Gilman's Eve, however, thwarts the harrowing, and resists patriarchal liberation, preferring perhaps to remain within the domain of her newly discovered Self. For "The Yellow Wallpaper" is very much a story about psychogenesis, about the creation of a new identity. It charts a Jungian discovery of the Self, a movement towards wholeness achieved through the ordeal of the individuation process -- hence the activation of the archetypal motifs associated with the nekyia, which emerge spontaneously during periods of transition and crisis.

But "The Yellow Wallpaper" is also an allegory of poesis and hermeneusis, a metaphorical image of the writing and interpretation of texts. For the protagonist spends a great deal of time 'reading' the wallpaper, and this activity catalyzes her writing the story. There is a kind of hermeneutic circle at work here (reading leads to writing leads to re-reading). Like the wallpaper, which is composed of sequences of "lame uncertain curves for a little distance" that end suddenly in "suicide" (1214), the story is composed of sequences of very short paragraphs (sometimes eight in a row composed of single sentences). The protagonist is a 'reader' of the paper's "florid arabesque" (1218), a hermeneutic act which leads to her own activity as a writer. Her task is to trace the "pointless pattern to some sort of conclusion," and to discover its "principle of design," which, looked at one way, seems to violate all the laws of "radiation, or alteration, or repetition, or symmetry," and hence to be "a kind of 'debased Romanesque' with delirium tremens, consisting of "isolated columns of fatuity" (1216). But from the diagonal perspective, the floral patterns connect in a consistent (if horrifying) "optic horror, like a lot of wallowing sea-weeds in full chase" (1216).

The quest for one's destiny, for the shape and significance of history and the cosmos, is, of course, one of the standard themes of the descent into Hades -- Odysseus talks to his mother there, who reveals what lays ahead for him in Ithaka; Aeneas talks to his father, who discloses the imperial destiny of Rome; and Dante talks to those souls who reveal the essence of Providential design. Hades may even be etymologically linked to the notion of pattern or design, since the epithet "aidoneus" connects with "eidos," the Platonic term for form (Hillman 51). But for Gilman, the primary tenor of the metaphorical descent has to do with the creation and interpretation of a new kind of text, one which has a "pattern" (1218) or "sub-pattern" (1219), let's say, if not strictly speaking a "principle of design" (1218). Like the woman in the wallpaper, Gilman must "shake the pattern" (1218) of traditional patriarchal symmetries, in order to create her own voice and feminine sense of literary design. She does so by re-visioning the myths of the maze, the goddess, and the descent to the underworld, very much in the way of her Modernist compatriots.

Jorge Luis Borges

The descent to the underworld is a central motif in the short stories of Jorge Luis Borges, many of which were written during the 1940's at the peak of late Modernism. These little gems exemplify the way the nekyia catalyzes the revelation of what Borges called "ancient forms, forms incorruptible and eternal" ('formas antiguas, formas incorruptibles y eternas') (*Labyrinths* 170; *Obras* 117). These "ancient forms" are portrayed variously, but almost always in the context of the underworld.

In "The Aleph" by Borges, the descent is into the cellar beneath the dining room in the home of Carlos Argentino Danieri, poet and first cousin of Beatriz Viterbo, with whom the narrator (Borges) is still in love some five years after her death in 1929. It is the lure of the many photographs of Beatriz that eventually leads Borges to his descent into the cellar: the names Beatriz and Danieri surely meant to evoke Dante's *Inferno*. While objecting to the pedantry and pretentiousness of Danieri, Borges the narrator is nevertheless drawn to the Viterbos home "one day toward the end of October," the time of the year associated with the Celtic underworld, celebrated as All Soul's Day in the Catholic Church, and as the Day of the Dead in Mexico. Danieri calls to say that the house which for the narrator "would always stand for Beatriz" is going to be torn down. Carlos Argentino tells Borges that this is terrible because he will be unable to finish his long poem "The Earth" "without the house because down in the cellar there was an Aleph. He explained that an Aleph is one of the points in space that contains all other points" (*Borges* 159).

The revelation of the Aleph is predicated upon a rather humorous version of the descent, here down a cellar stairway so steep as to have been forbidden the young Carlos Danieri, who, compelled by the suggestion that "there was a world down there," nevertheless takes the plunge, stumbling and falling before seeing the Aleph for the first time. When Borges the narrator arrives at the house to see the Aleph for himself, he first addresses a portrait of his "darling Beatriz, Beatriz now gone forever" (*Borges* 160), before undertaking his descent (just as Dante's descent into the *Inferno* is preceded by a vision of Beatrice). Borges has his Virgil too: Carlos prepares him for the *nekyia* with a glass of pseudo-cognac and instructions. The scene suggests one of

Poe's many versions of Hades (such as the "Cask of Amontillado" or "The Pit and the Pendulum"): Borges swallows his libation and descends the narrow stairway into a cellar which "was something of a pit" (*Borges* 160). After lying prone in a blackness rendered nearly absolute after Carlos shuts the trapdoor, Borges hilariously fantasizes a literal descent to the realm of the dead: he has been "locked in a cellar by a lunatic, after gulping down a glassful of poison!" (*Borges* 160). Immediately after the shocked suspicion that "*Carlos had to kill me*," the Aleph reveals itself to Borges.

That the revelation of the archetypal form of the Aleph succeeds upon a realistically portrayed descent to a place familiarly ordinary to us as readers is absolutely characteristic of the journey into Hades as depicted in such Modernist works as *Ulysses*, where the underworld is a cemetery and a brothel, *The Magic Mountain*, where the underworld is a Swiss sanitarium, or Lawrence's "The Horse Dealer's Daughter," where the underworld is a cemetery and a pond in the meadow outside a coal mining town in Northern England. Equally typical is the sense of the revelation of all life's secrets in those various netherly *topoi*: for the Aleph is "the microcosm of the alchemists and Cabalists" (*Borges* 160), "the only place on earth where all places are seen from every angle, each standing clear" (*Borges* 159), "one of the points in space that contains all other points" (*Borges* 159), "the first letter of the Hebrew alphabet" which stands for "the pure and boundless godhead" (*Borges* 162) which is the source of all Creation. The Aleph, that is to say, is the *eidos* of all *eidola*, Broch's "*Urbild aller Bilder*," that ultimate pattern which gives shape and significance to all things. It is the part which contains the whole, a kind of holograph of the universe analogous to what the Hindu's called the *bindu*, that ineffable point in space (Eliot's "still point of the turning world" and the "Fearful Sphere of Pascal" of which Borges writes in the essay of that title) where the Divine energy roars into manifestation, creating the world of phenomenality. Hence, when looking into the Aleph, Borges sees all minute particulars in their universality (the "awful omneity of all in each" as Coleridge put it), just as Dante, after his descent through the Inferno, sees "the universal form / that binds these things" as the "single volume" of a divine book "bound by Love, of which the universe is the scattered leaves" (*Paradiso* 33. 91-2; 86-7). Additionally, however, the Aleph is a source of inspiration, specifically providing the material of Danieri's poem about the earth, and a source of "the numberless texts" revealed to Danieri in his cellar. The descent into the underworld of the cellar, that is to say, is an image of *poesis*, a metaphor for the way texts are created: for it is in the cellar that Danieri, "the master," develops his pictures (*Borges* 159).

In "The Garden of Forking Paths" of 1941 the key to the text which is in itself the entire world and all of time also occurs in the con-

text of a journey to the underworld, although here Hades is set in a little
train stop outside of London called Ashgrove. The hero of the tale, Dr.
Yu Tsun, travels to this appropriately named destination (grove of
ashes) by train at dusk on what he tells us is the day of his death. That
Dr. Tsun "was going to the village of Ashgrove but [I] bought a ticket
for a more distant station" (*Labyrinths* 21) is a coy way of remarking
that the journey is one that proceeds beyond the grove of ashes into
eternity. The ferryboat of classical myth and of Dante has here been replaced by the train, upon which Dr. Tsun rides like "a man already dead"
(22), fleeing the man who will be in fact instrumental in his death, one
Captain Richard Madden. Getting off the train, Dr. Tsun asks some
boys if he has arrived in Ashgrove, then gives them his last coin after
they direct him to Dr. Stephen Albert's house: the way is long they
say, but he won't get lost if turns left at every crossroad. All souls on
their journey into the afterlife must offer a coin to Charon; hence, after
doing so, Dr. Tsun immediately <u>descends</u> towards his end, going <u>down</u>
some stone steps, then "<u>downhill</u>" along a solitary road in the darkness,
details which evoke the imagery of Hades.

One of the oldest mythological images of the underworld which
we know anything about is the symbol of the labyrinth, which appears
over the gateway into Virgil's Hades in the *Aeneid*, and, much further
back in time, at the entrance to the stone earthmound of Newgrange,
outside of Dublin. As Eliade remarks, the labyrinth "was at one and the
same time the theater of initiation and the place where the dead gathered" (75). Hence it is logical that Dr. Tsun, after arriving in Ashgrove
and paying his coin for the crossing at dusk, should be reminded that
the instruction to turn left "was the common procedure for discovering
the central point of certain labyrinths" (22). The "central point" here is
analogous to the Aleph, that place where all the various points on the
compass of the world originate and terminate. As Dr. Tsun proceeds to
this point where his destiny will be met, his ancestral past enlightened,
and the mysteries of the world revealed, realistic details associated with
the *nekyia* continue to assert themselves. The road continues to descend,
and eventually forks "among the now confused meadows" to bring him
to the "tall rusty gate" outside the "grove and pavilion" (23); similarly,
the road Virgil has Aeneas follow diverges towards either Tartarus or the
Elysian fields "beneath the ramparts of great Dis," with its "giant gateway" and "solid, adamantine pillars" (6. 715-730).

After being led across the threshold by a man bearing a lantern
whose face is later described has having "something unalterable about
it, even immortal" (26), Tsun experiences a sequence of revelations
which eventually lead to murder and death on the gallows. The heart of
these revelations has to do with the book and maze which Dr. Tsun's
great grandfather, Ts'ui Pên, has famously left behind him. The maze,

Dr. Stephen Albert (our immortal) informs us, is the novel itself, which Dr. Tsun has until now cursed as "an indeterminate heap of contradictory drafts" (24), and that novel turns out to be an image of time. As I have shown in another work, one of the most persistent features of the *nekyia* retained by the Modernists is the encounter with the ancestral past in the crypt of the underworld. Odysseus meets his mother, and Aeneas his father, in scenes set in the underworld where their fates are revealed. In Eliot, Pound, and Joyce all the great voices of their literary forefathers are echoed in complex patchworks of quotations.[11] Co-incidentally with this encounter with the ancestors is the notion of revelation: hence, Dr. Albert offers the great grandson of Ts'ui Pên "the explanation of the novel's contradictions" (26), and says that he has "re-established the primordial organization" of the novel, and hence of the world of time which is the hidden theme of the novel. This sense of "primordial organization" corresponds to that revelation of the informing archetype which shapes life and art associated with the *nekyia* in the Modernist works cited above. In Borges, the revelation provides a key to deciphering a text (Ts'ui Pên's *The Garden of Forking Paths*) which is in itself an "image of the universe" which "embraces *all* possibilities of time" (28). Like the Aleph, the text bears within itself the entirety of the Creation (as the Kabbalists argued the biblical texts do). In order to decipher its mysteries, however, we must descend into that "humid garden ... infinitely saturated with invisible persons" where lurks the "enemy" of death and fate (28).

Another Borges story in which the deciphering of a cryptic text coincides with a realistically presented descent into the underworld is the detective story called "Death and the Compass." While this is not the place to explore the complexities of Kabbalistic speculation in the story, we can at least note that the revelation of the key to the sequence of murders which the protagonist Erik Lönnrot is investigating occurs in a ruined mansion which Borges takes pains to set in a modernistic, urban underworld.[12] Like Dr. Tsun, Lönnrot arrives at the place of revelation and death via train, which takes him to the south side of the city into an industrial suburb which lies on the other side of a "blind little river of muddy water" surely meant to evoke Virgil's "Tartarean Acheron," just as the "turbid, puddled plain" and the dogs which populate the deserted landscape seem suggestive of the "melancholy marshland" which Aeneas encounters on the other side of the "whirlpool thick / with sludge" in the *Aeneid* (6. 578; 391-92). Trees also inform the fabled iconography of Hades: "poplars and the drooping willow" outside the "crumbling homes of Death" in Homer (10. 482-84); oak forest, golden bough, and "myrtle grove" in Virgil (6. 275-282; 585); a dark wood in Dante; and the "black eucalypti" which surround the "villa of

The Hero Journey in Literature

Triste-le-Roy" in Borges (83). The entrance to this appropriately name villa, "a rusty wrought-iron fence" and "insurmountable gate" which seems to swing open of its own accord (83) recalls the "tall, rusty gate" of "The Garden" (23), and both evoke the iconography of doorways omnipresent in descriptions of Hades: from Virgil's "giant gateway" and "sacred doors" which open with "hinges grating horribly" (6. 731; 760-61), to Dante's gates with "Abandon all Hope" inscribed above them; to Milton's doorway out of Pandemonium, guarded by Sin and Death; and at last to Borges' "insurmountable gate" which creaks open with a "laborious passivity" (83).

Once through the gateway and in amongst the eucalypti of the courtyard, it is appropriate that Lönnrot find a "two-faced Hermes" which casts a "giant shadow" (83), appropriate because Hermes is the guide of souls (*psychopompos*) to the land of the dead in the *Odyssey* (24. 1-15). To enter the villa, Lönnrot must descend to a vault and open a trap door at the far end, which leads up to the place of revelation and death. For in the villa, Lönnrot is accosted by Red Scharlach, who reveals the mysteries of the planned sequence of murders before killing the detective. That the secrets of plot informing the story are revealed in the underworld is consistent with the linkage between Hades and the *eidola* which give shape and significance to life noted above. And indeed, Lönnrot expects to discover that "Secret Name" of the Kabbalists, in which the "immediate knowledge of all things that will be, which are and which have been in the universe" is encoded (78). This refers to the "Tetragrammaton--the name of God, JHVH" (86) which Scharlach has used as the clue to the sequence of murders executed to lure Lönnrot to his death. Scharlach presumably has special access to the secret mysteries of names and letter, not only because he is a kind of debased Kabbalist, but also because he is a type of Odin, Norse God of wisdom and possessor of the runes, those "holy words " which "provide the necessary link between human beings and the other world" (Leeming 102). In Norse myth, Odin acquires the runes via a descent into the underworld: he hangs nine days and nights from the windy world tree, Yggdrasil, during which time he peered downwards and "grasped the runes" (Leeming 102). In "Death and the Compass," Red Scharlach tells Lönnrot that for "Nine days and nine nights I lay in agony in this desolate, symmetrical villa" (84), during which time the world is revealed to him as a "labyrinth, from which it was impossible to flee" (85). He then conceives the plan of weaving "a labyrinth around the man who had imprisoned my brother" upon which the plot of the story is based (84).

Borges uses the labyrinth, geometrical figures, and elaborate symmetries in his plot to suggest those "ancient forms, forms incorruptible and eternal" revealed in the underworld: the "equilateral triangle" sent to Treviranus; the four cardinal points of the compass on the paint shop sign where the first murder occurs; the "pointless symmetries" and "maniacal repetitions" of the villa (83); the fourth point of the "perfect rhomb" where a "punctual death" awaits Lönnrot (86); and the "diamonds" of yellow, green, and red which divide the sky above the villa (86). All of these figures are meant to suggest that symmetry in time and symmetry in space (82) which comprises the universal order encoded in the Secret Name, which, like the Aleph and like Ts'ui Pên's labyrinthine novel, is a holograph, a part which contains the whole, and which is revealed to Lönnrot just before his death in an abandoned villa, belonging to the King of Sadness, Red Scharlach, Mafioso Lord of an industrial underworld.

Two other *invenciones* by Borges elaborate on the fable of the underworld, without however, strictly speaking, employing the mythical method, since they are set not in the ordinary context of daily life, but in fantastic landscapes of the imagination. In "The Immortal," the magnificent Piranesiesque temple where, the narrator tells us, "Everything was elucidated" for him (113), is reached by a journey which suggests the imagery of the *nekyia*. After wandering across deserts of black sand and encountering peoples "who worship only Tartarus," the narrator (later identified as Homer) collapses and dreams of a labyrinth with a water jug in the center. He awakens "in an oblong stone niche no larger than a common grave," dug out in the slope of a mountain, at the foot of which is "an impure stream ... clogged with debris and sand" (108). (Given the setting of this story in the ancient Near East, it is important to note that for the Sumerians, the Egyptians, and the Babylonians, the entrance to the underworld, through which the sun journeys nightly, is situated in the mountains.)[13] Across from the mountain, and across the sluggish, stygian river is the City of the Immortals, to which the narrator crosses at sunset after drinking the "dark water" of the river which reminds him of the "'black water of the Aisepos'" (108). Imagery of the descent continues on the yonder shore, as the narrator takes refuge from the sun in a cave, in the rear of which is a pit and "stairway which sank down abysmally into the darkness below" (109). He then finds himself lost in an infernal complex of circuitous chambers, each with nine doors linking and multiplying into a "deep stone network" (109) resembling the Cretan labyrinth below the Palace of Knossos. He finally discovers a well shaft leading upwards out of "the blind region of dark interwoven labyrinths into the resplendent City" (110). The imagery here suggests Dante's ascent up Satan's leg from the infernal pit to the purgatorial mountain. What follows then is that sense of the revelation of the "invisible design" or "secret form" of the world, of which the City is a "last symbol" forged by the Immortals (114; 113), which is the traditional climax of the descent in Modernism.

"The God's Script" is set entirely in an infernal prison, vaguely Aztec in nature, in which a profound revelation of one of those "ancient forms, forms incorruptible and eternal" (170), with which we began our discussion, occurs. In the nearly absolute darkness of his prison, the narrator ("Tzinacácan, magician of the pyramid of Qaholom") meditates upon "a magical sentence" written by god on the first day of Creation. His reflections proceed from the "generic enigma of a sentence written by a god," to the concept of a "single word" in which the entire universe and the "sum of time" is contained (171). When the jailer interrupts the nightmare of being buried by grains of sand (an allusion to Blake's world in the grain of sand), the narrator experiences a vision, catalyzed by his eternity in the black underworld of the prison. Instead of an Aleph in the basement, a text in the garden, the Secret Name of God evoked by a charlatan, or a symbolic temple, he sees a version of Ezekiel's Wheel, a compound of water and fire which contains the "total fabric," "the intimate designs," and the "origins" of the universe (172-73). Once again, the revelation of these wheels within wheels, compounds of fire and water (the basic elements of the creation) suggests the imagery of Dante's *Paradiso*, where God manifests Himself to the spellbound poet in the form of three circles of differing color with a single circumference, exhalations of "pure fire," which the Dante contemplates "Like a geometer wholly dedicated / to squaring the circle" (33.115f.).

At the same time that Mann was incorporating Kerényi's labyrinth studies in the Joseph novels, and Picasso and Kazantzakis were transforming the iconography of the Minotaur, the Goddess, and the maze, Jorge Luis Borges was at work developing his own unique variations on the theme. The idea of the labyrinth is an obsession in the work of Borges, most thoroughly delineated in such stories as "The Immortal," "The Library of Babel," and "The Garden of Forking Paths" (1941). The narrator of the first story journeys through a desert, where, after being "lacerated by a Cretan arrow," he falls asleep within sight of the "pyramids and towers" of the Immortal City and dreams "of an exiguous and nitid labyrinth: in the center was a water jar" (107). (Mann and Broch also center their labyrinth with a symbolic water source). The next day he descends a stairway in a cave to a "vast circular chamber" beneath a mountainous and elaborately wrought city: "there were nine doors in this cellar; eight led to a labyrinth that treacherously returned to the same chamber; the ninth (through another labyrinth) led to a second circular chamber equal to the first," and so on through a vast "stone network" that the narrator eventually escapes climbing up a ladder (109-10). This ladder leads upward from the "blind region of dark interwoven labyrinths into the resplendent City" which itself turns out to be another "atrocious" and "complexly senseless" maze, full of "dead-end corridors, high unattainable windows, portentous doors," and "inverted stairways" (111).

The passage overall emphasizes the impenetrability, the inextricability, and the inexplicability of the maze which Doob amply demonstrates as traditional features of its symbolism. As she notes, these features may enclose the indecipherable mystery of either a divine or a demonic design; hence, the maze in "The Immortal" has a Minotaur at its center too, evoked as "a chaos of heterogeneous words, the body of a tiger or a bull in which teeth, organs and heads monstrously pullulate in mutual conjunction and hatred" (111). The Minotaur, that is to say, is not only the empty center of a meaningless universe, but also the text and its forest of symbolic words and chimerae.

Borges brings the text and the world together again as tenors of the metaphor of the maze in "The Library of Babel," in which the Library and the universe become indistinguishable in their impenetrability, inextricability, and inexplicability. The universe is compared to a library composed of "an indefinite and perhaps infinite number of hexagonal galleries," with a spiral stairway, and a mirror in the hallways, which replicates the infinite network of galleries and chambers (51). Within the hexagonal chambers of this infinite universe are textual mazes which reflect the "delirious divinity" (57) which seems to have constructed the architectural maze. These texts are labyrinthine permutations of the "same elements: the space, the period, the comma, the twenty-two letters of the alphabet," and the Library as a whole registers "all the possible combinations of the twenty-odd orthographical symbols," ultimately yielding "all that it is given to express, in all languages," from the "archangel's autobiographies" to the "true story" of the reader's death! (54).

In "The Garden of Forking Paths" (1941), the secrets of the labyrinth are revealed at the climax of the narrator's journey by train to a little village outside of London called Ashgrove, which Borges intends to his readers to recognize as Hades (the grove of ashes). Here, in an aristocratic, scholarly country home, the narrator meets a Sinologist, Dr. Stephen Albert, who has deciphered the mystery of the narrator's Grandfather, who had retired from life in order to build a labyrinth and to write a novel, endeavors always thought to have been separate, but which Albert now shows to have been aspects of one single opus. The labyrinth is the novel itself, the theme of which is the universal history of Time. The labyrinth is the book of the world (as it was for the Gnostics), and the reader gets lost in the maze of its symbols, just as the soul gets lost in the labyrinth of the material world.

This line of reasoning suggests that Borges follows a long line of speculation about the maze according to which Daedalus was an image of the "sublime Artificer of the Universe" (Boccaccio qtd. in Doob:

215), and an image of the human creator as well, whose work is a meager textual imitation of the complexities of God's cosmic labyrinth (Doob Chapter 7). The reader too becomes implicated by entering the maze: as Penelope Doob puts it, "labyrinthine art begets a hermeneutic labyrinth" (215). In the words of Borges, the maze, the book, and the world of time constitute a single structure: Ts'ui Pên finds in Stephen Albert's home that "the book and the maze were one .... the confusion of the novel suggested to me that *it* was the maze" (25). As such, the maze is "A labyrinth of symbols," but it is also "An invisible labyrinth of time" (25). That Borges should choose a garden of forking paths as a metaphor for the novel as a maze is also in line with traditional adaptations of the labyrinth as found in gardens from the Middle Ages and the Renaissance (Doob 103-112) to the Enlightenment gardens of Versailles (Bord 189). But Borges seems most concerned with the maze as a metaphor for time and the novel: as Stephen Albert suggests to the erstwhile Ts'ui Pên, *The Garden of Forking Paths* is composed of "an infinite series of times, in a growing, dizzying net of divergent , convergent, and parallel times. This network of times which approached one another, forked, broke off, or were unaware of one another for centuries, embraces all possibilities of time (28).

Compare Nietzsche's dazzling portrait of the universe in a long winding sentence from his notebooks which combines the Gnostic imagery of the mirror, the maze, and the maelstrom: "And do you know what the world is to me?, Nietzche asks," "Shall I show it to you in my mirror? This world: a monster of energy, without beginning, without end ... a sea of forces flowing and rushing together, eternally changing, eternally flooding back, with tremendous years of recurrence, with an ebb and a flood of its forms ... my *Dionysian* world of the eternally self-creating, the eternally self-destroying ... do you want a *name* for this world?" (550). Borges names it the labyrinth, and though he mentions Schopenhauer and Newton, he oddly leaves out the obvious impact of Nietzsche on his conception of the universe of time as an inextricable and multicursal maze, in which all moments branch off into opposing directions which eventually circle back to themselves in endlessly recurring cycles. As we will see in the paragraphs below, Nietzsche's linkage of the mirror and the maze in this extraordinary passage is typical of Modernist musings on the philosophic and aesthetic symbolism of the labyrinth. We find the metaphors of the mirror and the maze conflated with the mythologies of the Goddess and the underworld in works from 1946-1959 by Hermann Broch, Jean Cocteau, Vladimir Nabokov, Günter Grass, and Gabriel Garciá Márquez.

Another story by Borges which involves uses the hero journey as a allegory of poesis is "The Circular Ruins." First published in 1940,it is about a "silent man" from the South spends his last days in the middle of a ruined temple in an Oriental jungle where he attempts to "dream a man" and "insert him into reality" (46). His first successful attempt comes one night after he had "uttered the lawful syllables of a powerful name" and "dreamt of a "beating heart" (47). The next night, he "invoked the name of a planet and set about to envision another of the principle organs" and then continues during the course of the year all the way to "the skeleton, the eyelids" until he had "dreamt a complete man" (48). But here his work fails, as the youth created "could not rise nor did he speak" (48): he has created a golem, envisaged in "Gnostic cosmogonies" as a "red Adam who cannot stand alone; as unskillful and crude and elementary as this Adam of dust" (48). Scholem describes this "clump of earth" (287) as the "original form of Adam" (288), the "cosmic, gigantic Golem" before he was "shrunken down to customary size" (287).

The magician of "The Circular Ruins" creates a human being with the aid of sacred syllables, each one associated with one of the principle organs, and like Rabbi Loew's golem, this being is unable to speak. This means of creation by letters clearly implies links between God the golem maker and man the creator of *ficciones*. In Cabbalistic speculation, the golem (like every character in every literary work) is created, organ by organ, by the recitation of letters. As Scholem notes, "each member is presided over by one of the letters" (248), but the result is either "soulless," lacking "either reason or libido," or "speechless" (278-89). In the Borges story, the magician succeeds in creating a fully live being only with the help of the Fire god of the ruined temple, but his success coincides with a conflagration which consumes him. During his last moments, the man realizes that he too is a golem, the creature of some other being's dream (50). The metaphysical suggestion is that we are all golems, created by the sacred syllables of God, and the aesthetic suggestion is that the artist mimics God (and the Cabbalistic rabbi) by inventing living beings through the power of the written word.

Similar notions are suggested by Borges in his poem titled "El Golem," which begins with a meditation on the Platonic idea that "the name is the archetype of the thing," and that hence there "should exist some Name / Whose exact syllables and letters frame / Within them, terribly, Omnipotence" (110-111). As a result of "the corrosive rust / Of sin," that Name has long been forgotten; but the "Chosen People pursued the Name / Over the wakeful ghetto's midnight oil," until Rabbi Loew "turned to permutations / Of letters in complicated variations, / And finally pronounced the Name which is the Key" in order to bring a "dummy" to life (110). Although the rabbi struggles to teach the golem the "secrets of Letters, Time, and Space," it remains ignorant and incapable of speech (like the dream man in "The Circular Ruins"). As Borges amusingly puts it,

> Perhaps there was a faulty text, or breach
> In the articulation of the Name;
> The magic was the highest -- all the same,
> The apprentice person never mastered speech. (113)

Borges then focuses on the uncanny (cats disappear when the golem comes), and on the pathos of a being (much like ourselves) who can only ape "the devotions of God" with hollow shows of piety and "Orientalized salaams" (113). The poem ends with the rabbi's terrified and tender meditation on the being he has created, and with the poet's recognition that both the rabbi and the writer are golems created by God, ignorant of their origins, two more 'integers' in an infinite and futile 'series' of pain and 'cause and effect' (115). The final effect is Escher-like: "El Golem" is a poem written by a man who himself has been mysteriously created by a God whom he cannot comprehend, and who then creates a poem about a being created by a man whom he cannot comprehend. As Patricia Merivale puts it, Borges contemplates a world in which the poet "too is dreamed, a book in which he too is written" (220). While "Poetry can dream into existence only tigers stuffed or flimsy like the Golem," Merivale continues, Borges must persist in the adventure of writing, "since Artifice, the realest thing we can know, is the only thing that can make reality endurable" (223).

Charles Williams

Descent Into Hell, published in 1937 by Charles Williams, is a fine example of the use of the mythical method as a metaphor of poesis, by which the fundamental forms of the imagination are catalyzed. T. S. Eliot defined the "mythical method" as "a continuous parallel between contemporaneity and antiquity," with the result of "giving a shape and significance ... to the futility and anarchy which is contemporary history" (681). This method yielded a wide range of Modernist works written during the late 1930's and early 1940's (such as Eliot's *Four Quartets*, Mann's *Joseph* novels and *Dr. Faustus*, Hermann Broch's *The Death of Virgil*, Nikos Kazantzakis' *The Odyssey: A Modern Sequel*, and the stories in *Ficciones* by Jorge Luis Borges) which fuse realistic details with such myths as the apocalypse, the maze, and the descent to the underworld.[14] Several of these works use the threshold imagery of doorways, gates, windows, and staircases common to the iconography of the myths of the maze and the descent, and all of them share the central theme of the myths of the underworld and the apocalypse. The climax of the hero journey involves the revelation of those fundamental ideas which give shape and significance to life and art, ideas for which the Modernists developed a complex variety of terms.

Charles Williams developed his own vocabulary to express the revelation of fundamental forms effected by the descent into Hades. The character Wentworth, for example is preoccupied with geometrical configurations of the eidola. He develops abstract "diagrams" by which reality is "geometricized" (24), and the narrator tells us that his historical studies "reduced the world to diagrams" (35). This habit persists in Wentworths's death, which Williams presents in Madame Tussaud's House of Wax, where Wentworth struggles to rearrange the figures of history on "diagrams, squares and rectangles," looking for the "right" or the "real" diagram, which unfortunately constantly changes (217). Wentworth's journey is the most infernal in the novel, but he shares with the rather angelic Margaret Anstruther the notion that "the spirit of a man at death saw truly what he was and had been" by the "lucid power of intelligence" and "energy of knowledge" activated by death and dying (67), a process of revelation by which "another system of relations" is created (158). But it is Margaret's granddaughter Pauline who develops the most complex variety of synonyms for the fundamental forms of the soul which give shape and significance to life. With the help of the poet Stanhope, she discovers the "laws" of a universe the "very fundamentals" of which are altered by her communion with her dead martyred ancestor Struther (104). For Stanhope's Christian doctrine of "substituted love" bridges the gap between the living and the dead and contains "the hint of a new organization of all things: a shape, of incredible difficulty in the finding, of incredible simplicity found, an infinitely alien arrangement of infinitely familiar things" (150). The words "organization," "shape," and "arrangement" in this passage embody in simple and powerful terms that sense of revelation effected by the descent. During the performance of Stanhope's play, Pauline uses the phrases "fundamental thing," "essential nature of all," and "sacred order" to express her sense of a "mystery" revealed by the verse and her "communion with the dead" (180). All of these terms refer ultimately to "The central mystery of Christendom, the terrible substitution" of God's love on the Cross, which Williams calls the "root of a universal rule," rather than a "miraculous exception" (189).

This lovely vocabulary of form accords with the Modernist notion that the myth of the descent into Hades catalyzes the revelation of the root forms of the mind and soul. The underworld could be almost anywhere for the Modernists: the streets of Paris in Strindberg's *Inferno*; Byzantium in the poetry of Yeats; a pond, river, barn, or channel in Lawrence's "The Horse Dealer's Daughter," *Sons and Lovers, The Rainbow,* or *Women in Love*; a bazaar, park where truant boys play hookey, hotel room, beach, or cemetery in Joyce's *A Portrait,*

Dubliners, or *Ulysses*; an insane asylum in Leonora Carrington's *Down Below*; lotos pool, tube stop, or streets of London in Eliot's *Four Quartets*; or Venice or Alpine sanitorium in Mann's *Death in Venice* or *The Magic Mountain*. For Charles Williams it is a little suburb of London called Battle Hill, "a haunt of alien life" (21), a "huge grave in which so many others had been dug" (69), a place of "predestined sepulchre" where "the currents of mortality had been drawn hither from long distances to some whirlpool of invisible depth" (67), and a place where the houses stood on "graves and bones, and swayed from their foundations" (74). It is, most archetypally, the mount of Cavalry, a "Hill of skulls" (25), but as a mountain in Margaret Anstruther's dream vision of death, it looks back to a long line of mythological prototypes in which the underworld is situated at the "bottoms of the mountains" (as Jonah 2: 6 puts it). For the Egyptians, the sun set into the underworld of the western mountains across the Nile in the Valley of the Kings (Budge 179), while the Sumerian word *kur* in "The Descent of Inanna" means both mountain and underworld (Wolkstein and Kramer 157).

It was also in these early mythologies that the imagery of doorways and the labyrinth were first developed to describe the journey through the underworld. The Egyptians pictured the nightly journey of the Sun God Ra as a passage through a sequence of doorways connecting the twelve chambers of the underworld domain of Osiris, with a different set of demons guarding each threshold. The climax of the journey -- for Ra as well as for the departed soul -- came with a vision of Osiris, Lord of the Dead, enthroned in his coffin or pillar (Budge 170f.). In the somewhat earlier Sumerian "Descent of Inanna to the Great Below," the Goddess passes through a sequence of seven gateways, shedding an article of royal clothing at each, until she stands naked in front of the Goddess of Death, Ereshkigal (Wolkstein and Kramer 52-61). This archaic notion of the underworld as a labyrinthine mansion of many chambers also recurs in Virgil's Halls of Dis and in the illuminated manuscript traditions, which picture the gateway into Hell as the gaping jaws of the devil leading into an infernal palace. This imagery persists in Medieval and Renaissance paintings of the "Harrowing of Hell," in which we often see Jesus standing at the doorway into Hell, and sometimes, as in Dürer, beneath an archway, to rescue the souls of Adam and Eve. Dante has his famous gateway superscribed by the words "Abandon all Hope Ye Who Enter Here," while Blake often used doorways into caves to depict the journey of the soul. In Modernism, threshold imagery is central in the descents depicted in such works as *Death in Venice, The Death of Virgil*, "The Garden of Forking Paths," or, for that matter *Gravity's Rainbow*, or *Hopscotch*. The descent through a sequence of doorways is also invoked in such films as

Murnau's *Nosferatu*, Cocteau's *Belle et Bête* and *Orphée*, and Ingmar Bergman's *Wild Strawberries*.[15]

We find such doorway and gate motifs throughout *Descent into Hell*, in which Williams persistently uses threshold imagery to evoke the transition between worlds. There are several occasional uses of doorway imagery. The dying Margeret Anstruther sees Pauline "coming over the rock through a door of great stones like Stonehenge" (121), and the dead man descends "through the door" of the room where he hung himself in Wentworth's home, "down the stairs" to the "front door," which opens "of itself before him" (156), and on to the window of Margaret Anstruther's home. Wentworth himself descends to the bottom of the Hill to a "secret gate" where he will find his phantom Adela (85), and then passes on through "his door" into a "sealed garden" (85) which swings shut "after him" when he leaves (90). Williams calls this garden Wentworth's Eden, only it is another manifestation of Lilith, not Eve, with whom he mates. Pauline too has her first encounter with Lily Sammile at the "gate" in her garden to which we first see her run to escape her *"doppelgänger"* (22). It is at this gate that Lily surprises and tempts her later in the novel, when Pauline initially swings "the gate more wide" (110) to admit Lily, but then flings it shut where Lily stands "at the gate -- of garden or world or soul -- leaning to but not over it" (111).

The most consistent threshold imagery is in fact reserved for the encounters with Lily Sammile, who as the Lilith of the novel stands at the gateway to Gomorrah and to the underworld. The gate and doorway imagery becomes a kind of leit-motif in these scenes. Pauline's ultimate conquest of Lily will occur at the "door" of the cemetery shed (194), where Lily appears as an "ancient witch" (206) to tempt Adela Hunt, when she visits the graveyard with Hugh, after the performance of Stanhope's play. The couple stands before the "rough swinging door" of the shed with Adela "holding on to a bar of the gate" (194), before a terrible groan unleashes the whirlwind which seems to liberate the dead from their graves. Before the terrible sound ceases, Lily had "jerked from the gate, and thrown herself at the dark shed, and disappeared within, and the swinging door fell to behind her" (196). Adela then breaks free of Hugh and runs wildly up the road to Wentworth's house, where she collapses at the window, terrified by the sight of her own *doppelgänger* within, Hugh's phantom Adela (199). Wentworth must then drag her down through "the gate" leading from his home into the road, where he leaves Adela lying unconscious on the road (199). She comes to later, quite sick and "at death's door" (201).

Pauline's encounter with Lilith is more successful, and is presented to us as a Harrowing of Hell, only with a female Christ and a female devil. Those medieval paintings and manuscript illuminations which portray this legendary episode in the life of Christ during the time between the crucifixion and resurrection inevitably put Jesus at a gate, arch, or doorway which leads into Hell. He stands with staff in hand, sometimes impaling a devil at the gate, who tries to impede Christ's liberation of Adam and Eve, whom Jesus leads by the hand through the gateway out of Hell. Albrecht Dürer's Harrowings of 1510 and 1512 can be taken as representative: they show Jesus framed by a arch in the background from which devils hang while he rescues Adam and Eve at the gateway of Hell. Pauline, who must harrow Lilith's hell at Adela's sickbed request, recalls her first meeting with Lily "as something more than an old woman by a gate, or if, then a very old woman indeed by a very great gate, where many go in who choose themselves, the gate of Gomorrah in the Plain" (203). When Pauline arrives at the "rough door" of the cemetery shed after leaving Adela (205), she raps twice then lays "a hand on the door" and "gently" pushes it (206). It swings open to reveal a "very long and narrow and deep" underworld, the floor of which slides away into infinity, and the "doorway" of which is mobbed by the masses of the "occupiers of the broken-up graves" (206). These are the "people of infinite illusion," and their queen is Lilith, the "ancient witch" who sits huddled on the dirt floor inside the gate. The door swings further open to admit Pauline (207), but she refuses to enter, or to yield to the temptation of selfishness, and thrusts the door shut with such determination that the shed collapses (210).

The repeated imagery of doorways in these passages devoted to the Harrowing of Hell suggests not only the mythological background of the Sumerian, Egyptian, and Classical descents into the underworld (in which doorways are to be found in abundance), but also the iconography of the labyrinth, another motif Williams shares with many other novelists and poets of the Modernist era. In Thomas Mann's *Death in Venice*, for example, the maze is linked to the underworld by the portrayal of the "labyrinthine little streets, squares, canals, and bridges" "die Gäßchen, Gewässer, Brücken, Plätzchen des Labyrinthes' (433; 413); in *The Magic Mountain* it is the sanitorium which "becomes the Palace of Knossos (Crete), the Labyrinth with the sign of the Double Axe, where Minos and Rhadamanthus rule and where Ariadne lives" ('Das Sanitorium wird also zum Palast auf Knossos (Kreta) wo Minos und Rhadamanth herrschen, wo Ariadne lebt, es wird zum Labyrinth mit dem Wahrzeichen der Doppelaxt') (Sandt 72); and in *Joseph and His Brothers*, it is the "Cretan Loggia" in where Pharaoh learns the Lord's Prayer from Joseph (928-931). In Hermann Broch's *The Death of Virgil*, we are all, and the poet especially, imprisoned in "the voice-maze, in the maze of perception, in the mazes of time," which, however, contain within them a "starry map of unity of order" created by "that symbol of all symbols" hidden within (89). Similar mazes of the underworld, time, and art are to be found in the extraordinary *The Odyssey: A Modern Sequel* by Kazantzakis, "The Garden of Forking Paths" by Borges, *Hopscotch* by Julio Cortázar, *Pnin* by Vladimir Nabokov, and *One Hundred Years of Solitude*, by Gabriel García Márquez. Several of these works were published around 1935, when the fourth volume of *The Palace of Minos* was published in London by Sir Arthur Evans, and when Picasso was at work (from 1934-1937) on his own Minotaur sequence (Rubin 308-346), and Williams on his *Descent Into Hell*, first published in 1937. Of these, Borges and Márquez are particularly close to Williams, for they combine the imagery of the underworld and the maze with the imagery of the mirror. In "The Library of Babel" of 1941, Borges places a mirror over the entrance into a labryinth of "hexagonal galleries" which "feign and promise infinity" (79), while in "Death and the Compass" of 1944, the protagonist Lonnröt loses himself among the labyrinthine chambers, staircases, and "opposing mirrors" of a "desolate and symmetrical" villa called Triste-le-Roy (138-39). In the later novel *One Hundred Years of Solitude*, Gabriel García Márquez portrays the death of the old patriarch, José Arcadio Buendia, as a "dream of the infinite rooms," through which he wanders, "as in a gallery of parallel mirrors," until he gets lost and is unable to find his way back to waking life (143). We also find the mirror, the maze, the dream and the underworld combined in *La Fille de Rappacini* of 1956, by Octavio Paz. In Scene 4, Giovanni's "dream takes the form of a voyage into a labyrinth of mirrors through past time into the depths of his subconscious" (Orenstein 77).

In *Descent Into Hell*, we find the notion that death is a labyrinth through which the soul wanders after death in the portrayal of the dead man's peregrinations through the "twisting maze of streets and times" on the Hill, in Wentworth following his spectral Adela "round and round in some twisting path" towards his damnation at the bottom of the Hill (84), and, most significantly, in Pauline's memory of her life, before Stanhope's help, as a dream in which "she had played hide-and-seek with herself in a maze made up of the roads of Battle Hill" (190). It is during this time that Pauline had pursued her *doppelgänger*,

> some poor image of herself that fled into the houses to escape her. The dream had been long, for the houses had opened up, as that shadow entered, into long corridors and high empty rooms, and there was one dreadful room which was all mirrors, or what was worse than mirrors, for the reflections in those mirrors were living, though they hid for a while and had no being till the shadow at last came speeding into the room, but then they were seen, and came floating out of their flickering cellls, and danced the shadow into some unintelligible dissolution among them. (190)

Pauline finally catches up with this double image of herself, a "miserable fugitive" which she "sought to save" by running down "infinite halls and corridors" until, at the end of "the last long corridor," she hears a trumpet and awakens, to remember "only as a dream the division between herself and the glorious image by which the other was to be utterly ensouled" (191).

This is a most extraordinary sequence linking, the mirror, the maze, and the underworld in a way that calls to mind a series of commentaries on Gnosticism published in the *Eranos Yearbooks* in 1953 and 1963. Henry Corbin's article "Pour une Morphologie de la Spiritualité Shîite" 'Towards a Morphology of Shiite Spirituality' connects the maze and the mirror to Islamic mysticism, to the so-called "miracle of the octave" referred to by Zuckerkandl, and to Leonardo da Vinci's "genial invention" of a labyrinth with an octagonal chamber of mirrors which multiply to infinity on eight sides the image of the initiate, who has traversed the "interminable paths among the tortuous turnings" to penetrate to the central sanctuary, the place of revelation, which, Corbin writes, is neither the place of combat with the monstrous Minotaur, nor the celestial Jerusalem searched for by the Medieval pilgrim traversing the labyrinths figured on the pavements of the Cathedrals (such as Chartres in France, or Ely outside of Cambridge in England). Rather, it is the place where the initiate contemplates himself as the "Donateur des Formes" the 'Giver of Forms'. "Celui qui se connaît le *donateur*," Corbin concludes, "n'est plus l'esclave des *données*" ('He who knows the giver is no longer the slave of the givens') (101-02).[16]

Corbin pursues the image of the mirror in his delineation of the Gnosis of Islam, which we can also see as an image ("ein Gleichnis") of the creation of consciousness during the analytical process of individuation. For Corbin, the Minotaur that we find imprisoned in the middle of the maze of mirrors is essentially the image ("Urbild") of the Self, which we see reflected in sequences of infinite regressions ("Abbilder") upon the surfaces of the octagonal "chambre aux miroirs" surrounding the center. According to the tradition of Ibn Arabî, each of these reflections represents one of the seven spheres (celestial earths). In each of these seven spheres we see the reflected image of the self that belongs to that particular world. All seven spheres taken together represent Hûrqalyâ, the world of the archetypes, above this visible terrestrial world, into which the Self projects the forms and images of its reflections, just as a body reflects itself incorporally into a mirror. In the Gnosis of Iranian mystics like Sarkâr Aghâ, therefore, our incarnation into this world is comparable to the manner in which an image enters a mirror. The soul does not actually descend into the world; it simply projects its reflection into the mirror-maze of materiality (70). The world, that is to say, is the mirror which reflects the archetypal forms by which the Self projects itself into the seven worlds of the *mundus archetypus*. The center of the octagonal chamber of mirrors is "the place of self contemplation" ('le lieu de la contemplation de soi-même') (101).

In Gilles Quispel's article on "Der Gnostische Anthropos und die Jüdische Tradition" ('The Gnostic Anthropos and Jewish Tradition'), he cites a Naaseen Psalm about the world soul imprisoned in the labyrinth of matter and longing for the way out: "im Labyrinth irrend / sucht vergebens sie den Ausweg" ('wandering in the Labyrinth astray, the lost soul vainly searches for the way') (211). Another section of Quispel's article evokes the connection between the mirror and the maze. How did the soul become trapped in matter? By looking at itself in the mirror of darkness, or by projecting its reflection, an act which provokes the de- monic lust of the powers residing within the gloomy deeps ('die Finsternisse') (212). From the Gnostic perspective then (as for the Christian), the labyrinth is the world in which the soul is imprisoned, and from which it seeks release. Quispel suggests that it was not the Soul itself which fell into the material world of darkness, but the image of the Soul, variously referred to as its "Eidolon" (220), reflection ("Abbild") (232), or shadow ("Schattenbild") (213). It was as if the soul of the world (Sophia or anima mundi) had briefly glimpsed her reflec- tion in a mirror which retains her image and uses it as the basis for the creation of the world: "The Light had only thrown a glimpse into the darkness, as into a mirror. Consequently, it was only an image of the Light which came down into the darkness. The darkness had only re- ceived a glimpse, an image into its material realm" ('Das Licht hat nur einen Blick auf die Finsternisse geworfen, wie in einen Spiegel. Darum ist nur ein Bild des Lichtes unter die Finsternisse gekommen. Die Finsternisse haben nur einen Blick, ein Bild in der Materie bekommen') (232). This reflection of Sophia is torn apart, mixed with the forces of the darkness ("Schalengewalten"), and used to "shape a world which is only a likeness" ('eine Welt schaffen, welche ein Gleichnes ist') (232), a symbol of the higher realm of Light. The mirror becomes the maze of the material world, shaped by the powers of the complexes of the un- conscious, just as our fragile egos are formed largely by the forces from below.

We all then, it seems, like Pauline have a spiritual double, with whom we are reunited in death, a "glorious image" by which we are en- souled in this world and the next. Pauline finds this image at the center of the maze of streets and corridors and houses on Battle Hill, which is both the inferno (for Wentworth, Adela, and Lily), the purgatorial mountain (for the dead man and Pauline), and paradise (for Stanhope and Margaret Anstruther). It is a place of intersection, where the labyrinthine ways of the living and the dead cross, a place of revelation, where the archetypal forms of the Christian imagination are disclosed, and a place of redemption, where the Minotaur of self-love is trans- formed, by the doctrine of substituted love, into the "glorious image" of ourselves, at the center of the mirror maze of our redemption. Theologically, Williams connects this reunion of self and soul with the apocalypse, a mythic configuration often found, in Modernist works of the late 1930's and early 1940's, in association with the maze and the underworld.

At the end of *Descent Into Hell*, the poet Stanhope explains the sudden plague of illness on the Hill as "one of the vials of the Apocalypse" (211), and earlier, as Pauline had made her way into the dark night of her soul to encounter her double and to redeem her ances- tor Struther from the flames of his martyrdom, she had seen "a star -- Hesper or Phospor, the planet that is both the end and the beginning, Venus, omega and alpha" (163). The phrasing here suggests first and foremost the famous words of Jesus from Revelation: "I am Alpha and Omega, the beginning and the end, the first and the last" (22: 13). We find the same theme in Eliot's *Four Quartets*, in which the words "In my beginning is my end" become a leit-motive (23); in Hermann Broch's *The Death of Virgil*, especially in the last chapter, when "the ring of time had closed and the end was the beginning" (481); and in Thomas Mann's *Doctor Faustus*, in which the narrator Zeitblom speaks of "the curvature of the world, which makes the last return unto the first" (376). But the fact that Williams chooses Venus as the star guid- ing Pauline through her dark night evokes another set of mythological associations of great interest. For the Sumerians, Venus was the star of Inanna, the Goddess whose descent into and return from the underworld is the first literary version of the nekyia we know anything about. Her symbols (found on a cylinder seal in the British Museum dating back to 3000 B.C.E.) were the eight pointed rosette of the evening and morning star, and the doorposts of the temple and the underworld (Wolkstein and Kramer 184). Attention was drawn to the mythologies of Ancient Mesopotamia in general, and of Inanna in particular, by the dramatic ac- counts of the excavations of the royal cemetery of Ur by Sir Charles Leonard Wooley in 1934 (three years before the publication of *Descent Into Hell*). As Joseph Campbell has suggested, the number of tombs and the nature of the burial symbolism have to do with the cycles of Venus, a planet which had "long been associated in both Classical and Near Eastern mythologies with a great goddess by that name (known also as Aphrodite, Ishtar, and Inanna) (*Atlas* 2.1.80). Inanna descends into the underworld for three nights, during which time her body is hung up to rot on a peg (the first crucifixion on record, but of a female divinity!), before being revived by the water and bread of life (Wolkstein and Kramer 67). All of this seems most apt when applied to Pauline in *Descent Into Hell*: she is associated with the planet Venus, she passes through a labyrinthine sequence of doorways to redeem herself, she harrows hell during a dark night of the soul, and she returns to life at the end of a novel richly informed by all of the central myths of Modernism.

T.H. White

Anthony Burgess includes *The Once and Future King* in his *99 Novels: The Best in English since 1939*, citing the novel's excellence of characterization, events, and dialogue, and pointing out its relevance as a "lesson ... for our time" (72). Though he says that "this ambitious work is a true novel" (72), he does not mention the cunning use of the conventional devices of form that give extraordinary shape and significance to the novel's mythic materials. T.H. White has condensed the material into a narrative "whole .... It is the tragedy, the Aristotelian and comprehensive tragedy, of a sin coming home to roost" (312). He achieves this wholeness through a consistency of thematic development, a reconciliation of opposites in the plot structure of the individual books, and through a highly wrought scheme of parallelism between the books.

The plot structure of all four books is basically the same: each book oscillates between opposing settings in the progressive development of its plot, which culminates in a reconciliatory climax that recapitulates the entire action of the individual book. In Book I, "The Sword and the Stone," the action moves back and forth between the Castle, where Wart receives Ector's "eddication" appropriate to a young squire and civilized gentleman, and the Forest, where Wart experiences the "education" of Merlyn's magic transformations. When in the penultimate chapter he pulls the sword from the stone, the opposed realms of civilization and nature come together, a reconcilation that consecrates Arthur's coronation. In Book II, "The Queen of Air and Darkness," White balances the opposed settings of Gallic Camelot in the South, and Gaelic Dunlothian in the North, bringing the two realms together in the Battle of Bedegraine and the subsequent seduction of Arthur by Queen Morgause of Orkney. Book III, "The Ill-Made Knight," oscillates between the chambers of Camelot where Arthur, Guenever, and Lancelot enact their chivalric drama of courtly love, and the surrounding country where the various Quests occur. The action divides this longest book of the tetrology into three sections: before the appearance of the Grail, the Grail Quests, and the events after the Grail Quests conclude. The climactic moment that recapitulates the action comes with Lancelot's miraculous healing of Urre, on the plain outside the Castle walls. Finally, Book IV, "The Candle in the Wind," totters between the public chambers of Arthur's new Court of Justice, where the Orkney clan gathers to plot its conspiracy, and the private inner chambers of the Castle, where Lancelot and Guenever are trapped by Mordred and Agravain. The two realms of public 'justice' and private 'sin' are brought together during the ironically named "pageant of reconciliation" (596), during which Guenever is absolved and Lancelot banished. After this ironic 'reconciliation,' the chapters polarize Arthur in his tents and Mordred the usurper in Castle Carlisle.

The notion of the reconciliation of opposites is of course basic to the structure of comedy, where the marriage of male and female brings together the opposing factions within and without to make new life possible. The ineluctable severing of the opposites constitutes the motive of tragedy, where the death of the hero results from the triumph of internal and external schisms. T.H. White incorporates the structure of both genre in his "comprehensive" novel, relying on the rhythms of comedy in Books I and II, and modulating towards tragedy in Books III and IV. The novel as a whole is "both a comedy and a tragedy" (Crane 85), and divides itself into two halfs accordingly. Furthermore, although each of the books is a self-contained novel, each also functions "contrapuntally" as a movement within a symphonic whole.

The comedy of both Books I and II relies structurally on the reconciliation of carefully orchestrated oppositions (of character, of setting, and of theme). In "The Sword and the Stone," the opposition is between the "eddication" Sir Ector provides his son Kay in the environs of the Castle, and the "education" Merlyn gives Wart through a series of magic transformations. The former is largely concerned with the skills and virtues of a civilized country lord: a dose of rhetoric in the morning followed by horsemanship and tilting, hawking, fencing, archery, theories of chivalry, and the terminology and etiquette of hunting (9). The latter, however, constitutes Merlyn's rejection of these petty skills: Merlyn provides the Wart complex instruction in the ways of the nature, a kind of eccentric course in natural history during which the young King Arthur is transformed into a fish, a hawk, an owl, an ant, a goose, and a badger.

Each natural transformation, however, is meant to prepare Wart for the kingship of an ideal country, and each transformation introduces him to the variety of social and political systems he would be likely to encounter during a course in political philosophy. From the King of the Moat, the pike Wart meets in the watercourse around the Castle, Wart learns about an "absolute monarch" (51) whose philosophy is Power: "only Might is Right" (52) he tells Wart before nearly devouring him. Among the hawks in the mews at night he learns the ways of the military, with its boot camp initiations, complex pedigrees and hierarchies, and ritualized modes of social interaction. As an ant he experiences life in a totalitarian state: the ants have numbers instead of names, no language adequate to free thought, an unquestioned devotion to their "Mammy," a chant which goes "Antland, Antland Over All," and an hysterical craving for 'defensive' warfare. Opposing the facscist totalitarianism of the ants is the Utopia of the snow geese, a boundaryless democracy of pacifist individuals, and the academic circle of badgers who live in a tumulus like "a college" surrounded by portraits of "ancient ... departed badgers" in the Great Hall, and sip from decanters while their black gowns are hung up outside during the reading of a treatise about the embryonic origins of the species (189-190).

While this plot seems merely repetitive and circular (one transformation after another), it is actually linear and progressive, having to do with the education of the King. In this sense, the encounter with the badger is truly, as Merlyn says, "the end" of Wart's education (183): its treatise on the origins and development of animals leading up to Man (190) sums up everything Wart has learned under Merlyn's tutelage in Book I. In fact, the episodes of the Wart's transformations anticipate in microcosm the structure of the novel as a whole: we move from the "Might is Right" philosophy of the King of the Moat, which Arthur encounters and then fights in Books I and II, to the Utopian vision of a boundaryless world among the snow geese, a vision Arthur returns to in his monologue on the concluding page of Book IV, where he imagines a world "which had no corners ... without boundaries between the nations" (639). This first book is indeed "contrapuntally ominous" (75) as a "foundation for the three books that follow it" (Crane 85).

The tragic ending which it anticipates is lead into by the counterpoint of comedy, a "light and refreshing" tone (Crane 75) appropriate to springtime and youth. All of Book I is invigorated by the energy of satire: of politics, of academia, and of course of Malory. Yet it is a gentle, loving satire of the latter, and adds to the tradition of Arthurian literature a unique and extended view of Arthur's childhood, unlike anything before it. The only possible Arthurian source I am aware of for the techniques of Merlyn's education is the "Romance of Taliesin" from the *Red Book of Hergest*, a 13th century Welsh manuscript which Lady Charlotte Guest included in her well known edition of the *Mabinogion* of 1848. This romance concerns the education of Gwion, the apprentice of the witch Ceridwen, who cooks up a cauldron of inspiration to feed her youngest child, an ugly boy not favored (like Wart) by his father. By tasting her magic brew, Gwion transforms himself into a hare, fish, sparrow, and grain of wheat before being eaten by Ceridwen. He is then reborn from her as the poet Taliesin, an ancient Welsh poet of the 6th century who claimed that he had once been Merlin (Graves 27-28; Stone 58-60). Perhaps T.H. White adapted this mythological view of the education of poet and sage to his concerns with the education of the young boy King.

Between transformations, we see Wart in his adoptive father's Castle during chapters devoted to the ideals of Sir Ector's feudalism (Chapter 14), a glorious Dickensian Christmas feast (Chapter 15), boarhunts on Boxing Day for the gentry (Chapter 16), and the initiation of Kay into knighthood (Chapter 20). As in so many Arthurian works, the central opposition here is between the Courtly world of chivalry, and the Celtic world of natural magic, which the hero must unite within himself (Zimmer 67-201). The two come together in the Chapter devoted to the pulling of the sword from the stone in a church courtyard in London. It is to this climactic moment that all of Merlyn's transformations of the Wart were leading up to, and in this moment the opposites are reconciled. Although the setting (London, Church Yard, Jousting Tourney) represents the realm of chivalric concerns associated with Sir Ector's "eddication" of the boys, the actual moment of the pulling of the sword from the stone recapitulates all of the Wart's transformations under the tutelage of Merlyn. All of the animals encountered during Wart's "education" join together in this moment to encourage him in his efforts: the King of the Moat urges him to use the "power that springs from the nape of the neck;" the Badger calls him "my dear embryo" and reminds him of the forearms; a Merlin urges him never to let go and a tawny Owl suggests he "Keep up a steady effort;" finally, the snow goose says "Fold your powers together, with the spirit of your mind, and it will come out like butter" (204-205). What follows is the splendid coronation scene, the last grandly detailed chapter of Book I which brings together all of the major human characters of "The Sword and the Stone."

The second book of the tetrology, "The Queen of Air and Darkness," follows exactly this same structural principle based on the reconciliation of opposites. The chapters move back and forth between contrasting settings and characters: Camelot in the South, where Arthur and Merlyn discuss matters of statecraft and warfare, and Dunlothian in the Orkney islands of the North, where the sons of Morgause (Gawain, Agravain, Gareth, and Gaheris) struggle to win their mother's love and enjoy the stories of St. Toirdealbhach. Thematically, the book juxtaposes the concerns of War (Mars), the primary focus of Arthur's deliberations, and Love (Venus), the malady afflicting all the characters in the North. The plot gradually effects a union of the opposites in the last chapters of the book, when, after the Battle between Arthur and Lot, the elaborately wrought marriage of King Pellinore and Piggy of Flanders brings Mars and Venus together during the seduction of Arthur by Morgause.

The maladies of love unify the action in Castle Dunlothian. Book II begins with the young Gaelic clan recounting the story of Uther's seduction of their grandmother, the "chaste and beautiful Igraine" by means of the "infernal arts" of the "nigromancer" Merlyn (216). That Igraine was "forced into marrying the King of England -- the man who had slain her husband" sows the seeds of the revenge tragedy that the novel as a whole will inevitably come round to harvesting: "Gawaine said: 'Revenge!'" and so it will be (217). Meanwhile their mother, rightful daughter of Igraine and the Earl of Cornwall, amuses herself by boiling a cat to make herself invisible, and falls asleep in her usual state of sexual agitation. Her sons vow revenge because they love her (219), and they attempt to demonstrate their love by brutally slaughtering a unicorn, the poor beast falling prey to the charms of the chambermaid whose virgin lap he is tricked to laying his head into.

Morgause, however, is at this point completely indifferent to her children's efforts to win her love: she is much more interested in King Pellinore and Palomides, who have arrived from the south on a mystic barge, and who look to Morgause likely candidates as lovers while her husband Lot is away fighting Arthur. Pellinore, however, is preoccupied with Piggy of Flanders, with whom he had fallen in love before being swept off by the magic barge. Palomides attempts to alleviate his melancholy by dressing up as the Questing Beast, but Pellinore is as indifferent as Morgause was to her children. When Piggy arrives in Orkney, the real Questing Beast serendipitously arrives with her, and takes a such fancy to the fake Beast that it requires a psychoanalysis ("But not too much of Freud") to be cured (305). St. Toirdealbhach, the tutor to the Gaelic clan, is also afflicted by the urgings of love that rule the denizens of Dunlothian: he sits drinking whiskey in Mother Morlan's kitchen, cooking up a "new heresy" having "something to do with the celibacy of the clergy" (240). When Merlyn appears briefly during his walking tour of the North, he too is preoccupied by love, pondering the preparations for his "nuptial journey to the Sargasso Sea, for the time of Nimue was at hand" (304).

Back in Camelot, Mars rather than Venus reigns, as Arthur discusses history, military strategy, and political philosophy with Merlyn in preparation for the upcoming wars with King Lot of Orkney. Merlyn relates to Arthur the historical background of the opposition between the Norman Galls and the Celtic Gaels. His historical overview looks backward from the Norman to the Saxon to the Roman invasions to a prehistoric conflict between two Gaelic races, one wielding copper hatchets and the other bronze swords (229-231). Later in the novel, T.H. White will update the conflict by suggesting Mordred's connection to contemporary Gaelic groups like the I.R.A. (518). In dealing with this latest eruption of civil war in the United Kingdom (of which

Arthur is the first mythical king), Arthur develops a less feudal approach to battle, working out a revolutionary military strategy that requires attack by night, neglects slaughtering the serfs to take the brunt of charge directly against the barons, and the utilization of a foreign alliance with two French kings (298-302).

But the primary focus of the chapters in Book II set in Camelot is on Arthur's efforts to think out a new political philosophy that will reconcile the opposites of Might and Right. Merlyn criticizes the "Might is Right" motto of the feudal barons, which is devastating the country (225). This leads Arthur to work out an "order of chivalry" (248) for the "new ideal of the Round Table" (298). Its oath will be "that Might is only to be used for Right" (266), and it becomes the basis for justifying the current war with the Gaelic Confederation. Merlyn is at first enthusiastic, reciting the "first few words of the Nunc Dimitis" when Arthur communicates his plans (248), but as a philosopher, he is later sceptical, seeing Arthur's attempts "to impose his ideas on King Lot" (as Kay realizes) as parallel to Hitler's efforts at "reformation by the sword" (266-267).

The opposite realms of Gall and Gael come together on the plain of Bedegraine, where the battle is fought which will unite the Kingdom. The conflicting themes of Love and War merge in the chapters following the battle, when Morgause seduces Arthur shortly after arriving in Camelot with her four boys from Dunlothian (Gawain and his brothers). In the last chapter of Book II, all opposites are 'reconciled' in the grand manner of comedy, with a splendid marriage feast celebrating the nuptials of King Pellinore and Queen Piggy. Marriage of course is the end of all comic works, and it symbolizes the union of opposites (male and female) which resolves tensions in the society and makes new life possible. But among other opposites, this novel as a whole is also a mixture of comedy and tragedy; hence the marriage "reconciliation" is complicated by the fact that two other unions occur in Chapter 14: Merlyn falls asleep with "the image of Nimue already weaving itself in his sleepy brain" and Arthur falls asleep thinking "of being married himself one day" and awakens with his half-sister Morgause standing in front of him (311).

Morgause effects her illicit union with Arthur for partially martial ends, having had her husband defeated by the King and her grandfather killed by Arthur's father: the offspring of this union will be Mordred, the avenger of Gaelic wrongs. All is fair in love and war, and Morgause brings Venus and Mars together through the use of Celtic magic. As she stands before Arthur, she is folding up a Spancel, a strip of skin cut from a corpse on the battlefield to form a continuous silhouette of the body. When thrown over the head of the loved victim, it has the power to compel love, unless the victim awakens during the maneuver, in which case he will die within the year (306). Morgause, in other words, is an avatar of the ancient Celtic Triple Goddess, who brings the opposites together: she is the eternal mymph, the mother of four sons, and the hag whose magic can kill. Her seduction of Arthur evokes the "Liebestod," the love death motif of the Tristan romances here worked out so that the progeny of Arthur's love will be the instrumental cause of his death (Mordred).[17] The allusion to the triplicate nature of the Celtic Goddess is even clearer when we look carefully at the pedigree T.H. White provides us at the end of Book II: Igraine is the Grandmother (the one Great Goddess) of three daughters, all witches (Morgan le Fay, Elaine, and Morgause). There are three major female characters in the novel (Morgause, Elaine, and Guenevere), and Arthur becomes the lover consort of the Goddess under the spell of her magic.[18] With a Gallic father and a Gaelic mother, Arthur is ideally suited to unite the schisms in the Kingdom.

At this moment, the climax of Book II and the exact middle of the novel as a whole, the rhythm of comedy modulates towards tragedy. T.H. White concludes the chapter by telling us that "the pedigree is a vital part of the tragedy of King Arthur," and that "the narrative is a whole .... It is the tragedy, the Aristotelian and comprehensive tragedy, of sin coming home to roost" (312). Arthur's "sin" is of course incest (with Morgause his half-sister). His tragedy is both pagan Greek (Oedipal and Oresteian), and Christian. It is Oedipal in the sense that he is fated not to know who is mother was (Crane 94) and hence is subjected to "a set of inescapable circumstances, ones more fashioned by fate than by human error, which will doom the hero no matter how hard he tries to escape them (Crane 96); and it is "a regular greek doom, comparable to that of Orestes" in that Arthur must pay for the wrongs of his father and the transgressions against his mother (White, qtd. in Warner xi). It is Christian in the sense of being the inevitable consequence of original sin, and the novel as a whole proceeds according to the Biblical paradigm: from Arthur's childhood and youth, when "Like the man in Eden before the fall, he was enjoying his innocence and fortune" (White 226), to the fall effected by his incestuous union and the adultery of Lancelot and Guenever, to the descent of the instrument of redemption (the Grail as the Incarnation), to the apocalypse of the last battle with Mordred, after which Arthur hopes to see a new heaven and a new earth established with his return.

White tells us explicitly, however, that the tragedy is "Aristotelian" (312), and this provides the basis of the clever linkage between Books II and III. An Aristotelian tragedy is one rooted in the consequences of a tragic flaw ("hamartia"), usually pride ("hybris"). Hence when the eye moves from page 312 to the title of Book III oppo-

site (in the paper edition), one cannot fail to notice the connection between the title, "The Ill-Made Knight," and the notion of the tragic flaw
in Aristotelian theory. Lancelot, in Book III, is most predominately, in
White's characterization, a flawed, or ill-made knight, and when we read
the opening pages of Chapter 1 of Book III, we find the young Lancelot
contemplating his ugly face, which seems to suggest that something
"must have gone wrong in the depths of his spirit to make a face like
that" (317). It is of course this flaw in his nature that plays a major role
in the tragedy of Arthur. In fact, the entirety of Book III develops the
implications of the various flaws in the major characters which lead up
to the final tragedy: Lancelot's cupidity and pride, Guenever's selfishness, and Arthur's innocent avoidance of domestic problems (Crane 103-
108).

Book III, like its predecessors, oscillates between opposites of
character and setting, with its major focus being on the war within each
character, what the Middle Ages called "psychomachia." Guenever suffers from a dual love for both Arthur and Lancelot that produces a
"chaos of the mind and body" (379) which she struggles to "balance"
during her middle years (377). Her dual love enacts the Medieval theme
of the conflict between love ("amor") and honor ("armes"), a theme exhaustively treated by, among others, Chrétien de Troyes:[19] she feels
"respect ... gratitude, kindness, love and a sense of protection" for
Arthur, but none of the "passion of romance" (363). Lancelot, of
course, is caught in a similar but more complex "dilemma" (367) that
opposes logos (Christian and Chivalric ideals) and eros (367): he is
driven by a need to serve God and King, but even more compelled by
his obsessive love for Guenever, for whom he would sacrifice everything. Add to this his sense of responsibility in the complications that
result from his seduction by Elaine and the conception of Galahad, and
the capacity for cruelty which paradoxically makes him merciful, and
one begins to have a sense of Lancelot's "contradictory nature which
was far from holy" (339).

Externally, T.H. White uses the figure of the "Eternal Quadrangle"
to describe the conflict between paired sets of opposites in Book III:
Lancelot is caught between both Guenever and Arthur and Guenever and
God, and in both cases "the two objects of his affection were contradictory" (483). This figure might also be applied to the mutually interlocking of love triangles of Book III, which combined give us a four-
sided diamond, symbol of eternal love. Or perhaps the Pentangle would
be the appropriate figure, with God the fifth point of the star which the
Gawain poet calls "the Endlesse Knot" (623). If so, then we might have
to put a picture of Morgan le Fay on the inside of the shield, since she
is the one pulling the strings of fate in the novel. Or, we might put a
"God" or perhaps a "Goddess" in the center of this Eternal Quadrangle,

for it is a divine personification of the Self which makes the reconciliation of opposites possible, performing what Jung called the "transcendent function" of the psyche (273-300). If we focus on the Lancelot-Arthur-Guenever half of the Quadrangle, then a Christian God would be in the center, but if we focus on the Lancelot-Elaine-Guenever half, then it would be the opposing pagan counterpart of the Christian divine in the center, the Celtic Goddess Morgan le Fay. For it is "Queen Morgan le Fay" who, we learn, is responsible for putting Elaine in the boiling cauldron for five years, from which she might be rescued only by "the best knight in the world" (370), who everyone knows is Lancelot. It seems that Morgan has set this Celtic "miracle" up for Lancelot, perhaps out of revenge for being spurned by him four chapters earlier in White's narrative (Chapter 7).

The rest of the novel also implies that the nearly divine power the feminine rules the action from behind the scenes, as does Morgan le Fay in *Sir Gawain and the Green Knight*. In Book I, several of the major powers Wart encountered during his transformations were female: "the great peregrine falcon" (78) who rules in the mews is addressed with fear and respect as "Madam" (79), the ants sing a monotonous hymn of praise to "Mammy-mammy-mammy" (126-127), and the snow goose who gives Arthur the vision of a world with "no boundaries" (638) that the novel ends with is female. In Book II, the appearances of Morgause in the first and last chapters frame the narrative, suggesting that somehow its action falls within her dominion. In fact, White will in Book IV be quite explicit in identifying the feminine (specifically the mother) with "the heart of tragedy:" "It the mother's not the lover's lust that rots the mind. It is that which condemns the tragic character to his walking death. It is Jocasta, not Juliet, who dwells in the inner chamber. It is Gertrude, not the silly Ophelia, who sends Hamlet to his madness" (611).

White brings the four human actors of his tragic Quadrangle together in Chapter 16 of Book III in a masterful dissection of the "subtle motives" of his "interesting characters" (389). In a logical progression of paragraphs, he delineates the "artlessness" of Elaine, the "revolted elements" of Lancelot's character, the prescient intuition of Guenever, and the loving "simplicity" of Arthur (386-389). Each paragraph is detailed and carefully structured, moving point by point through the terms of its analysis. This shows that White's attention to the larger issues of form and structure in his treatment of Arthurian matters is consistently applied as well to the smaller building blocks of the novel: the microcosm of sentence and paragraph reflects "comprehensive" sense of order White applies to the macrocosm of the narrative as a "whole" (312). There are in fact many other examples of White's rigorous ordering of sentence and paragraph structures withing the context of clearly focused chapters of the novel, such as his splendid historical overviews of Medieval England in Book IV (Chapter 3), and his penetration into the "Inferno" of Arthur's pre-war monologue in the last chapter of the novel (627-634).

The plot structure of Book III follows the same oscillation between opposites we saw in the first two Books of the novel: the action moves back and forth between Castle and Quest. At Camelot, Lancelot and Guenever enact their drama of courtly love, while Lancelot and Arthur discuss the progress of Arthur's chivalric ideals of the Round Table. During his Quests, Lancelot seeks to impose those ideals upon the feudal barons (Chapters 7-8), to rescue and be seduced by Elaine (Chapters 11-12), to run naked as the Wild Man of the Wood and be healed by Elaine (Chapters 19-24), to go forth in quest of the Grail (Chapters 28-33), and to do battle as the Knight of the Cart with Meliagance (Chapter 42). The narrative of Book III is not "loosely structured" as Crane suggests (99), but divisible into three parts, each of which moves between Castle and Quest: the Quests before the appearance of the Grail, the Grail Quests themselves, and Lancelot's departure from Camelot to Corbin after the Grail Quests. In the first, Lancelot attempts to escape from his illicit passion for Guenever in Camelot by enforcing Arthur's chivalric ideals on the barons; in the second, the Grail quests by which Arthur attempts to direct the power of Might in the service of the spirit are recounted by the knights returning to Camelot; and in the third, Lancelot fights Mador and Meliagance at Camelot to absolve Geunever of adultery charges after he returns from Elaine.

As with the previous Books of the novel, a penultimate public ceremony serves as the climax of Book III, bringing together all of the major events and characters in a grand finale. This ceremony involves the healing of Sir Urre of Hungary, whose wounds "were to go on bleeding ... until the best knight in the world had tended them and salved them with his hands" (511). Lancelot privately dreads the ordeal of being chosen to perform this miracle, which he is certain will result in the "public demonstration" of his "treachery, adultery, and murder" (512). His honor, however, stands up to the test against his shame, and he heals Urre during the pageant in the pavilioned fields surrounding Camelot. When he does so a tremendous display of energetic joy is released by those looking on, among whom we notice all of the major characters encountered by Lancelot during his movements between Castle and Quest: Arthur, Gawaine, Bors, King Anguish of Ireland, Sir Belleus, Sir Bedivere, Sir Bliant, Sir Castor, Aglovale and Gareth, Sir Mador and King Pelles, Uncle Dap, and of course Guenever (514). Each character played his role in what we might call Lancelot's "education," and each appears in this scene, which parallels Arthur's miracle of pulling the sword from the stone at the end of Book I, when all of the animals of his previous quests appeared in his support.

Lancelot is able to perform this miracle through the grace of god: "The miracle," he says, "was that he had been allowed to do a miracle" (514). Unlike the pure Knights whose discovery of the Grail had led them to abandon life for the pure realms of the spirit (Bors, Galahad, and Percival), Lancelot is drawn back into the mortal realm of suffering and sin through his love for Guenever and Arthur. In so doing, he enacts the mythological role of the Boddhisattva, the enlightened one who out of compassion for the world returns from Nirvana to help others. Perhaps this is why Lancelot becomes a Christ figure in Chretien de Troyes "The Knight of the Cart:" like Christ, Lancelot endures the sorrows and sins of the world because of his love, unable to ascend with his son Galahad into the heaven of a distant God (note that the Arthurian material reverses this traditional equation of the incarnate son and the disincarnate Father).[20]

In the final Book of the tetrology, "The Candle in the Wind," the setting moves between two sections of the Castle at Camelot: the Justice Room and the inner chambers of the King and Queen, from the public to the private realms of court. In the early chapters, only Arthur moves between the two worlds, in both cases coming by surprise first on the feuding Gaelic clan in the Justice Room, where Mordred and Gawaine debate a public accusation of Lancelot and Guenever, and then upon Lancelot and Guenever, who are arguing in the inner chambers about a private confession of their affair to Arthur. Because of Arthur's new preoccupations justice and civil law, Mordred and Agravain determine to catch Lancelot in Guenever's bedroom and present the evidence in court for a trial by jury. They do so, and Lancelot kills everyone but Mordred, but Guenever is then tried and sentenced to be executed. Lancelot rescues her and takes her to his own castle, Joyous Garde, where he is besieged by Arthur and Gawaine, who believes Lancelot killed his innocent brothers Gareth and Gaheris when rescuing Guenever.

The public and private sectors then come together during the so called "pageant of reconciliation" (596) in Chapter 10, an attempt to unify the court effected by a Papal Bull, during which Lancelot is banished and Guenever absolved. The opposing factions are sharply drawn during this scene, and take on historical significance: Mordred and his anti-semitic Thrashers suggest the decadent corruption of Nazi nationalism (593), and are compared to the I.R.A. and all other Gaelic threats to the United Kingdom (518); Lancelot and Arthur represent the nobility of the older generation, upholders of the grandeur and grace of chivalric idealism. With Lancelot's exile, the unity of the Table is shattered. What had been devised as a celebration of "reconciliation" turns sadly

ironic, as what in the previous four books had been a climactic moment
of comic redemption in a public ceremony now turns towards the
tragedy demanded by the Arthurian apocalypse. The parallelism between
the Coronation at the end of Book I, the Marriage at the end of Book II,
and the healing of Urre at the end of Book III is broken in Book IV,
which must move from the "pageant of reconciliation" to the last battle
with Mordred.

White shies away from ending his tetrology with an apocalyptic
scene. Instead, he sums up the action of all four books with Arthur's
long monologue in Chapter 14, during which he broods over the causes
of war and the collapse of the Round Table. He recounts his life
achievements (Table, Chivalry, Grail, and Justice) as failures in his efforts to quell rule by Might (628), and struggles for explanations for
war: original sin, evolutionary determinism, wicked leaders, ancestral
feuds going back to Cain and Abel, greed, and suspicion (629-634). The
opposites of youth and age are brought together as Arthur summons his
13 year old page (Thomas Malory) and instructs him to tell his story to
later generations. He then dreams of Merlyn and the novel closes by circling back to its first book. the end and the beginning of the novel are
brought together during Arthur's reverie about the peaceful snow geese
living in a world without boundaries (638-639). Past and present are
brought together in the calm of Arthur's reconciliation with himself and
history: he goes forth to "meet the future with a peaceful heart" as the
once and future king (REGIS QUONDAM REGISQUE FUTURI) who
imagines a new dispensation to be inaugurated by his return. This is the
ultimate reconciliation of opposites, echoing Christ of Revelation, who
says "I am Alpha and Omega, the beginning and the end, the first and
the last" (Rev.22:13).[21] Hence the last words of White's novel are
"THE BEGINNING" (639)--instead of The End.

Saul Bellow

I remember hearing Saul Bellow say, on the Dick Cavett show a
number of years ago now, that he had read a review of his novel
Henderson the Rain King in the *Züricher Zeitung* arguing that the author had given himself a Jungian analysis by writing the book. Bellow
brushed the notion aside by saying that he wasn't aware of having done
so while writing. The context of his remark was a general irritation at
the literary criticism industry, with its unnecessary accumulation of
commentaries, on such works as *Moby Dick*, which bring us no closer
to a genuine appreciation or understanding of those works. As an under-
graduate struggling through the labyrinth of analytical treatises trying
to find a legitimate perspective of my own, I agreed with Bellow's ob-

jection to the excessive outpouring of dubious and sometimes superfluous criticism, but as a young writer and critic myself I was intrigued by the Jungian connection. Afterall, a certain degree of unconsciousness seems the sine qua non of both literary creativity and psychoanalysis, both of which fields I was then focusing on with the increasing intensity of a neophyte.

About ten years later, I decided to teach Bellow's novel in a course on the hero journey in myth and literature. I remembered from an earlier cursory reading of the novel that it fit precisely into the pattern of the monomyth outlined by Joseph Campbell, with its separation from the pig farm in Connecticut, its initiatory ordeals during the journey in Africa, and its return to the farm with the lion cub at the end of the novel. I needed a recent novel to use along with Thomas Pynchon's *The Crying of Lot 49* to bring the course (which began with *Gilgamesh* and included Arthurian material from the Middle Ages, Romantic poetry, and Modernist short stories) up to the present, and I had a lingering curiosity about Bellow's mildly belligerent reference to Jung in the interview with Dick Cavet. Contrary to Raymond Olderman's assertion that there were no hero journey novels in the 1950's, and contrary to Bellow's own scorn regarding the Jungian critic from Zurich, I found *Henderson* to be a wonderful updating of the monomyth that draws heavily on the archetypal symbolism associated with Jungian analysis. In fact, Henderson's heroic quest into the underworld of Africa exactly mirrors the journey into the unconscious characteristic of the Jungian process of individuation.

In a lecture to a large group of academics and therapists at UCLA, Joseph Campbell outlined the relationship between Jungian psychology and the hero journey as a circle with a horizontal line drawn through the center. The horizontal line bifurcating the two circles represents the border between the dayworld of reality and the underworld of mythic transformation in the hero journey, and the threshold separating the ego from the personal and archetypal unconscious in the Jungian model of the psyche. Both the hero journey and the individuation process of analysis require a de-substantiation of the ego and separation from its ordinary reality, an initiatory encounter with the archetypal powers of the underworld, and a return to domestic reality.

The first four chapters of *Henderson* offer an extended treatment of the internal and external conditions which precipitate Henderson's separation from his wife and journey to Africa. They attempt to answer the question Henderson asks in the first sentence of the novel: "What made me take this trip to Africa?" (3). His answer delineates the psychopathology of a midlife crisis in the late 1950's in America. Henderson's war years haunt him, and contribute to his sense of living in an age of madness in a land "under a curse" (38). Once divorced, alcoholic, alienated from his son and daughter, driven by an obscure inner voice that says "I want! I want!" relentlessly, he has a terrible temper that erupts in futile quarrels with his wife and neighbors that take the form of bizarre episodes such as holding target practice in the basement during a cocktail party, and trying to shoot the tenant's cat in his attic in revenge for their having left it behind when he evicted them for complaining about the stench of his beloved pigs. Henderson later sums himself up as "A regular bargain basement of deformities" (83), and his symptoms approach crisis proportions in a fake suicide attempt and during a horrible breakfast table scene with his wife, during which he yells so loudly and pounds the table with such violence that his old faithful housemaid, Mrs. Lenox, has a heart attack in the kitchen. Henderson finds her dead, pins a sign reading "DO NOT DISTURB" to her skirts, and is overwhelmed by an awareness of "pestilence" and "death" (40). He then decides it is time for his trip to Africa: "So Miss Lenox went to the cemetery, and I went to Idlewild and took a plane," Henderson tells us (40).

As in so many examples of the heroic quest in myth and literature, the departure on the journey coincides with death: in Gilgamesh, the death of Enkidu; in the Sumerian "Descent of Innana," the funeral rites of Gugulanna in the underworld; in the Homeric Hymn to Demeter, the abduction of Persephone by Hades; in "The Rime of the Ancient Mariner," the slaying of the albatross; in "The Occurrence at Owl Creek Bridge," the hanging of Peyton Farquhar; in "The Horse Dealer's Daughter" by D.H. Lawrence, the death of Mabel's father; in *The Crying of Lot 49*, the death of Pierce Inverarity; and in *Henderson*, the death of Mrs. Lenox. Death is the "demon who would separate consciousness from its life attachments" so that the archetypal figures of the underworld may reveal themselves (Hillman, *Dream* 166). The journey into the underworld is a journey into the archetypal psyche, during which the Self is renewed and transformed. Henderson's pathology suggests that he is subject "to powers beyond ego control," and it is through his wounds "that the Gods enter" his life (Hillman, *Archetypal* 39). These Gods take the form of archetypal personifications in the rich mythological symbolism catalyzed by Henderson's hero journey to Africa.

Henderson arrives in Africa with his friend Charlie, who is traveling honeymoon style on a plush safari. After becoming discontent with this mode of travel, Henderson discards as much baggage as he can, and goes off the beaten track with his African guide Romilayu to a place "so remote" it could only be reached on foot (44). Romilayu, of course, is the archetypal guide or helper in the hero journey cycle, and he takes Henderson on a long trek through the clean, simplified splendor of plains, mountains, stars, and sun. They arrive at the village of the

Arnewi tribe, after which they will proceed to the Wariri village. In both episodes, the symbolism evokes mythic resonance in description, plot, and characterization. It is among the Arnewi tribe that Henderson's first tests and initiatory ordeals begin. These tests become stages in the revelatory transformation of his consciousness: as his ego is deflated and humiliated by his failure to help the Arnewi rid themselves of the frog plague, the center of consciousness shifts towards the deeper more comprehensive perspective of the Self.

Approaching the Arnewi village, Henderson has the experience, characteristic of many heroic journeys (such as in Conrad's *Heart of Darkness*), that he is returning to the primal origins of the prehistoric past. He says the village "looks like the original place. It must be older than the city of Ur" (47). Here Henderson has come to "purge his fierceness" (49) by leaving the complexity of the world behind (53). The Jungian process of individuation often involves a regression to earlier, primitive stages of the collective unconscious, during which archaic symbols emerge in dreams and fantasies. These archetypal symbols facilitate the process of renewal and transformation, common both to the hero journey and the individuation process. In his autobiography, Jung refers to one of his own dreams of a house with many levels, each of which represents a different strata of human history, as an image of this multi-layered structure of the psyche.

For Henderson, the first archaic symbol emerges during his initiatory encounters with Mtalba and Willatale, the two Queens of the Arnewi. The two Queens wear lion skins and greet Henderson by placing his hand between their breasts, where he feels the heart beating "as regular as the rotation of the earth" and "as if I were touching the secrets of life" (72). Later he is asked to kiss Mtalba's navel, a "significant experience" of "a certain power ... which emanated from the woman's middle" (74). Both women have "risen above ordinary human limitations" (75) and Henderson is sure they can offer him insights into "the wisdom of life" (80): "I believed the Queen could straighten me out if she wanted to;" he says, "as if, any minute now, she might open her hand and show me the thing, the source, the germ--the cipher. The mystery, you know" (79). (These last words clearly echo Marlow's narrative in *Heart of Darkness*).

These two Queens, then, are avatars of the Great Goddess, incarnations of the mother archetype, identifiable as such by their lion skins, the symbolism of their navels, and the sense of renewed life they offer Henderson. Joseph Campbell has shown the enduring continuity of association between the Goddess and the lion, from its earliest known instance at Çatal Hüyük in Anatolia, where the Goddess is shown "enthroned, giving birth, flanked and supported by lions" (78), to the Greek ceramic plate picturing the Marriage of Peleus and Thetis (74), to the

Roman marble sculpture of Cybele, the Anatolian Goddess, "also enthroned and flanked by lions" (78). In the matriarchal mythologies of the Neolithic, the lion was a symbol of the feminine sun, the fire of the womb into which the male moon bull died to be reborn. Henderson's journey, of course, has much to do with a need for "Life anew!" as he puts it later in the novel (193), and "the wisdom of life" (80) offered by this African Queen has to do with "a vital experience" (100) of the desire for life, summed up in her words "Grun-tu-molani. Man want to live" (85). Henderson accepts these words as a revelation of his character (87). Amplifying the archetypal image of the Goddess as the source of renewed life is the allusion to her navel, which Henderson must kiss in a ritual of reverence. The navel, or omphalos, symbolizes that point through which the energies of the divine enter the material world. In kissing her navel, Henderson returns to the womb of the Goddess, a necessary stage in the search for renewal and rebirth.

After leaving this archaic realm of the Mothers, Henderson proceeds to the Wariri village, where his hero journey takes on features of the descent to the underworld. He is guided there by a mysterious herdsman "holding a twisted stick" (115-116). Henderson says that "Something about this figure struck me as Biblical, and in particular he made me think of the man whom Joseph met when he went to look for his brothers, and who directed him along toward Dothan" (116). In *Joseph and His Brothers*, Thomas Mann makes it clear that this weird personage is a Hermes figure, guide of souls to the underworld, which in Mann's interpretation is the well Joseph's brothers throw him into in Dothan. Henderson's Hermes leads him to the underworld of the Wariri, whom Romilayu calls the "chillen dahkness" (115). This is the mythological sense of the fact that Henderson is forced to spend his first night among the Wariri with a corpse (136) which he carries to a ravine, only to find it returned to its place by his side the next morning (144).

It turns out that Henderson's strength is being tested to see whether he is capable of moving a large statue of the Goddess Mummah during the Rain King ceremony the next day. The ritual involved is described in great detail, and its climactic moment comes when Henderson resolves to make the attempt after all others have failed. The tribe is ruled by King Dahfu, whose presence exerts a profound influence on Henderson. The King is a symbol of the Self, a "supraordinate personality" possessed of a certain "numinosity" that exerts a magical attraction upon the consciousness of the hero (Jung CW.6.460-461). Henderson says that "it comforted [him] unusually" to sit talking with King Dahfu, who sometimes "seemed to be three times his size, with the spectrum around him. Larger than life" (215). King Dahfu impresses Henderson as "some kind of genius" (216) with astonishing "personal beauty" (220): "He had such a relaxed way about him," Henderson says, "and every moment of his earthly life the extra shadow of brilliance was with him--the sign of an intenser gift of being" (224).

The new life which King Dahfu confers upon Henderson is entirely characteristic of the hero journey. It is a "regeneration" (197) won by the ordeal of the Lion's den, in which Henderson learns to spend a few hours every day, during King Dahfu's program of "transformation" (236), "resurrectibility" (261), "alteration" (260), and ultimately "Salvation, salvation" (217). Bellow alludes to a wide variety of archetypes of death and renewal to enrich his portrait of Henderson and establish the mythological and religious backgrounds of his hero journey: he is Daniel in the Lion's Den (21, 94), Lazarus returning from the dead (300), Jesus as the man of many sorrows, despised and rejected of men (8), Nebuchadnezzar (229, 267), Joseph in the vale of Dothan (116, 171), Ishmael (338), St. John the Baptist living on locusts in the wilderness (49, 326), Cain (213), and Oedipus at Colonnus (113). Many of these archetypal allusions revolve around the theme of death and rebirth, and many involve stories structured along the lines of the hero journey.

In addition to these archetypal allusions, Bellow uses a variety of secular terms to refer to more contemporary models of the hero journey, terms like "tourist," "wanderer," "restless seeker," "Mr. Traveler," "wayfarer," and "quester." All of these terms suggest a journey in progress, a man in the process of Becoming, rather than a man enjoying the stability of achieved Being. Whether we are to regard Henderson as a secular or sacred hero, his journey is certainly structured exactly by the cycle of the monomyth, for it ends where it began, as Henderson leaves Africa and returns to America.

F.W. Murnau

Nosferatu, Beauty and the Beast, Orpheus, and *Wild Strawberries* have in common plots structured by the hero journey cycle and a visual vocabulary of various passageways to the underworld (doorways, windows, stairways, corridors, mirrors, etc.). While the impact of Joseph Campbell's notion of the hero journey cycle (separation-initiation-return) is well known, no one to my knowledge has carefully examined the basic mythic structure of the descent to and return from Hades in these four films or connected the technical details of the cinematography (frame by frame) to this structure.

F.W. Murnau's film of 1922, *Nosferatu,* falls into that large category of literary and artistic works of the Modernist period which explore the myth of the descent to the underworld as a means of giving what T.S. Eliot called "shape and significance" to their material.[22]

Throughout the film, the two hero journeys of Jonathan Harker and Count Dracula are significantly juxtaposed -- Harker's from Bremen to Transylvania and back to Bremen, Dracula's from Transylvania to Bremen and back to Transylvania. This parallelism in the plot is reflected repeatedly in minute juxtapositions of imagery which link the domestic and the demonic realms together. Many of these juxtapositions, emphasized by the technique of montage, cut between frames from Harker's realm to Count Dracula's, and focus on imagery of doorways, arches, hatches, and windows, all suitable visual symbols of the movement between the two realms which shapes the plot.

The call to adventure which leads to Harker's separation from Bremen and the domestic security of his marriage to Nina comes in the form of a letter from Count Dracula requesting a copy of the contract outlining the terms of Dracula's proposed rental of an abandoned property across the river from Harker's home. Harker is then sent by his company to the remote corner of the Carpathian mountains where Dracula lives, and he sadly takes leave of his distraught wife. Mountains and the separation from home are thus the first archetypal symbols in the film. Mountains are associated not only with the demonic realm of witches and the supernatural in the German literary tradition (from *Faust* to *The Magic Mountain*), but also with the underworld of the mythological tradition (from the cedar mountains in *Gilgamesh* and the Sumerian *kur*, to the Egyptian, Semitic, and Islamic traditions (Budge 171), to the hollow hills of the Celtic faeryland). These conventional affiliations between mountains and the underworld are reinforced in Murnau's film by the related conventions that link river crossings to the heroic descent: in *Nosferatu*, Harker is driven by horse drawn coach at sunset to the edge of the "Land of Phantoms," where he must disembark and cross a bridge over a river before being met by the relay coach sent by Count Dracula. This is the threshold crossing over the river Styx into Hades.

Harker arrives at the Count's castle just before midnight, thus linking the German Romantic affiliation between night, death, sex, and dream to the symbolism of the underworld. A caption announces that the Land of the Phantoms begins here, as Harker crosses a bridge to be met by Count Dracula's coach. The coach takes him to the front of the castle, where Harker disembarks, and stands in front of the large arch that leads into the courtyard. The doors of the arch part mysteriously of their own accord, and the camera cuts to a shot of the Count coming beneath an arch inside the castle walls. We then cut back to a shot taken from inside now as Harker passes through the entrance arch, and once again pauses and turns around in astonishment, as the doorway closes again of its own accord. Harker then walks through a second internal archway, where Dracula stands waiting to meet him. Both doff their hats in salutation, framed by the large archway in the background. After the greeting, the Count leads Harker beneath a third arch, and the couple literally dissolves into the darkness this last doorway leads them into. All in all, it is a marvelously simple, yet powerfully evocative version of the descent to the underworld through a sequence of doorways.

In the castle, Harker will discover the vampire coffins in the basement and be infected by the bites of his hypnotic host: these two events constitute the revelation to, and transformation of, the hero characteristic of the initiation stage of the hero journey cycle. Murnau juxtaposes the initiatory scenes in the castle with Nina's nightmare back home in Bremen by focusing on imagery of doorways and windows in both: Dracula walks through a narrow pointed Gothic archway to get at Harker in his room in the Medieval castle, while Nina sleepwalks through a lovely rectangular patrician portal onto the balcony off her bedroom in the Westrena home in Bremen. The contrast between the Gothic arch and the patrician portals reinforces the opposition between the two realms, and establishes a visual symbol of the transit between them.

In the sequence immediately following, Harker wakes up and descends from his chamber in the upper story of the castle down through three doorways to a large gate that opens into a stairway to the basement of the castle where the coffins are stored. Here he discovers the body of the Count sleeping in his unconsecrated bed of dirt. This descent into the basement is achieved economically in a quick series of shots, in each of which we see Harker walking into or emerging from a doorway. These cinematographic details have a mythic background. The Egyptians pictured the nightly journey of the Sun God Ra as a passage through a sequence of doorways connecting the twelve chambers of the underworld domain of Osiris, with a different set of demons guarding each threshold. The climax of the journey -- for Ra as well as for the departed soul -- came with a vision of Osiris, Lord of the Dead, enthroned in his coffin or pillar. In the somewhat earlier Sumerian "Descent of Inanna to the Great Below," the Goddess passes through a sequence of seven gateways, shedding an article of royal clothing at each, until she stands naked in front of the Goddess of Death, Ereshkigal. This archaic notion of the underworld as a labyrinthine mansion of many chambers also recurs in Virgil's Halls of Dis and in the illuminated manuscript traditions, which picture the gateway into Hell as the gaping jaws of the devil leading into an infernal palace. Hence, Murnau has Jonathan Harker follow the footsteps of many a previous mythological hero during his descent into Dracula's cellar of vampires.[23]

Two further archetypal images of the underworld journey are spliced together in the subsequent juxtaposition of frames depicting the parallel journeys of Harker and Dracula from the Carpathian mountains of Transylvania to Bremen: Harker walks his horse over a stream crossing in a dark forest, while Dracula journeys by sea on board a ship called the *Demeter*. The image of Harker walking the riderless horse over the stream is a stroke of genius, for ritual processions of the dead typically include a riderless black stallion (as for example in John Kennedy's funeral). And the idea of the night sea journey as a symbol of the voyage to and from the underworld is extremely ancient and pervasive, from *Gilgamesh*, to Homer's *Odyssey*, to Coleridge's *Rime of the Ancient Mariner*, *to* Lawrence's poem "Ship of Death," to the last chapter of Hermann Broch's *The Death of Virgil*. For Count Dracula in Murnau's *Nosferatu*, the voyage proceeds on a barge loaded with coffins down a madly rushing mountain river, to a magnificently masted ship crossing the North Sea under full sail, and then to the eerily luffing vessel entering at twilight into the harbor at Bremen. To make certain the point is clear, Murnau informs us (in the written caption between the images of his silent film) that the name of the ship carrying Dracula and his cargo of vampire coffins is the *Demeter*. In Greek myth, of course, Demeter is the name of the mother of Persephone, whose yearly abduction into Hades was reenacted during the Classical Mysteries of Eleusis. Murnau's ship, then, is the mother of Death, and Nina, Harker's wife, will play the role of Persephone.

There are no more suitable symbols of this passage between the two worlds than doorways, windows, arches, hatches, holds, and the like, so that when Dracula arrives in the Bremen harbor, we see him crawling up slowly from the hold of the ship through the hatch, and then carrying his coffin through the arched gateway leading into a courtyard or plaza, with a large arch as its predominant background feature, and then finally across the river on a kind of English punt to the ruined mansion opposite the Harker's home -- the facade of this spooky domicile is all darkened windows and doorways, into one of which Dracula dissolves to enter his home. This wonderful progression from the hatch, through the arches of the city gate and courtyard to the multiple windows and doors of the mansion is then paralleled by the spreading of the news that plague has arrived in the next sequence of the film: as a town crier walks down the main street of the city, window after window is opened as Murnau zooms into a close-up of the inhabitants as they receive news of the epidemic. After hearing the news, the same windows are quickly shut in the next sequence of frames, as the children are pulled inside off of the sills and the windows carefully latched behind them.[24] The imagery of the film then shifts from windows to doors, as a health official paints white crosses on the doors of infected homes; in the last frame of this sequence, the official opens a door through which a coffin is carried out onto the plaza.

The recurrence of such visual details not only reiterates the symbolism of the descent to the underworld; it also establishes a remarkable coherence which links the architectural styles of Bremen and Transylvania into an elaborate interplay of echoes and contrasts. A final example of this technique retains our focus on the contrary worlds of the domestic and the demonic by situating Dracula's rented mansion directly across the river from Harker's home: when Nina opens the window after reading that a woman with a noble heart can redeem the curse of the vampires, she looks directly across the river at the facade of darkened windows in the ruined mansion inhabited by the Count. What connects the two realms separated now only by the river is the visual iconography of windows and doorways: Nina looks again through her window at the coffins carried below in the city streets, realizes she can prevent further deaths by sacrificing herself, and then sleepwalks to the same window, which she histrionically opens by splaying her arms out crosswise, only to see Dracula staring back at her from the window directly opposite. We then see Dracula pass through the doors of his mansion as Jonathan goes out the door to get a doctor for Nina; while Nina looks through her window over to the Count's window again, we see Dracula casting a long shadow on the door into Nina's room from the stairs up which he is sneaking. He then dissolves through the door into Nina's room. The next frames show us Dracula rising from Nina's body in the bed and walking over to the window, where the first rays of the rising sun strike him. As he evaporates, Harker plunges through the door into Nina's room, and the last image of the film shows us Dracula's castle, to which his spirit has presumably returned, completing its hero journey cycle.

Jean Cocteau

The vocabulary of windows, doorways, hatches, and arches as images of the descent to the underworld connects *Nosferatu* to a long mythic tradition going all the way back to Sumerian and Egyptian roots, and to films like Jean Cocteau's *Beauty and the Beast*. The plot of *Beauty and the Beast* is also modeled on the monomyth, and the hero journey which connects the two realms of the film together proceeds through elaborate sequences of doorways and corridors.[25]

The first of the two complete hero journey cycles in the film focuses on the father, who travels to town only to find that shipwreck has ruined his fortune. The jealous and greedy squabbling of his daughters at home and the depression that sets in as a result of poverty are typical of the kind of disruptions that catalyze the hero's departure. Lost in the forest at midnight between the village and his home, the father stumbles through an opening in a hedge onto the grounds of a mysterious chateau. The doorway to the stable opens magically for his horse, and the front portal of the chateau opens into a corridor of candles held by human arms that leads to a table in a firelit room lavishly set for dinner, during which the father is waited on by invisible servants and watched over by animated statuary faces puffing smoke on the capitals of the columns beside the fireplace. After awaking the next morning, the father plucks a rose for his daughter Beauty, and the Beast immediately appears from behind the bush to demand the father's or the daughter's life in return for the rose. The father then returns home, completing his heroic cycle, and initiating another by telling his story. This story is Beauty's call to adventure, since she clandestinely departs that night to offer herself to the Beast as payment for the rose.

It is Cocteau's marvelous use of doorways, corridors, and arched colonnades in this second hero journey cycle that I would like to focus on in some detail. Indeed, the related image of the window had been established at the beginning of the film, when Avenant (a friend of Beauty's brother who loves her) accidentally shoots an arrow into the sister's room, nearly killing their pet dog. Avenant and the sisters had then quarreled through the window (the arrow anticipates the climax of the film, when the statue of Diana in the Beast's pavilion shoots Avenant as he descends through the skylight window in its ceiling, and the dog on the floor represents a domesticated form of the Beast theme in the film). In the sequence where Beauty secretly departs on her journey to the magical realm of the Beast, doorways and corridors play a crucial role. The conditions leading up to her departure are again characteristic of the hero journey: a sudden collapse of fortune, intense sibling rivalry, and the need to redeem a debt by sacrifice. The sequence begins with Beauty emerging from a back door in the house, walking to a latticed gate entering into the barnyard, stopping at the door into the stable to look back briefly, and walking through the door to the Beast's white horse Magnifique.

Mounting Magnifique, Beauty then rides through the stable door, through the barnyard gate, and into the forest path that takes her to the concealed opening in the hedge that leads into the chateau grounds. We next see her from inside passing through the front portal and running down the corridor of candlelabrae. As soon as she passes through the portal, the film speed slows down so that Beauty seems to float into the realm of the Beast. She passes the dining room to ascend a long dark stairway to a large columned doorway at the top, where she pauses to turn back towards the camera (positioned below her at the bottom of the stairs), apparently blown by an invisible wind against the door frame. She then turns back through the dark doorway and the camera is repositioned to the end of the second floor corridor, down which Beauty liter-

ally floats in slow motion with the long white curtains of the four illuminated windows along the corridor to our right gently blowing in
time with her movement towards us. Her figure during this sequence is
framed by the large dark doorway in the background at the top of the
stairway she has just ascended.[26] The effect is of Beauty passing
through a sequence of four veils blown from the four windows (like
Inanna shedding her veils at each gateway into the underworld) until she
arrives at the doorway to our left leading into her room. Here she pauses
as a mysterious voice tells her that this is the door of her room.[27]

Passing through this door, she walks into her luxurious room and
goes to the wonderful large window, which is halfway open[28] and
frames Beauty as she sits down at a beautiful boudoir in front of the
window and looks into a mirror which reveals her father lying sick in
bed at home and calling out her name. Startled by this image and by the
rustling of the fur quilt on her lavish four-posted bed, Beauty jumps up
and begins her descent into the basement of the chateau (the film now
resumes normal speed). This descent takes her back through the door in
her room, out through the large portalled entrance to the chateau, and
down the curvilinear stairway on the left of a frame to a doorway beneath the stairway to the right. There she finally comes face to face
with the Beast, who emerges from another doorway into the basement.
Beauty then faints, and the camera is put behind a window in the basement to shoot the Beast as he picks her up and carries her back up the
curvilinear stairway to the portal entrance. He then proceeds with her
unconscious body down the front corridor of candelabra to the darkened
stairway leading up to the second floor. Light streams through a window on the lower right of this shot, as the Beast carries Beauty up the
darkened stairway on the left into the dazzling light coming from the
doorway at the top of the stairs. The camera then zooms into a close-up
of Beauty's body: as the Beast carries her through the door into her
room, three quick shots taken from inside, then just outside, and then
again from inside the door reveal the transformation of Beauty's clothing from the rags of her domestic servitude to the riches of her queenly
state in the Beast's chateau.

This magnificently detailed sequence devoted to Beauty's departure
from home and arrival at the chateau gives us approximately fifteen
passages through doorways in only a few minutes (some doorways, like
the entrance and gateway into the stable where Magnifique is and the
door into Beauty's room in the chateau, are passed through twice in the
same sequence). There are in fact exactly seven doorway-gate crossings
leading from Beauty's home to her room in the Beast's chateau (the
backdoor of her home, the gate into the barnyard from the house, the
door into the stable, the hole in the hedge, the main entrance of the

chateau, the door frame at the top of the stairs, and the doorway into her room). This is the exact number of gateways through which Inanna passes on her descent to Ereshkigal in the Sumerian underworld. A further connection is suggested by the change of clothing (an archetypal image in the hero journey) which occurs during the two journeys: Inanna is stripped down at each of the seven gateways, but Beauty is stripped down as she passes through the final door of the sequence, only to be reclothed in glory. Furthermore, Beauty collapses in a dead faint when the Beast emerges glaring from the basement, just as Inanna is killed when the Ereshkigal (the Queen of Death) fastens the "eye of wrath" upon her.

All of this is not to say that Cocteau was necessarily aware of the Sumerian material, but the intuitive imperatives of his artistic vision certainly informed the innovative techniques used to evoke an innate and archetypal response in his viewers: some level of our psyche responds spontaneously to Cocteau's linkage of doorways, stairways, corridors, descent, and death in this sequence, and that resonance between the imperatives of artistic technique and audience response greatly enriches our experience of the deeper layers of the film's visual symbolism.

Apart from the activation of archetypal levels of response, the doorway, corridor, and stairway sequences also serve to establish that pleasing relationship between the parts of an aesthetic whole that James Joyce (following Aquinas) designates with the terms *integritas, consonantia,* and *claritas*: we recognize the aesthetic object as one thing (*integritas*) composed of interrelated parts (*consonantia*), the perception of which releases that special quality of radiance (*claritas*) which emanates from its essence (*quidditas*) (*A Portrait*). Hence the repeated imagery of passageways in Cocteau's film not only serves to link frames in one particular sequence, but also to create parallelisms of visual and thematic detail between distinctly separate sequences. This is particularly evident in the second sequence in the film that takes Beauty from her home to the chateau. This occurs after Beauty has begged the Beast to allow her to return home to see her sick father, and subsequently resolved to return to the Beast by putting on her magic glove, which transports her from her bed at home to her bed at the chateau. When she arrives, she quickly rises from her bed and runs first through the door in her room, then through the corridor of candles to the front portal, and then through this door down the steps, pausing just outside the front portal to call out for the Beast (as she had paused in the earlier sequence depicting her arrival at the chateau, when she turned back to us at the top of the inner stairway). From the stars in front of the entrance, Beauty then runs down the curvilinear stairway from the earlier sequence (when the Beast emerged from the basement doorway), but this time turns to run along an outdoor colonnade. Moving left to right, with the camera fairly close to her, Beauty passes four rectangular frames of arches whose tops we cannot see (like the four windows in the second floor corridor into her room). Through the apertures of these arches we can see, in the distant background across a meadow, another colonnade of arches running parallel to this one. When Beauty turns to her left with her back towards us, she is on the right side of the screen running into the middle ground of the meadow, while to the left of the screen we see exactly four of the arches of the distant colonnade towards which she is running. A close up of the dying Beast is then spliced in, yielding quickly to the next shot (taken from below) of Beauty standing beneath a natural archway of bending boughs in the immediate foreground; to her right and above in the upper background across the meadow we see the colonnade of arches from which she has just descended into the little copse where she now stands. In the very next shot, Beauty turns a corner beneath the rock archway of a grotto, and then runs quickly to fall down upon the Beast lying on the grotto floor.

Hence, the movement throughout this sequence is one of sustained descent: through the door in her room down the corridor to the front door, down the steps in front of the entrance, down the curvilinear stairway to the colonnade, and down the sloping meadow to the grotto in the copse where the Beast lies dying. It is a visual descent to the underworld through passageways and chambers leading to a kind of transfiguration: the first sequence of descent ended with her fainting and falling to the ground in front of the Beast, who we then watched pick Beauty up to methodically carry back up the curvilinear stairway to the stairway into the brightly lit doorway to the second floor; in this last sequence of the film it is the Beast who lies nearly dead and Beauty who must stoop down to try to raise him up again. But this can only happen when Avenant, who has been shot by Diana while descending into her pavilion from the skylight window, is transformed into the Beast: as Avenant falls to the ground inside the pavilion, we see the Beast transformed into Avenant rising magically from the ground outside the pavilion where he had lain dying. Imagery of descent and ascent is beautifully synchronized in this last sequence, as if to illustrate Joyce's maxim from *Finnegans Wake*, "Phall if you will, but rise you must!" The Goddess of the pavilion where the Beast's riches are stored, Diana, therefore plays the role traditionally assigned the goddesses of the underworld in the hero journey, all the way back to Ereshkigal and Persephone: she is the agent of death and resurrection, the tomb and the womb, and consequently the means of transformation. Like Circe in the *Odyssey* or Isis in *The Golden Ass*, Diana's role in *Beauty and the Beast* is to turn animals into men, after having bewitched men into animals.

Cocteau's *Orpheus* (1950) also uses the hero journey pattern of descent-initiation-return to develop a complex allegory: the film is simultaneously about the psychodynamics of marriage, the creative process, and the journey towards psychic wholeness. What these three tenors of the film's allegory have in common is the theme of mediation between opposites (between male and female, Apollinian and Dionysian poetry, and conscious and unconscious). Cocteau explicitly frames the journey from the beginning to the end of the film in the form of a dream, hence underlining the analogy between the Orphic descent to the underworld and the integration of the archetypal energies of the unconscious (which is the common task of marriage, poetry, and the individuation process). This process of integration occurs through a sequence of four descents in the film, each of which relies heavily on the imagery of mirrors, doorways, ladders, corridors, and stairways to visualize the passage between worlds.

The first sequence occurs after Cegeste, a young and popular rival of the successful and middle-aged poet Orpheus, is killed during a Dionysian brawl in the Cafe des Poètes. Cégeste is then taken in a Rolls-Royce belonging to a mysterious dark lady who singles out Orpheus from the crowd to accompany her. Our first glimpse of this dark lady was through the doorway in the Cafe, which framed the black car as she stepped from it with Cégeste. When Orpheus gets into the car, he realizes Cégeste is dead, and looks at the lady in bewildered horror as the car proceeds into a twilight countryside beyond the city limits, pausing at a railway crossing as a locomotive screams by: beyond this threshold crossing the road narrows to a tree-lined avenue leading to a ruined country estate. Cocteau shoots the landscape rolling by through the car windows using negative film. This suggestion of an inverse reality, a realm of dark reflections, is reinforced by the camera shots taken from the back seat of Heurtebise (the Charon like chauffeur) glancing repeatedly in the mirror of the car. Two black clad motorcyclists precede the hearse like Rolls to a ruined mansion, where the body of Cégeste is removed from the car and carried upstairs.

The entrance into the ruined house takes us through the car door (first shot from inside framed by the front window of the house) as the two motorcycle police carry Cégeste cross like through the front door of the house then up a stairway with one 180 degree turn (shot from below where Orpheus stands looking up), reaching which the camera is repositioned at the top of the stairs to shoot the ascent from above. This shot frames the two motorcycle men carrying the dead Cégeste up the stairs, passing the dark lady on our left, against a square window divided in three parts on the wall in the background. When the men reach the top of the stairs, they turn right and carry Cégeste through a doorless portal into a paintless room where they lay him down on the floor. The lady in black then walks back through the portal across the hall to the bewildered Orpheus, whom she leads through a door into her room. She sits down first on her bed and then at her boudoir, on which a round mirror reflects her face and Orpheus standing behind her shoulder. The mirror shatters as the radio says "*Les miroires seraient reflechir d'avantage*" (translated in the subtitle as "Mirrors would do to reflect further"), and the dark lady petulantly stands up and pushes Orpheus down onto her bed, which has a full length mirror closet at its foot. The lady then leaves through another door which she must open and close, telling Orpheus to let his wife wait for him (she will be gladder to see him). Two Oriental servants then push a cart carrying champagne through another doorless portal, while we return immediately to the dark lady standing in front of a full length wall mirror that reflects her flanked by the two motorcyclists in black.

She then turns and walks over to the middle of the shot, framed exactly by the two doorways of the room she is in and the one in the background across the hall, which stands closed at the top of a short stairway. As she stands positioned against these doors and the hall as a background, she commands Cégeste to rise from the floor and to identify her as his death. The camera then shoots the full length wall mirror, which reflects Cégeste and the dark lady flanked by the cyclists. While she leads Cégeste through this mirror (a gateway to the underworld with threshold guardians on either side as in "The Descent of Inanna"), the camera moves back and forth through the mirror, shooting first from this and then from the other side. Just as the two cyclists pass through the mirror doorway to Hades, Orpheus comes and stands exactly positioned in the center of the door frame leading into the room, drops his champagne glass, and goes over to pound on the mirror. We see him from both sides of the mirror as he slumps down onto the floor, his contorted face reflected in the glass against which it presses in anguish. In the shot immediately following, Orpheus wakes up lying beside a reflecting pool of water in the sand dunes by the sea.

The overall purpose of the multiple doorways, windows, mirror frames, stairs, and hallways in this elaborate sequence is to visualize the descent into Hades as journey into the labyrinth. Orpheus, like the viewer, constantly passes through passageways between two worlds. His condition is genuinely liminal hermetic, between waking and sleeping, youth and middle age:[29] Orpheus is tired of his success, which he says stinks of death, and he wants to do something new that will "astonish" his audience. But to do that, new doorways need to be opened, new spaces entered, and new lines of communication opened up. Hence Orpheus begins moodily recording cryptic verses broadcast over the radio of the car the dark lady has sent Orpheus home in, verses which we later learn were written by Cégeste, now in the underworld: has Orpheus become a murderer and plagiarist, in addition to philanderer, during his midlife regression? To clear up these suspicions, Orpheus must visit the police inspector who is investigating the death of Cégeste. The journey from the home in the country where Orpheus lives, to the city offices of the Inspector is the second *nekyia* in the film, and once again doorways and corridors play a crucial role in the cinematography.

Orpheus is driven to the city by Death's chauffeur, Heurtebise, the Charon of the film who has been sent from the dead to watch over Orpheus and his wife Eurydice (here depicted as a domestic housewife frustrated by her imminent maternity). The sequence into the city begins with a phone call from the Inspector summoning Orpheus to town; Heurtebise gives him the message as Orpheus emerges from the garage door where he retreats to record the broadcasts from Hades. Heurtebise then enters the same door into the garage to prepare the car, and with the camera repositioned to the inside of the garage, he swings open the large stable like doors through which the car will pass. While Heurtebise swings these gates open, the camera jumps to Orpheus climbing the steps through the trap door on the floor of his bedroom, and then back down through the trap after arranging his tie in the mirror. The camera then returns to a position outside the garage gates, through the black portal of which Orpheus emerges before Heurtebise deliberately shuts and locks them. The two then open the doors of the car (now magically not a Rolls Royce but a little convertible sports car) and get in, the whole departure sequence having taken us up and down in and out through gates, doors, and traps in a few deft frames.

The ensuing trip to the city constitutes a complete hero journey cycle in itself, beginning and ending in the car driven by Heurtebise, and making use of the same visual icons of the Orphic descent to the underworld noted above. The convertible pulls up beneath a steep flight of twisting stairs ascending a city hillside to an arcade of windows in a large apartment building at the top background of the screen. Orpheus goes up the steep flight of stairs (as he had earlier ascended the stairway in the house where the dark lady had driven him and the dead Cégeste) to a plaza where he stops and suddenly sees the dark lady walking in front of a closed shop door across the street. He watches and then pursues as she walks directly into a large rectangular and cavernously darkened aperture that leads into an adjacent and labyrinthine plaza with a long corridor of arches on the right side of the screen. Emerging from the cavernous portal into this second plaza, Orpheus sees the dark lady disappear under the nearest of four arches into an interior corridor of the arcade. Orpheus runs after her, and the camera is repositioned to the inside of the arcade: we see patches of light streaming through the arches on the left, and a yawning darkened arch directly at the end of the interior arcade which frames Orpheus exactly as he runs towards it. Turning right at the end of the colonnade, Orpheus then pursues the dark lady through the labyrinthine alleys of a deserted marketplace. While trapped in a sequence of dead ends and empty stalls, Orpheus bumps into a man carrying a ladder (for ascents and descents, just as he will later bump into the glazier in the underworld proper), bothers a pair of lovers kissing in a corner, gets ridiculed by an old crone who accuses him of chasing after girls, and finds himself surrounded by a mob of maenadic admirers clamoring for an autograph while he watches the dark lady escape in the same convertible Heurtebise had driven him to town in. The last shot in the sequence show Orpheus returning to Heurtebise at the base of the stairs.

The gauntlet of stairways, avenues, arches, and alleys through which the lady has led Orpheus suggests the labyrinth, an extremely ancient icon of the underworld, and anticipates the climactic descents at the end of the film.[30] The first of these occurs after the death of Eurydice, who is killed when she attempts to leave the domestic prison of her house in the country and is run down on her bicycle by the demonic cyclists from Hades. Heurtebise sees this accident through the window of the house and then carries her up through the trap door to her bed as the dark lady walks in through the doors of the full length closet mirror, followed by Cégeste whom she must instruct to close the doors after he enters. While the dark lady closes the curtains of the windows and Cégeste closes the trap door on the floor, Heurtebise momentarily vanishes to warn Orpheus of the imminent death of Eurydice, and then reappears through the trap door before the dark lady crashes through the mirror to take Eurydice down into Hades. We then see Orpheus from above as he walks through the side door of the garage and looks up to Heurtebise in the window, who tells Orpheus to ascend the ladder and enter his room through the window. After closing the window, Orpheus turns to find Eurydice lying dead on her bed. Heurtebise then tells him that he can go in pursuit through the mirror.

Their journey proceeds through the watery mirror down through a corridor of a bombed out military school with numerous doorways, ruined walls, and the skeletons of dark window jambs. It is a difficult descent, impeded by a mysterious wind that blows through the hall of men's memories, and by a glazier who criss-crosses in front of Orpheus and Heurtebise as they move towards a very large dark portal at the end of the corridor. After the camera is repositioned to the other side of this doorway, we see the pair emerge from its cavernous darkness to descend a flight of some fifteen stairs that lead them, in the next shot, into the interrogation chamber where the Judges of the underworld have assembled (there are three of them plus a scribe). During the ensuing trial scene, Cégeste and the dark lady are escorted by the motorcyclists back and forth through a sequence of two doors and short steps as the Judges cross-examine them. Orpheus and Heurtebise arrive through a full length mirror which reflects the three Judges and the dark lady, who, after confessing her love for Orpheus, is escorted by the motorcyclists back through the same doorway that Eurydice subsequently enters to hear the similar confession that Heurtebise loves her. After a complex love scene between the dark lady and Orpheus, the two are summoned to return back through the two sets of doorways and steps that leads from her room to the inquisition chamber, where the verdict is passed granting Orpheus the right to return with Eurydice (accompanied by Heurtebise), providing he doesn't look at her.

The final descent and return begins after Orpheus glances at his wife while recording messages from the car radio. Eurydice immediately vanishes, and then the raving maenads of the film break through the front gateway into the driveway and shoot Orpheus. At this point Cocteau resumes his emphasis on passageways, having the two motorcyclists of Hades drag the dead Orpheus through the blackened side doorway into the garage, from the front gate of which we next see the Rolls Royce emerging to speed down a highway beneath a large roman arch in the next shot, under which the Rolls follows the two motorcycles. Just after passing beneath this arch, the Rolls comes to a halt, with the arch framing the car in the background. It then proceeds down the country road leading to the original ruined mansion where the dark lady had taken Orpheus and the dead Cégeste. From there, Orpheus and Heurtebise begin the final descent into Hades.

Once again they struggle along the outer wall of the bombed out military academy past a sequence of three heavily barred large window jambs, in the third of which a mysterious shade sits drumming. After turning a corner, both are swept down a conduit by the same mysterious wind that had impeded their progress earlier. Orpheus lands on his feet in front of a fourth now barless window, and the next shot shows him walking through the same slightly arched doorway to descend the same fifteen steps as he had in his first journey (though running in slow motion this time and with the camera at a different angle). The camera then returns to the dark lady, who runs to embrace Orpheus exactly in front of an empty doorway through which we see, in the background, a large ruined wall punctured by many dark windows. It is on the large stone sill of one of these empty ruined window doorways that the dark lady then orders Cégeste and Heurtebise to strangle Orpheus so he can be reunited in the upper world with his wife Eurydice. Orpheus then dies in the underworld in order to return to life: he passes back through the same labyrinthine passageways to the mirror leading into his room, which reflects the multiple windows in the ruined walls of Hades. Once through to this side of the looking glass, he is reunited with Eurydice as the two seem to awaken from and kind of midsummer night's dream.[31] As they kiss, Heurtebise fades back through the mirror, and the last shot of the film shows him with the dark lady escorted by the infernal cyclists down an enormous hall with great large arches at the top of a wall in the background. Then they turn of the right into a corridor which presumably leads them down into some inscrutably deeper circle of Hell.

All four of these journeys comprise an elaborate polysemous allegory, a kind of pilgrimage towards creativity and wholeness within the Self and within the relationships between the poet and his muse and between the husband and his wife.[32] As so often in the hero journey, this pilgrimage requires a reconciliation between the various oppositions which generate tension both in the Self and in the society. A Jungian model can help us to sort out these oppositions within and between the various characters in the film; polarities like anima/animus, persona/shadow, ego/archetype help delineate the fundamental duality between the upper and the lower world that structures the film as a whole. The basic maxim (derived from alchemy) that what is above reflects what is below applies to the central metaphor of mirroring in the film, and can be approximately diagrammed as follows:

	Inspector	Aglaonice	
Orpheus			Eurydice
Heurtebise			Dark Lady
	Judges	Cégeste	

This gives us an octagonal configuration for the major characters of the film, the octagon being an archetypal symbol representing the totality of the Self.[33] All of the characters above live in the upperworld of daily life (the conscious aspect of the personality), while those below represent the underworld figures in the film (the unconscious side of the personality). As Cocteau suggests by the iconography of mirrors in the film, what is above reflects what is below: the vertical lines connect the principal male and female characters of the upper and lower worlds, corresponding to the Jungian dichotomy between the persona and its shadow, while the diagonal lines link the contrasexual dialectic between the ego and its anima (Orpheus and the dark lady) or its animus (Eurydice and Heurtebise). As the film progresses, we witness the psychodynamics of what Jung called the alchemical marriage, during which the tensions between the conscious and the unconscious (caused by the reciprocal projections of the anima, animus, and shadow), are gradually integrated to produce moments of equilibrium within the Self which are the goal of the individuation process.

To begin with the vertical lines of reflection, linking the persona to the shadow, we find that the domestic kindness which Heurtebise exhibits throughout the film towards Eurydice contrasts sharply with the callous cruelty and egotism of Orpheus: Heurtebise repeatedly comforts Eurydice when she recoils from her husband's imperious selfishness, so that, in this case, Heurtebise represents a positive shadow of Orpheus, that loving and tender side of the obsessive poet which is repressed until the very end of the film. This duality between Orpheus and Heurtebise is inverted in their relationships with the dark lady: Orpheus the fawning and fascinated lover and Heurtebise the resentful and rebellious subject who relates to the dark lady much as Orpheus seems to relate to Eurydice. Moving to the female persona shadow relationships, we see that the dark side of the thoroughly domestic blond haired Eurydice, pregnant and confined to kitchen and bedroom (when she tries to leave she is killed), is the dark haired fury of the underworld, passionate, petulant, and bossy (she roams freely between the two worlds, until confined to the underworld by the Judges). The female ego-shadow opposition between Eurydice and the dark lady, therefore, embodies the more typical notion of the shadow as the negative side of the personality that must be repressed. That the male shadow is positive and the female negative contributes to the opposition between male and female in the film, and is another one of those reciprocal inversions caused by the reversal of images reflected in mirrors.

Hence the four couples mirror each other (as above, so below): Orpheus and Eurydice in the upper world reflect the animosity of Heurtebise and the dark lady in the lower, while the tenderness between Heurtebise and Eurydice reflects the tenderness between Orpheus and the dark lady. These reciprocal reflections are caused by the mutual projection of anima and animus figures, indicated along the diagonal lines of the diagram above. The dark lady is clearly an anima figure for Orpheus, a part of his underworld, i.e., his unconscious: she is the passionate psychopomp who leads him deeply into the labyrinth of his innermost dreams and fantasies. Like the dark haired lady of many romance novels, she is poetic, dangerous, deadly -- a *belle dame sans merci* who functions as a muse. Orpheus is obsessed with her, driven compulsively to pursue her through city streets and into the underworld. Yet, as he himself says, she is really the unknown to him, the mystery of the dark side of irrationality which nourishes his poetry and offers it the hope of renewal. She is, like Jung's mother archetype, loving and terrible, positive in her enrichment of his verse, negative in her disruptive impact on his domestic bliss (*Four Archetypes*). Heurtebise, on the contrary, as an animus figure for Eurydice (having committed suicide for rejected love, he reflects her own innermost feelings and ideals of masculinity), is almost wholly positive. He is everything she would probably wish

Orpheus to be: obsequious, tender, completely honorable, and devoted. He puts a shawl around her shoulder, lies her down into bed, not to make love, but to get her to take a nap, and he constantly tries to protect her both from death and the destructive 'artistic' temperament of her husband. His only negative attributes, in fact, are completely unconscious, coming out in his irritable relations with Eurydice's shadow side, the dark lady.

These complicated interrelationships between the four major characters in the film, therefore, represent aspects of what Jung called the alchemical marriage,[34] the purpose of which is to sort out the projected unconscious content from the conscious experience of the other person. The various reconciliations between opposites which constitute the essence of the alchemical analogy (between life and death, male and female, anima and animus, persona and shadow, conscious and unconscious) are gradually achieved during the individuation process of marriage, which moves towards (but perhaps never fully realizes) wholeness within the Self. In the film, this process of reconciling conscious with unconscious contents is represented by the sequence descents to and returns from the underworld, each of which, as the closing frames suggest, are aspects of a single archetypal dream. Though whether the dreamer is the living husband and poet Orpheus, his wife Eurydice, or the hidden god with whose nightmares the dark lady identifies herself, is a question left unanswered. We are left to walk through the yawning arches into the abyss of mystery from which the film's meaning emerges.

This depth of indecipherability is essential to the film and in fact to all poetry: only those symbols rooted in the unknown, as Jung remarked, live with the power to move us. Hence the film is not only an allegory of marriage or of the individuation process, but also an allegory of *poesis*.[35] The journey into the underworld also a journey into the archetypal depths of the imagination (into its granary of seed forms), where it becomes necessary not to comprehend (*comprendre*) but to believe (*croire*).[36] Orpheus must cease questioning death, accept his mortality and frustrated desire to know and control everything, in order to be renewed by the irrationalities of the muse. The broadcasts from Hades offer him lines he says he would give his life to have written. "Death," as Wallace Stevens says, "is the mother of beauty," and it has been the traditional task of the Orphic bard to charm death and to sing a particular kind of poetry that is haunted by the passionate suggestiveness of its metaphors and mysteries -- the kind of poetry that pierces the heart with that sense of the precious evanescence of life which makes the flesh tremble and the hair stand on end.[37] To write such poetry, the film suggests, one must go down, again and again, into the underworld of one's innermost vulnerabilities, and be relentlessly attentive to the psychopathology of daily life and to the chance messages from the unconscious which those symptoms communicate. One must, Cocteau suggests, surrender rationality and control to the painful processes of reverie and reflection which take us through the mirror of art into the realm of meaning.[38] Only such openness to the archetypal depths of the psyche allows the poet to astonish us.[39]

Ingmar Bergman

Ingmar Bergman's masterpiece, *Wild Strawberries*, would seem to owe a great deal to Cocteau's earlier films. "The external sequence of the plot is provided by a journey" (Taylor 159) into the underworld, and its vocabulary of images (doorways, city streets, and corridors) symbolize that journey. The film takes place within a twenty-four hour period, during which the character of the hero (Isak) is transformed by a sequence of initiatory revelations that ultimately reconcile him to his imminent death. Indeed, the "idea of death-in-life and a return to the past from which the central character arises reborn" (Taylor 149) is as characteristic of Bergman's work as it is of Modernism in general (think of Virginia Woolf or Marcel Proust) and of the hero journey itself. As in *Nosferatu, Beauty and the Beast,* and *Orpheus,* the mythic structure of the descent to the underworld is masterfully evoked in the three dream sequences at the beginning, middle, and end of the film. The first two of these, in particular, utilize the vocabulary of doorways, corridors, and streets that we have seen associated with the descent in Murnau and Cocteau, while the third dream sequence that closes the film evokes the night sea journey to the Promised Land.

While the external call to adventure that precipitates Isak's departure from home comes as a summons to receive an award for his scientific achievement in the city of Lund, the internal call comes in the form of the death dream with which the film begins. As so often in the monomyth, it is the awareness of mortality that initiates the journey that will transform the hero's identity through a sequence of trials, ordeals, and revelations. Isak's initial dream evokes the archetypal imagery associated with the underworld, and anticipates much of the action of the rest of the film (it is a kind of overture). The dream begins with Isak wandering lost through the streets of an unknown city; during the entire sequence, Isak walks up and down a short segment of sidewalk, framed throughout by the darkened doorways, arches, and boarded windows of the city's buildings, which the considerably complicated camera work uses as a symbolic background to all of his movements.[40]

In the first shot, Isak walks down the sidewalk with his back to us towards the tall dark doorways in the background, one of which directly at the end of the walk frames his dark suited figure exactly, while one larger doorway stands immediately at the end of the walk to the left. After pausing beneath a lamppost that has a pair of eyes with a handless clock above them in the position of a third eye, the camera is repositioned from our end of the sidewalk to the other side of the street midway down the walk, so that we now see Isak framed to the right by a large completely darkened doorway, and to the left by boarded windows and another dark doorway which he now moves directly in front of, before pausing and turning back to walk again beneath the lamppost to stand again in front of the large black basement entrance to the right. The camera then zooms in to a profile shot against the entirely black basement entrance, as Isak slowly turns again back towards the lamppost. The camera is then put back in its original position at our end of the sidewalk, so we see a strange black coated man standing with his back to us and Isak in the midground beneath the lamppost, with the large arched and darkened doorway at the end of the walk to his far left and the thin strip of a smaller dark door to his immediate left.

After this strange man turns towards Isak with a doll-like contorted face, he falls dead onto the street and his body fluids seep out under his hat. The camera meanwhile has been moved up the sidewalk closer to Isak, accentuating the large dark doorways at the end of the walk which frame Isak to the right and to the left as he approaches the mysterious stranger.[41] Isak then walks once more to the far end of the sidewalk, turns to look right up the street running perpendicular to the one he is on, and sees a horse drawn hearse turning towards him from another street at the end of the frame. With the camera now in its original position at our end of the sidewalk (where we see a shop entrance bifurcated by a pole and a noontime shadow), Isak stands directly in front of the two doorways at the end of the walk, where the hearse turns into the street beside Isak to the left. As the hearse proceeds up the street down which Isak has been walking, the camera is put behind it as it bangs against the lamppost and dislodges a wheel which rolls back towards Isak, breaking its rim after nearly knocking Isak over. A quick shot shows Isak pressed up against a wall between a narrow dark doorway to our right and a large square dark door towards which the wheel rolls to our left. With the camera now opposite the street from Isak again, we see him standing by a sunlit wall to the left and a large black basement entrance to the right (dividing the screen exactly in half), as the coffin falls from the hearse onto the street. Isak then walks to the hand that he sees protruding from the coffin, and we see him framed exactly by the black basement doorway in the background as he stoops to grasp the hand and be pulled down towards the coffin. A close up taken from below frames his white head against a the boarded dark edge of a window halfway up the wall behind him. The sequence ends as the now demonically animated corpse slips out of the coffin and comes closer and closer to Isak, eyes glaring and filling the frame with a face we now recognize as Isak's own.

The doorways, windows, and basement entrances in this sequence clearly configure a visual iconography of the journey into the Halls of Dis which sets the scene for the conventional folkloric imagery of death that permeates the film (carriage, coffin, mysterious stranger, meeting one's double, the alien city, etc.). The entire sequence is literally framed against the background of these labyrinthine streets and gaping doorways into a cavernous urban Hades. In addition, the details of the sequence look forward to the action of the rest of the film: the procession of the hearse and the loss of its wheel to the car journey and accident on the road to Lund during the day that follows the dream; the large eyes and handless clock on the lamppost to Isak's eyes beneath the microscope in the examination scene and to his father's watch given him by his mother in her home; and the strange man and animated corpse again to the examination scene, during which a female corpse will spring to life.

This examination scene is the second major dream sequence of the film. It comes after a series of trials and revelations (during the drive south to Lund) which are characteristic of the initiation stage of the hero journey. During the drive, Isak's daughter-in-law Marianne tells him how much she dislikes his coldness and impecunious insistence not to relieve his son Evald from the obligation of paying back a loan made several years earlier. She also chastises Isak for having been a poor father earlier in Evald's childhood, which she sees as having been crippled by Isak's acrimonious marriage to Evald's mother Karin, who is now dead. In fact, Marianne severely concludes, Isak's failure to father Evald has led to Evald's decision to divorce Marianne if she refuses to abort the child she is now carrying. Marianne's painful accusations are intensified from within by Isak's memories of his own adolescence, largely evoked by the synchronistic similarity between a young hitchhiker, who they pick up on the grounds of the cottage where Isak's family spent many of its summers, and the young cousin with whom he first fell in love, only to be rejected in favor of his brother Sigfrid: both girls are named Sara and both share the same dilemma about whom they should marry. The trauma of Isak's rejection, from which he never recovered (the lingering attachment to his cousin Sara, the film suggests, having been partly responsible for the failure of Isak's marriage to Karin) is relived during Isak's reveries and dreams on the drive south. Hence, the combination of Marianne's painful accusations about Isak's failure as a father and the renewed recollection of first love and rejection chips away at Isak's ego until he is rendered intensely vulnerable. This progressive humiliation leads to the second major dream sequence in the film. The dream is the climactic revelation of Isak's initiatory descent into himself, and it holds out the hope of a redemptive transformation of his character. The stripping down of Isak's complacent self-esteem and review of the major failings of his life leads to an archetypal dream of death, judgment, and rebirth which utilizes many of the visual icons of the descent to the underworld analyzed above.

In the first part of this long dream sequence, Isak confronts his own reflection in a mirror held up to him by his cousin Sara as she tells him of her decision to marry his brother Sigfrid.[42] Sara then gets up and runs to a cradle beneath a pine tree, swaying in the long Scandinavian dusk. She picks the baby up and rocks it in her arms, whispering comforting words against the danger of the wind and water, and assuring the baby that the day is near. This powerful image of mother and child reflects, on a Freudian level, Isak's Oedipal longings (in the Bible Sara is the name of Isak's mother, not of his wife or first love), but on a deeper Jungian level the assurance that day is near suggests rebirth from the darkness of death and last judgment which Isak now faces. After standing beside the empty cradle (into which he gazes as he had gazed into the coffin in the opening dream of the film), Isak goes to the door length windows of a lakeside country cottage, looking through which he sees his cousin Sara sharing a romantic dinner with his brother Sigfrid. This painful revelation of their marital bliss -- from which he is excluded, like Ishmael cast into the wilderness outside the cottage -- is so intense that Isak sighs heavily, leans his head against the wall, and puts his hand on a protruding nail (the only heavy handed touch in the film, the nail symbolizes the Crucifixion).

Then begins the descent into limbo sequence of the dream (quite appropriately, since we have just seen the Crucifixion), during which the imagery of doorways, corridors, and basement chambers is picked up from the first dream, only now the dreamer actually goes through these passageways into the buildings which he remained outside before. After Isak cuts his palm on the nail and holds it up in front of a window pane to examine the wound, we see his reflection in the glass of the pane as he moves slowly to the left side of the screen. Then a man (who resembles the vicious husband he had picked up after the accident on the drive south) comes to the window. With the camera repositioned to the inside of the cottage (now empty of romantic accoutrements), we watch as Isak walks first through the outer door which the man opens for him, through a doorless portal separating the living room from the hall stairs (lit one flight above around a corner), beneath which Isak pauses to remove his overcoat for the first time during the journey (a divestiture characteristic of the stripping down phase of the hero's descent, leading to a re-investiture in the royal robes of the award ceremony in the Cathedral at the end of the film), before passing through a third door unlocked for him by his severe inquisitor. As Isak walks through this third door in the sequence, the camera is repositioned to the viewer's end of a basement corridor into which the third door opens, and down which Isak is now led by his inquisitor to a fourth door to the right. This corridor (like Cocteau's candle-lit corridor in the Beast's chateau) is lined with four electric lamps along the right side, and one lamp suspended in the darkness of the extreme mid-background of the screen. This image of a dark corridor with a light at the end of the tunnel is another image suggestive of rebirth, an image quite common in the near death narratives recorded by researchers like Kenneth Ring. After proceeding down this corridor, the severe inquisitor unlocks the fourth door on the right, and the camera zooms in to a close up of Isak's profile (reminiscent of the profiles frame by darkened doorways in the opening dream) as he passes through the door into an examination chamber.

It is appropriate that the series of doorways in this sequence leads from outside to inside, and from upstairs to downstairs to a basement chamber where Isak will fail an examination and be condemned to relive the day he discovered his wife's adultery, to which he had driven her by his coldness (Karin's lover looks like a vile mature version of Isak's brother Sigfrid, to whom he had lost Sara, as if Isak were compelled to repeat the trauma of his first rejection in his marriage with Karin). During the examination in the basement (representing the inner, lower world of Isak's psychic burial ground), Isak fails to decipher an inscription on the blackboard and then fails to identify a bacterial specimen under a microscope (instead he sees his own eye reflected, as if the specimen to be examined is himself; the image recalls the eyes above the clock and the close up of the corpse face and eyes from the opening dream sequence).[43] After this he must diagnose a woman in a chair who resembles the abused wife he had picked up after the accident during his drive south; she bursts out into demonic laughter after he pronounces her dead (paralleling the risen corpse of the opening sequence and again suggesting a continuation of life after death -- and the refusal of our buried complexes to stay dead). The severity of this last judgment sequence (appropriate to a journey into Hades) yields to a kind of rebirth or redemption when Isak finally arrives at his destination in Lund (a sort of promised land).

It is in his son's home after the long day celebrating his scientific achievements in the Cathedral of Lund that Isak has the final archetypal dream or reverie sequence in the film. This sequence adapts a vocabulary of images different from the doorways and corridors of the previous dreams, but still derived from the mythic journey to the underworld.

Unlike the first two dream sequences, images of nature predominate in this last vision. Furthermore, reconciliations replace painful revelations and confer an ultimate sense of peace and understanding that helps Isak prepare for the final passage into death: he apologizes to his house-keeper for his rudeness the morning before, encourages a truce between Evald and Marianne by suggesting he will not insist on the redemption of his loan, and kisses Marianne in a very touching gesture of genuine affection before falling asleep. Watching these last scenes of the film and of Isak's life it is difficult not to think of Rembrandt's painting of the dying Jacob blessing the sons of Joseph. As in that famous painting, we see here the old Isak in bed blessing Evald and then Marianne who come to the bedside. Earlier touches in the film, of course, have prepared us for this biblical conclusion: Isak's rivalry with his brother Sigfrid recasts the sibling conflicts with Ishmael in the Old Testament, only in the film the brothers compete for the love of their cousin Sara, not for their father's blessing. Furthermore, the cousin is named Sara, the biblical name of Isak's mother, Bergman's way of underscoring the Oedipal complications of Isak's love life. Indeed, the last image before Isak falls into reverie is of the gently maternal Marianne kissing the old Isak as a mother kisses a child in bed, and the kiss immediately evokes Isak's memories of childhood.

After the kiss, Isak settles down into bed and remarks that after a trying day it calms him to "recall childhood memories," though the sequence which follows quickly achieves the intensity of a visionary dream in which the actual memory has been modified by archetypal lenses. The first shot shows the children rushing out of the country estate (visited earlier in the film) and heading down to the dock with a boy carrying a long slender fishing pole in the lead. Isak's cousin Sara detaches herself from the group and runs towards Isak, who stands off to the side dressed in his habitual funereal overcoat. Sara tells Isak that there are no strawberries left (life's feast having been consumed) and asks him to go look for his mother and father, while the children sail around to them on the lake (the children's time, that is to say, has not yet come round, but Isak is ready to join his dead father). When Isak says he doesn't know where his parents are (they are in the *terra incognita* of the afterlife), Sara offers help and guides him through meadow and forest to a little rocky promontory by the side of the lake. Then Sara turns homeward (back into life, as she had done in the scene before Isak fell asleep of the erstwhile Sara serenading the old man beneath his window before saying good-bye), after pointing across a little inlet to another promontory where Isak's father sits fishing and his mother pic-nicking and knitting. Sara's role in these initial frames of the last sequence is to guide Isak towards the underworld, both the literal under-world of his imminent death, and the underworld of his own buried memories and longings. Like Circe in the *Odyssey*, Sara is a psychopomp, directing the hero to the land of shades, where he will encounter a male sage and the image of his departed mother.

This last shot of Isak's father and mother fishing and knitting across the inlet is a beautiful impressionistic still, a serenely paradisal landscape evocative of those visions reported by people who have undergone near-death experiences: the father sits on a rock right by the waterline where the lake meets the inlet, exactly in the middle of the composition. Above him and to the right, Isak's mother sits knitting and waves warmly to her son on the other side of the water (goddesses of fate and death always sit knitting, as do Circe, Calypso, and Penelope in the *Odyssey*, or the weaving *moirai* of Hades). Beyond the father, the lake stretches away indeterminately into the far left background of the still, so that the composition is divided exactly in half between lake and land, with the father's long slender fishing pole linking the two halves and upper and lower segments of the shot. The influx of water from the lake into the little inlet in the foreground also links the two halves of the composition and separates Isak (and the viewer) from the midground just across the inlet where his father and mother sit on the yonder shore of the afterlife (the father down closest to the water since he is already dead).

The promontory across the water where the departed ancestors sit waiting for their son is a kind of Promised Land. The near-death narratives recorded by Moody and Ring nearly always include such an encounter with a departed relative who serves as a guide for the newly dead soul, and the image of the father fishing on the shores of the lake suggests Christ, the fisher of souls, on the shores of Galilee. The bliss of the return to the long lost father, which suggests the biblical theme of atonement so dear to Joyce's *Ulysses*, is reflected by the radiant serenity of Isak's face, the birdsong in the background, and the harp music of the score.[44] That Isak is approaching the end of his life and the beginning of his night sea journey to the land beyond the waves is underscored by the fact that he stands on the edge of the land this side of the inlet, and by a quick shot, earlier in the sequence, of the family boat at the end of the dock, with its sail hanging halfway hoisted up the mast, rocking in the brisk breeze, and ready for departure. As the children walk excitedly down to the boat, one falls into the water and must be thrown a circular life preserver by his screaming siblings. This dream memory, of course reflects Isak the dreamer, who is also drowning, and who yet has had life-lines tossed out to him at several points during his trying day: by his daughter in law Marianne, who has broken through his pedantic shell of repressed memories and failures; by the erstwhile and recollected Saras, who have stirred up the sorrows and joys of his adolescence; and by his own unconscious, which has thrown a life raft of images out to a dying old man, to help him prepare for his last journey to the Promised Land.

Alifa Rifaat

Like many hero and heroine journey narratives, the nameless narrator of "My World of the Unknown," by the Egyptian feminist Alifa Rifaat, undertakes a "night sea journey" through the underworld (Frobenius 85) -- a characteristic image of the descents of Gilgamesh, Odysseus, Aeneas, Dante, the Ancient Mariner, and, most cogently perhaps, of the Pharaohs of the Egyptian Books of the Dead, passing on the solar barge up the river of the dead. The narrator's journey takes her from Cairo by train to a small country town in rural Egypt, and on across a "broad canal" past "swans" and "sailing boats" to a "white house" on the "opposite bank" (1911). The river crossing marks her passage into the unknown world of dreams, the "garden door" to which is, however, guarded, by a young woman with a fat child on her shoulders. She stands "barring the door," and refuses to give way, bracing her hands "resolutely against the door," until the narrator's male companion knocks her down, which enables the narrator to rush "through the door into the house" and to explore the rooms (1911-12). The threshold battle at the gateway to the underworld is an old Egyptian motif, going all the way back to the illustrated tombs of the Pharaohs, and to the Books of the Dead, in which each chamber of the underworld (called the Tuat) is guarded by a serpent (Budge 170-262; Wilkinson 138), with which, as we shall see, the "mad woman" in Rifaat's tale is intimately related (1912). The same "mad woman" appears after the narrator has moved into the house, and gives her "a ring on which were several keys" (1913), keys which seem to imply access to the hidden chambers of the "bottom of the house" where its secret resides (1914). As the tale progresses, the narrator feels herself "tumbling down into a bottomless pit and being destroyed" (1918), as the snake lures her into the beautiful but terrifying underworld beneath the house.

As in Tagore's "Hungry Stones," Hoffman's "Mines of Falun," and Gilman's "Yellow Wallpaper," the secret of the house emanates from a symbol of the archetypal feminine, goddess of the underworld. In Rifaat's tale, she takes the form of a snake, which the narrator first sees "twisting and turning" from the "limb of a nearby tree" in the garden surrounding the house (1914). As the snake curls "round on itself in spiral rings," the narrator is gripped by terror and desire; she remains hypnotized, completely captivated, until the "snake coyly twisted round and gently, gracefully glided away," to pass silently through a crack in the wall into the bottom of the house (1915). The connection between the spiraling coils of the serpent and the imagery of the maze is an old one, very much evident in Milton's *Paradise Lost*, to cite just one example. The linkage between the tree, the garden, the serpent, sacred vessels, and the great goddesses of the Ancient Near East, during the Bronze ages, is even more firmly archetypal, one of the most persistent icons of the mythologies of Egypt, Sumeria, Greece, and Rome. Joseph Campbell shows how this archetypal iconography permeated the prebiblical cultures the Near East and the Indus river valleys, until its message of joyful participation in the rhythms of life and death was transformed by the patriarchs of the Old Testament, of the *Theogony*, and of the Vedas into an image of the Fall (*Occidental Myth* 9-41; *Mythic Image* 281-301). Campbell's work acknowledges the seminal work of Jane Ellen Harrison on the pre-Olympian deities of Greece, and has recently been amplified by Marija Gimbutas, whose *Language of the Goddess* devotes an entire chapter to the icon of the goddess and the serpent (121-37).

The realm of the serpent in Rifaat's story combines Gnostic, Egyptian, Zoroastrian, Arabic, and Muslim images into a composite allegory of poesis. Rifaat's snake is like the Gnostic Sophia, imprisoned in the labyrinthine underworld of matter (Quispell 211), and like the Hindu jiva, trapped in that realm of illusion (maya) which is generated and sustained by fear and desire (kama-mara) (Zimmer 205-06; 263-68; 460-61). In such important Gnostic documents as the Syrian "Hymn of the Pearl," the serpent and the sea represent the underworld of matter, in which the soul (symbolized by the pearl) lies imprisoned, having been seduced by the sensual delights of a foreign country or town (another typical Gnostic symbol of the material world) (Jonas 112-129). It is curious then to note that the narrator's journey in Rifaat's tale takes her to a town far out in the countryside, to a house beside the water, where the snake appears to seduce her with the promise of secret delights in "the depths of the azure sea of pleasure," on a bed "inlaid with pearls newly wrenched from their shells" (1917). It is a realm of sleep, of dream, of forgetting -- precise and frequent symbols of the material world among the Gnostics. Yet, as seductively erotic as the snake's promise is -- "to prise out your pearl from its shell that I may polish it and bring forth its splendor" (1917) -- it is also creatively spiritual, and replaces the patriarchal condemnation of the serpent with the promise of the soul's liberation from (not imprisonment in) the shell of materialism. The assignment of such a positive role to the serpent is entirely consistent with the Bronze mythologies of the Ancient Near East -- in which the serpent is celebrated as a symbol of the knowledge that immortality brings, when the soul sheds its mortal coil (Campbell, *Occidental Myth* Figs. 1-10) -- and it reemerges in the Gnostic exaltation of the serpent in Genesis as the force which liberates the souls of Adam and Eve from the demonic Demiurge of the Creation (Jonas 93). Hence, the Gnostic serpent stands at the doorway which out of the material world into the imaginal realm, properly inhabited by the inspired poet.

The imagery linking the serpent goddess of the otherworld with doorways persists when a Sheik comes to explain that the snake is the "sovereign of the house" and "one of the monarchs of the earth" (1915). He encourages the narrator to pray for an "increase" in "knowledge," to be gained in communion with the snake, who will open "doors" leading to "other worlds known only to their Creator" (1915). In her dreamlike state of spiritually charged eroticism, the narrator feels herself "on the brink of a new world, a new destiny, or rather, if you wish, the threshold of a new love" (1915). It is entirely archetypal, particularly so for the iconography of the Ancient Egyptians, for the passage into another world to be represented by doorways, and, it is important to note, the doorway in this story leads to a realm associated not only with sex, but with aesthetic inspiration as well: the underworld is a realm of poesis, as well as of coitus (perhaps the most elemental symbol of human creativity). The snake's "golden tongue" (1914) is afterall is not only a sexual organ (1917), but also a linguistic organ, the source of "the tenderest of words" and of "gentle," "soft," and "musical whisperings" (1917). Her realm is one in which acts of poesis coincide with cunnilingus: it is an intensely imaginative underworld "on the horizon of dreams," down in "the depths of the azure sea of pleasure" (1917). Its very existence is testimony of God's power to "create worlds and living beings ... other than that of matter and the transitory" (1918), worlds "fashioned of jewels, a world whose every moment was radiant with light and formed a thousand shapes, a thousand colors" (1919). But the creative power which shapes intangible worlds of the imagination is not only divine, it is also literary.

For the snake's otherworld is the realm of what Henry Corbin referred to as the mundus imaginalis, a concept central to Arabic and Persian mystical traditions, extending from the Mazdaism to Islam. The story gives us a fascinating glimpse of that world, mixing Arabic folklore and Muslim mysticism, when the Sheik arrives to chant "verses from the Qur'an as he tapped the ground with his stick" (1915), and later when the snake instructs the narrator to "Bring a container of water" to recite some "verses from the Qur'an" while sprinkling water over the places where the other snakes live, thus closing "the doors on them" (1918). A typical feature of the ancient Egyptian Books of the Dead involved the recitation of cryptic incantations at the gateways of the Tuat, all guarded by serpents, as the soul passes through the underworld (Budge 170-232). The linkage between poesis and the descent is, therefore, primordial, perhaps the oldest of all our stories. In "My World of the Unknown," the snake's world inspires the recitation of verses and the activation of the primary powers of the imagination, associated with the creation of new worlds and living beings which transcend the physical. The Sheiks called this imaginal "universe *âlam al-mithâl*, world of the archetypal images" ("Terre-Céleste" 159; my trans.), a "world of symbols and archetypal images" (*Avicenna* 76). It is the "the Paradise of Hûrqalyâ ... the Earth in its purified state, since it directly reflects the premeditated Image of the soul" ("Terre-Céleste" 159; my trans.). The primary activity of the soul in this realm is an imaginal act of poesis, whereby "spirits embody and bodies spiritualize" ("Terre-Céleste" 168; my trans.).

Rifaat narrator herself suggests this is a world generated by "the echo of some image that my unconscious had stored up and was chewing over" (1911), and that is surely so, if we extend our notion of the unconscious to the archetypally collective realm which the mystics called *âlam al-mithâl*. It is a world ruled by the serpent goddess, a matriarchal power the Arabic and Persian mystics associated with the Angel of the Earth, "Spenta Armaiti, "feminine Archangel of the Earth," and with the emerald cities of her Earth (Corbin, "Terre-Céleste" 236, 156). The Zoroastrian Rivâyat refers to her as "daughter of the Lord of Wisdom," and as the "mistress of the household" (Corbin, "Terre-Céleste" 138; my trans.). Curiously enough, these are terms very close to the narrator's language in Rifaat's wonderful tale, in which the snake is referred to as "one of the daughters of the monarchs of the djinn" (1916), and as "the guardian of the house" (1917). But this spiritual mistress soon succumbs to the energies of the patriarchy, as the old matriarchal cultures of the Near Eastern world did, annihilated by the thunderbolts of Zeus, Jahweh, and Indra (Campbell, *Occidental Myth* Fig. 10), and as Alifa Rifaat did herself, for some ten years in her life, when her father and husband forced her stop writing (like Charlotte Gilman's husband). The story of the love affair ends when the narrator's husband kills a snake in the garden, thus closing the door on the "sovereign of the house" (1915), mistress of unknown worlds, muse of tender words and gentle whisperings.

Black Elk

As strange as it may seem, *Black Elk Speaks* was published in 1932, just after the first peak of the Modernist, and a few years before its great second period of fulfillment, during the years of the Second World War. Black Elk's narrative -- the story of a Holy man of the Oglala Sioux -- is perhaps the greatest spiritual autobiography ever produced on American soil, and surely one of the most precious treasures of world mythology. It is a narrative based on a sequence of hero journeys, which take the form of Black Elk's visionary cycles. These take him from the body, to the spirit world, and back to the body. Many of the revelations of the initiatory stage of the journey draw upon the wellspring of iconography which is the subject of this book.

The first of these hero journey cycles is known as "The Great Vision," which Black Elk experienced when he was only nine years old. The separation stage of the journey began with those psychosomatic symptoms frequently associated with the shamanic vocation.[45] Black Elk was traveling by horseback when his arms and legs began to swell up. The call to adventure came that night, when Black Elk lay inside the teepee of his camp, and saw two men "coming from the clouds, head first like arrows slanting down" (22). Strangely analogous to the Angel Messengers of Sufi mysticism, these men -- each carrying spears with jagged lightning flashing from the tips -- initiate the boy's ascent to the spirit world with a literal vocation: "Hurry! Come! Your Grandfathers are calling you!" (22). The lightning bolts flashing from the spear tips recall the Tibetan vajra, the symbol of enlightenment associated with the revelations of Buddhist meditation. After this dramatic call to adventure, Black Elk gets up in a visionary state, and walks to a "little cloud coming very fast," which then carries him up into the sky. He looks back down at his mother and father, sorry to leave them -- a moment recalling the out-of-body sequence at the beginning of near-death narratives. The little cloud takes Black Elk to a destination familiar to students of the hero journey -- great "snowy hills and mountains" made of towering white clouds, where the thunder beings live (22).

The revelations of the initiation stage of the hero journey begin when a bay horse appears to carry Black Elk on his ascent (rather like Mohammed's mule during the Miraj Namah!). The bay horse announces his intention to tell his "life history" (23), a moment recalling the life review stage of the near-death narrative. As the bay horse wheels about to the west, north, east, and south, twelve horses of differing colors come riding forth from each of the four cardinal points: from the west, twelve black horses, "with necklaces of bison hoofs," manes of lightning, and "thunder in their nostrils"; from the north, twelve white horses, manes flowing like blizzards, noses roaring, and white geese soaring and circling around them; from the east, twelve sorrel horses, with necklaces of elk's teeth, manes of morning light, and eyes shining like the morning star; and from the south, twelve buckskins, with horns and manes sprouting trees and grasses (23-24). Together, these forty eight horses form a mandala, a quaternity radiating out from a central point. Not only reminiscent of the Heavenly City in The Book of Revelation (in which the numbers 3, 4, 12, and 48 play central roles), this vision recalls all those ancient cosmographies of the High Neolithic which divided the world into sacred quadrants (Campbell, *Flight* 93-95, 138-143; *Atlas*, 2.1.28). Among these is to be included the visions of the Tibetan Book of the Dead, in which the post-mortem soul encounters Buddhas associated with the four directions, radiating out from Vairocana, the white Buddha of consciousness and space, in the center, holding an eight-spoked wheel in his hand, and sitting on a lion throne: Vajrasattva, the blue Buddha of form and water, from the East, holding a five-pointed vajra, and sitting on an elephant throne; Ratnasambhava, the yellow Buddha of earth and feeling, from the South, holding a wish-fulfilling jewel, and sitting on a horse throne; Amitabha, the red Buddha of fire and perception, from the West, holding a yellow lotus, and sitting on a peacock throne; and Amoghasiddhi, the green Buddha of air and conceptualization, from the North, holding a double vajra, and sitting on a throne of shang-shang birds (41-48). The Tibetan Book of the Dead, of course, forms a complete hero journey cycle, from life, to the otherworld of the mind after death, and back to life when the soul is reincarnated.

Black Elk's vision of the sacred quaternity will also eventually come full circle, when he returns to his body lying in the teepee. In between, however, we have the revelations of the journey. Like the ritual objects the various Buddhas hold in their hands (wheel, vajra, lotos, jewel), the necklaces of the horses of the four directions in Black Elk's vision have iconographic significance. We know, for example, that both the bison hoof and elk's teeth necklaces worn by the horses indicate the dynamic of death and rebirth represented by the sacrificial animals upon which the hunting peoples of the Paleolithic depended for survival. The bison is unique to the Plains Indians, but it recalls the importance of the bull in the rituals of the Ancient Mediterranean, Egyptian, and Mesopotamian cultures. The deer also, as we have seen, played a key role in such hero journey cycles as *The Quest of the Holy Grail*, and the ballad of "The Three Ravens," in which hind and doe were associated with the otherworld. Black Elk's vision also summons the symbolism of birds, here the wild geese circling around the white horses from the north. The migratory patterns of these marvelous birds has long been associated with the hero journey of the soul: shamanistic artifacts from Lake Baikal, of geese carved in mammoth ivory, have been recovered from burial sites dated around 16, 000 B.C.E. (Campbell, *Atlas* 1.1.72); and in Hinduism, the wild gander (Hamsa) represents both the universal and the individual soul, Brahman and Atman (Zimmer, *Myths* 47-50). Furthermore, the eyes of the sorrel horses of the east, glimmering like the morning star, recall the imagery of the Sumerian Goddess Inanna, who survives Ereshkigal's "eye of wrath" in the underworld, to emerge at dawn as Hesperus, symbol of rebirth.

After the boy in Black Elk's vision summons the forty eight horses of the four quarters, they all line up to form a grand procession (rather like the forty eight horses in Aladdin's wedding). They then

march four by four, with wild herds of animals of kinds cavorting behind them, proceeding to a large teepee of piled up clouds, which represents the source of life. At this point in Black Elk's visionary journey,
threshold symbolism emerges, as the procession stops in front of the
"open door" of the teepee: the door is made of a rainbow, and through it
Black Elk sees "six old men sitting in a row" (25). The rainbow door
represents the boundary between the material and the spiritual worlds. In
Norse myth, for example, the rainbow forms a bridge linking heaven to
earth, a bridge by which the gods ascend to Valhalla in Wagner's
"Rheingold." In Tibetan Buddhism, the pious enter the paradise of the
Amitabha Buddha (Sukhavati) via a rainbow of five colors, at the end of
which another buddha stands guarding a gate (Lauf 49). Another rainbow encircles the eight Boddhisattvas seated inside the confines of paradise, awaiting the souls ascending from the earth. In Black Elk's vision, six elders sit inside the circle formed by the teepee with the rainbow door, and the two angel messengers with spears escort the boy into
their presence. The six Grandfathers look "older than men can ever be --
old like hills, like stars" (25), and they are called "the Powers of the
World," sitting at the "high and lonely center of the earth" (26). Like
the horses, they represent the four cardinal points of the compass, plus
the Sky and the Earth, and from them the further revelations of the hero
journey issue forth.

Each of the six Grandfathers bestows a boon and a vision upon
Black Elk, and these increase his "understanding" of the world he lives
in, a simple but crucial purpose of the initiations of the hero journey.
The first Grandfather, of the West, gives the boy a cup and a bow, with
the powers to "make live" and "to destroy" (26). The cup recalls the
Grail, and a wide variety of other sacred vessels encountered during the
hero journey (cauldrons, lamps, bowls, chalices). The second
Grandfather, of the North, gives Black Elk an "herb of power," which
he then uses to heal the skinny black horse into which the Grandfather
of the West has transformed himself (27). Then the Grandfather of the
North changes into a "white goose wheeling" through the sky and
singing two songs, acts of poesis which the hero (Black Elk) memo-
rizes (27). The third Grandfather, of the East, gives Black Elk a sacred
pipe with living eagle feathers and the power of healing. Then he shows
the boy two men flying beneath the daybreak star -- like Boddhisattvas,
they have the power to awaken "all the beings of the earth with roots
and legs and wings" (27). The fourth Grandfather, of the South, bestows
a very special gift upon the boy: he gives Black Elk a "bright red stick
that was alive," and it immediately sprouts "branches and leaves where
birds begin to sing, and it gives shade to the villages which circle round
beneath it. It is an axis mundi: like Yggdrasil, like the Cross, like the
Boddhi Tree, like the Huluppu Tree, the flowering rod is "the center of

the nation's circle" (28), and it later stands at the crossroads, where the red and black roads intersect (29).

The flowering of the "holy stick" is an old and lovely symbol of regeneration, one found in an enormous range of biblical and pagan sources from all over the world. An extremely beautiful page from the illuminated Psalter of Robert de Lindesey, of about 1220, shows Christ crucified upon a "'Living Cross' from which sprigs of foliage sprout. The idea conveyed is that the wood of the Cross is a symbolic Tree of Life through the redemption from sin and promise of resurrection given to man by the sacrifice of Christ. This imagery is used in hymns on the Cross, most particularly of the liturgy of Good Friday" (Marks and Morgan 45). The imagery of the 'Verdant Cross' goes back at least as far as the fourth century A.D., to the Holy Sepulchre at Jerusalem, where the emperor Theodosius I "had erected a large golden cross, encrusted with gems and in the form of a burgeoning, flowering plant" (Schama 214). Shortly thereafter, in Palestine, small ampoules appeared (said to contain drops of holy oil, pressed from the wood of the Cross), inscribed with a palmate form of the cross, possibly derived from those Mesopotamian peoples who saw the palm as a symbol of renewal and immortality (Schama 214-15). Since the words "palm" and "phoenix" were "interchangeable in both Greek and Egyptian Coptic," an early Christian mosaic at Santa Prassede in Rome shows the phoenix perched on a palm tree with the adoring apostles below (Schama 15). From then on, "The botanical cross was rapidly translated into the iconography of the Christian West," appearing in illuminated manuscripts like the Lindesey Psalter, in Books of Hours as the Tree of Jesse, in Breviaries like the one by the Ermengau Master, which shows Christ on a tree-cross, in Taddeo Gaddi's spectacular fresco for the refectory of Santa Croce in Florence, in which the cross has twelve branches for each of the apostles, and in woodcuts like Heinrich Vogtherr's "Glaubensbaum" of 1524, which shows Jesus on a flowering cross rooted in "gottes Wort" (Schama 219-23). Albrecht Dürer left us a particularly splendid example in his Crucifixion of 1500, which shows Joseph spading, and Mary watering the twin stems of a tree rooted at the foot of the Cross, with the branches exfoliating and bearing fruit as they coil up around the figure of Jesus (Campbell, *Mythic Image* 190). At about the same time the Psalter of Robert de Lindesey was being illuminated, , an anonymous Cistercian monk in France added a long chapter on the "Legend of the Tree of Life" to his magnificent *Quest of the Holy Grail.*

It is very interesting, given the well known importance of trees in the lore of the Celtic druids and in Celtic verse,[46] that the Cistercian monk should develop the image of the Tree of Knowledge in such extraordinary detail: perhaps it was the residual element of Celtic mythology in European society (which played such an important role in the origins and development of the Arthurian romances in general)[47] that contributed to the formation of this fantastic midrash (one is tempted to call it) about the Tree. In fact, tree cults and various aspects of an archetypal arboretum permeated much of pagan European culture, in such forms as the green men sculpted over the portals at Chartres (Anderson 76-81), to the flowering hawthorn of Glastonbury Abbey, said to have been planted by Joseph of Arimathea after bringing the Grail to England (Schama 220). These legendary images are rooted in a variety of biblical versions of the flowering branch motif, prefigurations of the miracle of the cross in the Old Testament, such as Job's evocation of the "hope of a tree, if it be cut down, that it will sprout again, and that the tender branch thereof will not cease. Though the root thereof wax old in the earth, and the stock thereof die in the ground; Yet through the scent of water it will bud, and bring forth boughs like a plant" (14: 7-9).

The last two gifts of the Grandfathers in Black Elk's vision also bring up some interesting amplifications: Grandfather Sky appears as an eagle, and Grandfather Earth appears as a very old man, with long white hair, a wrinkled face, and eyes "deep and dim" (30). In one of the most astonishing moments of revelation in the history of the hero journey: Time reverses itself, as the old man grows "backwards into youth," and Black Elk gradually recognizes the old man as himself (30). This vision brings two important analogous moments to mind. One is Henry Corbin's discussion of an octagonal maze drawn by Leonardo in one of his notebooks. It is characteristic of the journey into the maze, Corbin writes, for the hero to find in the central chamber the "great priest who reveals the symbolic meaning of the wanderings and of the figures encountered" during his quest ("Morphologie" 101; my trans.). And so it is with Black Elk, who confronts the elders in the teepee, who reveal the symbolic significance of his vision. On a deeper level, however, Corbin suggests that Leonardo's labyrinth has an octagonal mirror maze in the central sanctuary, which reflects the initiate's own image into the infinity of all eight sides. Hence, in the center of the maze, at the climax of the hero journey, the initiate (like Black Elk) finds himself, instead of a Minotaur.

A similar moment came to Jung, during a near-death experience in 1944, when, after breaking his foot, he endured several nights of delirious visions, hanging on the "edge of death (*Memories* 289). The first vision involved a celestial ascent, like Black Elk's, or like Mohammed's Miraj Namah. Jung felt himself going high up into space, looking down at Ceylon, India, Arabia, and the Mediterranean. As he turned to the south, a "tremendous dark block of stone, like a meteorite" entered his vision (290). At this point the imagery of doorways and divestiture emerge, as Jung describes a staircase leading up to an entrance into the stone, which leads to a small ante-chamber inside a kind of Hindu temple. Once through the doorway, as Jung approaches a yogi meditating in a small niche, surrounded by candles, he had "the feeling that everything was being sloughed away; everything I aimed at or worked for or thought, the whole phantasmagoria of earthly existence, fell away or was stripped from me -- an extremely painful process" (291). Jung reiterates the imagery of divestiture, when he remarks upon the sense "of having been stripped or pillaged" as he steps through the doorway into the temple (291), and when he remarks that the stripping down was a "painful process of defoliation" (292), using a metaphor that also occurs in Black Elk's vision (leaves falling from trees). Like Inanna being disrobed as she steps through the gateways during her journey into the underworld, Jung is relentlessly stripped down, defoliated, during his own visionary journey. Just before he steps into the next chamber, which seems to hold out the hope of complete understanding, Jung's vision is interrupted by his doctor, who has come to call him back to life, bringing the journey full circle: bed, to the heavens, and back to bed (much like Black Elk).

Jung's visionary dreams shortly after this experience focus on a key point that connects them to Black Elk's Great Vision. Jung dreamt that he was walking through a hilly landscape when he came upon a small chapel, with its door standing ajar -- imagery of the mountain destination and doorways coming together in this dream journey. After walking through the open door, Jung found a wonderful flower arrangement, and, instead of images of the Virgin Mary and the Crucifixion, he found a yogi, sitting in a lotos posture in deep meditation, on the floor in front of an altar! This was the yogi inside the door of the stone temple in his near-death vision, only this time Jung is able to go closer. To his astonishment, and indeed terror, Jung finds that the yogi has his face, and he is shocked awake (323). Like Black Elk, or like the mystagogue wandering to the center of Leonardo's octagonal mirror maze, Jung has journeyed into the otherworld to find himself, sitting at the center of the psyche.

Similar threshold imagery emerges at this point in Black Elk's Great Vision, when, after seeing the last Grandfather turn into himself, Black Elk gets up and walks back through the rainbow door of the teepee, where the bay horse is waiting for him. The bay summons all the forty eight horses of the four quarters, who come up bearing the gifts Black Elk has received from the elders: the black horses bearing cup and bow; the sorrels the sacred pipe; the buckskins the holy stick; and the white horses the wing and herb (31). A grand procession then moves along the black road to the east, and the trial phase of the hero journey begins. Like Lancelot, Yvain, Galahad, or the boy in "The

Devil and the Three Golden Hairs," Black Elk must now heal the waste land of its various afflictions, the first of which is drought. Looking down upon the earth, Black Elk sees a "sick green light," frightened birds, and a blue man rising in flames from the place where three streams converge. He personifies drought, which Black Elk defeats when his black horses shake hail from their manes, snort thunder and lightning, and plunge torrentially earthwards. Black Elk then kills the blue man by impaling him with his lightning-tipped spear. The effect of these heroic deeds is both literal and symbolic, for the drought is removed by releasing the waters at the place where the rivers meet, an archaic symbol of the source of life. Like the dried-up fountain in "The Devil and the Three Golden Hairs," the releasing of the waters requires the slaying of the demonic forces of death.

Waste land condition prevail in the second ordeal of the journey, when Black Elk comes to a village "filled with moaning and with mourning for the dead" (33). A fierce southwind blows fever inside every teepee, where the "women and the children and the men lay dying with the dead" (33). The conventions of the hero journey demand the conquest of death itself, as when Lancelot lifts the stone slab in Chrétien's "Knight of the Cart," thereby releasing the captives in that land from which no traveler returns. Black Elk performs a similar feat by thrusting the flowering stick into the "center of the nation's hoop" (34). Like the withered apple tree in "The Three Golden Hairs," the holy stick bursts into bloom, a veritable Tree of Life, "full of leafy branches and of all birds singing" (34), like the tall pine beside the fountain in Chrétien's "Yvain," to which all the birds of the forest return after the devastation of the hailstorm.

After these two triumphs (the drought and the dying village) come the trials of the four ascents, as the horses proceed along the red road. Black Elk says the four ascents represent the four generations of his own lifetime, and the procession moves slowly towards an apocalyptic destination. That the journey proceeds through the underworld is clear, for Black Elk notes among the throng behind him the "ghosts of people like a trailing fog as far as I could see -- grandfathers of grandfathers and grandmothers of grandmothers without number" (36). The barriers separating the living and the dead have broken down, as all proceed on the journey of the four ascents. Conditions get bad after the second, when the animals get restless and the holy tree is defoliated (as in Jung's vision) (37). Things grow rapidly worse during the third ascent, when "all the animals and fowls that were the people ran here and there, for each one seemed to have his own little vision that he followed and his own rules" (37). If that sounds like a familiar diagnosis of our own times, Black Elks' vision of the winds of war beginning to blow all over the universe is even more uncanny, given his identification of the time of that vision and 1932, shortly before World War II. The fourth ascent is purely apocalyptic: the people have haggard faces, their ponies shrivel up into "hide and bone," the holy tree disappears, and it seems that "all the winds of the world were fighting," and that women and children and horses are screaming and wailing "all over the world" (39).

The resolution of this apocalyptic crisis involves rituals of dance and poesis, at the climax of the hero journey. First, Black Elk sees a red man holding a spear who walks into the "center of the people," turns himself into a fat bison by lying down and rolling over, and stamping on the ground, where sacred herb springs up. It has four blossoms on a single stem of four different colors (white, scarlet, yellow, and blue), the rays of which flash up to the heavens. Then the flowering tree stands "there again at the center of the nation's hoop where the four-rayed herb had blossomed," and it catalyzes the regeneration of horses and people. An act of poesis follows, as Black Elk sings a "song of power," and gets on his bay horse to take the healing herb to a skinny brownish black horse dying in the west (40). Black Elk regenerates that horse with the herb, and it then wheels around to all four directions, bringing all the horses back to life (one thinks here of the horsemen of the Apocalypse). They are "beautiful" and "terrible" (41). Further rituals of regeneration then follow, and they combine the imagery of virginity, the dance, and poesis, in a way that recalls the marvelous procession of virgins in Wolfram's Grail Castle. After the horses of the four quarters stop and stand around a black stallion in the center of the nation's hoop, "four virgins, more beautiful than women of the earth can be, came through the circle, dressed in scarlet, one from each of the four quarters, and stood about the great black stallion in their places" (41). Each holds one of the gifts Black Elk received from the Grandfathers: cup, wing, pipe, and nation's hoop. The dance then turns to poesis, as all the universe listens to a song with two stanzas, each repeated four times. It is "more beautiful than anything can be. It was so beautiful that nothing anywhere could keep from dancing" (42). The virgins dance, the horses dance, the leaves and grasses dance, the waters in the creeks and rivers dance, the birds dance, and all four-legged and two-legged animals dance. When they stop, a flaming rainbow in the east consecrates this marvelous ritual of annihilation, renewal, and poesis.

The imagery of poesis, doorways, and divestiture characteristic of the hero journey continue in the climax and conclusion of Black Elk's vision, when he returns to the place from which he has departed. Before he does, the bay horse takes him to a mountain top, from which he surveys the "whole hoop of the world" (43). The mountain top is the axis mundi, the place where the heavens and the earth come together, and the place where the ultimate revelations of the hero journey occur, as in the story of Moses. Black Elk says that "while I stood there I saw more than I can tell and I understood more than I saw; for I was seeing in a sacred manner the shapes of all things in the spirit, and the shape of all shapes as they must live together like one being" (43). The language here is at once Platonic and biblical, an archetypal language of form and revelation associated with the initiation stage of the hero journey. One thinks of Paul's evocation, "the eye of man hath not seen, the ear of man hath not heard," which Bottom botches to describe his vision of Titania in *A Midsummer Night's Dream*; one thinks of Plato's notion of the eidola, as the pure shape of all shapes, the one Form of all forms, existing in the mind of God. This revelation of the ultimate form of forms, of the archetypes from which all things come, is typical of all the great hero journeys of Modernist literature, in which the descent to the underworld leads to a precise vocabulary and symbolic iconography of form. Black Elk's phrase, "the shape of all shapes," curiously recalls such Modernist formulations as Hermann Broch's "symbol of all symbols" ('Sinnbild aller Sinnbild')(89; 85), or "first image of all archetypes" ('Urbild aller bilder') (481; 453).

The imagery of divestiture and of doorways follows this revelation of the pure spiritual forms of all things. After Black Elk sees the healing four-rayed herb fall to and take root in the earth, dispelling the darkness all around it, he notices for the first time how he was dressed: painted red all over, joints black and with white stripes connecting them. It is curious to note the connection between these three colors (black, white, and red) with the three essential qualities (called gunas) of matter in Hindu mythology: sattva, rajas, and tamas (essence, energy, and mass; white, red, and black) (Mookerjee, *Tantric* 17). Like the cosmic man, called the Anthropos, Black Elk is now clothed with the essential elements of the entire creation. He is also a kind of Messiah, or redeemer, for when he strides back "through the rainbow door" into the teepee where the six Grandfathers sit, he is greeted by voices "cheering from all over the universe," and the Grandfathers cry out in unison, "He has triumphed!" in voices "making thunder" (45), rather like the voice of the Word in John's Apocalypse. As he passes before each of the elders, each gives again the gift each had given before -- cup and bow, white wing and healing herb, sacred pipe, and flowering stick (45). The hero journey then comes full circle, as Black Elk looks down below to the earth, and sees himself "lying like the dead" in his teepee (45). As the "flaming rainbow door" of the celestial teepee begins to grow dim, Black Elk steps through it, and descends to the next doorway: the entrance to the earthly teepee, where he is reunited with his father and mother, who don't seem to know how "far away" he has been (47).

Eudora Welty

I would like to finish this book with one of the most "transcendently beautiful" of all hero journeys, both for its simplicity and for the human profundity of its wisdom. Various critics have argued that Eudora Welty should be regarded as a contemporary American master of the mythical method, and have used this approach to account for the subtle richness of her surface realism, which consistently points beyond itself to deeper realms of archetypal symbolism.[48] "A Worn Path" indeed provides an excellent example of a short story which enriches the ordinary details of daily life with a mythological background that confers shape and significance upon the work.

This is a realistic portrayal of one old woman's heroic devotion to her Grandchild, a profoundly human story about love, faith, and hope in the face of discouraging odds. Its plot is simple: Phoenix Jackson departs from her woodland shack one winter morning to walk into the city to get medicine for the boy, who has swallowed lye some years earlier. Her walk through the woods is vividly evoked through precisely observed realistic details with mythological overtones: this is a Modernist nekyia, but one in which the old heroine conquers death through the power of love (for a day at least). The name Phoenix immediately triggers these allusions, referring as it does to the mythical bird that is periodically reborn from its own ashes, an ancient symbol of resurrection and rebirth. The time of year -- midwinter season, Christmas time -- reinforces the allusion of the name, since the time of the solstice also revolves around the yearly cycles of death and rebirth in the natural world, and since the birth of Jesus is an expression of God's love for humanity, which redeems us from death.

Many of the details noted by the narrator during the forest journey into town follow naturally from the theme of death and rebirth established by the name and temporal setting. First, Phoenix gets entangled in a thorn bush and then must crawl through some barbed wire fencing, both of which ordinary details of rural life in Mississippi are common enough. But the age of the old woman greatly adds to the heroic nature of these trials, and the Christian setting suggests they may allude to the crown of thorns and humiliations of the Passion. Rather more pagan allusions enrich the imagery of the stream crossing and vision of the mistletoe boughs hanging in the oak trees which follow immediately thereafter (326-27). In the context of the winter season and dead landscape, the stream crossing marks the threshold into the underworld, as it does in the Classical symbol of the river Styx. So also the mistletoe hanging in the oak trees, a common enough sight in the woods, evokes the Virgilian golden bough which Aeneas needed as a source of light during his passage into Hades. The fact that oak trees were sacred to the Celtic Druids, in as much as their branches reached into the heavens while their roots wriggle down into the underworld, may also be significant in the overall context of the story's concern with death and rebirth. Pliny mentions a "festival on the sixth day of the moon, when the druids climbed a sacred oak, cut down a branch of mistletoe and sacrificed two white bulls, in a fertility rite" (Green 164), and it was of course in an oak grove on Lake Nemi that Frazer's famous ritual of the golden bough was enacted.

By crossing the stream and passing by the oaks, Phoenix has entered the underworld. She immediately notices "Big dead trees, like blackmen with one arm" (327). The "field of dead corn" which she then passes through is a "maze" with "no path" but with a kind of Minotaur: a "tall, black and skinny" scarecrow that Phoenix thinks is a ghost (327). The word "maze" of course puns on "maize," the Mayan word for corn, the seasonal cultivation of which is one our oldest symbols for the cycles of death and rebirth, and for the resurrection (as we know from the Gospel of John). Corn maiden rituals associated with the harvest in the old Celtic world of rural England are also among the most intriguing festivals discussed by Frazer. Eudora Welty's woodland Mississippi therefore is a labyrinth haunted by the Minotaur of the Cretan past, here a symbol of death which Phoenix will overcome by virtue of her heroine's journey. In order to do so, she herself must die, a sacrificial victim.

She does so shortly after traversing the maze of the cornfield to pass on into a dark road so heavily overhung by oak trees that it looks like a "cave" (328). A black dog appears out of nowhere and scares Phoenix so badly that she falls over into a little ditch on the side of the road. Lying in the ditch, looking upward, she has a dream vision of a man reaching down to help her up, a hunter who is passing through the woods with his dog. The blackness of the animal corresponds to the blackness of the scarecrow in the field of dead corn, and its kind suggests Cerberus, the dog who guards the entrance to Hades in Classical myth. After Phoenix lives up to her name by climbing out of the grave in which she lies, she snatches a shiny nickel lying on the ground before the hunter can realize he has dropped it by leaning over the ditch to help the old woman out. Roman corpses were buried with coins for Charon under their tongues, payment for the crossing to the yonder shore of the river Styx, but Phoenix cheats the infernal ferryman in this scene, just as she will cheat death with the medicine she eventually retrieves from the clinic in the city.

It is characteristic for the heroine of the journey to procure an elixir or some other symbol of immortality, which is sometimes lost on the return journey (as Gilgamesh loses his flower and Eldest Lady her husband). This is the ultimate feat Phoenix performs by getting medicine for her little boy at the clinic. Her journey has taken her from the woods into town, and will end when she completes the cycle by returning home to her shack in the woods. As nurse to a dying boy, Phoenix is a kind of Pièta, but as mother child whose very life is a marvel, she is a Madonna. She buys a little toy with the nickel stolen from the hunter to take with the medicine, and we gather from the nurses at the clinic that the boy's survival is something of a miracle. But with grandmothers like Phoenix, miracles are possible.

Notes

[1] See Gregory Lucente's *The Narrative of Realism and Myth* for one of many fine studies of the method.

[2] See my article "The Descent to the Underworld in Borges and Cortázar" for a discussion of this terminology.

[3] I quote the original because of the intense controversy surrounding translations of Mann's work:

> er die Brunnentiefe nicht denken konnte, ohne daß die Idee der Unterwelt und des Totenreiches sich in den Gedanken, ihn vertiefend und heligend, einmengte, -- diese Idee, die zwar nichte in seinen religiösen Meinungen, wohl aber in den Tiefen seiner Seele und Einbildungskraft, uralt mythisches Erbgut der Völker, das sie war, eine wichtige Rolle spielte: die Vorstellung der unteren Landes, in dem Usiri, der Zerstückelte, herrschte, des Ortes Namtars, des Pestgottes, des Königsreichs der Schrecken, woher alle üblen Geister und Seuchen stammten. Es war die Welt, wohin die Gestirne hinabtauchten bei ihrem Untergange, um zur geregelten Stunde wieder daraus emporzusteigen, währen kein Sterblicher, der zu diesem Hause den Pfad gewandelt, ihn wieder zurückfand. Es war der Ort des Kotes under Exkremente, aber auch des Goldes un Reichtums; der Schoß, in dem man das Samenkorn bettete und aus dem es also nährendes Getreide emporsproßte, das Land des Schwarzmondes, des Winters und verkohlten Sommers, wohin Tammuz, der lenzliche Schäfer, gesunken war und alljährlich wieder sank, wenn ihn der Eber geschlagen, so daß alle Zeugung versiegte und die beweinte Welt dürre lag, bis Ischtar, di Gattin und Mutter, Höllenfahrt hielt, ihn zu suchen, die staubbedeckten Riegel des Gefängnisses brach und den geliebten Schönen unter großen Lachen aus Höhle und Grube hervorführte, als Herrn der neuen Zeit und der frisch beblümten Flur. (68).

[4] This was apparent right from the first translations of the Gilgamesh tablets in 1872, but has become increasingly evident in our century, in which the biblical debt to both Egyptian and Mesopotamian mythologies

has been delineated by such scholars as Frazer, Gaster, Pritchard, and many others. Mann, no doubt, drew upon this scholarship extensively in his creation of a somewhat optimisitically tolerant and syncretic Joseph, for whom it all seems prety much the same whether it is Adonis, Osiris, or Abraham who makes the descent.

5 For a terrific article on the Jungian aspects of the Dionysus archetype in the story, see Gary Astrachan.

6 See Penelope Doob for a discussion of "the labyrinth of sin" in Dante's *Inferno* (Chapter 10).

7 See Anthony Roche on the Celtic callings during this scene.

8 The quotation is from Penelope Reed Doob's fine book, *The Idea of the Labyrinth: From Classical Antiquity Through the Middle Ages*, (12).

9 For a discussion of the way Frost uses sonnet form and sentence sounds in his linkage of Eve and poetry, see my article in *The Explicator*.

10 See M. H. Abrams, *Natural Supernaturalism*, on the apocalyptic symbolism of weddings and homecomings in the literature of Romanticism.

11 See the "Introduction" to *Rape and Revelation* on the four chambers of the underworld (temenos, crypt, granay, and inferno). The phrase "patchwork of quotations" comes from Aizenberg's paraphrase of Kristeva (73), but long before Kristeva's "mosaic of citations," intertextuality, or Bloom's precursor and ephebe, we had Eliot's "Tradition and the Individual Talent," Joyce's *Ulysses*, and Pound's *Cantos*.

12 On the Kabbalah in Borges, see Edna Aizenberg and the sources she compiles in her notes.

13 The Sumerian word for underworld, *kur*, also means mountain (see Wolkstein and Kramer). Gilgamesh reaches the Land of the Living, where the immortal Utnapishtim lives, via a journey through the twelve leagues of darkness beneath the mountains. In Egyptian myth, the sun god Ra begins his journey with a descent into the mountains of the west (the tombs of the Pharaohs are on the west side of the Nile, in the Valley of the Kings, up in the mountains) (see Budge).

14 See Gregory Lucente's *The Narrative of Realism and Myth* for one of many fine studies of the method. My publications discuss in detail the descent to the underworld in many of the works of Modernism, while a work in progress has chapters on the maze, the underworld, the great goddess, alchemical imagery, and the apocalypse.

15 For an image of the Medieval inferno, see, among many others, *The Hours of Catherine of Cleves* (Plate 99). See also Arnold van Gennep's discussion of the Egyptian rites of Osiris as developed in *The Book of the Doors*, in which the underworld was imagined as an immense temple divided into rooms separated by doors, each door guarded by a baboon, spirit, mummy, or uraeus serpent spitting fire (157 f.). (Note the heads puffing smoke on the capitals of the fireplace in Beast's chateau in Cocteau's film, which I discuss in my article "Framing the Underworld").

16 All translations from the Eranos Yearbook are my own. I include the original citation for those readers who wish to verify them.

17 For the "Liebestod" as the mystical reconciliation of opposites, see of course Wagner's libretto for *Tristan und Isolde,* in which "Love's Goddess" weaves together joy and grief, love and hate, death and love (66). In Wagner's source, Gottfried von Strassburg, the notion of opposites occurs in the thematic figure of the oxymoron, so popular in Medieval poetry: Tristan muses on the multiple implications of Isolde's pronunciation of "lameir," which could mean bitter, love, and the sea (199). Joseph Campbell discusses the implied meanings uniting love ("l'amour") and death (la morte") as a basic theme in Arthurian mythology (*Creative Myth* 175-257).

18 On the triple powers of the Goddess to bestow, sustain, and destroy life see Robert Graves in *The White Goddess* and "Joseph Campbell on the Great Goddess" in *Parabola.*

19 On the "conjointure" of "armes" (honor) and "amours" (love) in Chretien, see William Kibler (xiii-xvii).

20 On the linkage between the Boddhisattva and Christ, see Joseph Campbell (*Mythic Image* 415-419; *Oriental Myth* 304-310).

21 See Valerie Lagorio, who suggests that "one critical approach to the Vulgate cycle of Arthurian romances should consider the apocalyptic outlook which prevailed in the era of its composition" (1).

22 See my other books for a thorough discussion of a large range of Modernist and Postmodernist works in which the myth of Hades occurs. T. S. Eliot's phrase is from his 1922 review of James Joyce's *Ulysses,* reprinted in *The Modern Tradition,* edited by Ellmann and Feidelson.

23 For images of the Egyptian underworld see Wallis Budge (170f.), for the Sumerian gateways see Wolkstein and Kramer's *Inanna: Queen of Heaven and Earth,* and for an image of the Medieval inferno, see, among many others, *The Hours of Catherine of Cleves.*

24 In this context it is interesting to find James Hillman note that "One epithet of Hades was 'he who closes the door'" (180).

25 Robert Hammond's edition of the shooting script of *Beauty and the Beast* reproduces many shots that illustrate the importance of arches and doorways in the film, though he does not reproduce entire sequences.

26 See shot 142 in Hammond's edition of the shooting script.

27 Shot 144 in Hammond.

28 Hillman notes that "The double Janus nature of the gate was also expressed as a door, neither open nor closed, ajar, waiting, always an open possibility; c.f. B. Haarlov, *The Half-open Door. A common symbolic motiv within Roman sepulchral sculpture* (Odense, Denmark: Odense University Classical Studies 10, 1977). As Beauty walks into her chamber (Shot 144 in Hammond) the door is halfway open.

[29] See Murray Stein's *In MidLife* for a discussion of the descent to Hades as a period of liminality during the midlife crisis. His use of the term "floating" to describe the movements of the psyche during this phase is literally visualized by Cocteau both in *Orpheus* and in the sequence where Beauty goes to her room in the Beast's chateaux for the first time. See also Livingston Paisley's discussion of liminality and the ritual scapegoat who threatens both violence and redemption in Bergman's films (92-100).

[30] See for example the spiral labyrinths carved on the entrance stones of the tumulus of Newgrange outside of Dublin, dating back to approximately 3,000 B.C.E. For a quick overview of images of the labyrinth see Janet Bord.

[31] Louis Carroll's *Through the Looking Glass* also conflates the journey to the otherworld with the labyrinth.

[32] Jean Decock also suggests a multilevel and psychological approach to the use of myth anf folktale in Cocteau's films: "the fairy tale genre expresses myths; that is crystallizations of psychological virtualities. Thus, every fairy tale can be interpreted on three levels: anecdotal, the miraculous adventure with an historical or profane moral; sacred, with a lesson attributable to psychology, be it conscious or unconscious; and finally initiatory, with a meaning acceding to metaphysics" (vii.).

[33] See Jung's discussion of the number eight in *Mysterium Coniunctionis* and *Psychology and Alchemy.*. The octagon is also important in Freemasonry and architectural forms of sacred space, such as in the Baptistery in Florence

[34] See *The Psychology of the Transference* throughout, and especially the diagram on page 59 which outlines the complex dynamics of the relations between the conscious and unconscious contents of the personality during marriage.

[35] See my *Rape and Revelation* for an analysis of the descent to the underworld in Modernist literature as a metaphor for the creative process.

[36] Note the echo of Theseus in Shakespeare's *A Midsummer Night's Dream*: "Lovers and madmen have such seething brains, / Such shaping fantasies, that apprehend / More than cool reason ever comprehends" (5.1.4-6)

[37] On the Orphic poet in the European tradition see Walter Strauss, *Descent and Return*, in which he argues that the journey downward is into nothingness.

[38] With respect to mirrors and reflection, Hillman notes "entering the underworld is like entering the mode of reflection, mirroring, which suggests that we may enter the underworld by means of reflection, by reflective means" (52).

[39] Ingmar Bergman acknowledged that Cocteau's work, while technically unsophisticated, remained "perfectly astounding" (*Bergman on Bergman 45*).

[40] For still shots of most of the images in this sequence see *Bergman on Bergman* (142-145).

[41] The mysterious stranger is one of the many archetypal images of death in dreams and folklore discussed in *Psyche and Death* by Edgar Herzog. M.L von-Franz also writes that "the other who comes to take away the living" most often appears in its "terror-filled, uncanny aspect ... when the dreamer has as yet *no relation to death or does not expect it*" (72; italics hers).

[42] In the *Tibetan Book of the Dead*, the mirror of karma reflects all of the deeds and events to the dead soul on its journey towards enlightenment or rebirth: "Then the Lord of Death will say, 'I will look in the mirror of karma,' and when he looks in the mirror all your sins and virtues will suddenly appear in it clearly and distinctly, so although you have lied it is no use" (77).

[43] Edgar Herzog discusses the strangeness of the speech of the dead in *Psyche and Death* (143, 191): "'speaking with tongues' suggests ... wisdom which can only be understood by those already in the beyond" (191). The idea that the dead speak a special indecipherable language is a common one in literature: think of the whispering voices in Ambrose Bierce's "Occurrence at Owl Creek Bridge," of Eliot's *Four Quartets*, or of the knowledge of the mysterious language of the dead given the young D.H. Lawrence in his poem on his mother's death.

[44] Birdsong is of course another archetypal image of the afterlife, from the birdsouls of Egyptian papyri, to the golden bird on the golden bough" and crowing cocks of the underworld in Yeats's Byzantium poems, and the woodthrushes singing on the yonder shore in Eliot's "Marina."

[45] In her book, *Shamanic Voices*, Joan Halifax calls these initiatory symptoms the "Underworld of Disease" (10-13), and Mircea Eliade devotes an entire chapter of his great study, *Shamanism*, to "Initiatory Sicknesses and Dreams" (33-67). See also Stephen Larsen, *The Shaman's Doorway* (59-82).

[46] See Robert Graves *The White Goddess* on the relation between the alphabet and tree lore in Celtic poetry.

[47] See R.S. Loomis for the classic study of the diffusion of Celtic myths via the minstrel traditions of the Middle Ages into the great literary legacy of the Arthurian stories.

[48] See for example Guy Davenport.

Conclusion:
Into the Labyrinth

The hero journey cycle (separation-initiation-return) has been discussed from a variety of perspectives, and its diverse ramifications from
the fields of religion, comparative mythology, anthropology, psychology, thanatology, and comparative literature have attracted much attention since the publication of *The Hero With a Thousand Faces*.

The anthropological study of the shamans of the Siberian, Ural-
Altaic, and Native American traditions have uncovered initiatory ordeals which follow the hero journey cycle of separation from home or
village, ritual annihilation and rebirth, with visions of the otherworld
that give the shaman the power of healing and make them guides of the
living to the land of the dead. Arnold van Gennep's rites of passage,
enacted at time of biological transitions in life, such as birth, puberty,
marriage, death, also follow the pattern of the monomyth: separation
(removal from social matrix), transition (sleep deprivation, fasting,
physical and psychological stress, drugs used to induce altered states
often involving death and rebirth), incorporation (reintegration of the
transformed individual into the community with a new role). The end
result is the death of an old social self and the birth of a new. Variations
on the initiation rites include the Classical Mysteries of the Ancient
World: in the rituals associated with Tammuz and Ishtar, Isis and
Osiris, Demeter and Persephone, Dionysos, Orpheus, and others, the
neophytes experienced ritual death and rebirth which often employs fertility images as metaphors of spiritual transformation.

Comparative religion and mythology have added a great deal to
our understanding of the hero journey. Our knowledge of the eschato-
logical systems of Egypt, Tibet, Greece, and the Ars Moriendi of the
Middle Ages has given us a new understanding of the iconography of
the hero journey. The archetypal patterns of the Egyptian Book of the
Dead, which is about the posthumous journey of the soul, and of the
Sun God Ra, on a barge through the twelve regions of underworld; and
the symbolism of the Tibetan Book of the Dead, with the Chikai Bardo
(Primary Clear Light of Reality), the Chonyid Bardo (Peaceful and

Wrathful Deities and realms of rebirth), and the Sidpa Bardo (King and Judge of Dead's mirror of karma, reflecting all deeds as manifestations of the mind) both establish a narrative sequence and cluster of images frequently encountered in literary versions of the journey. Greek Myth and the Mystery rites of Eleusis have both laid the foundations for the literary itinerary of the soul's journey in works from Homer, to Virgil, to Apuleius, to Dante. to the Ars Moriendi, (The Art of Dying) of the Middle Ages, books written for as guides through stages of dying. These enriched the cluster of motifs with practical experience of the emotional, physical, and spiritual stages of the dying process, often depicted in symbolic versions of the hero journey.

Psychological approaches to the journey have flourished, for the basic diurnal rhythms of sleep-dream-waking follow the stages of the monomyth. Death and rebirth have become Jungian archetypes of transformation at midlife. In humanistic and transpersonal psychology, the hero journey is an image of intense growth and powerful change. Stanislav Grof's birth trauma theory of psychosis, psychedelic experience, and the near death narratives as being residues of actual experience of biological birth is one of the most profound additions to our concept of the journey: The perinatal stages of engulfment, no exit, struggle, and death and rebirth typically follow the patterns and evoke the symbolism of the monomyth.

The new study of thanatology has also enriched our understanding of the psychology of the monomyth, and opened up new vistas of discussion. The work of Raymond Moody, Kenneth Ring and Stanislav Grof on the Near Death Experience (NDE) -- clinical death followed by revival -- suggests a pattern much like the heroic cycle, with the stages of separation (clinical death, out of the body sensation), threshold crossings (vortex or dark tunnel), guides or helpers (being of light or ancestral spirit at the end of the tunnel), initiatory revelations (life review, emanation of ineffable love, paradisal landscapes or cityscapes, revelation of ultimate knowledge), and finally the return to life following resuscitation. Carol Zaleski prefers to call these experiences near death narratives, a designation which brings the connection between the hero journey and poesis into the foreground: whatever else may be said about the near death experiences, or about the visionary literature typical of the monomyth, it is clear that both involve great stories, with powerful images, language, characters and themes.

All of these approaches are important, and work together to shape our total response to the hero journey narratives. But for me, the most significant aspects of the archetypal cycle are personal and poetic: the stories provide us with myths to live by, giving shape and significance to our lives; and they serve as parables of poesis, providing a mythical reflection of the mysteries of the creative process. I would therefore like to conclude with some personal reflections on the hero journey, which tsummarize its key themes. One of the ways we experience the individuation process is as a hero journey: we have to go down into the Inferno before even thinking about the ascent up the Purgatorial mountain towards Paradise; or we have to tread the steps and stops of the labyrinth, winding our way towards maturity. Being held captive in the grips of archetypal complexes beyond our conscious control is like being sucked down by a maelstrom into the labyrinth of the unconscious, where we wander through a hall of mirrors which reflect grotesque images of our true selves at every painful turning of the way. When these archetypal levels of the psyche are activated (and when, it seems, are they not?), curious and not always joyful synchronicities pop up like poltergeists to keep our feet to the fire -- and to drag us down into the depths or through the tortuous turnings of the maze.

I recently read, for the first time, Poe's story "Descent into the Maelstrom," which describes in vivid detail a shipwreck which the narrator escapes by throwing himself with a barrel into a tremendous vortex off the coast of Norway. The story evokes the steep swirling journey down the walls of the whirlpool, and then the rapid ascent, as the barrel, but not the ship on which the narrator's brother goes down, is spit out into the frothy circles surrounding the center of the maelstrom. The next day I watched a Disney animated feature with my little daughter, in which a girl must descend through a narrow hole on a bucket to retrieve a large diamond called the Devil's Eye from the skull of a dead pirate. The skull is on the other side of a cavernous geyser which erupts periodically and then sucks everything in its path down into the depths of the maelstrom. The girl is compelled to make the journey by a wicked middle aged woman who greedily exploits and imprisons everyone around her out of her lust for power. The girl succeeds in retrieving the diamond from the skull guarded by the geyser and whirlpool with the help of two little mice on their honeymoon. By the end of the film the diamond is safely ensconced in the Smithsonian Museum, and the little girl has found the adoptive parents she has so longed for.

I recognized several of the motifs of this fine little film, called "The Rescuers," from my teaching in folklore, myth, and literature. First of all there is the light in the skull motif: the diamond as a symbol of the immortal soul which survives the rotting of the gray matter behind the eyes, whose vision it had animated in life. On a mystical level, the girl's journey is a Gnostic journey of deliverance (rescue) of the soul from the darkness of the underworld, comparable to the journey undertaken by the heroine of the Russian folktale "Vasilisa the Beautiful" to the witch Baba Yaga, who gives Vasilisa a skull on a stick with bright laser light shining through its eyes. In "The Second Voyage

of Sinbad" from the *Arabian Nights*, the diamonds stuck to the carcasses in the valley of serpents are similar symbols of the soul stitched
to the rotting corpse we carry around with us. On a psychological level,
however, the girl's search for the diamond in "The Rescuers" involves
an encounter with what Jung called the Terrible Mother in her Ogress
aspect, which is balanced by the Loving Mother the girl finds at the end
of the film. Retrieving the diamond from the underworld involves a
conquest of the Terrible Mother, and the release of the positive energies
of the Self which she has imprisoned: in the center of this maelstrom, at
least, lies the archetype of the Great Mother in her dual aspect.

A sequence of familial synchronicities underscored the archetypal
significance of my obsession with the maze: my son came home from
his Bible school at the Baptist Church this past Friday with a folder of
things he had done, including two mazes. One was a prayer maze,
traversing which reminded you of things to say prayers for, and the
other was a maze illustrating the Creation in Genesis, with the creation
of man in the center and the five other days surrounding arranged in the
corridors of the circumference. It reminded me of the famous Atrium
Mosaic on the ceiling of San Marco in Venice, which depicts the
Creation and the Fall in concentric bands radiating outwards from the
still point of the divine in the middle of the maze, and of the labyrinths
on the floor of the Cathedrals of Chartres and Ely which depict the life
of man as a spiritual pilgrimage. More secular associations were evoked
when my daughter Angela brought home a kid's meal from
"Whataburger" with a Map Maze on the bag (meat of the Minotaur inside!). Several days later I took my son Carly to lunch at the Italian
eatery in the mall. It is a restaurant with mirrors on both walls, so that
one witnesses the infinite repetition of one's own image (eating pizza)
reflected in the mirrors on both walls.

One more piece of the puzzle was inserted on the weekend after
these first two threads began to weave themselves together into an intricate knot (my dream-group partner had said that he felt all knotted up
inside). On Saturday there was a Native American gathering and dance
contest in the Coliseum at the University where I teach, to which I took
my children. While sitting in the amphitheater, I watched my children
run endless circles around the circumference in the upper tiers, and
running up and down and in and out of the many interlinked but confus-
ing hallways. After each circle they would come briefly back to me,
children going forth from, and eventually returning to, the father, I suddenly realized, as souls circle too, going forth eternally from, and returning eternally to, the Father. Then I noticed there were exactly eight
corridor stairs entering the coliseum, and the whole was much like
Leonardo's octagonal maze, only without the mirror chamber. Instead,
in the center of the building was the basketball circle with MSU written

in it as a signature (just as Leonardo's knot has his signature in the middle). The brilliantly colored Indians were dancing in an elaborate spiral around this central axis, to the pounding beat of the drums and high keening of the Chippewa singers. I thought of the axis mundi or world omphalos, the point at which the divine energy enters the world to be broken up into pairs of opposites, in this case two quaternities, which then revolve spiral or swaztika like around the *bindu* point. The dance also recalled the Crane Dance of Delos, in which "The dancers, having danced into the labyrinth from right to left, the direction of involution and death, turn round in the centre and, following their leader dance out again, now in the opposite direction, that of evolution and birth" (Wosien, qtd. in Bord 60).

It was therefore very interesting to find Coomaraswamy connect the spiral dance and the maze: "Compare the winding and unwinding of the ribbons by which the dancers are connected to the Maypole. The history of the labyrinth is intimately connected with that of dancing" (30). The winding and unwinding of the spiral dance here become images of incarnation (birth) and dis-incarnation (death), the opposing swirls of those "spiral forms to which labyrinths approximate" (29). One thinks also in this context of Yeats' great poem "Byzantium," in which the dance beneath the Emperor's dome becomes a means of liberation from "all complexities of mire or blood". Coomaraswamy calls these "complexities" the "'knots (granthi) of the heart' ... of which the ego complex ... is the tightest and the hardest to be undone" (28). The whole task of spiritual liberation and release (*moksha*) is then seen as an effort to untie the knots binding the soul to its endless cycles of incarnation (endless cycles of projection we might say, endless cycles of the repetition compulsion). Those who succeed are called "the Nirgrantha, 'whose knot is undone'" (28). For Yeats, it is the dance of departed souls in the holy city which serves to "unwind the winding path" (244). It is on the "Marbles of the dancing floor" that the "bitter furies of complexity" are broken, and the "blood-begotten spirits" liberated from the labyrinthine "complexities, / The fury and the mire of human veins"(244). Such also is the job of therapy -- to untie the knots of our complexes.

Such meditations on the spiral dance and the labyrinth as a metaphor for spiritual incarnation and release led me to think of the hoop dance of the native Americans, which I had seen in the Baltimore Museum of Art, and which I began to see as a performance version of the initiatory descent of the soul into the labyrinth of the world. In the hoop dance, a single dancer approaches a circle in which nine wooden hoops have been laid out. His task while dancing is to pick up each of the nine hoops, one by one, somehow stabilize them on his body by passing them over his head and around his arms, without ever touching one with his hands. This involves complex maneuvers and contortions of the body, until the dancer appears to be inextricably entangled by the maze of hoops. The beautiful trick is to gracefully situate the hoops around the body so as to suggest the various shapes and forms (referred to by Quispel as 'Schalengewalten,' shells (here hoops) which imprison the world soul) into which the soul of the dancer has figuratively descended. The high point for me was when, completely entangled in the hoops, the dancer so linked them together as to suggest the wings of a great eagle fully extended, while continuing the gyrations of the dance. From this point on he gradually shed the hoops, one by one, until he was once again totally unencumbered, and was able to step out of the other side of the circle. He had turned the torment of a soul completely entangled in the hoops of life into a celebratory gesture of escape on the wings of the eagle.

As I watched this dance and absorbed the vibrations of the drum, I experienced a gradually dawning epiphany regarding the meaning of the dance, an epiphany which I felt very personally before thinking more universally about its symbolism. Personally, the dance evoked my sense of being caught in life's various entanglements: like the dancer in the hoops, I had entered the circle naked and unencumbered, but now felt all tangled up in a kind of knot of fate. How was I to regain the freedom of my earlier days? The dancer seemed to show me the way both into and out of the maze of entanglements, as he joyfully wrapped himself up in one hoop after another, and, instead of enacting the rat caught in the maze, transformed the hoops into wings with which to escape the labyrinth. Like Daedalus after having reached the center of his own "genial construction," the dancer "turned his mind to unknown arts"[1], become an eagle and proceeded to fly out of the labyrinth by shedding the hoops one by one.

More universally, the hoop dance symbolized a complete cycle of incarnation and deliverance, as the naked soul makes its way into life at one end of the circle, assumes the various forms of earthly life or carries the burdens applied to it (represented by the hoops and the shapes the dancer made them take), until reaching a kind of turning point at the center, where an enantiodromia takes place: at the nadir of the soul's descent, when the dancer is most entangled in the hoops and the soul most painfully trapped in the complexes of life, the hoops turn to wings, the dancer remembers his celestial source, and begins to systematically shed each hoop before, at the end of the cycle, returning naked to his father by stepping out of the circle at death. Christianity celebrated such an escape of the soul from the tangled complexities of life in such rituals as the Easter dances performed by the dean and the canons on the pavement labyrinths of the Cathedrals of the Middle

Ages, dances which brought together the symbolism of the signs of the zodiac with the resurrection and the harrowing of hell (Doob 123-127).

As Coomaraswamy suggests, the clockwise and counterclockwise revolutions of the dance represent the "paired motions of evolution and involution, birth and death" (30). He comments also on the symbolism of the thread, which is related to the imagery of the dance -- in such rituals as "the winding and unwinding of the ribbons by which the dancers are connected to the Maypole" (30)[2] -- and to the maze -- Ariadne's thread leads Theseus into and out of the Cretan labyrinth. Maria-Gabriele Wosien illustrates this point with the Crane Dance of Delos, which Sir James G. Frazer relates to the Cretan maze and Ariadne's dance, which both Frazer and Graves interpret as a form of sun worship (qtd. Bord 60-61). Symbolism associating the solar journey and the escape from the maze persisted into the Middle Ages: Penelope Reed Doob has shown how the "Easter labyrinth dances during the latter Middle Ages" performed on the pavements of places like the Cathedral at Auxerre were symbolic representations of the cosmos and celebrations of "the harrowing of hell and the resurrection" (123; 125). Edgar Wind also notes a connection between mazes, knots, and dances during the Renaissance: "In Ben Jonson's *Pleasure Reconciled to Virtue*, a sequence of 'knots' is introduced by the dancing master Daedalus, who interweaves the two opposites in a perfect maze" (206). Hence it was greatly interesting to find that recent discoveries in the study of those mysterious patterns etched into the Nazca plains in South America have brought together the imagery of the spiral, the thread, the dance, and the journey of the sun through the signs of the zodiac. The spiral (and perhaps other forms like the spider) was probably created by a dancer wearing a piece of thread tied to stakes in the center which enabled, by the progressive shortening of the length of the thread with each turning of the circumference, the precise diminution of his or her path around the center necessary to the exact formulation of the spiral. Furthermore, an American astronomer has shown that the mysterious patterns and lines etched into the plains are lined up with the procession of the constellations of the night sky in such a way as to chart the solsticial journey of the sun through the labyrinth of the year and of the zodiac. The spider, for example, points to the position on the horizon of the rising Orion, the processional shifting of which has been adjusted by the sequence of straight lines added over the years to the original spider. Mythologically, we can guess that the spider weaving its web was seen to be analogous to the dancer who wove the spiral maze with the assistance of the thread, and that the entire ritual of the creation of the spiral on the plain through the dance and the thread gives us a clue to the meaning of other mazes around the world like Newgrange, outside Dublin, where the rising sun illuminates the inner corridor on the

Winter Solstice, or Silbury Hill near Avebury in England, in which
large quantities of thread were discovered.[3]
     These thoughts led to a kind of tentative conclusion for me. I
closed my discussion of synchronicity, serpents, dolphins, finches,
Ayatollahs, scarab beetles, wild rhododendrons, and the symbolism of
the moth in the essays by Annie Dillard and Virginia Woolf, with a
story about a funeral in Archer City, attended by a student named
Sonny. The funeral took place in the fall, the time when migrating
Monarch butterflies are to be found along the shores of the lakes and
dangling in the shadows of the Mesquite trees in the brush. I recalled
that the Greek word for butterfly is the same as the word for the soul
(Psyche), since the soul leaves the body at death like a butterfly molting
and shedding the gooey shroud of its chrysalis. In Crete, the spread
wings of the butterfly were associated with the sign of the labyrinth, a
double-bladed ax (Johnson 195), and impressions of butterflies are
common features of the beautiful golden seals, like the "Ring of
Nestor," unearthed by Sir Arthur Evans at Knossos, which depict
Elysian scenes of the "resurgence of the human spirit after death"
(Campbell, *Occidental* 51). To die, apparently, meant to escape from
the maze of life, to take flight from the cocoon of mortality. My friend
Sonny told me that after the funeral service in Archer city ended, when
the body had been lowered into the grave, on a bright, autumn afternoon, a migrating monarch butterfly settled briefly on one black corner
of the coffin. The silent mourners stared down from above in amazement as the butterfly rose gently from the grave and circled upwards in
spirals towards the sun, before a rising breeze carried it away south-
wards on its long journey to the hills of Cuernavaca.
     The symbolism of the hero journey is, in fact, frequently associ-
ated with death, with dreams, and with poesis. This is particularly clear
in the perfectly marvelous Hindu tale known as "The King and the
Corpse," with which I would like to conclude. Shortly after my grandfather died, I dreamt of taking trip by car to the edge of a lake or ocean,
where sat a little cabin in which my grandfather had taken residence.
After getting out of my car and beginning to prepare for the farther
journey across the lake, I suddenly found myself encumbered with the
gruesome corpse of my grandfather, who had shriveled up into a kind
of enlarged brown fetus, the arms of which clung irremovably around
my neck. Some years later I read the "The King and the Corpse,"
published in the posthumous collection, by Heinrich Zimmer, of the
same title. The story tells of a King who is tricked into going to a burial
ground by a wizard, who appears disguised as a beggar everyday for ten
years at the King's court, never failing to offer the King a piece of fruit.
The King throws the fruit into his storage chamber, until one day his
monkey snatches the beggar's offering out of the King's hand, and peels

the rind, revealing a magnificent gem inside. The King sends a servant to his storage room and finds a mass of gems piled up in the rotting heaps of fruit deposited over the ten year period. His interest in the beggar now aroused, the King talks to him the next day, and the beggar entices the King to the burial ground. Hence begins the King's hero journey, with the call to adventure taking some ten years of boring routine to penetrate the armor of the ego.

Once arrived at the burial ground, the wizard instructs the King to collect a corpse hanging from a tree on the far side of the cemetery, which is described in gruesome, ghoulish detail: there is a "tumult of the specters and demons hovering about the uncanny place, feasting upon the dead," and "the charred scattering of the blackened skeletons and skulls" among the "still smoldering funeral pyres" (203). He is clearly in the underworld, among corpses whose rotting flesh recalls the fruit decaying in his storage rooms: will the gemstones of the soul emerge from the rot?. He arrives at the tree and cuts the corpse down (the corpse hanging like fruit from the tree of death), taking it upon his back to traverse the ghoulish terrain. As he does so, the corpse begins to speak, telling a riddle in the form of a complex story. After the King solves the riddle, the corpse flies back to its perch on the tree, and the King must proceed once again, and again listen to "the unrelenting specter in the corpse spinning tale upon tale of twisted destinies and tangled lives" (208). This continues until twenty four stories are told, ending with riddles for which the King provides the answer to all but the last. Impressed by the King's determination and honesty, the specter offers the corpse to the King, who has admirably passed through the trials and ordeals of the monomyth, which have gradually, if imperceptibly, transformed his consciousness and prepared him for the great revelation of the initiation phase of the journey to come. The specter which had been an impediment on the journey now becomes a guide and helper, warning the King about the dangers to come.

For the beggar monk is a wizard in disguise, who plans to place the corpse in the center of a magic circle, and then to decapitate the King after ordering him to prostrate himself before the idol. The King then follows the specter's instructions. The wizard uses a "kind of paste composed of the whitish meal of ground bones mixed with the blood of dead bodies" to inscribe the magic circle with the corpse inside (214). As instructed, the King then asks the wizard to demonstrate the proper posture of worship. When he does so, the King swiftly decapitates the sorcerer, splits the chest, and rips the heart out to offer up, "together with the head, as an oblation to the specter in the corpse" (215). The specter in the corpse then adds its voice to the "mighty sound of jubilation" lifted by innumerable invisible spirits in celebration of their liberation from the necromancer, who sought to gain power over all souls, ghouls, and "spiritual presences of the supernatural domain" (215). When asked what reward the King would like to have for performing his feat, the King answers simply that he would like the twenty five tales told during the course of his infernal peregrinations to become eternally famous. This answer precipitates the climactic revelation of the initiation phase of the journey, as Shiva appears in all of his glory, "attended by a multitude of gods" (216). Shiva declares that whosoever recites a single one of the twenty five tales will be "free from sin," and he then lifts "the veil of ignorance" that had been concealing the King's consciousness from the "immortal essence of his human life" (216): the soul, like the gemstones in the fruit, survives the rotting of the rind, as the specter does the degradation of the corpse. The King's hero journey ends full circle, as he returns to his throne "full of knowledge and transformed" by his ordeal (216).

This precious version of the hero journey situates the activities of storytelling (poesis) and interpretation (hermeneusis) in the underworld of the burning ground. The corpse constructs a labyrinthine network of riddles which the King must 'read' in order to solve. His salvation, in fact, depends upon the quality of his 'reading': For, in the midst of the maze (as in the midst of all good stories), he finds himself, and he finds Shiva, lord of the beginning, and of the end.

Notes

[1] The words of Ovid which serve as the epigraph to James Joyce's *A Portrait of the Artist as a Young Man.*

[2] Maria-Gabriele Wosien connects the imagery of the bird and the opposing directions of the of the Crane Dance of Delos in her book *Sacred Dance.*

[3] The information about the discoveries on the Nazca plains comes from the PBS series called "The New Explorers," the broadcast on Saturday evening 1/30/93 I saw after delivering a lecture on the maze that afternoon. Penelope Reed Doob has shown how, in the mazes of the Middle Ages, "the labyrinth imitates the concentric circles of the cosmos," and suggested that the "twelve concentric circles of "virtually all French labyrinths" may possibly allude "to the zodiac" (130).

Works Cited

Anderson, William. *Green Man: The Archetype of our Oneness with the Earth.* Photographs by Clive Hicks. London and San Francisco: HarperCollins, 1990.

Anderson, William S. "Calypso and Elysium." *Essays on the Odyssey: Selected Modern Criticism.* Ed. Charles H. Taylor Jr. Bloomington and London: Indiana University Press. 1963.

Apollonius of Rhodes. *The Voyage of the Argo.* Trans. E.V. Rieu. Penguin Books. 1971.

Apuleius. *The Golden Ass.* Trans. Jack Lindsay. Bloomington: Indiana UP, 1962.

Astrachan, Gary. "Dionysos in Thomas Mann's Novella, *Death in Venice.*" *Journal of Analytical Psychology.* 35 (1990): 59-78.

---, "Hermes der Argustöter." *Gorgo: Zeitschrift für archetypische und bildhaftes Denken.* 20 (1991): 29-46.

Athanassakis, Apostolos. N., Trans. *The Homeric Hymns.* Baltimore: The Johns Hopkins UP, 1976.

Aziz, Robert. *C.G. Jung's Psychology of Religion and Synchronicity.* Albany: State University of New York Press, 1990.

Bachofen, J.J. *Myth, Religion, and Mother Right: Selected Writings of J.J. Bachofen.* Trans. Ralph Mannheim. Preface by George Boas and Introduction by Joseph Campbell. Bollingen Series LXXXIV. Princeton: Princeton UP. 1967.

Baigent, Michael, et. al. *Holy Blood, Holy Grail.* New York: Dell, 1982.

Barber, Richard. *The Arthurian Legends: An Illustrated Anthology.* Totowa, NJ: Littlefield, Adams, and Company 1979.

Baym, Nina. Introduction. *The Scarlet Letter.* Nathaniel Hawthorne. New York: Viking Penguin Books, 1983.

Bergman on Bergman: Interviews with Ingmar Bergman. by Stig Bjorkman, Torsten Manns, Jonas Sima. Trans. Paul Britten Austin. New York: Simon and Schuster, 1973.

Bettelheim, Bruno. *The Uses of Enchantment: The Meaning and Importance of Fairy Tales.* New York: Alfred A. Knopf, 1976.

Biedermann, Hans. *Dictionary of Symbolism*. Trans. James Hulbert. New York and Oxford: Facts on File, 1992.

Bilibin, Ivan, illustrator. *Four Russian Folktales*. Trans. Robert Chandler. Boulder: Shambhala, 1980.

Bjelajac, David. *Millennial Desire and the Apocalyptic Vision of Washington Allston*☐ Washington: Smithsonian Institution Press, 1988.

Black Elk Speaks: Being the Life Story of a Holy Man of the Oglala Sioux. With John G. Neihardt. Lincoln: University of Nebraska Press, 1961.

Bonnefoy, Yves. *Roman and European Mythologies*. Translated Under the Direction of Wendy Doniger. Chicago and London: The University of Chicago Press, 1992,

Bord, Janet. *Mazes and Labyrinths of the World*. New York: E.P. Dutton, 1975.

Borges, Jorge Luis. "Death and the Compass." *Ficciones*. Ed. Anthony Kerrigan. New York: Grove Press, 1962.

---, "The Garden of Forking Paths." *Ficciones*. Ed. Anthony Kerrigan. New York: Grove Press, 1962.

---, *Labyrinths: Selected Stories and Other Writings*. Ed. Donald A. Yates and James E. Irby. New York: New Directions, 1964.

---, *Obras Completas*. Vol. 2. Buenos Aires: Emecé Editores, 1954.

---, *Selected Poems: 1923-1967*. Ed. Norman Thomas Di Giovanni. New York: Delta, 1972.

Branston, Brian. *The Lost Gods of England*. New York: Oxford UP, 1974.

Briggs, Katherine. *An Encyclopedia of Fairies: Hobgoblins, Brownies, Bogies, and Other Supernatural Creatures*. New York: Pantheon Books, 1976.

Broch, Hermann. *Der Tod des Vergil*. Ed. Paul Michael Lützeler. Frankfort am Main: Suhrkamp Verlag, 1976.

---, *The Death of Virgil*. Trans. Jean Starr Untermeyer (1945). San Francisco: North Point Press, 1983.

Bromiley, Geoffrey W. *Theological Dictionary of the New Testament*. Grand Rapids: William B. Eerdmans Publishing Company, 1985.

Brontë, Charlotte. *Villette*. Ed. Mark Lilly. New York: Penguin Books, 1983.

Brown, Norman. O. *Hermes the Thief*. Madison: The University of Wisconsin Press, 1947.

Budge, E.A. Wallis. *Amulets and Talismans*. New York: University Books, 1968.

---, *The Gods of the Egyptians*. Vol.1. New York: Dover, 1969.

Burkert, Walter. *Ancient Mystery Cults*. Boston: Harvard UP, 1987.

---, *Structure and History in Greek Mythology and Ritual*. Berkeley: The University of California Press, 1979.

Byatt, A.S. *Possession: A Romance*. New York: Vintage International, 1990.

Cacciari, Massimo. *The Necessary Angel*. Trans. Miguel E. Vatter. Albany: State University of New York Press, 1994.

Campbell, Joseph. *The Flight of the Wild Gander. Explorations in the Mythological Dimension*. New York: The Viking Press, 1969.

---, "Folkloristic Commentary." *Grimm's Fairy Tales*. New York: Pantheon Books, 1944.

---, *The Hero With a Thousand Faces*. Princeton: Princeton UP, 1949.

---, *Historical Atlas of World Mythology*. 2 Volumes, 5 Parts. New York: Harper and Row, 1988.

---, Introduction. *Bullfinch's Mythology*. Compiled by Bryan Holme. New York: The Viking Press, 1979.

---, *The Hero With a Thousand Faces*. Bollingen Series XVII.. Princeton: Princeton UP, 1968.

---, *The Inner Reaches of Outer Spaces: Metaphor as Myth and as Religion*. New York: Alfred van der Marck Editions, 1985.

---, *Joseph Campbell and The Power of Myth with Bill Moyers*. Ed. Sue Flowers. New York: Doubleday, 1988.

---, "Joseph Campbell on the Great Goddess." *Parabola: Myth and the Quest for Meaning*. 5.4 (1980): 74-85.

---, *The Masks of God: Occidental Mythology*. New York: The Viking Press., 1964.

---, *The Mysteries: Papers From the Eranos Yearbooks*. Bollingen Series XXX. Ed. Joseph Campbell. Princeton: Princeton UP, 1955.

---, *The Mythic Image*. Princeton: Princeton UP, 1974.

---, *Occidental Mythology*. New York: Penguin Books, 1964.

Caracciolo, Peter L. "Introduction." *The Arabian Nights in English Literature*. Ed. Peter L. Caracciolo. New York: St. Martin's Press, 1988.

Carrington, Leonora. *Down Below*. (1944). Chicago: Black Swan Press, 1983.

Chailley, Jacques. *The Magic Flute, Masonic Opera*. Trans. Herbert Weinstock. New York: Alfred A. Knopf, 1971.

Clark, R.T. Rundle. *Myth and Symbol in Ancient Egypt*. London: Thames and Hudson, 1959.

Clayton, Peter. *Great Figures of Mythology*. Introduction by Joseph Campbell. Greenwich: Crescent, 1990.

Cocteau, Jean. *Beauty and the Beast: Scenario and Dialogs by Jean Cocteau*. Ed. Robert M. Hammond. New York: New York UP, 1970.

---, *Beauty and the Beast.* Lopert Films 1946. Embassy Home Entertainment.

---, *Orpheus.* (1950). Video Images.

Coleridge, S. T. C. *The Rime of the Ancient Mariner.* Introduction by Millicent Rose. New York: Dover Publications, 1970.

Coomaraswamy, Ananda K. *Coomaraswamy: Selected Papers 1: Traditional Art and Symbolism.* Ed. Roger Lipsey. Bollingen Series LXXXIX. Princeton: Princeton UP, 1977.

---, *Coomaraswamy: Selected Papers 2: Metaphysics.* Ed. Roger Lipsey. Bollingen Series LXXXIX. Princeton: Princeton UP, 1977.

---, *The Dance of Shiva: Fourteen Indian Essays.* Revised Edition. New York: The Noonday Press, 1957.

---, "The One Thread." *Parabola: Thge Magazine of Myth and Tradition: Labyrinth.* Summer 1992. 17 (2): 26-34.

Corbin, Henry. *Avicenna and the Visionary Recital.* Trans. Williard R. Trask. Princeton: Princeton UP, 1960.

---, "Pour une Morphologie de la Spiritualité Shîite." *Eranos-Jahrbuch 1960: Mensch und Gestaltung.* Vol. 29. Ed. Olga Fröbe-Kapteyn. Zürich: Rhein Verlag, 1961.

---, "Terre Céleste et Corps de Résurrection d'après quelques Traditions Iraniennes." *Eranos-Jahrbuch 1953: Mensch und Erde.* Vol. 22. Ed. Olga Fröbe-Kapteyn. Zürich: Rhein-Verlag, 1954.

Crane, John. K. *T.H. White.* Boston: Twayne Publishers, 1974.

Cortázar, Julio. *Hopscotch.* Trans. Gregory Rabassa. New York: Pantheon Books, 1966.

Crossley-Holland, Kevin. *The Norse Myths.* New York: Pantheon Books, 1980.

Cunliffe, Barry. *The Celtic World.* New York: McGraw Hill, 1979.

Curtis, J.E. and J.E. Reade, eds. *Art and Empire: Treasures From Assyria in the British Museum.* The Metropolitan Museum of Art. New York: Harry N. Abrams, 1995.

Davidson, H.R. Ellis. *Scandinavian Mythology.* London: Paul Hamlyn, 1975.

Decock, Jean. "Preface." *Beauty and the Beast: Scenario and Dialogs by Jean Cocteau.* Ed. Robert M. Hammond. New York: New York UP, 1970.

De Rola, Stanislas Klossowski. *Alchemy: The Secret Art.* New York: Avon Books, 1973.

Dimmit, Cornelia and J.A.B. van Buitenen. *Classical Hindu Mythology: A Reader in the Sanskrit Puranas.* Philadelphia: Temple UP, 1978.

Di Stasi, Lawrence. *Mal Occhio (Evil Eye): The Underside of Vision.* San Francisco: North Point Press, 1981.

Doob, Penelope Reed. *The Idea of the Labyrinth: From Classical Antiquity to the Middle Ages.* Ithaka: Cornell UP, 1990.

Downing, Christine. *The Goddess: Mythological Images of the Feminine.* New York: Crossroad, 1981.

Drew, Elizabeth. *T.S. Eliot: The Design of His Poetry.* New York: Charles Scribner's Sons, 1949.

Drucker, Johanna. *The Alphabetic Labyrinth: The Letters in History and Imagination.* London: Thames and Hudson, 1995.

Edinger, Edward F. *Anatomy of the Psyche: Alchemical Symbolism in Psychotherapy.* La Salle: Open Court, 1985.

---, *"Romeo and Juliet:* A Coniunctio Drama." *The Shaman From Elko: Papers in Honor of Joseph L. Henderson on His Seventy-Fifth Birthday.* San Francisco: C.G. Jung Insitute of San Francisco, 1978.

---, *Melville's Moby Dick: A Jungian Commentary.* New York: New Directions, 1978.

Eco, Umberto. *Foucault's Pendulum.* Trans. William Weaver. San Diego, New York, London: Harcourt Brace Jovanovich, 1989.

Eliade, Mircea. *The Forge and the Crucible: The Origins and Structures of Alchemy.* Second Edition. Trans. Stephen Corrin. Chicago and London: The University of Chicago Press, 1978.

---, *Myths, Dreams, and Mysteries.* New York: Harper and Row, 1960.

---, "La Terre-Mère et les Hiérogamies Cosmiques." *Eranos Jahrbuch 1953: Band XXII: Mensch und Erde.* Herausgegeben von Olga Fröbe-Kapteyn. Zürich: Rhein-Verlag, 1954.

---, *Shamanism: Archaic Techniques of Ecstasy.* Trans. Williard R. Trask. Bollingen Series LXXVI. Princeton: Princeton UP, 1964.

Eliot, Alexander, et. al. *Myths.* New York: McGraw-Hill Book Company, 1976.

Eliot, T.S. *Four Quartets.* New York: HBJ, 1971.

---, "Ulysses, Order and Myth." (1923). *The Modern Tradition.* Ed. Richard Ellmann and Charles Feidelson. New York: Oxford UP, 1965.

---, *The Waste Land and Other Poems.* New York: Harcourt, Brace, Jovanovich, 1962.

---, *Four Quartets.* New York: HBJ, 1971.

Epic of Gilgamesh. Trans. N.K. Sandars. New York: Penguin,

Eschenbach, Wolfram von. *Parzival.* Trans. A.T. Hatto. New York: Penguin Books, 1980.

Evans, Sir Arthur. *The Palace of Minos.* 4 Vols. London: Macmillan and Company, 1921 and 1934.

Fabricius, Johannes. *Alchemy: The Medieval Alchemists and Their Royal Art.* Copenhagen: Rosenkilde and Bagger, 1976.

Fontenrose, Joseph. *Python: A Study of Delphic Myth and Its Origin.* Berkeley: The University of California Press, 1959.

Foreman, Clifford William Willis. "Typology in the Fiction of Nathaniel Hawthorne." DAI. 1987 Mar; 47 (9): 3427A.

Foster, Michael. "The Christian Doctrine of Creation and the Rise of Modern Natural Science." *Creation: The Impact of an Idea.* Ed. Daniel O'Connor and Francis Oakley. New York: Charles Scribner's Sons, 1969.

Faivre, Antoine. *The Golden Fleece and Alchemy.* Albany: State University of New York Press, 1993.

Feldman, Burton and Robert D. Richardson. *The Rise of Modern Mythology: 1690-1860.* Bloomington: Indiana UP, 1972.

Franz, Marie-Louise von. *Alchemy: An Introduction to the Symbolism and the Psychology.* Toronto: Inner City Books, 1980.

---, *Creation Myths.* Dallas: Spring Publications, 1972.

---, *On Dreams and Death: A Jungian Interpretation.* Boulder and London: Shambhala, 1984.

---, *A Psychological Interpretation of Apuleius' Golden Ass With the Tale of Eros and Psyche.* Dallas: Spring Publications, 1980.

Frobenius, Leo. *Das Zeitalter des Sonnengottes.* Berlin, 1904.

Friedman, Albert B., ed. *The Penguin Book of Folk Ballads of the English Speaking World.* New York: Penguin Books, 1978.

Fromm, Erich. *The Forgotten Language: An Introduction to the Study of Dreams, Fairy Tales, and Myths.* New York: Grove Press, 1951.

Frye, Northrop. "The Argument of Comedy." *Shakespeare: Modern Essays in Criticism.* Ed. Leonard F. Dean. London: Oxford UP, 1967.

Gennep, Arnold van. *The Rites of Passage.* Trans. Monika B. Vizedom and Gabrielle L. Caffee. Chicago: The University of Chicago Press, 1960.

Gilman, Charlotte Perkins. "The Yellow Wallpaper." *Western Literature in A World Context: Volume Two: The Enlightenment through the Present.* Ed. Paul Davis, et. al. New York: St. Martin's Press, 1995.

Gimbutas, Marija. *The Civilization of the Goddess: The World of Old Europe.* San Francisco: HarperSanFrancisco, 1991.

---, *The Language of the Goddess.* San Francisco: Harper and Row, 1989.

Gittes, Katherine Slater. "The Canterbury Tales and the Arabic Frame Tradition." PMLA. March (1993): 237-51.

Godwin, Joscelyn. *Athanasius Kircher: A Renaissance Man and the Quest for Lost Knowledge.* London: Thames and Hudson, 1979.

Grass, Günter. *The Tin Drum.* (1959). Trans. Ralph Mannheim. New York: Vintage Books, 1990.

Graves, Robert. *The White Goddess.* Amended and Enlarged Edition. New York: Farar, Straus and Giroux, 1948.

Green, Miranda J. *Dictionary of Celtic Myth and Legend.* London: Thames and Hudson, 1992.

Grof, Stanislav. *Realms of the Human Unconscious: Observations from LSD Research.* New York: E.P. Dutton, 1976.

Guénon, René. "The Language of the Birds." *The Sword of Gnosis.* Ed. Jacob Needleman. Baltimore: Penguin Books, 1974.

Halifax, Joan. *Shamanic Voices: A Survey of Visionary Narratives.* New York: E.P. Dutton, 1979.

Harrison, Jane Ellen. *Prolegomena to the Study of Greek Religion.* London: Merlin Press, 1980.

Haskins, Susan. *Mary Magdalen: Myth and Metaphor.* New York: Harcourt, Brace, and Company, 1993.

Hawthorne, Nathaniel. *The Scarlet Letter.* Columbus: Ohio State University Press, 1962.

---, *Tales and Sketches.* Ed. Roy Harvey Pearce. New York: The Library of America, 1982.

Hillman, James. *The Dream and the Underworld.* New York: Harper and Row, 1979.

---, *Healing Fiction.* Preface by George Quasha. Barrytown: Station Hill, 1983.

---, *The Myth of Analysis: Three Essays in Archetypal Psychology.* New York: Harper and Row, 1972.

---, "Pothos." *Loose Ends: Primary Papers in Archetypal Psychology.* Dallas: Spring Publications, 1976.

---, "Puer Wounds and Ulysses' Scar." *Puer Papers.* James Hillman et.al. Dallas: Spring Publications, 1979.

Hoffman, E.T.A. "Die Bergwerke zu Falun." *Sämtliche poetischen Werke.* Zweiter Band. Berlin and Darmstadt: Der Tempel Verlag, 1963.

---, "The Mines of Falun." *Western Literature in A World Context: Volume Two: The Enlightenment through the Present.* Ed. Paul Davis, et. al. New York: St. Martin's Press, 1995.

Homer. *The Odyssey.* Trans. Robert Fitzgerald. New York: Anchor Books, Doubleday and Company, 1963.

Hornung, Erik. "Auf den Spuren der Sonne: Gang durch ein äegyptis-ches Königsgrab." *Eranos Jahrbuch (1981): Aufstieg und Abstieg.* Ed. Adolph Portmann and Rudolf Ritsema. Frankfort am Main: Insel Verlag, 1982.

470   *The Hero Journey in Literature*

Irwin, John T. *American Hieroglyphics: The Symbol of the Egyptian Hieroglyphics in the American Renaissance*. New Haven: Yale UP, 1980.

Irwin, Robert. *The Arabian Nights: A Companion*. New York: Penguin Press, 1994.

Johnson, Robert. *He: Understanding Masculine Psychology*. New York: Harper and Row, 1977.

---, *She: Understanding Feminine Psychology*. New York: Harper and Row, 1976.

---, *We: Understanding the Psychology of Romantic Love*. San Francisco: Harper and Row, 1983.

Jonas, Hans. *The Gnostic Religion*. Second Edition. Boston: Beacon Press, 1963.

Joyce, James.. *Finnegans Wake*. New York: The Viking Press, 1976.

---, *A Portrait of the Artist as a Young Man*. Chester Anderson, ed. New York: Viking Press, 1968.

---, *Ulysses*. New York: Random House, 1961.

Jung, C.G. *Four Archetypes*. Princeton: Princeton UP, 1964.

---, *Memories, Dreams, Reflections*. Ed. Aniela Jaffé. Trans. Richard and Clara Winston. New York: Pantheon Books, 1963.

---, *Mysterium Coniunctionis: An Inquiry Into the Separation and Synthesis of Psychic Opposites in Alchemy*. Second Edition Trans. R.F.C. Hull. Bollingen Series XX. Princeton: Princeton UP, 1970.

---, *The Practice of Psychotherapy . (The Collected Works of C.G. Jung, Volume 16)*. Princeton: Princeton UP, 1966.

---, "A Psychological Commentary on The Tibetan Book of the Dead." 1935. *Psychology and Religion: West and East*. New York: Pantheon Books, 1958.

---, *Psychology and Alchemy*. Second Edition. Princeton: Princeton UP, 1980.

---, *Psychology of the Transference*. Princeton: Princeton UP, 1966.

---, *Symbols of Transformation . (The Collected Works of C.G. Jung, Volume 5)*. Princeton: Princeton UP, 1967.

---, "The Transcendent Function." *The Portable Jung*. Ed. Joseph Campbell. New York: The Viking Press, 1971.

Jung, C.G. and C. Kerényi. *Essays on a Science of Mythology: The Myth of the Divine Child and the Mysteries of Eleusis*. Bollingen Series XXII. Princeton: Princeton UP, 1973.

Jung, Emma and Marie-Louise von Franz. *The Grail Legend*. New York: G.P. Putnam's Sons, 1970.

Kazantzakis, Nikos. *The Odyssey: A Modern Sequel*. Trans. Kimon Friar. New York: Simon and Schuster, 1958.

Kerényi, Karl.

Kerényi, Karl. *Eleusis: Archetypal Image of Mother and Daughter*. Trans. Ralph Manheim. Princeton, NJ: Princeton UP, 1967.

---, *Goddesses of Sun and Moon*. Trans. Murray Stein. Dallas: Spring Publications, 1979.

---, *The Gods of the Greeks*. London: Thames and Hudson, 1979.

---, *Hermes: Guide of Souls*. Dallas and Zürich: Spring Publications, 1976.

---, "Kore." *Essays on a Science of Mythology: The Myth of the Divine Child and the Mysteries of Eleusis*. Jung, C.G. and C. Kerényi. Bollingen Series XXII. Princeton: Princeton UP, 1973.

---, Preface. *Mythology and Humanism: The Correspondence of Thomas Mann and Karl Kerenyi*. Trans. Alexander Gelley. Ithaca: Cornell UP, 1975.

Kilber, William. "Introduction." *Lancelot, or The Knight of the Cart*. Chrétien de Troyes. New York: Garland Publishing, Inc., 1984.

Lagorio, Valerie. "The Apocalyptic Mode in the Vulgate Cycle of Arthurian Romances." Philological Quarterly 57 (1978): 1-22.

Larsen, Stephen. *The Shaman's Doorway: Opening the Mythic Imagination to Contemporary Consciousness*. New York: Harper and Row, 1976.

The Larousse Encyclopedia of Mythology. Introduction by Robert Graves. New York: Barnes and Noble, 1994.

Lauf, Detlef-Ingo. *Verborgene Botschaft Tibetischer Thangkas: Secret Revelation of Tibetan Thangkas*. Freiburg im Breisgau: Aurum Verlag, 1976.

Lawrence, D.H. *Apocalypse*. Ed. Mara Kalnins. New York: The Viking Press, 1982.

---, *The Complete Poems of D.H. Lawrence*. Ed. Vivian de Sola Pinto and Warren Roberts. New York: Penguin, 1964.

---, "The Horse-Dealer's Daughter."*The Complete Short Stories*. Vol. 2. New York: Viking Press, 1969.

---, *Sons and Lovers*. Penguin Books, 1981.

---, *The Symbolic Meaning: The Uncollected Versions of Studies in Classic American Literature*. Ed. Armin Arnold. New York: The Viking Press, 1964.

---, *Women in Love*. Penguin Books, 1982.

Leisegang, Hans. "The Mystery of the Serpent." (1939). *The Mysteries: Papers From the Eranos Yearbooks*. Ed. Joseph Campbell. Bollingen Series XXV. Princeton: Princeton UP, 1955.

Lessing, Doris. *Briefing For a Descent Into Hell*. New York: Random House, 1981.

Lilly, Mark, ed. Notes. *Villette*. Charlotte Brontë. New York: Penguin Books, 1983.

Lindborg, Henry J. "Hawthorne's Enoch: Prophetic Irony in The Scarlet Letter." TWA. (1986) 74: 122-125.

Lord, George de F. "The Odyssey and the Western World." Essays on the Odyssey: Selected Modern Criticism. Ed. Charles H. Taylor, Jr. Bloomington and London: Indiana UP, 1963.

Lowry, Malcolm. Under the Volcano. New York: New American Library, 1965.

Lucente, Gregory L. The Narrative of Realism and Myth: Verga, Lawrence, Faulkner, Pavese. Baltimore: Johns Hopkins UP, 1981.

Lucretius. On the Nature of Things: De rerum natura. Anthony Esolen, Ed. and Trans. Baltimore: Johns Hopkins UP, 1995.

MacDonald, Ronald R. The Burial Places of Memory: Epic Underworlds in Vergil, Dante, and Milton. Amherst: The University of Massachusetts Press, 1987.

Maclagan, David. Creation Myths: Man's Introduction to the World. London: Thames and Hudson, 1977.

Mann, Thomas. "Death in Venice." Stories of Three Decades. Trans. H. T. Lowe-Porter. New York: Alfred Knopf, 1936.

---, Doctor Faustus: The Life of the German Composer Adrian Leverkühn as Told by a Friend. New York: Alfred Knopf, 1948.

---, Doktor Faustus: Das Leben des deustschen Tonsetzers Adrian Leverkühn erzählt von einem Freunde. Gesammelte Werke 12 Vols. Oldenburg: S. Fischer Verlag, 1960. Vol. 6.

---, Essays of Three Decades. New York: Alfred Knopf, 1976.

---, "Freud und die Zukunft." Reden und Aufsätze. Gesammelte Werke. 12 Vols. Oldenburg: S. Fischer Verlag, 1960. Vol 9.

---, Joseph and His Brothers. New York: Alfred Knopf, 1976.

---, Joseph und Seine Brüder. Frankfurt am Main: Fischer Verlag, 1964.

---, The Magic Mountain. New York: Alfred Knopf, 1966.

---, "Der Tod in Venedig." Sämtliche Erzählungen. Frankfort am Main: S. Fischer Verlag, 1963.

---, Der Zauberberg. (1922). Frankfurt am Main: Fischer Taschenbuch Verlag, 1972.

Mardrus, Dr. J. C. and Powys Mathers, Trans. The Book of the Thousand Nights and One Night. 4 Vols. London: The Folio Press, 1980. Vol. 1.

Marks, Richard and Nigel Morgan. The Golden Age of English Manuscript Painting: 1200-1500. New York: George Braziller and Company, 1981.

Márquez, Gabriel García. One Hundred Years of Solitude. Trans. Gregory Rabassa. New York: Harper and Row, 1970.

Matthews, John. The Grail: Quest for the Eternal. New York: Crossroad, 1981.

Melville, Herman. *Moby Dick, or The Whale*. Arion Press Edition. Berkeley: The University of California Press, 1979.

Meyer, Marvin, ed. *The Ancient Mysteries, A Sourcebook: Sacred Texts of the Mystery Religions of the Ancient Mediterranean World*. New York: Harper and Row, 1987.

Miller, J. Hillis. *Ariadne's Thread: Story Lines*. New Haven: Yale UP, 1992.

Miller, Mary and Karl Taube. *The Gods and Symbols of Ancient Mexico and the Maya: An Illustrated Dictionary of Mesoamerican Religion*. London: Thames and Hudson, 1993.

Milton, John. *Complete Poems and Major Prose*. Ed. Merritt Y. Hughes. Indianapolis: The Odyssey Press (Bobbs Merrill Educational Publishing), 1957.

Mookerjee, Ajit and Madhu Khanna. *The Tantric Way: Art, Science, Ritual*. Boston: New York Graphic Society, 1977.

---, *Yoga Art*. Boston: New York Graphic Society, 1975.

Moorman, Charles. "Myth and Medieval Literature: *Sir Gawain and the Green Knight*. *Myth and Literature: Contemporary Theory and Practice*. Ed. John B. Vickery. Lincoln: University of Nebraska Press, 1966.

Murdock, Maureen. *The Heroine's Journey: Woman's Quest for Wholeness*. Boston and London: Shambhala, 1990.

Nabokov, Vladimir. *Pnin*. New York: Random House (Vintage International), 1989.

Neumann, Erich. *Amor and Psyche: The Psychic Development of the Feminine*. Bollingen Series LIV. Princeton: Princeton UP, 1956.

Nicholl, Charles. The Chemical Theatre. London: Routledge & Kegan Paul, 1980.

Opie, Iona and Peter. *The Classic Fairy Tales*. New York: Oxford UP, 1974.

Orenstein, Gloria Feman. *The Theater of the Marvelous: Surrealism and the Contemporary Stage*. New York: New York UP, 1975.

Oswald, Victor A. Jr. "Full-Fathom Five: Notes on Some Devices in Thomas Mann's *Doktor Faustus*." *The Germanic Review* (49)

---, "Thomas Mann's *Doktor Faustus:* The Enigma of Frau von Tolna." *Germanic Review* Dec. 1948. (23): 249-253.

Paisley, Livingston. *Ingmar Bergman and the Ritual of Art*. Ithaca: Cornell UP, 1982.

Pater, Walter. *The Marriage of Cupid and Psyche*. Illustrated by Edmund Dulac. New York: The Heritage Press, 1951.

Panofsky, Erwin. *Studies in Iconology: Humanistic Themes in the Art of the Renaissance*. Icon Edition. New York: Harper and Row, 1972.

Pépin, Jean. "The Platonic and Christian Ulysses." *Neoplatonism and Christian Thought.* Ed. Dominic J. O'Meara. International Society for Neoplatonic Studies. Albany: State University of New York Press, 1982.

Poncé, Charles. *Kabbalah: An Introduction and Illumination for the World Today.* London: Theosophical Publishing House, 1973.

Popol Vuh. Trans. Dennis Tedlock. *The HarperCollins World Reader: Antiquity to the Early Modern World.* Ed. Mary Ann Caws and Christopher Prendergast. New York: HarperCollins College Publishers, 1994.

Porter, Howard. Introduction. *The Odyssey.* Trans. George Palmer. New York: Bantam, 1963.

Quasha, George. Preface. *Healing Fiction.* James Hillman. Barrytown: Station Hill, 1983.

Quispel, Gilles. "Der Gnostische Anthropos und Die Jüdische Tradition." *Eranos-Jahrbuch (1953): Mensch und Erde.* Vol. XXII. Ed. Olga Fröbe-Kapteyn. Zürich: Rhein Verlag, 1954.

Raine, Kathleen. *Blake and Antiquity.* Bollingen Series. Princeton: Princeton UP, 1977.

---, *William Blake.* New York: Praeger Publishers, 1970.

Rifaat, Alifa. "My Unknown World." Trans. Denys Johnson-Davies. *Western Literature in A World Context: Volume Two: The Enlightenment through the Present.* Ed. Paul Davis, et. al. New York: St. Martin's Press, 1995.

Ring, Kenneth. *Life at Death: A Scientific Investigation of the Near-Death Experience.* New York: Coward, McCann, and Geoghegan, 1980.

Roberts, Gareth. *The Mirror of Alchemy: Alchemical Ideas and Images in Manuscripts and Books From Antiquity to the Seventeenth Century.* Toronto: University of Toronto Press, 1994.

Robinson, Douglas. *American Apocalypses: The Image of the End of the World in American Literature.* Baltimore: The Johns Hopkins UP, 1985.

Roche, Anthony. "'The Strange Light of Some New World': Stephen's Vision in A Portrait." 25 : 3 (Spring 1988): 323-332.

Rubin, William, ed. *Pablo Picasso: A Retrospective.* Chronology by Jane Fluegel. New York: The Museum of Modern Art, 1980.

Sandt, Lotti. *Mythos und Symbolik im Zauberberg von Thomas Mann.* Bern und Stuttgart: Verlag Paul Haupt, 1979.

Schama, Simon. *Landscape and Memory.* New York: Alfred A. Knopf, 1995.

Scholem, Gershom. "Die Vorstellung vom Golem in ihren tellurischen und magischen Beziehungen." *Eranos Jahrbuch 1953: Mensch und Erde.* Vol. 22. Ed. Olga Fröbe-Kapteyn. Zürich: Rhein-Verlag, 1954.

Scott, Walter, ed. *Hermetica: The Ancient Greek and Latin Writings Which Contain Religious or Philosophic Teachings Ascribed to Hermes Trismegistus.* Boulder: Hermes House, 1982.

Shakespeare, William. *A Midsummer Night's Dream.* Ed. Madeleine Doran. *William Shakespeare: The Complete Works.* Ed. Alfred Harbage. Baltimore: Penguin Books, 1969.

Smith, Evans Lansing. "Alchemical Imagery in Modernism." *Cauda Pavonis.* Spring (1994) New Series 13 (1):11-18.

---, "The Arthurian Underworld of Modernism: Thomas Mann, Thomas Pynchon, Robertson Davies." *Arthurian Interpretations.* Spring, 1990. 4 (2): 50-64.

---, "The Descent to the Underworld: Jung and His Brothers" *C.G. Jung and the Humanities: Towards a Hermeneutics of Culture.* Ed. Karin Barnaby and Pellegrino D'Acierno. Princeton: Princeton UP, 1990.

---, "The Descent to the Underworld in Borges and Cortázar." *The Yearbook of Comparative and General Literature.* 40 (1992): 105-115.

---, "The Descent to the Underworld in Charles Williams' *Descent into Hell.*" *Mythlore,* Forthcoming.

---, "Form and Function in T.H. White's *The Once and Future King Quondam et Futurus: A Journal of Arthurian Interpretations.* Winter, 1991. 1 (4): 39-52.

---, *Rape and Revelation: The Descent to the Underworld in Modernism.* Lanham: University Press of America, 1990.

---, *Ricorso and Revelation: An Archetypal Poetics of Modernism.* Columbia, SC: Camden House, 1995.

Smith, Grover. *The Waste Land.* London: George Allen and Unwin, 1983.

Spearing, A.C. *The Gawain Poet: A Critical Study.* Cambridge: Cambridge UP, 1970.

Speirs, John. *Medieval English Poetry: The Non-Chaucerian Tradition.* London: Faber and Faber, 1971.

Spenser, Edmund. *The Faerie Queene.* in *The Literature of Renaissance England.* Ed. John Hollander and Frank Kermode. New York: Oxford UP, 1973.

Sproul, Barbara C. *Primal Myths: Creating the World.* New York: Harper and Row, 1979.

Stein, Murray. *In MidLife: A Jungian Perspective.* Dallas: Spring Publications, 1983.

Stevens, Wallace. *The Poem at the End of the Mind: Selected Poems and a Play.* Ed. Holly Stevens. New York: Random House, 1967.

Stone, Merlin. *Ancient Mirrors of Womanhood: Our Goddess and Heroine Tradition.* Volume 1. New York: New Sybylline Books, 1979.

Strassburg, Gottfried von. *Tristan and Isolde.* Trans. A.T. Hatto. New York: Penguin, 1960.

Strauss, Walter. *Descent and Return: An Orphic Pattern in Literature.* Cambridge: Harvard UP, 1971.

Strindberg, August. *Inferno and From an Occult Diary.* Trans. Mary Sandbach. New York: Penguin Books, 1984.

Swann, Charles. "Hester and the Second Coming: a note on the conclusion of *The Scarlet Letter.*" Journal of American Studies. (1987) (21): 264-268.

Tagore, Rabindrath. "The Hungry Stones." *Western Literature in A World Context: Volume Two: The Enlightenment through the Present.* Ed. Paul Davis, et. al. New York: St. Martin's Press, 1995.

Taylor, Charles Jr., Ed. *Essays on the Odyssey: Selected Modern Criticism.* Bloomington and London: Indiana UP, 1963.

Taylor, John Russell. *Cinema Eye, Cinema Ear: Some Key Film-Makers of the Sixties.* New York: Hill and Wang, 1964.

Thoreau, Henry David. *Walden; or Life in the Woods.* Ed. Robert F. Sayre. New York: The Library of America, 1985.

The Tibetan Book of the Dead: The Great Liberation Through Hearing in the Bardo. Trans. Francesca Fremantle and Chögyam Trungpa. Boulder and London: Shambhala, 1975.

The Times Atlas of World History. Ed. Geoffrey Barraclough. Revised Edition. Maplewood, NJ: Hammond Inc., 1984.

Treasures From the Bronze Age of China. New York: The Metropolitan Museum of Art and Ballantine Books, 1980.

Turner, Arlin. *Nathaniel Hawthorne: A Biography.* New York: Oxford UP, 1980.

Twain, Mark. *Adventures of Huckleberry Finn. Mississippi Writings.* Ed. Guy Cardwell. New York: The Library of America, 1982.

Ulanov, Ann and Barry. "Bewitchment." *Quadrant: Journal of the C.G. Jung Foundation for Analytical Psychology.* Winter (1978): 33-61.

Virgil. *The Aeneid of Virgil: A Verse Translation by Alan Mandelbaum.* Berkeley: The University of California Press, 1981.

Wagner, Richard. *Tristan and Isolde.* English National Opera Guide 6. New York: Riverrun Press, 1981.

Wakeman, Mary K. *God's Battle With the Monster.* Leiden: E.J. Brill, 1973

Walker, Barbara. *The Woman's Dictionary of Symbols and Sacred Objects.* San Francisco: HarperSanFrancisco, 1988.

---, *The Women's Encyclopedia of Myths and Secrets*. HarperSanFrancisco, 1983.

Warner, Sylvia. Prologue. *The Book of Merlyn*. T.H. White. Austin:University of Texas Press, 1977.

Wasson, Gordon, et. al. *The Road to Eleusis: Unveiling the Secret of the Mysteries*. New York: HBJ, 1978.

Westcott, Brooke Foss, and John Anthony Hort. *The Kingdom Interlinear Translation of the Greek Scriptures*. New York: Watchtower Bible and Tract Society of Pennsylvania, 1969.

Weston, Jessie. *From Ritual to Romance*. Mythos Series. Princeton: Princeton UP, 1993.

White, T.H. *The Once and Future King*. New York: Ace Books, 1987.

Whitman, Walt. *Complete Poetry and Collected Prose*. Ed. Justin Kaplan. New York: The Library of America, 1982.

Whitmont, Edward C. *Return of the Goddess*. New York: Crossroad, 1982.

Wilkinson, Richard H. *Reading Egyptian Art: A Hieroglyphic Guide to Ancient Egyptian Painting and Sculpture*. London: Thames and Hudson, 1992.

Williams, Charles. *Descent Into Hell*. (1937). Grand Rapids: William B. Eerdmans Publishing Company, 1985.

Wind, Edgar. *Pagan Mysteries in the Renaissance*. Revised and Enlarged Edition. New York: W. W. Norton & Company, 1968.

Wolkstein, Diane and Samuel Noah Kramer. *Inanna Queen of Heaven and Earth*. New York: Harper and Row, 1983.

Woodroffe, Sir John. *The Garland of Letters: Studies in the Mantra-S'astra*. 7th Ed. Pondicherry: Ganesh and Company, 1979.

Wooley, Sir Charles Leonard. *Publications of the Joint Expedition of the British Museum and of the Museum of the University of Pennsylvania to Mesopotamia*. 2 vols. London: Oxford University Press, 1934.

---, *Ur of the Chaldees*. London: Ernest Benn, Ltd., 1929.

Yates, Frances A. *Giordano Bruno and the Hermetic Tradition*. (1964). Midway Reprint. Chicago: The University of Chicago Press, 1979.

---, *Majesty and Magic in Shakespeare's Last Plays: A New Approach to Cymbeline, Henry VIII, and The Tempest*. Boulder: Shambhala, 1978.

---, *The Occult Philosophy in the Elizabethan Age*. London and Boston: (Routledge and Kegan Paul) Ark Paperbacks, 1983.

---, *The Rosicrucian Enlightenment*. (1972). Boulder: Shambhala, 1978.

Yeats, W.B. *The Complete Poems of W.B. Yeats*. Ed. Richard Finneran. New York: Macmillan Publishing Company, 1983.

Zamora, Lois Parkinson. "The Myth of Apocalypse and the American Literary Imagination." *The Apocalyptic Vision in America: Interdisciplinary Essays on Myth and Culture.* Ed. Lois Parkinson Zamora. Bowling Green: Bowling Green University Popular Press, 1983.

Zimmer, Heinrich. *The King and the Corpse: Tales of the Soul's Conquest of Evil.* Ed. Joseph Campbell. Bollingen Series XI. (1948). Princeton: Princeton UP, 1973.

---, *Myths and Symbols in Indian Art and Civilization.* Ed. Joseph Campbell. Bollingen Series VI. (1947). Princeton: Princeton UP, 1974.

---, *Philosophies of India.* Ed. Joseph Campbell. Bollingen Series XXVI. (1951). Princeton: Princeton UP, 1969.

Zipes, Jack. *Spells of Enchantment: The Wondrous Fairy Tales of Western Culture.* New York: Viking Penguin, 1991.

Index

Moby Dick 221, 290-308, 404
mock epic 168, 192, 195, 204, 234, 235
Mohammed 223, 437, 441
moksha 259, 260
Moody, Raymond 334, 335, 432, 454
Morgan Le Fay 84, 86, 87, 89, 93, 115, 117, 134, 398, 400
Moses 56, 248, 444
mountain symbolism 16, 18, 46, 58, 97, 156, 177, 200, 218, 223, 232, 255, 386
Mozart, Wolfgang Amadeus 163, 165
Müller, Max 91, 114
mundus archetypus 161, 227, 390
mundus imaginalis 226, 435
Munsalvaesche 136
Murnau, F.W. 23, 58, 354, 386, 409-13, 426
Musäus 210
Museum Hermeticum 183
Mut 219
"My World of the Unknown" 432, 433-36
Mylius 183
mystery rites 35, 64, 67, 69, 77, 81, 250, 453
mythical method 118, 168, 192, 195, 205, 234, 235, 341, 360, 384
Nabokov, Vladimir 382, 388
nagas 260
Naiades 32, 33, 86
Nanna 8, 9

Napoleon 245
Narrow Road Through the Provinces 233
Nazca plains 459
Nausicaa 27, 28, 30, 37
Navajo myth 232, 239
Near Death Experience 97, 333, 358, 429, 432, 454
Nebuchadnezzar 408
Nekhebet 219
nekyia 18, 31, 37, 56, 57, 60, 61, 62, 98, 198, 206, 225, 256, 259, 291, 293, 294, 304, 317, 322, 323, 330, 333, 335, 372, 373, 377, 379, 392
Nemi 111
Neoclassical 194
Neoplatonic 44, 52, 57, 86, 99, 100, 153, 160, 162, 167, 178, 179, 180, 184, 185, 186, 187, 190, 192
Nephthys 23, 24
Nestor 121
Nestorian Christianity 155, 162
net symbolism 44, 45, 235
netherworld 58
Neumann, Erich 4, 64, 75
"Never Again Would Birdsong Be the Same" 367
New Jerusalem 173, 223, 275
New Testament 40, 59, 125, 157
Newgrange 83, 261, 376, 459
Newton, Sir Isaac 189, 191, 202, 382